ALEXANDER WILLIAM KINGLAKE.

THE

# INVASION OF THE CRIMEA:

## ITS ORIGIN,

AND

## AN ACCOUNT OF ITS PROGRESS

DOWN TO THE DEATH OF

## LORD RAGLAN.

BY

ALEXANDER WILLIAM KINGLAKE.

VOLUME I.

NEW YORK:
HARPER & BROTHERS, PUBLISHERS,
FRANKLIN SQUARE.
1868.

# ADVERTISEMENT TO FOURTH EDITION.

In this Edition many notes have been added. The spelling of the names of several English officers, and of one foreigner, has been corrected. Not a word has been withdrawn from the text, and not a word has been added to it.

Of the notes, there are some few which correct or qualify the words of the text. For a book which chances to be a subject of controversy, this way of setting right all mistakes is, I think, the fairest and best. Far from hiding the mended spot, it makes the newly-found truth more conspicuous than it would have been if it had been allowed to glide quietly into the text. For example: In one of the lists of wounded officers, I or my printers chanced to leave out the name of Colonel Smith. Upon the omission becoming known to me, I attached to the passage a mark of reference, which seizes the eye of the reader and carries him to the foot of the page, where instantly he sees it stated that Colonel Smith was one of the wounded. In this way the omitted fact is presented to the reader more effectually than it would have been if the word 'Smith' had been blended with the text, standing there with thirteen other names.

But also, by this method, I acknowledge and publicly record against myself every single inaccuracy, however minute and trivial, which had struck me as requiring correction when last I went through the book. Whether I could have been so venturesome as to do thus, if the emendations required had been many and important, I will not undertake to say. As it is, I am enabled to take this method of courting any criticism which may be founded upon my confessions of error.

The plan, therefore, is a fair one; but it is also, I think, very needful to adopt it, and I will say why.

The book is undergoing discussion; and in order that the conflict it raises may be honestly waged, it seems right to take care that the subject of dispute shall not be a shifting thing—a thing shifting this way and that under stress of public scrutiny.

Again, there is a charge now pending. Rightly or wrongly, the accusers say that in public journals—in journals still sold under honorable titles—the writers are now and then suffered to misstate the tenor of books; and it seems that the printed accounts which have been given of this work are put forward as some of the instances in which misdescription has occurred. I have not myself taken the pains which would warrant me in declaring a resemblance, or a want of resemblance, between the book and its likenesses; but knowing that the charge has been brought, I see it to be right that all those who are called upon to judge the question should have before their eyes the very text of a book which is the subject of the alleged misdescriptions—the very text with all its sins and wickednesses, not having one single word added, nor one single word withdrawn.

But, besides his reasons for the course he is taking, a man may have his motive; and I acknowledge that, with me, a chief motive for declining to alter the text is this:—I wish to keep a check upon those who might like to be able to say that I had materially altered the book. If any body shall try to say such a thing in defiance of the plan I have adopted, he will find himself painfully tethered; for, the words of the text standing fast, he will be unable to range beyond the circle of those little matters—matters chiefly minute, and of detail—which are dealt with in a few corrective foot-notes. Either he must say what is not true under circumstances which make his exposure a simple task, or else he will have to browse upon such scant herbage as is afforded by notes of this sort:—'No [not a 'squadron]; only one troop.' 'No [not sixty years old]; 'only sixty-four.' 'Here the words "Laurence and" 'should be inserted.' 'Instead of "a wing," read "the '"whole."' The first of the commentators who found himself checked in this way was thrown into so angry a state, that when I stood observing his struggles, I was glad to think of the prudence which had led me to keep him tied up.

I said just now that some of the writings which purported to give the tenor of these volumes had been put forward as instances of unfaithful description. I have not enabled myself to assist this inquiry by comparing the accounts of things contained in the book with the book itself; and it is not desirable for me to do so, because an author can hardly expect to be looked upon as a good judge of what is, or is not, an honest abridgment or statement of his words; but I may be allowed to adduce two curious instances of the errors into which men may be led by looking to the accounts which have been given of a book instead of to the book itself.

On the 15th of February, a stranger, who had been present at the Battle of the Alma, addressed to me a letter from a distant foreign station, which began thus: 'Sir,—It has 'not been yet my good fortune to see a copy of your re'cent . . . work, the "Invasion of the Crimea," but a critique 'upon it in the' (here the writer of the letter gives the name of his newspaper) 'of the 27th of January last, purporting 'to give an outline of some parts of the narrative, contains 'an assertion, made with reference to a description of the 'Battle of the Alma—viz., that under the fire sustained by 'Lord Raglan's Head-Quarter Staff, "not a man of it re'"ceived a scratch,"—which I take to be incorrect.'

The writer proceeds to state, with admirable clearness, the circumstances which enabled him to speak as an eyewitness of what went on with the Head-Quarter Staff, and then says:—'I presume to detail these particulars, in 'order to show, Sir, that having thus, like yourself, taken 'part in, and been an eye-witness of, the movements of the 'Staff on the memorable day referred to, I may venture to 'point out how far the statement as to the Staff having 'come out of it scathless seems to be inaccurate;' and the writer then proceeds to prove to me, with great clearness and perspicuity, that on the two spots of ground which he rightly and carefully describes, two officers of the Head-Quarter Staff were wounded.

Supposing that his newspaper was guiding him faithfully, well indeed might this critic remonstrate with me for the inaccuracy of which he had been led to suppose me guilty, because the Staff, so far from coming off scathless, had been more than decimated. When my correspondent at that foreign station shall see the book itself, he will know that I disclose this fully, giving the names of the two wounded officers; and, indeed, it would have been strange if I had omitted to do so, for Leslie and Weare, the two Staff officers wounded, were both of them struck down on the part of the field where I was, and one of them fell within a few paces of me.

Thus, then, it appears that even a careful and accurate man who has to put up with his newspaper's account of a book, at a time when he remains debarred from access to the book itself, is so misled by this method of seeking for the real purport of a volume that he thinks it is his duty to address the author with a view to correct a gross error—a gross error not existing in the book itself, but appearing to do so in the mind of one who receives his account of it from a newspaper.

On the 18th of March last, another letter was written, which I doubt not to be also an instance of the effect produced upon a mind of fair intelligence by accounts purporting to give the tenor of a book. When Captain Mends thought it his duty to address his letter to the newspaper about the buoy, he introduced the subject by writing, and suffering to be printed and published, the following words:

'As I have been referred to by many as to the truth of 'Mr. Kinglake's statement in his "Invasion of the Cri-'"mea," "that the landing of our army at Old Fort was '"materially delayed by the willful displacement of a buoy '"by the French," I feel called upon in justice,' etc. Now Captain Mends not only made that statement, but suffered it to be printed in the newspaper with inverted commas, exactly as given above. Well, those words are not in the book. Not only is there no such passage in the book—not only is there no assertion that 'material delay was oc-'casioned by the willful displacement of the buoy by the 'French'—but the book actually makes light of the delay, saying that there was 'much less delay, and much less 'confusion, than might have been expected;' and, far from undertaking to assert that the displacement of the buoy was willful, it goes out of its way to suggest that one of the hypotheses which would account for the displacement was 'sheer mistake.' I can not doubt that Captain Mends intended to quote accurately; and I account for his mistake by supposing that, instead of copying from the book itself he must have been induced to give what purported to be a quotation, by taking his words from one of those printed representations of the contents of the book which were current at the time when he wrote his letter to the newspaper.

I repeat that I have done nothing toward that collation of passages which is necessary for determining whether any given account of the tenor of the book is an account given in good faith; but it struck me that the above two instances of men who trusted to printed versions of the contents of the book, instead of to the book itself, might possibly help the inquiry, and could hardly fail to serve as wholesome examples.

In the general controversy which the book has engendered I am not taking part,[1] but having in my hands

[1] And I have no present intention of doing so; but when I give my

large means of proof and disproof, I ought, of course, to aid toward the attainment of right conclusions upon disputed matters of fact; and it is only with that view that I am now going to speak—not of the nature and spirit, but—of the mere abundance of the scrutiny which the book has undergone.

The book treated of such subjects, and of a time so little removed from the present, that there were great numbers of public men—ministers, diplomatists, and military and naval officers—who were not only likely to have strong motives for narrowly scrutinizing the accuracy of the narrative, but were able to speak upon some or one of the subjects it touches with the authority of partakers or eye-witnesses. Thence, as was to be expected, there were addressed to me a quantity of communications, some personal, and some by letter. In these communications, the speakers and writers pointed out what they deemed to be errors or omissions. In almost every instance they made their representations with great precision, and with a strikingly rigid adherence to the subject-matter.[1]

But, besides the authoritative criticism of those numbers of men who had been actors in the scenes described, there was the criticism of the periodical press. This was applied to the book, both at home and abroad; and so diligently, that already the works of the commentators must be many times greater in bulk than the original book. Of the publications which yielded these floods of comment, there were

long-withheld Preface I shall say why I resolved to tell aloud 'the transac-'tions which brought on the war.' The Preface, I think, will be of the same purport as the one I was preparing when I determined that I would let the book appear without covering it by any prefatory statement, except what was needed for showing 'the sources of the narrative.'

[1] I include in this category of communications from individuals some few which also appeared in print; as, for instance, one about the age of Sir George Brown, and the way he carried his plumes—another about the exact rank with which Colonel Codrington went out—and one or two more of a less important kind; but I do so rightly, because these communications had reached me *before* the time when they got published. I also include in this category the communication from Colonel Norcott, because, though his letter appeared in a newspaper, it was a letter addressed to me.

some whose conductors trusted mainly to public sources for the information on which they rested, but there were other conductors of reviews and newspapers who placed themselves under the guidance of some public man—some minister, some soldier, some sailor—who had been what is called 'an actor in the scene.' The criticism resulting from this last method was of a composite sort, for it more or less covertly uttered the notions of some public man whose reputation was at stake, but expressed them in the name of the journal through whom he addressed the public. From causes to which I need not advert, the commentaries were delivered, not only with great animation and zeal, but with a persistency not often applied to the criticism of one mere book. Diligence of the most varied kinds was brought to bear; for since the book involved politics as well as history, it fairly enough became the subject—not merely of reviews, but also—of what they call 'articles;' and seeing that it touched things abroad, correspondents employed by the conductors of newspapers in foreign capitals were encouraged or suffered to remit their daily toil of gathering 'news,' and take part for a time with their colleagues at home in finding something to say about this book. Finally, it was made to appear, that if an officer would submit to the condition of writing to a newspaper, and would begin his letter with a criticism upon the book of a kind approved by the managers, he might append to his comments a narrative of his own achievements, with the certainty that his own account of his own deeds would be read in one day by thousands and thousands of people.

It may be imagined that the immense body, both of authoritative and anonymous criticism, thus brought to bear upon one book, could hardly fail to show that mistakes had crept in here and there; but if any reader shall take the pains to separate from the bulk of the notes every sentence which puts right an error, he will be able to judge and say whether the corrections are many and important, or whether they are scanty and slight.

Be that as it may, I must state that, with the exceptions which I shall presently enumerate, I owe all these corrections to the public men and officers who have done me the honor to communicate with me either personally or by letter.

For reasons of larger scope than those which only apply to the questioned worth of a book, the public, I imagine, has an interest in knowing what impression has been made upon these volumes by the exertions of the periodical press. Certainly my own reading of the criticisms brought to bear on the book has been not only very imperfect, but has been conducted without method; and although I have taken other means besides my own scanty reading for learning what statements of mine upon matters of fact have been disputed in respectable publications, I can not be sure, nor even indeed imagine, that I have dealt with every contradiction upon matters of fact which has been taken in print to my statements. All I can say is, that when last I went through these volumes I did not knowingly pass by any error; and it must be remembered that there is this safeguard—namely, that every public writer whose challenge upon a matter of fact I may have failed to notice, will not only be able to exclaim against me for my neglect of his strictures, but will even be likely to do so, because it is according to nature that any critic who may have taken pains to give to a book this kind of antagonistic assistance should be loth to see his industry wasted.

Now, then, to speak of the corrections upon matters of fact which I owe to the periodical press. In writing a book of this kind, one naturally glances at many things which are not in strictness the subject of the History. Thus, before I came to the time when their actions brought them strictly within the range of this narrative, I glanced at the antecedent career of several public men, and in referring to those 'tidings from the Danube,' which I spoke of as stirring the public mind in England, I suffered myself to linger awhile on the ground whence the tidings had come. Well, in the course of those retrospective glances, I treated Lord Stratford's antecedent absence from Constantinople as lasting full double the number of months that it really did; I said that, in 1836, St. Arnaud entered for the third time into 'the military profession,' when I ought rather to have said that he entered for the third time 'upon the career of an officer serving with troops;' I spoke of Lieutenant Glyn and his seamen as coming up from the sea with some gunboats, whereas I ought to have said that the gunboats they used at Giurgevo were lying in the river beforehand; and finally, I spoke of General Airey as returning from Canada to England upon the death of his uncle, whereas I ought to have said that he came back some months before. These four mistakes were pointed out, the first three of them by respectable English journals, and the fourth by an American newspaper. So far as concerns my retrospective glances at things not falling within the strict limits of the History, these are, I think, all the corrections which I owe to the zeal of the press.

Well, but what impression has public criticism made upon the rest of the book? What (properly) historical errors have owed their correction to the vigilance of the periodical press?

They are as follows:—'Garan' should be 'Gagarin;' Captain 'Schane' should be Captain 'Schaw;' 'Luxmore' should be 'Luxmoore;' 'Bisset' should be 'Bissett;' 'Wool-'combe' should be 'Wollocombe;' 'Montagu' should be 'Montague.'[1]

[1] The press also suggested four perfectly just corrections in regard to the following matters:—The rank with which Colonel Codrington went out; the wrongly-spelled name of 'Stacey;' the omission of Colonel Smith from the list of wounded; the misspelling which gave 'Wardlow' instead of 'Ward-'law;' and the error about Sir George Brown's exact age, and the way he carried his plumes; but these corrections had been previously supplied to me by means of private communication, and it is for that reason that I do not place them in the above enumeration of the corrections which I owe to the periodical press.

For these corrections I am indebted to the conductors of an eminent English newspaper.[1]

I will repeat that there may, and there must be, numbers of printed challenges upon questions of fact with which I have not become acquainted; and there may be others which I have heard of and forgotten; but the above, I believe, are the only corrections supplied by the periodical press which I have hitherto seen fit to adopt.

What then did I do with all the rest of those charges of error in matter of fact which were brought against me by the press? Well, I looked through the book, and where I observed a statement which I knew at the time to have been denied, I did this: By a note at the foot of the page where a challenged assertion occurred, I supplied a sufficing portion of the proofs by which I support my statement. Of the soundness and cogency of the proofs thus produced, it will be for the public to judge. They are all, or nearly all, documentary.

But, besides the unnumbered strangers and friends who have addressed to me private communications on the contents of the book, and besides the whole host of those who speak to the public through the medium of the periodical press, there is one persistent scrutinizer who (so far as concerns all questions of dry fact) has hitherto proved more formidable than all. He alone has succeeded in proving that, here and there, there is a mistake—slight enough perhaps in itself, but—occurring in a place where, to point to it, is to fix upon the part of the narrative in which it appears, a small, yet ugly blemish. For some years this caviler took an interest in the progress of the book, and it is believed that he still wishes well to it; but, in his determination to insist upon strict accuracy without the least regard for the flow of the narrative, he is steadfast and pit-

[1] The misspelling of the name of 'Garan' for 'Gagarin' was pointed out by the correspondent of the newspaper acting at Constantinople. The other misspellings of names were indicated in one of the many reviews of the book which appeared in the same journal.

iless. What makes his scrutiny so formidable is, that—without the least merit on his part—he has chanced to become possessed—nay, is every day becoming more and more possessed—of the knowledge, the constantly-accruing knowledge, which enables him to find fault with effect. This persistent, implacable critic is no other than the author himself.

Of the way in which I break in and find fault with the book wherever truth bids me do so, I can best speak by giving a single example. Guided by Sir Colin Campbell's narrative of the operations of his brigade at the Alma, I narrated the advance of the 79th Highlanders against the flank of a Russian column then marching across its front, and—catching animation from that strangely kindling power with which Lord Clyde used to speak of these scenes—I said that the 79th 'sprang at the flank' of the Russian column. I never knew of any body except myself who ever found fault with the accuracy of the sentence. But it happened that, long after the publication of the book, and for a purpose having nothing to do with the movement in question, Lord Clyde, one day, brought me a paper, written by an officer of the 79th, and containing more minute details of the advance of the regiment than had previously come to my knowledge. From these details I gathered that, although the 79th had advanced exactly in the direction I described, and against the flank of the Russian battalions then marching across its front, it had advanced more deliberately than I had supposed. I no sooner read this than I felt that my expression, 'sprang at the flank,' indicated a greater swiftness of attack than was consistent with the bare truth, and therefore needed to be qualified. Lord Clyde did not agree with me; he thought the expression sufficiently accurate, and deprecated the notion of my qualifying the words; but I was steadfast in my determination to show what I myself judged to be the very truth, and therefore it is that, by a qualifying note, I willfully mar and deface the sentence to which I append it. This is only one example of the rigor with which the book is treated by its author.

And here I may say that, in order to substantiate disputed statements, I have not been always obliged to reopen the stores of information on which I founded my assertions. In many, and I think in most instances, I was saved the need of going back to papers long out of my sight, by the firm love of justice which brought men who had observed that I was wrongly contradicted to come forward of their own accord and lay before me the private letters and journals of eye-witnesses in support of the statements I had made. Of the written documents on which I based the narrative, I can say that, for the most part, I have hitherto kept them in reserve.

Until after the publication of the book, I think I was as much inclined as the generality of men to be doubtful of the possibility of getting very close to historical truth ; and I knew, of course, that the occurrences of a battle-field are especially hard to seize; but I must acknowledge that the supply of fresh, confirming proof by which I now find myself supported, has done something toward lessening any tendency I had toward this kind of historical scepticism. When the first edition of the book was published, I had never seen the private journal and letters of Colonel Hood, the officer who commanded the Grenadier Guards at the Alma, nor the clear and straightforward narrative of Sir Charles Russell, of the same regiment. I was without that letter of Colonel Percy of the same regiment, to which (as will be gathered from the notes) I attach great worth. I had never seen that journal of Colonel Annesley of the Fusileer Guards, which tells me the story so naturally and so well, that to glance through the written words is more like listening than reading. I had never seen the rough, life-like letters of Colonel Yea, nor the short telling letter of Colonel Aldworth. Yet, when all this authentic testimony of eye-witnesses is laid before me, I find it confirming what I had asserted in print some months before. Seeing this, I can not but think that—even in the battle-field —there is truth, after all, to be found.

If I might be suffered to press this view for a moment more by giving a chosen instance of the way in which it applies to my own narrative, I would venture to speak of one only among those several pieces of testimony by which I now support my account of the operations of the Grenadier Guards at the Alma. I support what I say of the battalion by giving extracts from the journal and private letters of its honored chief, Colonel Hood. These extracts correspond so closely with the tenor of the narrative, that the reader would be likely to say—'That journal and 'those letters were evidently the authority on which the au-'thor based his account of the operations of the Grenadier 'Guards.' It is, however, a fact, that I never saw the journal, nor the letters, and never knew any thing of their tenor, until after the publication of the first and second editions of this book. It was then that Mrs. Grosvenor Hood (the widow of him whose achievement on the banks of the Alma had won so large a share of my attention) resolved to give me fresh means of substantiating the narrative, by placing in my hands the treasured words which were written to her from the banks of the Alma.[1]

Now, when it is seen that I make a series of statements —of statements planted thick with particulars—in regard to the operations of a given battalion at the Alma, and that, after the publication, there comes to light a private record written on the field of the battle by the officer who commanded the battalion—a record confirming almost sen-

[1] This she did with the full approval of Lord Hood, the present head of the family. I may here say (though I think I have clearly explained it in the foot-note, vol. ii. p. 441) that the order with respect to which Colonel Hood wrote, 'Thank God I disobeyed!' was not an order given by the Divisional General H.R.H. the Duke of Cambridge. Colonel Hood had been directed by General Bentinck to conform to any movements on his left, and it was only by being applied to the event which afterward happened—viz., the temporary retreat of the Fusileer Guards—that General Bentinck's order became in effect an order directing Colonel Hood to retreat.

tence by sentence the account I give in my narrative—it is plainly a sound deduction to say, that the coincidence between the two accounts must result from the accuracy of both. But I venture to think that an inference of wider scope than that may fairly be drawn; for surely in the mind of any body who shall be seeking after truth with the aid of accustomed principles, the appearance of new and confirmatory proofs of this sort will not only establish the particular assertion to which he finds them appended, but will even tend to strengthen his trust in other parts of the book.

NOTE.—The additional notes of the author in the second, third and fourth editions, will be found at the close of the volume, under the head of NOTES TO FOURTH EDITION.

# THE SOURCES OF THE NARRATIVE.

BEFORE I had determined to write any account of the war, there were grounds from which many inferred that a task of this kind would be mine; and I may say that, from the hour of their landing on the enemy's coast close down to the present time, men, acting under this conviction, have been giving me a good deal of their knowledge.

In 1856 Lady Raglan placed in my hands the whole mass of the papers which Lord Raglan had with him at the time of his death. Having done this, she made it her request that I would cause to be published a letter which her husband addressed to her a few days before his death.[1] All else she left to me. Time passed; and no history founded upon these papers was given to the world. Time still passed away; and it chanced to me to hear that people who longed for the dispersion of what they believed to be falsehoods, were striving to impart to Lady Raglan the not unnatural impatience which all this delay had provoked. But, with a singleness of purpose and a strength of will which remind one of the great soldier who was her father's brother, she answered that, the papers having once been placed under my control, she would not disturb me with expressions of impatience, nor suffer any one else to do so with her assent. I can not be too grateful to her for her generous and resolute trustfulness. If these volumes are late, the whole blame rests with me. If they are reaching the light too soon, the fault is still mine.

Knowing Lord Raglan's habits of business, knowing his

[1] I need hardly say that this letter will appear in its proper place, though not in this volume.

tendency to connect all public transactions with the labors of the desk, and finding in no part of the correspondence the least semblance of any thing like a chasm, I am led to believe that, of almost every thing concerning the business of the war which was known to Lord Raglan himself, there lies in the papers before me a clear and faithful record.

In this mass of papers there are—not only all the military Reports which were from time to time addressed to the Commander of the English army by the generals and other officers serving under him (including their holograph narratives of the part they had been taking in the battles), but also Lord Raglan's official and private correspondence with sovereigns and their ambassadors; with ministers, generals, and admirals; with the French, with the Turks, with the Sardinians; with public men, and official functionaries of all sorts and conditions; with adventurers, with men propounding wild schemes, with dear and faithful friends.[1] Circumstances had previously made me acquainted with a good deal of the more important information thus laid before me; but there is a completeness in this body of authentic records which enables me to tread with more confidence than would have been right or possible if I had had a less perfect survey of the knowledge which belonged to headquarters. And, so methodical was Lord Raglan, and so well was he served by Colonel Steele, his military secretary, that all this mass of authentic matter lies ranged in perfect order. The strategic plans of the much-contriving Emperor —still carrying the odor of the Havanas which aid the ingenuity of the Tuileries—are ranged with all due care, and can be got at in a few moments; but, not less carefully ranged, and equally easy to find, is the rival scheme of the enthusiastic nosologist who advised that the Russians should

[1] I have never looked at it since 1856, but it struck me then, that the letter which Mr. Sidney Herbert addressed to Lord Raglan in the winter of the first campaign was the very ideal of what, in such circumstances, might be written by an English statesman who dearly loved his friend, but who loved his country yet more.

be destroyed by the action of malaria, and the elaborate proposal of the English general who submitted a plan for taking Sebastopol with bows and arrows. Here and there, the neatness of the arranging hand is in strange contrast with the fiery contents of the papers arranged; for, along with reports and returns, and things precise, the most hurried scrawl of the commander who writes to his chief under stress of deep emotion lies flat, and hushed, and docketed. It would seem as though no paper addressed to the English Head-Quarters was ever destroyed or mislaid.

With respect to my right to make public any of the papers intrusted to me, I have this—and this only—to say: circumstances have enabled me to know who ought to be consulted before any State Paper or private letter hitherto kept secret is sent abroad into the world; and, having this knowledge, I have done what I judge to be right.

The papers intrusted to me by Lady Raglan contain a part only of the knowledge which—without any energy on my part—I was destined to have cast upon me; for, when it became known that the papers of the English Head-Quarters were in my hands, and that I was really engaged in the task which rumor had prematurely assigned to me, information of the highest value was poured in upon me from many quarters. Nor was this all. Great as was the quantity of information thus actually imparted to me, I found that the information which lay at my command was yet more abundant; for I do not recollect that to any one man in this country I have ever expressed any wish for the information which he might be able to give me, without receiving at once what I believe to be a full and honest disclosure of all he could tell on the subject.[1] This facility embarrassed me;

[1] In one of the Reviews for April, 1863, there appeared this:—'Indeed, we 'believe that access [to the unpublished portion of the political correspond- 'ence] was refused to him [Mr. Kinglake] by the Foreign Office.' In the number of the same Review which was published in the following July, there appeared a Postscriptum or Note in reference to the above statement. After showing my ground of complaint in regard to another misstatement of fact which I had called upon the editor of the Review to withdraw, the Postscriptum or Note says as follows:—'He [Mr. Kinglake] also informs us,

for I never could find that there was any limit to my power of getting at what was known in this country. I rarely asked a question without eliciting something which added, more or less, to my labor, and tended to cause delay.

And now I have that to state which will not surprise my own countrymen, but which still, in the eyes of the foreigner, will seem to be passing strange. For some years, our statesmen, our admirals, and our generals have known that the whole correspondence of the English Head-Quarters was in my hands, and very many of them have from time to time conversed and corresponded with me on the business of the war. Yet I declare I do not remember that any one of these public men has ever said to me that there was any thing which, for the honor of our arms, or for the credit of the nation, it would be well to keep concealed. Every man has taken it for granted that what is best for the repute of England is the truth.

I have received a most courteous, clear, and abundant answer to every inquiry which I have ventured to address to any French Commander; and indeed the willingness to communicate with me from that quarter was so strong, that an officer of great experience, and highly gifted with all the qualities which make an accomplished soldier, was dispatched to this country with instructions to impart ample statements to me respecting some of the operations of the French army. I seize upon this occasion of acknowledging the advantage I derived from the admirably lucid statements which were furnished to me by this highly-instructed officer; and I know that those friends of mine to whom I had the honor of presenting him will join with me in expressing the gratification which we all derived from his society.

I thought it right to apprise the authorities of the French War Department, that, if they desired it, the journals of

'that access to the unpublished political correspondence, relating to the 'causes of the war, was not refused to him by the Foreign Office (as we 'had been led to believe), inasmuch as he made no application to obtain it. 'As Mr. Kinglake has expressed to us his desire that these two points should 'be explained, we readily comply with his request.'

their divisions, and any other unpublished papers in their War-Office which they might be pleased to show, would be looked over by a gifted friend of mine, now a member of the House of Commons, who had kindly offered to undertake this task for me. The French authorities did not avail themselves of my offer; but any obscurity which might otherwise have resulted from this concealment has been effectually dispersed by the information I afterward obtained from Russian sources.

Of all the materials on which I found my account of the battle of the Alma, hardly any have been more valuable to me than the narratives of the three Divisional Generals who there held command under Prince Mentschikoff. The gifted young Russian officer who obtained for me these deeply interesting narratives, and who kindly translated them from their Russian originals, has not only conferred upon me an important favor, but has also done that which will uplift the repute of the far-famed Russian infantry, by helping to show to Europe the true character of the conflict which it sustained on the banks of the Alma.

My knowledge respecting the battles of Balaclava and Inkerman, and the subsequent fights before Sebastopol, is still incomplete, and I shall welcome any information respecting these conflicts which men may be pleased to intrust to me. From the Russians especially, I hope that I may receive communications of this kind. Their defense of Sebastopol ranges high in the annals of warfare, and I imagine that the more the truth is known, the more it will redound to the honor of the Russian arms.

I do not in general appeal for proof to my personal observation, but I have departed from this abstinence in two or three instances where it seemed to me that I might prevent a waste of controversial energy by saying at once that the thing told had been seen or heard by myself.

With regard to the portion of the work which is founded upon unpublished documents and private information, I had intended at one time—not to give the documents nor the names of my informants, nor the words they have written or spoken, but—to indicate the nature of the statements on which I rely; as, for instance, to say in notes at the foot of a page, 'The Raglan Papers,' 'Letter from an officer en-'gaged,' 'Oral statement made to me by one who was pres-'ent,' and the like. But, upon reflection, I judged that I could not venture to do this. When a published authority is referred to, any want of correspondence between the assertion and the proof can be detected by a reader who takes the trouble to ascend to the originals; but I do not like to assert that a document or a personal narrative withheld (for the present) from this wholesome scrutiny is the designated, yet hidden foundation of a statement which I make freely, in my own way, and in my own language. So although, when I found my statements upon a Parliamentary Paper or a published book, I commonly give my authority, yet, so far as concerns that part of the work which is based upon unpublished writings or private information—and this applies to an important part of the first, and to nearly the whole of the second volume—I in general make no reference to the grounds on which I rely. Hereafter it may be otherwise; but, for the present, this portion of the book must rest upon what, after all, is the chief basis of our historical knowledge—must rest upon the statement of one who had good means of knowing the truth. In the mean while, I shall keep and leave ready the clew by which in some later time, and without farther aid from me, my statements may be traced to their sources.

For a period of now several years my knowledge of what I undertake to narrate has been growing more and more complete. Far from gathering assurance at the sight of the progress thus made, I am rather led to infer that approaches which continued so long might continue perhaps still longer; and it is not without a kind of reluctance that I pass from the tranquil state of one who is absorbing the truth, to that of a man who at last stands up and declares it. But the time has now come.

A. W. KINGLAKE.

12 *St. James's Place, London,* 1*st January*, 1863.

# CONTENTS.

## TRANSACTIONS WHICH BROUGHT ON THE WAR.

## CHAPTER VII.



## CHAPTER VIII.



## CHAPTER IX.



## CHAPTER X.



## CHAPTER XI.



## CHAPTER XII.

## CHAPTER XIII.



## CHAPTER XIV.

## CHAPTER XV.



## CHAPTER XVI.

## CHAPTER XVII.



## CHAPTER XVIII.



## CHAPTER XIX.

## CHAPTER XX.



## CHAPTER XXI.



## CHAPTER XXII.



## CHAPTER XXIII.



## CHAPTER XXIV.



## CHAPTER XXV.



## CHAPTER XXVI.

## CHAPTER XXVII.



## CHAPTER XXVIII.



# INVASION OF THE CRIMEA.

## CHAPTER XXIX.



## CHAPTER XXX.

## CHAPTER XXXI.



## CHAPTER XXXII.



## CHAPTER XXXIII.



## CHAPTER XXXIV.



## CHAPTER XXXV.



## CHAPTER XXXVI.

## CHAPTER XLII.



## CHAPTER XLIII.



## CHAPTER XLIV.

## APPENDIX.

## PLANS AND ILLUSTRATIONS TO VOL. I.

# INVASION OF THE CRIMEA.

## CHAPTER I.

The Crimea.

In the middle of this century the peninsula which divides the Euxine from the Sea of Azoff was an almost forgotten land, lying out of the chief paths of merchants and travelers, and far away from all the capital cities of Christendom. Rarely any one went thither from Paris, or Vienna, or Berlin: to reach it from London was a harder task than to cross the Atlantic, and a man of office receiving in this distant province his orders dispatched from St. Petersburg was the servant of masters who governed him from a distance of a thousand miles.

Along the course of the little rivers which seamed the ground, there were villages and narrow belts of tilled land, with gardens, and fruitful vineyards; but, for the most part, the Chersonese was a wilderness of steppe or of mountain range much clothed toward the west with tall stiff grasses, and the stems of a fragrant herb like southernwood. The bulk of the people were of Tartar descent, but they were no longer in the days when nations trembled at the coming of the Golden Horde; and though they were of the Moslem faith, their religion had lost its warlike fire. Blessed with a dispensation from military service, and far away from the accustomed battle-fields of Europe and Asia, they lived in quiet, knowing little of war, except what tradition could faintly carry down from old times in low monotonous chants. In their husbandry they were more governed by the habits of their ancestors than by the nature of the land which had once fed the people of Athens, for they neglected tillage, and clung to pastoral life. Watching flocks and herds, they used to remain on the knolls very still for long hours together, and when they moved, they strode over the hills in their slow-flowing robes with something of the forlorn majesty of peasants descended from warriors. They wished for no change, and they excused their content in their simple way by saying that for three generations their race had lived happy under the Czars.[1]

But afterward, and for reasons unknown to the shepherds, the chief Powers of the earth began to break in upon these peaceful scenes. France, England, and Turkey were the invaders, and these at a later day were re-enforced by Sardinia. With the whole might which she could put forth in a province far removed from her military centre, Russia stood her ground. The strife lasted a year and a half, and for twelve months it raged.

And with this invasion there came something more than what men saw upon the battle-fields of the contending armies. In one of the Allied States, the people, being free of speech and having power over the judgment of their rulers, were able to take upon themselves a great share of the business of the war. It was in vain that the whole breadth of Europe divided this people from the field of strife. By means unknown before, they gained fitful and vivid glimpses of the battle and the siege, of the sufferings of the camp and bivouac, and the last dismal scenes of the hospital tent; and being thus armed from day to day with fresh knowledge, and feeling conscious of a warlike strength exceeding by a thousand fold the strength expressed by the mere numbers of their army, they thronged in, and made their voice heard, and became partakers of the counsels of State. The scene of the conflict was mainly their choice. They enforced the invasion. They watched it hour by hour. Through good and evil days they sustained it, and when by the yielding of their adversary the strife was brought to an end, they seemed to pine for more fighting. Yet they had witnessed checkered scenes. They counted their army on the main land. They watched it over the sea. They saw it land. They followed its march. They saw it in action. They tasted of the joy of victory. Then came the time when they had to bear to see their army dying upon a bleak hill from cold and want. In their anguish this people strove to know their General. They had seen him in the hour of battle, and their hearts had bounded with pride. They saw him now commanding a small force of wan, feeble, dying men, yet holding a strong enemy at bay, and comporting himself as though he were the chief of a strong besieging army. They hardly knew at the time that for forty days the fate of two armies and the lasting

[1] The villagers of Eskel (on the Katcha) declared this to me on the 23d of September, 1854, and the date gives value to the acknowledgment, for these villagers had been witnessing the confusion and seeming ruin of the Czar's army.

fame and relative strength of great nations were hanging upon the quality of one man's mind. Tormented with grief and anger for the cruel sufferings of their countrymen, they turned upon the Chief with questioning looks, and seeing him always holding his ground and always composed, they strove to break in upon the mystery of his calm. But there, their power fell short. Except by withstanding the enemy, he made them no sign, and when he was re-enforced and clothed once more with power, he still seemed the same to them. At length they saw him die. Thenceforth they had to look upon the void which was left by his death. They grew more patient. They did not become less resolute. What they hoped and what they feared in all these trials, what they thought, what they felt, what they saw, what they heard, nay, even what they were planning against the enemy, they uttered aloud in the face of the world; and thence it happened that one of the chief features of the struggle was the demeanor of a free and impetuous people in time of war.

Again, the invasion of the Crimea so tried the strength, so measured the enduring power of the nations engaged, that, when the conflict was over, their relative stations in Europe were changed, and they had to be classed afresh.

Moreover, the strife yielded lessons in war and policy which are now of great worth.

Ground for tracing the causes of the war.

But this war was deadly. It brought, they say, to the grave full a million of workmen and soldiers. It consumed a pitiless share of the wealth which man's labor had stored up as the means of life. More than this, it shattered the frame-work of the European system, and made it hard for any nation to be thenceforth safe except by its sheer strength. It seems right that the causes of a havoc which went to such proportions should be traced and remembered.

Europe in 1850.

For thirty-five years there had been peace between the great Powers of Europe. The outbreaks of 1848 had been put down. The wars which they kindled had been kept within bounds, and had soon been brought to an end. Kings, emperors, and statesmen declared their love of peace. But always while they spoke, they went on levying men. Russia, Germany, and France were laden with standing armies.

Standing armies.

Personal government. Comparison between this

This was one root of danger. There was another. Between a sovereign who governs for himself, and one who reigns through a council of statesmen, there are points of difference which make it more likely that

system and that of governing through a Council.

war will result from the will of the one man than from the blended judgments of several chosen advisers. In these days the exigencies of an army are vast and devouring. Also, modern society growing more and more vulnerable by reason of the very beauty and complexity of its arrangements is made to tremble by the mere rumor of an appeal to arms; and upon the whole the evils inflicted by war are so cruel, and the benefit which a Power may hope to derive from a scheme of aggression is commonly so obscure, so remote, and so uncertain, that when the world is in a state of equilibrium and repose it is generally very hard to see how it can be really for the interest of any one State to go and do a wrong, clearly tending to provoke a rupture. Here then there is something like a security for the maintaining of peace. But this security rests upon the supposition that a State will faithfully pursue its own welfare, and therefore it ceases to hold good in a country where the government happens to be in such hands that the interests of the nation at large fail to coincide with the interests of its ruler. This history will not dissemble—it will broadly lay open—the truth that a people no less than a prince may be under the sway of a warlike passion, and may wring obedience to its fierce command from the gentlest ministers of state; but upon the whole, the interests, the passions, and foibles which lead to war are more likely to be found in one man than in the band of public servants which is called a ministry. A ministry indeed will share in any sentiments of just national anger, and it may even entertain a great scheme of state ambition, but it can scarcely be under the sway of fanaticism, or vanity, or petulance, or bodily fear; for though any one member of the Government may have some of these defects, the danger of them will always be neutralized in council. Then again, a man rightly called a minister of state is not a mere favorite of his sovereign, but the actual transactor of public business. He is in close intercourse with those laborers of high worth and ability who in all great States compose the permanent staff of the public office, and in this way, even though he be newly come to affairs, he is brought into acquaintance with the great traditions of the State, and comes to know and feel what the interests of his country are. Above all, a ministry really charged with affairs will be free from the personal and family motives which deflect the state policy of a prince who is his own minister, and will refuse to merge the interests of their country in the mere hopes and fears of one man.

On the other hand, a monarch governing for himself, and

without responsible ministers, must always be under a set of motives which are laid upon him by his personal station as well as by his care for the people. Such a prince is either a hereditary sovereign or he is a man who has won the crown with his own hand. In the first case, the contingency of his turning out to be a man really qualified for the actual governance of an empire is almost, though not quite, excluded by the bare law of chances; and on the other hand it may be expected that a prince who has made his own way to the throne will not be wanting in such qualities of mind as fit a man for business of state. In some respects, perhaps, he will be abler than a council. He will be more daring, more resolute, more secret; but these are qualities conducive to war and not to peace. Moreover, a prince who has won for himself a sovereignty claimed by others will almost always be under the pressure of motives very foreign to the real interests of the State. He knows that by many he is regarded as a mere usurper, and that his home enemies are carefully seeking the moment when they may depose him, and throw him into prison, and ill-use him, and take his life. He commands great armies, and has a crowd of hired courtiers at his side; but he knows that if his skill and his fortune should both chance to fail him in the same hour, he would become a prisoner or a corpse. He hears from behind, the stealthy foot of the assassin; and before him he sees the dismal gates of a jail, and the slow, hateful forms of death by the hand of the law. Of course he must and he will use all the powers of the State as a defense against these dangers, and if it chance to seem likely—as in such circumstances it often does—that war may give him safety or respite, then to war he will surely go; and although he knows that this rough expedient is one which must be hurtful to the State, he will hardly be kept back by such a thought, for, being, as it were, a drowning man who sees a plank within his reach, he is forced by the law of nature to clutch it; and his country is then drawn into war, not because her interests require it, nor even because her interests are mistaken by her ruler, but because she has suffered herself to fall into the hands of a prince whose road to welfare is distinct from her own.

Personal government in Russia.

The power of All the Russias was centred in the Emperor, and it chanced that the qualities of Nicholas were of such a kind as to enable him to give a literal truth to the theory that he, and he alone, was the State.

In Austria.

In Austria the disasters of 1848 had broken the custom of government, and placed a kind of dictatorship in the hands of the youthful Emperor. And, although before the summer of 1853 the traditions of the state had regained a great deal of their force, still for a time the recovery was not so plainly evident as to compel an unwilling man to see it; and the notion that the great empire of the Danube had merged in the mere wishes of Francis Joseph lingered always in the mind of the Czar and drew him on into danger.

In Prussia.

Even in Prussia, though the country seemed to enjoy a constitutional form of government, the policy of the State was always liable to be deranged by the tremulous hand of the King; and the anticipation of finding weakness in this quarter was one of the causes which led the Czar to defy the judgment of Europe.

Administration of foreign affairs under the Sultan.

In the Ottoman dominions Abdul Medjid was accustomed to leave the administration of foreign affairs to responsible ministers; and it will be seen that this wholesome method of reigning gave the Turkish Government a great advantage over the diplomacy of other Continental States.

Constitutional system of England in its bearing upon the conduct of Foreign Affairs.

In England there was no evil trace of that Oriental polity which yields up the power of the state into the hands of one human being. Happy in the love of the people who surrounded her throne, and free from all motives clashing with the welfare of her realms, the Queen always intrusted the business of the monarchy to ministers of state enjoying the confidence of Parliament; and upon the whole, the polity of the English state was such that no Government could draw the country into a needless war unless its error came to be shared by the bulk of the people. Indeed the power of the Crown in England is so far from being a source of disturbance, that it is one of the safeguards of peace. There are circumstances in which an ancient reigning House gains a view of foreign affairs more tranquil and in some respects more commanding than any obtained by a Cabinet; and, although it is known that in these days ministerial responsibility can never be evaded by alleging the order of the Crown, the practice of the Constitution requires that the Foreign Secretary shall have the actual sanction of his Sovereign for every important step which he takes, and it requires also that, in order to the obtaining of this sanction, the explanations tendered to the Crown by the ministry shall be complete and frank.[1] The duty of rendering these explanations, and of asking for the Royal sanction can scarcely be fulfilled without giving a minister the advantage of seeing

[1] The existing practice of the Constitution in this respect is laid down in the debates which began the Session of 1852.

a question from a new point of view. Therefore, although the responsible Secretary for Foreign Affairs can never find shelter by setting up the overruling will of his Sovereign as the justification of his conduct, and although he must needs be supported by the advice or assent of Parliament, still he is not without means of guidance from sources of a less changeful kind; for whilst he has below him the tradition of the office, there is above him the tradition of the monarchy. By these means some steadfastness of purpose is generally, though not always, insured; and, except when it happens that the people are turned aside for a moment by some honest sentiment or moved by their innate desire to hear of instructions and battles, the foreigner has good grounds for inferring that, whatever the policy of England may be, it will not be altogether unstable. Certainly the transactions of the East so drew England away from her landmarks as to bring her at last into war, and this, too, at a time when the Queen was still blessed with the counsels of a husband, who was a wise and a gifted statesman; but it will be seen by-and-by how it came to happen that the forces of the Constitution were baffled.

And of France, down to the 2nd of December, 1851.

France down to the winter of 1851 was under parliamentary government, and although, as will be seen, the President was able to take steps which tended to generate troubles, the country was safe from the calamity of a wanton rupture with friendly States. The change wrought in the night of the 2nd of December, 1851, will be shown by-and-by, and its effects upon the peace of Europe will be traced, but the period now spoken of is the middle of the century, and at that time and so long as the Republic maintained a real existence it was not possible in France, any more than in England, that a war should be undertaken by the Executive Government without the approval of Parliament and of the nation at large.

Power of Russia.

It was believed that the Emperor Nicholas numbered almost a million of men under arms; and of these a main part were brave, steady, obedient soldiers. Gathering from time to time great bodies of troops upon his western frontier, he caused the minds of men in the neighboring states to be weighed down with a sense of his strength. Moreover, he was served by a diplomacy of the busy sort, always laboring to make the world hear of Russia and to acknowledge her might; and being united by family ties with some of the reigning Houses of Germany, he was able to have it believed that his favor might be of use to the courtiers and even sometimes to the statesmen of Central Europe. Down to the giving of trinkets and ribbons, he was not forgetful. His power was great; and when the troubles of 1848 broke out, the broad foundation of his authority was more than ever manifested; for, surrounded by sixty millions of subjects whose loyalty was hardly short of worship, he seemed to stand free and aloof from the panic which was overturning the thrones of the Western Continent, and to look down upon the terrors of his fellow-sovereigns, not deigning to yield his cold patronage to the cause of law and order. In the West, he said, and even in Central Europe, the storm might rage as it liked, but he warned and commanded that the waves should not so much as cast their spray upon the frontiers of 'Holy Russia;'[1] and when Hungary rose, he ordered his columns to pass the border, and forced the insurgent army to lay down its arms. Then, proudly abstaining from conditions and recompense, he yielded up the kingdom to his Ally. That day Russia seemed to touch the pinnacle of her greatness; for men were forced to acknowledge that her power was vast, and that it was wielded in a spirit of austere virtue, ranging high above common ambition.

But toward the South, Russia was the neighbor of Turkey.

Turkey.

The descendants of the Ottoman invaders still remained quartered in Roumelia and the adjoining provinces. They were a race living apart from the Christians who mainly peopled the land; for the original scheme of the Moslem invasions still kept its mark upon the country. When the Ottoman warriors were conquering a province, they used to follow the injunction of the Prophet, and call upon such of the nations as rejected the Koran, to choose between 'the tribute' and the sword; but the destiny implied by the first branch of the alternative was very different from that of a people whose country is conquered by European invaders. Instead of being made subject to all the laws of their conquerors, the people of the Christian Churches were suffered to live apart, governing themselves in their own way, furnishing no recruits to the army, and having few legal relations with the State, except as payers of tribute.

In cities, the people of the Christian Churches and of the Synagogue generally had their respective districts, apart from the Moslem quarter. They were not safe from lawless acts of tyranny; and there were usages which reminded them that they were a conquered people; but they were never interfered with, as the citizens of European States are, for the mere sake

[1] See the Manifesto issued by the Czar in 1848.

of method or uniformity. They were free in the exercise of their religion; and most of the customs under which they lived were so completely their own, and so many of the laws which they obeyed were laws administered by themselves, that they might almost be said to form tributary republics in the midst of a military empire. Indeed this distinct existence was so fully recognized as a result of Mahometan conquest that the Turkish Government was accustomed to give the title of a 'Nation' to the members of any Christian Church or Synagogue established within the Ottoman realm.

The subjects, or 'Rayahs,' as they are called, thus held under Mussulman sway numbered perhaps fifteen millions; and although the Mussulmans of the whole Empire might be computed at twenty-one millions, the great bulk of these were scattered over remote provinces in Asia and Africa. There were hardly more than two million Turks in Europe. These dominant Ottomans were in an earlier stage of civilization than most of the Christian States; and it had happened that their Government in straining to overtake and imitate the more cultivated nations, had broken down much of the strength which belongs to a warlike and simple people. Besides, amongst the Turks who clustered around the seat of government, a large proportion were men so spoilt by their contact with the metropolis of the Lower Empire, that, whilst the State suffered from the ignorance and simplicity of the governing race, it was suffering also in an opposite way under the evils which are bred by corruption.

Yet, notwithstanding the canker of Byzantian vice, and although they knew that they were liable to be baffled by the methods of high organization and ingenious contrivance now brought to bear upon the structure of armies, the Ottoman people still upheld the warlike spirit which belongs to their race and to their faith. It is true that Russia, seizing a moment when the Sultan was without an ally,[1] and almost without an army,[2] had invaded Bulgaria in 1828, and, passing the Balkan in the following year, had brought the campaign to an issue which seemed like a triumph. Yet men versed in the affairs of Eastern Europe always knew that the Treaty of Adrianople had not been won by the real strength of the invaders, but rather by a daring stratagem in the nature of a surprise, and

[1] The accustomed policy of England had been deranged by a sentiment in favor of Greece. Moreover, Lord Aberdeen was then at the Foreign Office.

[2] The Sultan had destroyed the Janissaries, and was beginning the formation of an army upon the European plan.

by a skillful feat of diplomacy. Experience showed that the Turks could generally hold their ground with obstinacy, when the conditions of a fight were of such a kind that a man's bravery could make up for the want of preparation and discipline. In truth they were a devoted soldiery, and fired with so high a spirit that when brought into the right frame of mind they could look upon the thought of death in action with a steadfast, lusty joy. They were temperate, enduring, and obedient to a degree unknown in other armies. They brought their wants within a very narrow compass, and, without much visible effort of commissariat skill or of transport power, they were generally found to be provided with bread and cartridges and even with means of shelter. Their arms were always bright. Their faith tended to make them improvident, but a wise instinct taught them that if there was one thing which ought not to be left to fate or to the precepts of a deceased prophet, it was the Artillery. Their guns were well served. The Empire was wanting in the classes from which a large body of good officers and of able statesmen could be taken, and therefore, with all their bravery, the Turks were liable to be brought to the verge of ruin by panic in the field, or by panic in the Divan; but where the men are of so warlike a quality as the Turks, the want of able officers can be remedied to an almost incredible degree by the presence of a foreigner, and indeed the Osmanlee is so strangely cheered and supported by the mere sight of an Englishman that aid rendered upon the spur of the moment by five or six of our countrymen has more than once changed despair into victory, and governed the course of events. Help of that sort, whatever our Government might do, was not again likely to be wanting to the Turks in a defensive war. Moreover, the vast and desolate tracts of country which lie between the Pruth and the Bosphorus can not easily be crossed by an army requiring large supplies, especially if it should be deprived of the sea communication. It is true that neither the warlike qualities of the Ottoman people nor the physical difficulties of the invasion were well understood in Europe, and it was commonly believed that Turkey, if left unsupported, would lie completely at the mercy of the Czar. This, however, was an error. Except in the possible event of their being overwhelmed by some panic, the Turks were not liable to be speedily crushed by an army forcing the line of the Danube and advancing through the passes of the Balkan.

But also, the conquest of European Turkey was obstructed by the very splendor of the prize. To have the dominion of the summer kiosks, and the steep shady gardens looking down on the straits between Europe and Asia is to have a command which carries with it nothing less than an Empire: and, since the strength of every nation is relative, and is liable to be turned to naught by the aggrandizement of another Power, it was plain that no one among the nations of Europe could be seen going in quest of dominion on the Bosphorus without awakening alarm and resistance on the part of the other great Powers. Certainly the Turks trusted much in Heaven; but being also highly skilled in so much of the diplomatic art as was needed for them in this temporal world, they knew how to keep alive the watchfulness of every Power which was resolved to exclude its rivals from the shores of the Bosphorus. Moreover, those descendants of the Ottoman conquerors still remained gifted with the almost inscrutable qualities which enable a chosen race to hold dominion over a people more numerous and more clever than their masters. There were a few English statesmen and several English travelers who had come to understand this; but the generality of men in the Christian countries found it hard to make out that a people could be wise without being keenly intelligent, and could see little strength in a civilization much earlier and more rude than their own.

So in the common judgment of the world it had long seemed natural that, as a result of the decay which was thought to have come upon the Ottoman Empire, its European provinces should revert to Christendom. By many, the conquest of them was thought to be an easy task: for the Turks were few and simple, and in peace-time very listless and improvident; and the bulk of the people held under their sway in Europe were Christians, who bore hatred against their Ottoman masters. And, to Russia these same provinces seemed to be of a worth beyond all kind of measurement, for they lay toward the warm South, and, commanding the Bosphorus and the Dardanelles, gave access to and fro between the Euxine and the Mediterranean. The Power which seemed to be abounding in might was divided from the land of temptation by a mere stream of water. No treaty stood in the way.[1] Was there in the polity of Europe any principle, custom, or law which could shelter the weak from the strong, and forbid the lord of eight hundred thousand soldiers from crossing the Pruth or the Danube?

[1] The preambles of the Treaties of 1840 and 1841 recognized the expediency of maintaining the Sultan's dominion, but there was nothing in the articles of either of those treaties which engaged the contracting parties to defend the empire from foreign invasion.

## CHAPTER II.

The Usage which tends to protect the weak against the strong.

THE supreme Law or Usage which forms the safeguard of Europe is not in a state so perfect and symmetrical that the elucidation of it will bring any ease or comfort to a mind accustomed to crave for well-defined rules of conduct. It is a rough and wild-grown system, and its observance can only be enforced by opinion, and by the belief that it truly coincides with the interests of every Power which is called upon to obey it; but practically, it has been made to achieve a fair portion of that security which sanguine men might hope to see resulting from the adoption of an international code. Perhaps under a system ideally formed for the safety of nations and for the peace of the world, a wrong done to one State would be instantly treated as a wrong done to all. But in the actual state of the world there is no such bond between nations. It is true that the law of nations does not stint the right of executing justice, and that any Power may either remonstrate against a wrong done to another State great or small, or may endeavor, if so it chooses, to prevent or redress the wrong by force of arms; but the duties of States in this respect are very far from being coextensive with their rights. In Europe, all States except the five great Powers are exempt from the duty of watching over the general safety; and even a State which is one of the five great Powers is not practically under an obligation to sustain the cause of justice unless its perception of the wrong is re-enforced by a sense of its own interests. Moreover, no State, unless it be combating for its very life, can be expected to engage in a war without a fair prospect of success. But when the three circumstances are present—when a wrong is being done against any State great or small, when that wrong in its present or ulterior consequences happens to be injurious to one of the five great Powers, and finally, when the great Power so injured is competent to wage war with fair hopes, then Europe is accustomed to expect that the great Power which is sustaining the hurt will be enlivened by the smart of the wound, and for its own sake, as well as for the public weal, will be ready to come forward in arms, or to labor for the formation of such leagues as may be needed for upholding the cause of justice. If a Power fails in this duty to itself and to Europe it suddenly becomes lowered in the opinion of mankind, and happily there is no historic lesson more true than that which teaches all rulers that a moral degradation of this sort is speedily followed by disasters of such a kind as to be capable of being expressed in arithmetic, and of being in that way made clear to even the narrowest understanding. The principle on which the safeguard rests will not be acknowledged by all, but those who will disown it can be designated beforehand. There are many who can not make out how society can justly be harsh upon a man for being tame under insult or injury; and the same class of moralists will encounter a like difficulty in their endeavor to understand the cogency and the worth of this Usage.

Instance of a wrong to which the Usage did not apply.

Perhaps the limit to which the Usage is subject may be best shown by first giving an example of circumstances in which it fails to take practical effect. When the Republic of Cracow was abolished by an arrangement concerted between Russia and Austria a clear wrong was done, and France and England protested against it, but it could hardly be said that their interests were grievously affected by the change, and therefore it was not the opinion of Europe that the Western Powers had been guilty of a great dereliction of duty because on this account they declined to go to war.

Instance in which the Usage was applicable and was disobeyed.

But, as an example of circumstances in which tame acquiescence would be clearly a breach of the great Usage and a defection from the cause of nations, one may cite the conduct of Prussia in 1805; for, when the First Napoleon suddenly came to a rupture with Austria, and broke up from his camp at Boulogne and poured his armies into Germany, advancing upon Ulm and finally upon Vienna itself, all men saw that it was not only for the interest of Europe at large, but also for the interest of Prussia herself that she should come forward to prevent the catastrophe. She hung back and stood still whilst Austria succumbed; but acting thus, Prussia incurred the ill opinion of Europe, and the ruin which follows degradation did not at all lag, for in the very next year Bonaparte was issuing his decrees from Berlin, and the Prussians were yielding up their provinces and their strong places to France, and handing over their stores of gold and silver, and of food and clothing, to cruel French intendants, and French soldiery were quartered upon them at their hearths. A brave and warlike people had been brought down into this abyss because their rulers had shrunk from taking up arms in obedience to the great Usage; and Europe set it down and remembered that Prussia's dereliction of duty in 1805 was followed by shame and ruin in the autumn of 1806.

Instances in which the Usage was faithfully obeyed.

But if the wars of 1805 and 1806 supplied a signal instance of this kind of defection and of its speedy chastisement, they also furnished examples of loyal obedience to the great Usage. From the rupture of the peace of Amiens to the summer of 1805, Bonaparte was at peace with the Continent and at war with this country. During that interval of more than two years he bent his whole energy, and devoted the vast resources at his command to the one object of invading and crushing England. It was against the interest of Europe that England should be ruined, but more especially it was for the interest of Austria that this disaster should be averted, because the great empire of the Danube is so situate that its interests are more closely identical with the interests of England than with those of any other Power. Moreover the indignation of Austria was whetted by seeing Bonaparte crowning himself at Milan and seizing Genoa. Therefore when Pitt turned to the Court of Vienna, he did not turn in vain. Supported by Russia and Sweden, Austria came forward in arms, and though she was for the time broken down by the disaster of Ulm, and the defeat of the Russian army at Austerlitz, her old ally was safe: nothing more was heard in those days of the invasion of England; and the islanders relieved from the duty of mere literal self-defense were set free to enter upon a larger scheme of action.[1] Thenceforth they defended England by toiling for the deliverance of Europe. The coalition of 1805 was shattered, but before it perished it had helped to secure the precious life of the nation which was destined to be the first to carry war into the territory of the disturber.

By Austria.

Again, in the same year it was perilous to central Europe that Bonaparte should be having dominion in Germany; but also it was against the interest of Russia that this should be, and the defection of Prussia threw upon the Czar the burden of having to be foremost in the defense of Austria. Therefore, in 1805, the Emperor Alexander came forward with his army to the rescue, and in the following year he refused to stand idle when Prussia was the victim, and again moved for-

By Russia.

[1] Of course it was the destruction of the French and Spanish fleets at Trafalgar, which prevented Bonaparte from resuming the idea of invading England, but that which caused him to abandon the enterprise which he had been planning for two years was the coalition. He broke up from the camp of Boulogne several weeks before the battle of Trafalgar.

ward his armies; and although he was worsted at Austerlitz in striving to defend Austria, and although after heroic struggles in defense of Prussia he at last was vanquished at Friedland and was obliged to make peace, still his faithful and valorous efforts gained him so much of the respect of Europe and even of his victorious adversary, that, beaten as he was, he was able to go to Tilsit and to negotiate with the great Conqueror of the day upon a footing which resembled equality.

By England.

It has fallen to the lot of England also to have some share of the honor which Europe bestows upon resolute defenders of right, for when Bonaparte wished to make himself master of Spain and Portugal, it was the interest of England to prevent this result if she could, and to endeavor to thwart and humble the French Emperor in the midst of his triumphs; but it was also for the interest of Europe that England should be able to do this. Nay, so crushing had been the disasters suffered by the Continental States that the glorious duty of standing foremost and alone in defense of the liberties of mankind was cast for a time upon England. The task might well seem a hard one, for all that the islanders could do was to send out in ships scanty bodies of troops, in order that the men, when they landed, might encounter the armies of the hitherto victorious Emperor. But England did not shrink from the undertaking. For more than six years she carried on the struggle, and during some three years of that time she stood alone against Napoleon, for he had put down all the other nations which had sought to resist him, and during that evil time it seemed that the vanquished people of the Continent had no hope left except when they were telling one another in whispers that England remained mistress of the seas, and in the Peninsula was still fighting hard. Times grew better, and although Bonaparte still held the language of a great potentate, he had so mismanaged the resources of the heroic and warlike country which he ruled, that an English army with its Portuguese auxiliaries was able to invade and hold his territory, and whilst he still pretended to the Germans that he was a proud and powerful sovereign, Wellington unmasked the whole imposture of the "French Empire" by establishing his army and his foxhounds in the south of France, and quietly hunting the country in the livery of the Salisbury hunt.[1] The effort had begun when Sir Arthur Wellesley land-

[1] Larpent's 'Private Journal' at Head-Quarters, vol. ii., p. 105. Wellington established himself in France in November, 1813. He sent back into the Peninsula his whole Spanish army, because it plundered. The invasion of France by the Continental Powers took place in the beginning of the following year.

ed upon the coast of Portugal in the year 1808, and it ended in 1814. In the spring of that last year, men of several nations were gathered together at the English head-quarters in Toulouse; and it was put into the heart of a man whose name is unknown, but who spoke in the French tongue, to confer the loftiest title that ever was truthfully given to man. In a moment his words were seized as though they were words from on High, and the whole assembly with one voice saluted Wellington the "Liberator of Europe."[1] The loyal soldier shrank from the sound of a title not taken exact from the Gazette,[2] but the voice which had spoken was nothing less than the voice of grateful nations. If the fame of England had grown to this proportion, it was because she had faithfully obeyed the great Usage, and had come to be the main prop of the rights of others by firmly defending her own.

The practical working of the Usage.

The obligation imposed upon a great State by this Usage is not a heavy yoke, for after all it does no more than impel a Sovereign by fresh motives and by larger sanctions to be watchful in the protection of his own interests. It quickens his sense of honor. It warns him that if he tamely stands witnessing a wrong which it is his interest and his duty to redress, he will not escape with the reckoning which awaits him in his own dishonored country, but that he will also be held guilty of a great European defection, and that his delinquency will be punished by the reproach of nations, by their scorn and mistrust, and at last perhaps by their desertion of him in his hour of trial. But on the other hand, the Usage assures a Prince that if he will but be firm in coming forward to redress a public wrong which chances to be collaterally hurtful to his own State, his cause will be singularly ennobled and strengthened by the acknowledgment of the principle that, although he is fighting for his own people, he is fighting also for every nation in the world which is interested in putting down the wrong-doer.

Of course, neither this nor any other human law or usage can have any real worth except in proportion to the respect and obedience with which it is regarded; but, since the Usage exacts nothing from any State except what is really for its own good as well as for the general weal, it is very much obeyed, and is always respected in Europe. Indeed, a virtual compliance with the Usage is much more general than it might seem to be at first sight, for the known or foreseen determination of

[1] Larpent's 'Private Journal,' vol. ii. p. 267.

[2] Sir George Larpent (who was present) says that Wellington "bowed confused," and abruptly put an end to the scene.

a great State to resist the perpetration of a wrong is constantly tending with great force to the maintenance of peace, and, peace being much less remarkable than war, the very success with which the principle works prevents it from being conspicuous. And, certainly, when the Usage is faithfully obeyed, it is a strong safeguard, for, the interests of different States being much intertwined, it commonly happens that a wrong done to a lesser State is in some way hurtful or dishonoring to one or other of the great Powers, and if the great Power which is thus aggrieved takes fire, as it ought to do, and determines to resist or avenge, it is generally able to embroil other States, and the result is that the Prince who is the wrong-doer finds himself in a war which—having a tendency to become greater and greater—can hardly be otherwise than formidable to him. It is the apprehension of this result which is the main safeguard of peace. Any prince who might be inclined to do a wrong to another State casts his eyes abroad to see the condition of the great Powers. If he observes that they are all in a sound state and headed by firm, able rulers who are equal, if need be, to the duty of taking up arms, he knows that his contemplated outrage would produce a war of which he can not foresee the scope or limit, and, unless he be a madman or a desperado desiring war for war's sake, he will be inclined to hold back. On the other hand, if he sees that any great nation which ought to be foremost to resist him is in a state of exceptional weakness or under the governance of unworthy or incapable rulers, or is distracted by some whim or sentiment interfering with her accustomed policy, then perhaps he allows himself to entertain a hope that she may not have the spirit or the wisdom to perform her duty. That is the hope, and it may be said in these days it is the one only hope which would drive a sane prince to become the disturber of Europe. To frustrate this hope—in other words, to keep alive the dread of a just and avenging war—should be the care of every statesman who would faithfully labor to preserve the peace of Europe. It is a poor use of time to urge a king or an emperor to restrain his ambition and his covetousness, for these are passions eternal, always to be looked for, and always to be combated. For such a prince, the only good bridle is the fear of war. Of course it is right enough to appeal to this wholesome fear under the courteous title of "deference to opinion," though in truth it is not for the ambitious disturber, but rather for those Princes who are showing signs of weakness and failing spirit, that the discipline of opinion is really needed. Happily this discipline is not often wanting, for the feelings of nations in regard to the toleration of a wrong coincide with the general weal, and if men can not always shame a prince from being guilty of an ignominious defection, they at least take care that the fruit of his delinquency shall be bitter. Europe is severe and slow of forgiveness toward any great Power which by shrinking from the defense of its own rights has suffered a harm to be done to another State.

It will be seen by-and-by that, in defiance of the opinion of Europe and without any color of right, a great Power invaded the territory of a weaker neighbor; but any one who keeps in mind the principle of the great Usage will have the means of seeing what resources Europe had for repressing this act of violence, and will hold a clew for finding out the quarter to which men had a right to look for the commencement of resistance.

Aspect of Europe in reference to the Turkish Empire. Policy of Austria.

The Power most exposed to harm from Russian encroachments upon European Turkey was Austria; for it was plain, that if her great neighbor of the North were to extend his empire in the direction of Moldavia, Wallachia, and Servia, and so come winding round her Southeastern frontier, she would be brought into grievous danger; and her motives for watchfulness in this quarter were quickened by a knowledge of the disturbing elements which existed in the border provinces, where the people were drawn toward Russia by the ties of religion and race, and even of language. If the prospect of the Czar's carrying his dominion to the shores of the Bosphorus was galling and offensive to the other Powers of Europe, the evil which such a change was calculated to bring upon Austria seemed hardly short of ruin. Moreover Austria, in her character as a representative of German interests, was charged to see that the Lower Danube, ordained by Nature to be the main outlet for the products of Central Europe, should not hopelessly fall under the control of the Northern Power. Thus upon Austria, before all other Powers, there attached the care of guarding against encroachments on the European provinces of the Sultan, and the cogency of this duty toward herself, toward Germany, and toward Europe, Austria has always acknowledged. When Turkey was invaded in 1828, Prince Metternich was the one statesman in Europe who strove to form a league for the defense of the Sultan, and it will be seen that, although the events of 1849 had tended to embarrass the free action of the Emperor Francis Joseph, the last war against the Sultan disclosed no change in Austrian policy.

Over the councils of Prussia at this time the Court of St.

Of Prussia. Petersburg had a dangerous ascendency; but by his actual station as a leading member of the Confederation and by his hopes of attaining to a still higher authority in Germany, the King was forced into accord with Austria upon all questions which touched the freedom of the Lower Danube, and it was certain that he would do all that he safely could to discourage schemes for the disturbance of the German Empire. Still he lived in awe of the Emperor Nicholas, and it was hard to say beforehand what course he would take if he should be called upon to choose between defection and war.

Of France. Among the very foremost of the great Powers of Europe was France; and she was well entitled, if her rulers should so think fit, to use her strength against any potentate threatening to alter the great territorial arrangements of Europe; and especially it was her right to withstand any changes which she might regard as menacing to her power in the Mediterranean. But French statesmen have generally thought that, as the Mediterranean after all is only a part of the ocean, a new maritime power in the Levant might be rather a convenient ally against England, than a dangerous rival to France; and, upon the whole, it was difficult to make out, either from the nature of things or from the general course of her policy, that France had any deep interest in the integrity of the Sultan's dominions. At all events, her interest was not of so cogent a sort as to oblige her to stand more forward than any of the other great Powers, or to bear in any greater proportion than they might do, the charge of keeping the Ottoman Empire untouched. Indeed, it was hard at that time to infer from the past acts of France that she had any settled policy upon the Eastern Question. She had clung with some steadiness to the idea of establishing French influence in Syria; and from time to time during the last half century she had been inclined to entangle herself in Egypt; but upon the question whether the elements constituting the Ottoman Empire should be kept together, she had generally seemed to be undecided; for, although she took part in the conservative arrangements of 1841, her conduct in the previous year, and at several other times of crisis, had disclosed no great reluctance on her part to see the empire dismembered. Upon the supposition, however, that she intended to pursue the policy which she afterward avowed, and to concur in the endeavor to maintain the Sultan's dominions, her duty toward herself and to Europe required that she should herself refrain from disturbing the quiet of the East; and that in the event of any wrongful aggression by Russia upon the dominions of the Sultan, she should loyally range herself with such of the four great Powers as might be willing to check the encroachment by their authority, or, in last resort, by force of arms; but it was not at all incumbent upon France to place herself in the van; and it was not consistent with the welfare of her people that she should take upon herself a share of the European burden disproportionate to her interest in the state of Eastern Europe. Nor was there at this time any reason to imagine that the country could be brought into strife, or engaged in warlike enterprises without sufficient cause; for the institutions of France had not then shriveled up into a system which subordinated the vast interests of the State to the mere safety and welfare of its ruler. The legislative power and the control of the supplies were in the hands of an Assembly freely elected; and both in the Chamber and in print, men enjoyed the right of free speech. Also the executive power rested lawfully in the hands of ministers responsible to Parliament; and therefore, although the President, as will be seen, could do acts leading to mischief and danger, he could not bring France to a rupture with a foreign State unless war were really demanded by the interests or by the honor, or at least by the passions of the country. And, the people being peacefully inclined, and the interests and the honor of the country being carefully respected by all foreign States, France was not at that time a source of disturbance to Europe.

Of England.

Next to Austria, England was of all the great Powers the one most accustomed to insist upon the maintenance of the Ottoman Empire. It might be a complex task to prove that the rule of the English in Hindostan is connected with the stability of the Sultan's dominions in a far distant region of the world; but, whether the theory of this curious inter-dependence be sound or merely fanciful, it is certain that the conquest of the shores of the Bosphorus and the Dardanelles by one of the great Continental Powers would straiten the range of England's authority in the world; and, even if it did not do her harm of a positive kind, would relatively lessen her strength. The effect, too, of Russia's becoming a Mediterranean Power could not be so clearly foreseen and computed as not to be a fitting subject of care to English statesmen. The people at large were not accustomed to turn their minds in this direction; but the "Eastern Question," as it was called, had become consecrated by its descent through a great lineage of Statesmen; and the traditions of the Foreign Office were re-enforced by English travelers: for these men, going to Eastern countries in early life, and becoming charmed with their glimpse of the grand, simple, violent world that they had read of in their Bibles, used soon to grow interested in the diplomatic strife always going on at Constantinople; and then coming home they brought back with their chibouques and their cimeters a zeal for the cause of Turkey which did not fail to find utterance in Parliament. In process of time the accumulated counsels of these travelers, coming in aid of diplomatists and statesmen, put straight the deflection which had been caused by a romantic sympathy with the Greek insurgents, and it may be said that after the year 1833 the Eastern policy of England was brought back into its ancient channel.

Abroad, no one doubted that the maintenance of the Sultan's authority at Constantinople was of high concern to England; and indeed the bearing of the Eastern question upon English interests seemed even more clear and obvious to foreigners than to the bulk of our countrymen at home. At this time Lord John Russell was the Prime Minister; and the Secretary of State for Foreign Affairs was Lord Palmerston. It is true that during the last Russian invasion of Turkey in 1828 Lord Palmerston, then out of office, had taken part with Russia; but from the period of the Treaty of Unkiar Skelessi in 1833 he had not swerved from the traditions of the Foreign Office; and upon the whole there was no fair ground for believing that under his counsels, and under the sanction of the then Prime Minister, Lord Aberdeen's acquiescent policy of 1829 would again be followed by England. It is true that strange doctrines were afloat; but after 1833 the Government had not forgotten that England was one of the great Powers of Europe, and had never confessed by any unpardonable inaction that this height and standing in the world gave their country mere rank and celebrity without corresponding duties. Upon the whole, there was not at this time any sound reason for doubting that England would pursue her accustomed policy with due resolution. Thus Europe was in repose; for in general, when the world believes that England will be firm, there is peace; it is the hope of her proving weak or irresolute which tends to breed war.

Of the lesser States of Europe.

Of the lesser States of Europe, there were some which, in the event of a war, might lean toward Russia; and more which would lean against her; and the divided opinion of the minor Courts of Germany might be reckoned upon by the Czar as tending to hamper the action of the leading States; but, upon the whole, the interests of the lesser Powers of Europe and the means of action at their command were not of such a kind as to exert much weight in retarding or accelerating Russian schemes of encroachment upon Turkey.

This was the quiet aspect of Europe in relation to the Eastern question when an ancient quarrel between the monks of the Greek and Latin Churches in Palestine began to extend to laymen and politicians, and even at last to endanger the peace of the world.

---

## CHAPTER III.

THE mystery of holy shrines lies deep in human nature. For, however the more spiritual minds may be able to rise and soar, the common man during his mortal career is tethered to the globe that is his appointed dwelling-place; and the more his affections are pure and holy, the more they seem to blend with the outward and visible world. Poets bringing the gifts of mind to bear upon human feelings have surrounded the image of love with myriads of their dazzling fancies, but it has been said that in every country, when a peasant speaks of his deep love, he always says the same thing. He always utters the dear name, and then only says that he "worships the ground she treads." It seems that where she who holds the spell of his life once touched the earth—where the hills and the wooded glen and the pebbly banks of the stream have in them the enchanting quality that they were seen by him and by her when they were together—there always his memory will cling; and it is in vain that space intervenes, for imagination transcendent and strong of flight can waft him from lands far away till he lights upon the very path by the river's bank which was blessed by her gracious step. Nay, distance will inflame his fancy; for if he be cut off from the sacred ground by the breadth of the ocean, or by vast endless desolate tracts, he comes to know that deep in his bosom there lies a secret desire to journey and journey far, that he may touch with fond lips some mere ledge of rock where once he saw her foot resting. It seems that the impulse does not spring from any designed culture of sentiment, but from an honest earthly passion vouchsafed to the unlettered and the simple-hearted, and giving them strength to pass the mystic border which lies between love and worship. For men strongly moved by the Christian faith it was natural to yearn after the scenes of the Gospel narrative. In old times this feeling

Holy shrines.

had strength to impel the chivalry of Europe to undertake the conquest of a barren and distant land; and although in later days the aggregate faith of the nations grew chill, and Christendom no longer claimed with the sword, still there were always many who were willing to brave toil and danger for the sake of attaining to the actual and visible Sion. These venturesome men came to be called Pelerins or Pilgrims. At first, as it would seem, they were impelled by deep feeling acting upon bold and resolute natures. Holding close to the faith that the Son of God being also in mystic sense the great God himself had for our sakes and for our salvation become a babe, growing up to be an anxious and suffering man, and submitting to be cruelly tortured and killed by the hands of his own creatures, they longed to touch and to kiss the spots which were believed to be the silent witnesses of his life upon earth, and of his cross and passion. And, since also these men were of the Churches which sanctioned the adoration of the Virgin, they were taught alike, by their conception of duty and by nature's low whispering voice, to touch and to kiss the holy ground where Mary, pure and young, was ordained to become the link between God and the race of fallen man. And, because the rocky land abounded in recesses and caves yielding shelter against sun and rain, it was possible for the Churches to declare, and very easy for trustful men to believe, that a hollow in a rock at Bethlehem was the Manger which held the infant Redeemer, and that a Grotto at Nazareth was the very home of the blessed Virgin.

Priests fastened upon this sentiment, and although in its beginning their design was not sordid, they found themselves driven by the course of events to convert the alluring mystery of the Holy Places into a source of revenue. The Mahometan invaders had become by conquest the lords of the ground; but, since their own creed laid great stress upon the virtue of pilgrimage to holy shrines, they willingly entered into the feeling of the Christians who came to kneel in Palestine. Moreover, they respected the self-denial of monks, and it was found that even in turbulent times a convent in Palestine surrounded by a good wall, and headed by a clever Superior, could generally hold its own. It was to establishments of this kind that the pilgrim looked for aid and hospitality, and in order to keep them up the priests imagined the plan of causing the votary to pay according to his means at every shrine which he embraced. Upon the understanding that he fulfilled that condition he was led to believe that he won for himself unspeakable privileges in the world to come, and thenceforth a pilgrimage to the holy shrines ceased to be an expression of enthusiastic sentiment, and became a common act of devotion.

But, since it happened that, because of the manner in which the toll was levied, every one of the Holy Places was a distinct source of revenue, the prerogative of the Turks as owners of the ground was necessarily brought into play, and it rested with them to determine which of the rival Churches should have the control and usufruct of every holy shrine. Here then was a subject of lasting strife. So long as the Ottoman Empire was in its full strength, the authorities at Constantinople were governed in their decisions by the common appliances of intrigue, and most chiefly, no doubt, by gold; but when the power of the Sultans so waned as to make it needful for them to contract engagements with Christian sovereigns, the monks of one or other of the Churches found means to get their suit upheld by foreign intervention. In 1740, France obtained from the Sultan a grant which had the force of a treaty, and its Articles or "Capitulations," as they were sometimes called, purported to confirm and enlarge all the then existing privileges of the Latin Church in Palestine. But this success was not closely pursued, for in the course of the succeeding hundred years the Greeks keenly supported by Russia obtained from the Turkish Government several firmans which granted them advantages in derogation of the treaty with France; and until the middle of this century France acquiesced.

Contest for the possession of the shrines.

Patronage of Foreign Powers.

In the contest now about to be raised between France and Russia, it would be wrong to suppose that, so far as concerned strength of motive and sincerity of purpose, there was any approach to an equality between the contending Governments. In the Greek Church the right of pilgrimage is held to be of such deep import that if a family can command the means of journeying to Palestine even from the far distant provinces of Russia, they can scarcely remain in the sensation of being truly devout without undertaking the holy enterprise; and to this end the fruits of parsimony and labor enduring through all the best years of manhood are joyfully devoted. The compassing of vast distances with the narrow means at the command of a peasant is not achieved without suffering so great as to destroy many lives. This danger does not deter the brave, pious people of the North. As the reward of their sacrifices, their priests, speaking boldly in the name of Heaven, promise them ineffable blessings. The advantages held out are not understood to be dependent upon the volition and motive of the pil-

Comparison between the claims of Russia and France.

grim, for they hold good, as baptism does, for children of tender years. Of course every man who thus came from afar to the Church of the Holy Sepulchre was the representative of many more who would do the like if they could. When the Emperor of Russia sought to gain or to keep for his Church the holy shrines of Palestine, he spoke on behalf of fifty millions of brave, pious, devoted subjects, of whom thousands for the sake of the cause would joyfully risk their lives. From the serf in his hut even up to the great Czar himself, the faith professed was the faith really glowing in the heart, and violently swaying the will. It was the part of wise statesmen to treat with much deference an honest and pious desire which was rooted thus deep in the bosom of the Russian people.

On the other hand, the Latin Church seems not to have inculcated pilgrimage so earnestly as its Eastern rival; and if it did, it obtained but slight compliance with its precept, for whilst the Greek pilgrim ships poured out upon the landing-place of Jaffa the multitudes of those who had survived the misery and the trials of the journey, the closest likeness of a pilgrim which the Latin Church could supply was often a mere French tourist, with a journal and a theory, and a plan of writing a book. It was true that the French Foreign Office had from time to time followed up those claims to protect the Latin Church in the East which had arisen in the times when the mistresses of the Most Christian kings were pious; but it was understood that by the course of her studies in the eighteenth century France had obtained a tight control over her religious feelings. Whenever she put forward a claim in her character as 'the eldest daughter of the Church,' men treated her demand as political, and dealt with it accordingly; but as to the religious pretension on which it was based, Europe always met that with a smile. Yet it will presently be seen that a claim which tried the gravity of diplomatists might be used as a puissant engine of mischief.

Measures taken by the French President.

There was repose in the empire of the Sultan, and even the rival Churches of Jerusalem were suffering each other to rest, when the French President, in cold blood, and under no new motive for action, took up the forgotten cause of the Latin Church of Jerusalem, and began to apply it as a wedge for sundering the peace of the world.

The French Ambassador at Constantinople was instructed to demand that the grants to the Latin Church which were contained in the treaty of 1740 should be strictly executed, and, since the firmans granted during the last century to the

Greek Church were inconsistent with the capitulations of 1740, and had long been in actual operation, the effect of this demand on the part of the French President was to force the Sultan to disturb the existing state of repose, to annul the privileges which (with the acquiescence of France) the Greek Church had long been enjoying, to drive into frenzy the priesthood of the Greek Church, and to rouse to indignation the Sovereign of the great military empire of the North, with all those millions of pious and devoted men who so far as regarded this question were heart and soul with their Czar. 'The Ambas-'sador of France,' said our Foreign Secretary, 'was the first to 'disturb the status quo in which the matter rested. Not that 'the disputes of the Latin and Greek Churches were not very 'active, but that without some political action on the part of 'France those quarrels would never have troubled the relations 'of friendly Powers. If report is to be believed, the French 'Ambassador was the first to speak of having recourse to force, 'and to threaten the intervention of a French fleet to enforce 'the demands of his country. We should deeply regret any 'dispute that might lead to conflict between two of the great 'Powers of Europe; but when we reflect that the quarrel is 'for exclusive privileges in a spot near which the heavenly 'host proclaimed peace on earth and good-will toward men—'when we see rival Churches contending for mastery in the 'very place where Christ died for mankind—the thought of 'such a spectacle is melancholy indeed. . . . . . Both parties 'ought to refrain from putting armies and fleets in motion for 'the purpose of making the tomb of Christ a cause of quarrel 'among Christians.'[1]

Still, in a narrow and technical point of view, the claim of France might be upheld, because it was based upon a treaty between France and the Porte which could not be legally abrogated without the consent of the French Government, and the concessions to the Greek Church, though obtained at the instance of Russia, had not been put into the form of treaty engagements, and could always be revoked at the pleasure of the Sultan. Accordingly M. de Lavalette continued to press for the strict fulfillment of the treaty, and being guided, as it would seem, by violent instructions, and being also zealous and unskilled, he soon carried his urgency to the extremity of using offensive threats, and began to speak of what should be done by the French fleet. The Russian Envoy, better versed in affairs, used wiser but hardly less cogent

By the Russian Envoy.

[1] 'Eastern Papers,' part i., p. 67.

words, requiring that the firmans should remain in force; and, since no ingenuity could reconcile the engagements of the treaty with the grants contained in the firmans, the Porte, though having no interest of its own in the question, was tortured and alarmed by the contending negotiators. It seemed almost impossible to satisfy France without affronting the Emperor Nicholas.

Embarrassment of the Porte.

The French, however, did not persist in claiming up to the very letter of the treaty of 1740, and, on the other hand, there were some of the powers of exclusion granted by the firmans which the Greeks could be persuaded to forego; and thus the subject remaining in dispute was narrowed down until it seemed almost too slender for the apprehension of laymen.

Mutual concessions.

Stated in bare terms, the question was whether, for the purpose of passing through the building into their Grotto, the Latin monks should have the key of the chief door of the Church of Bethlehem, and also one of the keys of each of the two doors of the sacred manger,[1] and whether they should be at liberty to place in the sanctuary of the Nativity a silver star adorned with the arms of France. The Latins also claimed a privilege of worshiping once a year at the shrine of the Blessed Mary in the Church of Gethsemane, and they went on to assert their right to have 'a cupboard and a lamp in the tomb of the Virgin,' but in this last pretension they were not well supported by France,[2] and virtually, it was their claim to have a key of the great door of the Church of Bethlehem instead of being put off with a key of the lesser door which long remained insoluble, and had to be decided by the advance of armies,[3] and the threatening movement of fleets.

The actual subject of dispute.

Diplomacy, somewhat startled at the nature of the question committed to its charge, but repressing the coarse emotion of surprise, 'ventured,' as it is said, 'to inquire whether in this case 'a key meant an instrument for opening a door, only not to be 'employed in closing that door against Christians of other 'sects, or whether it was simply a key—an emblem;'[4] but Diplomacy answered, that the key was really a key—a key for opening a door, and its evil quality was—not that it kept the Greeks out, but that it let the Latins come in.

After the change which was wrought in the institutions of France in the night between the 1st and the 2nd of December, 1851, increased violence seems to have been imparted to

1 'Eastern Papers,' part i., p. 84.
2 Ibid., p. 48.
3 See Count Nesselrode's Dispatches, ibid., p. 61.
4 Ibid., p. 79.

Increased violence of the French Government.

the instructions under which M. de Lavalette was acting, and his demand was so urgently pressed, that the Porte at length gave way, and acknowledged the validity of the Latin claims in a formal Note;[1] but the paper had not been signed more than a few days, when the Russian Minister, making hot remonstrance, caused the Porte to issue a firman,[2] ratifying all the existing privileges of the Greeks, and virtually revoking the acknowledgment just given to the Latins. Thereupon, as was natural, the French Government became indignant, and to escape its anger the Porte promised to evade the public reading of the firman at Jerusalem;[3] but, the Russian Minister not relaxing his zeal, the Turkish Government secretly promised him that the Pasha of Jerusalem should be instructed to try to avoid giving up the keys to the Latin monks.

Afif Bey's Mission.

Then again, under further pressure by France, the Porte engaged to evade this last evasion, and at length the duty of affecting to carry out the conflicting engagements thus made by the Porte was intrusted to Afif Bey. This calm Mahometan went to Jerusalem, and strove to temporize as well as he could betwixt the angry Churches. His great difficulty was to avert the rage which the Greeks would be likely to feel when they came to know that the firman was not to be read; and the nature of his little stratagem showed that, although he was a benighted Moslem, he had some insight into the great ruling principle of ecclesiastical questions. His plan was to inflict a bitter disappointment upon the Latins in the presence of the Greek priesthood, for he imagined that in their delight at witnessing the mortification of their rivals, the Greeks might be made to overlook the great question of the public reading of the firman. So, as soon as the ceremonial visits had been exchanged, Afif Bey, with a suite of the local Effendis, met the three Patriarchs, Greek, Latin, and Armenian, in the Church of the Resurrection just in front of the Holy Sepulchre itself and under the great dome, and there he 'made an oration upon the desire of his Majesty the Sultan to 'gratify all classes of his subjects,' and when M. Basily and the Greek Patriarch and the Russian Archimandrite were becoming impatient for the public reading of the firman which was to give to their Church the whole of the Christian sanctuaries of Jerusalem, the Bey invited all the disputants to meet him in the Church of the Virgin near Gethsemane. There he read

[1] Note of the 9th February, 1852.

[2] The firman of the mi-fevrier, 1852.

[3] Col. Rose to Lord Malmesbury. 'Eastern Papers,' part i., p. 46.

an order of the Sultan for permitting the Latins to celebrate a mass once a year, but then to the great joy of the Greeks, and to the horror of their rivals, he went on to read words, commanding that the altar and its ornaments should remain undisturbed. 'No sooner,' says the official account, 'were these 'words uttered, than the Latins, who had come to receive their 'triumph over the Orientals, broke out into loud exclamations 'of the impossibility of celebrating mass upon a schismatic 'slab of marble with a covering of silk and gold, instead of 'plain linen, among schismatic vases, and before a crucifix 'which has the feet separated, instead of one nailed over the 'other.' Under cover of the storm thus raised, Afif Bey perhaps thought for a moment that he had secured his escape, and for a while he seems to have actually disentangled himself from the Churches, and to have succeeded in gaining his quarters.

But when the delight of witnessing the discomfiture of the Latins had in some degree subsided, the Greeks perceived that, after all, the main promise had been evaded. The firman had not been read. M. Basily, the Russian Consul-General, called on Afif Bey, and required that the reading of the firman should take place. At first the Bey affected not to know what firman was meant, but afterward he said he had no copy of it; and at length, being then at the end of his stratagems, he acknowledged that he had no instructions to read it. Thereupon M. Basily sent off Prince Garari to Jaffa to convey these tidings to Constantinople in any Arab vessel that could be found, and then hurrying to the Pasha of Jerusalem, he demanded to have a special council assembled, with himself and the Greek Patriarch in attendance, in order that Russia and the Orthodox Church might know once for all whether the firman had been sent or not; but when the meeting was gathered, Hafiz Pasha only 'made a smooth speech on the well-known benevolence 'of his Majesty toward all classes of his subjects, and that was all that could be said.'[1] So the Greeks, though they had been soothed for a moment by the discomfiture of their Latin adversaries in the Church of the Virgin, could not any longer fail to see that their rivals were in the ascendant, and it soon turned out that the promise to evade the delivery of the keys was not to be faithfully kept.

The pressure of France was applied with increasing force, and it produced its effect. In the month of December, 1852, the silver star was brought with much

Delivery of the key and the star.

[1] Consul Finn to Earl of Malmesbury, Oct. 27, 1852. 'Correspondence,' part i., p. 44.

pomp from the coast. Some of the Moslem Effendis went down to Jaffa to escort it, and others rode out a good way on the road that they might bring it into Jerusalem with triumph; and on Wednesday, the 22nd of the same month, the Latin patriarch, with joy and with a great ceremony, replaced the glittering star in the sanctuary of Bethlehem, and at the same time the key of the great door of the church, together with the keys of the sacred manger, was handed over to the Latins.[1]

Indignation of Russia.

For the Czar and for the devout people of All the Russias it was hard to bear this blow. 'To the indignation,' Count Nesselrode writes, 'of the whole people following the Greek ritual, the key of the Church of Bethlehem 'has been made over to the Latins, so as publicly to demonstrate their religious supremacy in the East. The mischief 'then is done, M. le Baron, and there is no longer any question 'of preventing it. It is now necessary to remedy it. The immunities of the Orthodox religion which have been injured, 'the promise which the Sultan had solemnly given to the Emperor, and which has been violated, call for an act of reparation. It is to obtain this that we must labor. If we took for 'our example the imperious and violent proceedings which 'have brought France to this result, if like her we were indifferent to the dignity of the Porte, to the consequences which 'an heroic remedy may have on a constitution already so shattered as that of the Ottoman Empire, our course would be 'already marked out for us, and we should not have long to 'reflect upon it. Menace, and a resort to force would be our 'immediate means. The cannon has been called the last argument of kings, the French Government has made it its first. 'It is the argument with which at the outset it declared its 'intention to commence its proceedings at Tripoli as well as at 'Constantinople. Notwithstanding our legitimate causes of 'complaint, and at the risk of waiting some time longer for 'redress, we shall take a less summary course. . . . It may 'happen that France, perceiving any hesitation on the part of 'the Porte, may again have recourse to menace, and press upon 'it so as to prevent it from listening to our just demands. . . . 'The Emperor has therefore considered it necessary to adopt 'in the outset some precautionary measures in order to support 'our negotiations, to neutralize the effect of M. Lavalette's 'threats, and to guard himself in any contingency which may 'occur against a Government accustomed to act by surprises.'[2]

[1] Consul Finn to Earl of Malmesbury, Dec. 28, 1852; but see Mr. Pisani's note, p. 106.

[2] Count Nesselrode to Baron Brunnow, 14th January, 1853. Ibid., p. 61.

Nor were these empty words. The same authentic page[1] which tells of this triumph of Church over Church goes on to show how the Czar was preparing for vengeance. 'Orders,' says Sir Hamilton Seymour, 'have been 'dispatched to the 5th corps d'armée to advance to the fron- 'tiers of the Danubian provinces, without waiting for their 'reserves, and the 4th corps, under the command of General 'Count Dannenberg, and now stationed in Volhynia, will be 'ordered to hold itself in readiness to march if necessary. 'General Luder's corps d'armée, accordingly, being now 48,000 'strong, will receive a re-enforcement of 24,000 men soon after 'its arrival at its destination, and, supposing the 4th corps to 'follow, the whole force will amount at least, according to offi- 'cial returns, to 144,000 men.'

Advance of Russian forces.

Is it true that for this cause great armies were gathering, and that for the sake of the key and the silver star the peace of the nations was brought into danger? Had the world grown young once more?

The strife of the Churches was no fable, but after all, though near and distinct, it was only the lesser truth. A crowd of monks with bare foreheads stood quarreling for a key at the sunny gates of a church in Palestine, but beyond and above, towering high in the misty North, men saw the ambition of the Czars.

---

## CHAPTER IV.

MEN dwelling amidst the snows of Russia are driven by very nature to grow covetous when they hear of the happier lands where all the year round there are roses and long sunny days. And since this people have a sea-board and ports on the Euxine, they are forced by an everlasting policy to desire the command of the straits which lead through the heart of an empire into the midst of that world of which men kindle thoughts when they speak of the Ægean and of Greece, and the Ionian shores, and of Palestine and Egypt, and of Italy, and of France, and of Spain and the land of the Moors, and of the Atlantic beyond, and the path of ships on the Ocean. Gifted with the knowledge and the skill which are means of excellence in the diplomatic art, and excluded by their institutions from taking any but an official part in the home Government, the Russian nobles had long

Natural ambition of Russia.

[1] 'Eastern Papers,' part i., p. 56.

been accustomed to bend their minds to foreign policy, and the State, favoring this inclination, used to multiply the labors of its diplomatic service. Almost every gifted and accomplished Russian who might be traveling in foreign countries used to receive instructions of some kind from his Government, and was enabled to believe that, either by collecting information or in some still more important way, he was performing a duty toward the State. Men thus intrusted became eager partakers of a policy rather more enterprising than the policy avowed by their Government, and the result was that the natural ambition of the country was always being nurtured and subserved by a great Aristocracy.

But moreover the ambition of the Statesmen and the Nobles was re-enforced by the pious desire of the humbler classes. Some fifty millions of men in Russia held one creed; and they held it too with the earnestness of which Western Europe used to have experience in earlier times. In her wars Russia had always been engaged against nations which were not of her faith; and twice at least in the very agony of her national life, and when all other hope was gone, she had been rescued by the warlike zeal of her priesthood. By these causes love of country and devotion to the Church had become so closely welded into one engrossing sentiment, that good Muscovites could not sever the one idea from the other;[1] and although they were by nature a kind and good-humored race of men, they were fierce in the matter of their religion. They had heard of Infidels who had torn down the crosses from the Churches of Christ, and possessed themselves of the great city, the capital of the Orthodox Church; and, as far as they could judge, it would be a work of piety, with the permission of the Czar their father, to slaughter and extirpate the Turks. But this was not all. They knew that in the Turkish dominions there were ten or fourteen millions of men holding exactly the same faith as themselves, who were kept down in thraldom by the Moslems, and they had heard tales of the sufferings of these their brethren which seemed to call for vengeance. The very indulgence with which the Turks had allowed these Christians to have a distinct corporate existence in the Empire gave weight to their prayers; for, instead of being only a disorganized multitude of sufferers, they seemed to be, as it were, a suppliant nation, ever kneeling before the great Czar, and imploring him to deliver them from their captivity. It was not pos-

[1] I owe my perception of the causes which rendered the Russian Church so intensely national to Arthur Stanley's most interesting work upon the Greek Church.

sible for the Russian people to conceive any enterprise more worthy of their nation and their Church than to raise high the banner of the Cross, drive the infidel Turks out of Europe, and cause the broad provinces in which their Christian brethren lived and suffered to be blended with 'Holy Russia.' It is true that the Muscovite peasants were not an enterprising race of men, and it might be hard perhaps to find a villager, who, if he could have his choice, would rather be a soldier of the Cross than remain at home in his hut; but the people knew that, whether there were peace or whether there were war, the exigency of their Czar's military system would always go on consuming their youth, and, since this engine of a vast standing army was destined to be kept up and to be fed with their flesh and blood, they desired in their simple hearts that it should be used for a purpose which they believed to be holy and righteous. To a cause having all these sanctions, the voice of prophecy could not be wanting. Seers foretold the destruction of the Turks by the men of the yellow hair.

Yet, vast as it was in its aggregate force, the heart's desire of a whole nation would have been vague and dim of sight if it had not some famed city for its goal, or some outward and visible figure or sign to which the multitude could point as the symbol of its great intent. The people were not without their goal nor without their symbol, for the city whither they tended was the imperial city of Constantine, once mistress of the world, and the Cross that the Emperor had seen in the heavens was still the sign in which the Church said they must conquer. For such as were the politic few there was the Golden Horn with its command of the Bosphorus and the Dardanelles, and all its fair promise of wealth and empire. In the horizon of the pious multitude there rose the dome of St. Sophia. Ambition was sanctified by Religion. The most pious might righteously desire that the devotion of their militant Church should be aided by the wisdom of the serpent, and the most worldly-minded statesman could look with approval upon the scheme of a lucrative crusade. The Emperor Alexander the First, when he declared that for the time he was trying to withstand the ambition of his people, acknowledged that he was 'the only Russian who resisted the views of his subjects upon 'Turkey.'[1]

The Czar was the head of the Church. It was not without raising scruples in the minds of the pious that his predecessors had been able to attain ecclesiastical authority; but this shad-

[1] Quoted by Sir H. Seymour, 'Eastern Papers,' part v., p. 11.

ow of doubt upon the title of the lay Pontiff made it all the more needful for him to take care that his zeal should be above reproach. It is true that the great body of the Muscovite people were simple and docile, not partaking in cares of Government, and that even among the most powerful Nobles there were none who would be unwilling to leave the choice of time and of measures to the Chief of the State, but still the religious mind of the vast empire would have been dangerously shocked if the priests had been forced to know that the Czar failed to share the pious desire of his people; and the minds of men accustomed to bend their thoughts to the aggrandizement of the nation would be overclouded and chilled if they saw that the Emperor was growing forgetful of their favorite cause.

But the prospect of what would follow upon the realization of this scheme of ambition was dim. The sovereignty of European Turkey could scarcely be added to the possessions of the Czar without tending to dislocate the system of his empire, for plainly it would be difficult to sway the vast Northern territories of All the Russias by orders sent from the Bosphorus, and yet, by force of its mere place in the world, Constantinople seemed destined to be the capital of a great State. Therefore, in the event of its falling into the hands of the Romanoffs, it may be thought more likely that the imperial city would draw dominion to itself, and so become the metropolis of some new assemblage of territories than that it would sink into the condition of a provincial sea-port. The statesmen of St. Petersburg have always understood the deep import of the change which the throne of Constantine would bring with it; and it may be imagined that considerations founded on this aspect of the enticing conquest have mingled with those suggested by the physical difficulties of invasion, the obstinate valor of the Turks, and the hostility of the great Powers of Europe. Still, the prize was so unspeakably alluring to an aristocracy fired with national ambition, and to a people glowing with piety, that apparently it was necessary for the Czar to seem as though he were always doing something for furthering a scheme of conquest thus endeared to the nation. He was liable to be deemed a failing champion of the faith when he was not laboring to restore the insulted Cross to the Church of Constantine; he was chilling the healthy zeal of his ablest servants if he lived idle days making no approach to the Bosphorus.

Upon the whole, it resulted from the various motives tending to govern the policy of the State that the ambition of the Russian emperors in the direction of

Its irresolute nature.

Constantinople was generally alive and watchful, and sometimes active, but was always irresolute. The First Napoleon said in the early years of this century[1] that the Czars were always threatening Constantinople and never taking it; and what he said then had already been true for a long time, and his words continued to be a true description of the Russian policy for half a century afterward. Evidently it answered the purpose of the Czars to have it thought amongst their own people that they were steadily advancing toward the conquest, but they always suffered their reasons for delay to prevail. They had two minds upon the question. They were willing, but they were also unwilling, and this clashing of motives caused them to falter. At home they naturally tried to make their ambition apparent. Abroad, as might be expected, they were more careful to display the inclinations forced upon them by prudence; but it would seem that this double face was not simply a deceptive contrivance, but resulted from imperfect volition. The project against Constantinople was a scheme of conquest continually to be delayed, but never discarded, and, happen what might, it was never to be endured that the prospect of Russia's attaining some day to the Bosphorus should be shut out by the ambition of any other Power.

Of course it followed that a great State ambition of this watchful but irresolute kind would be stimulated to an increased activity by the disappearance of any of the chief obstacles lying in the way of the enterprise; and especially this would be the case whenever the course of affairs seemed to be unfavorable to an alliance against Russia between the other great Powers of Europe.

The Emperor Nicholas.

The Emperor Nicholas held an absolute sway over his Empire, and his power was not moderated by the salutary resistance of ministers who had strength enough to decline to take part in acts which they disapproved. The old restraints which used sometimes to fetter the power of the Russian monarchs had fallen away, and nothing had yet come in their stead. Holding the boundless authority of an Oriental Potentate, the Czar was armed besides with all the power which is supplied by high organization and the clever appliances of modern times. What he chose to do he actually did. He might be sitting al[illegible]nd reading a dispatch, and if it happened that its contents made him angry, he could touch a bell and kindle a war without hearing counsel from any living man. In the room where he labored he could hear over-

[1] 'La Russie a trop menacé Constantinople sans le prendre.'

head the clicking of machinery, and he liked the sound of the restless magnets, for they were giving instant effect to his will in regions far away. He was of a stern, unrelenting nature. He displayed, when he came to be tried, a sameness of ideas and of language and a want of resource which indicated poverty of intellect; but this dearth within was masked by the brilliancy of the qualities which adorned the surface, and he was so capable of business, and had such a vast activity, that he was able to arrogate to himself an immense share of the actual governance of his subjects. Indeed by striving to extend his management beyond the proper compass of a single mind he disturbed the march of business, and so far superseded the responsibility of his servants, that he ended by lessening to a perilous extent the number of gifted men who in former times had taken part in the counsels of the State. Still, this widely-ranging activity kept alive the awe with which his subjects watched to see where next he would strike; and made the nation feel that, along with his vast stature and his commanding presence, he carried the actual power of the State. He had been merciless toward the Polish nation; but whilst this sternness made him an object of hatred to millions of discomfited men, and to other millions of men who felt for them in their sorrows, it tended, perhaps, at the time to increase his ascendency, by making him an object of dread. And it trebled the delight of being with him in his gentle mood. When he was friendly or chose to seem so, there was a glow and frankness in his manner which had an irresistible charm. He had discarded in some measure his predecessor's system of governing Russia through the aid of foreigners; and took a pride in his own people, and understood their worth. In the great empire of the North religion is closely blended with the national sentiment, and in this composite shape it had a strong hold upon the Czar. It did not much govern him in his daily life, and his way of joining in the service of the Church seemed to disclose something like impatience and disdain, but no one doubted that faith was deeply rooted in his mind. He had the air of a man raised above the level of common worshipers who imagined that he was appointed to serve the cause of his Church by great imperial achievements, and not by humble feats of morality and devotion. It will be seen but too plainly that the Emperor Nicholas could be guilty of saying one thing and doing another, and it may be supposed therefore that at once and in plain terms he ought to be charged with duplicity: yet there are circumstances which make one falter in coming to such a conclusion. He had reigned, and had personally governed for some seven-and-twenty years, and although during that period he had done much to raise bitter hatred, the most sagacious statesmen in Europe placed faith in his personal honor. It is certain that he had the love of truth. When he sought to speak of what he deemed fair and honorable, he traveled into our language for the word which spoke his meaning, and claimed to have the same standard of uprightness as an English 'gentleman.' It is known also that his ideal of human grandeur was the character of the Duke of Wellington. No man could have made that choice without having truth in him.

It would seem, however, that beneath the virtues which for more than a quarter of a century had enabled the Czar to stand before Europe as a man of honor and truth there lurked a set of opposite qualities; and that when he reached the period of life which has often been found a trying one to men of the Romanoff family, a deterioration began to take place which shook the ascendant of his better nature. After the beginning of 1853 there were strange alternations in his conduct. At one time he seemed to be so frank and straightforward that the most wary statesmen could not and would not believe him to be intending deceit. Then, and even within a few hours, he would steal off and be false. But the vice which he disclosed in those weak intervals was not the profound deceit of statecraft, but rather the odd purposeless cunning of a gipsy or a savage, who shows by some sudden and harmless sign of his wild blood that even after years of conformity to European ways he has not been completely reclaimed. For the present, however, the Emperor Nicholas must be looked upon not merely as he was, but as he seemed to be; and what he seemed to be in the beginning of 1853 was a firm righteous man too brave and too proud to be capable of descending to falsehood.

Nicholas had a violent will; but of course when he underwent the change which robbed him of his singleness of mind, his resolves, notwithstanding their native force, could not fail to lose their momentum. He was a man too military to be warlike; and was not only without the qualities for wielding an army in the field, but was mistaken also as to the way in which the best soldiers are made: under his sway Russia was so oppressively drilled that much of the fire and spirit of enterprise which are needed for war was crushed out by military training. No man, however, could toil with more zeal than he did in that branch of industry which seeks to give uniformity and mechanic action to bodies of men. He was an unwearied inspector of troops. He kept close at hand great numbers of small wooden images clothed in various uniforms, and one of the rooms in his favorite palace was filled with these military dolls.

The Emperor Nicholas had not been long upon the throne when he showed that he was a partaker of the ambition of his people; for in 1828 he had begun an invasion of Turkey, and was present with his army in some of the labors of the campaign: but his experience was of a painful kind. The mechanical organization in which he delighted broke down under stress of real war carried on upon an extended line of operations. In the country of the Danube his soldiery perished fast from sickness and want; and although he had so well chosen his time that the Sultan was without an ally, and (having but lately put to death his own army) was in an ill condition for war, still he encountered so much of obstinate and troublesome resistance from the Turks, and was so ill able to cope with it, that at the instance, as it is said, of his own Generals, he retired from the scene of conflict, and went back to St. Petersburg, with the galling knowledge that he was without the gifts which make an able commander in the field; he could not but see, too, that the military reputation of Russia was brought into great peril; and although in the following year he was rescued from the dangerous straits into which he had run by the brilliant audacity of Diebitsch, by the skill of his diplomacy, and above all by indulgent fortune, still he was so chastened by the anxiety of the time, and by the narrowness of his escape from a great humiliation, that he ceased to entertain any hope or intention of dismembering Turkey, except in the event of there occurring a chain of circumstances which should enable him to act with the concurrence of other great Powers.

But the Emperor knew that the pride of his people would be deeply wounded if any great changes should take place in the Ottoman Empire without bringing gain to Russia and accelerating her march to Constantinople; and therefore he believed that, until he was prepared to take a part in dismembering the Empire, it was his interest to preserve it intact. For more than twenty years his actions as well as his declared intentions were in accordance with this view; and it would be wrong to believe that the policy thus shown forth to the world was only a mask. Just as the love of killing game generates a sincere wish to preserve it, so the very fact that the Czar looked upon Turkey as eventual booty, made him anxious to protect it from every other kind of danger. In 1833, the Emperor Nicholas saved the Sultan and his dynasty from destruction; and, although he accompanied this measure with an act offensive to the other maritime powers,[1] his conduct toward Turkey was loyal. In 1840 he again acted faithfully toward the Sultan, and joined with England and the leading Powers of Germany in preventing the disruption of the Ottoman Empire.

In 1844 the Czar came to England, and anxiously strove to find out whether there were any of our leading statesmen who had grown weary of a conservative policy in Turkey. He talked confidentially with the Duke of Wellington and Lord Aberdeen, and also no doubt with Sir Robert Peel; but evidently meeting with no encouragement, he covered his retreat by giving in his adhesion to England's accustomed policy, and, to do this with the better effect, he left in our Foreign Office a solemn declaration not only of his own policy, but likewise, strange to say, of the policy of Austria; and all this he blended in a somewhat curious manner with words which might be read as importing that his views had obtained the sanction of the English Government. It would seem that our Government agreed, as they naturally would, to that part of the Czar's memorandum which was applicable to the existing state of things, and which, in fact, echoed the known opinion of England; and they also assented to the obvious proposition that the event of a breaking up of the Ottoman Empire would make it important for the great Powers to come to an understanding amongst themselves; but it must be certain that the Duke of Wellington, Sir Robert Peel, and Lord Aberdeen refrained, as it is the custom of our Statesmen to do, from all hypothetical engagements. 'Russia and England,' said this Memorandum, 'are mutually penetrated with the conviction, 'that it is for their common interest that the Ottoman Porte 'should maintain itself in the state of independence and of territorial possession which at present constitutes that Empire. 'Being agreed on this principle, Russia and England have an 'equal interest in uniting their efforts in order to keep up the 'existence of the Ottoman Empire, and to avert all the dangers 'which can place in jeopardy its safety. With this object, the 'essential point is to suffer the Porte to live in repose, without 'needlessly disturbing it by diplomatic bickerings, and without interfering, without absolute necessity, in its internal affairs.' Then, after showing that the tendency of the Turkish Government to evade treaties and ill-use its Christian subjects ought to be checked rather by the combined and friendly remonstrance of all the Powers, than by the separate action of

[1] The Treaty of Unkiar Skelessi.

one, the Memorandum proceeded:—'If all the great Powers 'frankly adopt this line of conduct, they will have a well-found-'ed expectation of preserving the existence of Turkey. How-'ever, they must not conceal from themselves how many ele-'ments of dissolution that Empire contains within itself. Un-'foreseen circumstances may hasten its fall. . . . In the uncer-'tainty which hovers over the future, a single fundamental 'idea seems to admit of a really practical application: it is, 'that the danger which may result from a catastrophe in Tur-'key will be much diminished if, in the event of its occurring, 'Russia and England have come to an understanding as to the 'course to be taken by them in common. That understanding 'will be the more beneficial, inasmuch as it will have the full 'assent of Austria. Between her and Russia there exists al-'ready an entire accord.'

His policy from 1829 to 1853.

Upon the whole, it would seem that from the peace of Adrianople down to the beginning of 1853 the state of the Czar's mind upon the Eastern Question was this:—He was always ready to come forward as an eager and almost ferocious defender of his Church, and he deemed this motive to be one of such cogency that views resting on mere policy and prudence were always in danger of being overborne by it; but, in the absence of events tending to bring this fiery principle into action, he was really unwilling to face the troubles which would arise from the dismemberment of Turkey unless he could know beforehand that England would act with him. If he could have obtained any anterior assurance to that effect, he would have tried perhaps to accelerate the disruption of the Sultan's Empire; but, as England always declined to found any engagements upon the hypothesis of a catastrophe which she wished to prevent, the Emperor had probably accustomed himself to believe that Providence did not design to allot to him the momentous labor of governing the fall of the Ottoman Empire. He therefore chose the other alternative, and not only spoke, but really did much for the preservation of an Empire which he was not yet ready to destroy. Still, whenever any subject of irritation occurred, the attractive force of the opposite policy was more or less felt, for it is not every man, who, having to choose between two lines of action, can resolve to hold to the one and frankly discard the other. In general, the principle governing such a conflict is found to be analogous to the law which determines the composition of mechanic forces, and the mental struggle does not result in a clear adoption of either of the alternatives, but in a mean betwixt the two. It was thus with the Emperor Nicholas whenever it happened that he was irritated by questions connected with the action of the Turkish Government. At such times, his conduct, swayed in one direction by the notion of dismembering the Empire, and in the other direction by the policy of maintaining it, resulted in an endeavor to establish what the English Ambassador called 'a predominant influence over the counsels 'of the Porte, tending in the interest of absolute power to exclude all other influences, and to secure the means, if not of 'hastening the downfall of the Empire, at least of obstructing 'its improvement and settling its future destinies to the profit 'of Russia, whenever a propitious juncture should arrive.'[1]

---

## CHAPTER V.

Troubles in Montenegro.

IT happened that at a time[2] when the Emperor of Russia was wrought to anger by the triumph of the Latin over the Greek Church, there were troubles in one of the provinces bordering upon the Austrian territory, and Omar Pasha, at the head of a Turkish force, was operating against the Christians in Montenegro. The continuance of this strife on her frontier was, no doubt, alarming and vexatious to Austria; but with the Emperor Nicholas the tidings of a conflict going on between a Moslem soldiery and a Christian people of the Greek faith could not fail to kindle his religious zeal, and cause him to thirst for vengeance against the enemies of his Church. Of course the existence of this feeling on the part of the Czar was well understood at Vienna, and it was probably in order to anticipate his wishes and to remove his motives for interference that the Austrian Cabinet determined to address a peremptory summons to the Porte calling upon the Sultan to withdraw his forces immediately from Montenegro. The Czar secretly but studiously represented that upon this and every other matter touching his policy in Turkey he was in close accord with Austria.[3] This, however, the Austrian Government denies. Truthful men declare that the Czar was not even informed beforehand of the demand which Austria had resolved to press upon the Porte. It is certain, however, that the Czar determined to act as though he were in close concert with Austria. Count Leiningen was to be the bearer of the Austrian summons, and simultaneously

Count Leiningen's mission.

[1] 'Eastern Papers,' part i., p. 237. [2] The winter of 1852–3.
[3] 'Eastern Papers,' part v., in several places.

with the Count's departure from Vienna, the Emperor Nicholas resolved to dispatch to the Porte an Ambassador Extraordinary, who was to declare that a refusal to withdraw Omar Pasha's forces from Montenegro would be regarded by the Czar as a ground of war between him and the Sultan; and the Ambassador was also to be charged with the duty of obtaining redress for the change which had been made in the allotment of the Holy Sites to the contending Churches. It may seem strange that the Czar should propose to found a declaration of war upon a grievance which was put forward by the Cabinet of Vienna and not by himself, but he was always eager to stand forward as the protector of Christians of his own Church who had taken up arms against their Moslem rulers; and when, as now, his conservative policy was disturbed by anger and religious zeal, his ulterior views upon the Eastern Question became too vague, and also no doubt too alarming, to admit of their being made the subject of a treaty engagement with Austria.

The Czar's plan of sending another mission to the Porte at the same time.

Apparently, then, the plan of the Emperor Nicholas was this:—he would make the rejection of Count Leiningen's demand a ground of war against the Porte, and then acting under the blended motives furnished by the assigned cause of war and by his own separate grievance, he would avenge the wrong done to his Church by forcing the Sultan to submit to a foreign protectorate over all his provinces lying north of the Balkan. This, however, was only one view of the contemplated war. It might be applicable, if the occupation of the tributary provinces should evoke no element of trouble except the sheer resistance of the enemy; but the Czar, who did not well understand the Turkish Empire, was firmly convinced at this time that the approach of war would be followed by a rising of the Sultan's Christian subjects. On the other hand he feared, and with better reason, that if the angry Moslems should deem the Sultan remiss or faint-hearted in the defense of his territory, they might rise against their Government, and fall upon the Christian rayahs, whom they would regard as the abettors of the invasion. He could not fail to perceive that in the progress of the contemplated operations he might be forced by events to give a vast extension to his views against the Sultan, and that, even against his will, and without being prepared for the crisis, he might find himself called upon to deal with the ruins of the Ottoman Empire in the midst of confusion and massacre.

Plans of the Emperor Nicholas.

# CHAPTER VI.

Now therefore it became needful for the Emperor Nicholas to endeavor to divine the temper in which the other great Powers of Europe would be inclined to regard his intended pressure upon the Sultan and the eventual catastrophe which, even if he should wish it, he might soon be unable to avert. It was of deep moment to him to know what help or acquiescence he might reckon upon, and what hostility he might have to encounter, if he should be called upon to take part in regulating the collapse of the Turkish Empire, and controlling the arrangements which were to follow.

Position of Austria in regard to Turkey at the beginning of 1853.

He looked around. The policy of one of the great States of Europe was bent out of its true course, and in others there were signs of weak purpose. The Power most deeply interested in preventing the dismemberment of European Turkey had already determined to press upon the Sultan an unjust and offensive demand, and although the statesmen of Vienna might have resolved in their own minds to stop short at some prescribed stage of the contemplated hostilities, it was plain that Austria, when once engaged in war against the Sultan, would lose the standing ground of a Power which undertakes to resist change, and would become so entangled by the mere progress of events, that it would be difficult for her to extricate herself, and revert to a conservative policy. Indeed the Emperor Nicholas might fairly expect that Austria, having committed the original mistake of disturbing the peace, would afterward strive to cling to his friendship in the hope of being able to moderate his course of action, and avert or mitigate the downfall of the Turkish Empire.

Of Prussia.

With respect to Prussia, the Emperor Nicholas was free from anxiety. As long as the measures against the Sultan were carried on in alliance with Austria, the States of Germany had little ground for fearing that the interest which they had in the freedom of the Lower Danube would be forgotten; and, this object being secured or regarded as secure, Prussia had less interest in the fate of the Ottoman Empire than any of the other great Powers. There being therefore no reason of state obliging him to take a contrary course, it was to be expected that the King of Prussia would continue to live under the ascendency which his Imperial brother-in-law had long been accustomed to maintain.

Of France.

France having great military and naval forces, and a Mediterranean sea-board, was well entitled to frame for herself any honest system of policy which she might deem to be the best guide for her conduct in Eastern affairs, but the time for her having a policy of her own had passed away; for she had fallen under the mere control of the Second Bonaparte, and in order to divine what France would do, it was necessary to make out what scheme of action her ruler would deem to be most conducive to his comfort and safety. Even the supposition that he would copy the First Napoleon gave no sufficing clew for saying what his Eastern policy ought to be, or what it was, or what it was likely to be in any future week. France as wielded by a Bonaparte had been known to the Sultan, sometimes as a friendly Power, sometimes as a Power pretending to be friendly to him, but secretly bargaining for the dismemberment of his empire; sometimes as a mere predatory State seizing his provinces in time of peace and without the pretense of a quarrel,[1] and sometimes even as a rival Mahometan Power, for it is known that the First Bonaparte did not scruple to call himself in Egypt a true Mussulman;[2] and although he now and then claimed to be 'the eldest son of 'the Catholic Church,' he first introduced himself in the Levant as the soldier of a nation which had 'renounced the Messiah.'

Upon the whole, there seemed to be no reason why the new French Emperor should refuse to join with Russia in trying to bring about the dismemberment of the Turkish Empire, and to arrange the distribution of the spoil. Indeed, the great extension which France had given of late to her navy rendered views of this kind less chimerical than they were at the time of the Secret Articles of Tilsit. But, on the other hand, it was the French Government which had provoked the religious excitement under which Nicholas was laboring, and although it is believed that when his troubles increased upon him the Czar afterward made overtures to France, it would seem that in the beginning of 1853 he was too angry and too scornful toward the French Emperor to be able to harbor the thought of making him his ally. Of the danger lest France should suddenly adopt a conservative policy, and undertake to resist his arrangements in the East of Europe, the Emperor Nicholas made light,

[1] *e. g.* Bonaparte's predatory invasion of Egypt in time of peace.

[2] A falsified copy of the manifesto was sent to France. The one really issued represented Bonaparte as a Mahometan.

for he had resolved at this time not to place himself in conflict with England, and, the operations of any Western Power in Turkey being dependent upon sea communications, he did not think it to be within the wide compass of possible events that France, single-handed and without the alliance of her maritime neighbor, would or could obstruct him in the Levant. 'He 'cared,' he said, 'very little what line the French might think 'proper to take in Eastern affairs, and he had apprised the 'Sultan that if his assistance were required for resisting the 'menaces of the French it was entirely at the service of the 'Sultan.'[1] 'When we (Russia and England) are agreed, I am 'quite without anxiety as to the West of Europe: it is imma-'terial what the others may think or do.'[2]

Of England. Seeming state of opinion there.

There remained then only England, and upon the whole it had come to this: that the Emperor Nicholas would feel able to meet the emergency caused by the downfall of the Sultan, and might perhaps be inclined to do a little toward bringing about the catastrophe, if beforehand he could come to an understanding with the English Government as to the way in which Europe should deal with the fragments of the Turkish Empire. But he had learned, as he said, that an alliance with England must depend upon the feeling of the country at large,[3] and this he strove hard to understand.

England had long been an enigma to the political students of the Continent, but after the summer of 1851 they began to imagine that they really at last understood her. They thought that she was falling from her place among nations; and indeed there were signs which might well lead a shallow observer to fancy that her ancient spirit was failing her. An army is but the limb of a nation, and it is no more given to a people to combine the possession of military strength with an unmeasured devotion to the arts of peace than it is for a man to be feeble and helpless in the general condition of his body, and yet to have at his command a strong right arm for the convenience of self-defense. The strength of the right arm is as the strength of the man: the prowess of an army is as the valor and warlike spirit of the nation which gives it her flesh and blood. England having suffered herself to grow forgetful of this truth, seemed in the eyes of foreigners to be declining. It was not the reduction of the military and establishments which was the really evil sign: for — to say nothing of ancient times — the Swiss in Europe, and some of the States of the North American continent, have shown the world that a people which al-

[1] 'Eastern Papers,' part v., p. 10. [2] Ibid., p. 1. [3] Ibid., part iii.

most dispenses with a standing army, may yet be among the most resolute and warlike of nations; but there was in England a general decrying of arms. Well-meaning men harangued and lectured in this spirit. What they sincerely desired was a continuance of peace; but instead of taking the thought and acquiring the knowledge which might have qualified them to warn their fellow-countrymen against steps tending to a needless war, they squandered their indignation upon the deceased authors of former wars, and used language of such breadth that what they said was as applicable to one war as to another. At length they generated a sect called the 'Peace Party,' which denounced war in strong indiscriminate terms.

Moreover at this time extravagant veneration was avowed for mechanical contrivances, and the very words which grateful nations had wrought from out of their hearts in praise of tried chiefs and heroes were plundered, as it were, from the warlike professions, and given to those who for their own gain could make the best goods. It was no longer enough to say that an honest tradesman was a valuable member of society, or that a man who contrived a good machine was ingenious. More was expected from those who had the utterance of the public feeling, and it was announced that 'glory' and 'honor' —nay, to prevent all mistake, 'true honor' and 'true glory' were due to him who could produce the best articles of trade. At length in the summer of 1851 it was made to appear to foreigners that this singular faith had demanded and obtained an outward sign of its acceptance, and a solemn recognition by Church and State. The foreigners were mistaken. The truth is, that the English in their exuberant strength and their carelessness about the strict import of words are accustomed to indulge a certain extravagance in their demonstrations of public feeling, and this is the more bewildering to foreign minds because it goes along with practical moderation and wisdom. What the English really meant was to give people an opportunity of seeing the new inventions and comparing all kinds of patterns, but above all to have a new kind of show and bring about an immense gathering of people. Perhaps too in the secret hearts of many who were weary of tame life there lurked a hope of animating tumults. This was all the English really meant. But the political philosophers of the Continent were resolved to impute to the islanders a more profound intent. They saw in the festival a solemn renouncing of all such dominion as rests upon force. England, they thought, was closing her great career by a whimsical act of abdication, and it must be acknowledged that there was enough to confound men accustomed to lay stress upon symbols. For the glory of mechanic Arts, and in token of their conquest over nature, a cathedral of glass climbed high over the stately elms of Knightsbridge, inclosing them, as it were, in a casket the work of men's hands, and it was not thought wrong nor impious to give the work the sanction of a religious ceremony. It was by the Archbishop of Canterbury that the money-changers were brought back into the temple. Few protested. One man indeed, abounding in Scripture, and inflamed with the sight of the glass Babel ascending to the skies, stood up, and denounced the work, and foretold "wars" and "judgments."[1] But he was a prophet speaking to the wrong generation, and no one heeded him. Indeed it seemed likely that the soundness of his mind would be questioned, and if he went on to foretell that within three years England would be engaged in a bloody war springing out of a dispute about a key and a silver star, he was probably adjudged to be mad, for the whole country at the time felt sure of its peaceful temper. Certainly it was a hard task for the sagacity of a foreigner to pierce through these outward signs, and see that, notwithstanding them all, the old familiar 'Eastern Question' might be so used as to make it rekindle the warlike ardor of England. Even for Englishmen, until long after the beginning of 1853, it was difficult to foresee how the country would be willing to act in regard to the defense of Turkey, and the representatives of foreign Powers accredited to St. James's might be excused if they assured their Courts that England was deep in pursuits which would hinder her from all due assertion of her will as a great European Power.

Thus foreigners came to believe that the English nature was changed, and that for the future the country would always be tame in Europe, and it chanced that in the beginning of the year 1853 they were strengthened in their faith by observing the structure of the Ministry then recently formed, for Lord Palmerston, whose name had become associated with the idea of a resolute and watchful policy, was banished to the Home Office, and the Prime Minister was Lord Aberdeen, the same statesman who had held the seals of the Foreign Office in former years, when Austria was vainly entreating England to join with her in defending the Sultan. The Emperor Nicholas heard the tidings of Lord Aberdeen's elevation to the premiership with a delight which he did not suppress. Yet this very event, as will be seen, was a main link in the chain of causes

[1] This I witnessed.

which was destined to draw the Czar into war, and bring him in misery to the grave.

But if there was a phantasy in vogue which seemed likely to make England acquiesce in transactions adverse to her accustomed policy in the East, there were other counsels afloat which, although they were based on very different views, seemed to tend in the same direction, for some of our countrymen were beginning to perceive that the restoration of a Bonapartist Empire in France would bring back with it the traditions and the predatory schemes of the First Napoleon. These advisers were unwilling that the elements of the great alliance which thirty-eight years before had delivered Europe from its thraldom should now be cast asunder for the mere sake of giving a better effect to the policy which the Foreign Office was accustomed to follow upon the Eastern Qustion. And in truth, this same Eastern policy, though held by almost all responsible statesmen, was not so universally received in England as to go altogether unchallenged. The notion of England's standing still, and suffering the Turks to be driven from Europe, was not deemed so preposterous as to be unworthy of being put forward by men commanding great means of persuasion; and before the new year[1] was far advanced the Emperor Nicholas had means of knowing that the old English policy of averting the dismemberment of Turkey would be gravely questioned, and brought in an effective way to the test of printed discussion. Upon the whole, therefore, it seemed to the Czar that now, if ever, England might be willing to acquiesce in his encroachments upon Turkey, and even perhaps to abet him in schemes for the actual dismemberment of the Empire.

Sir Hamilton Seymour.

The Minister who represented the Queen at the Russian Court was Sir Hamilton Seymour. It is said that before there was a prospect of his being accredited at St. Petersburg he had conceived a high admiration of the qualities of the Emperor Nicholas, and that this circumstance becoming known to the Czar, tended, at first, to make the English Minister more than commonly welcome at the Imperial Court. Sir Hamilton was not so constituted as to be liable to the kind of awe which other diplomatists too often felt in the majestic presence of the Emperor; but his dispatches show that he was much interested and, so to speak, amused by the conversation of a prince who wielded with his own very hand the power of All the Russias. Moreover, Sir Hamilton had

[1] 1853.

the quickness and the presence of mind which enable a man to seize the true bearing and import of a sentence just uttered, and to meet it at the instant with the few and appropriate words which convey the needful answer, and provoke a still farther disclosure.

On the night of the 9th of January, 1853, the English Minister was at a party gathered in the palace of the Archduchess Helen, when the Emperor Nicholas approached him, and drew him into conversation.

His conversation with the Emperor.

'You know my feelings,' the Emperor said, 'with regard 'to England. What I have told you before I say 'again: it was intended that the two countries 'should be upon terms of close amity; and I feel 'sure that this will continue to be the case. . . . I repeat that 'it is very essential that the two Governments—that is, that 'the English Government and I, and I and the English Gov-'ernment—should be on the best terms; and the necessity was 'never greater than at present. I beg you to convey these 'words to Lord John Russell. When we are agreed, I am 'quite without anxiety as to the West of Europe; it is imma-'terial what the others may think or do. As to Turkey, that is 'another question: that country is in a critical state, and may 'give us all a great deal of trouble. And now I will take my 'leave of you.' The Emperor then shook hands with Sir Hamilton Seymour, and believed that he had closed the conversation, but the skilled diplomatist saw and grasped his opportunity, and, whilst his hand was still held by the Emperor, Sir Hamilton Seymour said, 'Sir, with your gracious permission, I 'would desire to take a great liberty.' 'Certainly,' his Majesty replied; 'what is it—let me hear.' Sir Hamilton said, 'I 'should be particularly glad that your Majesty should add a 'few words, which may tend to calm the anxiety with respect 'to the affairs of Turkey which passing events are so calculated 'to excite on the part of her Majesty's Government; perhaps 'you will be pleased to charge me with some additional assur-'ances of this kind.'

The Emperor's words and manner, although still very kind, showed that he had no intention of speaking to Sir Hamilton of the demonstration which he was about to make in the South. He said, however, at first with a little hesitation, but, as he proceeded, in an open and unhesitating manner: 'The affairs of 'Turkey are in a very disorganized condition; the country it-'self seems to be falling to pieces: the fall will be a great mis-'fortune, and it is very important that England and Russia 'should come to a perfectly good understanding upon these 'affairs, and that neither should take any decisive step of which 'the other is not apprised.' The Envoy answered, that this was certainly his view of the way in which Turkish questions should be treated; but the Emperor then said, as if proceeding with his remark, 'Stay! we have on our hands a sick man '—a very sick man; it will be, I tell you frankly, a great misfortune, if one of these days he should slip away from us, especially before all necessary arrangements were made. But, 'however, this is not the time to speak to you on that matter.'

On the 22nd of January another interview took place between the Emperor and the English Envoy. 'I found his Majesty,' writes Sir Hamilton Seymour, 'alone; he received me 'with great kindness, saying that I had appeared desirous to 'speak to him upon Eastern affairs; that, on his side, there was 'no indiposition to do so, but that he must begin at a remote 'period. You know, his Majesty said, the dreams and plans in 'which the Empress Catherine was in the habit of indulging; 'these were handed down to our time; but while I inherited 'immense territorial possessions, I did not inherit those visions, 'those intentions if you like to call them so. On the contrary, 'my country is so vast, so happily circumstanced in every way, 'that it would be unreasonable in me to desire more territory 'or more power than I possess; on the contrary, I am the first 'to tell you that our great, perhaps our only danger, is that 'which would arise from an extension given to an Empire already too large.

'Close to us lies Turkey, and in our present condition nothing better for our interests can be desired; the times have 'gone by when we had any thing to fear from the fanatical 'spirit or the military enterprise of the Turks, and yet the 'country is strong enough, or has hitherto been strong enough, 'to preserve its independence, and to insure respectful treatment from other countries.

'Well, in that Empire there are several millions of Christians 'whose interests I am called upon to watch over, while the 'right of doing so is secured to me by treaty. I may truly 'say that I make a moderate and sparing use of my right, and 'I will freely confess that it is one which is attended with obligations occasionally very inconvenient; but I can not recede 'from the discharge of a distinct duty. Our religion, as established in this country, came to us from the East, and there are 'feelings as well as obligations which never must be lost sight of.

'Now Turkey, in the condition which I have described, has 'by degrees fallen into such a state of decrepitude that, as I 'told you the other night, eager as we all are for the prolonged 'existence of the man (and that I am as desirous as you can be 'for the continuance of his life I beg you to believe), he may 'suddenly die upon our hands: we can not resuscitate what is 'dead; if the Turkish Empire falls, it falls to rise no more; and 'I put it to you, therefore, whether it is not better to be pro-'vided beforehand for a contingency, than to incur the chaos, 'confusion, and the certainty of a European war, all of which 'must attend the catastrophe if it should occur unexpectedly, 'and before some ulterior system has been sketched. This is 'the point to which I am desirous you should call the atten-'tion of your Government.'

Sir Hamilton Seymour adverted to the objection which the English Government habitually felt to the plan of taking engagements upon possible eventualities, and said that disinclination might be expected in England to the idea of disposing by anticipation of the succession of an old friend and ally. 'The rule is a good one,' the Emperor replied, 'good at all 'times, especially in times of uncertainty and change like the 'present; still it is of the greatest importance that we should 'understand one another, and not allow events to take us by 'surprise. Now I desire to speak to you as a friend and as 'a "gentleman:" if England and I arrive at an understanding 'in this matter, as regards the rest it matters little to me; it 'is indifferent to me what others do or think. Frankly then I 'tell you plainly, that if England thinks of establishing herself 'one of these days at Constantinople I will not allow it. I do 'not attribute this intention to you, but it is better on these 'occasions to speak plainly; for my part I am equally disposed 'to take the engagement not to establish myself there, as pro-'prietor that is to say, for as occupier I do not say: it might 'happen that circumstances, if no previous provision were made, 'if every thing should be left to chance, might place me in the 'position of occupying Constantinople.'

On the 20th of February the Emperor came up to Sir Hamilton Seymour at a party given by the Grand Duchess Hereditary, and in the most gracious manner took him apart, saying he desired to speak to him. 'If your Government,' said the Emperor, 'has been led to believe that Turkey retains any 'elements of existence, your Government must have received 'incorrect information. I repeat to you that the sick man is 'dying, and we can never allow such an event to take us by 'surprise. We must come to some understanding.'

Then Sir Hamilton Seymour felt himself able to infer that the Czar had settled in his own mind that the hour for bringing about the dissolution of the Ottoman Empire must be at hand.

The next day the Emperor again sent for Sir Hamilton Seymour, and after combating the determination of the English Government to persist in regarding Turkey as a Power which might, and which probably would remain as she was, he at length spoke out his long reserved words of temptation. He thought, he said, that in the event of the dissolution of the Ottoman Empire, it might be less difficult to arrive at a satisfactory territorial arrangement than was commonly believed, and then he proceeded: 'The principalities are, in fact, an independent State under my protection: this might so continue. 'Servia might receive the same form of government. So 'again with Bulgaria: there seems to be no reason why this 'province should not form an independent State. As to 'Egypt, I quite understand the importance to England of that 'territory. I can then only say, that if, in the event of a distribution of the Ottoman succession upon the fall of the Empire, you should take possession of Egypt, I shall have no 'objection to offer. I would say the same thing of Candia: 'that island might suit you, and I do not know why it should 'not become an English possession.'

'As I did not wish,' writes Sir Hamilton Seymour, 'that the 'Emperor should imagine that an English public servant was 'caught by this sort of overture, I simply answered that I had 'always understood that the English views upon Egypt did 'not go beyond the point of securing a safe and ready communication between British India and the mother country. 'Well,' said the Emperor, 'induce your Government to write 'again upon these subjects—to write more fully, and to do so 'without hesitation. I have confidence in the English Government. It is not an engagement—a convention which I ask 'of them; it is a free interchange of ideas, and in case of need 'the word of a "gentleman;" that is enough between us.'[1]

Reception of the Czar's overtures by the English Government.

In answer to these overtures, the Government of the Queen disclaimed all notion of aiming at the possession of either Constantinople or any other of the Sultan's possessions, and accepted the assurances to the like effect which were given by the Czar. It combated the opinion that the extinction of the Ottoman Empire was near at hand, and deprecated the discussions based on that supposition, as tending directly to produce the very result against which they were meant to provide. Finally, our Government, with abundance of courtesy, but in terms very stringent and clear, peremptorily refused to enter into any kind of

[1] 'Eastern Papers,' part v.

secret engagement with Russia for the settlement of the Eastern Question.

These communications of January and February, 1853, were carried on between the Emperor of Russia and the English Government upon the understanding that they were to be held strictly secret; and for more than a year this concealment was maintained. It will be for a later page to show the ground on which the engagement for secrecy was broken, and the effect which the disclosure wrought upon the opinion of Europe and upon the feelings of the people in England.

The Czar was baffled by the failure of his somewhat shallow plan for playing the tempter with the English Government; and an event which occurred at this same time still farther conduced to the abandonment of his half-formed designs against the Sultan.

When Nicholas came to the singular resolution of declaring war against the Sultan in the event of his rejecting Austria's demand respecting Montenegro, he imagined perhaps that his counsels were kept strictly secret; but it seems probable that a knowledge or suspicion of the truth may have reached the Turkish Government, and helped to govern its decision. What is certain is that the demand made by Austria was carried by Count Leiningen to Constantinople, and that, having been put forward in terms offensively peremptory, it was suddenly acceded to by the sagacious advisers of the Sultan.

Result of Count Leiningen's mission.

This contingency seems to have been unforeseen by the Emperor Nicholas; at first the tidings of it kindled in his mind strong feelings of joy, for he looked upon the deliverance of Montenegro as a triumph of his Church over the Moslem. But he soon perceived that this sudden attainment of the object to be sought would disconcert his plans. He found himself all at once deprived of the basis on which his scheme of action had rested; and, except in respect of the question of the key and the silver star, there was nothing that he had to charge against the Sultan. On the other hand, he had failed in his endeavor to win over England to his views. He therefore relapsed into the use of the conservative language which he had been accustomed to apply to the treatment of the Eastern Question; professed his willingness to labor with England to prolong the existence of the Turkish Empire; and even went so far as to join with our Government in declaring that the way to achieve this result was to abstain 'from harassing the Porte by imperious de-'mands, put forward in a manner humiliating to its independ-

Its effect upon the plans of the Czar.

He abandons the idea of going to war.

'ence and its dignity.'[1] He abandoned the intention of going to war, and even deprived himself of the means of taking such a step with effect; for immediately upon hearing the result of Count Leiningen's mission, he stopped the purchase of horses required for enabling him to take the field.

---

## CHAPTER VII.

The pain of inaction.

But when a man's mind has been once thrown forward toward action, it gains so great a momentum, that the ceasing of the motive which first disturbed his repose does not instantly bring him to a stand. The Czar had found himself suddenly deprived of his ground of war against the Porte by the embarrassing success of Count Leiningen's mission, and in the same week he was robbed of his last hope of the alliance which he most desired by the failure of his overtures to England. He gave up the idea of going to war, and policy commanded that for a while he should rest; but already he had so acted that rest was pain to him. He could not but be tortured with the thought that the furtive words which he had uttered to Sir Hamilton Seymour on the 21st of February were known to the Queen of England and to several of her foremost statesmen. Moreover, in a thousand forms, the bitter fruits of the delivery of the key and the Star of Bethlehem, and the tidings of the triumph which the Latins had gained over his Church, and of the agony which this discomfiture had inflicted upon pious zealots, were coming home upon him, and from time to time in a fitful way were tormenting him, and then giving him a little rest, and then once more rekindling his fury. So he began to turn this way and that, in order that by turmoil he might smother the past, win back the self-respect which he had lost, and gain some counter-victory for his Church. He had already gathered heavy bodies of troops in the south of his empire; he had a powerful fleet in the Euxine; the Bosphorus was nigh. The Turks, trusting mainly to heavenly power, were ill prepared. No French or English fleets were in the Levant. Above all, that shady garden at Therapia, commanding the entrance of the Euxine, and seeming to be the fit dwelling-place for a Statesman who watched against invasion from

[1] 'Eastern Papers,' part v., p. 25.

the North was no longer paced by the English Ambassador. The great Eltchi was away. Many thought it was possible for the Czar to seize the imperial city, and treat with the anger of Europe from the Seraglio Point.

But Nicholas, though he was capable of venturing a little way into wrong paths, and was often blinded to the difference between right and wrong by a sense of religious duty, was far from being a lawless prince. His conscience, warped by Faith, would easily reconcile him to an act of violence against a Mahometan Power; but he never questioned that the fate of Turkey was a matter of concern to other Christian States as well as to his own; and he did not at this time intend to take any steps which England would regard as an outrage. The plan which he resorted to as a means of giving vent to his anger, and satisfying that tendency to action which had been engendered by his preparations against the Sultan, was to go on with the scheme of sending an Extraordinary Embassy to Constantinople, to make up for the sudden loss of the Montenegro grievance by laying an increased stress upon the question of the Holy Places, and to force the Sultan to settle the dispute upon terms which, without wounding the Latins more than could be helped, should still do justice to the Greek Church. Any attempt at resistance which the Porte might make, by alleging the counter-pressure of France, was to be met by at once engaging that the Emperor of Russia, with all his forces, should defend the Sultan's territory against every attack by a Western Power; and, well knowing that protective aid of such a kind was a burden and not a gift, the Emperor seems to have directed that this alliance should be not merely offered, but pressed.

*The Czar's new scheme of action.*

But the secret purpose of the mission was to make the past defaults of the Turkish government in regard to the Holy Places of Palestine a ground for extorting a treaty engagement by which the Greek Church throughout all Turkey would be brought under the protection of Russia. It seemed to the Czar that his half-completed preparations for war would give to his demands exactly that kind of support which their offensive character required; for the position of the troops gathered in Bessarabia, and the activity of the last few months in Sebastopol would not fail to make the Turks see that force was at hand. The armaments in readiness were more than enough for the occupation of the Danubian Principalities; and as soon as they should become swollen by the unfailing aid of rumors, they might easily grow to be thought a sufficing force for some great enterprise against Constantinople.

For some time the Emperor Nicholas hesitated in the choice of the person to whom this extraordinary mission should be intrusted. He hesitated between Count Orloff and Prince Mentschikoff. He did not hesitate because he was doubting which of the two men would be the fittest instrument of his policy, but rather because he had not determined what his policy should be. Count Orloff was a wise and moderate man, much associated with the Czar, and accustomed to speak to him with becoming freedom. To make choice of this trusty friend was to avoid any such outrage as would lead to the isolation of Russia. To choose Prince Mentschikoff was to choose a man whose feelings and prejudices might cause him to embitter the Czar's dispute with the Porte, and who, to say the least, could have no pretension to moderate the zeal of his master. It was for this very reason perhaps that he was preferred. In an evil hour Nicholas brought his doubts to an end, and made choice of Prince Mentschikoff.

His choice of an Ambassador.

Mentschikoff was a Prince of the sort which Court almanacs describe as 'Serene.' He was a General, a High Admiral, the Governor of a great province, and in short, so far as concerns official and titular rank, was one of the chief of the Czar's subjects; but Russia has not disclosed the grounds on which it was thought fit to intrust to him, first the peace, and then the military renown of his country; for, when Russians are asked about the qualities of mind which caused a man to be chosen for a momentous embassy, and for the command of an army defending his country from invasion, they only say that the Prince was famous for the strange and quaint sallies of his wit. However, he was of the school of those who desired to govern the affairs of the State upon principles violently Russian, and without the aid and counsel of foreigners. It was understood that he held the Turks in contempt; and it was said also that he entertained a strong dislike of the English. He had not been schooled in diplomacy, but he was to be intrusted with the power of using a threatening tone, and was to be supported by a fleet held in readiness and by bodies of troops impending upon the Turkish frontiers. The Emperor Nicholas seems to have thought that harsh words and a display of force might be made to supply want of skill.

Prince Mentschikoff.

Great latitude was given to Prince Mentschikoff in regard to the means by which he was to attain the objects of his mission; but it is certain that the general tenor of his instructions contravened with singular exactness the honorable and generous language in which the Emperor Nicholas loved to mark out the duty of the great Powers of Europe toward Turkey. In the last Secret Memorandum solemnly placed in the hands of our Envoy at St. Petersburg as a record of the Emperor's determination, Nicholas, as we have seen, had laid it down that it was the duty of great Powers not 'to harass the Porte by 'imperious demands put forward in a manner humiliating to 'its independence and dignity;' and yet these very words, which so well point out what the Czar said ought not to be done, are a close description of that which he ordered his Ambassador to do.

The approach of Prince Mentschikoff to Constantinople was heralded by the arrival of staff officers, who were charged to prepare the way, and cause men to feel the import of the coming embassy. For many days rumor was busy. When for some time men's minds had been kept on the rack, it became known that the expected vessel of war was nearing the gates of the Bosphorus, and at length, surrounded with pomp, and supported by the silent menace of fleets equipped, and battalions marching on the Danube, Prince Mentschikoff entered the palace of the Russian embassy. The next day another war-steamer came down, bringing the Vice-Admiral Korniloff, the commander of the Black Sea fleet, and the Chief of the Staff of the land-forces under General Rudiger, with several other officers. All this warlike following went to show that the Ambassador had the control of the military and naval forces which were hovering upon the Turkish Empire. Then also came tidings that General Dannenburg, commanding the cavalry of the 5th corps d'armée, had pushed his advance-guard close up to the frontiers of Moldavia; that funds had been transmitted to merchants in Moldavia and Wallachia for the purchase of rations; and, finally, that the fleet at Sebastopol was getting ready to sail at the shortest notice.

Mentschikoff at Constantinople.

In the midst of the alarm engendered by these tidings, Prince Mentschikoff began the duties of his mission; and he so acted as to make men see that he was charged to coerce, and not to persuade. With his whole Embassy he went to the Grand Vizier's apartment at the Porte, but refused to obey the custom which imperatively required that he should wait upon Fuad Effendi, the Minister for Foreign Affairs. With him, as it was understood, the Ambassador declined to hold intercourse. Fuad Effendi, the immediate object of the affront, was the ablest member of the Government. He instantly resigned his office. The Sultan accepted his resignation. There was a panic. It was understood that Prince

Panic in the Divan.

Mentschikoff was going to demand terms deeply humiliating and injurious to the Sultan, and that a refusal to give way would be followed by an instant attack. The Grand Vizier believed that the mission, far from being of a conciliatory character, as pretended, was meant, on the contrary, 'to win some 'important right from Turkey, which would destroy her inde-'pendence,' and that the Czar's object was 'to trample under 'foot the rights of the Porte, and the independence of the 'Sovereign.'[1] In short, the Divan was so taken by surprise, and so overwhelmed by alarm, as to be in danger of going to ruin by the path of concession for the sake of averting a sudden blow. But there remained one hope—the English fleet was at Malta; and the Grand Vizier went to Colonel Rose, who was then in charge of our affairs at the Porte, and entreated that he would request our Admiral at Malta to come up to Vourla, in order to give the Turkish Government the support of an approaching fleet. Colonel Rose, being a firm, able man, with strength to bear a sudden load of responsibility, was not afraid to go beyond the range of common duty. He consented to do as he was asked; and although he was disavowed by the Government at home, and although his appeal to the English Admiral was rejected, it is not the less certain that his mere consent to call up the fleet allayed the panic which was endangering at that moment the very life of the Ottoman Empire. Happily, there was not a complete perfect communication by telegraph between London and Constantinople, and long before the disavowal reached the Bosphorus the Turkish statesmen had recovered their usual calm. On the other hand, the Russian Government was much soothed by the intelligence that the English Cabinet had declined to approve Colonel Rose's request to the Admiral; and it might be said with truth that both the act of the Queen's Representative and the disavowal of it by his Government at home were of advantage to the public service.[2]

Colonel Rose.

It would seem that in the middle of the month of March the anger of the Emperor Nicholas had grown cool. He had always felt the difficulty of basing a war upon the question of the Holy Places alone, and the language of his Government at this time was moderate and pacific.[3] But unhappily there were distinct centres of action

The Czar seemingly tranquillized.

[1] 'Eastern Papers,' part i., p. 88.

[2] Colonel Rose was the officer who afterward became illustrious for his career of victory in India, but at that later time he was known to his grateful country as Sir Hugh Rose.

[3] Lord Cowley's account of Count Nesselrode's Dispatch of the 15th March. 'Eastern Papers, part i., p. 96

in Paris, in London, in St. Petersburg, and in Constantinople, and it was constantly happening that when the fire seemed to be got down in three out of the four capitals, it would spring up with fresh strength in the fourth. Thus, at a moment when the panic of the Divan had entirely ceased, and when the Court of St. Petersburg, already inclining toward moderation, was about to be farther pacified by the welcome tidings which informed it of the disavowal of Colonel Rose by the Home Government, the Emperor of the French suddenly determined to send a naval force into the Levant, and, notwithstanding the opposition of our Government, the French fleet was ordered to Salamis. This was done without sound reason, for the panic which had induced Colonel Rose to appeal to the English Admiral at Malta had long ago ceased. The step gave deep umbrage to Russia.

The French fleet suddenly ordered to Salamis.

When the Emperor Nicholas learned that the advance of the French fleet had been disapproved by England, his anger was followed by gladness, and the relations between the Governments of St. Petersburg and London then seemed to be upon so friendly a footing as to exclude the fear of a disagreement. Count Nesselrode assured Sir Hamilton Seymour that Russia was alleging no grievance against the Turkish Government except in regard to the question of the Holy Places, and even this one remaining subject of complaint he began to treat as a slighter matter than it had hitherto appeared to be. It is hard to have to believe that all this good humor of the Court of St. Petersburg was simulated, and yet the assurances of Count Nesselrode distinctly went to exclude the belief that Russia could ever do that which she was actually doing. Yielding it would seem to an instinct of wild cunning, the Czar failed to understand that the chance of carrying a point at Constantinople by a diplomatic surprise could never be of such worth as to deserve to be set against his old reputation for truthfulness. If he thought at all, he would see that the difference between what he was saying and what he was doing would be laid bare in three weeks. Yet he gave way to the strange impulse which forced him to go and try to steal a trophy for his Church. He concealed from the French as well as from our Government all knowledge of his intention to endeavor to extort from the Sultan an engagement giving to Russia the protectorate of the Greek Church in Turkey. The Cabinets of the Western Powers were suffered to gather the first tidings of this scheme from their Constantinople dispatches, and the trust which the English Government had hitherto placed in the honor and good faith of the Emperor Nicholas was suddenly and forever destroyed.

His concealments.

Mentschikoff's demands.

Meanwhile Prince Mentschikoff brought forward the claims of the Greek Church in regard to the Holy Places; but he seemed disposed to be moderate in his demands respecting the shrines, if the Turkish Government should show any willingness to give way to him in regard to the other and more important object which he was to endeavor to compass. Striving to take advantage of the alarm created by his Embassy, he proposed to wring from the Porte a treaty engagement, conceding to the Emperor of Russia a protectorate over the Greek Church in Turkey. At first he spoke darkly, intimating that he had some great demand to press upon the Sultan, but not yet choosing to say what the demand might be. Then he began to say to the Turkish Ministers that if they would appease the anger of the Czar, and deliver their State from danger, it would be well for them at once to turn away from France and England, trust themselves wholly to the generosity of the Emperor of Russia, and begin by giving a solemn assurance that they would withhold from the representatives of the Western Powers all knowledge of the negotiation they were required to undertake. 'We are aware,' said the Grand Vizier, 'that the object of his (Prince Mentschi- 'koff's) mission is to make a secret treaty of alliance with us. 'He has not demanded it officially, but he has told some per- 'sons in his confidence, who (he knows) are in communication 'with us, that we do wrong to rely on the English and French 'Governments, for experience should at length have proved to 'us that we have lost much and gained nothing by following 'their policy and advice. By this language he seeks to gain 'their support and to insure their concurrence in the work of 'the secret treaty which he is seeking to conclude. His policy 'is most confused. At one time he would attract us to Russia 'by mildness, spreading abroad a report that the intentions of 'his Government are pacific. At another time he seeks to gain 'us over by pointing out the disadvantages and inutility of our 'reliance upon England and France, and how wrong we are in 'following the advice of those two Powers, to whom we ought 'not to be attached, especially if we consider that the nature 'of their Constitution differs from that of ours, which, on the 'contrary, resembles that of Russia and Austria. Prince Ments- 'chikoff had a conference with Rifaat Pasha two days ago. 'He told him that before communicating to the Sublime Porte 'the nature of his mission, and the demands of his Government, 'and before giving any explanation, he required from Rifaat 'Pasha the formal promise of the Porte, that it would not com- 'municate to the representative either of England or of France 'any thing whatever as to what he demanded or proposed; 'that it was his wish that it should be treated with the great- 'est secrecy, otherwise he would not enter upon the subject.'[1]

The Grand Vizier declared that the Turkish Government had at once refused to withhold from the Western Powers a knowledge of the impending negotiation, but it seems likely that some alarmed member of the Turkish Government may have been led to give the required promise of secrecy, for before the end of March Prince Mentschikoff vouchsafed to disclose the offers and the demands of his Sovereign. He verbally expressed the Emperor's wish to enter into a secret treaty with Turkey, putting a fleet and 400,000 men at her disposal, if she ever needed aid against any Western Power. As 'the 'equivalent for this proffered aid,' said the Grand Vizier, 'Rus- 'sia farther secretly demanded an addition to the treaty of 'Kainardji, whereby the Greek Church should be placed en- 'tirely under Russian protection without reference to Turkey. 'Prince Mentschikoff had stated that the greatest secrecy must 'be maintained relative to this proposition, and that, should 'Turkey allow it to be made known to England, he and his 'mission would instantly quit Constantinople.'[2]

This kind of pressure upon the Turkish Government was perhaps well fitted for the days of alarm which immediately followed Prince Mentschikoff's arrival at Constantinople; but it was now the end of March, and it was so long ago as the 6th of the month that Colonel Rose, by requesting the English Admiral to come into the Levant, had been able to stop the panic. Rifaat Pasha, the Minister who had succeeded to Fuad Effendi in the Department of Foreign Affairs, was firm. 'I am not a 'child,' said he, in his message to Colonel Rose; 'I am an old 'Minister, very well acquainted with the treaties which unite 'the Sublime Porte with the friendly Powers, and I understand, 'God be praised, too well the importance of our good relations 'with England and France, the full weight of the obligation to 'maintain treaties, the whole extent of the evil which would 'result to my Government if it departs from or infringes them, 'to hesitate a single instant to inform their respective repre- 'sentatives of every demand or proposal which Russia might 'be desirous of enforcing upon us, and which might not be in 'accordance with the rights recorded in those treaties.'[3]

Finding himself thus encountered, and being unskilled in negotiation, Prince Mentschikoff had already begun to draw to himself the support of an army. The English Vice-Consul

[1] 'Eastern Papers,' part i., p. 111. [2] Ibid., p. 112. [3] Ibid., p. 114.

at Galatz reported that preparations had been made in Bessarabia for the passage of 120,000 men, and that battalions were marching to the South from all directions. Though the time of mere panic was past, there was 'anxiety and alarm' in the Divan.[1]

But Prince Mentschikoff was destined soon to learn that there was a power in the world which could exert more governance over Turkish Statesmen than the march of the Czar's battalions. Before the week was past he had to undergo the sensation of encountering a formidable mind.

---

## CHAPTER VIII.

WHEN a great country is induced by virtue or by policy to refrain from using her physical strength against the Sovereign of a weaker State, she often solaces herself for this painful effort of moderation by showing her neighbor the error of his ways and giving him constant advice; and if it happen that two or more great Powers are thus engaged in tendering their rival counsels to the same State, they will be prone to struggle with one another for the ascendency, and to do this with a zeal scarcely intelligible to men who have never seen that kind of strife. The prize contended for is commonly known by the name of 'influence;' and although this moral sovereignty over foreign States may be a privilege of small intrinsic worth, the Princes and Statesmen who have once begun combating for the prize, and even the merchants and the travelers who have happened to be on the spot and to witness with any attention the animating incidents of the conflict, have generally had their zeal kindled. Now the Ottoman polity is of such a nature as almost to court this kind of interference. The practice of suffering the Christian Churches to live and thrive separate and apart, without being subjected to any attempt at amalgamation, has given to these communities so many of the privileges of distinct national existence that they long to make their independence still more complete, and to do this—not by attempting to lay their timid hands upon the government, but rather by becoming more and more separate, and at last dropping off from the Empire. Therefore, instead of harboring

Foreign 'influence.'

Grounds for foreign interference in Turkey.

[1] 'Eastern Papers,' part i., p. 124.

schemes for rising in arms against the Sultan, they have accustomed themselves to seek to form ties of a political and religious kind with foreign States, and to appeal to them for protection against their Ottoman rulers. Here then, of course, a gaping cleft was open to receive the wedge which diplomatists call a 'Protectorate.' Russia claimed a moral right to protect the ten or fourteen millions of Turkish subjects who constituted the Greek Church, and she availed herself of some loose words which had crept into the old treaty of Kainardji as a ground for maintaining that this moral claim was converted into a distinct right by treaty engagement. Austria, armed with treaties, was empowered to protect the Roman Catholic worship, but France had always been accustomed to busy herself in watching over that portion of the Latin Church which was connected with Palestine and Syria. It is true that the Armenian, the Coptic, and the Black Churches were without any recognized foreign patron, and flourished quite as well as their protected brethren, but the numbers composing these Churches were scanty in comparison with the worshipers following the Greek ritual, and it may be said that the bulk of the Christian population of Turkey had contracted the habit of looking abroad for support.

Again, the Turkish Government was always so sensible of the distinctness of the 'nations' held under its sway, and of the hardship of keeping Christians under the close subjection of the Moslem system, that even in the times when the Sultans were in the pride of their strength, they generously allowed humble foreigners, though living in Turkey, to have the protection of their country's flag, and to enjoy immunities which (except in the case of Sovereigns and their embassies) the Governments of Christian countries have never been accustomed to give to any of their foreign guests. These privileges had been granted to the principal States of Europe by treaty engagements which went by the name of 'capitulations,' and they were so extensive that, except in regard to one or two specified descriptions of crime and outrage, a foreigner in Turkey who was a native of any of the States to whom these capitulations had been granted, was exempt from the laws of the country in which he dwelt. And these privileges were not even confined to foreigners, for Ambassadors at the Porte claimed and exercised a right of withdrawing a Turkish subject from the laws of his country by taking him into their service, or even by a mere written grant of protection; and the streets of Pera and Galata were filled with Orientals of various races who had contrived to be turned into 'Russians,' or 'Frenchmen,' or 'Englishmen.' Thus it resulted that not only the great communities forming Churches or 'nations,' but also a great number of individuals, often clever, stirring, and unscrupulous men, were always laboring to attract the interference of some great Power, furnishing it with ready grounds of dispute, and stimulating its desirè for preponderance. But there was a broad difference between the protectorate of Russia and that of the other States of Europe; for whilst the Roman Catholic States could only reckon a few hundred thousands of clients, and whilst the Protestant subjects of the Porte were too few to form a body in the State, the number of Greek Christians who looked to Russia for protection amounted to from ten to fourteen millions. This fact gave great strength and substance to the pretensions of Russia, but on the other hand it made her interference in a high degree dangerous, for it was clear that if the guardianship of so vast a number of the Rayahs or Turkish subjects were to be suffered to lapse into the hands of a foreign Sovereign, the empire of the Sultans would pass away. All the great Powers of Europe were accustomed to press upon the Sultan the duty of conferring upon his people, and especially upon his Christian subjects, the blessing of good and equal government, but Russia urged these demands with the not unnatural desire to prepare for herself a firm standing-ground in the midst of her neighbor's territory, whilst Austria and England, being interested in averting the dismemberment of the Sultan's dominions, gave their counsel with a real view to make the Sultan do what they deemed to be for his own good.

Rivalry between Nicholas and Sir Stratford Canning.

Sir Stratford Canning.

For ascendency on this the favorite arena of diplomacy two men had long contended. They were altogether unequal in station, and yet were not ill matched. The first of the combatants was the Emperor Nicholas: the other was Sir Stratford Canning. This kinsman of Mr. Canning the Minister had been bred from early life to the career of diplomacy, and whilst he was so young that he could still perhaps think in smooth Eton Alcäics more easily than in the diction of 'High Contracting Parties,' it was given him to negotiate a treaty which helped to bring ruin upon the enemy of his country.[1] How to negotiate with a perfected skill never degenerating into craft, how to form such a scheme of policy that his country might be

[1] The Treaty of Bucharest in 1812. By enabling the Czar to withdraw from the South the forces commanded by Tchitchagoff, this treaty did much to convert the discomfiture of Napoleon's 'grand army' into absolute ruin.

brought to adopt it without swerving, and how to pursue this always, promoting it steadily abroad, and gradually forcing the home Government to go all lengths in its support, this he knew; and he was moreover so gifted by nature that, whether men studied his dispatches, or whether they listened to his spoken words, or whether they were only by-standers caught and fascinated by the grace of his presence, they could scarcely help thinking that if the English nation was to be maintained in peace or drawn into war by the will of a single mortal, there was no man who looked so worthy to fix its destiny as Sir Stratford Canning. He had faults which made him an imperfect Christian, for his temper was fierce, and his assertion of self was so closely involved in his conflicts that he followed up his opinions with his feelings and with the whole strength of his imperious nature. But his fierce temper, being always under control when purposes of State so required, was far from being an infirmity and was rather a weapon of exceeding sharpness, for it was so wielded by him as to have more tendency to cause dread and surrender than to generate resistance. Then, too, every judgment which he pronounced was enfolded in words so complete as to exclude the idea that it could ever be varied, and to convey therefore the idea of duration. As though yielding to fate itself, the Turkish mind used to bend and fall down before him.

But the counsels which Sir Stratford Canning had been accustomed to tender to the Sultan's Ministers, however wholesome they might be, were often very irksome to hear, and very difficult to adopt. Indeed it might be questioned whether his Turkish policy could be made to consist with the principle on which the Ottoman system was based. He sought to make the Ottoman rule seem tolerable to Christendom by getting rid of the differences which separated the Christian subjects of the Porte from their Mahometan fellow-subjects, and placing the tributaries on a footing with their masters. But the theory of Mahometan government rests upon the maintenance of a clear separation from the unbelievers, and to propose to a Mussulman of any piety that the Commander of the Faithful should obliterate the distinction between Mahometans and Christians would be proposing to obliterate the distinction between virtue and vice; the notion would seem to be not merely wrong and wicked, but a contradiction in terms. A virtuous Osmanlee would feel that if he were to consent to this leveling of the barriers between good and evil, he would lose the whole merit and comfort of being a Turk. Perhaps the opposite policy, namely, that of widening the separation of the Christians, and giving them (under a tenure less precarious than the present one) the character of tributary municipalities, would be more consonant with the scheme of a Mussulman Empire, and therefore more susceptible of complete execution. But, whether the reforms thus counseled were possible or not, it was hard to resist the imperious Ambassador to his face. If what he directed was inconsistent with the nature of things, then possibly the nature of things would be changed by the decree of Heaven, for there was no hope that the great Eltchi would relax his will. In the mean time, however, and by the blessing of God, the actual execution of the Ambassador's painful mandates might perhaps be suffered to encounter a little delay. So thought, so temporized the wise tranquil statesmen at the Porte.

Of course this kind of ascendency was often very galling to the Sultan's advisers. They knew that the English Ambassador was counseling them for the good of their country; but they felt that he humbled them by making his dictation too plainly apparent, and they were often very conscious that the motive which made them succumb to him was dread. Yet, if the Ambassador was unrelenting, and even harsh in the exercise of his dominion over the Turks, he was faithful to guard them against enemies from abroad. He chastened them himself, but he was dangerous to any other man who came seeking to hurt his children.

Now it happened that this was exactly the kind of ascendency over the Turks for which the Emperor Nicholas had long been craving. Some men imagine that the Emperor's designs in regard to Turkey were steadily governed by sheer desire for his neighbor's land; and they are not without specious materials for forming such an opinion; but perhaps a full knowledge of the truth would justify the belief that, from the Peace of Adrianople in 1829, down to the time of his death, the Czar would have preferred the ascendency which Sir Stratford Canning enjoyed at Constantinople to any scheme of conquest. And, what is more, if Nicholas had succeeded in gaining this ascendency, he would have been inclined to use it as a means of enforcing counsels somewhat similar to those which were pressed upon the Sultan by the English Ambassador; for, though his first care would have been always for his own Church, it would have suited his pride and his policy to extend his protection to all the Christian subjects of the Porte. But, just as similarity of doctrine often embitters the differences between contending sects, so the very resemblance between his and Sir Stratford Canning's views with regard to the Christian subjects of the Porte, made it the more intolerable to him to see that he, the powerful neighbor of Turkey who was able to hover over her frontiers and her shores with great armies and fleets, could never make an effort to force his counsels on the Porte without finding himself baffled or forestalled by the stronger mind.

Even in his very early life, it had been the fate of Sir Stratford Canning to have to resist and thwart the Russian Government; and during a great part of the years of his embassy at Constantinople he had been more or less in a posture of resistance to the Emperor Nicholas. Moreover, the feeling with which the Emperor carried on this long-standing conflict was quickened by personal animosity, and by a knowledge that diplomacy was watching the strife with interest and amusement; for he had once gone the length of declining to receive Sir Stratford Canning as the English Ambassador at St. Petersburg, and had thus marked him out before Europe as his recognized antagonist. The struggle had lasted for a long time, and with varying success; for many a Turkish ministry owed its frail existence and its untimely end to the chances of the combat going on between the Czar and the English Ambassador. The Turks could not help knowing that the counsels of the Ambassador were for their own good; and they had reason to surmise that the advice of the Emperor might spring from opposite motives; but there are times when the smooth speech and the wily promises of a political foe are more welcome than the painful lectures of an honest friend; and again, though it was hard to bear up with mere words against the personal ascendant of the Ambassador, the Emperor had the power of throwing the sword into the scale at any moment. The strife, therefore, had not been altogether unequal; but, upon the whole, Sir Stratford Canning had kept the upper hand, and the Czar had been forced to endure the agony of being what his representative called 'secondary,' so long as Sir Stratford Canning was in the palace of the English embassy.

Lord Stratford instructed to return to Constantinople.

For almost two years Sir Stratford Canning had been absent from Constantinople; but now, at a time when Europe had fastened its eyes upon the Czar, and was watching to see how the Ambassador of All the Russias would impose his master's will upon Turkey, the Emperor Nicholas was obliged to hear that his eternal foe, traveling by the ominous route of Paris and Vienna, was slowly returning to his embassy at the Porte.

It was on the 25th of February, 1853, that Lord Stratford

His instructions.

de Redcliffe[1] was instructed to return to his former post. The measure was not without significance. Read by foreigners, it imported that England clung to her ancient policy, and was proceeding to maintain it; and although the instructions addressed to Lord Stratford disclosed no knowledge of the spirit in which Prince Mentschikoff was about to conduct his embassy, or of the kind of proposals which he was about to press upon the Porte, they indicated that the Cabinet was alarmed for the fate of Turkey.

The dispatch which supplied Lord Stratford with his instructions, announced to him that, in the then critical period of the fate of the Ottoman Empire, he was to return to his Embassy at Constantinople for a special purpose. Then, after recording once more the fact that the duty of maintaining the integrity and independence of the Ottoman Empire was a principle solemnly declared and acknowledged by all the great Powers of Europe, the dispatch informed Lord Stratford that it was his mission to counsel prudence to the Porte, and forbearance to those Powers who were urging compliance with their demands. In Paris, he was to remind the French Government that the interests of France and England in the East were identical, and was to explain the fatal embarrassment to which the Sultan might be exposed if unduly pressed by France upon a question of such vital importance to the Power from which Turkey had most to apprehend. At Vienna, he was to give and elicit fresh declarations of the conservative views entertained by the two Governments. Then proceeding to Constantinople, the Ambassador was to inform the Sultan that his Embassy was to be regarded as a mark of Her Majesty's friendly feelings toward His Highness, but also as indicating the opinion which Her Majesty entertained of the gravity of the circumstances in which there was reason to fear the Ottoman Empire was placed. In regard to any part which he might be able to take in conducing to a settlement of the question of the Holy Places, the discretion of the Ambassador was left unfettered. The Ambassador was directed to warn the Porte that the Ottoman Empire was in 'a position of peculiar 'danger. The accumulated grievances of foreign nations,' continued Lord Clarendon, 'which the Porte is unable or unwill-'ing to redress; the mal-administration of its own affairs, and 'the increasing weakness of executive power in Turkey, have 'caused the allies of the Porte latterly to assume a tone alike 'novel and alarming, and which, if persevered in, may lead to a

[1] Sir Stratford Canning was created Viscount Stratford de Redcliffe in 1852.

'general revolt among the Christian subjects of the Porte, and 'prove fatal to the independence and integrity of the Empire '—a catastrophe that would be deeply deplored by Her Maj-'esty's Government, but which it is their duty to represent to 'the Porte is considered probable and impending by some of 'the great European Powers. Your Excellency will explain 'to the Sultan that it is with the object of pointing out these 'dangers, and with the hope of averting them, that Her Maj-'esty's Government have now directed you to proceed to Con-'stantinople. You will endeavor to convince the Sultan and 'his Ministers that the crisis is one which requires the utmost 'prudence on their part, and confidence in the sincerity and 'soundness of the advice they will receive from you, to resolve 'it favorably for their future peace and independence.' Then (and probably at the suggestion of Lord Stratford himself) the Ambassador was to press upon the Porte the adoption of the reforms which his intimate knowledge of the affairs of Turkey enabled him to recommend; and then—disclosing the effect already produced upon the mind of the Government by the challenge to which our accustomed policy in the East had just been subjected by the press—the dispatch went on: 'Nor 'will you disguise from the Sultan and his Ministers, that per-'severance in his present course must end in alienating the 'sympathies of the British nation, and making it impossible for 'Her Majesty's Government to shelter them from the impend-'ing danger, or to overlook the exigencies of Christendom, ex 'posed to the natural consequences of their unwise policy and 'reckless mal-administration.' Finally the Ambassador was told that, in the event of imminent danger to the existence of the Turkish Government, he was to dispatch a messenger at once to Malta, requesting the Admiral to hold himself in readiness; but Lord Stratford was not to direct him to approach the Dardanelles without positive instructions from the Government at home.

Thus, so far as concerned the power of turning for aid to physical force, the Ambassador went out poorly armed; but he was destined to have an opportunity of showing that a slender authority in the hands of a skilled diplomatist may be more formidable than the absolute control of great armaments intrusted to a less able Statesman. Lord Stratford was licensed to do no more than send a message to an Admiral, advising him to be ready to go to sea; and, slight as this power was, he never exhausted it; yet, as will be seen, he so wielded the instruction which intrusted it to him as to be able to establish a great calm in the Divan at a moment when Prince Mentschikoff was violently pressing upon its fears, with a fleet awaiting his orders, and an army of 140,000 men.

---

## CHAPTER IX.

Lord Stratford's return.

On the morning of the 5th of April, 1853, the Sultan and all his Ministers learned that a vessel of war was coming up the Propontis, and they knew who it was that was on board. Long before noon the voyage and the turmoil of the reception were over, and, except that a frigate under the English flag lay at anchor in the Golden Horn, there was no seeming change in the outward world. Yet all was changed. Lord Stratford de Redcliffe had entered once more the palace of the English Embassy. The event spread a sense of safety, but also a sense of awe. It seemed to bring with it confusion to the enemies of Turkey, but austere reproof for past errors at home, and punishment where punishment was due, and an enforcement of hard toils and painful sacrifices of many kinds, and a long farewell to repose. It was the angry return of a king whose realm had been suffered to fall into danger. Before a day was over, the Grand Vizier and the Reis Effendi had begun to speak, and to tell a part of what they knew to the English Ambassador. They did not yet venture to tell all. Things which they had told to Colonel Rose they did not yet dare to tell to the great Eltchi. They did not perhaps mean to conceal from him, but they shrank from the terror of seeing his anger when he came to know of Prince Mentschikoff's demands for a Protectorate of the Greek Church. If they were to confess that they had borne to hear such a proposal, the Eltchi might think that they had dared to listen to it. Lord Stratford, observing their fear, imagined that it was Prince Mentschikoff who had disturbed their equanimity. 'This combination,' said he, 'of alarm, seeking for advice, and of reluctance to intrust me frankly with the whole case, is attributable to the threatening language of Prince Mentschikoff, and to the character of his proposals.' But his view of the cause of this tendency toward suppression is displaced by observing the frankness of the disclosures which the Turkish Ministers had long before made to Colonel Rose;[1] the truth is, that Lord Stratford was unconscious of exercising the

[1] 'Eastern Papers,' part i., p. 107 *et seq.*

ascendency which he did, and, imagining that men gave way to him because he was in the right, he never came to understand the awe which he inspired. However, by degrees the Turkish Ministers went so far as to tell him that 'since the arrival of Prince Mentschikoff, the language held by the Russian Embassy to them had been a mixture of angry complaints and friendly assurances, accompanied with positive requisitions as to the Holy Places in Palestine, indications of some ulterior views, and a general tone of insistance bordering at times on intimidation.'[1] They declared that as to what the ulterior views were, 'there was still some uncertainty in the language of Prince Mentschikoff. In the beginning he had sounded the sentiments of the Porte as to a defensive alliance with Russia, but, receiving no encouragement, had desisted from the overture. His intentions were now rather directed to a remodeling of the Greek Patriarchate of Constantinople, to a more clear and comprehensive definition of Russian right under treaty to protect the Greek and Armenian subjects of the Porte in religious matters, and to the conclusion of a formal agreement comprising those points.' Then, eager to place themselves under Lord Stratford's guidance, but still shrinking from a disclosure of the whole truth, the Turkish Ministers entreated the Ambassador to tell them how to meet the demands which, although they only spoke of them hypothetically, had been already made by Prince Mentschikoff.

His plan of resistance to Mentschikoff's demands.

Lord Stratford instantly saw that he must cause the question of the Holy Places to be kept clear of all the other subjects of discussion which Prince Mentschikoff might be intending to raise, for it was plain that the vacillation of the Porte in regard to the sanctuaries (though it had sprung from a desire to avoid giving offense to either of two great Powers) had given Russia fair grounds of complaint on that subject; but the Czar had nothing else to complain of, and it was clear therefore that, if the one grievance which really existed could be settled, every hostile step which Russia might afterward take would place her more and more in the wrong. 'Endeavor,' said Lord Stratford, in charging the Turkish Ministers, 'to keep the affair of the Holy Places separate from the ulterior proposals (whatever they may be) of Russia. The course which you appear to have taken under the former head was probably the best, and I am glad to find that there is a fair prospect of its success. When-

[1] 'Eastern Papers,' part i., p. 125.

'ever Prince Mentschikoff comes forward with farther propo- 'sitions, you are at perfect liberty to decline entering into ne- 'gotiation without a full statement of their nature, extent, and 'reasons. Should they be found, on examination, to carry with 'them that degree of influence over the Christian subjects of 'the Porte in favor of a foreign Power which might eventual- 'ly prove dangerous or seriously inconvenient to the exercise 'of the Sultan's legitimate authority, His Majesty's Ministers 'can not be doing wrong in declining them.'[1] But then added the Ambassador—and his words portended some counsels hard to follow—this 'will not prevent the removal, by direct 'sovereign authority, of any existing abuse.'[1]

Gradually the Turkish Ministers told more, and on the 9th of April Lord Stratford knew that Russia was demanding a treaty engagement, giving her the protectorate of the Greek Church in Turkey; and being now in communication with Prince Mentschikoff, he succeeded, as he believed, in penetrating the real object which Russia had in view. 'That object,' he said, 'was to reinstate Russian influence in Turkey on an 'exclusive basis, and in a commanding and stringent form.' In other words, Prince Mentschikoff, with horse, and foot, and artillery, and the whole Sebastopol fleet at his back, was come to depose the man whom they called in St. Petersburg 'the English Sultan.' On the other hand, Lord Stratford was not willing to be deposed. The struggle began.

Commencement of the struggle between Prince Mentschikoff and Lord Stratford.

The severance of the question of the Holy Places from the ulterior demands of the Czar was not an object to be pursued for the sake of order and convenience only. On the contrary, it bid fair to govern the result of the diplomatic conflict; for, the Montenegro question having disappeared, and Russia having committed herself to the avowal that she had no complaints against the Sultan except in regard to the Holy Places, a settlement of that solitary grievance would leave the ulterior demand so baseless that any attempt to enforce it by arms would be a naked outrage upon the opinion of Europe. If Prince Mentschikoff had been a man accustomed to negotiate, he would have taken care to preserve the question of the Holy Places, and keep it blended with the ulterior demand until he saw his way to a successful issue, for he was in the position of having to found two demands upon one grievance, and it was clear, therefore, that he would be stranded if he allowed his one grievance to be disposed of without having good reason for

[1] 'Eastern Papers,' part i., p. 125.

knowing that his farther demand would be granted; but he was vain and confident, and perhaps his sagacity was blunted by the thought that he was able to threaten an appeal to force. Moreover, Prince Mentschikoff was in the hands of a practiced adversary.

Lord Stratford, knowing the full import of the decision toward which he was leading his opponent, did not fail to deal with him tenderly; and for several days the Prince had the satisfaction of imagining that the imperious and overbearing Englishman of whom they were always talking at St. Petersburg was become very gentle in his presence. The two Ambassadors, without being yet in negotiation, began to talk with one another of the matters which were bringing the peace of the world into danger. They spoke of the Holy Places. Far from seeming to be hard or scornful in regard to that matter, Lord Stratford was full of deference to a cause which, whether it were founded on error or on truth, was still the honest heart's desire of fifty millions of pious men. He showed by his language that if by chance he should be called upon to use his good offices in this matter, or to mediate between Russia and France, he would form his judgment with gravity and with care. Where he could do so with justice, he admitted the fairness of the Russian claims.

Prince Mentschikoff's tone became 'considerably softened.'[1] Then the Ambassadors ventured upon the subject still more pregnant with danger, for Lord Stratford now disclosed his knowledge of Prince Mentschikoff's 'ulterior propositions relative to the protectorate of the whole Greek Church and the 'priesthood in Turkey, and his conviction that they would meet 'with serious opposition from the Porte, and be regarded with 'little favor by Powers even the most friendly to Russia.'[2] Prince Mentschikoff tried to 'attenuate the extent and effect'[3] of his demands; and, on the other hand, Lord Stratford drew a clear line of 'distinction between the confirmation of special 'points already stipulated by treaty, and an extension of influence having the virtual force of a protectorate, to be exercised 'exclusively by a single foreign Power, over the most important and numerous class of the Sultan's tributary subjects;'[3] but, by common consent, the two Ambassadors 'avoided entering into a discussion which might have proved irritating upon 'this question.'[3] Prince Mentschikoff, however, committed the diplomatic error of intimating 'that, notwithstanding the great 'importance attached to it by his Government, there was no

[1] 'Eastern Papers,' part i., p. 134. [2] Ibid., p. 151. [3] Ibid., p. 139.

'danger of any hostile aggression as the result of its failure, 'but at most an estrangement between the two Courts, and 'perhaps, though it was not so said, an interruption of diplo- 'matic relations.'[1]

That, in these circumstances, and until he had succeeded in separating the question of the Holy Places, it was right for the English Ambassador to deal very temperately with the ulterior demands of the Czar, no diplomatist would doubt; and Lord Stratford acknowledges[2] that he carefully refrained from discussing the subject in a way tending to irritate, but the Russians imagine that he did more than abstain. They say that having been supplied with a copy of Prince Mentschikoff's draft of the convention embodying his demands in respect to the Greek Church and clergy, Lord Stratford struck out as inadmissible the clauses relating to the Greek Patriarch's tenure of office, and, sending back the draft with that and with no other alteration, induced the Turkish Ministers (and through them induced the Russian Embassy) to suppose that he entertained no objection to the proposed convention except that which he had indicated by his erasure; and that Prince Mentschikoff being in this belief, and being prepared to give way upon the question of the Greek Patriarch, had a right to expect Lord Stratford's acquiescence in that dangerous part of the Czar's demand which sought to establish a Protectorate over the Greek Church in Turkey. Nothing is more likely than that, in the process of endeavoring to penetrate Lord Stratford's intentions through the medium of the Turkish Ministers, Prince Mentschikoff may have received a wrong impression, and it is very likely that Lord Stratford, in reading the draft, may have at once struck out clauses which he regarded as totally inadmissible, reserving for separate discussion and for oral explanation the consideration of an ambiguous clause which, dangerous as it was, might easily be so altered as to become entirely harmless; but it is certain that there was never a moment in which Lord Stratford was willing or even would have endured that any Protectorate over the Greek Church in Turkey should be ceded to Russia,[3] and no one versed in the spirit of English diplomacy, or having a just conception of Lord Stratford's nature, will be able to accept the belief that the Queen's Ambassador intended to overreach his antagonist by any misleading contrivance.

But, whatever may have been the clew which led him into the wrong path, Prince Mentschikoff failed to see the danger

[1] 'Eastern Papers,' part i., p. 139. [2] Ibid., p. 134.
[3] See Lord Stratford's Dispatches, ib., p. 127 *et seq.* to p. 151.

in which he would place the success of his negotiation if he consented to let the question of the Holy Places be treated separately; and the angry dispatches which now came in from St. Petersburg[1] did not tend to divert him from his error. On the contrary, they tended to place him in hostility with France more distinctly than before; and since the question of the Holy Places was the one in which France and Russia were face to face, the Czar's Ambassador was not perhaps unwilling to enter upon a course which would place him for the time in distinct antagonism with France, and with France alone. He agreed to allow the question of the Holy Places to be treated first and apart from his other demands.

It must be acknowledged that so far as concerned the question of the Holy Places, the demands made by Russia were moderate. Notwithstanding all the heat of his sectarian zeal, the Emperor Nicholas had seen that to endeavor to enforce a withdrawal of the privileges which had been granted with public solemnity to the Latin Church would be to outrage Catholic Europe, and it may be believed too that his religious feeling made him unwilling to exclude the people of other creeds from those Holy Sites which, according to the teaching of his own Church, it was good for Christians to embrace. But, if the demands of the Russian Emperor in regard to the Holy Places were fair and moderate, he was resolved to be peremptory in enforcing them. And it seemed to him that in this matter he could not fail to have the ascendant, for his forces were near at hand. Also he had good right to suppose that France would be isolated, for it was not to be believed that England or any other Power would take a part or even acknowledge the slightest interest in a question between two sorts of monks.

On the other hand, the violent language of M. de Lavalette, his threats, the persistence of the French Government, and the advance of the Toulon fleet to the Bay of Salamis, all these signs seemed to exclude the expectation that the French Government would easily give way. Here was an error. Zealous himself, the Russiam Ambassador imagined a zeal in the Government and the Church to which he was opposing himself, and fancied that he saw in the French Ambassador's 'resist-'ance a proof of the encroaching spirit of that Church which 'proclaims itself universal, and looked for its real cause in the 'unceasing desire of the same Church to extend the sphere of 'its action.'[2] He failed to see that his French antagonist might

[1] 13th April.

[2] 'Eastern Papers,' part i., p. 139.

suddenly smile and throw off the cause of the Latin Church, and so rob the Czar of the signal triumph on which he was reckoning by the process of mere concession.

But whilst to the common judgment of men who watched this haughty Embassy it seemed that the Czar in all the pride of strength and firm purpose was descending on his prey, he was fulfilling the utmost hope of the patient enemy in the West, who had long pursued him with a stealthy joy, and was now keenly marking him down.

---

## CHAPTER X.

State of the dispute respecting the Holy Places.

MEANTIME the course of events affecting the question of the Holy Places had shifted the grounds of dispute; for the solemn act performed at Bethlehem in the foregoing December had converted the claims of the Latins into established privileges, and the Emperor Nicholas, notwithstanding his religious excitement, had still enough wisdom to see that, although he might have been able to prevent this result by a violent use of his power at an earlier period, he could not now undo what was done. Without outraging Catholic Europe, and even, it may be believed, his own sense of religious propriety, he could not now wrench the key of the Bethlehem Church from the hands of the Latin monks, nor tear down the silver star from the Holy Stable of the Nativity. Therefore all that Prince Mentschikoff demanded in regard to the key and the star was a declaration by the Turkish Government that the delivery of the key implied no ownership over the principal altar of the Church, that no change should be made in the system of the religious ceremonies or the hours of service, that the guardianship of the Great Gate should always be intrusted to a Greek priest, and finally that the silver star should be deemed to be a gift coming from the mere generosity of the Sultan, and conferring no sort of new rights.[1] In regard to the shrine of the Blessed Virgin at Gethsemane, Prince Mentschikoff required that the Greeks should have precedence at her tomb. He also insisted that the gardens of the Church of Bethlehem should remain in the joint guardianship of the Greeks and the Latins, and in demanding that some buildings which overlooked the terraces of the

[1] 'Eastern Papers,' part i., p. 129.

Church of the Holy Sepulchre should be pulled down, he required that the site of these buildings should never become the property of any 'nation,' but be walled off and kept apart as neutral ground. This last demand is curious. The Russian Government felt that even at Jerusalem it would be well to set apart one small shred of ground and keep it free from the strife of the Churches.

But the last of Prince Mentschikoff's demands in regard to the Holy Places was the one most hard to solve. It has been said that in comparing the ways of men in the East with the ways of men in the West there are found many subjects on which their views are not merely different, but opposite. One of these is the business of repairing Churches. Whilst the English Churchmen were contending that they ought not to be laden with the whole burden of keeping their sacred buildings in repair, the Christians in Palestine were willing to set the world in flames for the sake of maintaining their rival claims to the honor of repairing churches. The cupola of the Church of the Holy Sepulchre at Jerusalem was out of order. The Greeks, supported by Russia, claimed the right to repair it. The Latins denied their right. The dispute raged. Then, as usual, the wise and decorous Turk stepped in between the combatants, and said he would repair the Church himself. This did not content the Greeks, and Prince Mentschikoff now demanded that the ancient rights of the Greeks to repair the great Cupola and Church at Jerusalem should be recognized and confirmed, and, although he did not reject the Sultan's offer to supply the means for the repairs, he insisted that the work should be under the control of the Greek Patriarch of Jerusalem.[1]

Some of these demands were resisted by France; and, although M. de Lavalette had been long since recalled, M. de la Cour who succeeded him seemed inclined to be somewhat persistent, especially in regard to the question of the Cupola and the question of precedence at the tomb of the Blessed Virgin.

It seems probable, however, that although M. de la Cour may have been sufficiently supplied with instructions touching the immediate question in hand, he had not perceived so clearly as his English colleague the dawn of the new French policy. From the communications of his own Government before he crossed the Channel, from his sojourn at Paris, and from the tenor of the dispatches from England, Lord Stratford had gathered means of inferring that France no longer intended to keep

[1] 'Eastern Papers,' part i., p. 129.

herself apart from England by persisting in her pressure upon the Sultan, and, supposing that she had made up her mind to enter upon this new policy, Lord Stratford might well entertain a hope that the question whether a Greek priest should be allowed to control the repair of a Cupola at Jerusalem, or whether the door-keeper of a Church should be a Greek or a Latin, would not be fought with undue obstinacy by the quick-witted countrymen of Voltaire. He spoke with M. de la Cour, and found that he was prepared for concession, if matters could be so arranged as to satisfy what Lord Stratford, in his haughty and almost zoological way, liked to call 'French feelings of honor.'[1]

Lord Stratford's measures for settling it.

By means of his communications with the Turks, the English Ambassador easily ascertained the points on which Prince Mentschikoff might be expected to be inexorable. These were:—the repair of the Cupola, the question of precedence at the tomb of the Virgin, and the question about the Greek door-keeper in the Church of Bethlehem. Furnished with this clew, Lord Stratford saw M. de la Cour, and dissuaded him from committing himself to a determined resistance on any of these three questions. He also gave his French colleague to understand that in his opinion the Greek pretension upon these three points stood on strong ground, and urged him to bear in mind the great European interests at stake, the declared moderation of the French Government, and the triumph already achieved by France in regard to the key and the silver star. And then Lord Stratford gave M. de la Cour a pleasing glimpse of the discomfiture into which their Russian colleague would be thrown if only the question of the Holy Places could be settled.[2] The French Ambassador soon began to enter into the spirit of these counsels.

On the other hand, Prince Mentschikoff was also willing to dispose of this question of the Holy Places, for he had now seen enough to be aware that he would not encounter sufficient resistance upon this matter to give him either a signal triumph or a tenable ground of rupture, and the angry dispatches which he was receiving from St. Petersburg made him impatient to press forward his ulterior demand. The two contending negotiators being thus disposed, it was soon found that the hinderances which prevented their coming to terms were very slender. But it often happens that the stress which a common man lays upon any subject of dispute is proportioned to the energy which he has spent in dealing with it rather than to the

[1] 'Eastern Papers,' part i., p. 134.

[2] Ibid., p. 155.

real magnitude of the question itself; and when Prince Mentschikoff and M. de la Cour seemed to be approaching to a settlement, they allowed their minds to become once again so much heated by the strenuous discussions of small matters that 'the 'difficulty of settling the question of the Holy Places threat-'ened to increase. The French and Russian Ambassadors in-'sisted on their respective pretensions, while the Porte inclined 'but hesitated to assume the responsibility of deciding between 'them.'[1] Then at last the hour was ripe for the intervention of Lord Stratford de Redcliffe. 'I thought,' said he, 'it was 'time for me to adopt a more prominent part in reconciling 'the adverse parties.'

He was more than equal to the task. Being by nature so grave and stately as to be able to refrain from a smile without effort and even without design, he prevented the vain and presumptuous Russian from seeing the minuteness and inanity of the things which he was gaining by his violent attempt at diplomacy. For the Greek Patriarch to be authorized to watch the mending of a dilapidated roof, for the Greek votaries to have the first hour of the day at a tomb, and finally for the door-keeper of a Church to be always a Greek, though without any right of keeping out his opponents—these things might be trifles, but awarded to All the Russias through the stately mediation of the English Ambassador, they seemed to gain in size and majesty, and for the moment perhaps the sensations of the Prince were nearly the same as though he were receiving the surrender of a province or the engagements of a great alliance. On the other hand, Lord Stratford was unfailing in his deference to the motives of action which he had classed under the head of 'French feelings of honor,' and if M. de la Cour was set on fire by the thought that at the tomb of the Virgin, or any where else, the Greek priests were to perform their daily worship before the hour appointed for the services of the Church which looked to France for support, Lord Stratford was there to explain in his grand quiet way that the priority proposed to be given to the Greeks was a priority resulting from the habit of early prayer which obtained in Oriental Churches, and not from their claim to have precedence over the species of monk which was protected by Frenchmen. At length he addressed the two Ambassadors; he solemnly expressed his hope that they would come to an adjustment. His words brought calm. In obedience, as it were, to the order of Nature, the lesser minds gave way to the greater, and the

[1] 'Eastern Papers,' part i., p. 157.

contention between the Churches for the shrines of Palestine was closed. The manner in which the Sultan should guarantee this apportionment of the shrines was still left open, but in all other respects the question of the Holy Places was settled.[1]

*He settles it.*

According to the terms of the arrangement thus effected, the key of the Church of Bethlehem, and the silver star placed in the Grotto of the Nativity, were to remain where they were, but were to confer no new right on the Latins, and the door-keeper of the Church was to be a Greek priest as before, but was to have no right to obstruct other nations in their right to enter the building. The question of precedence at the tomb of the Blessed Virgin was ingeniously eluded by the device before spoken of, for the priority given to the Greeks was treated as though it resulted from a convenient arrangement of hours rather than from any intent to grant precedence, and it was accordingly arranged that the Greeks should worship in the Church every morning immediately after sunrise, and then the Armenians, and then the Latins, each nation having an hour and a half for the purpose. Perhaps it was in order to hinder the outgoing worshipers from coming into conflict with those who were about to begin their devotions, that the gentle Armenians were thus interposed between the two angry Churches. The gardens of the Convent of Bethlehem were to remain as before under the joint care of the Greeks and Latins. With regard to the cupola of the Church of the Holy Sepulchre, it was arranged that it should be repaired by the Sultan in such a way as not to alter its form; and if in the course of the building any deviation from this engagement should appear to be threatened, the Greek Patriarch of Jerusalem was to be authorized to remonstrate, with a view to guard against innovation. The buildings overlooking the terraces of the Church of the Holy Sepulchre were to have their windows walled up, but were not to be demolished, and therefore no effect could be given to the Russian plan of setting apart a neutral ground to be kept free from the dominion of both the contending Churches. All these arrangements were to be embodied in firmans addressed by the Sultan to the Turkish authorities at Jerusalem.[2]

*Terms on which it was settled.*

Thus, after having tasked the patience of European diplomacy for a period of nearly three years, the business of apportioning the holy shrines of Palestine between the Churches of the East and of the West was brought at last to a close. The

[1] April 22nd, 1853. 'Eastern Papers,' part i., p. 157.
[2] 'Eastern Papers,' part i., p. 248.

question was perhaps growing ripe for settlement when Lord Stratford reached Constantinople, but, whether it was so or not, he closed it in seventeen days. For the part which he had taken in helping to achieve this result he received the thanks of the Turkish Government, and of the Russian and the French Ambassadors. The Divan might well be grateful to him, and he deserved too the thanks of his French colleague; for, having more insight into the new policy of the French Government than M. de la Cour, he was able to place him in the path which turned out to be the right one. But when Lord Stratford received the thanks of Prince Mentschikoff he felt perhaps that the gravity which had served him well in these transactions was a gift which was still of some use.

---

## CHAPTER XI.

WHILST the question of the Holy Places was approaching the solution which was attained on the 22nd of April, Prince Mentschikoff went on with his demand for the protectorate of the Greek Church in Turkey, but the character of his mission was fitfully changed from time to time by the tenor of his instructions from home. On the 12th of April, the peaceful views which had prevailed at St. Petersburg some weeks before were still governing the Russian embassy at Constantinople, and Lord Stratford was able to report that the altered tone and demeanor of Prince Mentschikoff corresponded with the conciliatory assurances which Count Nesselrode had been giving in the previous month to Sir Hamilton Seymour. But on the following day all was changed. Fresh dispatches came in from St. Petersburg. They breathed anger and violent impatience, and of this anger and of this impatience the causes were visible. It was the measure adopted in Paris, several weeks before, which had rekindled the dying embers of the quarrel at St. Petersburg, and the torch was now brought to Constantinople. It has been seen that, without reason, and without communication with the English Ministers[1] (though it professed to be acting in unison with them), the French Government had ordered the Toulon fleet to approach the scene of controversy by advancing to Salamis;

Peaceful aspect of the negotiation.

Angry dispatches from St. Petersburg.

Cause of the change.

[1] 'Eastern Papers,' part i., p. 98.

and it was whilst the indignation roused by this movement was still fresh in the mind of the Emperor Nicholas that the dispatches had been framed. Moreover, at the time of sending off the dispatches, the Czar knew that by the day they reached the shores of the Bosphorus, the man of whom he never could think with temper or calmness would already be at Constantinople, and he of course understood that in the way of diplomatic strife his Lord High Admiral the Serene Prince Governor of Finland was unfit for an encounter with Lord Stratford. He seems therefore to have determined to extricate his Ambassador from the unequal conflict by putting an end to what there was of a diplomatic character in the mission, and urging him into a course of sheer violence which would supersede the finer labors of negotiation.

From the change which the dispatches wrought in Prince Mentschikoff's course of action, from the steps which he afterward took, and from the known bent and temper of the Czar's mind, it may be inferred that the instructions now received by the Russian Ambassador were somewhat to this effect: 'The 'French fleet has been ordered to Salamis. The 'Emperor is justly indignant. You must bring 'your mission to a close forthwith. Be peremptory 'both with the French and the Turks. If the French Ambas-'sador is obstinate enough upon the question of the Holy Places 'to give you a tenable ground on which you can stand out, then 'hasten at once to a rupture upon that business without farther 'discussion about our ulterior demands. But if the French 'Ambassador throws no sufficing difficulties in the way of the 'settlement of the question of the Holy Places, then press your 'demand for the protectorate of the Greek Church. Press it 'peremptorily. In carrying out these instructions, you have 'full discretion so far as concerns all forms and details, but in 'regard to time the Emperor grants you no latitude. You 'must force your mission to a close. By the time you receive 'this dispatch Stratford Canning will be at Constantinople. He 'has ever thwarted His Majesty the Emperor. The inscruta-'ble will of Providence has bestowed upon him great gifts of 'mind which he has used for no other purpose than to baffle 'and humiliate the Emperor, and keep down the Orthodox 'Church. In negotiation or in contest for influence over the 'Turks he would overcome you and crush you, but his instruc-'tions do not authorize him to be more than a mere peaceful 'negotiator. You, on the contrary, are supported by force. 'He can only persuade: you can threaten. Strike terror. Make 'the Divan feel the weight of our preparations in Bessarabia

Inferred tenor of the fresh dispatches.

'and at Sebastopol. Dannenburg's horsemen are close upon 'the Pruth. When the Emperor remembers the position of 'the 4th and the 5th corps d'armée and the forwardness of his 'naval preparations, he conceives he has a right to expect that 'you should instantly be able to take the ascendant over a man 'who, with all his hellish ability, is after all nothing more than 'the representative of a country absorbed in the pursuit of 'gain. The Emperor can not and will not endure that his Rep-'resentative, supported by the forces of the Empire, should re-'main secondary to the English Ambassador. Again the Em-'peror commands me to say you must strike terror. Use a 'fierce insulting tone. If the Turks remain calm, it will be be-'cause Stratford Canning supports them. Therefore demand 'private audiences of the Sultan, and press upon his fears. If 'your last demands, whatever they may be, are rejected, quit 'Constantinople immediately with your whole suite, and carry 'away with you the whole staff of our Legation.'

Mentschikoff's demand for a protectorate of the Greek Church in Turkey.

On the day after receiving his dispatches Prince Mentschikoff had a long interview with Rifaat Pasha, and strove to wrench from him the assent of the Turkish Government to the terms already submitted to the Porte as the project for a secret treaty. And, although it happened that in the course of the negotiations on this subject Russia submitted to accept many changes in the form or the wording of the engagement which she required, it may be said with accuracy that from the first to the last she always required the Porte to give her an instrument which should have the force of a treaty engagement, and confer upon her the right to insist that the Greek Church and Clergy in Turkey should continue in the enjoyment of all their existing privileges. It was clear, therefore, that if the Sultan should be induced to set his seal to any instrument of this kind,

Effect which would be produced by conceding it.

he would be chargeable with a breach of treaty engagements whenever a Greek bishop could satisfy a Russian Emperor that there was some privilege formerly enjoyed by him or his Church which had been varied or withdrawn. It was plain that for the Sultan to yield thus much would be to make the Czar a partaker of his sovereignty. This seemed clear to men of all nations, except the Russians themselves, but especially it seemed clear to those who happened to know something of the structure of the Ottoman Empire. The indolence or the wise instinct of the Mussulman rulers had given to the Christian 'nations' living within the Sultan's dominions many of the blessings which we cherish under the name of 'self-government,' and since the Greek Christians had exercised these privileges by deputing their bishops and their priests to administer the authority conceded to the 'nation,' it followed that the spiritual dominion of the priesthood had become blended with a great share of temporal power. So many of the duties of prefects, of magistrates, of assessors, of collectors, and of police were discharged by bishops, priests, and deacons, that a protectorate of these ecclesiastics might be so used by a powerful foreign Prince, as to carry with it a virtual sovereignty over ten or fourteen millions of laymen.

The negotiations which followed the demand.

All this had been seen by Lord Stratford and by the Turkish Ministers, and when Prince Mentschikoff pressed the treaty upon Rifaat Pasha he was startled, as it would seem, by the calmness, and the full knowledge which he encountered. 'The treaty,' said Rifaat Pasha, 'would be giving to Russia an exclusive protectorate over the 'whole Greek population, their clergy, and their Churches.'[1]

The Prince, it would seem, now began to know that he had to do with the English Ambassador, for he made the alteration before adverted to in the draft of his treaty, and on the 20th of April read it in its amended shape to Lord Stratford, and assured him that it was only an explanatory guarantee of existing treaties, giving to the co-religionists of Russia what Austria already possessed with regard to hers. Lord Stratford on that day had approached to within forty-eight hours of the settlement of the question of the Holy Places, which he deemed it so vital to achieve, and it may be easily imagined that in the remarks which he might make upon hearing the draft read he would abstain with great care from irritating discussion, and would not utter a word more than was necessary for the purpose of fairly indicating that his postponement of discussion on the subject of the ulterior demands was not to be mistaken for acquiescence; but all that for that purpose was needed he fairly said, for he observed to Prince Mentschikoff 'that the 'Sultan's promise to protect his Christian subjects in the free 'exercise of their religion differed extremely from a right con'ferred on any foreign Power to enforce that protection, and 'also that the same degree of interference might be dangerous 'to the Porte, when exercised by so powerful an empire as 'Russia on behalf of ten millions of Greeks, and innocent in 'the case of Austria, whose influence derivable from religious 'sympathy was confined to a small number of Catholics, in'cluding her own subjects.'[2] These remarks were surely not ambiguous, but it seems probable that Prince Mentschikoff,

[1] 'Eastern Papers,' part i., p. 153.

[2] Ibid., p. 156.

misled by his previous impression as to what Lord Stratford really objected to, may have imagined that the proposed convention in its altered form would not be violently disapproved by the English Ambassador. At all events, he seems to have instructed his Government to that effect.

On the 19th of April the Russian Ambassador addressed his remonstrances and his demands to the Turkish Minister for Foreign Affairs in the form of a diplomatic Note. In the first sentence of this singular document Prince Mentschikoff tells the Minister for Foreign Affairs that he must have 'seen the 'duplicity of his predecessor.' In the next he tells him he must be 'convinced of the extent to which the respect due to 'the Emperor had been disregarded, and how great was his 'magnanimity in offering to the Porte the means of escaping 'from the embarrassments occasioned to it by the bad faith of 'its Ministers;' and then, after more objurgation in the same strain, and after dealing in a peremptory way with the question of the Holy Places, the Note goes on to declare that 'in consequence of the hostile tendencies manifested for some years 'past in whatever related to Russia, she required in behalf of 'the religious communities of the orthodox Church an explanatory and positive act of guarantee.' Then the Note requested that the Ottoman Cabinet would 'be pleased in its 'wisdom to weigh the serious nature of the offense which it 'had committed, and compare it with the moderation of the 'demands made for reparation and guarantee, which a consideration of legitimate defense might have put forward at greater length and in more peremptory terms.' Finally the Note stated that 'the reply of the Minister for Foreign Affairs would 'indicate to the Ambassador the ulterior duties which he would have to discharge,' and intimated that those duties would be 'consistent with the dignity of the Government which he represented, and of the religion professed by his Sovereign.'[1]

It might have been politic for Prince Mentschikoff to send such a Note as this in the midst of the panic which followed his landing in the early days of March, but it was vain to send it now. The Turks had returned to their old allegiance. They could take their rest, for they knew that Lord Stratford watched. Him they feared, him they trusted, him they obeyed. It was in vain now that the Prince sought to crush the will of the Sultan and of his Ministers. Whether he threatened, or whether he tried to cajole; whether he sent his dragoman with angry messages to the Porte, or whether he went thither in person;

[1] 'Eastern Papers,' part i., p. 158.

whether he urged the members of the Government in private interviews, or whether he obtained audience of the Sultan, he always encountered the same firmness, the same courteous deference, and, above all, that same terrible moderation which day by day, and hour by hour, was putting him more and more in the wrong. The voice which spoke to him might be the voice of the Grand Vizier, or the voice of the Reis Effendi, or the voice of the Sultan himself, but the mind which he was really encountering was always the mind of one man.

Far from quailing under the threatening tone of the Note, the Turkish Government now determined to enter into no convention with Russia, and to reject Prince Mentschikoff's proposals respecting the protection of the Greek Church in Turkey. The Grand Vizier and the Reis Effendi calmly consulted Lord Stratford as to the manner in which they should give effect to the decision of the Cabinet, and Lord Stratford, now placed at ease by the settlement of the question of the Holy Places, contentedly prepared to encounter the next expected moves of Prince Mentschikoff.[1]

Rage of the Czar on finding himself encountered by Lord Stratford.

In strife for ascendency like that which was now going on between the Czar and Lord Stratford, the pain of undergoing defeat is of such a kind that the pangs of the sufferer accumulate; and far from being assuaged by time, they are every day less easy to bear than they were the day before. By the pomp and the declared significance of Prince Mentschikoff's mission, the Emperor Nicholas had drawn upon himself the eyes of Europe, and the presence of the religious ingredient had brought him under the gaze of many millions of his own subjects who were not commonly observers of the business of the state. And he who, in transactions thus watched by men, was preparing for him cruel discomfiture—he who kept him on the rack, and regulated his torments with cold unrelenting precision—was the old familiar enemy whom he had once refused to receive as the English Ambassador at St. Petersburg. People who knew the springs of action in the Russian capital used to say at that time that the whole 'Eastern Question,' as it was called, lay inclosed in one name—lay inclosed in the name of Lord Stratford. They acknowledged that the Emperor Nicholas could not bear the stress of our Ambassador's authority with the Porte.

And in truth, the Czar's power of endurance was drawing to a close. He wavered and wavered again and again. He was versed in business of state, and it would seem that when

[1] 24th April. Ibid., p. 160. The settlement of the question of the Holy Places was on the 22nd.

his mind was turned to things temporal he truly meant to be politic and just. But in his more religious moments he was furious. Even for Nicholas the Czar it was all but impossible to endure the Ambassador's political ascendency, but the bare thought of Lord Stratford's protecting Christianity in Turkey was more than could be borne by Nicholas the Pontiff. Men not jesting approached him with stories that the Ambassador had determined to bring over the Sultan to the Church of England. His brain was not strong enough to be safe against rumors like that. He almost came to feel that the Englishman who seemed to be endued with strange powers of compulsion always used for the support of Moslem dominion and for curbing the orthodox Russo-Greek Church was a being in his nature Satanic, and that resistance to him was as much a duty (and was a duty as thickly beset with practical difficulties) as resistance to the great enemy of mankind. Maddened at last by this singular kind of torment, the Czar broke loose from the restraints of policy, and was even so void of counsel, that, having determined to do violence to the Sultan, he did not take the common care of giving to his action any semblance of consistency with public law.

Its effect upon the negotiation.

The dispatches framed under the orders of a monarch in this condition of mind reached Prince Mentschikoff in the beginning of May. Breathing fresh anger, and enjoining haste, they fiercely drove him on. They urged him to an almost instantaneous rupture, without giving him a standing-ground for his quarrel. Yet at this time the condition of things was of such a kind that a good Cause, nay, even a specious grievance, would have helped Prince Mentschikoff better than the advance of the 4th and 5th corps or the patrolling of Dannenburg's cavalry.

Mentschikoff's difficulty.

In truth, what now befell the Russian Ambassador was this: —he found himself placed under the compulsion of violent instructions at a time when all ground for just resentment was wanting. He could obey his orders, and force on a rupture, but he could no longer do this upon grounds which Europe would regard as having a semblance of fairness. When he had dispatched his note of the 19th of April, the question of the Holy Places was still unsettled, and he was then able to blend that grievance with other matters, and make it serve as a basis for his ulterior demands; but now that that question was disposed of, his standing-ground failed him, for he alleged against the Sultan no infraction of a treaty, and the only grievance of which he had to complain had been redressed on the 22nd of April; and yet, passing straight from this smooth condition of things, he had to call upon the Sultan to sign a treaty which he disapproved, and to make his refusal to do so a ground for the immediate rupture of diplomatic relations.

He is baffled by Lord Stratford.

The natural hope of a diplomatist placed in a stress of this sort would have lain in the chance that the Government upon which he was pressing might be guilty of some imprudence, and it may be inferred that the Note of the 19th had been framed with a view of provoking the Turkish Ministers into a burst of anger. But every hope of this kind had been baffled. Turks were fanatical, Turks were fierce, Turks were quick to avenge, and, above all, Turks were liable to panic; but some spell had come upon the race. The spell had come upon the Sultan, it had come upon the Turkish Ministers, it had come upon the Great Council, it had come even upon the larger mass of the warlike people who bring their feelings to bear upon the policy of their Sultan. At every step of his negotiation Prince Mentschikoff encountered an adversary always courteous, always moderate, but cold, steadfast, wary, and seeming as though he looked to the day when perhaps he might wreak cruel vengeance. Who this was the Prince now knew, and he perhaps began to understand the nature of the torment inflicted upon his imperial Master by the bare utterance of the one hated name. Prince Mentschikoff found himself powerless as a negotiator, and it was clear that unless he could descend to the rude expedient of an ultimatum or a threat, he was a man annulled. Indeed, without some act of violence he could hardly deliver himself from ridicule.

He presses his demand in a new form.

Therefore, on the 5th of May, Prince Mentschikoff forwarded to the Minister for Foreign Affairs the draft of a Sened or Convention, purporting to be made between the Sultan and the Emperor of Russia. This proposed Sened confirmed with the force of a treaty engagement the arrangements respecting the Holy Places which had been made in favor of the Greek Church, and it also introduced and applied to the rival Churches a provision similar in its wording to that which often appears in commercial treaties, and goes by the name of 'the most favored nation clause.' But the noxious feature of the Convention was detected in the Article which purported to secure for ever to the Orthodox Church and its clergy all the rights and immunities which they had already enjoyed, and those of which they were possessed from ancient times.[1] Here, under a new form, was the old en-

[1] 'Eastern Papers,' part i., p. 167.

deavor to obtain for Russia a protectorate of the Greek Church in Turkey.

This draft of a Convention was annexed to a Note, in which Prince Mentschikoff pressed its immediate adoption, and urged the Sublime Porte, 'laying aside all hesitation and all mistrust, 'by which,' he declared 'the dignity and the generous senti-'ments of his august Master would be aggrieved,'[1] to delay its decision no longer. In conclusion, Prince Mentschikoff suffered himself to request that the Minister for Foreign Affairs would be good enough to let him have his answer by the following Tuesday, and to add, that he could not 'consider any 'longer delay in any other light than as a want of respect 'toward his Government, which would impose upon him the 'most painful duty.'[1]

Counsels of Lord Stratford.

Upon receiving this hostile communication, the Minister for Foreign Affairs appealed to Lord Stratford for counsel. He advised the Turkish Government to be still deferential, still courteous, still willing to go to the very edge of what might be safely conceded, but to stand firm.

His communications with Prince Mentschikoff.

At this time Lord Stratford received a visit from Prince Mentschikoff, and ascertained from him that he did not mean to recede from his demands. The Prince declared that he had run out the whole line of his moderation, and could go no farther, and that his Government would no longer submit to the state of inferiority in which he said Russia was held with reference to the co-religionists of the Emperor Nicholas.

A few days later Lord Stratford addressed a letter to Prince Mentschikoff, in which, with all the diplomatic courtesy of which he was master, he strove to convey to the Prince some idea of the way in which he was derogating from that justice and moderation toward foreign sovereigns which had hitherto marked the reign of the Emperor Nicholas. The answer of Prince Mentschikoff announced that it was impossible for him to agree in the views pressed upon him by Lord Stratford, and (after a little more of the wasteful verbiage in which Russia used to assert that her exaction was good and wholesome for Turkey) the Prince claimed a right to freedom of action. He said that he was not conscious of having failed in the loyal assurances given by his Government to the Cabinet of the Queen, declared that he had been perfectly sincere in his communications with Lord Stratford, and owned that he had expected a

[1] 'Eastern Papers,' part i., p. 165.

frank co-operation on his part. But when he had written these common things the truth broke out. 'The Emperor's 'legation,' said he, 'can not stay at Constantinople under the 'circumstances in which it has been placed. It can not sub- 'mit to the secondary position to which it might be wished to 'reduce it.'[1]

Lord Stratford, it would seem, had now little hope of being able to bring about an accommodation, and henceforth his great object was to take care that the Porte should stand firm, but should so act that in the opinion of England and of Europe the Sultan should seem justified in exposing himself to the hazard of a rupture with Russia.

His advice to the Turkish Ministers.

Late at night Lord Stratford saw the Grand Vizier at his country-house, and the Minister for Foreign Affairs and the Seraskier were present. During the day there had been a little failing of heart, and when the Turkish Ministers were in the presence of M. de la Cour, they had seemed 'disposed to shrink from encountering the 'consequences of Prince Mentschikoff's retiring in displeas- 'ure,'[2] but either they had dissembled their fears in the presence of the English Ambassador, or else, whilst Lord Stratford was in the same room with them, their fear of other Powers was suspended. They were unanimous in regarding the Convention as inadmissible. Lord Stratford's determination was that the demand of Prince Mentschikoff should be resisted, but that at the same time there should be shown so much of courtesy and of forbearance, and so great a willingness to go to the utmost limit of safe concession, and to improve the condition of the Christian subjects of the Porte, that the Turks should appear before Europe in a character almost angelic. 'I ad- 'vised them,' said he, 'to open a door for negotiation in the 'Note to be prepared, and to withhold no concession compati- 'ble with the real welfare and independence of the Empire. I 'could not in conscience urge them to accept the Russian de- 'mands, as now presented to them, but I reminded them of 'the guarantee required by Prince Mentschikoff, and strongly 'recommended that if the guarantee he required was inadmis- 'sible, a substitute for it should be found in a frank and com- 'prehensive exercise of the Sultan's authority in the promulga- 'tion of a firman, securing both the spiritual and temporal 'privileges of all the Porte's tributary subjects, and by way of 'farther security communicated officially to the five great Powers of Christendom.'[3] To all these counsels the Turkish Ministers listened with assenting mind.

[1] 'Eastern Papers,' part i., p. 217. [2] Ibid., p. 177. [3] Id. ibid.

But it was now late in the night, and the Ambassador rose. Perhaps the hour and the Ambassador's movement to depart cast a shadow of anxiety upon the minds of the Turkish Ministers. Perhaps the ripple of the waters (for the conference was in a house on the edge of the Bosphorus) called to mind the thought of the English flag. At all events, the Grand Vizier, in that moment of weakness, suffered himself to cast a thought after the arm of the flesh, and to ask whether the Porte might expect the eventual approach of the English squadron in the Mediterranean. Lord Stratford rebuked him. 'I replied,' said he, 'that I considered the position in its present stage to be one of a moral character, and consequently that its difficulties or hazards, whatever they might be, should be rather met by acts of a similar description than by demonstrations calculated to increase alarm and provoke resentment.' It was a new and a strange task for this Grand Vizier of a warlike Tartar nation to be called upon to defend a threatened empire by 'acts of a moral character,' but after all his reliance was upon the man. It might be hard for him to understand how the mere advantage of being in the right could be used against the Sebastopol fleet, or the army that was hovering upon the Pruth; but if he looked upon the close, angry, resolute lips of the Ambassador, and the grand overhanging of his brow, he saw that which more than all else in the world takes hold of the Oriental mind, for he saw strength held in reserve. And this faith was of such a kind that, far from being weakened, it would gather new force from Lord Stratford's refusal to speak of material help. The Turkish Ministry determined to reject Prince Mentschikoff's proposals, and to do this in the way advised by the English Ambassador. All this while Lord Stratford was unconscious of exercising any ascendency over his fellow-creatures, and it seemed to him that the Turks were determining this momentous question by means of their unbiased judgments.[1]

Prince Mentschikoff was soon made aware of the refusal with which his demand was to be met, and finding that all his communications with the Turkish Ministers gave him nothing but the faithful echo of the counsels addressed to them by Lord Stratford, he seems to have imagined the plan of overstepping the Turkish Ministers, and endeavoring to wring an assent to his demands from the Sultan himself. It seems probable that Lord Stratford had been apprized of this intention, and was willing to defeat it, for on the 9th he sought a private

[1] 'Eastern Papers,' part i., p. 213.

audience of the Sultan; he sought it, of course, through the legitimate channel. The Minister for Foreign Affairs went with Lord Stratford to the Sultan's apartment, and then withdrew.

His audience of the Sultan.

The Ambassador spoke gravely to the Sultan of the danger with which his Empire was threatened, and then of the grounds for confidence. He was happy, he said, to find that His Majesty's servants, both Ministers and Council, were not less inclined to gratify the Russian Ambassador with all that could be safely conceded to him, than determined to withhold their consent from every requisition calculated to inflict a serious injury on the independence and dignity of their Sovereign. 'I had waited,' said Lord Stratford, 'to know 'their own unbiased impressions respecting the kind of guar'antee demanded by Prince Mentschikoff, and I could not do 'otherwise than approve the decision which they appeared to 'have adopted with unanimity. My own impression is, that 'if your Majesty should sanction that decision, the Ambassa'dor will break off his relations with the Porte and go away, 'together perhaps with his whole embassy: nor is it quite im'possible even that a temporary occupation, however unjust, 'of the Danubian Principalities by Russia may take place; 'but I feel certain that neither a declaration of war nor any 'other act of open hostility is to be apprehended for the pres'ent, as the Emperor Nicholas can not resort to such extremi'ties on account of the pending differences without contradict'ing his most solemn assurances, and exposing himself to the 'indignant censure of all Europe. I conceive that under such 'circumstances the true position to be maintained by the Porte 'is one of moral resistance to such demands as are really inad'missible on just and essential grounds, and that the principle 'should even be applied under protest to the occupation of the 'Principalities, not in weakness or despair, but in reliance on 'a good cause, and on the sympathy of friendly and independ'ent Governments. A firm adherence to this line of conduct, 'as long as it is possible to maintain it with honor, will, in my 'judgment, offer the best chances of ultimate success with the 'least practicable degree of provocation, and prevent disturb'ance of commercial interests. This language,' writes Lord Stratford, 'appeared to interest the Sultan deeply, and also to 'coincide with His Majesty's existing opinions. He said that 'he was well aware of the dangers to which I had alluded; 'that he was perfectly prepared, in the exercise of his own free 'will, to confirm and to render effective the protection prom'ised to all classes of his tributary subjects in matters of relig'ious worship, including the immunities and privileges granted 'to their respective clergy. He showed me the last communi-'cations in writing which had passed between his Ministers 'and the Russian Embassy; he thanked me for having helped 'to bring the question of the Holy Places to an arrangement; 'he professed his reliance on the friendly support of Great 'Britain.'

But now Lord Stratford apprized the Sultan that he had a communication to make to him which he had hitherto withheld from his Ministers, reserving it for the private ear of his Majesty. The pale Sultan listened.

The disclosure which he had reserved for the Sultan's ear

Then the Ambassador announced that, in the event of imminent danger, he was instructed to request the Commander of Her Majesty's forces in the Mediterranean to hold his squadron in readiness.[1]

This order was of itself a slight thing, and it conferred but a narrow and stinted authority; but, imparted to the Sultan in private audience by Lord Stratford de Redcliffe, it came with more weight than the promise of armed support from the lips of a common Statesman. Long withheld from the Turkish Ministers, and now disclosed to them through their Sovereign, it confirmed them in the faith that, whatever a man might know of the great Eltchi's power, there was always more to be known. And when a man once comes to be thus thought of by Orientals, he is more their master than one who seeks to overpower their minds by making coarse pretenses of strength.

On the 10th the Secretary for Foreign Affairs sent his answer to Prince Mentschikoff's demand. The letter was full of courtesy and deference toward Russia: it declared it to be the firm intention of the Porte to maintain unimpaired the rights of all the tributary subjects of the Empire, and it expressed a willingness to negotiate with Russia concerning a church and a hospital at Jerusalem, and also as to the privileges which should be conceded to Russian subjects, monks, and pilgrims; but the Note objected to entertain that portion of the Russian demands which went to give Russia a protectorate of the Greek Church in Turkey.[2]

Turkish answer to Mentschikoff's demand.

On the following day Prince Mentschikoff sent an angry reply to this Note, declining to accept it as an answer to his demand. He stated that he was instructed to negotiate for an engagement guaranteeing the priv-

Mentschikoff's angry reply.

[1] 'Eastern Papers,' part i., p. 213.

[2] May 10th. 'Eastern Papers,' part i., p. 196.

ileges of the Greek Church, as a mark of respect to the religious convictions of the Emperor, and if the principles which formed the basis of this proposed mark of respect were to be rejected, and if the Porte by a systematic opposition was to persist in closing the very approaches to an intimate and direct understanding, then the Prince declared with pain that he must consider his mission at an end, must break off relations with the Cabinet of the Sultan, and throw upon the responsibility of his Ministers all the consequences which might ensue. The Prince ended his Note by requiring that it should be answered within three days.[1]

On the second day after sending this Note, Prince Mentschikoff was to have had an interview with the Grand Vizier at half past one o'clock; but before that hour came the Prince took a step which had the effect of breaking up the Ministry.

His private audience of the Sultan.

Without the concurrence, and apparently without the previous knowledge of the Ministers, he found means to obtain a private audience of the Sultan at 10 o'clock in the morning. The Sultan did wrongly when he submitted to receive a foreign Ambassador without the advice or knowledge of his Ministers, and the Grand Vizier had the spirit to resent the course thus taken by his Sovereign, for upon being sent for by the Sultan, immediately after the audience, he requested permission to stay at home, and at the same time gave up his seals of office.

This causes a change of ministry at Constantinople,

The new Ministry, however, was formed of men who, as members of the Great Council, had declared opinions adverse to the extreme demands of Russia.[2] Reshid Pasha became the Secretary of State for Foreign Affairs, and this was not an appointment which disclosed any intention on the part of the Sultan to disengage himself from the counsels of the English Ambassador.

If the Sultan had erred in granting an audience without the assent of his Ministers, he had carried his weakness no farther.

but fails to shake the Sultan.

It soon transpired that Prince Mentschikoff had failed to wring from the Sultan any dangerous words. It seems that when the Prince came to press his demands upon the imperial ear, he found the monarch reposing in the calmness of mind which had been given him by the English Ambassador five days before, and in a few moments he had the mortification of hearing that, for all answers to his demands, he was referred to the Ministers of State.[3] In the judgment of Prince Mentschikoff, to be thus answered

[1] May 11th. 'Eastern Papers,' part i., p. 197.
[2] 'Eastern Papers,' part i., p. 194. [3] Ibid., p. 195.

was to be remitted back to Lord Stratford. It was hard to bear.

Prince Mentschikoff began his intercourse with the new Foreign Secretary by insisting upon an immediate reply to his Note of the 11th of May. Reshid Pasha asked for the delay of a few days on the ground of the change of Ministry. This reasonable demand was met at first by a refusal, but afterward by a Note, which seems to have been rendered incoherent by the difficulty in which Prince Mentschikoff was placed; for, on the one hand, a request for a delay of a few days, founded upon a change of Ministry, was a request too fair to be refused with decency, and, on the other hand, the violent orders which had just come in from St. Petersburg enjoined the Prince to close the unequal strife with Lord Stratford, and to enforce instant compliance, or at once break off and depart. The Note began by announcing that Reshid Pasha's communication imposed upon the Russian Ambassador the duty of breaking off from the then present time his official relations with the Sublime Porte; but it added that the Ambassador would suspend the last demand, which was to determine the attitude which Russia would thenceforth assume toward Turkey. The Note farther declared that a continuance of hesitation on the part of the Ottoman Government would be regarded as an indication of reserve and distrust offensive to the Russian Government, and that the departure of the Russian Ambassador, and also of the Imperial Legation, would be the inevitable and immediate consequence.

Mentschikoff violently presses his demands.

By the voices of forty-two against three, the Great Council of the Porte determined to adhere to the decision already taken; and on the 18th Reshid Pasha called upon Prince Mentschikoff, and orally imparted to him the extreme length to which the Turkish Government was willing to go in the way of concession. The honor of the Porte required, he said, that the exclusively spiritual privileges granted under the Sultan's predecessors, and confirmed by His Majesty, should remain in full force, and he declared that the equitable system pursued by the Porte toward its subjects demanded that the Greek clergy should be on as good a footing as other Christian subjects of the Sultan. He added, that a firman was to issue, proclaiming this determination on the part of the Sultan. In regard to the shrine at Jerusalem, Reshid Pasha was willing to engage that there should be no change without communicating with the Russian and French Governments. Reshid Pasha also consented that a church and hospital for the Rus-

The Great Council determine to resist.

Offers made by the Porte under the advice of Lord Stratford.

sians should be built at Jerusalem; and in regard to all these last matters connected with the Holy Land, the Porte, he said, was willing to solemnize its promise by a formal convention. These overtures were made in exact accordance with a Paper of advice which Lord Stratford had placed in the hands of Reshid Pasha five days before.[1] Virtually Reshid Pasha offered Prince Mentschikoff every thing which Russia had demanded except the protectorate of the Greek Church in Turkey.[2] That he refused.

Mentschikoff replies by declaring his mission at an end.

Instantly, and without waiting for the written statement of the proposals orally conveyed to him by Reshid Pasha, Prince Mentschikoff determined to break off the negotiation. On the same day he addressed to the Porte an official Note, which purported to be truly his last. In this he declared that, by rejecting with distrust the wishes of the Emperor in favor of the orthodox Greco-Russian religion, the Sublime Porte had failed in what was due to an august and ancient ally. The refusal, he said, was a fresh injury. He declared his mission at an end; and after asserting that the Imperial Court could not, without prejudice to its dignity and without exposing itself to fresh insults, continue to maintain a mission at Constantinople, he announced that he should not only quit Constantinople himself, but should take with him the whole Staff of the Imperial Legation, except the Director of the Commercial Department. The Prince added, that the refusal of a guarantee for the orthodox Greco-Russian religion obliged the Imperial Government to seek in its own power that security which the Porte declined to give by way of treaty engagement; and he added, that any infringement of the existing state of the Eastern Church would be regarded as an act of hostility to Russia.[3]

The representatives of the four Powers assembled by Lord Stratford.

Policy involved in this step.

Prince Mentschikoff's departure did not immediately follow the dispatch of this Note, and on the morning of the 19th Lord Stratford took a step of great moment to the tranquillity of Europe, for it laid the seed of a wholesome policy, which, until it was ruined, as will be seen hereafter, by the evil designs of some, and by the weakness of other men, promised fair to enforce justice and to maintain truth without bringing upon the world the calamity of a war. Instead of putting himself in communication with one only of the other great Powers, and so preparing a road to hostilities, the English Ambassador assembled the representatives of Austria, France,

[1] 'Eastern Papers,' part i., p. 196. [2] Ibid., p. 205, and see p. 252.
[3] 18th May. Ibid., p. 206.

Unanimity of the four representatives.

and Prussia. It then appeared that there was no essential difference of opinion between the representatives of the four great Powers. None of them questioned the soundness of the Porte's views in resisting the extreme demands of Russia; all acknowledged the spirit of conciliation displayed by the Sultan's Ministers; all were agreed in desiring to prevent the rupture; all desired that the Emperor Nicholas should be enabled to recede without discredit from the wrong path which he had taken, and were willing to cover his retreat by every device which was consistent with the honor and welfare of other States. This union of opinion, followed close by concerted action, was surely a right example of the way in which it was becoming for Europe to regard an approach to injustice by one of the great Powers.

Their measures.

It was arranged that the Austrian Envoy should call upon Prince Mentschikoff; should apprize him of the sorrow with which the representatives of the four Powers contemplated the rupture of his relations with the Porte; should express the lively gratification which a friendly solution, if that were still possible, would afford them; and, finally, should ascertain whether the Prince would receive through a private channel the Porte's intended Note, and give it a calm consideration.[1] This appeal from the representatives of the four great Powers produced no effect on the mind of Prince Mentschikoff,[2] and Lord Stratford scarcely expected that it would do so; but it commenced, or rather it marked and strengthened, that expression of grave disapproval on the part of the four Powers, which was the true and the safe corrective of an outrage threatened by one.

After his official relations with the Porte had come to a close, Prince Mentschikoff received and rejected the Turkish Note[3] which embodied the concessions already described to him orally by Reshid Pasha; but on the evening of the 20th of May the Prince determined to make a concession in point of form, and to be content to have the engagement which he was demanding from the Porte in the form of a diplomatic Note, instead of a Treaty or Convention.

Russia's ultimatum.

In furtherance of this view, though his official capacity had ceased, he caused to be delivered to Reshid Pasha the draft of a Note to be given by the Porte. This draft purported to involve the Porte in engagements exactly the same as those which it had refused to contract, and to give to Rus-

[1] 'Eastern Papers,' part i., p. 205. [2] Ibid., p. 219.

[3] This Note, being the last offer made by the Turkish Government to Prince Mentschikoff, is printed in the Appendix, No. I.

sia (by means of a Note instead of a Convention) the protectorate of the Greek Church in Turkey.[1] Reshid Pasha immediately sent the Note to Lord Stratford for communication to the three other representatives of the four Powers, with a request that they would give an opinion as to the most advisable mode of proceeding. Early the next morning Lord Stratford ascertained that in the opinion of Reshid Pasha the altered form of the Russian demands left them as objectionable as ever.[2] The Russians imagined that Reshid Pasha was willing to give way to them, and that he even entreated Lord Stratford to let him yield, but that the English Ambassador was inexorable. There was no truth in this notion.[3] Lord Stratford's counsels had cut so deep into the mind of the Turkish Minister that he was well able to follow them without wanting guidance from hour to hour. The English Ambassador assembled the representatives of the three Powers, and found that they unanimously agreed with him 'in adopting an opin-'ion essentially identical with that of the Turkish Ministers.'[4] They all signed a memorandum, declaring that 'upon a ques-'tion which so closely touched the freedom of action and the 'sovereignty of His Majesty the Sultan, his Highness Reshid 'Pasha was the best judge of the course which it was fitting 'to take, and that they did not consider themselves authorized 'to pronounce an opinion.'[5]

Its rejection.

Prince Mentschikoff had caused it to be understood that this his last demand was only to be accepted by being accepted in full. It was rejected; and on the 21st of May the Prince was preparing to depart, when he heard that the Porte intended to issue and proclaim a guarantee for the exercise of the spiritual rights possessed by the Greek Church in Turkey. It was hard for Russia to endure the resistance which she had encountered, but it was more difficult still to hear with any semblance of calmness that the Porte, of its own free will, was doing a main part of that which the Emperor Nicholas had urged it to do. This was not tolerable. To Russian ears the least utterance about 'the free will of the 'Porte' instantly conveyed the idea that all was to be ordered and governed at the will and pleasure of the English Ambassador. The thought that the protectorate of the Greek Church was not only refused to the Czar, but was now passing quietly into the hands of Lord Stratford, was so maddening that Prince

[1] 'Eastern Papers,' part i., p. 220. As this Draft was Prince Mentschikoff's real ultimatum, it is printed in the Appendix, No. I.

[2] Ibid., pp. 219, 220.

[3] It is clearly disproved. Ibid., pp. 336–8.

[4] Ibid., p. 220.

[5] Ibid., p. 222.

Mentschikoff, forgetting or transcending the fact that he had formally announced the rupture of his relations with the Porte, now suffered himself to address a solemn Note to the Minister for Foreign Affairs, in which (basing himself upon a theory that the mention of the spiritual might be deemed to derogate from the temporal rights of the Church) he announced that any act having the effect which this theory attributed to the proposed guarantee, would be regarded as 'hostile to Russia and her religion.'[1] Having dispatched these last words of threat, he at length went on board and departed. On the same day the arms of Russia were taken down from the palace of the Imperial Embassy.

Final threats of Prince Mentschikoff.

His departure.

Thus ended the ill-omened mission of Prince Mentschikoff. It had lasted eleven weeks. In that compass of time the Emperor Nicholas destroyed the whole repute which he had earned by wielding the power of Russia for more than a quarter of a century with justice and moderation toward foreign States.[2] But, moreover, in these same fatal days the Emperor Nicholas did much to bring his good faith into question. The tenor of his previous life makes it right to insist that any imputation upon his personal honor shall be tested with scrupulous care, but it is hard to escape the conviction that during several weeks in the spring of the year he was giving to the English Government a series of assurances which misrepresented the instructions given by him to Prince Mentschikoff during that same period. Thus, almost at the very hour when Count Nesselrode was assuring Sir Hamilton Seymour that 'the adjustment of the difficulties respecting the Holy Places would settle all matters in dispute 'between Russia and the Porte,'[3] Prince Mentschikoff was striving to wring from the Porte a secret treaty, depriving the Sultan of his control over the Patriarchate of Constantinople, and ceding to Russia a virtual protectorate of the Greek Church in Turkey, and was enjoining the Turkish Ministers to keep this negotiation concealed from the 'ill-disposed Powers,' for so he called England and France;[4] and again, in the very week in which the Czar was joining with the English Government in a form more than usually solemn in denouncing the practice

Effect of the mission upon the credit of Nicholas.

[1] 'Eastern Papers,' part i., p. 253.

[2] Computed from the Peace of Adrianople in 1829. The reign of Nicholas commenced in 1825.

[3] 'Eastern Papers,' part i., p. 102. The slight qualification with which Count Nesselrode accompanied the assurance, tended to strengthen it by giving it greater precision.

[4] 'Eastern Papers,' part i., p. 108.

of 'harassing the Porte by overbearing demands, put forward 'in a manner humiliating to its independence and its dignity,'[1] he was shaping the angry dispatch which caused Prince Mentschikoff to insult the Porte by his peremptory Note of the 5th of May.

But, notwithstanding all this variance between what the Czar said and what he did, it must be acknowledged that it would be hard to explain his words and his course of action by imputing to him a vulgar and rational duplicity, for it was plain that the secrecy at which he aimed would be terminated by the success of the negotiation; and supposing him to have been in possession of his reason, and to have been acting on grounds temporal, he could not have imagined that, for the sake of extorting a new promise from the Sultan, and giving a little more semblance of legality to pretensions which he already maintained to be valid, it was politic for him to forfeit that reputation for honor which was a main element of his greatness and his strength. The dreams of territorial aggrandizement which he imparted to Sir Hamilton Seymour in January and February had all dissolved before the middle of March, and it is vain to say that after that time his actions were governed by any rational plan of conquest. Policy required that for encroachments against Turkey he should choose a time when Europe, engaged in some other strife, might be likely to acquiesce; far from doing this, the Czar chose a time when the four Powers had nothing else to do than to watch and restrain the aggression of Russia. Again, policy required that presure upon the Sultan of a hostile kind should be justified by narratives of the cruel treatment of the Christians by their Turkish masters; yet if any such causes existed for the anger of Christendom, the Emperor Nicholas never took the pains to make them known to Europe. From first to last his loose charges against the Turks for maltreatment of their Christian subjects were not only left without proof, but were even unsupported by any thing like statements of fact.

Still, the Czar was not laboring under any general derangement of mind. The truth seems to be that zeal for his Church had made greater inroads upon his moral and intellectual nature than was commonly known, and that when he was under the stress of religious or rather of ecclesiastic feelings he ceased to be politic, and even perhaps ceased to be honest. It was at such times that there came upon him that tendency to act in a

[1] Memorandum by the Emperor Nicholas confidentially delivered to Sir Hamilton Seymour, and dated the 15th April, 1853. 'Eastern Papers,' part v., p. 25.

spirit of barbaric cunning which was really inconsistent with the general tenor of his life. But if it happened that whilst his mind was already under one of these spiritual visitations, it was farther inflamed by any tidings which roused his old antagonism to Sir Stratford Canning, then instantly it was wrought into such a state that one must be content to mark its fitful and violent impact upon human affairs without undertaking to deduce the result from any symmetrical scheme of action.

But, whatever the cause, the fall was great. The polity of the Russian State was of such a kind that when the character of its monarch stood high, he exalted the empire, and when he descended, he drew the empire along with him. In the beginning of March, the Emperor Nicholas almost oppressed the continent of Europe with the weight of his vast power, conjoined with moderation and a spirit of austere justice toward foreign States. Before the end of May, he stood before the world shorn bare of all this moral strength, and having nothing left to him except what might be reckoned and set down upon paper by an inspector of troops or a surveyor of ships. In less than three months, the station of Russia amongst the Powers of Europe underwent a great change.

Position in which Lord Stratford's skill had placed the Porte.

The English Ambassador remained upon the field of the conflict. Between the time of his return to Constantinople and the departure of Prince Mentschikoff there had passed forty-five days. In this period Lord Stratford had brought to a settlement the question of the Holy Places, had baffled all the efforts of the Emperor Nicholas to work an inroad upon the sovereign rights of the Sultan, and had enforced upon the Turks a firmness so indomitable, and a moderation so unwearied, that from the hour of his arrival at Constantinople they resisted every claim which was fraught with real danger; but always resisted with courtesy, and yielded to every demand, however unjust in principle, if it seemed that they could yield with honor and with safety. Knowing that, if he left room for doubt whether Russia or the Porte were in the right, the controversy would run a danger of being decided in favor of the stronger, he provided with a keen foresight, and at the cost of having to put a hard restraint upon his anger, and even upon his sense of justice, that the concessions offered by the Turks should reach beyond their just liability: nay, should reach so far beyond it as to leave a broad margin between, and make it difficult even for any one who inclined toward the strong to deny that Russia was committing an outrage upon a weaker State, and was therefore offending against Europe. In truth, he placed the Moslem before the world in an attitude of Christian forbearance sustained by unfailing courage; and in proportion as men loved justice and were led by the gentle precepts of the Gospel, they inclined to the Mahometan Prince who seemed to represent their principles, and began to think how best they could help him to make a stand against the ferocious Christianity of the Czar. In England especially this sentiment was kindled, and already it was beginning to gain a hold over the policy of the State. Less than three months before, the dismemberment of the Turkish Empire had been thought a fair subject to bring into question, and now the firmness and the strange moderation with which the Turks stood resisting the demands of their oppressor was drawing the English people day by day into a steadfast alliance with the Sultan.

But if Lord Stratford had succeeded in gaining over to his cause the general opinion of Europe, or rather in adapting the policy of the Divan to what he knew would be approved by the people of the West, he did not neglect to use such means as he had for moving the Governments of the four Powers; and the concerted action to which he had succeeded in bringing them on the 21st of May was a beginning of the peaceful coercion with which it was fitting that Europe should withstand the encroachments of a wrong-doer. But this was not all that was effected by the Diplomatic transactions of the spring. It can not be concealed that, without the solemnity of a treaty, nay, without the knowledge of Parliament, and perhaps without the knowledge of her Prime Minister, England in the course of a few weeks had slided into all the responsibility of a defensive alliance with the Sultan against the Emperor of Russia. It may seem strange that this could be, but the truth is that the general scope of a lengthened official correspondence is not to be gathered by merely learning at intervals the import of each dispatch. Taken singly, almost every dispatch composed by a skilled diplomatist will be likely to seem wise and moderate, and deserving of a complete approval; but if a Statesman goes on approving and approving one by one a long series of papers of this sort without rousing himself to the effort of taking a broader view of the transactions which he has separately examined, he may find himself entangled in a course of action which he never intended to adopt. Perhaps this view tends to explain the reasons which caused a minister whose love of peace was passionate and almost fanatical to become gradually and imperceptibly responsible for a policy leading toward war. Lord

Engagements contracted by England.

Aberdeen did not formally renounce his neutral policy of 1828, and he did not at this time advise the Queen to conclude any treaty for the defense of Turkey, nor ask the judgment of Parliament upon the expediency of taking such a course; but day after day and week after week the cabinet-boxes came and went, and came and went again, and every day he passed his anxious and inevitable hour and a half at the Foreign Office; and at length it became apparent that the Government of which he was the chief had so acted that it could not with honor[1] recede from the duty of defending the home provinces of the Sultan against an unprovoked attack by Russia. The advice of a strong Power is highly valued, but it is valued for reasons which should make men chary of giving it. It is not commonly valued for the sake of its mere wisdom, but partly because it is more or less a disclosure of policy, and still more because it tends to draw the advising State into a line of action corresponding with its counsels. England by the voice of her Ambassador (approved from time to time by the home Government[2]) had been advising a weak Power to resist a strong one. Counsels of such a kind could not but have a grave import.

Obligations contracted by the act of giving advice.

The French Emperor had been more careful to keep himself free from engagements with the Porte, but he had long ago resolved to seize the coming occasion of acting in concert with England. And England now became bound. Within three days from Prince Mentschikoff's departure, France and England were beginning to concert resistance to Russia;[3] on the 26th of May the Sultan's refusal of the Russian ultimatum was warmly applauded by the English Government, and before the end of the month the Foreign Secretary instructed the English Ambassador that it was 'indispensable to take measures for 'the protection of the Sultan, and to aid his Highness in repel- 'ling any attack that might be made upon his territory;' and that 'the use of force was to be resorted to as a last and una- 'voidable resource for the protection of Turkey against an un- 'provoked attack and in defense of her independence, which 'England,' as Lord Clarendon declared, 'was bound to main- 'tain.'[4]

England, in concert with France, becomes engaged to defend the Sultan's dominions.

Lord Clarendon at the same time addressed a dispatch to St. Petersburg, setting forth with painful clearness the difference between the words and the acts of the Czar, and indig-

[1] So said by Lord Clarendon. 'Eastern Papers,' part i.
[2] 'Eastern Papers,' part i., p. 183. [3] 24th May. Ibid., p. 182.
[4] Ibid., p. 197.

nantly requiring to know what was the object which Russia had 'in view, and in what manner and to what extent the do-'minions of the Sultan and the tranquillity of Europe were 'threatened.'[1]

The process by which England became bound.

It was not by any one decisive act or promise, but by the tenor of expressions scattered through a long series of Dispatches, and by words used from time to time in conversations, that England had taken upon herself the burden of defending the Sultan against the Czar.

Slowness of the English Parliament.

Parliament was sitting when this momentous engagement was being contracted, and it may be thought that there was room for questioning whether England in concert with France alone, and without first doing her utmost to obtain the concurrence of the other Powers, should good-humoredly take upon herself a duty which was rather European than English, and which tended to involve her in war. There were eloquent members of the Legislature who would have been willing to deprecate such a policy, and to moderate and confine its action, but apparently they did not understand how England was becoming entangled until about nine months afterward, and, either from want of knowledge or want of promptitude, they lost the occasion for aiding the Crown with their counsels. Indeed, from first to last, the backwardness of the English Parliament in seizing upon the changeful phases of the diplomatic strife was one of the main causes of the impending evil, and this was only one of the occasions in which it failed in the duty of opportune utterance. When the Dispatch of the 31st of May was once on the road to Constantinople, England stood bound, and all that might be afterward said about it would be criticism rather than counsel.

So ended one phase of the ancient strife between the Emperor Nicholas and Lord Stratford de Redcliffe. Prince Mentschikoff, landing at Odessa, hastened to dispatch to his master the best account he could give of the causes of his discomfiture, and of the evil skill of that Antichrist in stately English form whom Heaven was permitting for a while to triumph over the Czar and his Church.

Powers intrusted to Lord Stratford.

Lord Stratford reaped the fruit of his toil and of the long endured pain of encountering violence with moderation. All his acts were approved by the Government, and, so far as they were known and understood, by the bulk of his countrymen at home. And now, when he paced the shady gardens, where often he had put

[1] 'Eastern Papers,' part i., p. 200.

upon his anger a difficult restraint, he could look with calm joy to the headland where the Straits opened out into the Euxine, for he knew that the Governments of the Western Powers, supporting his every word, and even overstepping his more sober policy, were coming forward to stand between Russia and her prey. The fleet at Malta was to be moved when and whither he chose, and, even to the length of war, the Admiral was ordered to obey any requisitions made to him by the Ambassador.[1] A few days later, the Governments of Paris and London, fearing the consequence of delay, ordered the fleets to move up at once to the neighborhood of the Dardanelles.[2] The power to choose between peace and war went from out of the Courts of Paris and London and passed to Constantinople. Lord Stratford was worthy of this trust; for being firm, and supplied with full knowledge, and having power by his own mere ascendency to enforce moderation upon the Turks, and to forbid panic and even to keep down tumult, he was able to be very chary in the display of force, and to be more frugal than the Government at home in using or engaging the power of the English Queen. He remained on the ground. Still, as before, he kept down the home dangers which threatened the Ottoman State. Still, as before, he obliged the Turks to deserve the good will of Europe; but now besides, with the arm of the flesh, and no longer with the mere fencing of words, he was there to defend their capital from the gathered rage of the Czar. In truth, at this time he bore much of the weight of empire. Intrusted with the chief prerogative of kings, and living all his time at Therapia, close over the gates of the Bosphorus, he seemed to stand guard against the North and to answer for the safety of his charge.

---

## CHAPTER XII.

Rage of the Czar.

THE mere sensation of being at strife with the English Ambassador at Constantinople had kindled in the bosom of the Emperor Nicholas a rage so fierce as to drive him beyond the bounds of policy; but when he came to know the details of the struggle, and to see how at every step his Ambassador had been encountered, and, finally, when he heard (for that was the maddening thought) that, by counsels

[1] 'Eastern Papers,' part i., p. 199. [2] Pp. 210, 225.

always obeyed, Lord Stratford was calmly exercising a protectorate of all the Churches in Turkey, including the very Church of him the Czar, him the Father, him the Pontiff of Eastern Christendom, he was wrought into such a condition of mind that his fury broke away from the restraint of even the very pride which begot it. Pride counseled the calm use of force, an order to the Admiral at Sebastopol, the silent march of battalions. But the Czar had so lost the control of his anger, that every where, and to all who would look upon the sight, he showed the wounds inflicted upon him by his hated adversary. 'He addressed,' said Lord Clarendon, 'to the different Courts of Europe unmeasured complaints of Lord Stratford. To him and to him alone he attributed the failure of 'Prince Mentschikoff's mission.'[1] 'An incurable mistrust, a 'vehement activity,' said Count Nesselrode,[2] 'had characterized the whole of Lord Stratford's conduct during the latter 'part of the negotiation.'

Even in formal dispatches the Czar caused his Minister to speak as though there were absolutely no government at Constantinople except the mere will of Lord Stratford. 'The English Ambassador,' Count Nesselrode said, 'persisted in refusing us any kind of guarantee;'[2] and then the Count went on to picture the Turkish Ministers as prostrate before the English Ambassador, and vainly entreating him to let them yield to Russia. 'Reshid Pasha,' said he, 'struck with the 'dangers which the departure of our Legation might entail 'upon the Porte, earnestly conjured the British Ambassador 'not to oppose the acceptance of the Note drawn up by Prince 'Mentschikoff, but Lord Redcliffe prevented its acceptance by 'declaring that the Note was equivalent to a treaty, and was 'inadmissible.'[2] This last story, it has been seen, was the work of mere fiction,[3] but in the Czar Nicholas, as well as in Prince Mentschikoff, there were remains of the Oriental nature which made him ready to believe in the boundless power of a mortal, and he seems to have received without question the fables with which the Eastern mind was portraying the unbending, implacable Eltchi. It was vain to show a monarch, thus wrought to anger, that the difference between him and the terrible Ambassador lay simply in the fact that the one was in the wrong and the other in the right. The thought of this only made the discomfiture more bitter. In the eyes of the Czar, Lord Stratford's way of keeping himself eternally in the right and eternally moderate was the mere contrivance,

[1] 'Eastern Papers,' part i., p. 268. [2] Ibid., p. 243.
[3] This is proved very clearly. Ibid., p. 336, *et seq.*

the mere inverted Jesuitism of a man resolved to do good in order that evil might come; resolved to be forbearing and just for the sake of doing a harm to the Church. It was plain that, to assuage the torment which the Czar was enduring, the remedy was action: yet, strange to say, this disturber of Europe, who seemed to pass his life in preparing soldiery, was not at all ready for a war, even against the Sultan alone. His preparations had been stopped in the beginning of March, and the movements which his troops had been making in Bessarabia were movements in the nature of threats. He wished to do some signal act of violence without plunging into war.

The Danubian Principalities.

The disposition of the Russian forces on the banks of the Pruth had long been breeding rumors that the Emperor Nicholas meditated an occupation of the Principalities called Wallachia and Moldavia. These provinces formed a part of the Ottoman dominions in Europe, but they were held by the Sultan under arrangements which modified their subjection to the Porte, and gave them the character of tributary States. Each of them was governed by a prince called a Hospodar, who received his investiture at Constantinople, but the Sultan was precluded by treaty from almost all interference with the internal government of the provinces, and was even debarred the right of sending any soldiery into their territories. Russia, on the other hand, had acquired over these provinces a species of protectorate, and, in the event of their being disturbed by internal anarchy, she had power to aid in repressing the disorder by military occupation. This contingency had not occurred in either of the provinces; but the anomalous form of their political existence caused the Emperor Nicholas to imagine that, by occupying them with a military force and professing to hold them as a pledge, he could find for himself a middle course betwixt peace and war; and the thought was welcome to him, because, being angry and irresolute, he had been painfully driven to and fro, and was glad to compound with his passion.

The Czar's scheme for occupying them.

On the 31st of May, Count Nesselrode addressed a letter to Reshid Pasha, urging the Porte to accept without variation the draught of the Note submitted to it by Prince Mentschikoff; and announcing that, if the Porte should fail to do this within a period of eight days, the Russian army within a few weeks would cross the frontier in order to obtain 'by force 'but without war' that which the Porte should decline to give up of its own accord. It was afterward explained that this plan of resorting to violence without war was to be carried into effect by occupying the Danubian Principalities and holding them as a security for the Sultan's compliance.

But in the second week of June the Dispatch which brought to the Sultan a virtual alliance with England was already at Constantinople, and the English fleet was coming up from Malta to the mouth of the Dardanelles, under orders to obey the word of the English Ambassador. Before the moment came for dispatching an answer to Count Nesselrode's summons, both the French and the English fleets were at anchor close outside the Straits in waters called Besica Bay. Thus supported, the Porte at once refused to give Russia the Note demanded; but under Lord Stratford's counsel it did this in terms of deferential courtesy, and in a way which left open a door to future negotiation.

Efforts to effect an accommodation.

In all the capitals of the five great Powers, as well as at Constantinople, great efforts were made to bring about an accommodation, and it is certain that at intervals, if not continually, the Emperor Nicholas sought the means of retreating without ridicule from the ground on which his violence had placed him. It might seem that this was a condition of things in which diplomacy ought to have been able to act with effect; but it is hard for any one acquainted with the Dispatches to say that the Statesmen intrusted with the duty of laboring for this end were wanting in energy or in skill. It was the Czar's ancient hatred of Sir Stratford Canning which defied the healing art. What Nicholas wanted was to be able to force upon the Porte some measure which was keenly disapproved by Lord Stratford; and if it could have been shown that the English Ambassador had led the Turks into an untenable ground, there would have been an opportunity of giving the Czar this gratification; but Lord Stratford's moderation had been so firmly maintained, his sight had been always so clear and just, and his advice had gone so close to the edge of what could safely be conceded by the Turks, that (without doing a gross wrong to the Sultan) it was hardly possible to contrive any way of giving the Czar a semblance of triumph over the English Ambassador.

Defective representation of France, Austria, and Prussia, at the Court of St. Petersburg.

From this time and thenceforth down to the final rupture between Russia and the Western Powers, there was a cause of evil at work which was every day tending to draw the Czar on into danger. Austria, Prussia, and France were unfitly represented at St. Petersburg. In order to understand the nature of this evil, it must be remembered that in the reign of Nicholas the society of the Russian capital was what in the last century used to go by the name of a 'Court.' It was a mere group of men and women, gathered always around one centre, bending always their eyes on one man, and striving to divine his will. Moreover the worshipers were always watching to see who was in favor and who was in disgrace; and whoever was seen to be in favor with the Czar was brought into favor with all; and whoever was believed to have incurred the Czar's displeasure was immediately forced to perceive that he had become displeasing to the rest of his fellow-creatures. Strange to say, the members of the diplomatic body were not exempt from these vicissitudes: if a foreign envoy felt obliged to offer resistance to the imperial will, his life was made cold and gloomy to him; and, on the other hand, he was sure to be well caressed if he chose to cringe to the Czar. This condition of society made it a matter of great moment for foreign States to be represented at St. Petersburg by men of high spirit, and endued with some strength of will. Unhappily for the peace of Europe, France was represented at St. Petersburg by M. Castelbajac, Austria by Count Mensdorf, and Prussia by Colonel Rochow; and at a time when the Governments which they professed to represent were laboring to repress the violence of Russia by a policy of almost hostile resistance, these three men had suffered themselves to become the mere courtiers of the Czar.[1]

Sir Hamilton Seymour alone held language corresponding with the disapproval which the acts of the Czar were exciting in Central Europe, as well as in France and England. He alone represented at St. Petersburg the judgment of the four Powers. From the moment when the occupation of the Principalities was first threatened, he always treated it as an act perilous to the tranquillity of Europe, and always declined to give any measure of the extent to which it was likely to affect the relations between Russia and England. In using this wholesome language he was left without support from any of his colleagues.

Of course, in a literal way, the representatives of Austria, Prussia, and France obeyed their orders, and remonstrated when they were directed to do so; but the Czar was so prone to believe what he wished to be true, that diplomatists who were forced to make painful communications to his Government could easily do a great deal to blunt the edge of their instructions. So, although in Europe the Czar was isolated, yet

[1] It is conceived that the facts which will be hereafter stated in connection with the names of these men are alone sufficient to justify the statement in the text.

in Europe, as represented at St. Petersburg, the true order of things was reversed. There it was Sir Hamilton Seymour who stood alone. More than this, it was believed at St. Petersburg that the delinquency of M. Castelbajac often went beyond mere inaction, and that when the Czar was pained and discouraged by the reserve or the warning language of the Queen's representative, he was accustomed to turn for solace to the complaisant Frenchman, who was always ready to assure him that Sir Hamilton Seymour's grave tone was the sheer whim of an obstinate Englishman.

The Czar's reliance upon the acquiescence of England.

The Emperor Nicholas had laid down for himself a rule which was always to guide his conduct upon the Eastern Question, and it seems to be certain that, at this time, even in his most angry moments, he intended to cling to his resolve. What he had determined was, that no temptation should draw him into hostile conflict with England. He did not know that already he was breaking away from England, and rapidly going adrift. Persisting in the belief that the opposition which he had been encountering at Constantinople was the work of the English Ambassador, and of him alone, or at worst of the Foreign Office, he refused to accept the conviction that he was falling out with the English people, or even with the English Government. It was in vain that Lord Clarendon, in words as clear as day, disclosed the anger and the growing determination of the Cabinet. It was in vain that by grave words and by pregnant reserve Sir Hamilton Seymour strove to warn the Czar of the danger which he was bringing upon his relations with England. The Czar imagined that he knew better. 'My dear Sir Hamilton,' Count Nesselrode seemed to say, 'you have lived away from your 'country so long, that, forgive me, you do not know its condi-'tion and temper. We do. We have studied it. Your For-'eign Office speaks as if we did not know that England has 'her weak point. My dear Sir Hamilton, we have mastered 'the whole subject of the "School of Manchester." Certainly 'it cost us some trouble, but we have now made out the dif-'ference between a "Meeting" on a Sunday morning and a '"Meeting" on a Monday night. Nothing escapes us. We 'comprehend the Society of Friends. Pardon me, Sir Hamil-'ton, for saying so, but your country is notoriously engaged in 'commerce. With that we shall not interfere.'

In truth, the Czar's theory was that the foreign policy of the English Government was dictated by the people, and that the people loved money, and for the sake of money loved peace. In other words, he thought that the English nation had undergone what historians term 'corruption.' As far as he could make out, the vast expanse of men and women which presented itself to his imagination under the name of 'the people' was the same sort of thing as the crowd which went to hear a fierce speech against princes, and statesmen, and parliaments, and armies, and navies, and taxes. He also thought that the cheers which this crowd uttered at the end of sentences denouncing war were proof of a settled determination to prevent any Government from ever again breaking the peace without stringent reasons. A deeper knowledge would have taught him that what the crowd applauded was—not the mere doctrine, but—the pure racy strenuous English, and the animating ferocity of the speaker; for, in speeches of this kind, praises of peace were always blended with rough attacks upon public men; and therefore, to a shallow observer, the hearers might seem to be lifting up their voices for peace and good-will among men, when in reality they were only acknowledging the pleasantness of the sensation which is produced by hearing good invective. A prince of the Russian Emperor's breed might have known that, even if it be given in praise or in joy, the 'hurrah' of a northern people has in it a sound of conflict. What it negatives and forbids is peace and rest. His battalions were destined to hear it some day, to know its import, and to blend it long afterward with recollections of mist and slaughter, and the breaking strength of Russia. But to the mind of the Czar at this time the cheering which greeted the thin phantom of the 'Peace Party' imported a determination of the English people to abdicate their place in Europe; and, in proportion as this belief fixed its hold upon his mind, the tranquillity of the world was brought into danger.

Another unhappy circumstance tended to keep the Czar in his fatal error. Lord Aberdeen was the Prime Minister. He was a pure and upright statesman, and it can be said that the more closely he was known the more he was honored; for his friends always saw in him higher qualities than he was able to disclose to the general world by writing, or by speech, or by action. It was his lot to do much toward bringing upon his country a great calamity. He drew down war by suffering himself to have an undue horror of it. With good and truly peaceful intentions, he was every day breaking down one of the surest of the safeguards which protected the peace of Europe. This he did by the dangerous language which he suffered himself to hold almost down to the time of Baron Brunnow's departure from London. If judges were to declare their horror of justice, and make it appear that they would be likely to shrink from the duty of passing sentence on one of their erring fellow-creatures, they would invite the world to pillage and murder; but they would be committing a fault less grave than that of which Lord Aberdeen was guilty. He was chief of the Government, intrusted with the forces of the State. To be chary of the use of means so puissant for good and for evil is one of the most solemn charges that can be cast upon man; but for a ruler to give out that the sword of the State will be in his hands a thing loathed and cast aside, is to be guilty of a dereliction of duty fraught with instant danger. To all who would listen, Lord Aberdeen used to say that he abhorred the very thought of war, and that he was sure it would not and could not occur. He caused men to believe that, except for weighty and solemn cause, no war would be undertaken with his concurrence. Relying on a Prime Minister's words, the Emperor Nicholas felt certain that Lord Aberdeen would not carry England into a war for the sake of a difference between the wording of a Note demanded by Prince Mentschikoff, and the wording of a Note proposed by the Turks. It is true that Baron Brunnow had the sagacity to understand that imprudent and timid language, though coming from the lips of a Prime Minister, would not necessarily be binding upon the high-spirited people of England, and he, no doubt, warned his master accordingly, even at the time when he was conveying to him Lord Aberdeen's words of peace; but it was so delightful to the Czar to remain under the impression produced by the language of the English Prime Minister, and, moreover, this language was so closely in harmony with the apparent feelings of the active little crowd which he had mistaken for 'the 'English people,' that he could not or would not forego his illusion.

It is believed that the errors of Lord Aberdeen did not end here. In a conversation between Lord Clarendon and Baron Brunnow, our Foreign Secretary, they say, spoke a plain firm sentence, disclosing the dangers which the occupation of the Principalities would bring upon the relations between Russia and England. The wholesome words were flying to St. Petersburg. They would have destroyed the Czar's illusion, and they therefore bid fair to preserve the peace of Europe; but when Lord Aberdeen came to know what had been uttered, he insisted, they say, and insisted with effect, that Baron Brunnow should be requested to consider Lord Clarendon's words as unspoken. Of course, after a fatal revocation like this, it would be hard indeed to convince the Czar that his encroachment was provoking the grave resistance of England.

The Emperor Nicholas was alone in his accustomed writing-room in the Palace of Czarskoe Selo, when he came to the resolve which followed upon the discomfiture of Prince Mentschikoff. He took no counsel. He rang a bell. Presently an officer of his staff stood before him. To him he gave his orders for the occupation of the Principalities. Afterward he told Count Orloff what he had done. Count Orloff became grave and said, 'This is war.' The Czar was surprised to hear that the Count took so gloomy a view. He was sure that no country would stir against him without the concurrence of England, and he was certain that because of her Peace Party, her traders and her Prime Minister, it was impossible for England to move.

Orders for the occupation of the Principalities.

It was thus that by rashness and want of moderation men truly attached to the cause of peace were encouraging the wrong-doer, and rapidly bringing upon Europe the calamity which they most abhorred.

On the 2nd of July, the Emperor Nicholas caused his forces to pass the Pruth, and laid hold of the two Principalities. On the following day a manifesto was read in the churches of All the Russias.[1] 'It is 'known,' said the Czar, 'to all our faithful subjects, that the 'defense of the orthodox religion was from time immemorial 'the vow of our glorious forefathers. From the time that it 'pleased Providence to intrust to us our hereditary throne, the 'defense of these holy obligations inseparable from it was the 'constant object of our solicitude and care; and these, based 'on the glorious treaty of Kainardji, confirmed by other solemn 'treaties, were ever directed to insure the inviolability of the 'orthodox Church. But to our great grief, recently in despite 'of our efforts to defend the inviolability of the rights and 'privileges of our orthodox Church, various arbitrary acts of 'the Porte have infringed these rights, and threaten at last the 'complete overthrow of the long-perpetuated order so dear to 'orthodoxy. Having exhausted all persuasion, we have found 'it needful to advance our armies into the Danubian Principalities, in order to show the Ottoman Porte to what its obstinacy may lead. But even now we have not the intention 'to commence war. By the occupation of the Principalities 'we desire to have such a security as will insure us the restoration of our rights. It is not conquest that we seek; Russia 'needs it not; we seek satisfaction for a just right so clearly 'infringed. We are ready even now to arrest the movement

The Pruth passed. Russian Manifesto.

[1] 'Eastern Papers,' part i., p. 357.

'of our armies, if the Ottoman Porte will bind itself solemnly 'to observe the inviolability of the orthodox Church. But if 'blindness and obstinacy decide for the contrary, then, calling 'God to our aid, we shall leave the decision of the struggle to 'Him, and in full confidence in His omnipotent right hand, we 'shall march forward for the orthodox Church.'[1]

Course taken by the Sultan.

By declaring that his military occupation of these provinces was not an act of war, the Emperor Nicholas did not escape from any part of the responsibility naturally attaching to the invasion of a neighbor's territory, and yet, by making this announcement, he committed the error of enabling the Porte to choose its own time for the final rupture. The Sultan was advised by Lord Stratford, and afterward by the Home Governments of the Western Powers, that, although he was entitled, if he chose, to look upon the seizure of the tributary provinces as a clear invasion of his territory, he was not obliged to treat it as an act which placed him at war, and that for the moment it was wise for him to hold back. Upon this counsel the Sultan acted, and in truth the latitude which it gave him was highly convenient, because he was ill prepared for an immediate encounter. Therefore, without yet going to a rupture, the Turkish Government exerted itself to make ready for war. In States religiously constituted, the preparation for war is begun by preaching it, and now in Europe, in Asia, and in Africa, wherever there were Turkish dominions, the Moslems were called to arms by a truculent course of sermons. In the churches of Russia there was a like appeal to the piety of the multitude. Of course the members of the two disputing Governments were much under the influence of temporal motives, but by the people of both Empires the war now believed to be impending was regarded as a war for Religion.

Religious character of the threatened war.

---

## CHAPTER XIII.

Effect of the Czar's threat upon European Powers.

THE Czar had no sooner uttered his threat to occupy the Principalities than he found himself met by the unanimous disapproval of the other great Powers of Europe. Nor was this a barren expression of opinion. From the time of the accomplishment of Count Leiningen's mission, Austria had never ceased to declare her adhe-

[1] 'Eastern Papers,' part i., p. 323.

sion to her accustomed policy, and the moment that she saw herself endangered by the Czar's determination to send troops into Wallachia and Moldavia, she became, as it was her interest and her duty to be, a resolute opponent of Russia. And her resistance was of more value than that of any other Power, because she was so placed in reference to the Principalities that at any moment and without any very hard effort she could make her will the law. Of course the Czar might resent the interference of Austria and declare war against her, but in such a case he would necessarily place the scene of hostilities upon another part of her frontier. It was not possible for him with common prudence to wind round the frontier of the Austrian Empire and attempt to keep troops in Wallachia if he were liable to attack from Transylvania and the Banat.

Its effect upon Austria.

Clearly then it rested with Austria to prevent or redress the threatened outrage. Her resolution was never doubtful. Before the end of May, Count Buol represented at St. Petersburg the danger of the proceedings adopted by Prince Mentschikoff,[1] and on the 17th of June he declared that he considered himself as 'entirely united' with England in her policy toward the Turkish Empire, that he regarded 'the maintenance of its 'independence and integrity as of the most essential import'ance to the best interests of Austria,' and that he would employ all the 'means in his power to effect that object.' He promised that he would take no engagement with Russia not to oppose her 'with arms,' and he added that, 'should he be 'called upon to carry out an armed intervention on the fron'tiers, it would be in support of the authority and independ'ence of the Sultan.'[2]

The opinion of Prussia was scarcely less decided. On the 30th of May Lord Bloomfield was able to report that the impression made upon the Government of Berlin by the last reports from Turkey was 'most unfavorable 'to the Russian Government,' and Baron Manteuffel declared that Prince Mentschikoff had gone far beyond every thing that the Prussian Government had been given to expect, and he could hardly believe but that the Prince would be disavowed.[3] Three days later the Prussian Government conveyed this impression to the Court of St. Petersburg,[4] and on the 7th Lord Clarendon expressed his satisfaction at the views taken and the course of the policy indicated both by the Court of Berlin and the Court of Vienna.[5]

Upon Prussia.

[1] 'Eastern Papers,' part i., p. 224. [2] Ibid., p. 291. [3] Ibid., p. 223.
[4] Ibid., p. 227. [5] Ibid., p. 230.

This was the effect produced by the threat contained in Count Nesselrode's summons; but when the invasion of the Principalities took place and came to be known in Europe, it quickly appeared that the uneasiness excited by the actual occurrence of the event was more than proportioned to that which sprang from the mere expectation of it. In Austria the uneasiness of the Government was so great that it dissolved the close relations of friendship lately subsisting between the Courts of Petersburg and Vienna; and within three days from the time when Russia crossed the Pruth, Count Buol, abandoning the notion of 'acting singly,' which had been entertained some days before,[1] began to lay the foundations of a league well fitted to repress the Czar's encroachment without plunging Europe in war.

Effect produced by the actual invasion of the Principalities.

In Austria.

'The entry of the Russian troops into the Principalities,' wrote Lord Westmoreland to the English Secretary of State, 'is looked upon with the greatest possible regret, and I am requested by Count Buol to state this to your Lordship, as also 'to announce to you his intention immediately to convey this 'feeling to the Russian Cabinet, together with the expression 'of the disappointment he has felt at the sudden adoption of 'this measure while there still existed the hope of an arrangement at Constantinople. Count Buol expressed his entire 'satisfaction with the language your Lordship had held to 'Count Colloredo, agreeing as he does with the policy you recommend, and with the necessity which would arise, in case 'the invasion of the Principalities took place, of concerting 'measures among the Powers parties to the treaties of 1841 'with the view of obtaining from the Russian Cabinet the most 'distinct declarations as to the objects of that movement and 'the term which would be fixed for its duration.'[2]

On the other hand, the Governments of France and England, with less cause for anxiety about countries so remote as the provinces of the lower Danube, were angrily impatient of the Czar's intrusion.

In France and England.

Prussia, hitherto supposed to be hardly capable of differing with the Emperor Nicholas, did not fear to express her disapproval in decisive terms, and the Cabinet of Berlin instructed the King's Envoy at Constantinople to 'unite cordially' with the representatives of Austria, France, and England.[3]

In Prussia.

In short, the attitude of Europe toward the Russian Empe-

[1] 'Eastern Papers,' part i., p. 320. [2] Ibid., p. 356. [3] Ibid., p. 355.

Attitude of Europe generally.

ror was exactly that which a lover of peace and of order might desire to witness; for the wrong-doer was left without an ally in the world, and was resisted by the four great Powers with the assent of the other States of Europe. It was plain, moreover, that this resistance would not evaporate in mere remonstrance or protest; for, if Austria was the country most endangered by the seizure of the Principalities, she was also the Power which could most easily extirpate the evil, because, whenever she chose, she could fall upon the flank and rear of the Russian invaders by issuing through the passes of the Eastern Carpathian range, or the frontier which touched the Banat. Moreover, France and England, by bringing their fleets into the Levant, by causing them to approach the Dardanelles, by passing the Straits, by anchoring in the Golden Horn, by ascending the Bosphorus, by cruising in the Euxine, and finally by interdicting the Russian flag from its waters, could always inflict a graduated torture upon the Czar, and (even without going to the extremity of war) could make it impossible that the indignation of Europe should remain unheeded.

Concord of the four Powers.

Their means of repression.

The concord of the States opposing the Czar's encroachment was already so well perfected that, on the very day[1] when the Russian advance-guard crossed the Pruth, the representatives of the four Powers, assembled in Conference, determined to address to Russia a collective Note pressing the Czar to put his claims against Turkey in conformity with the sovereign rights of the Sultan. Here was the very principle for which France and England had been contending; and it was obvious that if this concerted action of the four Powers should last, it would insure peace; for, in the first place, any resistance to their united will would be hopeless, and, on the other hand, a Prince whose spirit rebelled against the idea of yielding to States which he looked upon as adversaries might gracefully give way to the award of assembled Europe. In short, the four Powers could coerce without making war; and the business of a statesman who sought to maintain the peace and good order of Europe was to keep them united, taking care that no mere shades of difference should part them, and that nothing short of a violent and irreconcilable change on the part of one or more of the Powers should dissolve a confederacy which promised to insure the continuance of peace and a speedy enforcement of justice.

Their joint measures.

Importance of maintaining close concert between the four Powers.

[1] 2nd July, 1853.

How came it to happen that in the midst of all this harmony there supervened a policy which discarded the principle of a peaceful coercion applied by the whole of the remonstrant Powers, and raised up in its stead a threatening alliance which was powerful enough to wage a bloody and successful war, but was without that more wholesome measure of strength which can enforce justice without inflicting humiliation, and without resort to arms? How came it to happen that within six days from the date of the collective Note, and without the intervening occurrence of any new event, the concert of the four Powers was suddenly superseded and paralyzed by the announcement of a separate understanding between two of them?

It was not for reasons of State that by one of the high contracting parties this evil course was designed; and in order to see how it came to be possible that the vast interests of Europe should be set aside in favor of mere personal objects, it will presently be necessary to contract the field of vision, and, going back to the winter of 1851, to glance at the operations of a small knot of middle-aged men who were pushing their fortunes in Paris.

---

## CHAPTER XIV.

State of the French Republic in November, 1851.

IN the beginning of the winter of 1851 France was still a republic; but the Constitution of 1848 had struck no root. There was a feeling that the country had been surprised and coerced into the act of declaring itself a republic, and that a monarchical system of government was the only one adapted for France. The sense of instability which sprang from this belief was connected with an agonizing dread of insurrections like those which forty months before had filled the streets of Paris with scenes of bloodshed. Moreover, to those who watched and feared, it seemed that the shadow on the dial was moving on with a terrible steadiness to the hour when a return to anarchy was, as it were, pre-ordained by law; for the Constitution required that a new President should be chosen in the spring of the following year, and the French, being by nature of a keen and anxious temperament, can not endure that lasting pressure upon the nerves which is inflicted by a long impending danger. Their impulse under such trials is to rush forward, or to run back, and what they are least inclined to do is to stand still and be calm, or make a steady move to the front.

In general, France thought it best that, notwithstanding the Rule of the Constitution which stood in the way, the then President should be quietly re-elected; and a large majority of the Assembly, faithfully representing this opinion, had come to a vote which sought to give it effect; but their desire was baffled by an unwise provision of the Republican Charter which had laid it down that no constitutional change should take place without the sanction of three fourths of the Assembly. By this clumsy bar the action of the State system was hampered, and many whose minds generally inclined them to respect legality were forced to acknowledge that the Constitution wanted a wrench. Still, the republic had long been free from serious outbreak. The law was obeyed; and indeed the determination to maintain order at all sacrifices was so strong, that, even upon somewhat slight foundation, the President had been intrusted with power to place under martial law any districts in which disturbances seemed likely to occur. The struggles which went on in the Chamber, though they were unsightly in the eyes of military men and of those who love the decisiveness and consistency of despotism, were rather signs of healthy political action than of danger to the State. It is not true, as was afterward pretended, that the Executive was wickedly or perversely thwarted either by the votes of the Assembly or by the speeches of its members; still less is it true that the representative body was engaged in hatching plots against the President; and although the army, remembering the humiliations of 1848, was in ill humor with the people, and was willing upon any fit occasion to act against them, there was no general officer of any repute who would consent to fire a shot without what French Commanders deemed to be the one lawful warrant for action—an order from the Minister of War.

Prince Louis Bonaparte.

But the President of the republic was Prince Charles Louis Napoleon Bonaparte, the statutory heir of the first French Emperor.[1] The election which made him the chief of the State had been conducted with perfect fairness, and since it happened that in former years he had twice engaged in enterprises which aimed at the throne of France, he had good right to infer that the millions of citizens who elected him into the Presidency were willing to use his ambition as a means of restoring to France a monarchical form of government.

[1] *i. e.* by the Senatus-Consulte of 1804.

But if he had been open in disclosing the ambition which was almost cast upon him by the circumstances of his birth, he had been as successful as the first Brutus in passing for a man of a poor intellect. Both in France and in England at that time men in general imagined him to be dull. When he talked, the flow of his ideas was sluggish: his features were opaque; and after years of dreary studies, the writings evolved by his thoughtful, long-pondering mind had not shed much light on the world. Even the strange ventures in which he had engaged had failed to win toward him the interest which commonly attaches to enterprise. People in London who were fond of having gatherings of celebrated characters never used to present him to their friends as a serious pretender to a throne, but rather as though he were a balloon-man, who had twice had a fall from the skies, and was still in some measure alive. Yet the more men knew him in England, the more they liked him. He entered into English pursuits and rode fairly to hounds. He was friendly, social, good-humored, and willing enough to talk freely about his views upon the throne of France. The sayings he uttered about his 'destiny' were addressed (apparently as a matter of policy) to casual acquaintance, but to his intimate friends he used the language of a calculating and practical aspirant to Empire.

The opinion which men had formed of his ability in the period of exile was not much altered by his return to France; for in the Assembly his apparent want of mental power caused the world to regard him as harmless, and in the chair of the President he commonly seemed to be torpid. But there were always a few who believed in his capacity, and observant men had latterly remarked that from time to time there appeared a State Paper, understood to be the work of the President, which teemed with thought, and which showed that the writer, standing solitary and apart from the gregarious nation of which he was the chief, was able to contemplate it as something external to himself. His long, endless study of the mind of the first Napoleon had caused him to adopt and imitate the Emperor's habit of looking down upon the French people and treating the mighty nation as a substance to be studied and controlled by a foreign brain. Indeed, during the periods of his imprisonment and of his exile, the relations between him and the France of his studies were very like the relations between an anatomist and a corpse. He lectured upon it; he dissected its fibres; he explained its functions; he showed how beautifully Nature in her infinite wisdom had adapted it to the service of the Bonapartes; and how, without the fostering care of those same

Bonapartes, the creature was doomed to degenerate, and to perish out of the world.

If his intellect was of a poorer quality than men supposed it to be at the time of the Anglo-French alliance, it was much above the low gauge which people used to assign to it in the earlier period which began in 1836 and ended at the close of 1851. That which had so long veiled his cleverness from the knowledge of mankind was the repulsive nature of the science at which he labored. Many men before him had suffered themselves to bring craft into politics. Many more, toiling in humbler grades, had applied their cunning skill to the conflicts which engage courts of law; but no living man perhaps, except Prince Louis Bonaparte, had passed the hours of a studious youth and the prime of a thoughtful manhood in contriving how to apply stratagem to the science of jurisprudence. It was not perhaps from natural baseness that his mind took this bent. The inclination to sit and sit planning for the attainment of some object of desire—this indeed was in his nature; but the inclination to labor at the task of making law an engine of deceit, this did not come perforce with his blood. Yet it came with his parentage. It is true he might have determined to reject the indication given him by the accident of his birth, and to remain a private citizen; but when once he resolved to become a pretender to the imperial throne, he of course had to try and see how it was possible—how it was possible in the midst of this century—that the coarse Bonaparte yoke of 1804 could be made to sit kindly upon the neck of France; and, France being a European nation, and the yoke being in substance a yoke such as Tartars make for Chinese, it followed that the accommodation of the one to the other was only to be effected by guile.

Therefore, by the sheer exigencies of his inheritance rather than by inborn wickedness, Prince Louis was driven to be a contriver; and to expect him to be loyal to France, without giving up his pretensions altogether, would be as inconsistent as to say that the heir of the first Perkin might undertake to revive the fleeting glories of the House of Warbeck, and yet refrain from imposture.

For years the Prince pursued his strange calling; and by the time his studies were over, he had become highly skilled. Long before the moment had come for bringing his crooked science into use, he had learned how to frame a Constitution which should seem to enact one thing and really enact another. He knew how to put the word 'jury' in laws which robbed men of their freedom. He could set the snare which he called 'universal suffrage.' He knew how to strangle a nation in the night time with a thing he called a 'Plebiscite.'

The lawyer-like ingenuity which had thus been evoked for purposes of jurisprudence could, of course, be applied to the composition of State Papers and to political writings of all kinds; and the older Prince Louis grew, the more this odd accomplishment of his was used to subserve his infirmities. It was his nature to remain long in suspense, not merely between similar, but even between opposite plans of action: this weakness grew upon him with his years; and, his conscience being used to stand neuter in these mental conflicts, he never could end his doubt by seeing that one course was honest, and the other not; so, in order to be able to linger safely in his suspense, he had to be always making resting-places upon which for a time he might be able to stand undecided. Just as the indolent man becomes clever in framing excuses for his delays, so Prince Louis, because he was so often hesitating between the right and the left, became highly skilled in contriving—not merely ambiguous phrases, but—ambiguous schemes of action.

Partly from habits acquired in the secret societies of the Italian Carbonari, partly from long years passed in prison, and partly too, as he once said, from his intercourse with the calm, self-possessed men of the English turf, he had derived the power of keeping long silence; but he was not by nature a reserved nor a secret man. Toward foreigners, and especially toward the English, he was generally frank. He was reserved and wary with the French, but this was upon the principle which makes a sportsman reserved and wary with deer, and partridges, and trout. No doubt he was capable of dissembling, and continuing to dissemble through long periods of time, but it would seem that his faculty of keeping his intentions secret was very much aided by the fact that his judgment was often in real suspense, and that he had therefore no secret to tell. His love of masks and disguises sprang more perhaps from the odd vanity and the theatric mania which will be presently spoken of than from a base love of deceit, for it is certain that the mystery in which he loved to wrap himself up was often contrived with a view to a melo-dramatic surprise.

It is believed that men do him wrong who speak of him as void of all idea of truth. He understood truth, and in conversation he habitually preferred it to falsehood, but his truthfulness (though not perhaps contrived for such an end) sometimes became a means of deception, because after generating confidence it would suddenly break down under the pressure of a strong motive. He could maintain friendly relations with a man, and speak frankly and truthfully to him for seven years, and then suddenly deceive him. Of course, men finding themselves insnared by what had appeared to be honesty in his character, were naturally inclined to believe that every semblance of a good quality was a mask; but it is more consistent with the principles of human nature to believe that a truthfulness continuing for seven years was a genuine remnant of virtue, than that it was a mere preparation for falsehood. His doubting and undecided nature was a help to concealment; for men got so wearied by following the oscillations of his mind, that their suspicions in time went to rest; and then, perhaps, when he saw that they were quite tired of predicting that he would do a thing, he gently stole out and did it.

He had boldness of the kind which is produced by reflection rather than that which is the result of temperament. In order to cope with the extraordinary perils into which he now and then thrust himself, and to cope with them decorously, there was wanted a fiery quality which nature had refused to the great bulk of mankind as well as to him. But it was only in emergencies of a really trying sort, and involving instant physical danger, that his boldness fell short. He had all the courage which would have enabled him in a private station of life to pass through the common trials of the world with honor unquestioned; but he had besides, now and then, a factitious kind of audacity produced by long dreamy meditation; and when he had wrought himself into this state, he was apt to expose his firmness to trials beyond his strength. The truth is, that his imagination had so great a sway over him as to make him love the idea of enterprises, but it had not strength enough to give him a foreknowledge of what his sensations would be in the hour of trial. So he was most venturesome in his schemes for action, and yet, when at last he stood face to face with the very danger which he had long been courting, he was liable to be scared by it, as though it were something new and strange.

He loved to contrive and brood over plots, and he had a great skill in making the preparatory arrangements for bringing his schemes to ripeness; but his labors in this direction had a tendency to bring him into scenes for which by nature he was ill fitted, because, like most of the common herd of men, he was unable to command the presence of mind and the flush of animal spirits which are needed for the critical moments of a daring adventure. In short, he was a thoughtful, literary man, deliberately tasking himself to venture into a desperate path, and going great lengths in that direction, but liable to find himself balked in the moment of trial by the sudden and chilling return of his good sense.

He was not by nature bloodthirsty nor cruel, and besides that in small matters he had kind and generous instincts, he was really so willing to act fairly until the motive for foul play was strong, that for months and months together he was able to live amongst English sporting-men without incurring disgrace; and if he was not so constituted nor so disciplined as to be able to refrain from any object of eager desire merely upon the theory that what he sought to do was wicked, there is ground for inferring that his perception of the difference between right and wrong had been dimmed (as it naturally would be) by the habit of seeking an ideal of manly worth in a personage like the first Bonaparte. It would seem that (as a study, or out of curiosity, if not with a notion of being guided by it) he must have accustomed himself to hear sometimes what conscience had to say, for it is certain that, with a pen in his hand and with sufficient time for preparation, he could imitate very neatly the scrupulous language of a man of honor.[1]

What he always longed for was to be able to seize and draw upon himself the wondering attention of mankind; and the accident of his birth having marked out for him the throne of the First Napoleon as an object upon which he might fasten a hope, his craving for conspicuousness, though it had its true root in vanity, soon came to resemble ambition; but the mental isolation in which he was kept by the nature of his aims and his studies, the seeming poverty of his intellect, his blank wooden looks, and, above all, perhaps the supposed remoteness of his chances of success, these sources of discouragement, contrasting with the grandeur of the object at which he aimed, caused his pretension to be looked upon as something merely comic and odd. Linked with this his passionate desire to attain to a height from which he might see the world gazing up at him, there was a strong and almost eccentric fondness for the artifices by which the framer of a melo-drama, the stage-manager, and the stage-hero combine to produce their effects; and so, by the blended force of a passion and a fancy, he was

[1] See *inter alia* his address to the Electors, 29th Nov., 1848; his speech, read after taking the oath, 20th Dec., 1848; speech at Ham, 22nd July, 1849; ditto at Tours, 1st Aug., 1849; message to the Chambers, 3rd Dec., 1849; ditto 12th Nov., 1850. It will be seen (see *post*) that, according to my view, these declarations may have been composed at a time when he was really shrinking from treason; but if, as others suppose, they were intended to hoodwink the country, it must be owned that they counterfeited the sentiments of an honest man with extraordinary skill.

impelled to be contriving scenic effects and surprises in which he himself was always to be the hero. This bent was so strong and dominant as to be, not a mere taste for theatric arrangements, but rather what men call a propensity. Standing alone, it would have done no more perhaps than govern the character of his amusements; but, since his birth had made him a pretender to the throne of France, his desire to imitate and reproduce the Empire supplied a point of contact between his theatric mania and what one may call his rational ambition, and the result was that, so long as he was in exile, he was always filled with a desire to mimic Napoleon's return from Elba, and to do this in his own person and upon the stage of the actual world.

In some of its features his attempts at Strasburg in 1836 was a graver business than is commonly supposed. At that time he was twenty-eight years old. He had gained over Vaudrey, the officer commanding a regiment of artillery which formed part of the garrison. Early in the morning of Sunday the 30th of October the movement began. By declaring that a revolution had broken out in Paris, and that the king had been deposed, Vaudrey persuaded his gunners to recognize the prince as Napoleon II. Vaudrey then caused detachments to march to the houses of the Prefect, and of General Voirol, the General commanding the garrison, and made them both prisoners, placing sentries at their doors. All this he achieved without alarming any of the other regiments.

Supposing that there really existed among the troops a deep attachment to the name and family of Bonaparte, little more seemed needed for winning over the whole garrison than that the heir of the great Emperor should have the personal qualities requisite for the success of the enterprise. Prince Louis was brought into the presence of the captive General, and tried to gain him over, but was repulsed. Afterward the Prince, surrounded with men personating an imperial staff, was conducted to the barrack of the 46th Regiment, and the men, taken entirely by surprise, were told that the person now introduced to them was their Emperor. What they saw was a young man with the bearing and countenance of a weaver—a weaver oppressed by long hours of monotonous in-door work, which makes the body stoop and keeps the eyes downcast; but all the while—and yet it was broad daylight—this young man, from hat to boot, was standing dressed up in the historic costume of the man of Austerlitz and Marengo. It seems that this painful exhibition began to undo the success which Vaudrey had achieved; but strange things had happened in Paris before, and the soldiery could not, with certainty, know that the young man might not be what they were told he was—Napoleon II., the new-made Emperor of the French. Their perplexity gave the Prince an opportunity of trying whether the sentiment for the Bonapartes were really existing or not, and, if it were, whether he was the man to kindle it.

But by-and-by Talandier, the Colonel of the regiment, having been at length apprised of what was going on, came into the yard. He instantly ordered the gates to be closed, and then—fierce, angry, and scornful—went straight up to the spot where the proposed Emperor and his 'Imperial Staff' were standing. Of course this apparition—the apparition of the indignant Colonel whose barrack had been invaded—was exactly what was to be expected, exactly what was to be combated; but yet, as though it were something monstrous and undreamt of, it came upon the Prince with a crushing Power. To him, a literary man, standing in a barrack-yard, in the dress of the great conqueror, an angry Colonel, with authentic warrant to command, was something real, and therefore, it seems, dreadful. In a moment Prince Louis succumbed to him. Some thought that, after what had been done that morning, the Prince owed it to the unfortunate Vaudrey (whom he had seduced into the plot) to take care not to let the enterprise collapse without testing his fortune to the utmost by a strenuous, not to say desperate resistance; but this view did not prevail. One of the ornaments which the Prince wore was a sword; yet without striking a blow he suffered himself to be publicly stripped of his grand cordon of the Legion of Honor and all his other decorations.[1] According to one account, the angry Colonel inflicted this dishonor with his own hands, and not only pulled the grand cordon from the Prince's bosom, but tore off his epaulettes, and trampled both epaulettes and grand cordon under foot. When he had been thus stripped, the Prince was locked up. The decorated followers, who had been impersonating the Imperial Staff, underwent the same fate as their chief. Before judging the Prince for his conduct during these moments, it would be fair to assume that, the Colonel having once been suffered to enter the yard, and to exert the ascendency of his superior firmness, the danger of attempting resistance to him would have been great,

[1] Dispatch of General Voirol, *Moniteur*, 2nd November. After stating the arrival of Lt. Col. Talandier in the barrack-yard, the dispatch says, 'Dans 'une minute L. N. Bonaparte et les miserables qui avaient pris parti pour lui 'ont été arretés, et les decorations dont ils etaient revêtus ont été arrachées 'par les soldats du 46$^{me}$.'

would have been greater than any which the common herd of men are at all inclined to encounter. Besides, the mere fact that the Prince had willfully brought himself into such a predicament, shows that, although it might fail him in very trying moments, he had extraordinary daring of a particular kind. It would be unjust to say, flatly, that a man so willing as he was to make approaches to dangers was timid. It would be fairer to say that his characteristic was a faltering boldness. He could not alter his nature, and his nature was to be venturesome beforehand, but to be so violently awakened and shocked by the actual contact of danger as to be left without the spirit, and seemingly without the wish or the motives, for going on any farther with the part of a desperado. The truth is that the sources of his boldness were his vanity and his theatric bent; and these passions, though they had power to bring him to the verge of danger, were not robust enough to hold good against man's natural shrinking from the risk of being killed—being killed within the next minute. Conscious that in point of hat, and coat, and boots, he was the same as the Emperor Napoleon, he imagined that the great revoir of 1815, between the men and the man of a hundred fights, could be acted over again between modern French troops and himself; but it is plain that this belief had resulted from the undue mastery which he had allowed, for a time, to his ruling propensity, and not from any actual overthrow of the reason; for when checked, he did not, like a madman or a dare-devil, try to carry his venture through; nor did he even, indeed, hold on long enough to try, and try fairly, whether the Bonapartist sentiment to which he wished to appeal were really existent or not: on the contrary, the moment he encountered the shock of the real world, he stopped dead; and becoming suddenly quiet, harmless, and obedient, surrendered himself (as he always has done) to the first man who touched him. The change was like that seeming miracle which is wrought when a hysteric girl, who seems to be carried headlong by strange hallucinations, and to be clothed with the terrible power of madness, is suddenly cured and silenced by a rebuke and a sharp angry threat. Accepting a small sum of money[1] from the Sovereign whom he had been trying to dethrone, Prince Louis was shipped off to America by the good-natured King of the French.

But if he was wanting in the quality which enables a man to go well through with a venture, his ruling propensity had strength enough to make him try the same thing over and over

[1] £600.

again. His want of the personal qualifications for enterprises of this sort being now known in the French Army, and ridicule having fastened upon his name, he could not afterward seduce into his schemes any officers of higher rank than a lieutenant. Yet he did not desist. Before long he was planning another 'return from Elba,' but this time with new dresses and decorations. So long as he was preparing counterfeit flags, and counterfeit generals, and counterfeit soldiers,[1] and teaching a forlorn London bird to play the part of an omen, and guide the destiny of France, he was perfectly at home in that kind of statesmanship; and the framing of the plebiscites and proclamations which formed a large part of his cargo was a business of which he was master; but if his arrangements should take effect, then what he had to look for was, that, at an early hour on a summer morning, he would find himself in a barrack-yard at Boulogne surrounded by a band of armed followers, and supported by one of the officers of the garrison whom he had previously gained over; but also having to do with a number of soldiery of whom some would be for him, and some inclining against him, and others confused and perplexed. Now, this was exactly what happened to him: his arrangements had been so skillful, and fortune had so far lured him on, that whither he meant to go, there he was at last, standing in the very circumstances which he had brought about with long design aforethought. But then his nature failed him. Becoming agitated, and losing his presence of mind,[2] he could not govern the result of the struggle by the resources of his intellect; and being also without the fire and the joyfulness which come to warlike men in moments of crisis and of danger, he was ill qualified to kindle the hearts of the bewildered soldiery. So, when at last a firm, angry officer[3] forced his way into the barrack-yard, he conquered the Prince almost instantly by the strength of a more resolute nature, and turned him out into the street, with all his fifty armed followers, with his flag and his eagle,[4] and his counterfeit head-quarters Staff, as though he were dealing with a mere troop of strolling players.[5] Yet only a few weeks afterward this same Prince Louis Napoleon was able to show

[1] The dresses were made to counterfeit the uniform of the 42nd, one of the regiments quartered at Boulogne; and buttons having on them the number of the regiment were forged for the purpose at Birmingham.

[2] This is his own explanation of his state given before the Chamber of Peers. The flutter he was in caused him, as he explained, to let his pistol go off without intending it, and to hit a soldier who was not taking part against him.—*Moniteur* for 1840, pp. 2031–2034.

[3] Captain Col. Puygellier.

[4] The eagle here spoken of is the wooden one.

[5] *Moniteur*, ubi ante.

by his demeanor before the Chamber of Peers that, where the occasion gave him leisure for thought, and for the exercise of mental control, he knew how to comport himself with dignity, and with a generous care for the safety and welfare of his followers.

It was natural that a man thus constituted should be much inclined to linger in the early stages of a plot. But, since it chanced that by his birth and by his ambition Prince Louis Napoleon was put forward before the world as a pretender to the throne of France, he had always had around him a few keen adventurers who were willing to partake his fortunes; and if there were times when his personal wishes would have inclined him to choose repose or indefinite delay, he was too considerate in his feelings toward his little knot of followers to be capable of forgetting their needs.

His overtures to the gentlemen of France at the time when he was President.

In 1851 motives of this kind, joined with feelings of disappointment and of personal humiliation, were driving the President forward. He had always wished to bring about a change in the Constitution, but, originally, he had hoped to be able to do this with the aid and approval of some at least of the statesmen and eminent generals of the country; and the fact of his desiring such concurrence in his plans seems to show that he did not at first intend to trample upon France by subjecting her to a sheer Asiatic despotism, but rather to found such a monarchy as might have the support of men of station and character. But, besides that few people believed him to be so able a man as he really was, there attached to him at this period a good deal of ridicule. So, although there were numbers in France who would have been heartily glad to see the Republic crushed by some able dictator, there were hardly any public men who believed that in the President of the Republic they would find the man they wanted. Therefore his overtures to the gentlemen of France were always rejected. Every statesman to whom he applied refused to entertain his proposals. Every general whom he urged always said that for whatever he did he must have 'an order from the Minister of War.'

Is rebuffed and falls into other hands. Motives which pressed him forward.

The President being thus rebuffed, his plan of changing the form of government with the assent of some of the leading statesmen and generals of the country degenerated into schemes of a very different kind; and at length he fell into the hands of persons of the quality of Persigny, Morny, and Fleury. With these men he plotted, and strangely enough it happened that the character and the pressing wants of his associates gave strength and purpose to designs which without this stimulus might have long remained mere dreams. The President was easy and generous in the use of money, and he gave his followers all he could, but the checks created by the constitution of the Republic were so effective that, beyond the narrow limit allowed by law, he was without any command of the State resources. In their inveterate love of strong government, the Republicans had placed within reach of the Chief of the State ample means for overthrowing their whole structure, and yet they allowed him to remain subject to the same kind of anxiety and to be driven to the same kind of expedients as an embarrassed tradesman. This was the President's actual plight, and if he looked to the future as designed for him by the Constitution, he could see nothing but the prospect of having to step down on a day already fixed, and descend from a conspicuous station into poverty and darkness. He would have been content perhaps to get what he needed by fair means. In the beginning of the year he had tried hard to induce the Chambers to increase the funds placed at his disposal. He failed. From that moment it was to be expected that, even if he himself should still wish to keep his hands from the purse of France, his associates, becoming more and more impatient and more and more practical in their views, would soon press their chief into action.

He declares for universal suffrage.

The President had been a promoter of the law of the 31st of May, restricting the franchise, but he now became the champion of universal suffrage. To minds versed in politics this change might have sufficed to disclose the nature of the schemes upon which the Chief of the State was brooding; but from first to last, words tending to allay suspicion had been used with great industry and skill. From the moment of his coming before the public in February, 1848, the Prince laid hold of almost every occasion he could find for vowing, again and again, that he harbored no schemes against the Constitution. The speech which he addressed to the Assembly in 1850[1] may be taken as one instance, out of numbers, of these solemn and volunteered declarations.[2] He

His solemn declarations of loyalty to the Republic.

'considered,' he said, 'as great criminals, those 'who by personal ambition compromised the small 'amount of stability secured by the Constitution '. . . that if the Constitution contained defects and dangers, 'the Assembly was competent to expose them to the eyes of 'the country; but that he alone, bound by his oath, restrained

[1] 13th November. [2] See an enumeration of a few of these given *ante*.

'himself within the strict limits traced by that act.' He declared that 'the first duty of authorities was to inspire the people with respect for the law by never deviating from it themselves; and that his anxiety was not, he assured the Assembly, to know who would govern France in 1852, but to employ the time at his disposal so that the transition, whatever 'it might be, should be effected without agitation or disturbance; for,' said he, 'the noblest object, and the most worthy 'of an exalted mind, is not to seek when in power how to perpetuate it, but to labor inseparably to fortify, for the benefit 'of all, those principles of authority and morality which defy 'the passions of mankind and the instability of laws.'

It was thus that, in language well contrived for winning belief, he repudiated as wicked and preposterous the notion of his being the man who would or could act against the Constitution; and, supposing that when he voluntarily made these declarations he had resolved to do what he afterward did, he would have been guilty of deceit more than commonly black; but perhaps an appreciation of the room which he had in his mind for double and conflicting views, and a knowledge of his hesitating nature, and of the pressing wants of the associates by whom he was surrounded, may justify the more friendly view of those who imagine that, when he made all these solemn declarations, he was really shrinking from treason. Certainly, his words were just such as may have pictured the real thoughts of a goaded man at times when he had determined to make a stand against hungry and resolute followers who were keenly driving him forward.

It was natural that in looking at the operation which changed the Republic into an Empire, the attention of the observer should be concentrated upon the person who, already the Chief of the State, was about to attain to the throne; and there seems to be no doubt that what may be called the literary part of the transaction was performed by the President in person. He was the lawyer of the confederacy. He no doubt wrote the Proclamations, the Plebiscites, and the Constitutions, and all such like things; but it seems that the propelling power which brought the plot to bear was mainly supplied by Count de Morny, and by a resolute Major named Fleury.

Morny.

M. Morny was a man of great daring, and gifted with more than common powers of fascination. He had been a member of the Chamber of Deputies in the time of the monarchy; but he was rather known in the world as a speculator than as a politician. He was a buyer and seller of those fractional and volatile interests in trading adventures which go by the name of 'shares,' and since it has chanced that the nature of some of his transactions has been brought to light by the public tribunals, it is probable that the kind of repute in which he is held may be owing in part to those disclosures.[1] He knew how to found a 'company,' and he now undertook to establish institutions which were destined to be more lucrative to him than any of his former adventures. M. Morny was a practical man. If Prince Louis Napoleon was going to be content with a visionary life, thinking fondly of the hour when grateful France would come of her own accord and salute him Emperor, M. Morny was not the sort of person who would consent to stand loitering with him in the hungry land of dreams.

It seems, however, that the man who was the most able to make the President act, to drive him deep into his own plot, and fiercely carry him through it, was Major Fleury. Fleury was young, but his life had been checkered. He was the son of a Paris tradesman, from whom at an early age he had inherited a pleasant sum of money. He plunged into the enjoyments of Paris with so much ardor that that phase of his career was soon cut short; but whilst his father's friends were no doubt lamenting ten times a day that the boy had 'eaten his fortune,' young Fleury was at the foot of a ladder which was destined to give him a control over the fate of a mighty nation. He enlisted in the army as a common soldier; but the officers of his corps were so well pleased with the young man, and so admired the high spirit with which he met his change of fortune, that their good-will soon caused him to be raised from the ranks. It was perhaps his knowledge about horses which first caused him to be attached to the Staff of the President.

Fleury.

From his temperament and his experience of life, it resulted that Fleury cared a great deal for money or the things which money can buy, and was not at all disposed to stand still and go without it. He was daring and resolute, and his daring was of the kind which holds good in the moment of danger. If Prince Louis Bonaparte was bold and ingenious in designing, Fleury was the man to execute. The one was skillful in preparing the mine and laying the train; the other was the man standing by with a lighted match, and determined to touch the fuse. The support of such a comrade as Fleury in the barrack-yard at Strasbourg or at Boulogne might have

[1] The trials here referred to are the action for libel against M. Cabrol, Tribunal of the Seine, January 21, and June 30, 1853; and the suit instituted by the shareholders of the 'Constitutionnel' against Veron, Mirès, and Morny.

brought many lives into danger, but it would have prevented the enterprise from coming to a ridiculous end. In truth, the nature of the one man was the complement of the nature of the other; and between them they had a set of qualities so puissant for dealing a sudden blow, that, working together, and with all the appliances of the Executive Government at their command, they were a pair who might well be able to make a strange dream come true. It would seem that from the moment when Fleury became a partaker of momentous secrets, the President ceased to be free. At all events, he would have found it costly to attempt to stand still.

Fleury searches in Algeria and finds St. Arnaud.

The language held by the generals who declared that they would act under the authority of the Minister of War and not without it, suggested the contrivance which was resorted to. Fleury determined to find a military man capable of command, capable of secrecy, and capable of a great venture. The person chosen was to be properly sounded, and if he seemed willing, was to be admitted into the plot. He was then to be made Minister of War, in order that through him the whole of the land forces should be at the disposal of the plotters. Fleury went to Algeria to find the instrument required, and he so well performed his task that he hit upon a general officer who was christened, it seems, Jacques Arnaud Le Roy, but was known at this time as Achille St. Arnaud. Of some of the adventures of this person it will be right to speak hereafter.[1] There was nothing in his past life, nor in his then plight, which made it at all dangerous for Fleury to approach him with the words of a suborner. He readily entered into the plot. From the moment that Prince Louis Bonaparte and his associates had intrusted their secret to the man of Fleury's selection, it was perhaps hardly possible for them to flinch, for the exigencies of St. Arnaud, formerly Le Roy, were not likely to be on so modest a scale as to consist with the financial arrangements of a Republic governed by law, and the discontent of a person of his quality, with a secret like that in his charge, would plainly bring the rest of the brethren into danger. He was made Minister of War. This was on the 27th of October.

St. Arnaud is suborned and made Minister-of-War.

Maupas.

At the same time M. Maupas, or de Maupas, was brought into the Ministry. In the previous July this person had been Prefect of the Department of the Upper Garonne. Of him, his friends say that he had property, and that he has never been used to obtain money dishon-

[1] In chapter XXIX.

estly. His zeal had led him to desire that thirty-two persons, including three members of the Council-General, should be seized and thrown into prison on a charge of conspiring against the Government. The legal authorities of the department refused to suffer this, because they said there was no ground for the charge. Then this Maupas, or de Maupas, proposed that the want of all ground for accusing the men should be supplied by a stratagem, and with that view he deliberately offered to arrange that incriminating papers, and arms, and grenades should be secretly placed in the houses of the men whom he wanted to have accused. Naturally the legal authorities of the department were horror-struck by the proposal, and they denounced the Prefect to the keeper of the seals. Maupas was ordered to Paris.[1] From the indignant and scornful presence of M. Faucher he came away sobbing; and people who knew the truth supposed him to be for ever disgraced and ruined, but he went and told his sorrows to the President.

He is suborned and made Prefect of Police.

The President, of course, instantly saw that the man could be suborned. He admitted him into the plot, and on the 27th of October appointed him Prefect of Police.

Persigny.

Persigny, properly Fialin, was in the plot. He was descended on one side of an ancient family, and, disliking his father's name, he seems to have called himself for many years after the name of his maternal grandfather.[2] He began life as a non-commissioned officer. As he himself said,[3] his instinct was 'to serve;' and at first he served the Legitimists, but chance brought him into contact with Louis Bonaparte, and he very soon became the attached friend of the Prince, and his partner in all his plans and adventures. If Morny was merely taking up the Bonaparte cause as one of many other money speculations, Persigny could truly say that he had made it for years his profession, and had even tried, as well as he could, to raise it to the dignity of a real political principle. But the part intrusted to Persigny on this occasion, though possibly an important one, was not of a conspicuous sort. It is said that, the firmness of the Prince Louis Bonaparte being distrusted by his comrades, Persigny, who

[1] See the 'Bulletin Français,' pp. 98 et seq. This publication appeared under auspices which make it a safe authority. It is to be regretted that its statements extend to only a portion of the events connected with the 2nd of December.

[2] This, I think, was the account which he gave upon his trial in 1840. He was tried by the description of Fialin *dit* Persigny.

[3] Before the Chamber of Peers, 1840.

was of a sanguine, hopeful nature, was to remain constantly at the Elysée in order to receive the tidings which would be coming in during the period of danger, and prevent them from reaching the President in such a way as to shake him and cause despondency. At all events, it would seem that the hand of Persigny was not the hand employed to execute the measures of the Elysée, and to this circumstance he owes it that he will not always have to stand in the same sentences with Morny, and Fleury, and Maupas, and St. Arnaud, formerly Le Roy.

Contrivance for paralyzing the National Guard.

It was necessary to take measures for paralyzing the National Guard, but the force was under the command of General Perrot, a man whose honesty could not be tampered with. To dismiss him suddenly would be to excite suspicion. The following expedient was adopted: the President appointed as Chief of the Staff of the National Guard a person named Vieyra. The past life and the then repute of this person were of such a kind, that General Perrot, it seems, conceived himself insulted by the nomination, and instantly resigned. That was what the brethren of the Elysée wanted. On Sunday the 30th General Lawæstine was appointed to the command. He was a man who had fought in the great wars, but now in his gray hairs he was not too proud to accept the part designed for him. His function was—not to lead the force of which he took the command, but —to prevent it from acting. It was unnecessary to admit either Lawæstine or Vieyra to a complete knowledge of the plot, because all that they were to do was to frustrate the assembly of the National Guard by withholding all orders and preventing the drums from beating to arms.

The Army.

Of course the engine on which the brethren of the Elysée rested their main hopes was the army, and it was known that the remembrance of humiliating conflicts in the streets of Paris had long been embittering the temper in which the troops regarded the people of the capital. Moreover it happened that at this time the Legislative Assembly had been agitated by a discussion which inflamed the troops with fresh anger against civilians in general, but more especially against the Parisians, against the representatives of the people, and against statesmen and politicians of all kinds. A portion of the Chambers, foreseeing that the army might be used against the freedom of the Legislative body, had desired that the Assembly should avail itself of a provision in the Constitution which empowered it not only to have an armed force for its protection, but to have that force under the order of its

Its indignation at M. Baze's proposal.

own nominee. This was a scheme which shocked the mind of the army. In France, of late years, the Minister of War had always been a soldier, and an order from him (though it was in reality the order of a member of the civil Government) was habitually regarded by military men as the order of a general having supreme command. A proposal to change this system by giving to the Assembly a direct control over a portion of the land-forces could be easily represented to the soldiery as a plan for withdrawing the French army from the control of its generals, and placing it under the command of men whom the soldiers called 'lawyers.' Seen in this light, the project so exasperated the feelings of the troops, that, if it had been carried, they would probably have been stirred up at once to effect by force a violent change of the Constitution. The measure was rejected; but anger is not always appeased by the removal of the kindling motive; and the soreness created by the mere agitation of the question had been so well kept up by the means employed for the purpose, that the garrison of Paris now came to look upon the people with a well-defined feeling of spite.

Selection of regiments and of officers for the Army of Paris.

Magnan.

Care had been taken to bring into Paris and its neighborhood the regiments most likely to serve the purpose of the Elysée, and to give the command to generals who might be expected to act without scruples. The forces in Paris and its neighborhood were under the orders of General Magnan. At the time of Louis Napoleon's descent upon the coast near Boulogne, Magnan had had the misfortune to be singled out by the Prince as a person to whom it was fitting to offer a bribe of £4000. He had also had the misfortune to be detected in continuing his intercourse with the officer who had thought it safe to come with a proposal like that into the presence of a French general. Magnan did not conceal his willingness to go all lengths, and the brethren, it appears, wished to bring him completely into the plot,[1] but his panegyrist (not seeing, perhaps, the full import of his disclosure) causes it to be known that the General, though ready to act against Paris and against the Assembly, declined to risk his safety by avowedly joining in the plot. 'He expressly requested,' says Granier de Cassaignac, 'not to be apprized until the moment for 'taking the necessary dispositions and mounting on horseback.'[2] In other words, though he was willing to use the forces under his command in destroying the Constitution, and in effecting

[1] This is inferred from what follows.

[2] Granier de Cassaignac, vol. ii.

such slaughter as might be needed for the purpose, he refused to dispense with the screen afforded by an order from the Minister of War. In the event of the enterprise failing, he would be able to say, 'I refused to participate in any plot. 'The duty of a soldier is obedience. Here is the order which 'I received from General St. Arnaud. I did no more than 'obey my commanding officer.'

Meeting of twenty generals at Magnan's house.

On the 27th of November, however, this Magnan assembled twenty generals whom he had under his command, and gave them to understand that they might soon be called upon to act against Paris and against the Constitution. They promised a zealous and thorough-going obedience; and although every one of them, from Magnan downward, was to have the pleasing shelter of an order from his superior officer, they all seem to have imagined that their determination was of the sort which mankind call heroic, for their panegyrist relates with pride that when Magnan and his twenty generals were entering into this league and covenant against the people of Paris, they solemnly embraced one another.[1]

The army encouraged in its hatred of the people.

From time to time the common soldiery were gratified with presents of food and wine, as well as with an abundance of flattering words, and their exasperation against the civilians was so well kept alive that men used to African warfare were brought into the humor for calling the Parisians 'Bedouins.' There was massacre in the very sound. The army of Paris was in the temper required.

It was necessary for the plotters to have the concurrence of M. St. Georges, the director of the state printing-office. M. St. Georges was suborned. Then all was ready.

Assembly at the Elysée on Monday night.

On the Monday night between the 1st and the 2nd of December, the President had his usual assembly at the Elysée. Ministers who were loyally ignorant of what was going on were mingled with those who were in the plot. Vieyra was present. He was spoken to by the President, and he undertook that the National Guard should not be beat to arms that night. He went away, and it is said that he fulfilled his humble task by causing the drums to be mutilated. At the usual hour the assembly began to disperse, and by eleven o'clock there were only three guests who remained. These were Morny (who had previously taken care to show himself at one of the theatres), Maupas, and St. Arnaud, formerly

Vieyra's errand.

Before midnight several of the confederates assem-

[1] Granier de Cassaignac, vol. ii.

ble in an inner room.

Le Roy. There was, besides, an orderly officer of the President, called Colonel Beville, who was initiated in the secret. Persigny, it seems, was not present. Morny, Maupas, and St. Arnaud went with the President into his cabinet; Colonel Beville followed them.[1] Mocquard, the private secretary of the President, was in the secret, but it does not appear that he was in the room at this time. Fleury too, it seems, was away; he was probably on an errand which tended to put an end to the hesitation of his more elderly comrades and drive them to make the venture. They were to strike the blow that night. They deliberated, but in the absence of Fleury their council was incomplete; because at the very moment when perhaps their doubts and fears were inclining them still to hold back, Fleury, impetuous and resolute, might be taking a step which must needs push them forward. By-and-by they were apprized that an order which had been given for the movement of a battalion of gendarmerie had duly taken effect without exciting remark. It is probable that the execution of this delicate movement was the very business which Fleury had gone to witness with his own eyes, and that it was he who brought the intelligence of its complete success to the Elysée. Perhaps also he showed that after the step which had just been taken, it would be dangerous to stop short, for the plotters now passed into action. The President intrusted a packet of manuscripts to Colonel Beville, and dispatched him to the state printing-office.

The President intrusts a packet to Colonel Beville.

It was in the streets which surround this building that the battalion of gendarmerie had been collected. When Paris was hushed in sleep, the battalion came quietly out, and folded round the state printing-office. From that moment until their work was done the printers were all close captives, for no one of them was suffered to go out. For some time they were kept waiting. At length Colonel Beville came from the Elysée with his packet of manuscripts. These papers were the proclamations required for the early morning, and M. St. Georges the Director gave orders to put them into type. It is said that there was something like resistance, but in the end, if not at first, the printers obeyed. Each compositor stood whilst he worked between two policemen, and, the manuscript being cut into many pieces, no one could make out the sense of what he was printing. By these proclamations the President asserted that the Assembly was a hot-bed of plots; declared it dis-

Transaction at the state printing-office.

Tenor of the Proclamations.

[1] Granier de Cassagnac, vol. ii.

solved; pronounced for universal suffrage; proposed a new Constitution; vowed anew that his duty was to maintain the Republic; and placed Paris and the twelve surrounding departments under martial law. In one of the proclamations he appealed to the army, and strove to whet its enmity against civilians, by reminding it of the defeats inflicted upon the troops in 1830 and 1848.[1]

Letters dismissing Ministers not in the plot.

The President wrote letters dismissing the members of the Government who were not in the plot; but he did not cause these letters to be delivered until the following morning. He also signed a paper appointing Morny to the Home Office.

Hesitation at the Elysée.

The night was advancing. Some important steps had been taken, but still, though highly dangerous, it was not absolutely impossible for the plotters to stop short. They could tear up the letters which purported to dismiss the Ministers, and although they could not hope to prevent the disclosures which the printers would make as soon as they were released from captivity, it was not too late to keep back the words, and even the general tenor of the Proclamations. But the next steps were of such a kind as to be irrevocable.

Fleury drags them on.

It is said that at this part of the night the spirit of some of the brethren was cast down, and that there was one of them who shrank from farther action; but Fleury, they say, got into a room alone with the man who wanted to hang back, and then locking the door and drawing a pistol, stood and threatened his agitated friend with instant death if he still refused to go on.[2]

At three o'clock the order from the Minister of War was in the hands of Magnan.

What is certain is that, whether in hope or whether in fear, the plotters went on with their midnight task. The order from the Minister of War was probably signed by half past two in the morning, for at three it was in the hands of Magnan.[3]

Maupas's arrangements for the intended arrests.

At the same hour Maupas (assigning for pretext the expected arrival of foreign refugees) caused a number of Commissaries to be summoned in all haste to the Prefecture of Police. At half past three in the morning these men were in attendance; Maupas received each

[1] Granier de Cassaignac, vol. ii. See also the *Annuaire* for 1851. This last publication (which must be distinguished from the *Annuaire des Deux Mondes*) gives an account of the events of December, written in a spirit favorable to the Elysée; but the Appendix contains a full collection of official documents.

[2] I have thought it right to introduce this account under a form indicating that it is based on mere rumor, but I entertain no doubt that the incident has been declared to be true by one of the two persons who stood face to face in that room.

[3] Granier de Cassaignac, vol. ii.

of them separately, and gave to each distinct instructions. It was then that, for the first time, the main secret of the confederates passed into the hands of a number of subordinate agents. During some hours of that night every one of those humble Commissaries had the destinies of France in his hands; for he might either obey the Minister, and so place his country in the power of the Elysée, or he might obey the law, denounce the plot, and bring its contrivers to trial. Maupas gave orders for the seizure at the same minute of the foremost Generals of France, and several of her leading Statesmen. Parties of the police, each under the orders of a Commissary, were to be at the doors of the persons to be arrested some time beforehand, but the seizures were not to take place until a quarter past six.[1]

Disposition of the troops.

At six o'clock a brigade of infantry, under Forey, occupied the Quai d'Orsay; another brigade, under Dulac, occupied the garden of the Tuileries; another brigade, under Cotte, occupied the Place de la Concorde; and another brigade of infantry, under Canrobert, with a whole division of cavalry, under Korte, and another brigade of cavalry, under Reybell, was posted in the neighborhood of the Elysée.[2] It would seem that the main objects aimed at by those who thus placed the troops were—not at this moment to overawe the whole of Paris, but—rather to support the operations of Maupas, and to provide for the safety of the brethren at the Elysée by keeping them close under the shield of the army as long as they remained in Paris, and, if such a step should become necessary, by securing and covering their flight.

The arrests of the principal Generals and of prominent Statesmen.

Almost at the same time Maupas's orders were carefully obeyed, for at the appointed minute, and whilst it was still dark, the designated houses were entered. The most famous generals of France were seized. General Changarnier, General Bedeau, General Lamoricière, General Cavaignac, and General Leflô were taken from their beds, and carried away through the sleeping city and thrown into prison.[3] In the same minute the like was done with some of the chief members and officers of the Assembly, and amongst others with Thiers, Miot, Baze, Colonel Charras, Roger du Nord, and several of the democratic leaders. Some men believed to be the chiefs of secret societies were also seized.[4] The general object of these night arrests was that, when morning broke, the army should be without generals inclined to observe the law, that the Assembly should be without the machinery for convoking it, and that all the political

[1] Granier de Cassagnac, vol. ii. [2] Ibid. [3] Ibid. [4] Ibid.

parties in the State should be paralyzed by the disappearance of their chiefs. The number of men thus seized in the dark was seventy-eight. Eighteen of these were members of the Assembly.[1]

Morny takes possession of the Home Office, and begins to use its power.

Whilst it was still dark, Morny, escorted by a body of infantry, took possession of the Home Office, and prepared to touch the springs of that wondrous machinery by which a clerk can dictate to a nation. Already he began to tell forty thousand communes of the enthusiasm with which the sleeping city had received the announcement of measures not hitherto disclosed.

Newspapers seized and stopped.

When the light of the morning dawned, people saw the Proclamations on the walls, and slowly came to hear that numbers of the foremost men of France had been seized in the night time, and that every General to whom the friends of law and order could look for help was lying in one or other of the prisons. The newspapers, to which a man might run in order to know, and know truly, what others thought and intended, were all seized and stopped.

Meeting of the Assembly.

It is dispersed by troops.

The gates of the Assembly were closed and guarded, but the Deputies, who began to flock thither, found means to enter by passing through one of the official residences which formed part of the building. They had assembled in the Chamber in large numbers, and some of them having caught Dupin, their reluctant President, were forcing him to come and take the chair, when a body of infantry burst in and drove them out, striking some of them with the butt-ends of their muskets. Almost at the same time a number of Deputies who had gathered about the side entrance of the Assembly were roughly handled and dispersed by a body of light infantry. Twelve Deputies were seized by the soldiers, and carried off prisoners.[2]

The President's ride.

In the course of the morning the President, accompanied by his uncle Jerome Bonaparte and Count Flahault,[3] and attended by many general officers and a numerous staff, rode through some of the streets of Paris. It would seem that his theatric bent had led Prince Louis to expect from this ride a kind of triumph upon which his fortunes would hinge, and certainly the unpopularity of the assembly, and the suddenness and perfection of the blow which he had struck in the night gave him fair grounds for his hope, but he was hardly aware of the light in which his personal pretensions

[1] Granier de Cassaignac, vol. ii. [2] La Verité, 'Recueil d'Actes Officielles.'

[3] I imagine that, before the night of the 1st of December, Count Flahault had some knowledge of what was going to be done.

were regarded by the keen laughing people of Paris. The moment when they would cease to use laughter against him was very near, but it had not yet come. Moreover, he did not bring himself to incur the risk which was necessary for obtaining an acclaim of the people, for he clung to the streets and the quays which were close under the dominion of the troops. Upon the whole, the reception he met with seems to have been neither friendly nor violently hostile, but chilling, and in a quiet way scornful.

It seems that after meeting this check his spirit suffered collapse. Once again, though not so hopelessly as at Strasbourg and Boulogne, he had encountered the shock of the real world. And again, as before, the shock felled him. Nor was it strange that he should be abashed and desponding: obeying his old propensity, he had prepared and appointed for the Austerlitz day a great scenic greeting between himself on the one hand, and on the other a mighty nation. When, leaving the room where all this had been contrived and rehearsed, he came out into the free air, and rode through street after street, it became every minute more certain that Paris was too busy, too grave, too scornful to think of hailing him Emperor; nay, strange to say, the people, being fastidious or careless, or imperfectly aware of what had been done, refused to give him even that wondering attention which seemed to be insured to him by the transactions of the foregoing night; and yet, there they were, the proffered Cæsar and his long-prepared group of Captains sitting published on the backs of real horses with appropriate swords and dresses. Perhaps what a man in this plight might the most hate would be the sun — the cold December sun. Prince Louis rode home, and went in out of sight.

Seclusion and gloom of Prince Louis.

Thenceforth, for the most part, he remained close shut up in the Elysée. There, in an inner room, still decked in red trowsers, but with his back to the daylight, they say he sat bent over a fireplace for hours and hours together, resting his elbows on his knees and burying his face in his hands.

Measures for sheltering him from alarming messengers.

What is better known is that, in general, during this period of danger, tidings were not suffered to go to him straight. It seems that, either in obedience to his own dismal intellect, or else because his associates had determined to prevent him from ruining them by his gloom, he was kept sheltered from immediate contact with alarming messengers. It was thought more wholesome for him to hear what Persigny or the more resolute Fleury might think it safe to tell him, than to see with his own eyes an aid-de-camp fresh come from St. Arnaud or Magnan, or a commissary full fraught with the sensations which were shaking the health of Maupas.

Driven from their Chamber, the Deputies assembled at the Mayoralty of the 10th arrondissement. There, upon the motion of the illustrious Berryer, they resolved that the act of Louis Bonaparte was a forfeiture of the Presidency; and they directed the judges of the Supreme Court to meet and proceed to the judgment of the President and his accomplices. These resolutions had just been voted, when a battalion of the Chasseurs de Vincennes entered the court-yard of the Mayoralty, and began to ascend the stairs. One of the Vice-Presidents of the Assembly went out and summoned the soldiers to stop, and leave the Chamber free. The officer appealed to felt the hatefulness or the danger of the duty intrusted to him, and declaring that he was only an instrument, he said he would refer for guidance to his chief.[1]

Meeting of the Assembly in another building.

Its decrees.

Troops ascend the stairs, but hesitate to use force.

Presently afterward, several battalions of the line, under the command of General Forey, came up and surrounded the Mayoralty. The Chasseurs de Vincennes were ordered to load. By-and-by two Commissaries of Police came to the door, and, announcing that they had orders to clear the hall, entreated the Assembly to yield. The Assembly refused. A third Commissary came, using more imperative language, but he also seems to have shrank back when he was made to see the lawlessness of the act which he was attempting. At length an aid-de-camp of General Magnan came with a written order, directing the officer in command of the battalion to clear the hall; to do this, if necessary, by force, and to carry off to the prison of Mazas any Deputies offering resistance. By his way of framing this order, Magnan showed how he crouched under his favorite shelter, for in it he declared that he acted 'in consequence of the orders of the 'Minister of War.'[2] The number of Deputies present at this moment was two hundred and twenty. The whole Assembly declared that they resisted, and would yield to nothing short of force. In the absence of Dupin, M. Benoist d'Azy had been presiding over the Assembly, and both he and one of the Vice-Presidents were now collared by officers of police and led out. The whole Assembly followed, and, enfolded between files of soldiery, was marched through the

Written orders from Magnan to clear the hall.

The Assembly refuses to yield except to force. The whole Assembly taken prisoners by the troops and marched to the Quai D'Orsay.

[1] La Vérité, 'Recueil d'Actes Officielles.' [2] Ibid.

streets. General Forey rode by the side of the column. The captive Assembly passed through the Rue de Grenelle, the Rue St. Guillaume, the Rue Neuve de l'Université, the Rue de Beaune, and finally into the Quai d'Orsay. The spectacle of France thus marched prisoner through the streets seems to have pained the people who saw it, but the pain was that of men who, witnessing by chance some disagreeable outrage, feel sorry that some one else does not prevent it, and then pass on. The members of the Assembly, trusting too much to mere law and right, had neglected or failed to provide that there should be a great concourse of people in the neighborhood of the hall where they met. Those who saw this ending of free institutions were casual by-standers, and were gathered, it seems, in no great numbers. There was no storm of indignation. In an evil hour the Republicans had made it a law that the representatives of the people should be paid for their services. This provision, as was natural, had brought the Assembly into discredit, for it destroyed the ennobling sentiment with which a free people is accustomed to regard its Parliament. The Paris workman, brave and warlike, but shrewd and somewhat envious, compared the amount of his day's earning with the wages of the Deputies, and it did not seem to him that the right cause to stand up for was the cause of men who were hired to be patriots at the rate of twenty-five francs a day. Still, by his mere taste, and his high sense of the difference between what is becoming and what is ignoble, he was inclined to feel hurt by the sight of what he witnessed. In this doubtful temper the Paris workman stood watching, and saw his country slide down from out of the rank of free States.

The Assembly imprisoned in the d'Orsay barrack.

The gates of the d'Orsay barrack were opened, and the Assembly was marched into the court. Then the gates closed upon them.[1]

It was now only two o'clock in the afternoon, but darkness was wanted to hide the thing which was next to be done, and the members of the Assembly were kept prisoners all the day in the barrack. At half past four, three Deputies who had been absent came to the barrack and caused themselves to be made prisoners with the two hundred and twenty already there; and at half past eight in the evening the twelve Deputies who had been seized by the troops at the house of the Assembly were brought to the barrack, so that the number of Deputies there imprisoned was now raised to five hundred and thirty-two.

[1] La Vérité, 'Recueil d'Actes Officielles.'

At a quarter before ten o'clock at night a large number of the windowless vans which are used for the transport of felons were brought into the Court of the barrack, and into these the two hundred and thirty-five members of the Assembly were thrust. They were carried off, some to the Fort of Mount Valerian, some to the fortress of Vincennes, and some to the prison of Mazas. Before the dawn of the 3rd of December all the eminent members of the Assembly, and all the foremost generals of France were lying in prison, for now (besides General Changarnier, and General Bedeau, General Lamoricière, General Cavaignac, and General Leflô, and besides Thiers, and Colonel Charras, and Roger du Nord, and Miot, and Baze, and the others who had been seized the night before, and were still held fast in the jails) there were in prison two hundred and thirty-two of the representatives of the people, including amongst others of wide renown, Berryer, Odillon Barrot, Barthêlemy St. Hilaire, Gustave de Beaumont, Benoist d'Azy, the Duc de Broglie, Admiral Cecile, Chambolle, De Courcelles, Dufaure, Duvergier de Hauranne, De Falloux, General Lauriston, Oscar Lafayette, Lanjuinais, Lasteyrie, the Duc de Luines, the Duc de Montebello, General Radoult-Lafosse, General Oudinot, De Remusat, and the wise and gifted De Tocqueville. Amongst the men imprisoned there were twelve Statesmen who had been Cabinet Ministers, and nine of these had been chosen by the President himself.[1]

The members of the Assembly carried off to different prisons in felons' vans.

The quality of the men imprisoned.

These were the sort of men who were within the walls of the prisons. Those who threw them into prison were Prince Louis Bonaparte, Morny, Maupas, and St. Arnaud, formerly Le Roy, all acting with the advice and consent of Fialin de Persigny, and under the propulsion of Fleury. It is true that the army was aiding, but it has been seen that Magnan, who commanded it, had taken care to screen himself under the orders of the Minister of War, and in the event of his being brought to trial he would no doubt labor to show that in doing as he did, and in effecting the midnight seizure and imprisonment of his country's greatest commanders he was an instrument, and not a contriver.

Quality of the men who imprisoned them.

By the laws of the Republic, the duty of taking cognizance of offenses against the Constitution was cast upon the Supreme Court. The Court was sitting, when

Sitting of the Supreme Court.

[1] The facts mentioned in the above paragraph are not, I believe, controverted in any important point, but the most authoritative and succinct account of what passed will be found in the well-known letter of M. de Tocqueville.

The Judges forcibly driven from the bench.

an armed force entered the hall, and the Judges were driven from the bench, but not until they had made a judicial order for the impeachment of the President. Before the Judges were thrust down they adjourned the Court to a day 'to be named hereafter,' and they had the spirit to order a notice of the impeachment to be served upon the President at the Elysée.[1] If the process-server encountered Colonel Fleury at the Elysée, he would soon find that Fleury was not the man who would suffer his gloomy master to be depressed by the sight of a man with an ugly summons from a Court of Law.

Circumstances which rendered it imprudent to resort to insurrection for the defense of the laws.

The ancient courage of the Parisians had accustomed them to the thought of encountering wrong by an armed resistance; but there were many causes which rendered it unwise for them at that moment to appeal to force. The events of 1848, and the doctrines of the sect called Socialists, had filled men's minds with terror. People who had known what it was to be for months and months together in actual fear for their lives and for their goods, were brought down into a condition of mind which made them willing to side with any executive government however lawless, against any kind of insurrection however righteous. Moreover, the feeling of contempt with which the President had been regarded was not immediately changed by the events of the 2nd of December. It was effectually changed, as will be seen, by the carnage of the 4th; but before the afternoon of that day, the very extravagance of the outrage which had been perpetrated so reminded men of the invasion of Strasbourg and the grotesque descent upon Boulogne, that during the fifty-four hours which followed upon the dawn of the 2nd, the indignation of the public was weakened by its sense of the ridiculous. The contemptuous cry of 'Soulouque!' indicated that Paris was comparing Louis Napoleon to the negro Emperor who had travestied the achievements of the First Bonaparte; and there were many to whom it seemed that his mimicry of the 18th Brumaire belonged to exactly the same class of enterprises as his mimicry of the return from Elba. Plainly the difference was, that this time, instead of having only a few dresses and counterfeit flags, he commanded the resources of the most powerful executive government in the world, but still there was a somewhat wide-spread belief that the President was tumbling as fast as was necessary, and would soon be defeated and punished. Besides, by the contrivance

[1] 'Bulletin Français.'

already described, the plotters had paralyzed the National Guard. Moreover, it would seem that the great body of the working men did not conceive themselves to be hurt by what had been done. Universal suffrage, and the immediate privilege of choosing a dictator for France, were offerings well fitted to win over many honest though credulous laborers, and the baser sort, whose vice is envy, were gratified by what had been done, for they loved to see the kind of inversion which was implied in the fact, that men like Lamoricière, and Bedeau, and Cavaignac, like De Luines, like De Tocqueville, and the Duc de Broglie, could be shut up in a jail or thrown into a felon's van by persons like Morny, and Maupas, and St. Arnaud, formerly Le Roy. Thus there was no sufficing material for the immediate formation of insurgent forces in Paris. The rich and the middle classes were indignant, but they had a horror of insurrection; and the poor had less dread of insurrection, but then they were not indignant. It is known moreover that for the moment there was no fighting power in Paris. Paris has generally abounded in warlike and daring men, who love fighting for fighting's sake; but for the time, this portion of the French community had been crushed by the result of the great street-battle of June, 1848, and the seizures and banishments which followed the defeat of the insurgents. The men of the barricades had been stripped of their arms, deprived of their leaders, and so thinned in numbers as to be unequal to any serious conflict, and their helplessness was completed by the sudden disappearance of the street captains and the chiefs of secret societies, who had been seized in the night between the 1st and 2nd of December.

The Committee of Resistance.

Still, there was a remnant of the old insurrectionary forces which was willing to try the experiment of throwing up a few barricades, and there was, besides, a small number of men who were impelled in the same direction by motives of a different and almost opposite kind. These last were men too brave, too proud, too faithful in their love of right and freedom to be capable of acquiescing for even a week in the transactions of the December night. The foremost of these was the illustrious Victor Hugo. He and some of the other members of the Assembly who had escaped seizure, formed themselves into a Committee of Resistance, with a view to assert by arms the supremacy of the law. This step they took on the 2nd of December.

Several members of the Assembly went into the Faubourg St. Antoine, and strove to raise the people. These deputies were Schœlcher, Baudin, Aubry, Duval, Chaix, Malardier, and

Attempted rising in the Faubourg St. Antoine.

de Flotte, and they were vigorously supported by Cournet, whose residence became their head-quarters, and by Xavier Durrieu, Kesler, Ruin, Lemaitre, Wabripon, Le Jeune, and other men connected with the democratic press. More, it would seem, by their personal energy than by the aid of the people, these men threw up a slight barricade at the corner of the Rue St. Marguerite. Against this there marched a battalion of the 19th Regiment; and then there occurred a scene which may make one smile for a moment, and may then almost force one to admire the touching pedantry of brave men, who imagined that, without policy or warlike means, they could be strong with the mere strength of the law. Laying aside their fire-arms, and throwing across their shoulders scarfs which marked them as Representatives of the People, the Deputies ranged themselves in front of the barricade, and one of them, Charles Baudin, held ready in his hand the book of the Constitution. When the head of the column was within a few yards of the barricade, it was halted. For some moments there was silence. Law and Force had met. On the one side was the Code democratic, which France had declared to be perpetual; on the other a battalion of the line. Charles Baudin, pointing to his book, began to show what he held to be the clear duty of the battalion; but the whole basis of his argument was an assumption that the law ought to be obeyed; and it seems that the officer in command refused to concede what logicians call the 'major premiss,' for, instead of accepting its necessary consequence, he gave an impatient sign. Suddenly the muskets of the front rank men came down, came up, came level; and in another instant their fire pelted straight into the group of the scarfed Deputies. Baudin fell dead, his head being shattered by more than one ball. One other was killed by the volley, several more were wounded. The book of the Constitution had fallen to the ground, and the defenders of the law recurred to their fire-arms. They shot the officer who had caused the death of their comrade and questioned their major premiss. There was a fight of the Homeric sort for the body of Charles Baudin. The battalion won it. Four soldiers carried it off.[1] Plainly this attempted insurrection in the Faubourg St. Antoine was without the support of the multitude. It died out.

The barricade of the Rue St. Marguerite.

The Committee of Resistance now caused barricades to be thrown up in that mass of streets between the Hotel de Ville

[1] Xavier Durrieu, pp. 23, 24.

Barricades in central Paris.

and the Boulevard, which is the accustomed centre of an insurrection in Paris; but they were not strong enough to occupy the houses, and therefore the troops passed through the streets without danger, and easily took every barricade which they encountered. When the troops retired, the barricades again sprang up, but only to be again taken. This state of things continued during part of the 3rd of December; but afterward the efforts of the troops were relaxed, and during the night, and the whole forenoon of the next day, the formation of barricades in the centre of Paris was allowed to go on without encountering serious interruption.[1]

State of Paris at 2 o'clock on the 4th of Dec.

At two o'clock in the afternoon of the 4th, the condition of Paris was this:—The mass of streets which lies between the Boulevard and the neighborhood of the Hotel de Ville was barricaded, and held without combating by the insurgents; but the rest of the city was free from grave disturbance. The army was impending. It was nearly forty-eight thousand strong,[2] and comprised a force of all arms, including cavalry, infantry, artillery, engineers, and gendarmes. Large bodies of infantry were so posted that brigades advancing from all the quarters of the compass could simultaneously converge upon the barricaded district. Besides that, by the means already shown, the troops had been wrought into a feeling of hatred against the people of Paris; they had clearly been made to understand that they were to allow no consideration for by-standers to interfere with their fire, that they were to give no quarter, and that they were to put to death not only the combatants whom they might see in arms against them, but those also who, without having been seen in the act, might nevertheless be deemed to have taken part against them. When it is remembered that the duty—the judicial duty—of bringing people within this last category was cast upon raging soldiers, it will be clear that the army of Paris was brought into the streets with instructions well fitted to bring about the events which marked the afternoon of the 4th of December.[3] For reasons which then remained unknown, the troops were abstaining from action, and there was a good distance between the heads of the columns and the outposts of the insurgents.

Attitude of the troops.

Hesitation of Magnan.

It is plain that, either because of his own hesitation, or because of the hesitation of the President, or M. St. Arnaud, the General in command of the army was

[1] Magnan's Dispatch, *Moniteur*. [2] 47,928.

[3] My knowledge as to what the troops were made to understand is derived from a source highly favorable to the Elysée.

hanging back;[1] and in truth, though the mere physical task which he had to perform was a slight one, Magnan could not but see that politically he had got into danger. The mechanical arrangements of the night of the 2nd of December had met with a success which was wondrously complete; but in other respects the enterprise of the Elysian brethren seemed to be failing, for no one of mark and character had come forward to abet the President. There were many lovers of order and tranquillity who wished the President to succeed in overthrowing the Constitution, or giving it the needful wrench, but they had assumed that he would not engage in any enterprise of this sort without the support of some at least of the Statesmen who were the known champions of the cause of order. Those whose views had lain in this direction were shocked out of their hopes when, on the 2nd of December, they came to find that all the honored defenders of the cause of order had been thrown into prison, and that the persons who were sheltering the President by their concurrence and their moral sanction were Morny and Maupas or de Maupas, and St. Arnaud, formerly Le Roy. The list of the Ministry, which was published on the following day, contained no name held in honor; and the plotters of the Elysée, terrified, as it seems, at the state of isolation in which they were placed, resorted to a curious stratagem. They formed what they called a 'Consultative Commission,' and promulgated a decree which purported to appoint as members of the body, not only most of the plotters themselves, and others whose services they could command, but also some eighty other men who were eminent for their character and station.[2] In so far as it represented these eighty men to be members of the Commission, the decree was a counterfeit. One after another the men with the honored names repudiated the notion that they had consented to go and 'consult' with Louis Bonaparte, and Morny, and Fleury, and Maupas, and St. Arnaud, formerly Le Roy.[3] The Elysée derived great advantages from

Its probable grounds.

Apparent terror of the plotters on account of their continued isolation.

Stratagem of forming the 'Consultative Commission.'

[1] Magnan, in his dispatch, accounts for his delay in words which tend to justify the conclusion of those who believe that the opportunity of inflicting slaughter on the people of Paris was deliberately sought for and prepared; but I am not inclined to believe that for such an object a French General would throw away the first seven hours of a short December day, and therefore, so far as concerns his motives, I reject Magnan's statement. I consider that the disclosures made before the Chamber of Peers, in 1840, give me a right to use my own judgment in determining the weight which is due to this person's assertions.

[2] *Annuaire*, Appendix.

[3] Their letters to this effect appeared from time to time in the Eng. journals.

this stratagem, because for many precious hours, and even days, it kept the country from knowing what was the number and what was the quality of the persons who were really abetting the President; but Magnan of course knew the truth, and when he found, on the morning of the 4th of December, that even the complete success of all the arrangements of the foregoing Tuesday had not been hitherto puissant enough to bring to the Elysée the support of men of weight and character, he had grounds for the alarm which seems to have been the cause of his inaction.

For, regarded in connection with the state of isolation in which the plotters still remained, the insurrection, feeble as it was, became a source of grave danger to the General in command of the troops. It would have been no new thing to have to act against insurgents in vindication of the law, and under the orders of what had been commonly called a 'Government;' but this time the law was on the side of the insurgents, and the knot of men who had got the control of the offices of the State were not so circumstanced in point of repute as to be able to make up for the want of legal authority by the weight of their personal character. Therefore it was natural for Magnan, notwithstanding his cherished order from the Minister of War, to think a good deal of what might happen to him if perchance, at the very moment when he was taking upon his hands the blood of the Parisians, the plot of which he was the instrument should after all break down for want of support from men known and honored as Statesmen.

Magnan at length resolves to act.

But at length perhaps it was effectually explained to Magnan that he must stand or fall with those to whom he was now committed, and that, although he thought to keep himself under the shelter of the 'order of the Minister of War,' the testimony of any one out of the twenty Generals who met him on the 27th of November would suffice to bring him into nearly the same plight as any of the avowed plotters. A judicious application of this kind of torture would make it unnecessary for Colonel Fleury to show even the hilt of his pistol. At all events, Magnan now at last consented to act against the insurrection. He had thrown away the whole of the morning and the better part of the afternoon, and this on a short December day; but at two o'clock the troops were ordered to advance, and by three all the heads of columns which were converging upon the insurrection from different points were almost close to the several barricades upon which they had marched.

The advance post of the insurgents, at its northwestern ex-

Point of contact between the ground occupied by the troops and that occupied by the insurgents.

tremity, was covered by a small barricade, which crossed the Boulevard at a point close to the Gymnase Theatre. Some twenty men, with weapons and a drum taken in part from the 'property room' of the theatre, were behind this rampart, and a small flag, which the insurgents chanced to find, was planted on the top of the barricade.[1]

State of the Boulevard at three o'clock.

Facing this little barricade, at a distance of about a hundred and fifty yards, was the head of the vast column of troops which now occupied the whole of the western Boulevard, and a couple of field-pieces stood pointed toward the barricade. In the neutral space between the barricade and the head of the column the shops and almost all the windows were closed, but numbers of spectators, including many women, crowded the foot-pavement. These gazers were obviously incurring the risk of receiving stray shots. But westward of the point occupied by the head of the column the state of the Boulevards was different. From that point home to the Madeleine the whole carriage-way was occupied by troops; the infantry was drawn up in subdivisions at quarter distance. Along this part of the gay and glittering Boulevard the windows, the balconies, and the foot-pavements were crowded with men and women who were gazing at the military display. These gazers had no reason for supposing that they incurred any danger, for they could see no one with whom the army would have to contend. It is true that notices had been placed upon the walls recommending people not to encumber the streets, and warning them that they would be liable to be dispersed by the troops without being summoned; but, of course, those who had chanced to see this announcement naturally imagined that it was a menace addressed to riotous crowds which might be pressing upon the troops in a hostile way. Not one man could have read it as a sentence of sudden death against peaceful spectators.

At three o'clock one of the field-pieces ranged in front of the column was fired at the little barricade near the Gymnase. The shot went high over the mark. The troops at the head of the column sent a few musket-shots in the direction of the barricade, and there was a slight attempt at reply, but no one on either side was wounded; and the engagement, if so it

[1] The great barricade in this district was the one which crossed the Boulevard diagonally near the Porte St. Denis. It is not noticed in the text, because the object here is—not to describe in detail the preparations of the insurgents—but merely to show the state of the Boulevard at the point where their advanced post faced the troops.

could be called, was so languid and harmless that even the gazers who stood on the foot-pavement between the troops and the barricade were not deterred from remaining where they were. And, with regard to the spectators farther west, there was nothing that tended to cause them alarm, for they could see no one who was in antagonism with the troops. So, along the whole Boulevard, from the Madeleine to near the Rue du Sentier, the foot-pavements, the windows, and the balconies still remained crowded with men, and women, and children; and from near the Rue du Sentier to the little barricade at the Gymnase, spectators still lined the foot-pavement, but in that last part of the Boulevard the windows were closed.[1]

The massacre of the Boulevard.

According to some, a shot was fired from a window or a house-top near the Rue du Sentier. This is denied by others, and one witness declares that the first shot came from a soldier near the centre of one of the battalions, who fired straight up into the air; but what followed was this: the troops at the head of the column faced about to the south and opened fire. Some of the soldiery fired point-blank into the mass of spectators who stood gazing upon them from the foot-pavement, and the rest of the troops fired up at the gay crowded windows and balconies.[2] The officers in general did not order the firing, but seemingly they were agitated in the same way as the men of the rank and file, for such of them as could be seen from a balcony at the corner of the Rue Montmartre appeared to acquiesce in all that the soldiery did.[3]

The impulse which had thus come upon the soldiery near the head of the column was a motive akin to panic, for it was carried by swift contagion from man to man, till it ran westward from the Boulevard Bonne Nouvelle into the Boulevard Poissonière, and gained the Boulevard Montmartre, and ran swiftly through its whole length, and entered the Boulevard des Italiens. Thus, by a movement in the nature of that which tacticians describe as 'conversion,' a column of some sixteen thousand men facing eastward toward St. Denis was suddenly formed, as it were, into an order of battle fronting southward, and busily firing into the crowd which lined the foot-pavement, and upon the men, women, and children who stood at the balconies and windows on that side of the Boulevard.[4] What made the fire at the houses the more deadly was that,

[1] What I say as to the state of the Boulevard at this time is taken from many concurrent authorities, but Captain Jesse's statement (see *post*) is the most clear and satisfactory so far as concerns what he saw.

[2] Captain Jesse, *ubi post*. [3] Ibid. [4] Ibid.

even after it had begun at the eastern part of the Boulevard Montmartre, people standing at the balconies and windows farther west could not see or believe that the troops were really firing in at the windows with ball cartridge, and they remained in the front rooms, and even continued standing at the windows, until a volley came crashing in. At one of the windows there stood a young Russian noble with his sister at his side. Suddenly they received the fire of the soldiery, and both of them were wounded with musket-shots. An English surgeon who had been gazing from another window in the same house had the fortune to stand unscathed; and when he began to give his care to the wounded brother and sister, he was so touched, he says, by their forgetfulness of self, and the love they seemed to bear the one for the other, that more than ever before in all his life he prized his power of warding off death.

Of the people on the foot-pavement who were not struck down at first, some rushed and strove to find a shelter, or even a half-shelter, at any spot within reach. Others tried to crawl away on their hands and knees; for they hoped that perhaps the balls might fly over them. The impulse to shoot people had been sudden, but was not momentary. The soldiers loaded and reloaded with a strange industry, and made haste to kill and kill, as though their lives depended upon the quantity of the slaughter they could get through in some given period of time.

When there was no longer a crowd to fire into, the soldiers would aim carefully at any single fugitive who was trying to effect his escape, and if a man tried to save himself by coming close up to the troops and asking for mercy, the soldiers would force or persuade the suppliant to keep off, and hasten away, and then if they could, they killed him running. This slaughter of unarmed men and women was continued for a quarter of an hour or twenty minutes. It chanced that amongst the persons standing at the balconies, near the corner of the Rue Montmartre, there was an English officer; and, because of the position in which he stood, the professional knowledge which guided his observation, the composure with which he was able to see and to describe, and the more than common responsibility which attaches upon a military narrator, it is probable that his testimony will be always appealed to by historians who shall seek to give a truthful account of the founding of the Second French Empire.

At the moment when the firing began, this officer was looking upon the military display with his wife at his side, and was so placed, that if he looked eastward, he could carry his eye along the Boulevard for a distance of about 800 yards, and see as far as the head of the column, and if he looked westward he could see to the point where the Boulevard Montmartre runs into the Boulevard des Italiens. This is what he writes: 'I went to the balcony at which my wife was standing, and 'remained there watching the troops. The whole Boulevard, 'as far as the eye could reach, was crowded with them, princi- 'pally infantry in subdivisions at quarter distance, with here 'and there a batch of twelve-pounders and howitzers, some of 'which occupied the rising ground of the Boulevard Poisson- 'ière. The officers were smoking their cigars. The windows 'were crowded with people, principally women, tradesmen, 'servants, and children, or, like ourselves, the occupants of 'apartments. Suddenly, as I was intently looking with my 'glass at the troops in the distance eastward, a few musket- 'shots were fired at the head of the column, which consisted 'of about 3000 men. In a few moments it spread, and after 'hanging a little came down the Boulevard in a waving sheet 'of flame. So regular, however, was the fire, that at first I 'thought it was a feu de joie for some barricade taken in ad- 'vance, or to signal their position to some other division; and 'it was not till it came within fifty yards of me that I recog- 'nized the sharp ringing report of ball cartridge; but even then 'I could scarcely believe the evidence of my ears, for as to my 'eyes I could not discover any enemy to fire at; and I contin- 'ued looking at the men until the company below me were 'actually raising their firelocks, and one vagabond sharper 'than the rest — a mere lad without whisker or mustache — 'had covered me. In an instant I dashed my wife, who had 'just stepped back, against the pier between the windows, 'when a shot struck the ceiling immediately over our heads, 'and covered us with dust and broken plaster. In a second 'after I placed her upon the floor, and in another, a volley 'came against the whole front of the house, the balcony, and 'windows; one shot broke the mirror over the chimney-piece, 'another the shade of the clock; every pane of glass but one 'was smashed, the curtains and window-frames cut; the room, 'in short, was riddled. The iron balcony, though rather low, 'was a great protection; still fire-balls entered the room, and 'in the pause for reloading I drew my wife to the door, and 'took refuge in the back rooms of the house. The rattle of 'musketry was incessant for more than a quarter of an hour 'after this; and in a very few minutes the guns were unlim- 'bered and pointed at the "Magasin" of M. Sallandrouze, five 'houses on our right. What the object or meaning of all this 'might be was a perfect enigma to every individual in the 'house, French or foreigners. Some thought the troops had 'turned round and joined the Reds; others suggested that 'they must have been fired upon somewhere, though they cer- 'tainly had not from our house or any other on the Boulevard 'Montmartre, or we must have seen it from the balcony. . . . 'This wanton fusillade must have been the result of a panic, 'lest the windows should have been lined with concealed en- 'emies, and they wanted to secure their skins by the first fire, 'or else it was a sanguinary impulse. . . . The men, as I have 'already stated, fired volley upon volley for more than a quar- 'ter of an hour without any return; they shot down many of 'the unhappy individuals who remained on the Boulevard and 'could not obtain an entrance into any house; some persons 'were killed close to our door.'[1] The like of what was calmly seen by this English officer was seen with frenzied horror by thousands of French men and women.

If the officers in general abstained from ordering the slaughter, Colonel Rochefort did not follow their example. He was an officer in the Lancers, and he had already done execution with his horsemen amongst the chairs and the idlers in the neighborhood of Tortoni's, but afterward imagining a shot to have been fired from a part of the Boulevard occupied by infantry, he put himself at the head of a detachment which made a charge upon the crowd; and the military historian of these events relates with triumph that about thirty corpses, almost all of them in the clothes of gentlemen, were the trophies of this exploit.[2] Along a distance of a thousand yards, going eastward from the Rue Richelieu, the dead bodies were strewed upon the foot-pavement of the Boulevard, but at several spots they lay in heaps. Some of the people mortally struck would be able to stagger blindly for a pace or two until they were tripped up by a corpse, and this perhaps is why a large proportion of the bodies lay heaped one on the other. Before one shop-front they counted thirty-three corpses. By the peaceful little nook or court which is called the Cité Bergère they counted thirty-seven. The slayers were many thousands of armed soldiery: the slain were of a number that never will be reckoned; but amongst all these slayers and all these slain

[1] Letter from Captain Jesse, first printed in the 'Times,' 13th December, 1851, and given also in the 'Annual Register.'

[2] This was in the Boulevard Poissonière. Mauduit, p. 217, 218. Mauduit speaks of these thirty killed as armed men, but it is well proved that there were no armed men in the Boulevard Poissonière, and I have therefore no difficulty in rejecting that part of his statement.

there was not one combatant. There was no fight, no riot, no fray, no quarrel, no dispute.[1] What happened was a slaughter of unarmed men, and women, and children. Where they lay, the dead bore witness. Corpses lying apart struck deeper into people's memory than the dead who were lying in heaps. Some were haunted with the look of an old man with silver hair, whose only weapon was the umbrella which lay at his side. Some shuddered because of seeing the gay idler of the Boulevard sitting dead against the wall of a house, and scarce parted from the cigar which lay on the ground near his hand. Some carried in their minds the sight of a printer's boy leaning back against a shop-front, because, though the lad was killed, the proof-sheets which he was carrying had remained in his hands, and were red with his blood, and were fluttering in the wind.[2] The military historian of these achievements permitted himself to speak with a kind of joy of the number of women who suffered. After accusing the gentler sex of the crime of sheltering men from the fire of the troops, the Colonel writes it down that 'many an amazon of the Boulevard has 'paid dearly for her imprudent collusion with that new sort of 'barricade,' and then he goes on to express a hope that women will profit by the example, and derive from it 'a lesson for the 'future.'[3] One woman who fell and died clasping her child, was suffered to keep her hold in death as in life, for the child too was killed. Words which long had been used for making figures of speech recovered their ancient use, being wanted again in the world for the picturing of things real and physical. Musket-shots do not shed much blood in proportion to the slaughter which they work, but still in so many places the foot-pavement was wet and red, that, except by care, no one could pass along it without gathering blood. Round each of the trees in the Boulevards a little space of earth is left unpaved in order to give room for the expansion of the trunk. The blood, collecting in pools upon the asphalte, drained down at last into these hollows, and there becoming coagulated, it remained for more than a day and was observed by many. 'Their 'blood'—says the English officer before quoted—'their blood 'lay in the hollows round the trees the next morning when we 'passed at twelve o'clock. The Boulevards and the adjacent

[1] I speak here of the Boulevard from the Rue du Sentier to the western extremity of the Boulevard Montmartre.

[2] For accounts of the state of the Boulevard after the massacre, see the written statement of eye-witnesses, supplied to Victor Hugo and printed in his narrative. It will be seen that I do not adopt M. Victor Hugo's conclusions, but there is no reason for questioning the authenticity or the truth of the statements which he has collected.

[3] Mauduit, p. 278.

'streets,' he goes on to say, 'were at some points a perfect 'shambles.'[1] Incredible as it may seem, artillery was brought to bear upon some of the houses in the Boulevard. On its north side the houses were so battered that the foot-pavement beneath them was laden with plaster and such ruins as field guns can bring down.

The soldiers broke into many houses, and hunted the inmates from floor to floor, and caught them at last and slaughtered them. These things, no doubt, they did under a notion that shots had been fired from the house which they entered, but it is certain that in almost all these instances, if not in every one of them, the impression was false. One or two soldiers would be seen rushing furiously at some particular door, and this sight, leading their comrades to imagine that a shot had been fired from the windows above, was enough to bring into the accused house a whole band of slaughterers. The Sallandrouze carpet warehouse was thus entered. Fourteen helpless people shrank for safety behind some piles of carpets. The soldiers killed them crouching.

Whilst these things were being done upon the Boulevard, four brigades were converging upon the streets where resistance, though of a rash and feeble kind, had been really attempted. One after another the barricades were battered by artillery, and then carried without a serious struggle; but things had been so ordered that, although there should be little or no fighting, there might still be slaughter, for the converging movement of the troops prevented escape, and forced the people sooner or later into a street barred by troops on either side, and then, whether they were combatants or other fugitives, they were shot down. It was the success of this contrivance for penning in the fugitive crowds which enabled Magnan to declare, without qualifying his words, that those who defended the barricades in the quartier Beaubourg were put to death,[2] and the same ground justified the Government in announcing that of the men who defended the barricade of the Porte St. Martin the troops had not spared one.[3] Some of the people thus killed were men combating or flying, but many more were defenseless prisoners in the hands of the soldiery who shot them. Whatever may have been the cause of the slaughter of the unoffending spectators on the Boulevard,[4] it is certain that the shooting of the prisoners taken at the bar-

Slaughter in central Paris.

[1] Mauduit, p. 278.
[2] See his Dispatch dated, I think, the 9th December.—*Moniteur.*
[3] The *Patrie,* one of the official organs of the President, Dec. 6.
[4] See the discussion on this subject toward the close of the chapter.

ricades was brought about by causing the troops to understand that they were to give no quarter. Over and over again, no doubt, the soldiers, listening to the dictates of humanity, gave quarter to vanquished combatants, but their clemency was looked upon as a fault, and the fault was repaired by shooting the prisoners they had taken. Sometimes, as was natural, a house was opened to the fugitives, but this shelter did not long hold good. For instance, when the barricade near the Porte St. Denis was taken, a hundred men were caught behind it, and all these were shot, but their blood was not reckoned to be enough, for, by going into the houses where there were supposed to be fugitives, the soldiers got hold of thirty more men, and these also they killed.[1] The way in which the soldiery dealt with the inmates of houses suspected of containing fugitives can be gathered by observing what passed in one little street. After describing the capture of a barricade in the Rue Montorgueil, the military historian of these events says that searches were immediately ordered to be made in the public houses. 'A hundred prisoners,' he says, 'were made in them, the most of whom had their hands 'still black with gunpowder, an evident proof of their partici- 'pation in the contest. How then was it possible not to exe- 'cute with regard to a good many of them the terrible pre- 'scriptions of the state of siege?[2]

Slaughter of prisoners.

This killing was done under orders so stringent, and yet in some instances with so much of deliberation, that many of the poor fellows put to death were allowed to dispose of their little treasures before they died. Thus, one man, when told that he must die, entreated the officer in command to be allowed to send to his mother the fifteen francs which he carried in his pocket. The officer consenting, took down the address of the man's mother, received from him the fifteen francs, and then killed him. Many times over the like of this was done.

Great numbers of prisoners were brought into the Prefecture of Police, but it appears to have been thought inconvenient to allow the sound of the discharge of musketry to be heard coming from the precincts of the building. For that reason, as it would seem, another mode of quieting men was adopted. It is hard to have to believe such things, but, according to the statement of a former member of the Legislative Assembly, who declares that he saw them with his own eyes, each of the prisoners destined to undergo this fate was driven with his hands tied behind

Mode of dealing with some of the prisoners at the Prefecture.

[1] An officer engaged in the operation made this statement—not as confession of sins, but as a narrative of exploits.

[2] Mauduit, p. 248.

him, into one of the Courts of the Prefecture, and then one of Maupas's police-officers came and knocked him on the head with a loaded club, and felled him—felled him in the way that is used by a man when he has to slaughter a bullock.[1]

Gradations by which slayers of vanquished men may be distinguished.

Troops are sometimes obliged to kill insurgents in actual fight, and unarmed people standing in the line of fire often share the fate of the combatants; what that is the whole world understands. But also an officer has sometimes caused people to be put to death—not because they were fighting against him, nor even because they were hindering the actual operations of the troops, but because he has imagined that under some probable change of circumstance their continued presence might become a source of inconvenience or danger, and he has therefore thought it right to have them shot down by way of precaution; but generally such an act as this has been preceded by the most earnest entreaties to disperse, and by repeated warnings. This may be called a precautionary slaughter of by-standers, who are foolhardy or perverse, or willfully obstructive to the troops. Again, it has happened that a slaughter of this last-mentioned sort has occurred, but without having been preceded by any such request or warning as would give the people time to disperse. This is a willful and malignant slaughter of by-standers; but still it is a slaughter of by-standers whose presence might become inconvenient to the troops, and therefore perhaps it is not simply wanton. Again, it has happened (as we have but too well seen) that soldiers not engaged in combat, and exposed to no real danger, have suddenly fired into the midst of crowds of men and women, who neither opposed nor obstructed them. This is 'wanton massacre.' Again, it has sometimes happened, even in modern times, that when men, defeated in fight, have thrown down their arms and surrendered themselves, asking for mercy, the soldiery to whom they appealed have refused their prayers, and have instantly killed them. This is called 'giving no quarter.' Again, it has happened that defeated combatants, having thrown down their arms and surrendered at discretion, and, not having been im-

[1] M. Xavier Durrieu, formerly a member of the Assembly, is one of those who states that he was an eye-witness of these deeds, having seen them from the window of his cell. He says, 'Souvent quand la porte était renfermée 'les sergens de ville se jetaient comme des tigres sur les prisonniers attachés 'les mains derrière le dos. Ils les assommaient a coup de casse-tête. Ils 'les laissaient râlant sur la pierre ou plusieurs d'entre eux ont expiré. . . . 'Il en est ainsi ni plus ni moins; nous l'avons vu des fenètres de nos cellules 'qui s'ouvraient sur la cour.'—*Le Coup d''Etat*, par Xavier Durrieu, ancien Representant du peuple, pp. 39 40.

mediately killed, have succeeded in constituting themselves the prisoners of the vanquishing soldiery, but presently afterward (as for instance within the time needed for taking the pleasure of an officer on horseback at only a few yards' distance) they have been put to death. This is called 'killing prisoners.' Again, defeated combatants, who have succeeded in constituting themselves prisoners, have been allowed to remain alive for a considerable time, and have afterward been put to death by their captors with circumstances indicating deliberation. This is called 'killing prisoners in cold blood.' Again, soldiers after a fight in a city have rushed into houses where they believed that there were people who helped or favored their adversaries, and, yielding to their fury, have put to death men and women whom they had never seen in combat against them. This is massacre of non-combatants, but it is massacre committed by men still hot from the fight. Again, it has happened that soldiery seizing unarmed people, whom they believed to be favorers of their adversaries, have nevertheless checked their fury, and, instead of killing them, have made them prisoners; but afterward, upon the arrival of orders from men more cruel than the angry soldiery, these people have been put to death. This is called an 'execution of non-combatants in cold blood.'

Slaughter ranging under all those categories was caused by the confederates.

Here then are acts of slaughter of no less than nine kinds, and of nine kinds so distinct that they do not merely differ in their accidents, but are divided the one from the other by strong moral gradations. It is certain that deeds ranging under all these nine categories were done in Paris on the 4th of December, 1851, and it is not less certain that, although they were not all of them specifically ordered, they were every one of them caused by the brethren of the Elyseé. Moreover, it must be remembered that this slaughtering of prisoners was the slaughtering of men against whom it was only to be charged that they were in arms—not to violate, but to defend the laws of their country.

Inquiry as to the alleged shooting of prisoners who were in the hands of the civil power.

But there is yet another use to which, if it were not for the honest pride of its officers and men, it would be possible for an army to be put. In the course of an insurrection in such a city as Paris, numbers of prisoners might be seized either by the immense police force which would probably be hard at its work, or by troops who would shrink from the hatefulness of refusing quarter to men without arms in their hands, and the prisoners thus taken, being consigned to the ordinary jails, would be in the custody of the civil power. The Government, regretting that many of the prisoners should have been taken alive, might perhaps desire to put them to death, but might be of opinion that it would be impolitic to kill them by the hand of the civil power. In this strait, if it were not for the obstacle likely to be interposed by the honor and just pride of a warlike profession, platoons of foot-soldiers might be used—not to defend—not to attack—not to fight, but to relieve the civilians from one of the duties which they are accustomed to deem most vile, by performing for them the office of the executioner, and these platoons might even be ordered to help the Government to hide the deed by doing their work in the dead hours of the night.

Is it true that with the sanction of the Home Office and of the Prefecture of Police, and under the orders of Prince Louis Bonaparte, St. Arnaud, Magnan, Morny, and Maupas, a midnight work of this last kind was done by the army of Paris?

To men not living in the French capital, it seems that there is a want of complete certainty about the fate of a great many out of those throngs of prisoners who were brought into the jails and other places of detention on the 4th and 5th of December. The people of Paris think otherwise. They seem to have no doubt. The grounds of their belief are partly of this sort: A family, anxious to know what had become of one of their relatives who was missing, appealed for help to a man in so high a station of life that they deemed him powerful enough to be able to question official personages, and his is the testimony which records what passed. In order, if possible, to find a clew to the fate of the lost man, he made the acquaintance of one of the functionaries who held the office of a 'Judge-Substitute.' The moment the subject of inquiry was touched, the 'Judge-Substitute' began to boil with anger at the mere thought of what he had witnessed, but it seems that his indignation was not altogether unconnected with offended pride and the agony of having had his jurisdiction invaded. He said that he had been ordered to go to some of the jails and examine the prisoners with a view to determine whether they should be detained or set free, and that, whilst he was engaged in this duty, a party of non-commissioned officers and soldiers came into the room and rudely announced that they themselves had orders to dispose of those prisoners whose fingers were black. Then, without regard to the protesting of the 'Judge-Substitute,' they examined the hands of the prisoners whom he had before him, adjudged that the fingers of many of them were black, and at once carried off all those whom they so condemned, with a view (as the 'Judge-Substitute' understood) to shoot them or have them shot. That they were so shot the 'Judge-'Substitute' was certain, but it is plain that he had no personal knowledge of what was done to the prisoners after they were carried off by the soldiers. Again, during the night of the 4th and the night of the 5th, people listening in one of the undisturbed quarters of Paris would suddenly hear the volley of a single platoon—a sound not heard, they say, at such hours either before or since. The sound of this occasional platoon-firing was heard coming chiefly, it seems, from the Champ de Mars, but also from other spots, and in particular from the gardens of the Luxembourg, and from the esplanade of the Invalides. People listening within hearing of this last spot declared, they say, that the sound of the platoon-fire was followed by shrieks and moans; and that once, in the midst of the other cries, they caught some piteous words, close followed by a scream, and sounding as though they were the words of a lad imperfectly shot and dying hard.

Partly upon grounds of this sort, but more perhaps by the teaching of universal fame, Paris came to believe—and rightly or wrongly Paris still believes—that during the night of the 4th, and again during the night of the 5th, prisoners were shot in batches and thrown into pits. On the other hand, the adherents of the French Emperor deny that the troops did duty as executioners.[1] Therefore the value of an Imperialist denial, with all such weight as may be thought to belong to it, is set against the imperfect proof on which Paris founds her belief; but men must remember why it is that any obscurity can hang upon a question like this. The question whether on the night of a given Thursday and a given Friday, whole batches of men living in Paris were taken out and shot by platoons in such places as the Champ de Mars or the Luxembourg gardens—this is a question which, from its very nature, could not have remained in doubt for forty-eight hours, unless Paris at the time had lost her freedom of speech and her freedom of printing; and even now, after a lapse of years, if freedom were restored to France, the question would be quickly and righteously determined. Now it happens that those who took away from Paris her freedom of speech and her freedom of printing are the very persons of whom it is said that during two December nights they caused their fellow-countrymen to be shot by platoons and in batches. So it comes to this, that those who are charged have made away with the means by which the truth might be best established. In this stress, Justice is

[1] Granier de Cassaignac, vol. ii.

not so dull and helpless as to submit to be baffled. Wisely deviating in such a case from her common path, she listens for a moment to incomplete testimony against the concealer, and then, by requiring that he who hid away the truth shall restore it to light, or abide the consequence of his default, she shifts the duty of giving strict proof from the accuser to the accused. Because Prince Louis and his associates closed up the accustomed approaches to truth, therefore it is cast upon them either to remain under the charge which Paris brings against them, or else to labor and show, as best they may, that they did not cause batches of French citizens to be shot by platoons of infantry in the night of the 4th and the night of the 5th of December.

Uncertainty as to the number of people killed.

The whole number of people killed by the troops during the forty hours which followed upon the commencement of the massacre in the Boulevards will never be known. The burying of the bodies was done for the most part at night. In searching for a proximate notion of the extent of the carnage, it is not safe to rely even upon the acknowledgments of the officers engaged in the work, for during some time they were under an impression that it was favorable to a man's advancement to be supposed to be much steeped in what was done. The colonel of one of the regiments engaged in this slaughter spoke whilst the business was fresh in his mind. It would be unsafe to accept his statement as accurate or even as substantially true, but as it is certain that the man had taken part in the transaction of which he spoke, and that he really wished to gain credence for the words which he uttered, his testimony has a kind of value as representing (to say the least of it) his idea of what could be put forward as a creditable statement by one who had the means of knowing the truth. What he declared was that his regiment alone had killed two thousand four hundred men. Supposing that his statement was any thing like an approach to the truth, and that his corps was at all rivaled by others, a very high number would be wanted for recording the whole quantity of the slaughter.[1]

Total loss of the army in killed.

In the army which did these things, the whole number of killed was twenty-five.[2]

Of all men dwelling in cities the people of Paris are perhaps

[1] The number of regiments operating against Paris was between thirty and forty, and of these about twenty belonged to the divisions which were actively employed in the work.

[2] Including all officers and soldiers killed from the 3rd to the 6th of December. The official return, *Moniteur*, p. 3062.

Effect of the massacre upon the people of Paris.

the most warlike. Less almost than any other Europeans are they accustomed to overvalue the lives of themselves and their fellow-citizens. With them the joy of the fight has power to overcome fear and grief, and they had been used to great street battles; but they had not been used of late to witness the slaughter of people unarmed and helpless. At the sight of what was done on that 4th of December the great city was struck down as though by a plague. A keen-eyed Englishman, who chanced to come upon some of the people retreating from these scenes of slaughter, declared that their countenances were of a strange livid hue which he had never before seen. This was because he had never before seen the faces of men coming straight from the witnessing of a massacre. They say that the shock of being within sight and hearing the shrieks broke down the nervous strength of many a brave though tender man, and caused him to burst into sobs as though he were a little child.

Before the morning of the 5th the armed insurrection had ceased. From the first it had been feeble. On the other hand, the moral resistance which was opposed to the acts of the President and his associates had been growing in strength, and when the massacre began on the afternoon of the 4th of December, the power of this moral resistance was in the highest degree formidable. Yet it came to pass that, by reason of the strange prostration of mind which was wrought by the massacre, the armed insurrection dragged down with it in its fall the whole policy of those who conceived that by the mere force of opinion and ridicule they would be enabled to send the plotters to Vincennes. The Cause of those who intended to rely upon this scheme of moral resistance was in no way mixed up with the attempts of the men of the barricades, but still it was a Cause which depended upon the high spirit of the people, and it had happened that this spirit—perplexed and baffled on the 2nd of December by a stratagem and a night attack—was now crushed out by sheer horror.

For her beauty, for her grandeur, for her historic fame, for her warlike deeds, for her power to lead the will of a mighty nation, and to crown or discrown its monarchs, no city on earth is worthy to be the rival of Paris. Yet, because of the palsy that came upon her after the slaughter on the Boulevard, this Paris—this beauteous, heroic Paris—this queen of great renown, was delivered bound into the hands of Prince Louis Bonaparte, and Morny, and Maupas or de Maupas, and St. Arnaud, formerly Le Roy. And, the benefit which Prince Louis derived from the massacre was not transitory. It is a maxim of

French politics that, happen what may, a man seeking to be a ruler of France must not be ridiculous. From 1836 until 1848 Prince Louis had never ceased to be obscure except by bringing upon himself the laughter of the world; and his election into the chair of the Presidency had only served to bring upon him a more constant outpouring of the scorn and sarcasm which Paris knows how to bestow.[1] Even the suddenness and perfect success of the blow struck in the night between the 1st and the 2nd of December had failed to make Paris think of him with gravity. But it was otherwise after three o'clock on the 4th of December; and it happened that the most strenuous adversaries of this oddly fated Prince were those who, in one respect, best served his cause, for the more they strove to show that he, and he alone, of his own design and malice had planned and ordered the massacre,[2] the more completely they relieved him from the disqualification which had hitherto made it impossible for him to become the supreme ruler of France. Before the night closed in on the 4th of December, he was sheltered safe from ridicule by the ghastly heaps on the Boulevard.

Effect of the massacre in removing one of Louis Bonaparte's personal disqualifications.

The fate of the provinces resembled the fate of the capital. Whilst it was still dark on the morning of the 2nd, Morny, stealing into the Home Office, had intrusted his orders for instant and enthusiastic support to the zeal of every prefect, and had ordered that every mayor, every juge de paix, and every other public functionary who failed to give in his instant and written adhesion to the acts of the President should be dismissed. In France the engine of state is so constructed as to give to the Home Office an almost irresistible power over the provinces, and the means which the Office had of coercing France were re-enforced by an appeal to men's fears of anarchy, and their dread of the sect called 'Socialists.' Forty thousand communes were suddenly told that they must make swift choice between socialism and anarchy and rapine on the one hand, and on the other a virtuous dictator and lawgiver recommended and warranted by the authority of Monsieur de Morny. The gifted Montalembert himself was so effectually caught in this springe that he publicly represented the dilemma as giving no choice except between Louis Bonaparte and

The fate of the provinces.

[1] A glance at the *Charivari* for '49, '50, and the first eleven months of '51, would verify this statement. The stopping of the *Charivari* was one of the very first exertions of the supreme power which was seized in the night of the 2nd of December.

[2] It will be seen (see *post*) that I question the truth of this charge against him.

'the ruin of France.' In the provinces, as in Paris, there were men whose love of right was stronger than their fears of the Executive Government, and stronger than their dread of the Socialists; but the Department, being kept in utter darkness by the arrangements of the Home Office, was slower than Paris in finding out that the blow of the 2nd of December had been struck by a small knot of associates, without the concurrence of Statesmen who were the friends of law and order; and it would seem that although the proclamations were received at first with stupor and perplexity, they soon engendered a hope that the President (acting, as the country people imagined him to be, with the support of many eminent statesmen), might effect a wholesome change in the Constitution, and restore to France some of the tranquillity and freedom which she had enjoyed under the government of her last king. There were risings, but every department which seemed likely to move was put under martial law. Then followed slaughter, banishment, imprisonment, sequestration; and all this at the mere pleasure of Generals raging with a cruel hatred of the people, and glowing with the glow of that motive—so hateful because so sordid—which in centralized states men call 'zeal.' Of these Generals there were some who, in their fury, went beyond all the bounds of what could be dictated by any thing like policy, even though of the most ferocious kind. In the department of the Allier, for instance, it was decreed, not only that all who were 'known' to have taken up arms against the Government should be tried by Court Martial, but that 'those 'whose socialist opinions were notorious' should be transported by the mere order of the Administration, and have their property sequestered. The bare mental act of holding a given opinion was thus put into the category of black crimes, and either the prisoner was to have no trial at all, or else he was to be tried, as it were, by the hangman. This decree was issued by a man called General Eynard, and was at once adopted and promulgated by the Executive Government.[1]

Motives for the ferocity of the measures taken. Terror, and afterward a hope of gaining support from men afraid of anarchy.

The violence with which the brethren of the Elysée were raging took its origin, no doubt, from their terror, but now that they were able to draw breath, another motive began to govern them and to drive them along the same road; for by this time they were able to give to their actions a color which tended to bring them the support and good will of whole multitudes—whole multitudes distracted with

[1] *Moniteur*, 28th Dec.

General dread of the Socialists.

fear of the democrats, and only longing for safety. For more than three years people had lived in dread of the 'Socialists,' and though the sect, taken alone, was never so formidable as to justify the alarm of a firm man, still it was more or less allied with the fierce species of democrat which men called 'Red,' and, the institutions of the Republic being new and weak, it was right for the nation to stand on its guard against anarchy; though many have judged that the defenders of order, being upheld by the voice of the millions no less than by the forces of intellect and of property, might have kept their watch without fear. But, whether the thing from which the people ran flying was a danger or only a phantom, the terror it spread brought numbers down into a state which was hardly other than abject. Of course people thus unmanned would look up piteously to the Executive Government as their natural protectors, and would be willing to offer their freedom in exchange for a little more safety. So now, if not before, the company of the Elysée saw the gain which would accrue to them if they could have it believed that their enterprise was a war against Socialism.

The brethren of the Elysée take advantage of this.

After the subjugation of Paris, the scanty gatherings of people who took up arms against the Government were composed, no doubt, partly of Socialists, but partly also of men who had no motive for rising, except that they were of too high a spirit to be able to stand idle and see the law trampled down. But the brotherhood of the Elysée was master—sole master—of the power to speak in print, and by exaggerating the disturbances going on in some parts of France, as well as by fastening upon all who stood up against them the name of the hated sect, they caused it to be believed by thousands, and perhaps by millions, that they were engaged in a valorous and desperate struggle against Socialism. In proportion as this pretense came to be believed, it brought hosts of people to the support of the Executive Government; and there is reason to believe that, even among those of the upper classes who seemed to be standing proudly aloof from the Elysée, there were many who secretly rejoiced to be delivered from their fear of the Democrats at the price of having to see France handled, for a time, by persons like Morny and Maupas.

They pretend to be engaged in a war against Socialism.

Support thus obtained.

The truth is, that in the success of this speculation of the Elysée many thought they saw how to escape from the vexations of democracy in a safe and indolent way. When an Arab decides that the burnous which is his garment by day and by night has become unduly populous, he lays it upon an ant-hill in order that the one kind of insect may be chased away by the other; and as soon as this has been done, he easily brushes off the conquering genus with the stroke of a whip or a pipe-stick. In a lazy mood well-born men thought to do this with France, and the first part of the process was successful enough, for all the red sort were killed, or crushed, or hunted away; but when that was done it began to appear that those whose hungry energies had been made use of to do the work were altogether unwilling to be brushed off. They clung. Even now, after the lapse of years,[1] they cling and feed.

Commissaries sent into the provinces.

The army in the provinces closely imitated the ferocity of the army of Paris, but it was to be apprehended that soldiery, however fierce, might deal only with the surface of discontent, and not strike deep enough into the heart of the country. They might kill people in streets, and roads, and fields; they might even send their musket-balls through windows into the houses, and shoot whole batches of prisoners; but they could not so well search out the indignant friends of law and order in their inner homes. Therefore Morny sent into the provinces men of dire repute, and armed them with terrible powers. These persons were called Commissaries. In every spot so visited the people shuddered, for they knew by their experience of 1848 that a man thus set over them by the terrible Home Office might be a ruffian well known to the police for his crimes as well as for his services, and that from a potentate of that quality it might cost them dear to buy their safety.

The Church.

There have been times when the all but dying spark of a nation's life has been kept alive by the priests of her faith; and when this has happened, there has sprung up so deep a love between people and Church that the lapse of ages has not had strength to put the two asunder.[2] In France, it is true, the Church no longer wielded the authority which had belonged to her of old, but besides that the virtues of her humble and laboring priesthood had gained for her more means of guiding men's minds than Europe was accustomed to believe, she was a cohering and organized body. Therefore, at a moment when the whole temporal powers of the State had been seized by a small knot of men slyly acting in concert, and when the Parliamentary and judicial authority which might restrain their violence had been all at once overthrown, the Church of France, surviving in the midst of ruined

[1] Written in September, 1861.

[2] See Arthur Stanley's admirable account of the relations between Russia and her Church.

institutions, became suddenly invested with a great power to do good or do evil. She might stand between the armed man and his victim; she might turn away wrath; she might make conditions for prostrate France. Or, taking a yet loftier stand, she might resolve to choose—and choose sternly—between right and wrong. She chose.

The priesthood of France were upon the whole a zealous, unworldly, devoted body of men; but already the Church which they served had been gained over to the President by the arrangements which led to the siege and occupation of Rome. Therefore, although the priests perceived that Maupas, coming privily in the night time, had seized the generals and the statesmen of France, and had shut up the Parliament, and driven the judges from the judgment seat, still it seemed to them that, because of Rome, they ought to side with Maupas. So far as concerned her political action in this time of trial, they suffered the Church of France to degenerate into a mere sub-department of the Home Office. In the rural districts, when the time for the Plebiscite came, they fastened tickets marked 'Yes' upon their people, and drove them in flocks to the poll.

Every institution in the country being thus suborned, or enslaved, or shattered, the brethren of the Elysée resolved to follow up their victory over France. In the sense which will presently appear they resolved to disman her. It had resulted from the political state of France during several years that great numbers of the most stirring men in the country had belonged to clubs, which the law called 'secret societies.' A net thrown over this class would gather into its folds whole myriads of honest men, and indeed it has been computed that the number of persons then alive who at one time or other had belonged to some kind of 'secret society' amounted to no less than two millions. If French citizens at some period of their lives had belonged to societies forbidden by Statute, it was enough (and after a lapse of time much more than enough) that the penalties of the law which they had disobeyed should be enforced against them. But it was not this, nor the like of this that was done.

France dismanned.

Prince Louis Bonaparte and Morny, with the advice and consent of Maupas, issued a retro-operative decree, by which all these hundreds of thousands of Frenchmen were made liable to be instantly seized, and transported either to the penal settlements in Africa, or to the torrid swamps of Cayenne.[1]

[1] Decree of 8th December inserted in the *Moniteur* of the 9th.

The decree was as comprehensive as a law would be in England, if it enacted that every man who had ever attended a political meeting might be now suddenly transported; but it was a hundred times less merciful, for, in general, to be banished to Cayenne was to be put to a slow, cruel, horrible death. Morny and Maupas pressed and pressed the execution of this almost incredible decree with a ferocity which must have sprung in the first instance from terror, and was afterward kept alive for the sake of that hideous sort of popularity which was to be gained by calling men Socialists, and then fiercely hunting them down. None will ever know the number of men who at this period were either killed or imprisoned in France, or sent to die in Africa or Cayenne; but the panegyrist of Louis Bonaparte and his fellow-plotters acknowledges that the number of people who were seized and transported within the few

26,500 men transported.

weeks which followed the 2nd of December, amounted to the enormous number of twenty-six thousand five hundred.[2]

France perhaps could have borne the loss of many tens of thousands of ordinary soldiers and workmen without being visibly weakened; but no nation in the world—no, not even France herself—is so abounding in the men who will dare something for honor and liberty as to be able to bear to lose in one month between twenty and thirty thousand men seized from out of her most stirring and most courageous citizens. It could not be but that what remained of France when she had thus been stricken should for years seem to languish and to be of a poor spirit. This is why I have chosen to say that France was dismanned.

But besides the men killed and the men transported, there were some thousands of Frenchmen who were made to undergo sufferings too horrible to be here told. I speak of those who were inclosed in the casemates of the fortresses and huddled down between the decks of the *Canada* and the *Duguesclin*. These hapless beings were for the most part men attached to the cause of the Republic. It would seem that of the two thousand men whose sufferings are the most known, a great part were men whose lives had been engaged in literary pursuits, for amongst them were authors of some repute; editors of newspapers, and political writers of many grades, besides lawyers, physicians, and others whose labors in the field of politics had been mainly labors of the intellectual sort. The torments inflicted upon these men lasted from two to

[2] Granier de Cassagnac.

three months. It was not till the second week in March that a great many of them came out into the light and the pure air of Heaven. Because of what they had suffered they were hideous and terrible to look upon. The hospitals received many. It is right that the works which testify to these things should be indicated as authorities on which the narrator founds his passing words;[1] but, unless a man be under some special motive for learning the detailed truth, it would be well for him to close his eyes against those horrible pages; for if once he looks and reads, the recollection of the things he reads of may haunt him and weigh upon his spirit till he longs and longs in vain to recover his ignorance of what, even in this his own time, has been done to living men.

The Plebiscite.

At length the time came for the operation of what was called the Plebiscite. The arrangements of the plotters had been of such a kind as to allow France no hope of escape from anarchy and utter chaos, except by submitting herself to the dictatorship of Louis Bonaparte; for, although the President in his Proclamation had declared that if the country did not like his Presidency, they might choose some other in his place, no such alternative was really offered. The choice given to the elector sdid not even purport to be any thing but a choice between Louis Bonaparte and nothing. According to the wording of the Plebiscite, a vote given for any candidate other than Louis Bonaparte would have been null. An elector was only permitted to vote 'Yes,' or vote 'No;' and it seems plain that the prospect of anarchy involved in the negative vote would alone have operated as a sufficing menace. Therefore, even if the collection of the suffrages had been carried on with perfect fairness, the mere stress of the question proposed would have made it impossible that there should be a free election: the same central power which nearly four years before had compelled the terrified nation to pretend that it loved a republic, would have now forced the same helpless people to kneel, and say they chose for their one only lawgiver the man recommended to them by Monsieur de Morny.

Causes rendering free election impossible.

Having the army and the whole executive power in their hands, and having preordained the question to be put to the people, the brethren of the Elysée, it would seem, might have safely allowed the proceeding to go to its sure conclusion without farther coercing the vote; and if they had done thus, they would have given a color to the assertion that the result

[1] 'Le Coup d'Etat,' par Xavier Durrieu, ancien Representant du Peuple. 'Histoire de la Terreur Bonapartiste,' par Hippolyte Magen.

of the Plebiscite was a national ratification of their act. But remembering what they had done, and having blood on their hands, they did not venture upon a free election. What they did was this: they placed thirty-two departments under martial law; and, since they wanted nothing more than a sheet of paper and a pen and ink in order to place every other department in the same predicament, it can be said without straining a word that potentially, or actually, the whole of France was under martial law.

The election under martial law.

Therefore men voted under the sword. But martial law is only one of the circumstances which constitute the difference between an honest election and a Plebiscite of the Bonaparte sort. Of course, for all effective action on the part of multitudes, some degree of concert is needful, and on the side of the plotters, using as they did the resistless engine of the executive government, the concert was perfect. To the adversaries of the Elysée, all effective means of concerted action were forbidden by Morny and Maupas. Not only could they have no semblance of a public meeting, but they could not even venture upon the slightest approach to those lesser gatherings which are needed for men who want to act together. Of course, in these days, the chief engine for giving concerted and rational action to bodies of men is the Press. But, except for the uses of the Elysée, there was no Press. All journals hostile to the plot were silenced. Not a word could be printed which was unfavorable to Monsieur Morny's candidate for the dictatorship. Even the printing and distributing of negative voting tickets was made penal; and during the ceremony which was called an 'election' several persons were actually arrested and charged with the offense of distributing negative voting tickets, or persuading others to vote against the President. It was soon made clear that, so far as concerned his means of taking a real part in the election, every adversary of the Elysée was as helpless as a man deaf and dumb.

Violent measures taken for coercing the election.

In one department it was decreed that any one spreading reports or suggesting fears tending to disquiet the people should be instantly arrested and brought before a court-martial.[1] In another, every society, and, indeed, every kind of meeting, however few the persons composing it might be, was in terms prohibited,[2] and it was announced that any man disobeying the order would be deemed to be a member of a secret society

[1] Arrêté du Général d'Alphonse, Commandant l'état de siège dans le Departement du Cher, Article 4.

[2] Arrêté du Préfet de la Haute Garonne, Articles 1, 2, 3.

within the meaning of the terrible decree of the 8th of December, and liable to transportation.[1] In the same department it was decreed that every one hawking or distributing printed tickets, or even manuscripts, unless authorized by the mayor or the juge de paix, should be prosecuted; and the same prefect, in almost mad rage against freedom, proclaimed that any one who was caught in an endeavor to 'propagate an opinion' should be deemed guilty of exciting to civil war, and instantly handed over to the judicial authority.[2] In another department the sub-prefect announced that any one who threw a doubt on the loyalty of the acts of the Government should be arrested.[3]

These are samples of the means which generals, and prefects, and sub-prefects adopted for insuring the result; but it is hardly to be believed that all this base zeal was really needed, because from the very first the brethren of the Elysée had taken a step which, even if it had stood alone, would have been more than enough to coerce the vote. They fixed for the 20th and 21st of December the election to which civilians were invited; but long before this the army had been ordered to vote (and to vote openly without ballot), within forty-eight hours from the receipt of a dispatch of the 3rd of December. So, all the land forces of France had voted, as it were, by beat of drum, and the result of their voting had been made known to the whole country long before the time fixed for the civilians to proceed to election. France, therefore, if she were to dare to vote against the President, would be placing herself in instant and open conflict with the declared will of her own army, and this at a time when, to the extent already stated, she was under martial law.

Contrivance for coercing the election by the vote of the army.

Surprised, perplexed, affrighted, and all unarmed and helpless, France was called upon either to strive to levy a war of despair against the mighty engine of the French executive government, and the vast army which stood over her, or else to succumb at once to Louis Bonaparte, and Morny, and Maupas, and Monsieur Le Roy St. Arnaud. She succumbed. The brethren of the Elysée had asked the country to say 'Yes' or 'No:' should Louis Bonaparte alone build a new Constitution for the governance of the mighty nation? and when, in the way already told, they had obtained the 'Yes,' from herds and flocks of men whom they ventured to number at nearly eight millions, it was made known to Paris that the person who had long been the favorite subject of her jests was

France succumbed.

[1] Arrêté du Préfet de la Haute Garonne, Article 3. [2] Ibid., Article 4.
[3] Arrêté du Sous-préfet de Valenciennes.

now become sole lawgiver for her and for France. In the making of such laws as he intended to give the country, Prince Louis was highly skilled, for he knew how to enfold the creation of a sheer Oriental autocracy in a nomenclature taken from the polity of free European States. With the advice and consent of Morny, and no doubt with the full approval of all the rest of the plotters, he virtually made it the law that he should command, and that France should pay him tribute and obey.

Prince Louis sole lawgiver of France.

The laws he gave her.

It has been seen that the success of the plot of the 2nd of December resulted from the massacre which took place in the Boulevard on the following Thursday; and, since this strange event became the foundation of a momentous change in the polity of France, and even in the destinies of Europe, it is right for men to know, if they can, how and why it came to pass. At three o'clock on the afternoon of the 4th of December, the ultimate success of the plot had seemed to become almost hopeless by reason of the isolation to which Prince Louis and his associates were reduced. But at that hour the massacre began, and before the bodies were cleared away, the brethren of the Elysée had Paris and France at their mercy. It was natural that wronged and angry men, seeing this cause and this effect, should be capable of believing that the massacre was willfully planned as a means of achieving the result which it actually produced. Just as the Cambridge theologian maintained that he who looked upon a watch must needs believe in a watchmaker, so men who had seen the massacre were led to infer a demon. They saw that the massacre brought wealth and blessings to the Elysée, and they thought it a safe induction to say that the man who gathered the harvest as though it were his own must have sown the seed in due season. Yet, so far as one knows, this argument from design is not very well re-enforced by external proof; and perhaps it is more consistent with the principles of human nature to believe that the slaughter of the Boulevard resulted from the mixed causes which are known to have been in operation, than from a cold design on the part of the President to have a quantity of peaceful men and women killed in order that the mere horror of the sight might crush the spirit of Paris. Without resorting to this dreadful solution, the causes of the massacre may be reached by fair conjecture.

Importance of the massacre on the Boulevard.

Inquiry into its cause.

The army, as we have seen, was burning with hatred of the civilians, and its ferocity had been carefully whetted by the President and by St. Arnaud. This feeling, apart from other motives of action, would not have induced the brave soldiery of France to fire point-blank into crowds of defenseless men and women; but a passion more cogent than anger was working in the bosoms of the men at the Elysée and the Generals in command, and from them it descended to the troops.

The passion of terror.

According to its nature, and the circumstances in which it is placed, a creature struck by terror may either lie trembling in a state of abject prostration, or else may be convulsed with hysteric energy; and when terror seizes upon man or beast in this last way, it is the fiercest and most blind of all passions. The French unite the delicate, nervous organization of the south with much of the energy of the north, and they are keenly susceptible of the terror that makes a man kill people, and the terror that makes him lie down and beg. On that 4th of December Paris was visited with terror in either form. The army raged, and the people crouched; but army and people alike were governed by terror. It is very true, that in the Boulevard there were no physical dangers which could have struck the troops with this truculent sort of panic, for even if it is believed that two or three shots were fired from a window or a house-top, an occurrence of that kind, in a quarter which was plainly prepared for sight-seeing, and not for strife, was too trivial of itself to be capable of disturbing prime troops. But the President and his associates, though they had succeeded in all their mechanical arrangements, had failed to obtain the support of men of character and eminence. For that reason they were obviously in peril; and if Morny and Fleury still remained in good heart, there is no reason for doubting that on the 4th of December the sensations of the President, of the two other Bonapartes, of Maupas, of St. Arnaud, and of Magnan, corresponded with the alarming circumstances in which they were placed.

State of Prince Louis Bonaparte during the period of danger.

The state of the President seems to have been very like what it had been in former times at Strasbourg and at Boulogne, and what it was years afterward at Magenta and Solferino.[1] He did not on any of these five occasions so give way to fear as to prove that he had less self-control in moments of danger than the common run of peaceful citizens; but on all of them he showed that, though he had chosen to set himself heroic tasks, his temperament was ill fitted for the hour of battle and for the crisis of an adventure. For, besides that (in common with the bulk of mankind) he was without resource and presence of mind when

[1] See Note IV. in Appendix.

he imagined that danger was really quite close upon him, his complexion and the dismal looks he wore in times of trial were always against him. From some defect perhaps in the structure of the heart or the arterial system, his skin, when he was in a state of alarm, was liable to be suffused with a greenish hue. This discoloration might be a sign of high moral courage, because it would tend to show that the spirit was warring with the flesh; but still it does not indicate that condition of body and soul which belongs to a true king of men in the hour of danger, and enables him to give heart and impulsion to those around him. It is obvious too that an appearance of this sort would be damping to the ardor of the by-standers. Several incidents show that between the 2nd and the 4th of December the President was irresolute, and keenly alive to his danger. The long-pondered plan of election which he had promulgated on the 2nd of December he withdrew the next day, in obedience to the supposed desire of the Parisian multitude. He took care to have always close to his side the immense force of cavalry to which he looked as the means of protecting his flight, and it seems that during a great portion of the critical interval the carriages and horses required for his escape were kept ready for instant use in the stable-yard of the Elysée. Moreover, it was at this time that he suffered himself to resort to the almost desperate resource of counterfeiting the names of men represented as belonging to the Consultative Commission. But perhaps his condition of mind may be best inferred from the posture in which history catches him whilst he nestled under the wing of the army.

He gave all he had to the soldiers.

When a peaceful citizen is in grievous peril, and depending for his life upon the whim of soldiers, his instinct is to take all his gold and go and offer it to the armed men, and tell them he loves and admires them. What in such stress the endangered citizen would be impelled by his nature to do is exactly what Louis Bonaparte did. The transaction could not be concealed, and the imperial historian seems to have thought that upon the whole the best course was to give it an air of classic grandeur by describing the soldiers as the 'conquerors' of a rugged Greek word, and by calling a French coin an 'obolus.' 'There remained,' said he, 'to the President out of all his personal fortune, out of all his 'patrimony, a sum of fifty thousand francs. He knew that in 'certain memorable circumstances the troops had faltered in 'the presence of insurrection, more from being famished than 'from being defeated; so he took all that remained to him, 'even to his last crown-piece, and charged Colonel Fleury to 'go to the soldiers, conquerors of demagogy, and distribute to 'them, brigade by brigade, and man by man, this his last obo- 'lus.'[1] The President had said, in one of his addresses to the army of Paris, that he would not bid them advance, but would himself go the foremost and ask them to follow him. If it was becoming to address empty play-actor's words of that sort to real soldiers, it certainly was not the duty of the President to act upon them, for there could not well be any engagement in the streets of Paris as would make it right for a literary man (though he was also the chief of the state) to go and affect to put himself at the head of an army inured to war; but still there was a contrast between what was said and what was done, which makes a man smile as he passes. The President had vowed he would lead the soldiers against the foe, and instead, he sent them all his money. There is no reason to suppose that the change of plan was at all displeasing to the troops, and this bribing of the armed men is only adverted to here as a means of getting at the real state of the President's mind, and thereby tracing up to its cause the massacre of the 4th of December.

He even signed the decree of the 5th of December.

Another clew, leading the same way, is to be found in the Decree by which the President enacted that combats with insurgents at home should count for the honor and profit of the troops in the same way as though they were fought against a foreign enemy.[2] It is true that this decree was not issued until the massacre of the 4th was over, but of course the temper in which a man encounters danger is to be gathered in part from his demeanor immediately after the worst moment of trial; and when it is found that the chief of a proud and mighty nation was capable of putting his hand to a paper of this sort on the 5th of December, some idea may be formed of what his sensations were on the noon of the day before, when the agony of being in fear had not as yet been succeeded by the indecorous excitement of escape.

State of Jerome Bonaparte.

Whilst Prince Louis Bonaparte was hugging the knees of the soldiers, his uncle, Jerome Bonaparte, fell into so painful a condition as to be unable to maintain his self-control, and he suffered himself to publish a letter in which he not only disclosed his alarm, but even showed that he was preparing to separate himself from his nephew; for he made it appear (as he could do perhaps with strict truth) that although he had got into danger by showing him-

[1] Granier de Cassaignac, vol. ii., p. 431.

[2] Decree of the 5th, inserted in the *Moniteur* of the 7th Dec.

self in public with the President on the 2nd of December, he was innocent of the plot, and a stranger to the counsels of the Elysée.[1] His son (now called Prince Napoleon) was really, they say, a strong disapprover of the President's acts, and it was natural that he should be most unwilling to be put to death or otherwise ill treated upon the theory that he was the cousin, and therefore the accomplice of Louis, for of that theory he wholly and utterly denied the truth. Any man, however firm, might well resolve that, happen what might to him, he would struggle hard to avoid being executed by mistake; and it seems unfair to cast blame on Prince Napoleon for trying to disconnect his personal destiny from that of the endangered men at the Elysée, whose counsels he had not shared. Still, the sense of being cast loose by the other Bonapartes could not but be discouraging to Prince Louis, and to those who had thrown in their lot with him.

Natural anxiety of Napoleon, son of Jerome.

Maupas, or de Maupas, was a man of a fine large robust frame, and with florid healthy looks; but it sometimes happens that a spacious and strong-looking body of that sort is not so safe a tabernacle as it seems for man's troubled spirit. It is said that the bodily strength of Maupas collapsed in the hour of danger, and that at a critical part of the time between the night of the 2nd of December and the massacre of the 4th he had the misfortune to fall ill.

Bodily state of Maupas.

Finally, it must be repeated that on the 4th of December the army of Paris was kept in a state of inaction during all the precious hours which elapsed between the earliest dawn of the morning and two o'clock in the afternoon.

These are signs that the brethren of the Elysée were aghast at what they had done, and aghast at what they had to do. And it is obvious that Magnan and the twenty Generals who had embraced one another on the 27th of November were now more involved in the danger of the plot than at first they might have expected to be, for the isolation in which the President was left, for want of men of character and station who would consent to come and stand round him, must have made all these

Grounds for the anxiety of the plotters, and of Magnan and the generals under him.

[1] The letter will be found in the 'Annual Register.' It seems to have been sent at 10 o'clock at night on the 4th of December; but the writer evidently did not know that the insurrection at that time was so near its end as it really was, and his letter may therefore be taken as a fair indication of the state of his mind in the earlier part of the day. The advice and the mild remonstrance contained in the letter might have been given in private by a man who had not lost his calm, but the fact of allowing such a letter to be public discloses Jerome's motives.

Generals feel that even the sovereign warrant of 'an order 'from the Minister of War' was a covering which had become very thin.

Effect of anxious suspense upon French troops.

Now, by nature the French people are used to go in flocks, and in their army there is not that social difference between the officers and the common soldiers which is the best contrivance hitherto discovered for intercepting the spread of a panic or any other bewildering impulse. With their troops, any impulse, whether of daring or fear, will often dart like lightning from man to man, and quickly involve the whole mass. Generally, perhaps, a panic in an army ascends from the ranks. On this day, the panic, it seems, went downward. For six hours the army had been kept waiting and waiting under arms within a few hundred yards of the barricades which it was to attack. The order to advance did not come. Somewhere there was hesitation; and the Generals could not but know that even a little hesitation at such a time was both a sign and a cause of danger; but when they saw it continuing through all the morning hours of a short December day, they could hardly have failed to apprehend that the plot of the Elysée was collapsing for want of support, and they could not but know that, if this dread were well founded, their fate was likely to be a hard one.

The temperament of Frenchmen is better fitted for the hour of combat than for the endurance of this sort of protracted tension; and the anxiety of men of their race, when they are much perturbed and kept in long suspense, will easily degenerate into that kind of alarm which is apt to become ferocious. This was the kind of stress to which the troops were put on that 4th of December, and in the case of Magnan and the Generals under him, the pangs of having to wait upon the brink of action for more than two thirds of a day were sharpened by a sense of political danger; for they felt that if, after all, the scheme of the Elysée should fail, their meeting of the 27th might cause them to be brought to trial. Any one knowing what those twenty-one Generals had on their minds, and being also somewhat used to the French army, will almost be able to hear the grinding of the teeth and the rumbling of the curses which mark the armed Frenchman, when he rages because he is anxious. Even without the utterance of any words, the countenances of men thus disturbed would be swiftly read in a body of French troops; and though the soldiery and the inferior officers would not be able to make out very well what it was that was troubling the minds of the Generals, the sense of not knowing all would only make them the more susceptible of infection. On the other hand, it is certain that the instructions given to the troops prescribed the ruthless slaughtering of all who resisted or obstructed them; and although it is of course true that these directions would not compel or sanction the slaughter of peaceful crowds not at all obstructing the troops, still they would so act upon the minds of the soldiery that any passion which might chance to seize them would be likely to take a fierce shape.

Surmised cause of the massacre.

Upon the whole, then, it would seem that the natural and well-grounded alarm which beset the President and some of his associates was turned to anxiety of the raging sort when it came upon the military commanders, and that from them it ran down, till at last it seized upon the troops with so maddening a power as to cause them to face round without word of command, and open fire upon a crowd of gazing men and women.

If this solution were accepted, it would destroy the theory which ascribes to Prince Louis Bonaparte the malign design of contriving a slaughter on the Boulevard as a means of striking terror and so crushing resistance, but it would still remain true that, although it was not specifically designed and ordered, the massacre was brought about by him, and by Morny, Maupas, and St. Arnaud, all acting with the concurrence and under the encouragement of Fleury and Persigny. By them the deeds of the 2nd of December were contrived and done. By them, and in order to the support of those same deeds, the army was brought into the streets. By their industry the minds of the soldiery were whetted for the slaughter of the Parisians, and finally by their hesitation, or the hesitation of Magnan their instrument, the army, when it was almost face to face with the barricades, was still kept standing and expectant, until its Generals, catching and transmitting in an altered form the terror which had come upon them from the Elysée, brought the troops into that state of truculent panic which was the immediate cause of the slaughter. It must also be remembered that the doubt which I have tried to solve extends only to the cause which brought about the massacre of the peaceful crowds on the Boulevard; for it remains unquestioned that the killing of the prisoners taken in the barricaded quarter was the result of design, and was enforced by stringent orders. Moreover, the persons who had the blood upon their hands were the persons who got the booty. St. Arnaud is no more; but Louis Napoleon Bonaparte, Morny, Fleury, Maupas, Magnan, and Persigny—all these are yet alive, and in their possession the public treasures of France may still be abundantly found.

It is known that the most practised gamesters grow weary sometimes of their long efforts to pry into the future which chance is preparing for them, and that in the midst of their anxiety and doubt they are now and then glad to accept guidance from the blind, confident guess of some one who is younger and less jaded than themselves; and when a hot-headed lad insists that he can govern fortune, when he 'calls the main,' as though it were a word of command, and shakes the dice-box with a lusty arm, the pale doubting elders will sometimes follow the lead of youth's high animal spirits, and if they do this and win, their hearts are warm to the lad whose fire and willfulness compelled them to run the venture. Whether it be true, as is said, that in the hour of trial any of the brethren of the Elysée were urged forward by Colonel Fleury's threats, or whether, abstaining from actual violence, he was able to drive them on by the sheer ascendency of a more ardent and resolute nature, it is certain that he well earned their gratitude, if by any means, gentle or rough, he forced them to keep their stake on the table. For they won. They won France. They used her hard. They took her freedom. They laid open her purse, and were rich with her wealth. They went and sat in the seats of Kings and Statesmen, and handled the mighty nation as they willed in the face of Europe. Those who hated freedom, and those also who bore ill will toward the French people, made merry with what they saw.

Gratitude due to Fleury.

The use the Elysée made of France.

These are the things which Charles Louis Napoleon Bonaparte did. What he had sworn to do was set forth in the oath which he took on the 20th of December, 1848. On that day he stood before the National Assembly, and lifting his right arm toward heaven thus swore:—'In the presence 'of God, and before the French people represented 'by the National Assembly, I swear to remain faith- 'ful to the democratic Republic one and indivisible, and to ful- 'fill all the duties which the Constitution imposes upon me.' What he had pledged his honor to do was set forth in the promise, which of his own free will he addressed to the Assembly. Reading from a paper which he had prepared, he uttered these words:—'The votes of the nation, and the 'oath which I have just taken, command my future 'conduct. My duty is clear. I will fulfill it as a 'man of honor. I shall regard as enemies of the country all 'those who endeavor to change by illegal means that which all 'France has established.'

The oath which the President had taken.

His added promise as a 'man of honor.'

In Europe at that time there were many men, and several

millions of women, who truly believed that the landmarks which divided good from evil were in charge of priests, and that what Religion blessed must needs be right.

The Te Deum.

Now on the thirtieth day computed from the night of the 2nd of December, the rays of twelve thousand lamps pierced the thick wintry fog that clogged the morning air, and shed their difficult light through the nave of the historic pile which stands marking the lapse of ages and the strange checkered destiny of France. There waiting, there were the bishops, priests, and deacons of the Roman branch of the Church of Jesus Christ. These bishops, priests, and deacons stood thus expecting, because they claimed to be able to conduct the relations between man and his Creator, and the swearer of the oath of the 20th of December had designed to apprize them that again, with their good leave, he was coming into 'the presence of God.' And he came. Where the kings of France had knelt, there was now the persistent manager of the company that had played at Strasbourg and Boulogne, and with him, it may well be believed, there were Morny rejoicing in his gains, and Magnan soaring high above sums of four thousand pounds, and Maupas no longer in danger, and St. Arnaud, formerly Le Roy, and Fialin, more often called 'Persigny,' and Fleury the propeller of all, more eager perhaps to go and be swift to spend his winnings, than to sit in a cathedral and think how the fire of his temperament had given him a strange power over the fate of a nation. When the Church perceived that the swearer of the oath and all his associates were ready, she began her service. Having robes whereon all down the back there was embroidered the figure of a cross, and being, it would seem, without fear, the bishops and priests went up to the high altar, and scattered rich incense, and knelt and rose, and knelt and rose again. Then in the hearing of thousands there pealed through the aisles that hymn of praise which purports to waft into heaven the thanksgivings of a whole people for some new and signal mercy vouchsafed to them by Almighty God. It was because of what had been done to France within the last thirty days that the Hosannas arose in Notre Dame. Moreover the priests lifted their voices and cried aloud, chanting and saying to the Most High, Domine salvum fac Ludovicum Napoleonem—Oh Lord! save Louis Napoleon.

What is good and what is evil? and who is he that deserves the prayers of a nation? If any man, being scrupulous and devout, was moved by the events of December to ask these questions of his Church, he was answered that day in the Cathedral of our Lady of Paris.

In the next December the form of the state system was accommodated to the reality, and the President of the Republic became what men call a 'French Emperor.' The style that Prince Louis thought fit to take was this: 'Napoleon the Third, by the Grace of God 'and by the will of the people, Emperor of the French.'

The President becomes Emperor of the French.

Of course, when any one thinks of the events of December, 1851, the stress of his attention is apt to be brought to bear upon those who were actors, and upon those who, desiring to act, were only hindered from doing so by falling into the pits which the trappers had dug for them; but no one will fail to see that one of the main phenomena of the time was the willful acquiescence of great numbers of men. It may seem strange that during a time of danger the sin of inaction should be found in a once free and always brave people. The cause of this was the hatred which men had of democracy. A sheer democracy, it would seem, is so unfriendly to personal liberty, and therefore so vexing or alarming, not only to its avowed political enemies, but to those also who in general are accustomed to stand aloof from public affairs, that it must needs close its frail existence as soon as there comes home a general renowned in arms, who chooses to make himself king. This was always laid down as a guiding principle by those who professed to be able to draw lessons from history, but even they used to think that, until some sort of hero could be found, democratic institutions might last. France showed mankind that the mere want of such a hero as will answer the purpose is a want which can be compensated by a little ingenuity. She taught the world that when a mighty nation is under a democracy, and is threatened with doctrines which challenge the ownership and enjoyment of property, any knot of men who can get trusted with a momentary hold of the engine of State (and somebody must be so trusted) may take one of their number, who never made a campaign except with counterfeit soldiers, and never fired a shot except when he fired by mistake, and may make him a dictator, a lawgiver, and an absolute monarch, with the acquiescence if not with the approval of a vast proportion of the people. Moreover France proved that the transition is not of necessity a slow one, and that, when the perils of a high centralization and a great standing army are added to the perils of a sheer democracy, then freedom, although it be hedged round and guarded by all the contrivances which clever, thoughtful, and honest republicans can devise, may be stolen and made away with

The inaction of great numbers of Frenchmen at the time when their country was falling.

Its cause.

in one dark winter night, as though it were a purse or a trinket.

Although France lost her freedom, it would be an error to imagine that upon the ruins of the commonwealth there was founded a monarchy like that, for instance, which governs the people of Russia. In empires of that kind the Sovereign commands the services of all his subjects. In France, for the most part, the gentlemen of the country resolved to stand aloof from the Government, and not only declined to vouchsafe their society to the new occupant of the Tuileries, but even looked cold upon any stray person of their own station who suffered himself to be tempted thither by money. They were determined to abide their time, and in the mean while to do nothing which would make it inconsistent for them, as soon as it suited their policy, to take an opportunity of laying cruel hands on the new Emperor and his associates. It was obvious that because of the instinct which makes creatures cling to life, a monarch thus kept always standing on the very edge of a horrible fate, but still having for the time in his hands the engine of the State, would be driven by the very law of his being to make use of the forces of the nation as means of safety for himself and his comrades; and that to that one end, not only the operations of the Home Government, but even the foreign policy of the country, would be steadily aimed. And so it happened. After the 2nd December, in the year 1851, the foreign policy of France was used for a prop to prop the throne which Morny and his friends had built up.

The gentlemen of France resolved to stand aloof from the Government.

The constant peril in which the confederates were kept.

The foreign policy of France was used to prop the new throne.

Therefore, although I have dwelt a while upon a singular passage in the domestic history of France, I have not digressed. The origin of the war with Russia could not be traced without showing what was the foreign policy of France at the time when the mischief was done; and since it happened that the foreign policy of France was new to the world, and was governed in all things by the personal exigencies of those who wielded it, no one could receive a true impression of its aim and purpose without first gathering some idea of the events by which the destinies of Europe were connected with the hopes and fears of Prince Louis, and Morny, and Fleury, of Magnan, and Persigny, and Maupas, and Monsieur Le Roy St. Arnaud.

## CHAPTER XV.

Immediate effect of the coup d'état upon the tranquillity of Europe.

Almost instantly the change which was wrought by these French transactions began to act upon Europe. The associates of the Elysée well understood that if they had been able to trample upon France and her laws, their success had been made possible by the dread which the French people had of a return to tumult; and it was clear that, until they could do something more than merely head the police of the country, their new power would be hardly more stable than the passing terrors on which it rested. What they had to do was to distract France from thinking of her shame at home, by sending her attention abroad. For their very lives' sake they had to make haste, and to pile up events which might stand between them and the past, and shelter them from the peril to which they were brought whenever men's thoughts were turned to the night of the 2nd of December and the Thursday the day of blood. There could be no hesitating about this. Ambition had nothing to do with it. It was matter of life and death. If Prince Louis, and Morny, and Fleury, if Maupas, St. Arnaud, and Magnan, were to continue quartered upon France instead of being thrown into prison and brought to trial, it was indispensable that Europe should be disturbed. Without delay the needful steps were taken.

The policy which it necessitated.

It must have been within a week or two after the completion of the arrangements consequent on the night of the 2nd of December that the dispatches went from Paris which caused M. de Lavalette to wring from the Porte the Note of the 9th of February,[1] and forced the Sultan into engagements unfair and offensive to Russia. The French President steadily continued this plan of driving the Porte into a quarrel with the Czar until at length he succeeded in bringing about the event,[2] which was followed by the advance of the Russian armies; but the moment the Czar was wrought up into a state of anger which sufficed to make him a disturber of Europe, Prince

The French Government coerced the Sultan into measures offensive to Russia.

[1] 1852. See *ante*.

[2] The delivery of the key and the star to the Latin monks at Bethlehem in December, 1852. See *ante*.

Louis, now Emperor of the French, sagaciously perceived that it might be possible for him to take violent means of appeasing the very troubles which he himself had just raised; and to do this by suddenly declaring for a conservative policy in Turkey, and offering to put himself in concert with one of the great settled States of Europe.[1] England, he knew, had always clung to a conservative policy in the East. France, he also knew, of late years had generally done the reverse, but then France was utterly in his power, and it seemed to him that, by offering to thrust France into an English policy, he might purchase for himself an alliance with the Queen, and win for his new throne a sanction of more lasting worth than Morny's well warranted return of his eight millions of approving Frenchmen. Above all, if he could be united with England he might be able to enter upon that conspicuous action in Europe which was needful for his safety at home, and might do this without bringing upon himself any war of a dangerous kind.

And then sought an alliance with England.

Another motive of a narrower sort was urging him in the same direction. Hating freedom, hating the French people, and delighting in an incident which he looked upon as reducing the theory of Representative Government to the absurdum, Nicholas had approved and enjoyed the treatment inflicted upon France by throwing her into the felon's van and sending her to jail; but he had objected to the notion of the second Napoleon being called 'the 'Third;'[2] and in a spirit still more pedantic, he had refused to address the French sovereign in the accustomed form. He would call him his 'good friend,' but no earthly power should make him add the word 'brother.' The taunting society of Petersburg amused itself with the amputated phrase, and loved to call the ruler of France their 'good friend.' The new Emperor chafed at this, for his vanity was hurt; but he abided his time.

Personal feelings of the new Emperor.

At length, nay so early as the 28th of January, 1853, the

[1] December, 1852.

[2] It is said, I know not with what truth, that the style of the new Emperor was the result of a clerical error. In the course of its preparations for constituting the Empire the Home Office wished the country to take up a word which should be intermediate between 'President' and 'Emperor,' so the minister determined to order that France should suddenly burst into a cry of 'Vive Napoleon,' and he wrote, they say, the following order, 'Que le mot d'ordre soit Vive Napoleon!!!' The clerk, they say, mistook the three notes of admiration for Roman numerals, and in a few hours the forty thousand communes of France had cried out so obediently for 'Napoleon III.,' that the Government was obliged to adopt the clerk's blunder.

The French Emperor's scheme for superseding the concord of the four Powers by drawing England into a separate alliance with himself.

French Emperor perceived that his measures had effectually roused the Czar's hostility to the Sultan, and he instantly proposed to England that the two Powers should act together in extinguishing the flames which he himself had just kindled, and should endeavor to come to a joint understanding, with a view to resist the ambition of Russia. Knowing beforehand what the policy of England was, he all at once adopted it, and proposed it to our Government in the very terms always used by English statesmen. He took, as it were, an 'old copy' of the first English speech from the throne which came to his hand, and following its words, declared that the first object should be to 'preserve the integrity of the Otto-'man Empire.'[1] From that moment until the summer of 1855, and perhaps even down to a still later period, he did not once swerve from the great scheme of forming and maintaining an offensive alliance with England against the Czar, and to that object he subordinated all other considerations. He had at that time the rare gift of being able to keep himself alive to the proportionate value of political objects. He knew how to give up the less for the sake of attaining and keeping the greater. Governed by this principle, he gradually began to draw closer and closer toward England; and when the angry Czar imagined that he was advancing in the cause of his Church against a resolute champion of the Latins, his wily adversary was smiling perhaps with Lord Cowley about the 'key' and the 'cupola,' and preparing to form an alliance on strictly temporal grounds.

It would have been well for Europe if the exigences of the persons then wielding the destinies of France would have permitted the State to rest content with that honest share of duty which fell to the lot of each of the four Powers when the intended occupation of the Principalities was announced. Neither the interest nor the honor of France required that in the Eastern question she should stand more forward than any other of the remonstrant States; but the personal interest of the new Emperor and his December friends did not at all coincide with the interest of France; for what he and his associates wanted, and what in truth they really needed, was to thrust France into a conflict, which might be either diplomatic or warlike, but which was at all events to be of a conspicuous sort, tending to ward off the peril of home politics, and give to the fabric of the 2nd of December something like station and ce-

[1] 'Eastern Papers,' part i., page 68.

lebrity in Europe. In order to achieve this, it clearly would not suffice for France to be merely one of a conference of four great Powers quietly and temperately engaged in repressing the encroachments of the Czar. Her part in such a business could not possibly be so prominent, nor so animating as to draw away the attention of the French from the persons who had got into their palaces and their offices of State. On the other hand, a close, separate, and significant alliance with England, and with England alone, to the exclusion of the rest of the four Powers, would not only bring about the conflict which was needed for the safety and comfort of the Tuileries, but would seem in the eyes of the mistaken world to give the sanction of the Queen's pure name to the acts of the December night and the Thursday the day of blood. The unspeakable value of this moral shelter to persons in the condition of the new French Monarch, and St. Arnaud, Morny, and Maupas, can never be understood except by those who look back and remember how exalted the moral station of England was in the period which elapsed between the 10th of April, 1848, and the time when she suffered herself to become entangled in engagements with the French Emperor.

It would have been right enough that France and England, as the two great maritime Powers, should have come to an understanding with each other in regard to the disposition of their fleets, but, even if they had been concerting for only that limited purpose, it would have been right that the general tenor and object of their naval arrangements should have received the antecedent approval of the two other Powers with whom they were in cordial agreement. The English Government, however, not only consented to engage in naval movements which affected—nay, actually governed—the question of peace or war, but fell into the error of concerting these movements with France alone, and doing this—not because of any difference which had arisen between the four Powers, but—simply because France and England were provided with ships; so that in truth the Western Powers, merely because they were possessed of the implement which enabled them to put a pressure upon the Czar, resolved to act as though they were the only judges of the question whether the pressure should be applied or not; and this at a time when, as Lord Clarendon declared in Parliament, the four Powers were 'all acting cordial-'ly together.' Of course, this wanton segregation tended to supersede or dissolve the concord which bound the four Powers, and, as a sure consequence, to endanger yet more than ever the cause of peace. Some strange blindness prevented

Lord Aberdeen from seeing the path he trod, or rather prevented him from seeing it with a clearness conducive to action. But what the French Emperor wanted was even more than this, and what he wanted was done. It is true that neither admiration nor moral disapproval of the conduct of princes ought to have any exceeding sway over our relations with foreign States, and if we had had the misfortune to find that the Emperor of the French was the only potentate in Europe whose policy was in accord with our own, it might have been right that closer relations of alliance with France (however humiliating they might seem in the eyes of the moralist) should have followed our separation from the other States of Europe. But no such separation had occurred. What the French Emperor ventured to attempt, and what he actually succeeded in achieving, was to draw England into a distinct and separate alliance with himself—not at a time when she was isolated, but —at a moment when she was in close accord with the rest of the four Powers.

Toward the close of the Parliamentary session of 1853, the determination on the part of Austria to rid the Principalities of their Russian invaders was growing in intensity. Prussia also was firm; and in principle the concord of the four Powers was so exact, that it extended, as was afterward seen, not only to the terms on which the difference between Russia and Turkey should be settled, but to the ulterior arrangements which might be pressed upon Russia at the conclusion of the war which she was provoking. 'The four great Powers,' said Lord Aberdeen on the 12th of August, 'are now acting in con-'cert.'[1] 'In all these transactions,' said Lord Clarendon,[2] 'Aus-'tria, England, Prussia, and France are all acting cordially to-'gether, in order to check designs which they consider incon-'sistent with the balance of power, and with those territorial 'limits which have been established by various treaties.'

The nature of the understanding of Midsummer, 1853, between France and England.

Yet it can not be doubted that in the midst of this perfect concord of the four Powers, the English Government was induced to enter into a separate understanding with the Emperor of the French.[3] This was the fatal transaction which substituted a cruel war for the peaceful but irresistible pressure which was exerted by the four Powers. The purport of this arrangement still lurks in private notes, and in recollections of private interviews, but it can be seen that (for reasons never yet explained) France and England were engaging to move in ad-

[1] 129 Hansard, p. 1650. [2] Ibid., p. 1423. [3] Ibid., pp. 1424, 1768, 1826.

vance of the other Powers. The four Powers, being all of one mind, were still to remain in concert, so far as concerned the discussion and adjudication of the questions pending between Russia and Turkey; but France and England were to volunteer to enforce their judgment. The four Powers were to be judges, and two of them, namely, France and England, were to be the executioners. What made this arrangement the more preposterous was that the outrage of which Europe complained was the occupation of two provinces which abutted upon the Austrian dominions. Of all the great Powers, Austria was the chief sufferer. Austria was upon the spot. Austria was the one Power which instantly and in a summary way could force the Czar to quit his hold; and yet the charge of undertaking a duty which pressed upon her more than upon any other State in Europe, was voluntarily taken upon themselves by two States whose dominions were vastly distant from the scene of the evil deed. It was much as though the forces of the United States and of Brazil were to come across the Atlantic to defend Antwerp from the French, whilst the English looked on and thanked their enterprising friends for relieving them of their duty.

There was not perhaps more than one of the members of the English Cabinet who desired the formation of this singular alliance on grounds like those which moved the French Emperor; and it is believed that Lord Aberdeen and several other members of the Government were much governed by a shallow theory which had prevailed for some years amongst public men. The theory was that close union between France and England was a security for the peace of Europe. 'Sure I am,' said one confident man, who echoed the crude thought of many, 'sure I am that if the advisers of the Crown in this country act 'in cordial concert with the government of the Emperor of the 'French, and if the forces of the two countries in the Mediter- 'ranean are to act in concert, then it will be almost impossible 'that any war can disturb the peace of Europe.' But of course, to men of more statesmanlike views, the main temptation was the prospect of seeing France dragged into the policy which England had always entertained upon the Eastern Question.

Perhaps it will be thought that the practice of hiding away momentous engagements between States in the folds of private notes may now and then justify an endeavor to infer the nature of an agreement secretly made between two Governments from the tenor of their subsequent actions, and from a knowledge of surrounding facts. If this license were to be granted, and if also it were to be assumed that the English as well as the French Government was negotiating with open eyes, it might, perhaps, be laid down that the compact of Midsummer, 1853, was virtually of this sort:—'The Emperor of the French 'shall set aside the old views of the French Foreign Office, and 'shall oblige France with all her forces to uphold the Eastern 'policy of England. In consideration of this sacrifice of French 'interests by the French Emperor, England promises to give 'her moral sanction (in the way hereinafter prescribed) to the 'arrangements of December, 1851, and to take the following 'means for strengthening the throne and endeavoring to es-'tablish the dynasty of the Emperor of the French:—1st. En-'gland shall give up the system of peaceful coercion which is 'involved in the concerted action of the four Powers, and shall 'adopt in lieu of it a separate understanding with France, of 'such a kind as to place the two Powers conspicuously in ad-'vance of the others, and in a state of more immediate antag-'onism to Russia with a prospect of eventual war. 2nd. Even 'before any treaty of alliance is agreed upon, the Queen of En-'gland shall declare before all Europe that the Emperor of the 'French is united with Her Majesty in her endeavors to allay 'the troubles now threatening Europe with war; and it shall 'not be competent to the English Government to weaken the 'effect of this announcement by advising Her Majesty to in-'clude any other Sovereigns in the same statement. If Her 'Majesty should continue to be closely in accord with the rest 'of the four Powers, she may be advised to speak of them in 'general terms as her allies, but they are not to be named. 3rd. 'If hostilities should become necessary, the two Governments 'will determine upon the measures to be adopted in common, 'and in that case also it is distinctly understood that the En-'glish Government will advise the Queen not to shrink from 'the gratification of receiving the Emperor of the French as 'her guest. It is, of course, to be understood (*il va sans dire*) 'that the reception of His Majesty at the English Court is to 'be in all respects the same as would be the reception of any 'other great Sovereign in alliance with the Queen. Whenever 'occasion requires it, the other actors in the operations of De-'cember, 1851, shall be received and treated by the English 'authorities with the honors due to the trusted servants of a 'friendly Power, and without objections founded on the trans-'actions of December, or any of the circumstances of their past 'lives.' These are only imaginary words, but they show what the French Emperor was seeking to achieve, and they represent but too faithfully what the English Government did.

Every state is entitled to regard a foreign nation as represented by its Government. The principle is a sound one; but it must be owned that by this alliance the theory was pushed to an ugly conclusion. What happened was the like of this:—There came to us five men heavily laden with treasure, but looking hurried and anxious. They wanted to speak to us. Upon inquiring who they were, and comparing their answers with our other means of knowing the truth, we found that two of them bore names resulting in the usual way from marriages and baptisms,[1] and that the other three had been going by names which they had chosen for the sake of euphony. They said that suddenly they had become so struck with the soundness of our old-fashioned opinions, that they asked nothing better than to be suffered to devote the immense resources which they could command to the attainment of the object which we had always desired. All they wanted in return was that, in pursuing our own object side by side with them, we would promise not to suffer ourselves to be clogged by our old scruples against breaches of the peace; that we would admit them to our intimacy, allowing ourselves to be much seen with them in public; and that, in order to make our favor the more signal, we would consent to turn aside a little from our old friends. That was all. With regard to the question of how they had come by their treasure, and all the vast resources they offered us, their story was that they had all these things with the express consent of the former owner. There was something about them which made us fear that, if we repulsed them, they would carry their treasures to the very man who, at that moment, was giving us trouble. In truth, it seemed that, either from us or from somebody else, they must and they would have shelter. Upon their hands there was a good deal of blood. We shrank a little, but we were tempted much. We yielded. We struck the bargain. What we did was not unlawful, for those with whom we treated had for the time a real hold upon the people in whose great name they professed to come, and, by the custom of nations, we were entitled to say that we would know nothing of any France except the France that was brought to us by these five persons to be disposed of for the purposes of our 'Eastern Question;' but when we had done this thing, we had no right to believe that, to Europe at large—still less to the gentlemen of France—the fair name of England would seem as it seemed before.

But, whatever were the terms of the understanding between the two Governments, the result of it was that, the English

[1] These two were Prince Louis Bonaparte and Maupas.

Announcement of it to Parliament.

Cabinet, disregarding the policy which only six days before had united it in a concerted action with the Powers represented at the Conference, now announced through the lips of Lord Palmerston,[1] 'that England 'and France were agreed, that they continued to follow the 'same policy, and that they had the most perfect confidence in 'each other.' These words were enough to show any one used to foreign affairs that England was advancing with France into an adventurous policy, and then (though even then they were dangerously late) Members of Parliament might have stood forward with some hope of being able to check their country in her smooth descent from peace to war. They lost the occasion. It did not recur.

Failure of Parliament to understand the real import of the disclosure.

At the close of the session, the Queen's Speech announced to Europe 'that the Emperor of the French had 'united with Her Majesty in earnest endeavors to 'reconcile differences the continuance of which 'might involve Europe in war, and She declared that, acting 'in concert with her Allies, and relying on the exertions of the 'Conference then assembled at Vienna, Her Majesty had good 'reason to hope that an honorable arrangement would speedily 'be accomplished.'[2]

The Queen's Speech, August, 1853.

It would seem at first sight that this language had been occasioned by some accidental displacement of words, and that it could not have been intended for the Queen of England to say that she was acting in concert with her Allies assembled at Vienna, and to declare in another limb of the same sentence that she was 'united' with one of them. Unhappily, the error was not an error of words. The speech accurately described the strange policy which our Government had adopted; for it was strictly true that, in the midst of a perfect concord between the four great Powers, the English Cabinet had been drawn into a separate union with France, and into a union of such a kind as to require the distinguishing phrase which disclosed the new league to Europe.

This speech from the throne may be regarded as marking the point where the roads of policy branched off. By the one road England, moving in company with the rest of the four Powers, might insure a peaceful repression of the outrage which was disturbing Europe. By the other, she might also enforce the right, but, joined with the French Emperor, and parted from the rest of

This marks where the roads to peace and to war branched off.

[1] 8th July, 1853, in the House of Commons.

[2] 129 Hansard, p. 1826.

the four Powers, she would reach it by passing through war. The Cabinet of Lord Aberdeen desired peace and not war; but seeing dimly, they took the adventurous path. They so little knew whither they were going, that they made no preparation for war.[1]

---

## CHAPTER XVI.

Count Nesselrode.

THE difference between a servant and a Minister of State lies in this:—that the servant obeys the orders given him, without troubling himself concerning the question whether his master is right or wrong; whilst a Minister of State declines to be the instrument for giving effect to measures which he deems to be hurtful to his country. The Chancellor of the Russian Empire was sagacious and politic; and his experience in the business of the State, and in the councils of Europe, went back to the great days when Nesselrode and Hardenburg, and Metternich and Wellington, set their seals to the same charter. That the Czar was wrong in these transactions against Turkey, no man in Europe knew better than Count Nesselrode; and at first he had the courage to speak to his master so frankly that Nicholas, when he had heard a remark which tended to wisdom and moderation, would cry out, 'That is what the Chancellor is perpetually 'telling me.' But, unhappily for the Czar and for his empire, the Minister did not enjoy so commanding a station as to be able to put restraint upon his Sovereign, nor even perhaps to offer him counsel in his angry mood. He could advise with Nicholas the Czar; but there were reasons which made his counsels unwelcome to a heated defender of the Greek faith. He was a member of the Church of England, and the maddening rumors of the day made out that into the jaws of this very Church of England Lord Stratford was dragging the Sultan and all his Moslem subjects. Then, too, Count Nesselrode was worldly; but, after all, the quality most certain to make him irksome to a Prince in a high state of religious or ecclesiastic excitement was his good sense. It was dangerous for a wise, able sinner like him to go near holy Nicholas the Pontiff, the Head of God's Orthodox Church upon earth, when he was hearing the voices from Heaven, when he was raging against the enemies of the Faith, and struggling to enforce his will

[1] See Lord Aberdeen's evidence before the Sebastopol Committee.

upon mankind by utterances of the hated name of Canning,[1] and interjections, and gnashing of teeth. Far from being able to make a stand against this consuming fury, Nesselrode did not even decline to be the instrument for disclosing to all the world his master's condition of mind.

State of the Czar after knowing that the fleets of France and England were ordered to the mouth of the Dardanelles.

When the Czar knew that the fleets of the Western Powers were coming up into the Levant, and that the sword of England was now in the hands of Lord Stratford, he was thrown into so fierce a state, that his notions of what was true and what was not true; of what was plausible and what was ascertainably false; of what was a cause and what was an effect; of what happened first and what happened last—nay, almost, it would seem, his notions of what was the Bosphorus and what was the Hellespont,[2] became as a heap of ruins. He was in the condition imagined by the Psalmist when he prayed the Lord that his enemy might be 'confounded.' Count Nesselrode was forced to gather up his master's shivered thoughts, and putting them as well as he could into the language of diplomacy, to address to all the Courts of Europe a wild remonstrance against the measures of the Western Powers. The approach of their fleets to an anchorage in the Ægean outside the Straits of the Dardanelles was treated in this dispatch as though it were little less than a seizure of Constantinople; and it was represented that this was an act of violence which had entitled and compelled the Czar, in his own defense, to occupy the Principalities.[3] Lord Clarendon seized this weak pretense and easily laid it bare, for he showed that Nicholas, in his anger, was transposing events; and that the Czar's resolve to cross the Pruth was anterior to the occurrence which he now declared to have been the motive of his action. Then, in language worthy of England, our Foreign Secretary went on to vindicate her right to send her fleets whither she chose, so long as they were on the high seas, or on the coasts of a Sovereign legitimately assenting to their presence. Nearly at the same time the writer of the French Foreign Office dispatches pursued the Czar through Europe with his bright, cutting, pitiless logic.[4]

His complaints to Europe.

Their refutation.

[1] The Czar used to call Lord Stratford 'Lord Canning.'

[2] The dispatch which gave utterance to this raving treated an anchorage in the Ægean, outside the Dardanelles, as almost a virtual occupation of Constantinople.

[3] 'Eastern Papers,' part i., p. 342.

[4] These dispatches bear the signature of M. Drouyn de Lhuys, but it was commonly believed at the time that they were written by a man on the permanent staff of the French Foreign Office.

Of course, the vivacity of France and England tended to place Austria at her ease, and to make her more backward than she would otherwise have been in sending her troops into the Banat; and moreover, the separate action of the Western Powers was well calculated, as will be seen by-and-by, to undo the good which might be effected by the Conference of the four Powers at Vienna. The Conference, however, did not remit its labor. The mediating character which belonged to it in its original constitution was gradually changed, until at length it represented what was nothing less than a confederacy of the four Powers against Russia. It is true that it was a confederacy which sought to exhaust persuasion, and to use to the utmost the moral pressure of assembled Europe before it resorted to arms; and it is true also that it was willing to make the Czar's retreat from his false moves as easy and as free from shame as the nature of his late errors would allow: but these were views held by the English Cabinet, as well as by the Conference; and it is certain that, if our Government had seen clear, and had been free from separate engagements, it would have stood fast upon the ground occupied by the four Powers, and would have refused to be drawn into measures which were destined to be continually undoing the pacific work of the diplomatists assembled at Vienna.

The Vienna Conference.

But partnership with the midnight associates of the 2nd of December was a heavy yoke. With all his heart and soul Lord Aberdeen desired the tranquillity of Europe; but he had suffered his Cabinet to enter into close friendly relations with one to whom the tranquillity of Europe portended jail, and ill usage, and death. The French Emperor had consented to engage France in an English policy; and he thought he had a right to insist that England should pay the price, and help to give him the means of such signal action in Europe as might drive away men's thoughts from the hour when the parliament of France had been thrown into the felons' van.

The effect upon England of becoming entangled in a separate understanding with France.

The object at which the French Emperor was aiming stands clear enough to the sight; but at this time the scheme of action by which he sought to attain his ends was ambiguous. In general, men are prone to find out consistency in the acts of rulers, and to imagine that numberless acts, appearing to have different aspects, are the result of one steady design: but those who love truth better than symmetry will be able to believe that much of the conduct of the French Emperor was rather the effect of clashing purposes than of duplicity. There are philosophers who im-

The French Emperor's ambiguous scheme of action.

agine that the human mind (corresponding in that respect with the brain) has a dual action, and that the singleness of purpose observed in a decided man is the result of a close accord between the two engines of thought, and not of actual unity. Certainly it would appear that the Emperor Louis Napoleon, more than most other men, was accustomed to linger in doubt between two conflicting plans, and to delay his final adoption of the one, and his final rejection of the other, for as long a time as possible, in order to find out what might be best to be ultimately done by carrying on experiments for many months together with two rival schemes of action.

But, whether this double method of action was the result of idiosyncrasy or of a profound policy, it was but too well fitted for the object of drawing England into a war. The aim of the French Emperor was to keep his understanding with England in full force, and yet to give the alliance a warlike direction. If he were to adopt a policy frankly warlike, he would repel Lord Aberdeen and endanger the alliance. If he were to be frankly pacific, there would be a danger of his restoring to Europe that tranquillity which could not fail to bring him and his December friends into jeopardy. In this strait he did not exactly take a middle course. By splitting his means of action, he managed to take two courses at the same time. There are people who can write at the same time with both hands. Politically, Louis Napoleon had this accomplishment. With his left hand he seemed to strive after peace; with his right he tried to stir up a war. The language of his diplomacy was pacific, and yet, at the very same time, he contrived that the naval forces of France and England should be used as the means of provoking a war. The part which he took in the negotiations going on at Vienna, and in the other capitals of the great Powers, was temperate, just, and moderate; and it is probable that the Dispatches which indicated this spirit long continued to mislead Lord Aberdeen, and to keep him under the impression that an Anglo-French alliance was really an engine of peace; but it will be seen that, as soon as the French Emperor had drawn England into an understanding with him, he was enabled to engage her in a series of dangerous naval movements, which he contrived to keep going on simultaneously with the efforts of the negotiators, so as always to be defeating their labors.

His diplomacy seems pacific. At the same time he engages England in naval movements tending to provoke war.

In order to appreciate the exceeding force of the lever which was used for this purpose, a man ought to have in his mind the political geography of southeastern Europe and the configuration of the seas which flow with a ceaseless current into the waters of the Ægean.

The Euxine is connected with the Mediterranean by the Straits of the Bosphorus, the Sea of Marmora, and the Straits of the Dardanelles. The Bosphorus is a current of the sea, seventeen miles in length, and, in some places, hardly more than half a mile broad; but so deep, even home to the shores on either side, that a ship of war can almost, as it were, find shade under the gardens of the European shore—can almost mix her spars with the cypresses which darken the coast of Asia. At its southern extremity the Bosphorus mingles with the waters of the great inlet or harbor which still often goes by the name of the Golden Horn; and at length, after passing between Constantinople and its beautiful suburb of Scutari, the straits open out into the land-locked basin—now known as the Sea of Marmora—which used to be called the Propontis. At the foot of this inland sea the water is again contracted into a deep channel, no more, in one place, than three quarters of a mile in breadth, and is not set free till, after a course of some forty miles, it reaches the neighborhood of the Troad and spreads abroad into the Ægean. These last are the famous straits between Europe and Asia, which used to be called the Hellespont, and are now the Dardanelles. The Bosphorus and the Dardanelles are both so narrow that even in the early times of artillery they could be commanded by guns on either side, and it followed that these waters had not the character of 'high seas.' And, since the land upon either side belonged to the Ottoman Empire, the Sultans always claimed and always enjoyed a right to keep out foreign ships of war from both the straits. Now on the Black Sea Russia had as much sea-board as Turkey, and, nevertheless, like every other Power, she was shut out from all right to send her armed navy into the Mediterranean through the Bosphorus and the Dardanelles. There being no other outlet, her Black Sea fleet was pent up in an inland basin. Painful as this duress must needs be to a haughty State having a powerful fleet in the Euxine, it would seem that Russia has been more willing to submit to the restriction than to see the war flag of other States in the Dardanelles or the Bosphorus. The presence of a force greater than her own, or even rivaling it, did not comport with the kind of ascendency which she was always seeking to establish at Constantinople and on the sea-board of the Euxine. Russia, therefore, had been a willing party to the treaty of 1841. By this treaty the five

The Bosphorus and the Dardanelles.

The Sultan's ancient right to control them.

Policy of Russia in regard to the straits.

The rights of the Sultan and the five Powers under the Treaty of 1841.

great Powers acknowledged the right of the Sultan to exclude armed navies from both the straits; and, on the other hand, the Sultan engaged that in time of peace he would always exercise this right of exclusion. Moreover, the five Powers promised that they would all respect this engagement by the Sultan. The result, therefore, was that, whether with or without the consent of the Sultan, no foreign squadron, at a time when the Sultan was at peace, could lawfully appear in either of the straits.[1] But when the Emperor Nicholas forcibly occupied the Principalities, it was clear that this act was a just cause of war whenever the Sultan might think fit so to treat it; and there was fair ground for saying that, even before a declaration of war, the invasion of the Sultan's dominions was such a violation of the state of peace contemplated by the treaty that the Sultan was morally released from his engagement, and might be justified in asking his allies to send their fleets up through the straits. On the other hand, the appearance of foreign navies in the Dardanelles was regarded as so destructive to Russian ascendency that the bare prospect of it used to fill Russian statesmen with dismay; and the Emperor Nicholas held the idea in such horror that the mere approach of the French and English fleets to the Levant wrought him, as we have seen, to a state of mind which was only too faithfully portrayed by his Chancellor's Circular.

How these rights were affected by the Czar's seizure of the Principalities.

It is plain, therefore, that the power of advising the Sultan to call up the French and English fleets was an engine of immense force in the hands of the Western Powers, but it is also certain that this was a power which would put a much harder stress upon Russia whilst it was kept suspended over her than it was likely to do when it came to be physically used. To subject Nicholas to the fear of having to see foreign war-flags in the straits was to apply a pressure well fitted for coercing him; but actually to exert the power was to break its spell, and to change the Czar's wholesome dread into a frenzy of anger hardly consistent with hopes of peace.

Powerful means of coercing the Czar.

Importance of refraining from a premature use of the power.

The French Emperor had no sooner engaged the English Government in a separate understanding than he began to insist upon the necessity of using the naval power of France and England in the way which he proposed — a way bitterly offensive to Russia. Having at length succeeded in forcing this measure

The naval movements in which the French Emperor engages England.

[1] There were exceptions in favor of vessels having on board the Representatives of foreign States.

upon England, he, after a while, pressed upon her another movement of the fleets still more hostile than the first, and again he succeeded in bringing the English Government to yield to him. Again, and still once again, he did the like, always in the end bringing England to adopt his hostile measures; and he never desisted from this course of action until at last it had effected a virtual rupture between the Czar and the Western Powers.

Proofs of this drawn (in anticipation of a later part of the narrative) from transactions subsequent to the date of the Queen's Speech.

Not yet as part of this narrative, but by way of anticipation, and in order to gather into one page the grounds of the statement just made, the following instances are given of the way in which the English Government was from time to time driven to join with the French Emperor in making a quarrelsome use of the two fleets: — On the 13th of July, 1853, the French Emperor, through his Minister of Foreign Affairs, declared to the English Government that if the occupation of the Principalities continued, the French fleet could not longer remain at Beshika Bay; on the 19th of August he declared it to be absolutely necessary that the combined fleets should enter the Dardanelles, and he pressed the English Government to adopt a resolution to this effect. On the 21st of September he insisted that the English Government, at the same moment as the French, should immediately order up the combined squadrons to Constantinople. On the 15th of December he pressed the English Government to agree that the Allied fleets should enter the Euxine, take possession of it, and interdict the passage of every Russian vessel. It will be seen that, with more or less reluctance, and after more or less delay, these demands were always acceded to by England; and the course thus taken by the Maritime Powers was fatal to the pending negotiations, for, besides that in the way already shown the Czar's wholesome fears were converted into bursts of rage, the Turks, at the same time, were deriving a dangerous encouragement from the sight of the French and English war-flags; and the result was, that the negotiators, with all their skill and all their patience, were never able to frame a Note in the exact words which would allay the anger of Nicholas without encountering a steadfast resistance on the part of the Sultan.

Some men will believe that a long series of acts all having a tendency in the same direction, and ending at length in war, were deliberately planned by the French Emperor as a means of bringing about the result which they effected, and that the temperate and sometimes conciliatory negotiations which were carried on during the same period were a mask to the real intent. It is perhaps more likely to be true that the French Emperor was all this time hesitating, and keeping his judgment in suspense. What he needed for his very life's sake was to become so conspicuous, whether as a disturber or as a pacifactor of other nations, that Frenchmen might be brought to look at what he was doing to others instead of what he had done to them; and if he could have reached to this by seeming to take a great ascendant in the diplomacy of Europe, it is possible that for a while at least he might have been content to spare the world from graver troubles; but, whether he acted from design or under the impulse of varying and conflicting wishes, it is certain that that command of naval power which was an engine of excellent strength for enforcing the restoration of tranquillity, was so used by his orders and under his persuasion as to become the means of provoking a war.

Means well fitted for enforcing a just peace were so used as to provoke war.

---

## CHAPTER XVII.

Lord Stratford's scheme of pacification.

LORD STRATFORD, it would seem, was unconscious of his power over the mind of Nicholas, and did not understand that it rested with him to determine whether the Czar should be politic or raging. He did not know that as long as he was at Therapia, every deed, every word of the Divan was regarded as coming from the English Ambassador, and that the bare thought of the Greek Church in Turkey being under the protection of 'Canning,' was the very one which would at any moment change the Czar from an able man of business to an almost irresponsible being. Taking the complaints of Russia according to their avowed meaning, the English Ambassador faithfully strove to remove every trace of the foundation on which they rested; and having caused the Porte to issue firmans perpetuating all the accustomed privileges of the Greek Church, he proposed that copies of these firmans should be sent to the Court of St. Petersburg, together with a courteous Note from the Porte to Count Nesselrode, distinctly assuring the Chancellor that the firmans confirmed the privileges of the Greek Church in perpetuity, and virtually, therefore, engaging that the grants should never be revoked.[1] This was doing exactly what Rus-

[1] 20th July, 1853. 'Eastern Papers,' part ii., p. 15.

sia ostensibly required; but it was also doing exactly that which the Czar most abhorred, for to his mind it indicated nothing less than that the Greek Church was passing under the gracious protection of Lord Stratford. The polished courtesy of the Note imparting this concession only made it the more hateful, by showing on its face whence it came. However, Lord Stratford obtained for his plan the full approval of his French, Austrian, and Prussian colleagues, as well as of the Porte, and the Note, signed by Reshid Pacha, and inclosing copies of the new firmans, was dispatched to Vienna, with a view to its being thence transmitted to St. Petersburg. The packet which held these papers contained the very ingredients which were best fitted for disturbing the reason of the Czar. It happened, however, that at Vienna there were men who knew something of the psychological part of the Eastern Question, and they took upon themselves to arrest the maddening Note in its transit.

And now the representatives of the four Powers conferring in the Austrian capital succeeded in framing a document which soon became known to Europe under the name of the 'Vienna 'Note.' This paper, framed originally in Paris, was perfected and finally approved by all the four Powers conferring at Vienna. It was a draught of a Note understood to be brought forward by Austria in her mediating capacity, and proposed to be addressed by the Porte to the Russian Government. The parties to the Conference believed that the engagements purporting to be made by the Note made on the part of the Sultan might satisfy the Czar without endangering the true interests of Turkey. Indeed, the Austrian Government, somewhat forgetting its duty as a faithful mediator, had used means of ascertaining that the Note would be acceptable to Russia,[1] but without taking a like step in favor of the other disputant. Copies of the Note thus framed were sent for approval to St. Petersburg and to Constantinople, and the acceptance of the arrangement was pressed upon the Governments of the two disputing States with all the moral weight which the four great Powers could give to their unanimous award.

*The 'Vienna 'Note.'*

*Agreed to by the four Powers, and*

*Accepted by Russia.*

And here it ought to be marked, that at this moment the French Emperor did nothing to thwart the restoration of tranquillity. He perhaps believed that if a Note which had originated in Paris were to be-

*The French Emperor does nothing to thwart the suc-*

[1] 'Eastern Papers,' part ii., p. 27.

cess of the Note.

come the basis of a settlement, he might found on this circumstance a claim to the glory of having pacified Europe, and in that wholesome way might achieve the sort of conspicuousness which he loved and needed. Perhaps he was only obeying that doubleness of mind which made him always prone to do acts clashing one with another. But, whatever may have been the cause which led him for a moment to intermit his policy, it is just to acknowledge that he seems to have been faithfully willing to give effect to the means of pacification which were proffered by the 'Vienna 'Note.' It soon became known that the Note was agreed to by the Emperor Nicholas. Men believed that all was settled. It was true that the courier who was expected to be the bearer of the assent of the Porte had not yet come in from Constantinople, but it was assumed that the representatives of the four Powers had taken the precaution of possessing themselves of the real views of the Turkish Government, and besides, it was thought impossible that the Sultan should undertake to remain in antagonism to Russia, if the support which he had hitherto received from the four great Powers were to be transferred from him to the Czar.

Lord Stratford had not been consulted.

Those who dwell far away from great cities can hardly perhaps believe that the touching signs of simplicity which they observe in rural life may be easily found now and then in the councils of assembled Europe. The Governments of all the four Powers, and their representatives assembled at Vienna, fondly imagined that they could settle the dispute and restore tranquillity to Europe without consulting Lord Stratford de Redcliffe. They framed and dispatched the Note without learning what his opinion of it was, and it is probable that a knowledge of this singular omission may have conduced to make the Czar accept the award of the mediating Powers, by tempting him with the delight of seeing Lord Stratford overruled. But, on the other hand, the one man who was judge of what ought or ought not to be conceded by the Turks was Lord Stratford, and it is plain that any statesmen who forgot him in their reckoning must have been imperfect in their notion of political dynamics. It would be wrong to suppose that a sound judgment by the four Powers would be liable to be overturned by Lord Stratford from any mere feeling of neglect. He was too proud, as well as too honest, to be capable of such a littleness. What was to be apprehended was that, until it was ratified by the English Ambassador at the Porte, the decision of a number of men in Vienna, and Paris, and London, and Berlin, might turn out to be really erroneous, or might seem to be so in the eyes of one who was profoundly versed in the subject; and no man had a right to make sure that, even at the instance of all Europe, this strong-willed Englishman would consent to use his vast personal ascendency as a means of forcing upon the Turks a surrender which he held to be dangerous.

Early in August the Vienna Note reached Constantinople; and the Turkish Government soon detected in it, not only a misrecital of history, but words of a dangerous sort, conveying, or seeming to convey to Russia, under a new form, that very protectorate of the Greek Church in Turkey which had brought about the rupture of the negotiation conducted by Prince Mentschikoff. The four Powers, however, had determined to press the acceptance of the arrangement upon the Porte, and on the 12th it became known at Constantinople that the Note had been accepted by the Emperor Nicholas. On the same day the English Ambassador received instructions from London, which informed him that the English Government 'adhered to the Vienna Note, and considered that it 'fully guarded the principle which had been contended for, and might therefore with perfect safety 'be signed by the Porte,' and Lord Clarendon went on to express a hope that the Ambassador would have 'found no difficulty in procuring the assent of the Turkish Government to a 'project which the allies of the Sultan unanimously concurred 'in recommending for his adoption.'[1]

The 'Vienna 'Note' in the hands of Lord Stratford.

It can not be doubted that Lord Stratford's opinion as to the effect of the Vienna Note was opposed to that of his Government,[2] but it was his duty to obey. He obeyed. He 'scrupulously abstained from expressing any private opinion of his 'on the Note whilst it was under consideration at the Porte,' and he conveyed to the Turkish Government the desire of Europe. 'I called the attention of Reshid Pacha,' said he, 'to 'the strong and earnest manner in which the Vienna Note was 'recommended to the acceptance of the Porte, not only by Her 'Majesty's Government, but also by the Cabinets of Austria, 'France, and Prussia. I reminded him of the intelligence which 'had been received from St. Petersburg, purporting that the 'Emperor of Russia had signified his readiness to accept the 'same Note. I urged the importance of his engaging the Porte 'to come to a decision with the least possible delay. I repeatedly urged the importance of an immediate decision, and 'the danger of declining, or only accepting with amendments,

[1] 'Eastern Papers,' part ii., p. 27.

[2] Ibid., pp. 72, 82.

'what the four friendly Powers so earnestly recommended, and 'what the Cabinet of St. Petersburg had accepted in its actual 'state.'[1]

These were dutiful words. But it is not to be believed that, even if he strove to do so, Lord Stratford could hide his real thoughts from the Turkish Ministers. There was that in his very presence which disclosed his volition; for if the thin disciplined lips moved in obedience to constituted authorities, men who knew how to read the meaning of his brow, and the light which kindled beneath, would gather that the Ambassador's thought concerning the home Governments of the five great Powers of Europe was little else than an angry 'quos 'ego!' The sagacious Turks would look more to these great signs than to the tenor of formal advice sent out from London; and if they saw that Lord Stratford was in his heart against the opinion of Europe, they would easily resolve to follow his known desire, and to disobey his mere words. The result was that, without any signs of painful doubt, the Turkish Government determined to stand firm. They quietly introduced into the draft the modifications which they deemed to be necessary for extracting its dangerous quality, and resolved that unless these changes were admitted they would altogether reject the Note. They were supported by the unanimous decision of the Great Council.

The Turkish Government determines to reject it unless altered.

It might seem that with Lord Stratford and the Turkish Government on one side, and all the rest of Europe, including England herself, on the other, the preponderance would be soon determined; and Lord Clarendon remonstrated against the obstinacy of the Turks in terms which approached to a disapproval of all that had lately been done at Constantinople;[2] but Europe was in the wrong, and Lord Stratford and the Turks were in the right; and, happily for the world, a strong man and a good Cause make a formidable conjunction. Lord Stratford did not fail to show his Government that the objections of the Turks to the proposed Note were well founded; and Europe was compelled to remember that the Russian demand still had in it the original vice of wrongfully seeking to extort a treaty in time of peace.

Lord Stratford and the Turks stand alone in Europe.

On the 19th of August, the Porte declined to accept the Vienna Note without introducing into it the required alterations.[3] These alterations were rejected by

They are firm.

[1] 'Eastern Papers,' part ii., p. 69. [2] Ibid., p. 91.

[3] Ibid., p. 80. A copy of the 'Vienna Note,' and of the alterations insisted upon by the Turks, is given in the Appendix, in order to show the exact

Russia; and, for a moment, Europe was threatened with the mortification of seeing that the question of peace or war was to depend upon a mere verbal criticism, and a criticism, too, in which the English Government at first supposed that the Turks were wrong.[1] It happened, however, that, in the course of the discussion, Count Nesselrode argued against the alterations proposed at Constantinople in language which avowed that the meaning and intent of Russia coincided with that very interpretation which had been fastened upon the Note by the sagacity of the Turks; and, the Governments of the four Powers being then obliged to acknowledge that they were wrong, and that Lord Stratford and the Turks were right, the question which brought about the final rupture between Russia and the Porte was virtually the same as that which had caused the departure of Prince Mentschikoff from Constantinople. What Russia still required, and what the Porte still refused to grant, was the protectorate of the Greek Church in Turkey.

Nesselrode uses language which shows the soundness of Lord Stratford's objection to the Note.

The Protectorate of the Greek Church in Turkey was still the thing in question.

At length, with the advice of a Great Council attended by a hundred and seventy-two of the foremost men of the Empire, the Porte determined upon war. A declaration was issued, which made the farther continuance of peace dependent upon the evacuation of the Principalities; and the Russian General there commanding was summoned to withdraw his troops from the invaded provinces within fifteen days. He did not comply with the demand; and, on the 23rd of October, 1853, the Sultan was placed in a state of war with the Emperor of Russia.

The Porte declares war.

But meanwhile the preachers of the Orthodox Church, and the preachers of Islam, had not been idle. In Russia, the piety and the spirit of the people had been forestalled by the consuming evil of a vast standing army, and crushed down by police and by drill. The Government had already taken so much by sheer compulsion, that the people, however brave and pious, had little more that it was willing to offer up in sacrifice. It was not thus in the Ottoman Empire. Through the vast and scattered dominions of the Sultan, the holy war had not been preached in vain. There, religion, and love of country, and warlike ardor were blent into one ennobling sentiment, which was strong enough, as was soon shown, to make men arise of their own free will, and endure long toil and cruel

Warlike spirit of the belligerents. In Russia this had been forestalled.

Warlike ardor of the people of the Ottoman Empire.

difference of words which brought about the final rupture between Russia and the Porte.

[1] 'Eastern Papers,' part ii., p. 91.

hardships, that they might attain to some battle-field or siege, and there face death with joy. And, under the counsels and ascendency of Lord Stratford, this ardor was so well guided that it was kept from breaking out in vain tumult or outrage, and was brought to bear in all its might upon the defense of the State. 'A spirit of self-devotion,' wrote the Ambassador, 'unaccompanied with fanatical demonstrations, and showing 'itself amongst the highest functionaries of the State, bids 'fair to give an extraordinary impulse to any military enter-'prise which may be undertaken against Russia by the Turk-'ish Government. The corps of Ulema are preparing to ad-'vance a considerable sum in support of the war. The Grand 'Vizier, the Minister for Foreign Affairs, and other leading 'members of the Administration, have resigned a large pro-'portion of their horses for the service of the artillery. Re-en-'forcements continue to be directed toward the Danube and 'the Georgian frontier. If hostilities commence, they will be 'prosecuted in a manner to leave, on one side or on the other, 'deep and durable traces of a truly national struggle.'[1]

Moderation of the Turkish Government.

But if the Turkish Empire was still the Caliphate; and if religion still gave the watchword which brought many races of men to crowd to the same standard, yet the Porte, chastened by the adversity of the latter century, and disciplined by the English Ambassador, had become so wise and politic, that it governed the beating heart of the nation, and suffered no fanatic words to go out into Christendom. The duty of the Moslem now called to arms, for his Faith was preached with a fervor sufficing for all military purposes; but the Proclamation which announced that the Sultan was at war abstained from all fierce theology. Reiterating the poignant truths which placed the Porte in the right and the Czar in the wrong, it kept to that tone of moderation which had hitherto marked all the State Papers of the Turkish Government. But this very moderation seemed always to kindle fresh rage in the mind of the Emperor Nicholas, and to fetch out his religious zeal. The reason perhaps was, that in all wisdom, and all moderation evinced by the Divan, he persisted in seeing the evil hand of Lord Stratford. In his Proclamation, he ascended to ecstatic heights:—'By the grace of 'God, We, Nicholas I., Emperor and Autocrat of All the Russias, make known:—By our Manifesto of the 14th of June, 'we acquainted our well-beloved and faithful subjects with the

Its effect on the mind of the Czar.

The Czar's Proclamation.

[1] 'Eastern Papers,' part ii., p. 167.

'motives which have compelled us to demand of the Ottoman 'Porte inviolable guarantees in favor of the sacred rights of 'the Orthodox Church . . . Russia is challenged to the fight; 'nothing therefore farther remains for her but, in confident re- 'liance upon God, to have recourse to arms, in order to compel 'the Ottoman Government to respect treaties, and obtain from 'it reparation for the offenses by which it has responded to our 'most moderate demands, and to our legitimate solicitude for 'the defense of the Orthodox faith in the East, which is equally 'professed by the Russian people. We are firmly convinced 'that our faithful subjects will join the fervent prayers which 'we address to the Most High, that His hand may be pleased 'to bless our arms in the holy and just cause which has ever 'found ardent defenders in our pious ancestors. "In Thee, O '"Lord, have I trusted; let me not be confounded for ever!"'[1]

---

## CHAPTER XVIII.

The Czar announces that unless he shall be farther provoked he will be content to hold his 'material guarantee' and refrain from taking the offensive.

THE Emperor Nicholas still sought to prolong the ambiguity of his relations with Turkey. On the 31st of October, Count Nesselrode issued a Circular to the representatives of Russia at foreign Courts, in which he declared that, notwithstanding the declaration of war, and as long as his master's dignity and his interests would permit, Russia would abstain from taking the offensive, and content herself with holding her position in the Principalities until she succeeded in obtaining the satisfaction which she required. This second endeavor to contrive a novel kind of standing-ground between real peace and avowed war was destined, as will be seen, to cause fresh discord between Russia and the Western Powers.

The negotiations are continued, and are ripening toward a settlement, when they are ruined by the Western Powers.

The negotiations for a settlement were scarcely interrupted, either by the formal declaration of war or by the hostilities which were commenced on the banks of the Danube; and the Conference of the four Powers represented at Vienna had just agreed to the terms of a collective Note, which seemed to afford a basis for peace, when the English Government gave way to the strenuous urgency of the French

[1] 'Eastern Papers,' part ii., p. 228.

Emperor, and consented to a measure which ruined the pending negotiations, and generated a series of events leading straight to a war between Russia and the Western Powers.

In the month of September, some weeks before the Sultan's final rupture with the Czar, the pious and warlike ardor then kindled in the Turkish Empire had begun to show itself at Constantinople. A placard, urging the Government to declare war, was pasted on one of the mosques. Then a petition for war was presented to the Council and to the Sultan himself, by certain muderris, or theological students. The paper was signed by thirty-five persons, of no individual distinction, but having the corporate importance of belonging to the 'Ulemah.' Though free from menace, the petition, as Lord Stratford expressed it, was worded in 'serious and impressive terms, implying a strong sense 'of religious duty, and a very independent disregard of conse-'quences.' The Ministers professed to be alarmed, and to believe that this movement was the forerunner of revolution; and Lord Stratford seems to have imagined that their alarm was genuine. It is perhaps more likely that they were skillfully making the most of these occurrences, with a view to embroil their maritime allies in the approaching war; for, when they went to the Ambassadors, and asked them to take part in measures for the maintenance of public tranquillity, their meaning was that they wished to see the fleets of France and England come up into the Bosphorus; and they well knew that if this naval movement could be brought to pass before the day of the final rupture between Russia and the Porte, it would be regarded by the Czar as a flagrant violation of treaty.

Movement at Constantinople.

The use made of this by the Turkish Ministers.

A curious indication of the sagacity with which the Turkish Ministers were acting is to be found in the difference between their language to the English Ambassador and their language to M. de la Cour. In speaking to Lord Stratford, they shadowed out dangers impending over the Eastern world, the upheaving of Islam, the overthrow of the Sultan's authority. Then they went straight to M. de la Cour, and drew a small vivid picture of massacred Frenchmen. They did not, said M. de la Cour, conceal from him, 'that the persons and 'the interests of his countrymen would be exposed to grave 'dangers, which they were sensible they were incapable of 'preventing, by reason of the want of union in the Ministry 'and the threats directed against themselves.'[1] This skillful

[1] 'Eastern Papers,' part ii., p. 115.

discrimination on the part of the Turkish Ministers seems to show that they had not at all lost their composure.

They succeed in alarming the French Ambassador.

Either by their real dread, or by their crafty simulation of it, the Turkish statesmen succeeded in infecting M. de la Cour with sincere alarm. He was easily brought to the conclusion that 'the state of the 'Turkish Government was getting worse and worse; and that 'matters had got to such a state as to cause dread of a ca-'tastrophe, of which the inhabitants, Rayahs or Europeans, 'would be the first victims, and which would even threaten 'the Sultan's throne.'[1] He called upon the English Ambassador to consult as to what was best to be done; and both he and the Austrian Internuncio expressed their readiness to join with him in adopting the needful measures.

Composure of Lord Stratford.

Lord Stratford does not seem to have suspected that the use which the Turkish Ministers were making of their Divinity students was in the nature of a stratagem; but, assuming and believing their alarm to be genuine, he was still proof against the infection, and retained his calm. Indeed, he seems to have understood that a cry for war on the part of the religious authorities was a healthy sign for the Empire. He expressed to his colleagues his readiness to act in concert with them; but he said he was reluctant to take any step which was not clearly warranted by the necessities of the case, and that he desired to guard against mistake and exaggeration, by gaining a more precise knowledge of the grounds for alarm. He deprecated any joint interference with the Turkish Government; and was still less inclined to join in bringing up the squadrons to Constantinople, without more proofs of urgent peril than had been yet obtained; but he suggested, as an opinion of his own, that the representatives of the maritime Powers should obtain from their respective Admirals such an addition of steam force as would secure them from any immediate attack, and enable them to assist the Government in case of an outbreak threatening its existence, without attracting any unusual attention, or assuming an air of intimidation.[2] This was done.[3] A couple of steamers belonging to each of the great Western Powers quietly came up to Constantinople. Tranquillity followed. Every good end was attained, without ostentation or disturbance, without the evil of seeming to place

His wise and guarded measures for preserving the peace of the capital.

[1] 'Eastern Papers,' part ii., p. 115.

[2] The steam force of the maritime Powers already in the Golden Horn consisted of vessels which had passed the Dardanelles by virtue of exceptions contained in the treaty of 1841.

[3] 'Eastern Papers,' part ii., p. 121.

the Sultan's capital under the protection of foreign Powers; and above all, without breaking through the Treaty of 1841 in a way which, however justifiable it might be in point of international law, clearly tended to force on a war.

The French Emperor. His means of putting a pressure upon the English Cabinet.

But the moderate and guarded policy of Lord Stratford at Constantinople was quickly subverted by a pressure which the French Emperor found means of putting upon the advisers of the Queen. Of course an understanding with a foreign Power is in its nature an abatement of a nation's free agency; and a statesman may be honest and wise in consenting to measures which have no other excuse than that they were adopted for the sake of maintaining close union with an Ally. England had contracted a virtual alliance, and when once she had taken this step, it was needful and right that she should do and suffer many things rather than allow the new friendship to be chilled. But this yoke was pressed hard against her. It was not the wont of England to be causelessly led into an action which was violent and provoking of violence. It was not her wont to rush forward without need, and so to drive through a treaty that many might say she broke it. It was not her wont to be governed in the use of her fleets by the will of a foreign Sovereign. It was not her wont to hear from a French Ambassador that a given movement of her Mediterranean squadron was 'indispensably necessary,' nor to be requested to go to such a conclusion by 'an immediate decision.' It was not her wont to act with impassioned haste, where haste was dangerous and needless. It was not her wont to found a breach with one of the foremost Powers of Europe upon a mere hysterical message addressed by one Frenchman to another. But the French Emperor had a great ascendant over the English Government, for the power which he had gained by entangling it in a virtual alliance was augmented by the growing desire for action now evinced by the English people. He knew that at any moment he could expose Lord Aberdeen and his colleagues to a gust of popular disfavor by causing it to be known or imagined that France was keen, and that England was lagging behind.

When M. de la Cour's account of his sensations reached Paris, it produced so deep an impression that the French Emperor, either feeling genuine alarm, or else seeing in his Ambassador's narrative an opportunity for the furtherance of his designs, determined to insist in cogent terms that the English Government should join him in overstepping the treaty of 1841, and ordering the Allied squadrons to pass the Dardanelles and anchor in the Bosphorus. On the 23rd of September, Count Walewski had an interview with Lord Aberdeen and Lord Clarendon at the same time, and then, after speaking of the crisis at Constantinople which M. de la Cour's dispatch had led the French Government to expect, he said that his Government thought it 'indispensably necessary that both 'fleets should be ordered up to Constantinople;' and his Excellency added, 'that he was directed to ask for the immediate 'decision of Her Majesty's Government, in order that no time 'might be lost in sending instructions to the Ambassadors and 'Admirals.'[1]

Violent urgency of the French Emperor for an advance of the fleets to Constantinople.

Now, at the time of listening to these peremptory words, the English Government had received no account from their own Ambassador of the apprehended disturbances, but they knew that the fleets at the mouth of the Dardanelles, being already under orders to obey the requisitions of the Ambassadors, could be instantly brought up to Constantinople without any farther orders for that purpose being sent from home. Moreover, the very dispatch which brought the alarm showed that the Ambassadors knew how to meet the danger, and that they had already called up that portion of the fleet which they deemed it prudent to have in the Golden Horn. From first to last, the power which France and England had intrusted to their representatives at the Porte had been used with admirable prudence, and it is hard to understand how it could have seemed right to withdraw, or rather supersede, the discretion hitherto committed to the Ambassadors by sending out an absolute order for the advance of the fleets. As it stood, the fleets would go up the moment they were wanted; and what the French Emperor now required was that, whether they were wanted or not, and in defiance of the treaty of 1840, they should immediately pass the Dardanelles. Either the Queen's Government had lost its composure, or else, when they gave way to this demand of the French Emperor, and consented to a needless[2] measure which operated as a sharp provocative of war, the Queen's Government went through the bitter duty of taking a step not right in itself, but forced upon them by the stringency of the new alliance.

Needlessness of the measure.

Its tendency to bring on war.

'I told Count Walewski,' says Lord Clarendon, 'that no in'telligence of the nature referred to by M. de la Cour had been

[1] 'Eastern Papers,' part ii., p. 114.

[2] Needless, because the authority to call up the fleets when they were wanted was already vested in the ambassadors.

'received from Lord Stratford de Redcliffe, and that so long 'as the Porte did not declare war against Russia, and desire 'the presence of the British fleet, it was the intention of Her 'Majesty's Government to observe the treaty of 1841; but 'Lord Aberdeen and I concurred in stating to Count Walewski that under such circumstances as those reported by M. de 'la Cour the provisions of any treaty must necessarily, and as 'a matter of course, be set aside.' And then, unhappily, Lord Aberdeen and Lord Clarendon went on to tell Count Walewski 'that they would, without hesitation, take upon 'themselves to agree to the proposal of the French 'Government that the Ambassadors should be in'structed to call up the fleets to Constantinople for 'the security of British and French interests, and if necessary 'for the protection of the Sultan.'[1]

The English Government yields to the French Emperor.

In compliance with the promise thus obtained from him, Lord Clarendon on the same day addressed a dispatch to Lord Stratford, saying: 'Your Excellency 'is therefore instructed to send for the British fleet 'to Constantinople,'[2] thus depriving the Ambassador of the discretion which had hitherto been used with singular care and wisdom, and with great advantage to the public service.

Fleet ordered up to Constantinople.

Want of firmness and discretion evinced in the adoption of the measure.

What makes the course of the English Government the more extraordinary is that they rushed into the hostile policy which is involved in this stringent order to Lord Stratford without having received any dispatch of their own from Constantinople, and without any knowledge of the events which had been there occurring, except what was conveyed by a telegraphic message from a French Ambassador to his own Government. If the English Ministers had paused five days,[3] they would have received Lord Stratford's calm dispatch, showing that he looked with more pleasure than alarm upon the petition of the theological students; and that he knew how to avail himself of force without using violence. If they had waited four days more,[4] they would have found that the hour was at hand when the fleets might enter the Dardanelles without any violation or seeming violation of treaty; and in fact it happened that this ill-omened order for the entry of the squadrons into the Dardanelles was carried into effect at a moment when a delay of less than twenty-four hours would have made their entry clearly consistent with a due observance of the treaty of 1841; for they

[1] 'Eastern Papers,' part ii., p. 114. [2] Ibid., p. 116.
[3] *i. e.* till 28th September. Ibid., p. 121.
[4] *i. e.* till 2nd October. Ibid., p. 127.

entered the Dardanelles on the 22nd, and on the following day the Sultan, being then at war with Russia, was released from the engagement which precluded him (so long as he was at peace) from suffering foreign fleets to come up through the Straits.

Baron Brunnow's remonstrance.

Baron Brunnow remonstrated in strong terms against the entry of the fleets into the Dardanelles as a breach of the treaty of 1841; and although he was well answered by Lord Clarendon so far as concerned the mere question of right, no endeavor was made to mitigate by words the true import of the measure, and, in truth, it was of so hostile a nature as not to be susceptible of any favorable interpretation; for, although the apprehension of disturbance at Constantinople might be a sufficing ground for the step, the order to the Ambassadors was not made dependent upon the occurrence of any such disturbances, nor even upon any alleged fear of them, but was peremptory and absolute in its terms, and was made applicable—not to such a portion of the naval forces as might be requisite for insuring the peace of the city, but—to the whole of the Allied squadrons.

Effect of the measure at St. Petersburg.

When the tidings of this hostile measure reached St. Petersburg they put an end for the time to all prospect of peace, and even Count Nesselrode, who had hitherto done all he could venture in the way of resistance to his master, now declared with sorrow that he saw in the acts of the British Government a 'settled purpose to humiliate Russia.' He spoke in sorrow, and his thoughts, it would seem, went back to the times when he had sat in great councils with Wellington. 'He spoke,' says Sir Hamilton Seymour, 'with much feeling of the horrors of war, and particularly of war between two powerful countries—two old allies like England and Russia—countries which, whilst they might be of infinite use to one another, possessed each the means of inflicting great injury upon its antagonist, and ended by saying that if for any motives known to him war should be declared against Russia by England, it would be the most unintelligible and the least justifiable war ever undertaken.'[1]

Count Nesselrode's sorrow.

The Czar's determination to retaliate with his Black Sea fleet.

The Czar received tidings of the hostile decision of the maritime Powers in a spirit which, this time at least, was almost justified by the provocation given. In retaliation for what he would naturally look upon as a bitter affront, and even as a breach of treaty,

[1] 'Eastern Papers,' part ii., p. 180.

he determined, it would seem, to have vengeance at sea whilst vengeance at sea was still possible, and it was under the spur of the anger thus kindled that orders for active operations were given to the fleet at Sebastopol.[1] The vengeance he meditated he could only wreak upon the body of the Turks, for the great offenders of the West were beyond the bounds of his power.

Error of the notion that the disaster of Sinope was a surprise achieved by stealth.

It was long believed in England that the disaster at Sinope was a surprise stealthily contrived by the Emperor Nicholas, and it is certain that the event fell upon the maritime Powers as a sudden shock; but it is not true that concealment was used by Russia. On the contrary, it seems that the attack was preceded by a long-continued ostentation of naval force. In the middle of the month of November, and at a time when the Allied squadrons were anchored in the Bosphorus, the Sebastopol fleet came out and was ranged in a kind of cordon, stretching from north to south across the centre of the Black Sea. So early as the 20th of November the Russian cruisers captured the 'Medora,' a Turkish steamer,[2] and about the same time they boarded a merchantman, and relieved the captain of a portion of his cargo, and of the whole of his cash;[3] and the Russians were so far from entertaining any idea of secrecy or concealment, that they seem to have hailed neutral merchantmen for the purpose of inquiring about the French and English fleets in the Bosphorus, and asking 'exultingly' if the captures which the Russian fleet had effected were known at Constantinople.[4]

Ostentatious publicity of the Russian operations in the Black Sea.

Tidings of an impending attack by the Russian fleet.

Full ten days[5] before the fatal 30th of November, a Russian force of seven sail and one war-steamer was cruising in sight of Sinope, and hovering over the Turkish squadron which lay there at anchor. An express, dispatched from Samsoon by land on the 22nd, bore tidings of this to Lord Stratford, and it must have reached him, it would seem, by the 25th or 26th. On Wednesday the 23rd

[1] This conclusion is drawn from dates. The hostile resolution of the Western Powers was known to the Czar a little before the 14th of October, and about the middle of the following month the Black Sea fleet was at sea. If allowance be made for distance and preparation, it will be seen that the sequence of one event upon the other is close enough to warrant the statement contained in the text. In the absence, however, of any knowledge to the contrary, it is fair to suppose that the Czar remembered his promise, and did not sanction any actual attack upon the enemy unless his commanders should be previously apprized that the Turks had commenced active warfare.

[2] 'Eastern Papers,' part ii., p. 315. [3] Ibid., p. 316. [4] Ibid., p. 315.

[5] Ibid. So early as the 22nd the appearance of the squadron was described as having occurred "some days back."

the Commander of the Turkish squadron descried a Russian force of seven sail and two steamers coming down under a northeast wind toward Sinope. The Turkish ships were cleared for action, but after some manœuvring, the Russian force stood out to windward and gained an offing. On the following day six Russian ships of the line, with a brig and two steamers, again made their appearance, and three of them under easy sail stood toward the port of Sinope until the evening. 'In fine,' writes the Turkish Commander, 'six sail of the 'line, a brig, and two steamers, are constantly off the port above 'mentioned, and at one time they lie-to, and another they beat 'about. From six to eight frigates, and two steamers, have 'been seen off the port of Bartin and Amasbre, and this news 'is certain. Besides, the great naval port of the enemy is near. 'He may, therefore, receive re-enforcements or attack us with 'fire-ships. That being the case, if re-enforcements are not sent 'to us, and our position continues the same for some time—'may God preserve us from them!—it may well happen that 'the Imperial fleet may incur disasters.'[1]

Inaction of the Ambassadors and the Admirals.

The power and habit of concentrating all energy in a single channel of action was one of the qualities which gave force and grandeur to Lord Stratford in the field of diplomacy, but it also seems to have had the effect of preventing him from casting a glance beyond the range of his profession, and it is curious that when the exigencies of the time called upon him to perform duties not commonly falling within the sphere of a diplomatist, his mind refused to act. England and France, without the wholesome formality of a treaty, had glided into an engagement to defend 'Constantinople, or any other part of the Turkish territory, 'whether in Europe or in Asia, that might be in danger of at-'tack.'[2] So much of this grave duty as consisted in originating a resolve to put forth the naval strength of the Allies remained committed to the two Ambassadors, but it was of course understood that any plans for active measures would be concerted between them and the Admirals; and since the nature of the duty which they might be called upon to undertake was known of course to the Admirals, it must be adjudged that it was incumbent upon them, as well as upon the two Ambassadors, to take measures for ascertaining whether the Russians were preparing to operate against the coasts of Turkey. Moreover the English Ambassador had been instructed by his Government that 'if the Russian fleet were to come out of Sebas-

[1] 'Eastern Papers,' part ii., p. 313.

[2] Ibid., p. 143.

'topol, the fleets would then as a matter of course pass through 'the Bosphorus,'[1] and, implicitly, this instruction required that measures should be taken for ascertaining whether the Czar's naval forces were in harbor or at sea, for if they were gone to sea, that was an event which (according to the orders from home) was to be the ground of a naval operation.

Yet not only were no measures taken for ascertaining the truth, but the rumors of great naval operations in the Black Sea, and the dispatch of the 22nd, announcing that the Russian squadron was hovering over Sinope, and even the dispatch containing the touching appeal of the Turkish Commander at Sinope, all alike failed to draw men into action. This last dispatch was communicated to Lord Stratford on the 29th. Even then an instant advance of the steam squadrons might not have been altogether in vain; for, though the attack commenced on the 30th, the Russian fleet did not quit Sinope until the 1st of December. Yet nothing was done. Nothing but actual intelligence of the disaster was cogent enough to lift an anchor. What Lord Stratford says of the causes of all this inaction ought to be stated in his own words. Writing on the 4th of December, he says, 'Rumors of Russian ships of the line being 'at sea have occasionally prevailed for some time. Uncertain-'ty of information, a wish to avoid as long as possible the 'chances of a collision, the arrival of a new French Ambassa-'dor, and the state of the weather, were natural causes of de-'mur in coming to a decision as to sending the squadrons into 'the Black Sea at this time of the year;'[2] but even supposing that there were reasons which justified hesitation in sending the squadrons to sea, the Home Governments of the Western Powers were entitled to ask why some humbler means of ascertaining the truth were never resorted to, and why no measures followed upon the receipt of the alarming dispatch from Samsoon, or even upon the appeal for help which had come from the Turkish Commander at Sinope.

The disaster of Sinope.

On the 30th of November, Admiral Nachimoff, with six sail of the line, bore down upon the Turkish squadron still lying at anchor in the port of Sinope. There was no ship of the line in the Turkish squadron. It consisted of seven frigates, a sloop, a steamer, and some transports. The Turks were the first to fire, and to bring upon their little squadron of frigates the broadsides of six sail of the line; and, although they fought without hope, they were steadfast. Either they refused to strike their colors, or else, if their colors

[1] 'Eastern Papers,' part ii., p. 143. [2] Ibid., p. 311. [3] Ibid., p. 305.

went down, the Russian Admiral was blind to their signal and continued to slaughter them. Except the steamer, every one of the Turkish vessels was destroyed. It was believed by men in authority that 4000 Turks were killed, that less than 400 survived, and that all these were wounded.[1] The feeble batteries of the place suffered under the enemy's fire, and the town was much shattered.[1] The Russian fleet did not move from Sinope until the following day.[1]

This onslaught upon Sinope and upon vessels lying in port was an attack upon Turkish territory, and was therefore an attack which the French and English Ambassadors had been authorized to repel by calling into action the fleets of the Western Powers. Moreover this attack had been impending for many days, and all this while the fleets of the Western Powers had been lying still in the Bosphorus, within easy reach of the scene of the disaster. The honor of France was wounded. England was touched to the quick.

---

## CHAPTER XIX.

Chasm in the instructions furnished to the Admirals of the Western Powers.

EITHER from sheer want of forethought, or else in tenderness to the feelings of men who shunned the bare thought of a collision, the Governments of France and England had omitted to consider the plight in which they would stand if, under the eyes of their naval commanders, a Russian admiral should come out from Sebastopol and crush a Turkish squadron in the midst of the Black Sea. It is true that this was not the event which had occurred, for the onslaught of Sinope was 'an attack upon 'Turkish territory,' and was therefore within the scope of the instructions from home. But it is also true that the Governments of Paris and London had not committed, either to their Ambassadors or their Admirals, any power to take part in a naval engagement against Russia upon the open sea; and it was obvious that this chasm in the instructions furnished a ground of palliation to the Ambassadors and the naval commanders; for, after all the angry negotiations that had taken place between Russia and the Western powers, a French or an English Admiral might naturally be loth to go watching the movements of a fleet which, so long as it was upon the

[1] 'Eastern Papers,' part ii., p. 305.

open sea, he was not empowered to strike, and might be honorably reluctant to move out into the Euxine and run the risk of having to witness a naval engagement between the ships of the Czar and of the Sultan, without being at liberty to take part in it, unless it chanced to be fought within gunshot of the Turkish coast. But exactly in proportion as this excuse for the Ambassadors and Admirals was valid, it tended to bring blame upon the home Governments of France and England. The honest rage of the English people was about to break out, and there were materials for a rough criticism of men engaged in the service of the State. Some might blame the home Government, some the Ambassador, some the Admiral; but, plainly, it would fare ill with any man upon whom the public anger might light.

In proportion as this would palliate the inaction of the Admirals, it would tend to bring blame upon the home Government.

On the 11th of December, the tidings of Sinope reached Paris and London. The French Government felt the bitterness of a disaster 'endured, as it were, 'under the guns of the French and English fleets.'[1] In England, the indignation of the people ran to a height importing a resolve to have vengeance, and if it had been clearly understood that the disaster had resulted from a want of firm orders from home, the Government would have been overwhelmed. But the very weight and force of the public anger gave the Government a means of eluding it. The torrent had so great a volume that it was worthy to be turned against a foreign State. The blaming of Ministers, and Ambassadors, and Admirals, and the endless conflict which would be engendered by the apportionment of censure, all might be superseded by suggesting instead a demand for vengeance against Russia. The terms of Count Nesselrode's Circular of the 31st of October[2] had given ground for expecting that, until provoked to a contrary course, the Czar, notwithstanding the Turkish declaration of war, would remain upon the defensive; and the people in England were now taught, or allowed to suppose, that Russia had made this attack upon a Turkish squadron in breach of an honorable understanding virtually equivalent to a truce, or, at all events, to an arrangement which would confine the theatre of active war to the valley of the Lower Danube. This charge against Russia was unjust; for, after the issue of the Circular, the Government of St. Petersburg had received in-

Reception of the tidings of Sinope by the French Government and by the people in England.

The anger of the English people is diverted from official personages, and brought to bear on the Czar.

An unjust charge against the Czar gains

[1] M. Drouyn de Lhuys. 'Eastern Papers,' part ii., p. 299. [2] See *ante*.

full belief in England.

telligence not only that active warfare was going on in the valley of the Lower Danube, but that the Turks had seized the Russian fort of St. Nicholas, on the eastern coast of the Euxine, and were attacking Russia upon her Armenian frontier. After acts of this warlike sort had been done, it was impossible to say with any fairness that Russia was debarred from a right to destroy her enemy's ships; and it must be acknowledged also, as I have already said, that the destruction of the Turkish squadron at Sinope was not a thing done in stealth. But the people of England, not knowing all this at first, and hearing nothing of the Russian fleet until they heard of the ravage and slaughter of Sinope, imagined that the blow had come sudden as the knife of an assassin. They were too angry to be able to look upon the question in a spirit of cold justice. It was therefore an easy task to turn all attention from the faults of public functionaries and fasten it upon a larger scheme of vengeance. Ministers, Ambassadors, and Admirals went free, and, in a spirit of honest, inaccurate justice, the Emperor Nicholas was marked for sacrifice. This time, it was his fate to be condemned on wrong grounds; but his sins against Europe had been grievous, and the rough dispensations of the tribunal which people call 'opinion' have often enough determined that a man who has been guilty of one crime shall be made to suffer for another. There were few men in England who doubted that the onslaught of Sinope was a treacherous deed.

First decision of the English Cabinet in regard to Sinope.

When the Cabinet met to consult upon the questions raised by the tidings from Sinope, it came to the conclusion that the fleets of the Western Powers would forthwith enter the Euxine, and the majority were of opinion that the instructions addressed to the English Admiral on the 8th of October, re-enforced by a warning that such a disaster as Sinope must not be repeated, would be still a sufficing guide. But Lord Palmerston saw that, even if this resolution was suited to the condition of things on the shores of the Bosphorus, it would find no mercy at home. In truth, he was gifted with the instinct which enables a man to read the heart of a nation. He saw, he felt, he knew that the English people would never endure to hear of the disaster of Sinope, and yet be told that nothing was done. He resigned his office. The residuum of the Cabinet determined to leave the English Admiral under the guidance of his own instructions.

Lord Palmerston resigns office.

But on the 16th of December the Emperor of the French once more approached the Government of the Queen with his subtle

Proposal of the French Emperor.

and dangerous counsels. The armed conflict of States in these times is an evil of such dread proportions that it seems wise to uphold the solemnity of a transition from peace to war, and to avoid those contrivances which tend to throw down the great landmark; for experience shows that statesmen heartily resolved upon peace, may nevertheless be induced to concur in a series of gentle steps which slowly and gradually lead down to war. The negotiations for a settlement between Russia and Turkey had not only been revived, but were far from being at this time in an unpromising state; and it is probable that if Lord Aberdeen and Mr. Gladstone had been called upon to say whether they would observe peace faithfully, or frankly declare a war, they would scarcely have made the more violent choice. But the alternative was not presented to the minds of the Queen's Ministers in this plain and wholesome form.

Danger of breaking down the old barriers between peace and war.

The ingenious Emperor of the French devised a scheme of action so ambiguous in its nature that, at the option of any man who spoke about it, it might be called either peace or war, but so certain nevertheless in its tendency that the adoption of it by the maritime Powers would blot out all fair prospect of maintaining peace in Europe. He proposed to give Russia notice 'that France and 'England were resolved to prevent the repetition of the affair 'of Sinope, and that every Russian ship thenceforward met in 'the Euxine would be requested, and if necessary constrained, 'to return to Sebastopol, and that any act of aggression after-'ward attempted against the Ottoman territory or flag would 'be repelled by force.'[1] This proposal involved, without expressing it, a defensive alliance with Turkey against Russia, and, if it were adopted, the Emperor of Russia would have to see his flag driven from the waters which bounded his own dominions. It was so framed that Lord Palmerston would know it meant war, whilst Lord Aberdeen and Mr. Gladstone might be led to imagine that it was a measure rather gentle than otherwise, which perhaps would keep peace in the Euxine. Indeed the proposal seemed made to win the Chancellor of the Exchequer, for it fell short of war by a measure of distance which, though it might seem very small to people with common eyesight, was more than broad enough to afford commodious standing-room to a man delighting, as he did, in refinements and slender distinctions.

Ambiguous character of the proposal.

[1] 'Eastern Papers,' part ii., p. 307.

The Emperor of the French pressed this scheme upon the English Cabinet with his whole force. He not only urged it by means of the usual channels of diplomatic communication, but privately desired Lord Cowley 'to recommend it in the strongest terms to 'the favorable attention of Her Majesty's Government as a 'measure incumbent upon himself and them to take,' and he avowed 'the disappointment which he should feel if a differ-'ence of opinion prevented its adoption.'[1] This language is cogent. It is also significant; and to one who can read it by the light of a little collateral knowledge it may open a glimpse of the relations subsisting between the French Court and public men in England.

The French Emperor presses upon the English Cabinet.

On the 17th, the English Government had taken a step in pursuance of the decision to which the majority of the Cabinet had come; but on the following day they were made acquainted with the will of the French Emperor. It would seem that there was a struggle in the Cabinet, but by the 24th all resistance had broken down, and the first decision of the Government was overturned. The proposal of the French Emperor closed in like a net round the variegated group which composed Lord Aberdeen's Ministry, and gathered them all together in its supple folds. Some submitted to it for one reason, and some for another; but the pressure of the French Emperor was the cogent motive which governed the result. Still, this time, though the pressure was inflicted by the hand of a foreign sovereign, it was after all from the English people themselves that the French Emperor drew his strongest means of coercion. Their indignation at the disaster of Sinope made him sure that he could bring ruin on Lord Aberdeen's Administration, by merely causing England to know that her Government was shrinking from the hostile scheme of action which he had proposed.

Lord Aberdeen's Cabinet yields, and adopts, with a slight addition, the French Emperor's scheme.

The result however was that now, for the second time, France dictated to England the use that she should make of her fleet, and by this time perhaps submission had become more easy than it was at first. The Ministry, with much openness, acknowledged that they were acting without the warrant of their own judgment, and in deference to the will of the French Emperor. 'The Government,' said Lord Clarendon, 'having announced that the recurrence of a disaster such as 'that at Sinope must be prevented, and that the command of

[1] 'Eastern Papers,' part ii., p. 307.

'the Black Sea must be secured, would have been content to 'have left the manner of executing those instructions to the 'discretion of the Admirals; but they attach so much import'ance not alone to the united action of the two Governments, 'but to the instructions addressed to their respective agents 'being precisely the same, that they are prepared to adopt 'the specific mode of action now proposed by the Government 'of the Emperor.'[1] This being resolved, Lord Palmerston consented to return to office.[2] With the addition of a proviso that for the present the Sultan should be engaged to abstain from aggressive operations on the Euxine, instructions exactly in accord with the French Emperor's proposal were forthwith sent out to the Bosphorus, and at the same time the French and English representatives at St. Petersburg were ordered to communicate this resolution to Count Nesselrode.

Lord Palmerston withdraws his resignation.

Orders to execute the scheme and to announce it at St. Petersburg.

---

## CHAPTER XX.

AFTER much labor, the representatives of the four Powers at Constantinople had agreed upon a scheme of settlement, which they deemed likely to be acceptable to the Emperor Nicholas, and they pressed its adoption by the Porte. The warlike spirit of the Ottoman people had been rising day by day; and it became very hard and dangerous for the Government to venture upon entertaining a negotiation for peace; but Lord Stratford had power over the minds of Turkish Statesmen; and he exerted it with so great a force, that, although it was now impossible for them to obey him without having to face a religious insurrection, they obeyed him nevertheless. The fury of the armed divines, insisting upon the massacre of worldlings, was less terrible to them than the anger of the Eltchi. To his

Terms of settlement agreed to by the four Powers and forced upon the acceptance of the Turks by Lord Stratford.

[1] 'Eastern Papers,' part ii., p. 321.

[2] His secession during these ten or twelve days was afterward stated by him to have been based upon a question of home politics, but it would not of course follow from this statement that no other motives were governing him, and when it is remembered that his resignation was simultaneous with the first resolution of the Cabinet, and that his return to office coincided with the Cabinet's adoption of the French Emperor's scheme, it will hardly be questioned that the four events may be fairly enough placed in an order which suggests the relation of cause and effect.

will they bent. Not only the Turkish Cabinet, but even the Great Council of State, was brought to accept the terms proposed.[1] The difficulty, nay, the peril of life which had thus been encountered by the Turkish Ministry for the sake of making peace with Russia; the success achieved at Sinope; and some victories gained over the Turks on the Armenian frontier—all these were circumstances tending to assuage the mortification inflicted upon the Czar by the failure of Prince Mentschikoff's mission. Again, it had long been plain that the time was ill fitted for the promotion of any scheme of Russian ambition; and it was known that the English Ambassador had brought the Turks to the utmost verge of possible concession. Moreover, terms of arrangement, agreed to by the Turkish Government, were about to be pressed upon the Czar, with all the authority of the four great Powers. It might seem, therefore, that all things were conducing toward an amicable settlement. Nor was this hope at all shaken when the Government of St. Petersburg was made acquainted with the first and unbiased decision to which the English Government had come after hearing of the disasters of Sinope. Apprized by his private letters of the tenor of this decision, Sir Hamilton Seymour gathered or inferred that the Admirals of the Western Powers being enjoined to prevent the recurrence of an attack like the attack of Sinope, would assert the command of the Black Sea; and when he imparted to the Russian Government the impression thus produced on his mind, his communication was received in a wise and friendly spirit by Count Nesselrode; for after hearing that the Western Powers would be likely to assume the command of the Black Sea, the Count 'expressed his belief that the Russian fleet would, 'in consequence of the advanced season, be little 'likely to leave Sebastopol;' and he then went on to suggest that, if the Russians were to be hindered from attacking the Turks, it would be fair that the Turks should be restrained from molesting the coast of Russia. The rest of the conversation related to the pending negotiations; and, upon the whole, it was plain that the first decision of the English Cabinet was looked upon as the natural result of the engagement at Sinope, that it would certainly not lead to a rupture,[2] and that at length the Russian Government was in a fit temper to receive the proposals for peace which the four Powers (with the concurrence, this time, of Lord Stratford, and with the extorted assent

Grounds for expecting an amicable solution.

Friendly reception by the Russian Government of the news of the first decision of the English Cabinet.

[1] The terms were finally accepted on the 31st of December, 1853. 'Eastern Papers,' part ii., p. 362.
[2] Ibid., p. 359.

of the Turks) were now again bringing to St. Petersburg. But, whilst this fair prospect was opened by the unceasing toil of the negotiators, there were messengers then journeying from Paris and from London to the Court of St. Petersburg; and they carried an announcement that the Western Powers were resolved to execute the harsh and insulting scheme of action which had been forced upon the acceptance of Lord Aberdeen's Cabinet by the Emperor of the French. Of course it was not to be expected that the friendly spirit in which the Russian Government had received the first and unbiased decision of the English Cabinet would even for one moment survive an announcement of the scheme which only some ten days later our Government had been brought to adopt. It was one thing for the Western Powers to enforce the neutrality of the Black Sea; and another, and a very different thing, to announce to the sovereign of a haughty State, that, even though he might be bent on no warlike errand, still, upon the very sea which washed his coast—upon the very sea which filled his harbors—he was forbidden to show his flag.

Announcement at St. Petersburg of the scheme finally adopted by the Western Powers.

On the 12th of January, 1854, the Emperor Nicholas was forced to hear—to endure to hear—that, upon peril of an unequal conflict with the combined fleets of the Western Powers, every ship that he had in the Euxine must either be kept from going to sea, or else must sail by stealth, and be liable to be ignominiously driven back into port. The negotiation, which had seemed to be almost ripe for a settlement, was then ruined. The Emperor Nicholas did not declare war against the Western Powers; but, as soon as he received the hostile announcement in a form which he deemed to be official, he withdrew his representatives from Paris and London. The Governments of France and England followed his example; and on the 21st of February, 1854, the diplomatic relations between Russia and the Western Powers were brought to a close. Moreover, the Czar prepared to undertake an invasion of the Ottoman dominions.

The negotiations are ruined.

Rupture of diplomatic relations.

The Czar prepares to invade Turkey. Fleets enter the Euxine.

On the 4th of January, 1854, the fleets of England and France moved up and entered the Euxine.

Diagram indicating the nature of the straits in which the Czar placed himself by attempting to maintain a hostile occupation of the Danubian Principalities without the assent of Austria.

*The tapering of the lines which show the route of the Czar's intruding forces is intended to remind the reader of the hourly decreasing strength of an invader who operates at a vast distance from his main resources.*

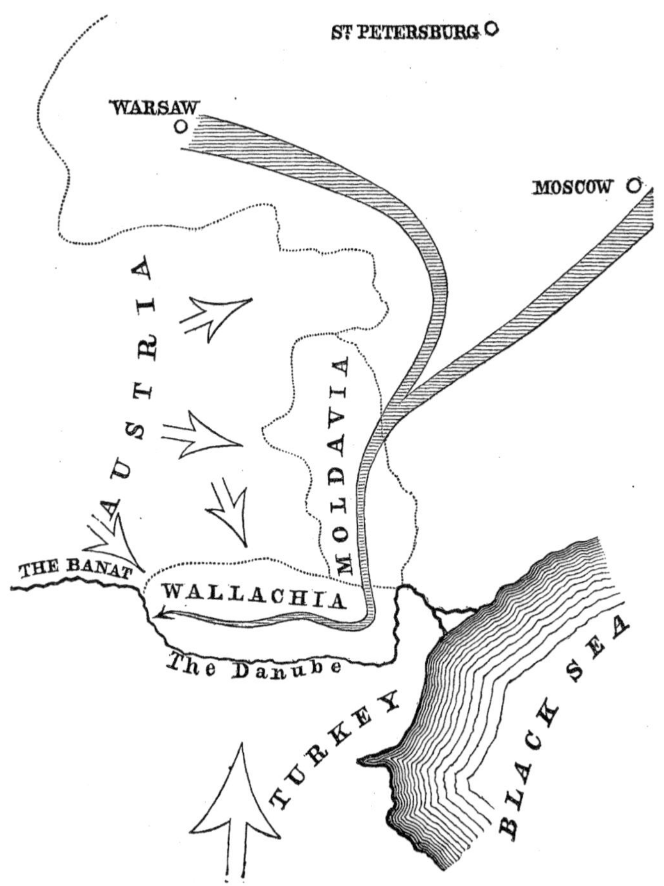

# CHAPTER XXI.

Military error of the Czar in occupying Wallachia.

IN a military point of view, and upon the supposition of there being no understanding between Russia and Austria, the seizure of the whole of Wallachia by a Russian army is a dangerous measure; for, after reaching Bucharest, the line of occupation has to bend at right angles, ascending the northern bank of the Danube between an enemy expectant and an enemy already declared, till at length it touches the frontier of the Banat at a distance from Moscow of not less than a thousand miles. To be in fitting strength at a point thus situate would imply the possession of resources beyond those which Russia could command.

Of this Omar Pasha takes skillful advantage.

The General at the head of the Turkish army was Omar Pasha; and it chanced that he was a man highly skilled in the art of bringing political views to bear upon the operations of an army in the field. He knew that, in protruding his forces into Lesser Wallachia, the Emperor Nicholas was committing a military fault; and he also inferred that political reasons and imperial vanity would make the Czar cling to his error. He also knew that, for the rest of that year, the Czar, being kept back by the engagements which he had taken, by his fear of breaking with the four Powers, and, above all, by the insufficiency of his means, would abstain from any farther invasion of Turkey, and would even be reluctant to alarm Europe by allowing the least glimpse of a Russian uniform to appear on the right bank of the Danube. Omar saw that the river had thus become a political barrier which protected the Turks from the Russians, without protecting the Russians from the Turks. He could therefore overstep the common rules of the art of war; and disporting himself as he chose on the line of the Danube, could concentrate forces on his extreme left, without any fear for his centre or his right.

His autumn and winter campaigns.

Therefore, in the early part of the autumn, a large portion of the Turkish army was quietly drawn to Widdin, a town on the right bank of the river, in the westernmost angle of Bulgaria; and, on the fifth day from the declaration of war, Omar Pasha was over the Danube, intrenching himself at Kalafat, and so established that he faced toward the east, and confronted the extreme flank of the intruding army.[1] From that moment Nicholas ceased to be the undisturbed holder of the territory which he had chosen to call his 'material guarantee.' His pride was touched. Tortured by the thought that his power to hold the pledge was challenged by a Turkish officer, he began to exhaust his strength in efforts to assemble a force at the westernmost point of his extended flank. This was the error which Omar Pasha wished him to commit. At the close of the year, the Czar had succeeded in pushing a heavy body of troops into Lesser Wallachia; and in the beginning of January the lines of Kalafat were attacked by General Aurep. The struggle lasted four days; but it ended in the retreat of the Russian forces; and, considering the vast distance between the lines of Kalafat and the home of the Russian army, it may be inferred that this fruitless effort of imperial pride must have worked a deep cavity in the military strength of the Czar.

Moreover, Omar Pasha took another, and a not less skillful advantage of the political considerations which prevented the Russians from passing the Danube; for, during the winter, he fleshed his troops by indulging them with enterprises against the enemy's posts along the whole line of the Lower Danube from Widdin to Rassova; and since these attacks were often attended with success, and could never be signally repressed by an enemy who had precluded himself from the right of crossing the river, they gave the Turks that sense of strength in fight which is at the root of warlike prowess.

Embarrassment and distress of the Czar.

Early in the winter the Emperor Nicholas came to understand the fault which he had committed in prescribing the Danube as a boundary—a boundary to be observed by himself, without the least right for expecting that it would be observed by his adversary. So now he would do the contrary of what he had done. Because he had committed a military fault in forbidding himself from all enterprises against the slowly-assembling forces of the Porte in 1853, he would now in 1854 undertake an invasion which must bring him into conflict with the gathered strength of the Ottoman Empire; and that, too, when it had become certain that the armed support of France and England would not be wanting to the Sultan. But perhaps, after all, it was hardly tolerable for a haughty monarch to have to stand passive, under the insulting coercion which was now to be applied to him by the Western Powers; and the Czar having no means of

[1] 28th October, 1853. The declaration of war became absolute on the 23rd.

hostile action against the territories or the ships of either France or England, could only strike at his greater foes by striking at the ally whom they had undertaken to befriend. Upon the whole, therefore, he could not so school himself as to be able to abstain from attempting an invasion of Turkey; but the wholesome trials which he had now undergone had so far disciplined his spirit that at length, after bitter anguish, he felt and acknowledged to himself the want of a firm adviser.

He resorts for aid to Paskievitch.

Russia owned a great General who had never sanctioned by his counsel the errors of the previous year; and now—baffled—agitated—driven hither and thither by alternating impulses till his brain had become a guide more blind than chance—the Czar abated his personal claims to the conduct of a war, and came for help and counsel to the veteran Paskievitch. The evil was almost beyond the old man's hope of cure; for how could Russia march upon Constantinople—nay, how, in strict prudence, could she march upon the Balkan whilst England and France were in full command of the Euxine? But was the Czar then simply powerless against Turkey? Had his million of soldiers been torn from their homes in vain? Had he not busied himself all his days in organizing armies, and reviewing drilled men, and grinding down his people into the mere fractional components of an army, until the very faces of soldiers in the same battalion were brought to be similar and uniform?—had his life been utter foolishness, and was the labor of his reign so barren that he could not now make a campaign against the simple Turks, who never took pains about any thing until the hour of battle? Had he not spoken in the councils of Europe as though he were a potentate so great that the Empire of the Ottomans existed by force of his magnanimity? And now—had it come to this—that at the mere bidding of the Western Powers, and without their firing a shot, he was to stand arrested in the presence of scoffing Europe like a prisoner who had delivered his sword?

Paskievitch's counsels.

Well, Paskievitch, in a painful, soldierly way, could tell him what would be the least imprudent plan for attacking the inner dominions of the Sultan. The principles of the art of war have a great stability; and although there is an infinite variety in the methods of applying them, it results, that the invasion of one nation by another is repeatedly undertaken upon the same accustomed route.

By the route which Paskievitch recommended, the invader crossed the Danube in the neighborhood of its great bend toward the north; makes himself master of Silistria; encounters and overcomes the assembled strength of the Ottoman Empire in front of the great intrenched camp of Shoumla; then advancing, forces the difficult passes of the Balkan as best he may; marches upon Adrianople; and thence on—thence on if he can and dares—to the shore of the Bosphorus. Erivanski[1] could hardly have believed that his master's military power was equal to so great an undertaking as that; but if it succeeded only in some of its early stages, diplomacy might come to the rescue of the Czar, as it had done in 1829; and the plan had this in its favor—that it placed a broad tract of country between Austria and the right flank of the invading army; and another, though less extended, territory between its left flank and the fleets of the Western Powers.

But, in the counsels of a wise and faithful soldier there is a pitiless candor—a dreadful precision. He comes in his hard way to weights, and to numbers, and to measurements of space and of time. Without mercy to the vanity of his suffering master, Paskievitch defaced the cherished form of the 'material guarantee' by insisting that the Czar should cease from trying to hold the Principalities entire, and that all his forces should be quickly withdrawn from the Lesser Wallachia. This done, he promised the Czar an invasion of the Ottoman Empire; but the carrying of the enterprise beyond the valley of the Danube was to be only upon condition that Silistria should fall, and should fall before the 1st of May.[2]

Movement of troops in the Russian empire.

So now, the streams of battalions rumored to be setting in upon the Lower Danube, from the confines of All the Russias, woke up the mind of Europe, and portended a great invasion.

---

## CHAPTER XXII.

Sir John Burgoyne and Colonel Ardent dispatched to the Levant.

It has been seen that without treaty, and without the advice or knowledge of Parliament—nay, even, perhaps, without a distinct conception of what it was doing —the English Government had been gradually contracting engagements which were almost equiva-

[1] This was Paskievitch's title. It denoted that he was the conqueror of Erivan, a province conquered from the Persians.

[2] My knowledge of the counsels tendered to the Emperor by Paskievitch is derived from papers in the possession of the late Lord Raglan.

lent to a defensive alliance with the Sultan. France, by virtue of her new understanding with England, had come under the same obligations; and now that an invasion of the Ottoman Empire was threatened, it became necessary that the Western Powers should take measures for its defense. At first, however, their views were limited to the defense of the Sultan's home territories, and especially those which gave the control of the Dardanelles and the Bosphorus. Two Engineer officers—Colonel Ardent on the part of France, and Sir John Burgoyne on the part of England—were dispatched to Turkey, with instructions to report upon the best means of aiding the Sultan to defend his home dominions; and, almost at the same time, it was agreed between the two Western Powers, that each of them should prepare to send a small body of troops into the Levant.

The English force was collected at Malta. Of the Ministers

Troops sent to Malta.

who joined in adopting this measure, some foresaw that the few battalions which they were dispatching to the East were the nucleus of an army which might have to operate in the field; but others looked upon them as a force

Tendency of this measure.

intended to support our negotiations. This ambiguity of motive was a root of evil; for the collateral arrangements which are requisite for enabling an army to live, to move, and to fight, bear a vast proportion to the mere business of collecting the men; and there is always a danger that a body of troops, sent toward the scene of action with a diplomatic intent, will be unsupported by the measures which are requisite for actual war, and yet, upon the rupture of the negotiations, will be prematurely hurried into the field. On the other hand, the councilors of a great military State are so well accustomed to know the cost and the labor which must precede the advance of an army, that the mere protrusion of a body of well-equipped troops, unsupported by the collateral appliances of war, does not tell upon their minds as a proof of an intention to act. By dispatching a few battalions to Malta, without instructing Commissaries to go to the Levant and begin buying up the agricultural wealth of the country, we not only subjected our troops to the danger of their being brought into the field before supplies were ready, but also convinced the Russians that we could not be sincerely intending to en-

Ministers determine to propose but a small increase of the army.

gage in a war. Moreover, the slenderness of the addition which the Government proposed to make to our army tended to prolong the Czar's fond confidence in the weight and strength of the English Peace party; and perhaps this dangerous error was strengthened if Baron Brunnow was able to tell him that in proposing to the Cabinet a material increase of our land forces the Duke of Newcastle stood almost alone.

Continuance of Lord Aberdeen's imprudent language.

The Prime Minister's continued persistency in the use of hurtful language was another of the causes which still helped to keep the Czar blindfold. Lord Aberdeen abhorred the bare thought of war; and he would not have suffered his country to be overtaken by it, if the coming danger had been of such a kind that it could be warded off by hating it and shunning its aspect. But it is not by intemperate hatred of war, nor yet by shunning its aspect, that war is averted. Almost to the last, Lord Aberdeen misguided himself. His loathing of war took such a shape, that he could not and would not believe in it; and when at last the spectre was close upon him, he covered his eyes and refused to see. Basing himself upon the thoughtless saying of a statesman, who had laid it down that there could be no war in Europe when France and England were agreed, he seems to have imagined that although he was suffering himself to be drawn on and on into measures which were always becoming less and less short of war, still he could maintain peace by taking care to be always along with the French Emperor; and he so clung to the paradise created by a false maxim, that he could not be torn from it. He would not be roused from a dream which was sweeter than all waking thoughts; and even now, to any man to whom he chanced to speak, he continued to say that there could not, there would not be war. Coming from a Prime Minister, such words as these did not fail to have a noxious weight with many who heard them. Baron Brunnow, we have seen, had looked deeper even at a much earlier period, and now again no doubt he took care to warn his master that Lord Aberdeen was under a passionate hatred of war which deprived him of his competence to speak in the name of his country; but by other channels the words of our Prime Minister were carried to the Emperor of Russia, and, being very welcome to him, and coinciding with his long cherished notions, they tended to keep him in the perilous belief that Lord Aberdeen was speaking with knowledge, and that England, still clogged by her Peace Party, was unable to go to war.

# CHAPTER XXIII.

The French Emperor's letter to the Czar.

A NEW opportunity of making his way back to peace was now thrown away by the Czar. The exigencies of a throne based upon the deeds of the 2nd of December were always driving the French Emperor to endeavor to allay the remembrance of the past by creating a stir in Europe and endeavoring to win celebrity. When Europe was quiet, he was obliged for his life's sake to become its disturber; but when it was at war or threatened with war, he was willing, it seems, to take an exactly opposite method of attaining the required conspicuousness, for he was not a bloodthirsty nor even a very active-minded man; and there seems no good reason to doubt that, having brought Europe to the state in which it was at the close of January, he was sincere in the pacific step which he then took. At a moment when war was already kindled and seemed to be on the point of involving the great Powers, the odd vanity and the theatric bent which had so strangely governed his life, might easily make him wish to come upon the scene and bestow the blessing of peace upon the grateful, astonished nations. On the other hand, an English Minister would be careless of this kind of celebrity, and, so that peace could be restored to Europe, would be well pleased that the honor of the achievement should seem to belong to the French Emperor.

There is no reason to doubt that the English Government assented to the somewhat startling plan under which the French Emperor conceived himself entitled to speak for the Queen of England as well as for himself, and certainly the license, however strange it may appear, was in strict consistency with the spirit of the understanding which seems to have been established between the two Western Powers.[1]

On the 29th of January the French Emperor addressed an autograph letter to his 'good friend' of All the Russias. The letter in many parts of it was ably worded and moderate in its tone, but it was mainly remarkable for the language in which the French Emperor took upon himself to speak, and even to threaten war in the name of the Queen of England. After

[1] See the inferred purport of this understanding as stated *ante*, p. 216.

suggesting a scheme of pacification, he said to the Czar: 'Let 'your Majesty adopt this plan, upon which the Queen of England and myself are perfectly agreed, and tranquillity will be 're-established and the world satisfied. There is nothing in 'the plan which is unworthy of your Majesty—nothing which 'can wound your honor; but if, from a motive difficult to understand, your Majesty should refuse this proposal, then 'France as well as England will be compelled to leave to the 'fate of arms and the chances of war that which might now be 'decided by reason and justice.'[1] The French Emperor permitted himself to write this at a time when, so far as is known, no threat like that which he chose to utter in the name of the Queen had been addressed by the English Cabinet to the Court of St. Petersburg.

With the feelings which might be expected from them, English Ministers of State have generally been slow to use threatening words, and they have been chary, too, in putting forward the name of their Sovereign. Our Government could not have been willing that England should be thrust upon the attention of the world in a way which the too fastidious Court of St. Petersburg would be sure to regard as grotesque. No one can doubt the pain with which the members of Lord Aberdeen's Cabinet must have seen the French Emperor come forward upon the stage of Europe, and publicly menace the Emperor of Russia in the name of their Queen. The process by which they were brought to suffer this is unknown to me. What seems probable is that a draft of the letter was submitted to them, accompanied with significant representations of the importance which the French Emperor attached to it, and that the Cabinet yielded to the pressure because it feared that resistance might chill the new alliance, and might even perhaps cause it to be suddenly abandoned for an alliance between Russia and France.

The letter proposed an armistice in order to leave open a free course for negotiation. It would seem that in a military point of view, an armistice for a limited period, commencing in the early days of February, could not have been inconvenient to a Sovereign whose main difficulty at that time lay in the immense marches which he had to effect within his own dominions; and, on the other hand, to any one acquainted with the French Emperor's personal weakness, it was obvious that, by a little harmless play upon his vanity, Russia might hope to obtain a great diplomatic advantage, and to effect a decorous

[1] 'Annual Register,' 1854.

escape from her troubles. But the Czar was not politic, and, instead of seizing the proffered occasion, he not only rejected the overture, but aggravated his refusal by an unwise allusion to the French disasters of 1812.

Mission to St. Petersburg from the English Peace Party.

In his quest after this sort of fame the French Emperor was not without rivals. We have seen the share which the English Peace Party had had in misleading the Emperor of Russia, and tempting him to become a disturber by withdrawing the wholesome fear which deters a man from venturing upon outrage. Certain brethren of the Society of Friends, who had been prominent members of this Party, now thought it becoming or wise to proceed to St. Petersburg and request the Emperor of All the Russias to concur with them in preserving Europe from the calamity of war.

A little later, and the Czar would have stamped in fury and driven from his sight any hapless aid-de-camp who had come to him with a story about a deputation from the English Peace Party, for the hour was at hand when his curses were about to fall heavy on the men who had led him on into all his troubles by pretending that England was immersed in trade and resolved to engage in no war.[1] But at this time his hope of seeing our Government held back by the Peace Party had not altogether vanished, and he resolved to give this strange mission a genial welcome.

Of course the political conversation between the booted Czar and the men of peace was sheer nothingness; but what followed shows the care with which Nicholas had studied the middle classes of England. When he thought that the first scene of the interlude had lasted long enough, he suddenly said to his prim visitors, 'By-the-by, do you know my wife?' They said they did not. The Czar presented them to the Empress. She charmed them with her kindly grace. They came away sorrowing to think that their wrong-headed countrymen in England should be seeking a quarrel with so good and well-meaning a man as friend Nicholas Romanoff, but perhaps what more than all else laid hold of their hearts was the thought that the Czar called his Empress so naturally by her dear homely title of wife.

[1] The scene of violence here prospectively alluded to will be mentioned hereafter. It occurred in the autumn.

## CHAPTER XXIV.

Temper of the English an obstacle to the maintenance of peace.

WELCOME or unwelcome, the truth must be told. A huge obstacle to the maintenance of peace in Europe was raised up by the temper of the English people. In public, men still used forms of expression implying that they would be content for England to lead a quiet life among the nations, and they still classed expectations of peace amongst their hopes, and declared in joyous tones that the prospects of war were gloomy and painful; but these phrases were the time-honored canticles of a doctrine already discarded, and they who used them did not mean to deceive their neighbors, and did not deceive themselves. The English desired war; and perhaps it ought to be acknowledged that there were many to whom war, for the sake of war, was no longer a hateful thought. Either the people had changed, or else there was hollowness in some of the professions which orators had made in their name.

Their desire for war.

Causes of the apparent change in their feeling.

When by lapse of years the glory of the great war against France had begun to fade from the daily thoughts of the people, they inclined to look more narrowly than before into the origin of taxes, and were not unwilling to hear that their burdens were the result of wars which might have been easily avoided. Moreover it chanced that from after Marlborough's time downward, or at all events from after the period of Chatham's ascendency, the wars in which England found herself engaged had been originated and conducted for the most part under the auspices of the Tory party, and it followed naturally that the Whig or Liberal party, being in antagonism to the party which had long kept the country under arms, should charge itself with the duty of expressing a just hatred of all wars which are needless or unjust. If speakers in the performance of this duty often used extravagant or fanatical language, they did not perhaps mean to inculcate much doctrine, but rather to display the vehemence of their hostility to the opposite faction. The applause which greeted these denunciations had the same meaning. On the other hand, the Tories declared that they did not yield to their adversaries in hatred of all needless wars; and thus for near forty years there was a chorus and an anti-chorus engaged in a continual chant, and denouncing wars in the abstract at times when no war seemed impending. To men skimming the surface of English politics it was made to appear that the people had a rooted love of peace.

These signs of a peaceful determination had increased in abundance after the great constitutional change which obliged the ruling classes to share their power with the people at large; and thence it was inferred that the desire of England to remain at peace was not the mere whim of any administration or of any political party, but was based upon the solemn determination of the whole people; and it has been seen that the Emperor Nicholas had deliberately founded his policy upon this belief. A deeper knowledge might have taught him that a fiery generous people is more quick to plunge into war than a cold, worldly, politic oligarchy, and that even if the policy of England were as much under the control of the masses of the people as he believed it to be, there would be all the more likelihood of her being prone to take up arms, because in states which are much under the governance of the democratic principle a proposal to make war against the foreigner is often resorted to by one of the contending factions as a stratagem for baffling the others. But these truths lay below, and what appeared upon the surface of English politics was a sincere devotion to the cause of peace. Over and over again it was laid down with the seeming concurrence of unanimous thousands, that war, if it were not for mere defense, was not only foolish, but was also in a high degree wicked.

But the English can hardly ever be governed by a dogma; for although they are by nature wise in action, yet, being vehement and careless in their way of applauding loud words, they encourage their orators and those also who address them in writing to be strenuous rather than wise; and the result is that these teachers, trying always to be more and more forcible, grow blind to logical dangers, and leap with headlong joy into the pit which reasoners call the Absurdum. Then, and not without joyous laughter, reaction begins.

All England had been brought to the opinion that it was a wickedness to incur war without necessity or justice; but when the leading spirits of the Peace Party had the happiness of beholding this wholesome result, they were far from stopping short. They went on to make light of the very principles by which peace is best maintained; and although they were conscientious men, meaning to say and do what was right, yet, being unacquainted with the causes which bring about the fall of empires, they deliberately inculcated that habit of setting comfort against honor, which historians call 'corruption.' They made it plain, as they imagined, that no war which was not engaged in for the actual defense of the country could ever be right; but even there they took no rest, for they went on and on, and still on, until their foremost thinker reached the conclusion that, in the event of an attack upon our shores, the invaders ought to be received with such an effusion of hospitality and brotherly love as could not fail to disarm them of their enmity, and convert the once dangerous Zouave into the valued friend of the family.[1] Then, with great merriment, the whole English people turned round, and, although they might still be willing to go to the brink of other precipices, they refused to go farther toward that one. The doctrine had struck no root. It was ill suited to the race to whom it was addressed. The male cheered it, and forgot it until there came a time for testing it, and then discarded it; and the woman, from the very first, with her true and simple instinct, was quick to understand its value. She would subscribe, if her husband required it, to have the doctrine taught to charity children, but she would not suffer it to be taught to her own boy. So it proved barren. In truth, the English knew that they were a great and a free people, because their fathers, and their fathers' fathers, and all the great ancestry of whom they come, had been men of warlike quality; and deeming it time to gainsay the teaching of the Peace Party, but not being skilled in dialectics and the use of words, they unconsciously came to think that it would be well to express a practical opinion of the doctrine by taking the first honest and fair opportunity of engaging in war. Still, the conscience of the nation was sound, and men were as well convinced as ever of the wickedness of a war wrongly or wantonly incurred. They were in this mind: they would not go to war without believing that they had a good and a just cause, but it was certain that tidings importing the necessity of going to war for duty's sake would be received with a welcome in England.

State of feeling in the Spring of 1853.

Therefore, when the people gradually came to hear of the fierce oppression attempted by Prince Mentschikoff, and the wise, firm, moderate resistance of the Turks, they believed that there might be coming in

Effect of the Czar's aggression upon the public mind.

[1] I have no copy of this curious pamphlet before me, but it has been quoted (I believe by Lord Palmerston) in the House of Commons, and therefore the passage alluded to in the text might no doubt be found in Hansard. The writer, I remember, went farther than is above stated. He argued that the French people would be so shamed by the kindness shown to their troops that they would never rest until they had paid us a large pecuniary indemnity for any losses or inconvenience which the invasion may have caused.

sight once more that very thing for which they longed in their hearts—namely, a just cause of war. And when at length the seemingly unequal conflict began, the bravery of the Turks on the Danube and the skill of their General quickly roused that sympathy which England hardly ever refuses to a valiant combatant who is weaker than his foe; but when they came to know of the catastrophe of Sinope, and to hear of it as a slaughter treacherously and stealthily committed upon their old ally by an enemy who had engaged to observe neutrality in the Euxine,[1] they were inflamed with a desire to execute justice, and nothing was now wanting to fill the measure of their righteous anger except a disclosure of the Czar's cold scheme for the spoliation of the 'sick man's' house.

Still, in foreign affairs, the nation looks for guidance to public men.

But after all, and especially in questions of foreign policy, the bulk of a nation must lean for guidance upon public men; and unless it appear that there were Statesmen deserving the ear of the country who faithfully tried to make a stand against error and failed for want of public support, it is unfair to charge the fault upon the people.

There were two Statesmen high in office, and high in the confidence of the nation, who, more than most other men, were known to be attached to the cause of peace. To them every man looked who desired that his country should not be drawn into war without stringent need.

The impression produced upon the Court of St. Petersburg by the heedless language of our Prime Minister has been already described; but the effect which he wrought upon the public mind of England by remaining at the head of the Government is still to be shown.

Lord Aberdeen.

Lord Aberdeen's hatred of war was so honestly and piously entertained, and was, at the same time, so excessive and self-defeating, that in one point of view it had the character of a virtue, and in another it was more like disease. His feelings, no less than his opinions, turned him against all war; but against a war with Russia he was biased by the impressions of his early life, by the relation of mutual esteem which had long existed between the Emperor Nicholas and himself; and perhaps by a dim foresight of the perils which might be brought upon Europe by a forcible breaking up of the ties established by the Congress of Vienna and riveted by the Peace of Paris. In an early stage of the dispute, he resolved that he would not remain at the head of the Government unless he could maintain peace;

[1] The erroneousness of this impression has been already shown. See *ante*.

and he anxiously sought to choose a moment for making his stand against the farther progress toward war. Far from wishing to prolong his hold of power, he was always laboring to make out when, and on what ground, he could lay down the burden which oppressed him. Every day he passed his sure hour and a half in the Foreign Office, and came away more and more anxious perhaps, but without growing more clear-sighted. If he could ever have found the point where the road to peace diverged from the road to war, he would instantly have declared for peace; and, failing to carry the Government with him, would have joyfully resigned office, and for his deliverance would have offered up thanksgiving to Heaven. But his intellect, though not without high quality in it, was deficient in clearness and force. In troubled times it did not yield him light enough to walk by, and it had not the propelling power which was needed for pushing him into opportune action. In politics, though not in matters of faith, he wanted the sacred impulse which his Kirk is accustomed to call 'the word of 'quickening.' Lord Clarendon's polished dispatches so forced his approval, that he could never lay his hand upon one of them, and make it the subject of a ministerial crisis. Yet, day by day, without knowing it, the Prime Minister was assenting to a course of policy destined to end in a rupture. Lord Clarendon's pithy phrase was less applicable to the country at large than to the Prime Minister. It was strictly true that Lord Aberdeen drifted. He steadfastly faced toward peace, and was always being carried toward war. He remained at the head of the Government; and, the papers being withheld from Parliament, the country was led to imagine that all which it was possible to do or suffer for the sake of peace would be done and suffered by a Cabinet of which Lord Aberdeen was the chief.

Mr. Gladstone.

But there was another member of the Cabinet who was supposed to hold war in deep abhorrence. Mr. Gladstone was Chancellor of the Exchequer, and, since he was by virtue of his office the appointed guardian of the public purse, those pure and lofty principles which made him cling to peace were re-enforced by an official sense of the harm which war inflicts by its costliness. Now it happened that, if he was famous for the splendor of his eloquence, for his unaffected piety, and for his blameless life, he was celebrated far and wide for a more than common liveliness of conscience. He had once imagined it to be his duty to quit a Government, and to burst through strong ties of friendship and gratitude, by reason of a thin shade of difference on the subject of white or brown sugar. It was believed that, if he were to commit even a little sin, or to imagine an evil thought, he would instantly arraign himself before the dread tribunal which awaited him in his own bosom; and that, his intellect being subtle and microscopic, and delighting in casuistry and exaggeration, he would be likely to give his soul a very harsh trial, and treat himself as a great criminal for faults too minute to be visible to the naked eyes of laymen. His friends lived in dread of his virtues as tending to make him whimsical and unstable, and the practical politicians, conceiving that he was not to be depended upon for party purposes, and was bent upon none but lofty objects, used to look upon him as dangerous — used to call him behind his back a good man — a good man in the worst sense of the term. In 1853, it seemed only too probable that he might quit office upon an infinitely slight suspicion of the warlike tendency of the Government; but what appeared certain was, that if, upon the vital question of peace or war, the Government should depart by even a hair's breadth from the right path, the Chancellor of the Exchequer would instantly refuse to be a partaker of their fault. He, and he before all other men, stood charged to give the alarm of danger; and there seemed to be no particle of ground for fearing that, like the Prime Minister, he would drift. The known watchfulness and alacrity of his conscience, and his power of detecting small germs of evil, led the world to think it impossible that he could be moving for months together in a wrong course without knowing it.

Lord Aberdeen and Mr. Gladstone remained in office.

Now, from the beginning of the negotiations until the final rupture, Lord Aberdeen continued to be the Prime Minister, and Mr. Gladstone the Chancellor of the Exchequer. The result was, that, during the session of 1853, and the autumn which followed it, the presence of these two Ministers in the Cabinet was regarded as a guarantee of the peaceful tendency of the Government; and when, after the catastrophe of Sinope, it became hardly possible to doubt that war was at hand, the continuing responsibility of these good men seemed to dispense the most anxious lovers of peace from the duty of farther questioning; for if Lord Aberdeen continued to head the Ministry which was leading the country into war, people thought he must have attained the bitter certainty that war was needed; and, on the other hand, it was clear that Mr. Gladstone remaining in office, and taking it upon his conscience to prepare funds for the bloody strife, was giving to the public a sure guarantee that the enterprise in which he helped to

Effect of this in paralyzing the efforts of those who wished to prevent a war.

engage the country was blameless at the very least, and even perhaps pure and holy. It was thus that the conscience of the people got quieted. It was a hard task to have to argue that peace could be honestly and wisely maintained when Lord Aberdeen was levying war. None but a bold man could say that the war was needless or wicked whilst Mr. Gladstone was feeding it with his own hand.

It was thus that, by the course which Lord Aberdeen and Mr. Gladstone had been taking, the efforts of those who loved peace were paralyzed. No doubt a cold retrospect, carried on with the light of the past, may enable a political critic to fix upon more than one occasion when, holding the opinions which they did, these two Ministers might have resolved to make a stand for peace; and it is believed that long before his death Lord Aberdeen saw this and grieved; but if any man will honestly recall the state of his own feelings and opinions in the year 1853, he will find perhaps that he himself at the time was carried down by the flood of events; and, when he has submitted to this self-discipline, he will be better able to understand that others, though honest and able, might easily lose their footing. At all events, the errors of Lord Aberdeen and Mr. Gladstone, if errors they were, were only errors of judgment. The scrupulous purity of their motives has never been brought into question.

The ruin of their cause was not for want of ample grounds to stand upon.

But, if these were the causes which inclined the bulk of the English people to desire or to assent to the war, they hardly yield reasons sufficing to show why the lesser number of men, who honestly thought that peace ought to be maintained, should suffer themselves to be overpowered, without making stand enough to prove that they clung to their old faith, and that England, however warlike, was, at all events, not of one mind. The hottest defenders of the war policy could hardly refuse to acknowledge that there was much semblance of reason on the side of their adversaries. No one could say that the interest which England had in the perfect independence of the Ottoman Empire was so obvious and so deep as to exclude all questioning; and, even if a man were driven from that first ground, still, without being guilty of paradox, he might fairly dispute and say that the independence of the Sultan was not really brought into peril by a form of words which, during some weeks, had received the approval of every one of the five great Powers.

But, if these views were only plausible, there was another which was sound. It could be fairly maintained that the intrusion of Russia into two provinces, lying far away on the southeastern frontiers of Austria, was no cause why England alone, nor why England and France together, should undertake to stand forward and perform, at their own charge and cost, a duty which attached upon Austria in the first place, and next upon Europe at large.

Not for want of oratorical power.

Of course the actual and immediate success of any such struggle for the maintenance of peace was grievously embarrassed, in the way already shown, by the course which had been taken by Lord Aberdeen and Mr. Gladstone; but it is not the custom of the English to be utterly disheartened by political losses; and it happened that outside the Government Offices the cause of peace was headed by two men who had been powerful in their time, and who retained the qualities of mind and body by which, in former years, they had gained a great sway.

Mr. Cobden and Mr. Bright.

Mr. Cobden and Mr. Bright were members of the House of Commons. Both had the gift of a manly strenuous eloquence, and their diction, being founded upon English lore rather than upon shreds of weak Latin, went straight to the mind of their hearers. Of these men the one could persuade, the other could attack; and, indeed, Mr. Bright's oratory was singularly well qualified for preventing an erroneous acquiescence in the policy of the day; for, besides that he was honest and fearless, besides that with a ringing voice he had all the clearness and force which resulted from his great natural gifts, as well as from his one-sided method of thinking, he had the advantage of being generally able to speak in a state of sincere anger. In former years, whilst their minds were disciplined by the almost mathematical exactness of the reasonings on which they relied, and when they were acting in concert with the shrewd traders of the north who had a very plain object in view, these two orators had shown with what a strength, with what a masterly skill, with what patience, with what a high courage they could carry a great scientific truth through the storms of politics. They had shown that they could arouse and govern the assenting thousands who listened to them with delight—that they could bend the House of Commons—that they could press their creed upon a Prime Minister, and put upon his mind so hard a stress that after a while he felt it to be a torture and a violence to his reason to have to make stand against them. Nay, more. Each of these two gifted men had proved that he could go bravely into the midst of angry opponents, could show them their fallacies one by one, destroy their favorite theories before their very faces, and triumphantly argue them down. Now these two men were honestly devoted to the cause of peace. They honestly believed that the impending war with Russia was a needless war. There was no stain upon their names. How came it that they sank and were able to make no good stand for the cause they loved so well?

The answer is simple.

Reasons why they were able to make no stand.

Upon the question of peace or war (the very question upon which more than any other a man might well desire to make his counsels tell) these two gifted men had forfeited their hold upon the ear of the country. They had forfeited it by their former want of moderation. It was not by any intemperate words upon the question of this war with Russia that they had shut themselves out from the counsels of the nation; but in former years they had adopted and put forward in their strenuous way some of the more extravagant doctrines of the Peace Party. In times when no war was in question, they had run down the practice of war in terms so broad and indiscriminate that they were understood to commit themselves to a disapproval of all wars not strictly defensive, and to decline to treat as defensive those wars which, although not waged against an actual invader of the Queen's dominions, might still be undertaken by England in the performance of a European duty, or for the purpose of checking the undue ascendency of another Power. Of course the knowledge that they held doctrines of this wide sort disqualified them from arguing with any effect against the war then pending. A man can not have weight as an opponent of any particular war if he is one who is known to be against almost all war. It is vain for him to offer to be moderate for the nonce, and to propose to argue the question in a way which his hearers will recognize. In vain he declares that for the sake of argument he will lay aside his own broad principles and mimic the reasoning of his hearers. Practical men know that his mind is under the sway of an antecedent determination which dispenses him from the more narrow but more important inquiry in which they are engaged. They will not give ear to one who is striving to lay down the conclusions which ought, as he says, to follow from other men's principles. He who altogether abjures the juice of the grape can not usefully criticize the vintage of any particular year; and a man who is the steady adversary of wars in general upon broad and paramount grounds, will never be regarded as a sound judge of the question whether any particular war is wicked or righteous, nor whether it is foolish or wise.

It must be added that there was another cause which tended to disqualify Mr. Bright from taking an effective part in the maintenance of peace. For one who would undertake a task of that kind at a time when warlike ardor is prevailing in the country, it is above all things necessary that he should be a statesman so truly attached to what men mean when they talk of their country, and so jealous of its honor, that no man could ascribe his efforts in the cause of peace to motives which a warlike and high-spirited people would repudiate. Mr. Bright sincerely desired the welfare of the traders and workmen in the United Kingdom; and if he desired the welfare of the other classes with less intensity, it may fairly be believed that to all he wished to see justice done; so, if this worthy disposition of mind were equivalent to what a man calls his "love of his country," no one could fairly say that Mr. Bright was without the passion. But, in another, and certainly the old and the usual sense, a man's love "of his country" is understood to represent something more than common benevolence toward the persons living within it. For if he be the citizen of an ancient State blessed with freedom, renowned in arms, and holding wide sway in the world, his love of his country means something of attachment to the institutions which have made her what she is, means something of pride in the long suffering, and the battle, and the strife which have shed glory upon his countrymen in his own time, and upon their fathers in the time before him. It means that he feels his country's honor to be a main term and element of his own content. It means that he is bent upon the upholding of her dominion, and is so tempered as to become the sudden enemy of any man who, even though he be not an invader, still attempts to hack at her power. Now in this, the heathen but accustomed sense of the phrase, Mr. Bright would be the last to say that he was a lover of his country. He would rather, perhaps, acknowledge that, taking 'his country' in that sense, he hated it. Yet at a time when the spirit of the nation was up, no man could usefully strive to moderate or guide it unless his patriotism were believed to be exactly of that heathen sort which Mr. Bright disapproved. Thus by the nature of his patriotism, no less than by the immoderate width of his views on the lawfulness of wars, this powerful orator was so disabled as to be hindered from applying his strength toward the maintenance of peace.

The country was impassioned, but it was not so mad as to be deaf to precious counsels; and a statesman who had shown by his past life that he loved his country in the ancient way, and that he knew how to contemplate the eventuality of war with a calm and equal mind, might have won attention for views which questioned the necessity of the war then threatened; and if in good time he had brought to bear upon his opinions a sufficing power and knowledge, he might have altered the policy of his country.[1] But outside the Cabinet the real tenor of the negotiations of 1853 was still unknown, and, Lord Aberdeen and Mr. Gladstone consenting to remain members of a war-going Government, and Mr. Cobden and Mr. Bright being disqualified for useful debate by the nature of their opinions, no stand could be made.

By these steps, then, the English people passed from a seeming approval of the doctrines of the Peace Party to a state of warlike ardor; and it was plain that, if the Queen should send down to the Houses of Parliament a message importing war, the Royal appeal would be joyfully answered by an almost unanimous people.

---

## CHAPTER XXV.

WHEN the English Parliament assembled on the 31st of January, there was still going on in Europe a semblance of negotiation; but amongst men accustomed to the aspect of public affairs, there was hardly more than one who failed to see that France and England had gone too far to be able to recede, and that by the very weight of their power and its inherent duties, they were now at last drawn into war.

*Meeting of Parliament.*

This condition of things was fairly enough disclosed by the Queen's Speech, and Parliament was asked to provide for an increase of the military and naval forces with a view to give weight to the negotiations still pending. But the English Government was not suffered to forget its bond with the French Emperor, and the Prime Minister, whilst still indulging a hope of peace, consented to record and continue the error which had brought him to the verge of war. It

*The Queen's Speech.*

[1] This was in print before that curious and interesting confirmation of my statement—my statement of the relations between the Peace Party and their country—which Mr. Cobden has since given to the world. Mr. Cobden has said that at the time of the war, neither he nor Mr. Bright could win any attention to their views, and he added that he (Mr. Cobden) will never again try to withstand a warlike ardor once kindled, because, when a people are inflamed in that way, they are no better than 'mad dogs.'—*Speech in the autumn of 1862.* He sees no defect in the principles of a Peace Party which is to suspend its operations in times of warlike excitement.

seems that for good reasons it was of some moment to the French Emperor to be signally named in the Queen's Speech, and Lord Aberdeen again submitted to a form of words which carefully distinguished the posture of France and England from that of the four Powers. The Queen was advised to say: 'I 'have continued to act in cordial co-operation with the Em'peror of the French, and my endeavors in conjunction with 'my Allies to preserve and to restore peace between the con'tending parties, although hitherto unsuccessful, have been un'remitting.'

The policy which it indicated.

Like the similar paragraph which had marked the Royal Speech at the close of the preceding session, this phrase, strange as it was, gave a true though somewhat dim glimpse of the policy which was leading England astray. In principle, she was marching along with all the rest of the four Powers; and yet, all the while, she was engaged with the French Emperor in a separate course of action. If the aims of Austria and Prussia had been seriously at variance with those of the Western Powers, this difference might have been a good reason for separate action on the part of France and England. But the contrary was true. So deep was the interest of Austria in the cause, and so closely were her views approved by Prussia, that, although for several months France and England had been pressing forward in a way which seemed to endanger the coherence of the quadruple union, still even this dangerous course had hitherto failed to destroy the unanimity of the four Powers. If the French Emperor sought to use his alliance with England as a means of strengthening his hold over France, and if England was beginning to love the thought of war for war's sake, Austria, from motives of a higher and more cogent sort (for she saw her interests vitally touched, and her safety threatened) was eager and determined to take such steps as might be needed for delivering the Principalities. Prussia agreed with her. It was nothing but the impatience and forwardness of France and England which relieved Austria from the necessity of taking the lead; for the wrong which had to be redressed was one from which she, of all the great Powers, was the most a sufferer, and she had the concurrence of Prussia, not only in regard to the existing state of things, but even as to the ulterior objects of the war which her resolve might bring upon Germany.

The separate understanding with France not justified by any difference of opinion between England and the German Powers.

Unswerving resolve of Austria (and Prussia supports her) to rid the Principalities of Russian troops.

The proofs of all this abound. By the repeated words of

Proofs of this drawn from transactions anterior to the Queen's Speech.

responsible statesmen, by dispatches, by collective notes, by protocols, by solemn treaty of offensive and defensive alliance against Russia, by peremptory summons addressed to the Czar, and, finally (so far as concerns Austria), by the application of force, the German Powers disclosed and executed their policy; and the policy which they disclosed and executed was the same policy as had been avowed by the Western Powers. It has been seen that in that early period of the troubles, when the Czar was but beginning to cross the Pruth, Austria took upon herself to endeavor to form a league for forcing the Czar to relinquish the Principalities; and, from that hour down to the time when Nicholas gave way and re-entered his own dominions, her efforts to bring about this end were unceasing and restless.

Of the spirit in which Austria was acting through all the early stages of the negotiations, many a proof has been already given. With time, her impatience of the Czar's intrusion upon her southern frontier increased and increased. It is true that she did not desire war. She anxiously wished to avoid it. She wished, if it were possible, to achieve the end without war, but to achieve it she was resolved; and, if a vestige of the mediating character which had belonged to her in the summer of 1853, or her legitimate anxiety to spare the Czar's personal feelings, was a motive which tended to soften her language, it did not deflect her policy. Count Buol declared that, although in treating with Russia, 'more management of terms'[1] was required from Austria than from the Western Powers, the objects sought by all the four Powers were the same, and that they ought to be compassed by 'a general concordance in the 'way of putting them forward.'[2] But even the notion of using a gentler form of expression than the one employed by the Western Powers was quickly abandoned, and Austria found no difficulty in adopting the exact words of the collective Note framed by Lord Clarendon in concert with the French Government. So anxious was Austria to remain on the same ground with the rest of the four Powers, that she came into every term of the firm and wise scheme of action laid down by Lord Clarendon on the 16th of November,[3] and bitterly offended the Czar by agreeing, at Lord Clarendon's instance, that the Porte should not be even asked to accept any condition which it had already rejected, and by affirming the determination of the four Powers to intervene in any settlement of the dispute between Russia and Turkey.

[1] 'Eastern Papers,' part vii., p. 231. [2] Ibid., p. 278. [3] Ibid., pp. 238, 258.

Prussia also gave her unreserved adhesion to the plan of action laid down by Lord Clarendon, and to the measures resulting from it.[1] By the Protocol of the 5th of December, 1853,[2] both Austria and Prussia joined with the Western Powers in declaring that the existence of Turkey in the limits assigned to it by existing treaties was one of the necessary conditions of the European equilibrium.

By the Protocol of the 13th of January, the four Powers recorded their approval of the terms agreed to by the Turkish Government, and resolved to submit them to the Court of St. Petersburg. At the very time when the English Government were framing the Speech from the throne, which ostentatiously separated France and England from the rest of the four Powers, the two great Courts of Germany were sending back Count Orloff and Baron Budberg to St. Petersburg, not only with a refusal on their part to give any engagement to stand neutral, but with a plain avowal that they intended to remain faithful to the principles which the four Powers had adopted in concert. Prussia told Baron Budberg that she should have to devise means without Russia for maintaining the equilibrium of Europe. In significant words, the Emperor Francis Joseph told Count Orloff that he should have to be guided by the interests and the dignity of his Empire.

It is said that by the tidings which forced him to know that he was alienated from the Austrian Emperor the Czar was wounded deep. He had conceived a strong affection for Francis Joseph, and wherever he went he carried with him a small statuette which recalled to his mind the features of the youthful Kaiser. It would seem that his affection was of the kind which a loving and yet stern father bears his son, for it was joined with a sense of right to exact a great deference to his will. Nicholas had been strangely slow to believe that Francis Joseph could harbor the thought of opposing him in arms, and when at last the truth was forced upon him, he desired that the marble should be taken from his sight. But he did not, they say, speak in anger. When he had spoken, he covered his face with his hands and was wrung with grief.

What we are showing just now is the complete union of opinion which was existing between England and the two great Courts of Germany on the 31st of January, 1854, and in order to this we have already referred to a variety of diplomatic transactions coming down to the time in question; but the policy of the courts of Vienna and Berlin at the close of the

[1] 'Eastern Papers,' part ii., p. 263. [2] Ibid., p. 296.

month of January is to be inferred of course from the transactions which followed this date, as well as from those which preceded it; and therefore it will be convenient to go forward a little in advance of the general progress of the narrative, in order to bring under one view the grounds which support our proposition.

Proofs drawn from transactions subsequent to the Queen's Speech.

Day by day the joint pressure of the four Powers became more cogent. By the Protocol of the 2nd of February the four Powers unanimously rejected the counter-propositions made by Russia. On the 14th of March both Austria and Prussia addressed circulars to the Courts of the German Confederation, in which they pointed out that the interests in question were essentially German interests, and that the active co-operation of Germany might be needed. On the 18th of March the King of Prussia asked his Chamber for an extraordinary credit of thirty million of thalers, and he at the same time declared that he would not swerve from the principles established by the Vienna Conference, and would faithfully protect every member of the Confederation who, at an earlier moment than Prussia, might be called on to draw the sword for the defense of German interests.

Nor were these bare words. Austria, it has been already said, was so placed that, whatever dangers she might draw upon her other frontiers, she could act with irresistible pressure upon the invader of the Principalities. On the 6th and 22nd of February she re-enforced her army on the frontier of Wallachia by 50,000 men, and thus placed the Russian army of occupation completely at her mercy. On the day when she sent that last re-enforcement into the Banat, she had grown so impatient of the farther continuance of the Russians in the Principalities that she actually pressed France and England to summon Russia to quit the Principalities under pain of a declaration of war, and undertook to support their summons.[1] Prussia was approving, and on the 25th Baron Manteuffel wrote to Count Arnim at Vienna 'on the subject of the more 'decided policy which it was supposed the Austrian Govern-'ment was about to adopt in the affairs of the East, and ex-'pressed the satisfaction of the Prussian Government at the 'interests of Germany on the Danube being likely to be so 'warmly espoused.'[2] On the 2nd of March the French Emperor had so little doubt of the concurrence of Austria and Germany, that he announced it in his speech from the throne.

[1] 'Eastern Papers,' part vii., p. 53.

[2] Ibid., p. 64.

'Germany,' said he, 'has recovered her independence, and has 'looked freely to see whither her true interests led her. Austria especially, who can not see with indifference the events 'going on, will join our alliance, and will thus come to confirm 'the morality and justice of the war which we undertake. We 'go to Constantinople with Germany.'

On the 20th of March the four Powers were so well agreed that, when Greece sought to make a diversion in favor of Russia, the representatives of Austria, Prussia, France, and England all joined in a collective Note which called upon the Greek Government in terms approaching menace to give way to the demands of the Porte. On the very day which followed the English declaration of war, the Emperor of Austria appointed the Archduke Albert to the command of the forces on the frontier of Wallachia, and at the same time the 'Third 'Army' was put upon the war footing. A little later[1] the Emperor of Austria ordered a new levy of 95,000 men for the defense of his frontiers. Later still, but within one day[2] of the time when France and England were making their alliance, Austria and Prussia joined with France and England in a Protocol which not only recorded the fact that the hostile step then just taken by France and England was 'supported by 'Austria and Prussia as being founded in right,' but went on to declare that 'at that solemn moment the Governments of 'the four Powers remained united in their object of maintaining the integrity of the Ottoman Empire, of which the fact of 'the evacuation of the Danubian Principalities is and will remain one of the essential conditions,' and that 'the territorial 'integrity of the Ottoman Empire is and remains the *sine quâ* '*non* condition of every transaction having for its object the 're-establishment of peace between the belligerent Powers.' Finally, the Protocol stipulated that none of the 'four Powers 'should enter into any definitive arrangement with the Imperial Court of Russia which should be at variance with the 'principles declared by the Protocol without first deliberating 'thereon in common.'[3]

On the 20th of April Austria and Prussia contracted with each other an offensive and defensive alliance, by which they guaranteed to each other all their respective possessions, so that an attack upon the territory of one should be regarded by the other as an act of hostility against his own territory, and engaged to hold part of their forces in perfect readiness for war. By the Second Article they declared that they stood

[1] May 15th. [2] April 9th, 1854.

[3] 'Eastern Papers,' part viii., p. 2.

'engaged to defend the rights and interests of Germany against 'all and every injury, and to consider themselves bound ac- 'cordingly for the mutual repulse of every attack on any part 'whatsoever of their territories; likewise also in the case 'where one of the two may find himself in understanding with 'the others obliged to advance actively for the defense of Ger- 'man interests.'[1]

By the Additional Article they declared 'that the indefinite 'continuance of the occupation of the territories on the Lower 'Danube under the sovereignty of the Ottoman Porte by im- 'perial Russian troops would endanger the political, moral, and 'material interests of the whole German Confederation, as also 'of their own States, and the more so as Russia extends her 'warlike operations on Turkish territory;' and then went on to stipulate 'that the Austrian Government should address a 'communication to the Russian Court with the object of ob- 'taining from the Emperor of Russia the necessary orders for 'putting an immediate stop to the farther advance of his armies 'upon the Turkish territory, as also to request of His Imperial 'Majesty sufficient guarantees for the prompt evacuation of 'the Danubian Principalities, and that the Prussian Govern- 'ment should again in the most energetic manner support 'these communications.' Finally, the high contracting parties agreed that, 'if, contrary to expectation, the answer of the 'Russian Court should not be of a nature to give them entire 'satisfaction, the measures to be taken by one of the contract- 'ing parties according to the terms of Article II. signed on 'that day, would be on the understanding that every hostile 'attack on the territory of one of the contracting parties should 'be repelled with all the military forces at the disposal of the 'other.'[2]

Of the intent and the meaning of this treaty and the use which Austria and Prussia were about to make of it no doubt could exist. Failing the peremptory summons which was to be addressed to Russia, the forces of Austria alone were to execute the easy task of expelling the troops of the Czar from the Principalities, and, in order to withstand the vengeance which this step might provoke, Austria and Prussia together stood leagued.

By the Protocol of the 23rd of May the four Powers declared the Anglo-French treaty and the Austro-Prussian treaty bound the parties in the relative situations to which they applied to secure the same common object, namely, the evacua-

1 'Eastern Papers,' part ix., p. 3. 2 Ibid., part x.

tion of the Principalities and the integrity of the Ottoman Empire.[1]

Now the mind and the solemn determination of Austria and Prussia being such as are shown by the Protocol of the 9th and the treaty of the 20th April, where was there such a difference of opinion—where was there even such a shadow of a difference—as to justify the Western States in pushing forward and separating themselves from the rest of the four Powers? The avowed principles and objects of the four Powers were exactly the same. If they had acted together, the very weight of their power would have given them an almost judicial authority, and would have enabled them to enforce the cause of right without wounding the pride of the disturber, and without inflicting war upon Europe.

Was Austria backward? Was she so little prone to action that it was necessary for the Western Powers to move to the front and fight her battles for her? The reverse is the truth. The Western Powers indeed were more impatient than Germany was, to go through the forms which were necessary for bringing themselves legally into a state of war, but for action of a serious kind they were not yet ready. Whilst they were only preparing, Austria was applying force. On the 3rd of June, with the full support of Prussia, she summoned the Emperor Nicholas to evacuate the Principalities. Her summons was the summons of a Power having an army on the edge of the province into which the Russian forces had been rashly extended. Such a summons was a mandate. The Czar could not disobey it. He could not stand in Wallachia when he was called upon to quit the province by a power which had assembled its forces upon his flank and rear. He sought indeed to make terms, but the German Powers were peremptory. On the 14th Austria entered into a convention with the Porte, which not only legalized her determination to drive the Russian forces from the Principalities, and to occupy them with her own troops, but which formally joined Austria in an alliance with the Porte against Russia; for, by the 1st Article of the convention, the Emperor of Austria 'engages to exhaust 'all the means of negotiation and all other means to obtain 'the evacuation of the Danubian principalities by the foreign 'army which occupies them, and even to employ, in case they 'are required, the number of troops necessary to attain this 'end.'[2] And, since Russia could not invade European Turkey by land without marching through the Principalities, this un-

[1] 'Eastern Papers,' part ix., p. 1.

[2] Ibid., part xii.

dertaking by Austria involved an engagement to free the Sultan's land frontiers in Europe from Russian invasion. Exactly at the same time,[1] Austria and Prussia addressed notes to the Powers represented at the Conference of Bamberg, in which the liberation of the commerce and navigation of the Danube was held out to Germany as the object to be attained.

The time when the interests of Austria and Prussia began to divide them from the Western Powers.

Austria was upon the brink of war with Russia, was preparing to take forcible possession of the Principalities, and had dispatched an officer to the English Head-Quarters with a view to concert a joint scheme of military operations, when the Czar at length gave way, and abandoned the whole of the territory which, under the nauseous description of a 'material 'guarantee,' had become the subject of war. Other causes, as will be seen, were conducing to this result, but none were so cogent as the forcible pressure which Austria had exerted, by first assembling forces in the Banat, and then summoning the Czar to withdraw from the invaded provinces.

Of course, when the object which called forth the German Powers was attained, and when it transpired (as it did at the same time) that the Western Powers were resolved to abandon the common field of action, and to undertake the invasion by sea of a distant Russian province, inaccessible to Austria and Prussia, then at last, and then for the first time, the German Powers found that their interests were parting them from the great maritime States of the West, for in one and the same week they were relieved from the grievance which was their motive for action, and deprived of all hope of support from the Western Powers; but it is certain that from the moment when the Czar first seized the Principalities, to that in which he recrossed the Pruth, the determination of Austria to put an end to the intrusion was never languid, and was always increasing in force. It is certain, also, that up to the time when the relinquishment of the Principalities began, there was no defection on the part of Prussia,[2] and that

From first to last Austria and Prussia never swerved from their resolve to secure the Czar's relinquishment of the Principalities.

[1] 14th and 16th of June.

[2] Prussia began to hang back, it seems, on about the 21st of July, 'Eastern Papers,' part xi., p. 1; and this was exactly the time when her interests counseled her to do so, for by that day she knew that the deliverance of the Principalities was secured and in process of execution, and had also no doubt learned of the determination of the Western Powers to move their forces to the Crimea, thereby uncovering Germany. Austria, with similar motives for separation, was less inclined to part from the Western Powers. See her Note of the 8th August, 1854, and the various diplomatic transactions in which she took part down to the close of the war.

the minor States of Germany, fully alive to the importance of a struggle which promised to free the great outlet of the Danube from Russian dominion, were resolved to support Austria and Prussia with the troops of the Confederation.[1] As soon as the Principalities were relinquished by the Czar they were occupied by Austrian troops, in pursuance of the convention with the Porte; and thus the outrage, which during twelve months had disturbed the tranquillity of Europe, was then at last finally repressed.

---

## CHAPTER XXVI.

FOR the sake of bringing under one view the course of action followed by the German powers, down to the moment when their object was achieved by the deliverance of the Principalities, it has been necessary, as we have said, to go forward in advance of the period reached by the main thread of the narrative. The subject thus quitted for a moment and now resumed, is the policy which was disclosed by the English Government upon the opening of Parliament.

Spirit of warlike adventure in England.

Distinct from the martial ardor already kindled in England, there had sprung up amongst the people an almost romantic craving for warlike adventure, and this feeling was not slow to reach the Cabinet. Now, without severance from the German Powers there could plainly be little prospect of adventure; for, besides that the German monarchs desired to free the Principalities with as little resort to hostilities as might be compatible with the attainment of the end, it was almost certain that the policy of keeping up the perfect union and co-operation of the four Powers would prevent war by its overwhelming force. Like the power of the law, it would operate by coercion, and not by clangor of arms. This was a merit, but it was a merit fatal to its reception in England. The popularity of such a policy was nearly upon the same modest level as the popularity of virtue. All whose volitions were governed by the imagined rupture of freeing Poland, or destroying Cronstadt, and lording it with our flag in the Baltic; or taking

The bearing of this spirit upon the policy of the Government.

[1] 20th July, 1854. The relinquishment of the Principalities virtually began on the 26th of June—the day when the siege of Silistria was raised, and before the end of July the Russian forces had quitted the capital of Wallachia. On the 2nd of August they repassed the Pruth.

command of the Euxine, and sinking the Russian fleet under the guns of Sebastopol; all who meant to raise Circassia and cut off the Muscovite from the glowing South by holding the Dariel Pass, and those also who dwelt in fancy upon deeds to be done on the shores of the Caspian; all these and many more saw plainly enough that separation from the German Powers and alliance with the new Bonaparte was the only road to adventure. Lord Aberdeen was not one of these; but it was his fate to act as though he were. He was not without a glimmering perception that the firmly-maintained union of the four Powers meant peace;[1] but he saw the truth dimly, and, there being a certain slowness in his high intellectual nature, he was not so touched by his belief as to be able to make it the guide of his action. He seems to have gone on imagining that, consistently with the maintenance of a perfect union of the four Powers, there might be a separate and still more perfect union between two of them, and that this kind of alliance within alliance was a structure not fatal—nay, even perhaps conducive to—peace.

England was under engagements with the French Emperor.

And after all, England was not free. She was bound to the French Emperor. No treaty of alliance had been signed, but the understanding disclosed in the summer of the year before was still riveted upon the members of the English Government. They had been drawn into a weighty engagement in 1853, and now they had to perform it. In the midst of perfect concord between her and her three allies, England had to stand forward with one of them in advance of the rest, and thus ruin that security for the maintenance of peace which depended upon the united action of the four great Powers. As the price of his consenting to join reluctant France in an alliance with Turkey, the French Emperor was justly entitled to insist on the other terms of the bond, and not only to be signally coupled with England in a course of action which was to separate her from the great German States, but to have it blazoned out to the world beforehand that, distinctly from the concord of the four Powers, the Queen of England and he were acting together. The Royal Speech of January, 1854, was as clear in this as the Speech of the previous August. Both disclosed a separate understanding with the French Emperor. In both, as any one could see who was used to state writings, the mark was set upon England with the same branding-iron.

To a man looking back upon the past, it seems strange that

[1] 129 Hansard, p. 1650.

a Cabinet of English statesmen could have been led to adopt this singular policy. It would seem that with many of the Cabinet the tendency of the measures which they were sanctioning was concealed from them by the gentleness of the incline on which they moved; and if there were some of them who had a clearer view of their motives, it must be inferred that they acted upon grounds not yet disclosed to the world. Of course, what the welfare of the State required was a ministry which shared and honored the public feeling without being so carried down by it as to lose the statesman's power of understanding and controlling events. But this was not given. Of the bulk of the Cabinet, and possibly of all of them except one, Lord Clarendon's pithy phrase was the true one. They drifted. Wishing to control events, they were controlled by them. They aimed to go in one direction, but, lapsing under pressure of forces external and misunderstood, they always went in the other.

Into this policy the bulk of the Cabinet drifted.

The statesman who went his own way was one whose share in the governance of events was not much known. He was supposed to be under a kind of ostracism. He had not been banished from England nor even from the Cabinet; but, holding office under a Prime Minister whose views upon foreign policy were much opposed to his own, and relegated to duties connected with the peaceful administration of justice, it seemed to the eye of the common observer that for the time he was annulled; and the humorous stories which floated about Whitehall went to show that the deposed Lord of Foreign Affairs had consented to forget his former greatness and to accept his Home Office duties in a spirit of half-cynical, half-joyous disdain, but without the least discontent. And in truth he had no ground for ill humor. In politics he was without vanity. What he cared for was power, and power he had. Indeed, circumstanced as he then was, he must have known that one of the main conditions of his strength was the general belief that he had none. The light of the past makes it easy to see that the expedient of trying to tether him down in the Home Office would alleviate his responsibility and increase his real power. To those who know any thing of Lord Palmerston's intellectual power, of his boldness, his vast and concentrated energy, his instinct for understanding the collective mind of a body of men and of a whole nation, and, above all, his firm, robust will; nay, even to those who only know of his daring achievements—achievements half peaceful, half warlike, half righteous, half violent in many lands and on many a sea—the notion of causing him to

The Minister who went his own way.

be subordinated to Lord Aberdeen in Foreign Affairs seems hardly more sound than a scheme providing that the greater shall be contained in the less. Statesmen on the Continent would easily understand this, for they had lived much under the weight of his strenuous nature; but at that time he had not been much called upon to apply his energies to the domestic affairs of England. Besides, he had been more seen in his own country than abroad, and for that very reason he was less known, because there was much upon the mere outside which tended to mask his real nature. His partly Celtic blood, and perhaps too in early life his boyish consciousness of power, had given him a certain elation of manner and bearing which kept him for a long time out of the good graces of the more fastidious part of the English world. The defect was toned down by age, for it lay upon the surface only, and in his inner nature there was nothing vulgar nor unduly pretending. Still, the defect made people slow—made them take forty years—to recognize the full measure of his intellectual strength. Moreover, the English had so imperfect a knowledge of the stress which he had long been putting upon foreign Governments, that the mere outward signs which he gave to his countrymen at home—his frank speech, his offhand manner, his ready banter, his kind, joyous, beaming eyes—were enough to prevent them from accustoming themselves to look upon him as a man of stern purpose. Upon the whole, notwithstanding his European fame, it was easy for him at this time to escape grave attention in England.

He was not a man who would come to a subject with which he was dealing for the first time with any great store of preconceived opinions, but he wrote so strenuously—he always, they say, wrote standing—and was apt to be so much struck with the cogency of his own arguments, that by the mere process of framing dispatches, he wrought himself into strong convictions, or rather perhaps into strong resolves; and he clung to these with such a lasting tenacity, that, if he had been a solemn, austere personage, the world would have accused him of pedantry. Like most gifted men who evolve their thoughts with a pen, he was very clear, very accurate. Of every subject which he handled gravely he had a tight, iron grasp. Without being inflexible, his will, it has been already said, was powerful, and it swung with a great momentum in one direction until, for some good and sound reason, it turned and swung in another. He pursued one object at a time without being distracted by other game. All that was fanciful or for any reason unpractical, all that was the least bit too high for him, or the least bit too deep for him, all that lay, though only by a little, beyond the immediate future with which he was dealing, he utterly drove from out of his mind; and his energies, condensed for the time upon some object to which they could be applied with effect, were brought to bear upon it with all their full volume and power. So, during the whole period of his reign at the Foreign Office, Lord Palmerston's method had been to be very strenuous in the pursuit of the object which might be needing care at any given time, without suffering himself to be embarrassed by what men call a 'comprehensive' view of our foreign policy; and, although it was no doubt his concentrative habit of mind and his stirring temperament which brought him into this course of action, he was much supported in it by the people at home; for, when no enterprise is on foot, the bulk of the English are prone to be careless of the friendship of foreign States, and are often much pleased when they are told that by reason of the activity of their Foreign Secretary they are without an ally in Europe.

Other statesmen had been accustomed to think that the principle which ought in general to determine the closeness of our relations with foreign States was 'community of interests;' and that in proportion as this principle was departed from, under the varied impulses of philanthropy or other like motives, disturbance, isolation, and danger would follow; but Lord Palmerston had never suffered this maxim to interfere with any special object which he might chance to have in hand at the moment, nor even with his desire to spread abroad the blessings of constitutional government.

As long as Lord Gray was at the head of the Government the energy of the Foreign Office was kept down, and even after the first five years of Lord Melbourne's Administration the disruption toward which it was tending had made so little way, that when, in 1840, the Ottoman Empire was threatened with ruin by France and her Egyptian ally, Lord Palmerston, with a majority of only two or three in the House of Commons, but having a bold heart and a firm, steady hand, had been able to gather up the elements of the great alliance of 1814, and to prevent a European war by the very might, and power, and swiftness with which he executed his policy; but at the end of eleven more years,[1] when his career at the Foreign Office

[1] It is not forgotten that during a large portion of this last period Lord Aberdeen was at the Foreign Office, but he was of course much bound by what his predecessors had been doing before him, and, speaking roughly, it may be said that from the spring of 1835 until the close of 1841, our foreign policy bore the impress of Lord Palmerston's mind. In the period between

was drawing to a close, his energy had cleared a space round him, and he seemed to be left standing alone.

His system by that time had fairly disclosed its true worth. Pursued with great vigor and skill, it had brought results corresponding with the numerous aims of its author, but corresponding also with his avowed disregard of a general guiding principle. Without breaking the general peace of Europe, it had produced a long series of diplomatic enterprises, pushed on in most instances to a successful issue; but, on the other hand, it had ended by making the Foreign Office an object of distrust, and in that way withdrawing England from her due place in the composition of the European system; for the good old safe clew of 'community of interests' being visibly discarded, no Power, however closely bound to us by the nature of things, could venture to rely upon our friendship. States whose interests in great European questions were exactly the same as our own, States which had always looked to the welfare and strength of England as main conditions of their own safety, found no more favor with us than those who consumed much of their revenue in preparing implements for the slaughter of Englishmen and the sinking of English ships. They were therefore obliged to shape their policy upon the supposition that any slight matter in which the Foreign Office might chance to be interesting itself at the moment—nay, even a difference of opinion upon questions of internal government (and this, be it remembered, was an apple which could always be thrown) would be enough to make England repulse them. From this cause, perhaps, more than from any other, there had sprung up in Germany that semblance of close friendship with the Court of St. Petersburg which had helped to allure the Czar into dangerous paths.

From the Emperor Nicholas Lord Palmerston was cut off not only by differences arising out of questions on which the policy of Russia and of England might naturally clash, but also because he was looked upon as the promoter of doctrines which the Court of St. Petersburg was accustomed to treat as revolutionary. Even to Austria, although we were close bound to her by common interests, although there was no one national interest which tended to divide us from her, he had in this way become antagonistic. He had too much lustiness of mind, too much simplicity of purpose to be capable of living on terms of close intelligence with the philosophical statesmen of Berlin. To the accustomed foreign policy of French statesmen—

November 1830, and the autumn of 1834, it was much governed by the then Prime Minister, Lord Gray.

in other words, to the France that he had been used to encounter in the Foreign Office—he was adverse by very habit. He spurned the whole invention of the French Republic. But his favorite hatred of all was his hatred of the House of Bourbon.[1] In short, by the 1st of December, 1851, though still at the Foreign Office, he had become isolated in Europe. But fortune smiles on bold men. The next night Prince Louis Bonaparte and his fellow venturers destroyed the French republic, superseded the Bourbons, and suppressed France. Plainly this Prince and Lord Palmerston were men who could act together—could act together until the Prince should advise himself to deceive the English Minister. Not longer: not an hour beyond the time when the momentous promise which was made —if I mistake not—before the events of December, should remain unbroken.

So, when the Czar began to encroach upon the Sultan, there was nothing that could so completely meet Lord Palmerston's every wish as an alliance between the two Western Powers, which should toss France headlong into the English policy of upholding the Ottoman Empire; and the price of this was a price which—far from grudging—he would actually delight to pay; for, desiring to have the Governments of France and England actively united together for an English object, desiring to prevent a revival of the French republic, and, above all, to prevent a restoration of the House of Bourbon, he was only too glad to be able to strengthen the new Emperor's hold upon France by exalting his personal station, and giving him the support of a close, separate, and published alliance with the Queen of England. And, in regard to the dislocation which such a new policy might work, he seems not to have set so high a value upon the existing framework of the European system as to believe that its destruction would be a portentous evil. If he thought it an evil at all, he thought it one which a strong man might repair. He yet lives, and now this very task is upon him. He meets it without suffering himself to be distracted by the remnant of any old illusion. He meets it, too, as becomes him, without shrinking or fear. A resolute people stand round him. Upon the issue of this, his last and mightiest labor, his fame, he well knows, will have to rest.

Lord Palmerston had been at the head of the Foreign Office during so many years of his life, and he had brought to bear upon its duties an activity so restless, and (upon the whole) so much steadfastness of purpose, that the more recent foreign

[1] This feeling probably drew its origin from the business of the 'Spanish Marriages.'

policy of England, whether it had been right or whether it had been wrong, was in him almost incarnate. It was obvious therefore that, whilst he was in the Cabinet, he would always be resorted to for counsel upon foreign affairs by any of his colleagues who were not divided from him by strong difference of opinion, by political antagonism, or by personal dislike. Again, it was scarcely wise to believe that the relations which had subsisted between Lord Palmerston and the President of the French Republic would be closed by the fact that they had led to Lord Palmerston's dismissal from the Secretaryship of Foreign Affairs. On the contrary, it was to be inferred that communications of a most friendly kind would continue to pass between the French Emperor and an English Minister who had suffered for his sake; and the very same manliness of disposition which would prevent him from engaging in any thing like an underhand intrigue against his colleagues, would make him refuse to sit dumb when, in words brought him fresh from the Tuileries, an ambassador came to talk to him of the Eastern Question, came to tell him that the new Emperor had an unbounded confidence in his judgment, wished to be governed by his counsels, and, in short, would dispose of poor France as the English minister wished.

Here, then, was the real bridge by which French overtures of the more secret and delicate sort would come from over the Channel. Here was the bridge by which England's acceptance or rejection of all such overtures would go back to France.

Thus, from the ascendency of his strong nature, from his vast experience, and from his command of the motive-power which he could bring at any moment from Paris, Lord Palmerston, even so early as the spring of 1853, was the most puissant member of Lord Aberdeen's Cabinet; and when, with all these sources of strength, he began to draw support from a people growing every day more and more warlike, he gained a complete dominion. If, after the catastrophe of Sinope, his colleagues had persevered in their attempt to resist him, he would have been able to overthrow them with ease upon the meeting of Parliament.

Therefore, in the transactions which brought on the war, Lord Palmerston was not drifting. He was joyfully laying his course. Whither he meant to go, thither he went; whither he chose that others should tend, thither they bent their reluctant way. If some Immortal were to offer the surviving members of Lord Aberdeen's Government the privilege of retracing their steps with all the light of experience, every one of them perhaps, with only a single exception, would examine the official papers of 1853 in order to see where he could most wisely diverge from the course which the Cabinet took. Lord Palmerston would do nothing of the kind. What he had done before, he would do again.

His way of masking the tendency of the Government.

Lord Palmerston's plan of masking the warlike tendency of the Government was an application to politics of an ingenious contrivance which the Parisians used to employ in some of their street engagements with the soldiery. The contrivance was called 'a live 'barricade.' A body of the insurgents would seize the mayor of the arrondissement and a priest (if they could get one), and also one or two respectable bankers devoted to the cause of peace and order. These prisoners, each forced to walk arm-in-arm between able-bodied combatants, were marched in front of a body of insurgents, which boldly advanced toward a spot where a battalion of infantry might be drawn up in close columns of companies, but when they got to within hailing distance, one of the insurgents, gifted with a loud voice, would shout out to the troops: 'Soldiers! respect the cause of order! 'Don't fire on Mr. Mayor! Respect property! Don't level 'your country's muskets at one who is a man and a brother, 'and also a respectable banker! Soldiers! for the love of God 'don't imbrue your hands in the blood of this holy priest!' Confused by this appeal, and shrinking, as was natural, from the duty of killing peaceful citizens, the battalion would hesitate, and mean time the column of the insurgents, covered always by its live barricade, would rapidly advance and crowd in upon the battalion, and break its structure and ruin it. It was thus that Lord Palmerston had the skill to protrude Lord Aberdeen and Mr. Gladstone, and keep them standing forward in the van of a Ministry which was bringing the country into war. No one could assail Lord Palmerston's policy without striking at him through men whose conscientious attachment to the cause of peace was beyond the reach of cavil.

Debates upon the Address.

Parliament still in the dark as to the real tendency of the Government.

In the debates which took place upon the Address, the speeches of the unofficial members of Parliament in both Houses disclosed a strange want of acquaintance with the character and spirit of the negotiations which had been going on for the last eight months. Confiding in the peaceful tendency of a Government headed by Lord Aberdeen, and having Mr. Gladstone for one of its foremost members, Mr. Bright, in the summer of 1853, had deprecated all discussion, and, under his encouragement, the Government, after some hesitation, determined to withhold the production of the papers.

With the lights which he then had, Mr. Bright was perhaps entitled to believe that the course he took was the right one, and the intention of the Government was not only honest, but in some degree self-sacrificing, for it can not be doubted that the disclosure of the able and high-spirited dispatches of Lord Clarendon would have raised the Government in public esteem. It is now certain, however, that the disclosure of the papers in the August of 1853 would have enabled the friends of peace to take up a strong ground, to give a new turn to opinion whilst yet there was time, and to save themselves from the utter discomfiture which they underwent in the interval between the prorogation and the meeting of Parliament.

The Cabinet of Lord Aberdeen was not famous for its power of preventing the leakage of state matters, but the common indiscretion by which simple facts are noised abroad does not suffice to disclose the general tenor and bearing of a long and intricate negotiation. Besides, in the absence of means of authentic knowledge, there were circumstances which raised presumptions opposite to the truth. Of course the chief of these was the retention of office by two men whose attachment to the cause of peace was believed to be passionately strong; but it chanced, moreover, that publicity had been given to a highly-spirited and able dispatch, the production of the French Foreign Office; and, since there had transpired no proof of a corresponding energy on the part of England, it was wrongly inferred that Lord Aberdeen's Government was hanging back. Accordingly, Ministers were taunted for this supposed fault by almost all the speakers in either house. What the Government were chargeable with was an undue forwardness in causing England to join with France alone in the performance of a duty which was European in its nature, and devolving in the first instance upon Austria. What they were charged with was a want of readiness to do that which they had done. Therefore every one who spoke against the Ministry was committing himself to opinions which (as soon as their real course of action should be disclosed) would involve him in an approval of their policy.

Production of the papers.

But now at last, and within a day or two from the conclusion of the debate on the Address, some of the papers relating to the negotiations of 1853 and the preceding years were laid upon the table of both Houses. As soon as the more devoted friends of peace were able to read these documents, and in some degree to comprehend their scope and bearing, they began to see how their cause had fared under the official guardianship of

Their effect.

Lord Aberdeen and Mr. Gladstone. They began to see that for near eight months the Government had been following a course of action which was gently leading toward war. They did not, however, make out the way in which the deflection began. They did not see that the way in which the Government had lapsed from the paths of peace was by quitting the common ground of the four Powers for the sake of a closer union with one, and by joining with the French Emperor in making a perverse use of the fleets.

Mr. Cobden fastened upon the 'Vienna Note,' and, with his views, he was right in drawing attention to the apparent narrowness of the difference upon which the question of peace or war was made to depend; but he surely betrayed a want of knowledge of the way in which the actions of mankind are governed when he asked that a country now glowing with warlike ardor should go back and try to obtain peace by resuming a form of words which its Government had solemnly repudiated four months before. Of course this effort failed; it could not be otherwise. Any one acquainted with the tenor of the negotiations, and with enough of the surrounding facts to make the papers intelligible, may be able to judge whether there were not better grounds than this for making a stand against the war. The evil demanding redress was the intrusion of the Russian forces into Wallachia and Moldavia, and it would seem that the judgment to be pronounced by Parliament upon a Government which had led their country to the brink of war should have been made to depend upon this question:

The question on which the judgment of Parliament should have been rested.

Was it practicable for England to obtain the deliverance of the Principalities by means taken in common with the rest of the four Powers, and without resorting to the expedient of a separate understanding with the French Emperor?

It may be that to this question the surviving members of Lord Aberdeen's Administration can establish a negative answer, but in order to do this they will have to make use of knowledge not hitherto disclosed to Parliament.

A belief, nay, even a suspicion that there was danger of a sudden alliance between the French Emperor and the Czar would gravely alter the conditions upon which Lord Aberdeen's Cabinet was called upon to form its judgment; but, so far as the outer world knows, no fear of this kind was coercing the Government. Upon the papers as they stand, it seems clear that, by remaining upon the ground occupied by the four Powers, England would have obtained the deliverance of the Principalities without resorting to war.

# CHAPTER XXVII.

THE last of the steps which brought on the final rupture between Russia and the Western Powers was perhaps one of the most anomalous transactions which the annals of diplomacy have recorded. The outrage to be redressed was the occupation by Russia of Wallachia and Moldavia. Of all the States of Europe, except Turkey itself, the one most aggrieved by this occupation was Austria. Now Austria was one of the great Powers of Europe. She was essentially a military State. She was the mistress of a vast and well-appointed army. She was the neighbor of Russia. Geographically, she was so placed that (whatever perils she might bring upon her other frontiers) her mere order to her officer commanding her army of observation would necessarily force the Czar to withdraw his troops. On the other hand, France and England, though justly offended by the outrage, and though called upon in their character as two of the great Powers to concur in fit measures for suppressing it, were far from being brought into any grievous stress by the occupation of the far distant Principalities, and moreover the evil, such as it was, was one which they could not dispel by any easy or simple application of force.

Austria proposes that France and England should summon the Czar to quit the Principalities, and threaten war as the result of his refusal.

It was in this condition of things that Austria suddenly conveyed to France, and through France to England, the intimation of the 22nd of February. In conversation with Baron de Bourqueny, Count Buol said, 'If England and France will fix a day for the 'evacuation of the Principalities, the expiration of 'which shall be the signal for hostilities, the Cabi-'net of Vienna will support the summons.'[1] The telegraph conveyed the tenor of this intimation to London on the same day. Naturally, it was to be expected that Austria would join in a summons which she invited other Powers to send, and to this hour it seems hardly possible to believe that the Emperor of Austria deliberately intended to ask France and England to fix a day for going to war without meaning to go to war himself at the same time. Lord Claren-

[1] 'Eastern Papers,' part vii., p. 53.

don, however, asked the question. Apparently he was not answered in terms corresponding with his question, but he was again told that Austria would 'support' the summons. Then all at once, and without stipulating for the concurrence of the Power which was pressing them into action, the Governments of France and England prepared the instruments which were to bring them into a state of war with Russia.

Importance of avoiding haste.

Austria at this period had plainly resolved to go to war, if the Principalities should not be relinquished by the Czar; but, before she could take the final step, it was necessary for her to come to an understanding with Prussia. This she succeeded in doing within twenty-four days from the period of the final rupture between Russia and the Western Powers; but France and England could not bear to wait. The French Emperor, rebuffed by the Czar in his endeavor to appear as the pacificator of Europe, was driven to the opposite method of diverting France from herself; and although the crisis was one in which a little delay, and a little calmness, would have substituted the coercive action of the four Powers for an adventurous war by the two, he once more goaded our Government on, and pressed it into instant action. M. Drouyn de Lhuys declared that in his opinion the sending of the proposed summons was a business which 'should be done immediately, and that the two 'Governments should write to Count Nesselrode to demand 'the immediate' withdrawal of the Russian troops from the Principalities—'the whole to be concluded by a given time, 'say the end of March.'[1] It must be owned, however, that the English people were pressing their Government in the same direction. Inflamed with a longing for naval glory in the Baltic, they had become tormented with a fear lest their Admiral should be hindered from great achievements for want of the mere legal formality which was to constitute a state of war. The majority of the Cabinet, though numbering on their side several of the foremost statesmen of the day, were collectively too weak to help being driven by the French Emperor, too weak to help being infected by the warlike eagerness of the people, too weak to resist the strong man who was amongst them without being of them. It is likely enough that statesmen so gifted as some of them were must have had better grounds for their way of acting than have been hitherto disclosed; but, to one who only judges from the materials com-

Pressure of the French Emperor.

Eagerness of the people in England.

The Government loses its composure.

[1] 'Eastern Papers,' part vii., p. 53.

municated to Parliament, it seems plain that at this time they had lost their composure.

The summons dispatched by England.

By the summons dispatched on the part of England Lord Clarendon informed Count Nesselrode that, unless the Russian Government within six days from the delivery of the summons should send an answer engaging to withdraw all its troops from the Principalities by the 30th of April, its refusal or omission so to do would be regarded by England as a declaration of war. This summons was in accordance with the suggestion of Austria, and what might have been expected was that the Western Powers, in acceding to her wish, should do so upon the understanding that she concurred in the measure which she herself proposed, and that they would consult her as to the day on which it would be convenient for her to enter into a state of war; in other words, that they would consult her as to the day on which a continued refusal to quit the Principalities should bring the Czar into a state of war with Austria, France, and England. Instead of taking this course, Lord Clarendon forwarded the summons (not as a draught or project, but as a document already signed and complete) to the Court of Vienna, and it was dispatched by a messenger who (after remaining for only a 'few hours' in the Austrian capital) was to carry on the summons to St. Petersburg. Therefore Austria was made aware that, whether she was willing to defend her own interests or not, England was irrevocably committed to defend them for her; and, instead of requiring that Austria should take part in the step which she herself had advised, Lord Westmorland was merely instructed to express a hope that the summons 'would meet with 'the approval' of the Austrian Cabinet, and that their opinion of it would be made known by Count Buol to the Cabinet of St. Petersburg. Such a step as this on the part of Austria was preposterously short of what the Western Powers would have had a right to expect from her, if they had been a little less eager for hostilities, and had consulted her as to the time for coming to a rupture.

Instructions to the messenger.

And to Lord Westmorland. Austria not required to take part in the summons which she had herself suggested.

Of course the impatience of France and England was ruinous to the principle of maintaining concert between the four Powers, and what made it the more lamentable was that it did not spring from any sound military views. It is true that the Western Powers were sending troops to the Levant and fitting out fleets for the Baltic; but there was nothing in the state of their preparations, nor in the position of the respective forces, which could justify their eagerness to accelerate the declaration of war.

The counter-proposals of Russia reach Vienna at the same time as the English messenger.

It chanced that simultaneously with the arrival of the English messenger at Vienna, there came thither from St. Petersburg the counter-propositions of Russia. Count Buol saw the importance of disposing of these before the summons went on to St. Petersburg; so, after persuading Lord Westmorland to detain the English messenger, he instantly assembled the Conference of the four Powers. By this Conference the counter-propositions of Russia were unanimously rejected,[1] and the bearer of the summons carried this decision of the four Powers to St. Petersburg, together with a dispatch from the Austrian Government instructing Count Esterhazy to support the summons, and throwing upon Russia the responsibility of the impending war.[2] The dispatch, however, fell short of announcing that the refusal to quit the Principalities would place the Czar in a state of war with Austria as well as with the Western Powers. Prussia supported the summons in language corresponding with the language of the Vienna Cabinet. Baron Manteuffel's dispatch to St. Petersburg 'was drawn up in very pressing language. It 'urged the Russian Government to consider the 'dangers to which the peace of the world would 'be exposed by a refusal, and declared that the re'sponsibility of the war which might be the conse'quence of that refusal would rest with the Emperor.'[3]

They are rejected by the Conference of the four Powers.

Austria and Prussia 'support' the summons, but without taking part in the step.

The French summons.

The summons addressed by France to the Russian Government was in the same terms as the summons dispatched by Lord Clarendon, and was forwarded at the same time.

France and England brought into a state of war with Russia.

After receiving the summons of the two Governments, Count Nesselrode took the final orders of his master; and then informed the Consuls of France and England that the Emperor did not think fit to send any answer to their Notes. A refusal to answer was one of the events which under the terms of the announcement contained in the summons was to be regarded by the Western Powers as a declaration of war. This refusal was uttered by Count Nesselrode on the 19th of March, 1854. The peace between the great Powers of Europe had lasted more than thirty-eight years, and now at length it was broken.

[1] The Conference unanimously agreed that it was impossible to 'proceed 'with those propositions.'—Protocol of Conference of March 5th. 'Eastern 'Papers,' part vii., p. 80. [2] Ibid., p. 64. [3] Ibid., p. 72.

Message from the French Emperor to the Chambers.

On the 27th of March a message from the Emperor of the French informed his Senate and Legislative Assembly that the last determination of the Cabinet of St. Petersburg had placed France and Russia in a state of war. In his speech from the throne at the opening of the session[1] he had already declared that war was upon the point of commencing. 'To avoid a conflict,' he said, 'I have gone 'as far as honor allowed. 'Europe now knows that if France 'draws the sword, it is because she is constrained to do so. 'Europe knows that France has no idea of aggrandizement. 'She only wishes to resist dangerous encroachments. The 'time of conquests has passed away, never to return. This 'policy has had for its result a more intimate alliance between 'England and France.' It is curious to observe that only a few hours after the time when England became inextricably engaged with him in a joint war against Russia, and in the same speech in which he announced the fact, the French Emperor acknowledged the value and the practicability of the wholesome policy which he had just then superseded by drawing the Cabinet of London into a separate alliance with himself; but when he was declaring, in words already quoted, that 'Germany had recovered her political independence, that Aus-'tria would enter into the alliance, and that the Western Pow-'ers would go to Constantinople along with Germany,' he had the happiness of knowing that the baneful summons which was to bring France and England into a separate course of action, and place them at last in a state of war, had been signed by the English Minister for Foreign Affairs, and was already on the way to St. Petersburg.[2]

Message from the Queen to Parliament.

On the same 27th of March a message from the Queen announced to Parliament that the negotiations with Russia were broken off, and that her Majesty, feeling bound to give active aid to the Sultan, relied upon the efforts of her faithful subjects to aid her in protecting the states of the Sultan against the encroachments of Russia.

Declaration of War.

On the following day the English declaration of war was issued. The labor of putting into writing the grounds for a momentous course of action is a wholesome discipline for statesmen; and it would be well for mankind if, at a time when the question were really in suspense, the friends of a policy leading toward war were obliged to come out of the mist of oral intercourse and private notes, and to put their

[1] March 2nd.

[2] The messenger had reached Berlin on the day of the French Emperor's Speech from the throne.

view into a firm piece of writing. It does not follow that such a document ought necessarily to be disclosed, but it ought to exist, and ought to be official. In the summer of 1853, the draft of a document fairly stating the grounds of that singular policy of alliance within alliance, which was shadowed out in the Royal Speech at the close of the session, would have been a good excuse for the members of Lord Aberdeen's Cabinet, and would have protected them against that sensation of 'drifting,' which was afterward described by the Foreign Secretary. It is known that when the English declaration announcing the rupture with Russia was about to be prepared, it was found less easy than might be supposed to assign reasons for the war. The necessity of having to state the cause of the rupture in a solemn and precise form disclosed the vice of the policy which the Government was following, for it could not be concealed that the grievance which was inducing France and England to take up arms was one of a European kind, which called for redress at the hands of the four Powers rather than for the armed championship of the two.

Difficulty of framing it.

Of course the difficulty was overcome. When the faith of the country was pledged, and fleets and armies already moving to the scene of the conflict, it was not possible that war would be stayed for want of mere words. The Queen was advised to declare that by the regard due to an ally, and to an empire whose integrity and independence were essential to the peace of Europe, by the sympathies of her people for the cause of right against injustice, and from a desire to save Europe from the preponderance of a Power which had violated the faith of treaties, she felt called upon to take up arms, in concert with the Emperor of the French, for the defense of the Sultan.

On the 11th of April the Emperor of Russia issued his declaration of war. He declared that the summons addressed to him by France and England took from Russia all possibility of yielding with honor, and he threw the responsibility of the war upon the Western Powers. It was for Central and Western Europe that Diplomacy shaped these phrases; but in the manifesto addressed to his own people the Czar used loftier words. 'Russia,' said he, 'fights not for the things of this world, but for the Faith.'[1] 'England and France have ranged themselves by the side of 'the enemies of Christianity against Russia fighting for the 'orthodox faith. But Russia will not alter her divine mission, 'and if enemies fall upon her frontier, we are ready to meet

The Czar's declaration and War manifesto.

[1] 23rd April.

'them with the firmness which our ancestors have bequeathed 'to us. Are we not now the same Russian nation of whose 'deeds of valor the memorable events of 1812 bear witness? 'May the Almighty assist us to prove this by deeds! And 'in this trust, taking up arms for our persecuted brethren pro- 'fessing the Christian faith, we will exclaim with the whole of 'Russia with one heart, "O Lord our Savior, whom have we '"to fear." "May God arise and his enemies be dispersed!"'[1]

The Czar's invasion of Turkey is commenced.

On the fourth day after the delivery of the message which placed Russia in a state of war with France and England, Prince Gortschakoff passed the Lower Danube at three points, and, entering into the desolate region of the Dobrudja, began the invasion of Turkey.[2]

Treaty between the Sultan and the Western Powers.

Nearly at the same time, France and England entered into a treaty with the Sultan, by which they engaged to defend Turkey with their arms until the conclusion of a peace guaranteeing the independence of the Ottoman Empire and the rights of the Sultan, and upon the close of the war to withdraw all their forces from the Ottoman territory. The Sultan, on his part, undertook to make no separate peace or armistice with Russia.[3]

Treaty between France and England.

On the 10th of April, 1854, there was signed that treaty of alliance between France and England which many men had suffered themselves to look upon as a security for the peace of Europe. The high contracting parties engaged to do what lay in their power for the reestablishment of a peace which should secure Europe against the return of the existing troubles, and, in order to set free the Sultan's dominions, they promised to use all the land and sea forces required for the purpose. They engaged to receive no overture tending to the cessation of hostilities, and to enter into no engagement with the Russian Court without having deliberated in common. They renounced all aim at separate advantages, and they declared their readiness to receive into their alliance any of the other Powers of Europe.

This great alliance did not carry with it so resistless a weight as to be able to execute justice by its own sheer force, and without the shedding of blood; but it was a mighty engine of war.

[1] 21st February.

[2] 24th March. By thus passing that part of the river which incloses the Dobrudja, a General does not effect much. He must cross it at and above Rassova before he can be said, in the military sense, to have 'broken through 'the line of the Danube.'

[3] 10th of March.

# CHAPTER XXVIII.

THE train of causes which brought on the war has now been followed down to the end. Great armies kept on foot, and empires governed by princes without the counsel of statesmen, were spoken of in the outset as standing elements of danger to the cause of peace, and their bearing upon the disputes of nations has been seen in all the phases of a strife which began in a quarrel for a key and a trinket, and ended by embroiling Europe. Upon the destinies of Russia the effect of this system of mere personal government has been seen at every step. From head to foot a vast empire was made to throb with the passions which rent the bosom of the one man Nicholas. If for a few months he harbored ambition, the resources of the State were squandered in making ready for war. If his spirit flagged, the ambition of the State fell lame, and preparations ceased. If he labored under a fit of piety, or rather of ecclesiastical zeal, All the Russias were on the verge of a crusade. He chafed with rage at the thought of being foiled in diplomatic strife by the second Canning, and instantly, without hearing counsel from any living man, he caused his docile battalions to cross the frontier, and kindled a bloody war.

Recapitulation.

Standing causes of disturbance.

Effect of personal Government by the Czar.

Nor was the personal government of the Emperor Francis Joseph without its share of mischief; for it seems clear that this was the evil course by which Austria was brought into measures offensive to the Sultan, but full of danger to herself. More than once, in the autumn of 1852, Nicholas and Francis Joseph came together; and at these ill-omened meetings the youthful Kaiser, bending, it would seem, under a weight of gratitude, overwhelmed by the personal ascendency of the Czar, and touched, as he well might be, by the affection which Nicholas had conceived for him, was led, perhaps, to use language which never would have been sanctioned by a cabinet of Austrian statesmen; and, although it is understood that he abstained from actual promises, it is hard to avoid believing that the general tenor of the young Emperor's conversations with Nicholas must have been the chief cause which led the Czar to imagine that he could enter upon

By the Emperor of Austria.

a policy highly dangerous to Austria, and yet safely count upon her assent. The Czar never could have hoped that Austrian councilors of state would have willingly stood still and endured his seizure of the country of the Lower Danube from Orsova down to the Euxine; but he understood that Francis Joseph governed Austria, and he imagined that he could govern Francis Joseph as though he were his own child. 'He 'could reckon,' he said, 'upon Austria.'[1]

Even in Prussia the policy of the State seemed to be always upon the point of being shaken by the fears of the King; and, although up to the outbreak of the war she was guilty of no defection,[2] it is certain that the anticipation of finding weakness in this quarter was one of the causes which led the Czar into danger.

By the King of Prussia.

In France, after the events of the 2nd of December, the system of personal government so firmly obtained that the narrator, dispensed from the labor of inquiring what interests she had in the question of peace and war, and what were the thoughts of her orators, her statesmen, and her once illustrious writers, was content to see what scheme of action would best conduce to the welfare and safety of a small knot of men then hanging together in Paris; and when it appeared that, upon the whole, these persons would gain in safety and comfort from the disturbance of Europe, and from a close understanding with England, the subsequent progress of the story was singularly unembarrassed by any question about what might be the policy demanded by the interests or the sentiments of France. Therefore, the bearing of personal government upon the maintenance of peace was better illustrated by the French Government than by the Emperor Nicholas; for in the Czar, after all, a vast people was incarnate. His ambition, his piety, his anger were, in a sense, the passions of the devoted millions of men of whom he was, indeed, the true chief. The French Emperor, on the contrary, when he chose to carry France into a war against Russia, was in no respect the champion of a national policy, nor of a national sentiment, and he therefore gave a vivid example of the way in which sheer personal government comes to bear upon the peace of the world.

By the French Emperor.

Perhaps, if a man were to undertake to distribute the blame of the war, the first Power he would arraign might be Russia.

[1] Memorandum by the Emperor of Russia, delivered to the English Government *ubi ante*.

[2] It was more than three months after the outbreak of the war that Prussia halted.

Share which Russia had in bringing about the War.

Her ambition, her piety, and her Church zeal were ancient causes of strife, which were kindled into a dangerous activity by the question of the Sanctuaries, and by events which seemed for a moment to show that the time for her favorite enterprise against Constantinople might now at last be coming. Until the month of March, 1853, these causes were brought to bear directly against the tranquillity of Europe, and even after that time they were, in one sense, the parents of strife, because, though they ceased to have a direct action upon events, they had set other forces in motion. But it would be wrong to believe that, after the middle of March, 1853, Russia was acting in furtherance of any scheme of territorial aggrandizement, for it is plain that, by that time, the Czar's vague ambition had dwindled down into a mere wish to wring from the Porte a protectorate of the Greek Church in Turkey. He had gathered his troops upon the Turkish frontier, and it seemed to him that he could use their presence there as a means of extorting an engagement which would soothe the pride of the Orthodox Church, and tighten the rein by which he was always seeking to make the Turks feel his power. The vain concealments and misrepresentations by which this effort of violent diplomacy was accompanied were hardly worthy to be ranked as acts of statecraft, and were rather the discord produced by the clashing impulses of a mind in conflict with itself.

Originally the Czar had no thought of going to war for the sake of obtaining this engagement, and least of all had he any thought of going to war with England. At first he thought to obtain it by surprise; and, when that attempt failed, he still hoped to obtain it by resolute pressure, because he reckoned that, if the great Powers would compare the slenderness of the required concession with the evils of a great war, there could be no question how they would choose.

As soon as the diplomatic strife at Constantinople began to work, the Czar got heated by it; and when, at length, he found himself not only contending for his Church, but contending, too, with his ancient enemy, he so often lost all self-command, that what he did in his politic intervals was never enough to undo the evil which he wrought in his fits of pious zeal and of rage. And when, with a cruel grace, and before the eyes of all Europe, Lord Stratford disposed of Prince Mentschikoff, it must be owned that it was hard for a proud man in the place of the Czar to have to stand still and submit. Therefore, without taking counsel of any man, he resolved to occupy the Principalities; but he had no belief that even that grave step would involve him in war, for his dangerous faith in Lord Aberdeen, and in the power of the English Peace Party, was in full force, and grew to a joyful and ruinous certainty when he learned that the Queen's Prime Minister had insisted upon revoking the grave words which had been uttered to Baron Brunnow by the Secretary of State. This illusory faith in the peacefulness of England long continued to be his guide; and, from time to time, he was confirmed in his choice of the wrong path by the bearing of the persons who represented France, Austria, and Prussia at the Court of St. Petersburg; for, although in Paris, in London, in Vienna, in Berlin, and in Constantinople, the four great Powers seemed strictly united in their desire to restrain the encroachments of the Czar, this wholesome concord was so masked at St. Petersburg by the demeanor of Count Mensdorf, Colonel Rochow, and M. Castelbajac, that Sir Hamilton Seymour, though uttering the known opinion of the other three Powers as well as of his own Government, was left to stand alone.

After his acceptance of the Vienna Note, the Emperor Nicholas enjoyed for a few days the bliss of seeing all Europe united with him against the Turks, and he believed perhaps that Heaven was favoring him once more, and that now at last 'Canning' was vanquished; but in a little while the happy dream ceased, and he had the torment of hearing the four Powers confess that, if for a moment they had differed from Lord Stratford, it was because of their erring nature. Then, fired by the Turkish declaration of war, and stung to fury by the hostile use of the Western fleets which the French Emperor had forced upon the English Government, the Czar gave the fatal orders which brought about the disaster of Sinope. After his first exultation over the sinking of the ships and the slaughter, he apparently saw his error, and was become so moderate as to receive in a right spirit the announcement of the first decision that had been taken by the English Cabinet when the news of the catastrophe reached it. But only a few days later he had to hear of the grave and hostile change of view which had been forced upon Lord Aberdeen's Government by the French Emperor, and to learn that, by resolving to drive the Russian flag from the Euxine, the maritime Powers had brought their relations with his empire to a state barely short of war. After this rupture it was no longer possible for him to extricate himself decorously, unless by exerting some skill and a steady command of temper. He was unequal to the trial; and, although in politic and worldly moments he must have been almost hopeless of a good result, he could not bear to let go his hold of the occupied provinces under the compulsion of a public threat laid upon him by England and France.

Share which Turkey had in causing it.

With the conduct of the Turkish Government little fault is to be found. It is true that in the early stage of the dispute about the Sanctuaries the violence of the French and the Russian Governments tormented the Porte into contradictory engagements, and that the anger kindled by these clashing promises was one of the provocatives of the war; but from the day of the delivery of the Bethlehem key and the replacement of the star, the Turkish Government was almost always moderate and politic. And, after the second week of March, 1853, it was firm, for the panic struck by Prince Mentschikoff in the early days of his mission was allayed by the prudent boldness of Colonel Rose, and the Czar, with all his hovering forces, was never able to create a second alarm.

It has been seen that by their tenacity of all those sovereign rights which were of real worth, by the wisdom with which they yielded wherever they could yield with honor and safety, by their invincible courtesy and deference toward their mighty assailant, and at last and above all by their warlike ardor and their prowess in the field, the Turks had become an example to Christendom, and had won the heart of England. And although it has been acknowledged that some of the more gentle of these Turkish virtues were contrived and enforced by the English Ambassador, still no one can fairly refuse to the Ottoman people the merit of appreciating and enduring this painful discipline.

Besides, there was a period when it might be supposed that the immediate views of the Turkish Government and of the English Ambassador were not exactly the same; for, as soon as the Turkish statesmen became aware that their appeal to the people had kindled a spirit which was forcing them into war, it of course became their duty to endeavor to embroil the other Powers of Europe, and they labored in this direction with much sagacity and skill. They saw that if they could contrive to bring up the Admirals from Besika Bay, the Western Powers would soon get decoyed into war by their own fleets, and, in order to this, we saw Reshid Pasha striving to affect the lofty mind of Lord Stratford by shadowing out the ruin of the Ottoman dominion; then mounting his horse, going off to the French Ambassador, and so changing the elevation of his soul, whilst he rode from one Embassy to the other, that in the presence of M. de la Cour he no longer spoke of a falling empire, but pictured to him a crowd of Frenchmen of all ranks cruelly massacred on account of their well-known Christianity by a host of fanatical Moslems. And, although the serenity of Lord Stratford defeated the sagacious Turk for the time, and disappointed him in his endeavor to bring up more than a couple of vessels from each fleet, still, in the end, the Turkish statesmanship prevailed, for M. de la Cour, disturbed by the bloody prospect held out to him, communicated his excitement to the French Emperor, and the French Emperor, as we have seen, then put so hard a pressure upon Lord Aberdeen as to constrain him to join in breaking through the treaty of 1841; and, since this resolve led straight into the series of naval movements which followed, and so on to the outbreak of war, the members of the Sultan's Cabinet had some right to believe that, even without the counsels of the great Ambassador, they knew how to govern events.

Share which Austria had.

In so far as the origin of the war was connected with Count Leiningen's mission, Austria is answerable; and although it must needs be true (for so she firmly declares[1]) that the Czar's reiterated account of his close understanding with her in regard to Montenegro was purely fabulous, she still remains open to the grave charge of having sent Count Leiningen to Constantinople armed with a long string of questionable claims, yet debarred by his orders from all negotiation, and instructed to receive no answer from the Turkish Government except an answer of simple consent or simple refusal. This offensive method of pressing upon an independent Sovereign was constantly referred to by the Czar as justifying and almost compelling his determination to deal with the Sultan in a high-handed fashion, and in this way (even upon the supposition of there being no pernicious understanding between the two Emperors) Count Leiningen's mission had an ill effect upon the maintenance of peace.

Again, Austria must bear the blame of employing servants who, notwithstanding the firm and right part which she took in the negotiations, were always causing her to appear before Europe as a Power subservient to the Czar; and especially

[1] I have a statement to this effect. To those who have not been called upon to test the relative worth of statements coming from different parts of Europe, it may seem that I am facile in accepting this one; and the more so when I acknowledge, as I do, that surrounding facts give an appearance of probability to the opposite assertion. The truth is that, like our own countrymen, the public men of Austria are much accustomed to subordinate their zeal for the public service to their self-respect. To undertake to disbelieve a statesman of the Court of Vienna is the same thing as to undertake to disbelieve an English gentleman.

she ought to suffer in public repute for the baneful effect produced at St. Petersburg by Count Mensdorf's shameful presence at the thanksgivings which the Czar and his people offered up to the Almighty for the sinking of the ships and the slaughter of the Turks at Sinope.

There is also a fault of omission for which it would seem that Austria is chargeable. The interests of Austria and England, both present and remote, were so strictly the same, that for the welfare of both States there ought to have been going on between them a constant interchange of friendly counsels. Our statesmen are accustomed to proffer advice without stint to foreign States, but it is remarkable that their frankness is not much reciprocated by words of friendly counsel from abroad. Yet there are times when such counsels might be wholesome. It would surely have been well if Austria had advised the English Government not to quit the safe, honest ground held by the four Powers for the sake of an adventure with the new Bonaparte. There is no trace of any such warnings from Vienna; and indeed it would seem that Austria, tormented by the presence of the Russian forces on her southern frontier, was more prone to encourage than to restrain the imprudence of her old ally.

In other respects Austria discharged her duty.

These were the faults with which Austria may fairly be charged. In other respects she was not forgetful of her duty toward herself and toward Europe; and it has been seen that from the day when the Czar crossed the Pruth down to the time when he was obliged to relinquish his hold, Austria persisted in taking the same view of the dispute as was taken by the Western Powers, and was never at all backward in her measures for the deliverance of the Principalities.

Share which Prussia had in causing the War.

In the nature and temperament of the King of Prussia there was so much of weakness that his Imperial brother-in-law was accustomed to speak of him in terms of ruthless disdain; and it seems that this habit of looking down upon the King caused the Czar to shape his policy simply as though Prussia were null. When he found his Royal brother-in-law engaged against him in an offensive and defensive alliance, he perhaps understood the error which he had committed in assuming that the policy of an enlightened and a high-spirited nation would be steadily subservient to the weakness of its Sovereign; but, until he was thus undeceived, or, at all events, until the failure of Baron Budberg's mission in the beginning of 1854, he seems to have closed his eyes to all the long series of public acts in which Prussia had engaged, and to have cheated himself into the belief that she would never take up such a ground as might enable Austria to act freely on her southern frontier, and so drive him out of the Principalities. And, although until after the outbreak of the war between Russia and the Western Powers Prussia did not at all hang back,[1] it is nevertheless true that the Czar's policy was shaped upon a knowledge of the King's weak nature. Therefore the temperament and mental quality of the Prussian monarch must be reckoned among the causes of the war.

Prussia also, in the same degree as Austria, must bear the kind of repute that was entailed upon her by the conduct of her representative; and the name of Colonel Rochow and his thanksgiving for the slaughter of Sinope will long be remembered against her.

Another fault attributable to Prussia was her invincible love of metaphysical, or rather mere verbal refinements. When this form of human error is brought into politics it chills all human sympathies, and tends to bring a country into contempt by giving to its policy the bitter taste of a theory or a doctrine, and so causing it to be misunderstood. An instance of this vice was given by the First Minister of the Prussian Crown in a speech of great moment which he addressed to the Lower Chamber on the 18th of March, 1854. After an abundance of phrases of a pacific tendency, Baron Manteuffel said that Prussia was resolved 'faithfully to aid any member of the 'Confederation who from his geographical position might feel 'himself called upon sooner than Prussia to draw the sword in 'defense of German interests.' Now this, to the ear of any diplomatist, foreshadowed—or rather announced—an offensive and defensive alliance with Austria against the Czar for the delivery of the Principalities; and accordingly the alliance so announced was actually contracted by Prussia some four weeks afterward. But, in the minds of the common public, a disclosure couched in this diplomatic phraseology was smothered under the intolerable weight of the pacific verbiage which had gone before; and the result was, that a speech which announced a measure of offense and hostility to Russia was looked upon as the disclosure of a halting, timid, and worthless policy.

In other respects Prussia discharged her duty.

But, except upon the grounds here stated, there was no grave fault to find with the policy of Prussia down to the outbreak of the war between the Czar and the Western Powers. Distant as she was from

[1] The state of war began on the 19th of March. Prussia first began to hang back about the 21st of July. See *ante*.

the scene of the Czar's encroachment, she was nevertheless compelled, as she valued her hold upon the good will of Germany, to be steadfast in hindering Russia from establishing herself in provinces which would give her the full control of the Lower Danube; and, up to the time of the final rupture, she always so accommodated her policy to the views of the Western Powers as to be able to remain in firm accord with them, both as to the adjudication of the dispute between Russia and Turkey, and as to the principles which should guide the belligerents in the event of their being forced into a war by the obstinacy of the Emperor Nicholas.

Of course the Czar's relinquishment of the Principalities took away from Prussia, as well as from Austria, her ground of complaint against the Czar, and with it her motive for action. Nor was this all; for, determining to quit the main land of Europe and make a descent upon a remote maritime province of Russia, the Western Powers deprived themselves of all right to expect that Austria and Prussia would favor a scheme of invasion which they did not and could not approve. Down to the time when the Czar determined to repass the Pruth, the policy followed by Prussia, as well as by Austria, was sound and loyal toward Europe.

As did also the German Confederation.

The German Confederation was brought into the same views as Austria and Prussia; and thus, so long as the object in view was the deliverance of the Principalities, the whole of central Europe was joined with the great Powers of the West in a determination to repress the Czar's encroachments. I repeat that the papers laid before the Parliament have not yet disclosed the ground on which the English Government became discontent with this vast union, and was led to contract those separate engagements with the Emperor of the French which ended by bringing on the war.

Share which the French Government had in causing the war.

The blame of beginning the dispute which led on to the war must rest with the French Government; for it is true, as our Foreign Secretary declared, that 'the 'Ambassador of France at Constantinople was the 'first to disturb the status quo in which the matter 'rested, and without political action on the part of France 'the quarrels of the Churches would never have troubled the 'relations of friendly Powers.'[1] For this offense against the tranquillity of Europe the President of the Republic was answerable in the first instance; but it must be remembered

[1] *Ubi ante.*

that, at the time, France was under a free Parliamentary Government, and it is just therefore to acknowledge that the blame of sanctioning the disinterment of a forgotten treaty more than a hundred years old, and of violently using it as an instrument of disturbance, must be shared by an Assembly which had not enough of the statesmanlike quality to be able to denounce a wanton and noxious policy. It was the weakness of the gifted statesmen and orators who then adorned the Chambers that, like most of their countrymen, they were too easily fascinated by the pleasure of seeing France domineer.

But at the close of the year 1851 the France known to Europe and the world was bereaved of political life, and thenceforth her complex interests in the affairs of nations were so effectually overruled by the exigency of personal considerations, that in a little while she was made to adopt an Anglo-Turkish policy, and, as the price of this concession to the views of our Foreign Office, the venturers of the 2nd of December were brought under the sanctions of an alliance with the Queen of England. It has been seen that, by superseding that conjoint action of the four Powers which was the true safeguard of peace and justice, the separate compact of the two became a main cause of the appeal to arms. Moreover it has been shown how, when once he had entangled Lord Aberdeen's Government in this understanding, the French Emperor gained so strong a hold over it that he became able to guide and overrule the counsels of England even in the use to be made of her Mediterranean fleet; and how thenceforth, and from time to time, he so used the English navy as well as his own, that at the moments when the negotiations seemed ripe for peace, they were always defeated by an order sent out to the Admirals. The real tendency of this perturbing and dislocating course of action was concealed by the moderation which characterized the French dispatches, and, in another and very different way, by the demeanor of the personage who represented the French Government at St. Petersburg; so that, at the very times when Lord Aberdeen was brought to consent to a hostile and provoking use of our naval forces, he was able to derive fatal comfort from the language of the French diplomacy; and, whenever the grave tone of Sir Hamilton Seymour was beginning to produce wholesome effect at St. Petersburg, his efforts were quickly baffled by the prostrations of his French colleague.

It was thus that, by generating the original dispute, by drawing England from the common ground of the four Powers into a separate understanding with himself, by causing a persistently hostile use to be made of the fleets, and, finally, by his ambiguous ways of acting and speaking, the French Emperor came to have a chief share in the kindling of the war.

Share which England had in causing it.

The stake which England holds in the world makes it of deep moment to her to avert disorder among nations; and, on the other hand, her insular station in Europe, joined with the possession of more than sufficing empire in other regions of the world, keeps her clear of all thought of territorial aggrandizement in this quarter of the globe. And, although it is the duty of all the rest of the great Powers as well as of England to endeavor toward the maintenance of peace and order, yet, inasmuch as there is no other great State without some sort of lurking ambition which may lead it into temptation, the fidelity of the Continental guardians of the peace can always be brought into question. Suspicions of this kind are often fanciful, but the fears from which they spring are too well founded in the nature of things to be safely regarded as frivolous, and the result is that the great island Power is the one which by the well informed statesmen of the Continent is looked to as the surest safeguard against wrong. Europe leans, Europe rests on this faith. So, the moment it is made to appear that for any reason England is disposed to abdicate, or to suspend for a while, the performance of her European duties, that moment the wrong-doer sees his opportunity and begins to stir. Those who dread him, missing the accustomed safeguard of England, turn whither they can for help, and, failing better plans of safety, they perhaps try hard to make terms with the spoiler. Monarchs find that to conspire for gain of territory, or to have other princes conspiring against them, is the alternative presented to their choice. The system of Europe becomes decomposed, and war follows. Therefore, exactly in proportion as England values the peace of Europe, she ought to abstain from every word and from every sign which tends to give the wrong-doer a hope of her acquiescence. Unhappily, this duty was not understood by the more ardent friends of peace, and they imagined that they would serve their cause by entreating England to abstain from every conflict which did not menace their own shores—nay, even by permitting themselves to vow and declare that this was the policy truly loved by the English race. Moreover, by blending their praises of peace with fierce invective against public men, they easily drew applause from assembled multitudes, and so caused the foreigner to believe that they really spoke the voice of a whole people, or, at all events, of great masses, and that England was no longer a Power which would interfere with spoliation in Europe. The fatal effect which this belief produced upon the peace of Europe has been shown. But the evil produced by the excesses of the Peace Party did not end there. It is the nature of excesses to beget excesses of strange complexion; and, just as a too rigid sanctity has always been followed by a too scandalous profligacy, so, by the law of reaction, the doctrines of the Peace Party tended to bring into violent life that keen warlike spirit which soon became one of the main obstacles to the restoration of tranquillity. Therefore England, it must be acknowledged, did much to bring on the war, first by the want of moderation and prudence with which she seemed to declare her attachment to the cause of peace, and afterward by the exceeding eagerness with which she coveted the strife.

We have seen the steps by which England was brought from her seeming peacefulness into a temper impatiently warlike; but, considering the much-avowed attachment of England to the maintenance of peace, the indirect, not to say remote way in which the Eastern dispute came to bear upon English interests, and, on the other hand, the immense concurrence of opinion which sanctioned, and at last almost compelled the appeal to arms, it is hard at first sight to understand how it came to happen that the cause of peace was—not merely defeated, but—brought to ruin. The truth is, that in a free country the fate of a cause must depend for the time on its leaders, and if several of the foremost of these chance to stumble and fall disabled at nearly the same time, they leave their followers helpless. Now the more strenuous lovers of peace had placed their trust in four men; and it might seem, at first sight, that any political cause would at least be safe from ruin when under the charge of Lord Aberdeen the Prime Minister, Mr. Gladstone the Chancellor of the Exchequer, and, besides these, Mr. Cobden and Mr. Bright, two of the most gifted orators in the country with seats in the House of Commons.

Loving peace, with a purity of motive and a devotedness of heart which no man has ever questioned, Lord Aberdeen and Mr. Gladstone had the misfortune to remain members of a Government which went out of the safe paths of peace. They went wrong; and although it is true that they went wrong at a slow rate, still they so moved for a period of eight months, and at last, to their grief and dismay, they found that they had been leading the country into a cruel war. Deceived by the crude notion that France and England, acting together, could secure peace, they did not understand that the way to maintain peace and order was to hold to the alliance of the four

Powers, and to avoid impairing it by a separate understanding with one of them. For want of this guiding principle they always failed to see the point at which they could make their stand, and they never could choose the day on which it would become them to retire from office. So they lingered on in a Cabinet which was becoming more and more warlike, and their presence there was in two ways hurtful to the cause of peace, for even the more earnest friends of peace were quieted by seeing that the trusted champions of the cause were still members of the Government; and at last, when they could no longer help seeing that this same Government was going to a rupture with the Czar, the more rational of them thought that there must really be some great State necessity for a war in which Lord Aberdeen and Mr. Gladstone were reluctantly engaging their country. Moreover, there was a great and good portion of the community who, retaining their theoretic disapproval of a needless war, were nevertheless fired with a secret longing for the clash of arms, and these men were relieved from the pain of a conflict between duty and inclination by finding that for the righteousness of the impending war Lord Aberdeen and Mr. Gladstone were their sponsors.

It has been seen also that by their continuance in office these two statesmen kept alive in the mind of the Emperor Nicholas that dangerous belief which has often been a source of European troubles—the belief that England would not go to war. The Czar's belief on this subject was so sweet to him that perhaps nothing short of the resignation of the Prime Minister could have undeceived him. Still, to a common observer it would seem that some effort might have been made to disperse the error which Lord Aberdeen and Mr. Gladstone had graven into the mind of the Czar by consenting to remain in office, and that, as the danger was caused in great measure by the continuance of old impressions upon the mind of the Emperor Nicholas, a special mission to St. Petersburg might have been usefully resorted to as a means of rousing the Czar to a sense of the danger which was threatening his relations with England. Nothing of this kind was done. Nothing was done to break the fatal smoothness of the incline.

But if the cause of peace was paralyzed by the friends whom it had in the Cabinet, it was brought to mere extinction by the disqualification inflicted upon its popular leaders as the result of their former excesses.

Mr. Cobden and Mr. Bright, as we have seen, had shut themselves out from the counsels of the nation. They were powerless. By their indiscriminate denunciations of war in general they had destroyed the worth of any criticism which they might be able to bring to bear upon the pending dispute. Their arguments, however well pruned and shaped out to suit the occasion, were sure of being treated by an English audience as the offspring of their doctrines, and, their doctrines being repudiated, they could make no good use of their privilege of speech. It was impossible to consult with them upon the question whether the country was bound in honor to take up arms for the Sultan, because they had spent their lives in teaching that the country could never be bound in honor to take up arms for any body. If they had not thus disqualified themselves for useful argument, they would surely have been able to make a becoming stand against what Count Nesselrode called 'the 'most unintelligible war' ever known. But because they had been extravagant before, therefore now they were null; and because they were null, the cause intrusted to their hands was brought to destruction.

The whole Cabinet of Lord Aberdeen must share the responsibility of that ill-fated policy which brought England to cast aside the blessings insured by the unanimity of the four Powers, and to enter into a separate understanding with France. It is true that, because this policy was novel and adventurous, it was highly approved by a people glowing with warlike ardor, and seeking for fields of enterprise; but, although for the time an Administration may be thus borne harmless, it would be wrong to allow that in questions of high policy the complicity of the public has power to absolve. A Minister who has fashioned out a new policy leading his country into a war ought to be able to show—not necessarily that the policy was a wise one (for man is of an erring nature), but—that at the time of its adoption there were better grounds than its mere popularity for believing it to be right. That some such grounds exist may be fairly imagined by those who have heard of the ability and the varied experience of the members of Lord Aberdeen's Cabinet; but hitherto, so far as I know, these grounds have not been disclosed.

Again, blame attaches upon Lord Aberdeen's Cabinet for yielding up its own better judgment under pressure from the French Government, and consenting to those hostile movements of the Allied fleets which baffled the patient labors of diplomacy, and twice rekindled the strife. When the warlike spirit in England had once arisen, the French Emperor knew that he could at any moment subject Lord Aberdeen's Cabinet to an access of popular disfavor by causing or allowing it to appear in England that the Government of the Queen was less eager than himself in the defense of the Sultan; and it is true therefore that, although the hand which touched the lever was foreign, the instrument of pressure was English. It is probably true, also, that the pressure was never inflicted without the consent of at least one great English Statesman. Still, because this facile yielding to the French Emperor in the use of naval forces was popular, or rather was a means of avoiding unpopularity, the propriety of it is not the less in question. It is possible, however, that the hitherto unknown grounds on which the separate understanding with France may come to be defended will extend to justify the plan of deferring in naval transactions to the Emperor of the French, and consenting at his instance to make our fleet an instrument for the disturbance of the pending negotiations.

In so far as concerns the general policy of the Government in these transactions, the merits of Lord Clarendon must be tried, of course, by the tests applicable to the whole body of the Cabinet; but it has been seen that personally he was not blind to the danger of allowing the Czar to continue in his belief of England's insuperable peacefulness, and that his firm, wholesome words were flying, as they say, to St. Petersburg,[1] when unhappily they were revoked at the instance of Lord Aberdeen. Lord Clarendon's dispatches were written with so much of grace and vigor, and in a tone so fair and manly, that any one who is familiar with them will understand something of the process by which Lord Aberdeen was from time to time forced into an approval of these able writings, and in that way hindered from finding the happy moment in which he could establish his divergence from the governing member of the Cabinet and effect his retreat from office.

The volitions which governed events.

Looking back upon the troubles which ended in the outbreak of war, one sees the nations at first swaying backward and forward like a throng so vast as to be helpless, but afterward falling slowly into warlike array. And when one begins to search for the man or the men whose volition was governing the crowd, the eye falls upon the towering form of the Emperor Nicholas. He was not single-minded, and therefore his will was unstable, but it had a huge force; and, since he was armed with the whole authority of his Empire, it seemed plain that it was this man—and only he—who was bringing danger from the North. And at first,

[1] I have avoided the obvious step by which this statement might be verified or disproved, because it seemed to me that a question upon the subject would be hardly fair; and I have preferred, therefore, to give it under cover of the *ὡς φασιν*. I do not, however, doubt that it is true.

too, it seemed that within his range of action there was none who could be his equal; but in a little while the looks of men were turned to the Bosphorus, for thither his ancient adversary was slowly bending his way. To fit him for the encounter, the Englishman was clothed with little authority except what he could draw from the resources of his own mind and from the strength of his own willful nature. Yet it was presently seen that those who were near him fell under his dominion, and did as he bid them, and that the circle of deference to his will was always increasing around him; and soon it appeared that, though he moved gently, he began to have mastery over a foe who was consuming his strength in mere anger. When he had conquered, he stood, as it were, with folded arms, and seemed willing to desist from strife. But also in the West there had been seen a knot of men possessed for the time of the mighty engine of the French State, and striving so to use it as to be able to keep their hold, and to shelter themselves from a cruel fate. The volitions of these men were active enough, because they were toiling for their lives. Their efforts seemed to interest and to please the lustiest man of those days, for he watched them from over the Channel with approving smile, and began to declare, in his good-humored, boisterous way, that so long as they should be suffered to have the handling of France, so long as they would execute for him his policy, so long as they would take care not to deceive him, they ought to be encouraged, they ought to be made use of, they ought to have the shelter they wanted; and, the Frenchmen agreeing to his conditions, he was willing to level the barrier —he called it perhaps false pride—which divided the Government of the Queen from the venturers of the second of December. In this thought, at the moment, he stood almost alone; but he abided his time. At length he saw the spring of 1853, bringing with it grave peril to the Ottoman State. Then, throwing aside with a laugh some papers which belonged to the Home Office, he gave his strong shoulder to the leveling work. Under the weight of his touch the barrier fell. Thenceforth the hinderances that met him were but slight. As he from the first had willed it, so moved the two great nations of the West.

## CHAPTER XXIX.

The commanders of the French and the English armies.

WHEN it had been resolved that the French and the English forces already dispatched to the East should be raised to a strength which might enable them to be more than auxiliary to the defense of the Turkish dominions, the French Emperor named an officer to the command of his army in the field, and the General who was to have charge of the Queen's land forces had already been chosen. It seems right for me now to say something of these two commanders; and, the better to make each of them known, I am willing to speak of some of the transactions which brought them together between the time of their meeting in Paris, and the day when they received their instructions for the invasion of the Crimea.

Marshal St. Arnaud.

The officer intrusted with the command of the French army in the East was a Marshal of France, and was the person before spoken of who had changed his name from Le Roy to 'St. Arnaud,' and from James to 'Achilles.' He impersonated with singular exactness the idea which our forefathers had in their minds when they spoke of what they called 'a Frenchman;' for although (by cowing the rich, and by filling the poor with envy) the great French Revolution had thrown a lasting gloom on the national character, it left this one man untouched. He was bold, gay, reckless, and vain; but beneath the mere glitter of the surface there was a great capacity for administrative business, and a more than common willingness to take away human life. In Algerine warfare he had proved himself from the first an active, enterprising officer, and in later years a brisk commander. He was skilled in the duties of a military governor, knowing how to hold tight under martial law a conquered or a half-conquered province. The empire of his mind over his actions was so often interrupted by bodily pain and weakness, that it is hard to say whether, if he had been gifted with health, he would have been a firm, steadfast man; but he had violent energies, and a spirit so elastic, that when for any interval the pressure of misery or of bodily pain was lifted off, he seemed as strong and as joyous as though he had never been crushed. He chose to subordinate the lives and the rights of other men to his own advancement. Therefore he was ruthless; but not in any other sense cruel. No one, as he himself said, could be more good-natured. In the interval between the grave deeds that he did, he danced and sung. To men in authority no less than to women, he paid court with flattering stanzas and songs. He had extraordinary activity of body, and was highly skilled in the performance of gymnastic feats; he played the violin; and, as though he were resolved in all things to be the Frenchman of the old time, there was once at least in his life a time of depression, when (to the astonishment of the good priest, who fell on his knees and thanked God as for a miracle wrought) he knelt down and confessed himself, seeking comfort and absolution from his Church.

He thrice went through a career in the army. First he entered it in 1816 as a sub-lieutenant of the Royal Guard. He soon plunged into a course of life which was of such a kind as to cause him to cease from being an officer. He kept away from France for many years, and became acquainted with several languages. For a long time he was in England, and he spoke our language very well; but in later years he was accustomed to be silent in regard to the time of his exile, and there is no need to lift the veil which he threw over this part of his life.

When the Revolution of 1830 broke out, he returned to France, and being then thirty-three years of age, he again entered the French army as a sub-lieutenant. He wrote some stanzas to Meunier, and gained a step by it. 'Tell me, after 'that,' said he, 'that songs are good for nothing!' His next enterprise was in prose. It chanced that Bugeaud, then the General in command of the district, had printed a small military work on the camping of troops. St. Arnaud or Le Roy (for the time of the change of name is not certain) translated the book into several languages, and presented the fruit of his labor with, no doubt, an appropriate letter of dedication to the General. Bugeaud was pleased; and from that time until his death he never lost sight of the judicious translator. St. Arnaud was immediately put upon the General's staff, and soon became one of his aids-de-camp. When the Duchess of Berri fell a prisoner into the hands of the Government, M. St. Arnaud, whose regiment was on duty at the place of her detention, found means to make himself useful to the Government without incurring the dislike of his captive, and he seemed to be in a fair road to promotion. But again the clouds passed over him.

In 1836, for the third and last time, being then near forty years of age, he entered the military profession. He began this his third career as a lieutenant in the 'Foreign Legion,' and joined the corps in Algeria. Every man of the corps, St. Arnaud said, had passed through a wild youth;[1] but with comrades of that quality a man might entertain better hopes of gaining renown than with a mere French regiment of the line; and St. Arnaud at this time made a strong resolve. He said, 'I will be remarkable, or die.' And he remained so faithful to this his covenant with himself, that even by acute illness he could not be kept out of action. When he lay upon the sick-bed, if it chanced that the Arabs or the Kabyles were offering any prospect of a fight upon ground within reach of the hospital, he almost always managed to drag his helpless, tortured body toward the scene of the conflict, and this he would do, not with an idea of being able to take an active part, but simply in order that the list of officers present might not fail to comprise his name. At the storming of Constantine, however, he really helped to govern the event; for when a great explosion took place, and many were blown into the air, the French soldiers ran back with a cry that all was ruined; but Bedeau and Combes, withstanding the madness of the common terror, strove hard to rally the crowd, and St. Arnaud, having with him in his company of the legion some bold, reckless outcasts of the North, he bethought him of the shout, very strange to the ears of Frenchmen, which he had heard in other climes. Skilled in the art of imitation, he uttered the warlike cry. Instantly from the Northmen around him, whether Germans or Swedes, or English, Scots, Irish, or Danes, there sprang their native 'Hurrah!' and with it came the thronging of men who must and would go forward. It was mainly the torrent of this new onslaught by St. Arnaud and his men of the 'stormy youth' which carried the breach, and brought about the fall of the city.

Even if for the recruiting of his health he were passing a few weeks of holiday in France, he would still seek personal distinction with a singular strength of will. If, for instance, there chanced to be a fire at night, he would fly to the spot, would scale the ladders, mount the roof, and contrive to appear aloft in seeming peril, displayed to a wondering crowd by the lurid glare of the flames. Then he would disappear, and then suddenly he would be seen again suspended in the air, and passing athwart the sky that divided one roof from another by the help of a rope or a pole. In the early part of his

[1] "Jeunesse orageuse." I translate this by the words "wild youth;" but I believe the phrase in the mouths of Frenchmen generally implies that the things done by the person spoken of are closely bordering upon crime.

service in Algeria, his old patron, General Bugeaud, was in command there, and was still a warm friend to him. Of course this circumstance helped to open a path for him, and the result was that, first by acts of bravery and vigor, and then by a display of administrative ability, the all but desperate lieutenant of the foreign legion rose in eight years to be intrusted with a General's command.[1] In 1845 he commanded in the valley of the Chelif, and he was so dire a scourge to the neighboring tribes that the force which obeyed his orders was called the 'Infernal Column.'

When first I saw him in that year he was moving with his force to wreak vengeance on a revolted tribe, and he was to march five weeks deep into the desert. He spoke with luminous force, and with a charming animation; and it seemed to me, as we rode along by the side of the heavy-laden soldiery, that the clear incisive words in which he described to me the mechanism of the 'movable column' were a model of military diction; but his keen, handsome, eager features so kindled with the mere stir and pomp of war, he seemed so to love the swift going and coming of his aids-de-camp, and the rolling drums, and the joyful appeal of the bugles; he was so content with the gleam of his epaulettes, half hidden and half revealed by the graceful white cabaan; so happy in the bounding pride of his Arab charger, that he did not seem like a man destined to be chosen from out of all others as the instrument of a scheme requiring grave care and secrecy. Yet of secrecy he was most capable; and at that very time he had upon his mind,[2] and was concealing, not from me only (for that would be only natural), but from every officer and man around him, a deed of such a kind that few men perhaps have ever done the like of it in secret.

We saw that, before the December of 1851, the enterprising and resolute Fleury was in Algeria, seeking out a fit African officer who would take the post of Minister of War, with a view of joining the President in his plans for the overthrow of the Republic. Monsieur St. Arnaud, formerly Le Roy, had not so lived as to occasion any difficulty in approaching him with dishonoring proposals; and there was ground for inferring that he might prove equal to the task which was to be set before him. The able administrator of a great district in Algeria might be competent to head a department. The commander of the 'Infernal Column' was not likely to be wanting in the

[1] But up to that time with the rank of Colonel only.

[2] The act here alluded to is spoken of farther on. It took place about six weeks before the time when I first saw Colonel St. Arnaud.

ruthlessness which was needed, and if his vanity made it seem doubtful whether he was a man who could keep a secret, there was a confidential paper in existence which might tend to allay the fear.

St. Arnaud had warmly approved the destruction of life which had been effected in 1844 by filling with smoke the crowded caves of the Dahra; but he had sagaciously observed that the popularity of the measure in Europe was not coextensive with the approbation which seems to have been bestowed upon its author by the military authorities. These counter views guided M. St. Arnaud. In the summer of 1845 he received private information that a body of Arabs had taken refuge in the cave of Shelas. Thither he marched a body of troops. Eleven of the fugitives came out and surrendered; but it was known to St. Arnaud, though not to any other Frenchman, that five hundred men remained in the cave. All these men Colonel St. Arnaud determined to kill, and so far he perhaps felt that he was only an imitator of Pelissier,[1] but the resolve which accompanied the formation of this scheme was original. He determined to keep the deed secret even from the troops engaged in the operation. Except his brother, and Marshal Bugeaud, whose approval was the prize he sought for, no one was to know what he did. He contrived to execute both his purposes. 'Then,' he writes to his brother, 'I had 'all the apertures hermetically sealed up. I made one vast 'sepulchre. No one went into the caverns. No one but my-'self knew that under there there are five hundred brigands 'who will never again slaughter Frenchmen. A confidential 'report has told all to the Marshal without terrible poetry or 'imagery. Brother, no one is so good as I am by taste and 'by nature. From the 8th to the 12th I have been ill, but my 'conscience does not reproach me. I have done my duty as a 'commander, and to-morrow I would do the same over again; 'but I have taken a disgust to Africa.'[2]

The officer who could cause French soldiery to be the unconscious instruments for putting to death five hundred fugitive men, and could afterward keep concealed from the whole force all knowledge of what it had done, was likely to be the very person for whom Fleury was seeking. He was brought back to Paris, and made Minister of War with a view to the great plot of the 2nd of December. France knows how well,

[1] It is believed, however, that Pelissier left open some of the entrances to the cave, and that he only resorted to the smoke as a means of compelling the fugitives to come out and surrender.

[2] St. Arnaud's letters published by his relatives after his death.

sooner or later, he answered to Fleury's best hopes. He kept his counsel close until the appointed night, and then (whatever faltering there may have been between midnight and three in the morning) he was out in time for the deed, and before the daylight came he had stabbed France through in her sleep.

Amongst men who make a great capture, there will often spring up questions concerning the division of the spoil. When he helped to make prize of France, St. Arnaud, of course, got much, but his wants were vast, and he had earned a clear right to extort from his chief accomplice, and to go back again, and again, and yet again, with the terrible demand for 'more!' He was in such a condition of health as to be unfit to command an army in the field; for, although during intervals he was free from pain and glowing with energy, he was from time to time utterly cast down by his recurring malady. It is possible that, notwithstanding his bodily state, he may have sincerely longed to have the command of an army in a European campaign; but whether he thus longed or not, he unquestionably said that he did, and the French Emperor took him at his word, consenting, as was very natural, that his dangerous, insatiate friend should have a command which would take him into the country of the lower Danube. Apparently it was not believed that in point of warlike skill M. St. Arnaud was well fitted to the command, for the French Emperor, as will be seen, resorted to the plan of surrounding him with men who were virtually empowered to guide him with their overruling counsels.

To try to understand the relations between the allied Generals of France and England without knowing something of the repute in which Marshal St. Arnaud was held by his fellow-countrymen would be to go blindfold; and a narrator keeping silence on this subject would be hiding a fact which belongs to history, and a fact, too, which is one of deep moment, and fruitful of lessons. Paris, stripped of the weapons which kill the body, and robbed of her appeal to honest print, was more than ever pitiless with the tongue; and M. St. Arnaud being laid open by the tenor of the life that he had led, his reputation fell a prey to cruel speech. The people of the capital knew of no crime too vile to be imputed to the new Marshal of France now intrusted with the command of her army in the field. Yet, so far as I know, they failed to make out that he had ever been convicted, or even arrested on a criminal charge; and when I look at the affectionate correspondence which almost through his life M. St. Arnaud seems to have maintained with his near relatives, I am led to imagine that they at least —and they would have been likely to know something of the truth—could have hardly believed his worst errors to be errors of the more dishonoring sort. Therefore there is ground for surmising that the Marshal was a man slandered. But in these times the chief defense against slanders upon public men is to be found in the award that results from free printing, and the right of free printing in France Marshal St. Arnaud, with his own midnight hand, had stealthily helped to destroy. Whether he was a man bitterly wronged by his fellow-countrymen, or whether what he suffered was mere justice, the state of his repute in the spring of 1854 is a thing lying within the reach of historical certainty. He had an ill name.

But state policy is a shameless leveler—is a leveler of even that difficult steep which seems to divide the man of high honor from those of mean repute. The plotters of the 2nd of December had overturned the social structure of France. They had stifled men's minds, and had made their eloquence mute. They had forced those who were of high estate by character, or by intellect, or by birth, or by honorable wealth, to endure to see France handled at will by persons of no account, and to submit to be governed by them, and to pay taxes into their hands, and to maintain them in luxury, and in all so much of pomp as can be copied from the splendor of kings. The new Emperor could not but know that he was breaking down yet another of the world's barriers, and was carrying subversion across the Channel when he contrived that all Europe should see him presenting his fellow-venturer of the December night to the appointed commander of an English army.

But when he knew who the English General was to be, he might well give the rein to his cynic joy. He could have been sure that the General, placed in command of our army, would be an officer of unsullied name; but he who had been chosen was one whose life was mixed with history—the friend, the companion of Wellington. It is true this Englishman was known to be very simple, very careless of self, a man hardly capable of imagining that he could be humbled by obeying the orders of his sovereign; and it is true, also, that the mass of the English people, being eager in the war, and little used to lay stress, as the French do, on the impersonation of a principle, were blind to the moral import of what their Government was doing; but the French Emperor understood England, and he remembered that his coming guest was one of a great and powerful body of nobles, who were proud on behalf of this favorite member of their class, and fenced him round with honor. For the leveling of these heights, and for the bringing down of those in Europe who were tall with the pride which sustains man's old strife between good and evil, no dreamer could dream of a solemnization more signal than the coming together of Marshal Le Roy St. Arnaud, and him whom old friends still called Lord Fitzroy Somerset. The French Emperor knew that the mind of Germany and France would be swift to interpret this public contact, and would see in it the terms of a great surrender.

Lord Raglan.

I conceive that in these latter times the scale upon which we measure warlike prowess has been brought down too low by the custom of awarding wild, violent praise to the common performance of duty, and even now and then to actual misfeasance; so if I keep from this path, it is not because I think coldly of our army or our navy, but because I desire—as I am very sure our best officers do—that we should return to our ancient and more severe standard of excellence. There is another reason which moves me in the same direction. Not only is the utterance of mere praise a lazy and futile method of attempting to do justice to worthy deeds, but it even intercepts the honest growth of a man's renown by serving as a contrivance for avoiding that labor of narration upon which, for the most part, all lasting fame must rest.

Too often the repute of a soldier who has done some heroic act is dealt with by a formal report, declaring that he has been 'brave,' or 'gallant,' or 'has conducted himself to the perfect 'satisfaction of his commanding officer.' The cheap, sugared words are quickly forgotten, and nothing remains; whereas, if his countrymen were told—not of the mere conclusion that the man had done bravely, but—of the very deed from which the inference was drawn, the story, however simple, might dwell perhaps in their minds, and they might tell it to their children, and the soldier would have his fame. Now this history will virtually embrace the whole of the short period in which Lord Raglan's quality as a General was tried, and it seems to me, therefore, that if, in narrating what happened, I can reach to near the truth; if I give honest samples of what our General said and of what he wrote—of his manner of commanding men, and his way of maintaining an alliance; if I show how he dealt with armies in the hour of battle, and how he comported himself in times of heavy trial, his true nature, with its strength and with its human failings, will be so far brought to light, that I may be dispensed from the need of striving to portray it; and, contenting myself with speaking of some of the mere outward and visible signs which showed upon the surface, may leave it to his countrymen to ascend by the knowledge of what he did to the knowledge of what he was. Where I think Lord Raglan's measures were right, I suppose I shall allow my belief to appear, and where I think they were wrong, I shall be likely to speak with an equal freedom; but it is not for me, who am no soldier, to undertake to compute the great account between the English people and a General who commanded their Queen's army in the field. Still, it must be remembered that the less I take upon myself in this regard, the graver will be the task of those who read. When the countrymen of Lord Raglan shall believe that they have in their hands sufficing means of knowledge, they will pass judgment—not, as I should, with the slender authority of a single by-stander, but with the weight of an honest nation in time of calm, judging firmly, yet not ungenerously, the career of a public servant.

Lord Fitzroy Somerset, afterward Lord Raglan, was a younger son of the fifth Duke of Beaufort and of a daughter of Admiral Boscawen. He was born in 1788. He entered the army in 1804. In 1807, Sir Arthur Wellesley, being about to depart for the expedition against Copenhagen, attached the young Lord Fitzroy Somerset to his staff, and during his career in the Peninsula he kept him close to his side, first as his aid-de-camp, and then as military secretary. Between the time of the first restoration of the Bourbons in 1814 and the flight of Louis XVIII. in the spring of the following year, Lord Fitzroy Somerset was secretary of the embassy at Paris. It was during this interval of peace that he married Emily Wellesley, a daughter of the third Earl of Mornington and a niece of the Duke of Wellington. When the war was renewed he again became military secretary and aid-de-camp to the Duke of Wellington, and served with him in his last campaign. At Waterloo—he was riding at the time near the farm of La Haie Sainte—he lost his right arm from a shot. But he quickly gained a great facility of writing with his left hand; and, the war being ended, he resumed his function as secretary of embassy at Paris. There he remained until 1819. He then returned to England and became secretary to the Master-General of the Ordnance. In 1825 he went with the Duke of Wellington to St. Petersburg as secretary of embassy. In 1827 he was appointed military secretary to the Commander-in-Chief at the Horse-Guards, and there he remained until the death of the Duke of Wellington in 1852. After that event he was made Master-General of the Ordnance, was appointed a Privy Councilor, and raised to the peerage. In February, 1854, he became a full General.

Thus from his very boyhood until the autumn of 1852, Lord Fitzroy Somerset had passed his life under the immediate guidance of the Duke of Wellington. The gain was not without its drawback; for in proportion as the great Duke's comprehensive grasp and prodigious power of work made him independent and self-sufficing, his subordinates were of course relieved from the necessity, and even shut out from the opportunity of thinking for themselves; but still, to have been in the close presence and intimacy of Wellington from the very rising of his fame in Europe—to have toiled at the desk where the immortal dispatches were penned—to have ridden at his side, and carried his orders in all the great campaigns—and then, when peace returned, to have engaged in the labors of diplomacy and military administration under the auspices of the same commanding mind—all this was to have a wealth of experience which common times can not give.

But for more than thirty years of his life Lord Raglan had been administering the current business of military offices in peace time, and this is a kind of experience which, if it be very long protracted, is far from being a good preparative for the command of an army in the field; because a military office, in time of peace, is impelled by its very constitution to aim at uniformity; and, on the other hand, the genius of war abhors uniformity, and tramples upon forms and regulations.

An armed force is a means to an end. The end is victory over enemies, and this is to be achieved partly, indeed, by a due use of discipline and method, but partly, also, by keeping alive in those who may come to have command a knowledge and love of war, and by cherishing that unlabeled, undocketed state of mind which shall enable a man to encounter the unknown. In England, however, and in all the great states of Europe, except France, the end had been so much forgotten in pursuit of the means, and the industry exerted in the regulation of troops in peace time had become so foreign to the business of war, that the more a man was military, in the narrowed sense of the term, the less he was likely to be fitted for the perturbing exigencies of a campaign. In one country, this singular perversity of busy, 'cold, formal man,' had been carried so far that an army and a war had been actually treated as things antagonistic the one to the other; for the late Grand Duke Constantine of Russia once declared that he dreaded a war, because he was sure it would spoil the troops, which, with ceaseless care and labor, he had striven to bring to perfection.

It is to be observed also that, partly from the way in which our military system was framed and partly from political causes, the sympathy which England ought ever to have with her troops had been materially lessened after the first few years of the peace. The Duke of Wellington, dreading lest our forces should be dangerously reduced by the House of Commons, made it his policy to withdraw the army as much as possible from public observation. This method had tended still farther to dissociate the country from its armed defenders; but naturally the Duke of Wellington's view was law, and it became the duty of those who were employed in the military administration—not to cause the country to practice itself heartily for the eventuality of another war, but—simply to maintain, as far as they could, a monotonous quiet in the army. For half a lifetime Lord Fitzroy Somerset was engaged in preventing and allaying discussion, and making the wheels of office run smooth. Against the baneful effect of this sort of experience, and against the habit of mind which it tended to generate, Lord Raglan had to combat with all the fire and strength of his nature.

When Lord Raglan was appointed to the command he was sixty-six years old. But, although there were intervals when a sudden relaxation of the muscles of the face used to show the impress of time, those moments were few; and, in general, his well-braced features, his wakeful attention, his uncommon swiftness of thought, his upright, manly carriage, and his easy seat on horseback, made him look the same as a man in the strong mid-season of life.

He had one peculiarity which, although it went near to being a foible, was likely to give smoothness to his relations with the French. Beyond and apart from a just contempt for mere display, he had a strange hatred of the outward signs and tokens of military energy. Versed of old in real war, he knew that the clatter of a General briskly galloping hither and thither with staff and orderlies did not of necessity imply any momentous resolve—that the aids-de-camp, swiftly shot off by a word like arrows from a bow, were no sure signs of dispatch or decisive action. And, because such outward signs might mean little, he shrank from them more than was right. He would have liked, if it had been possible, that he and his army should have glided unnoticed from the banks of the Thames to their position in the battle-field. It was certain, therefore, that although a French General would be sure to find himself checked in any really hurtful attempt to encroach upon the just station of the British army, yet that if, as was not unnatural, he should evince a desire for personal prominence, he would find no rival in Lord Raglan until he reached the enemy's presence.

He was gifted with a diction very apt for public business, and of a kind rarely found in Englishmen; for, though it was so easy as to be just what men like in the intercourse of private friendship, it was still so constructed as to be fit for the ear of all the world; and whether he spoke or whether he wrote, whether he used the French tongue, or his own clear, graceful English, it seemed that there had come from him the very words which were the best, and no more. It was so natural to him to be prudent in speech, that he avoided dangerous utterance without seeming cautious or reserved.

He had the subtle power to draw men along with him. To say that he was persuasive might mean that he could adduce reasons which tended to bring men to his views. His was a power of another sort; for, without pressure of argument, his mind, by its mere impact, broke down resistance for the moment; and, although the easy graciousness of his manner quickly set people free from all awkward constraint, it did not so liberate men's minds that, while they were still in his presence, they at all liked the duty of trying to uphold their own opinions against him. This dominion, however, was in a great degree dependent upon his actual personal presence; for, with all the power and grace of his pen, he could not, at a distance, work effects proportioned to those which he wrought when he dealt with men face to face.

It is plain that, in one respect, his empire over those who were in his presence was of a kind likely to become dangerous to him in the command of an army, because it prevented men from differing from him, and even made them shrink from conveying to him an unwelcome truth. Indeed, after the death of the Duke of Wellington, the proudest Englishman, if only he had intellect and a little knowledge of his country's latter history, had generally the grace to understand that, unless he, too, were a soldier who had taken his orders from the lips of Sir Arthur Wellesley, he could hardly be the equal of one whose mere presence was a record of England's great days. Thence it followed that, without pretension on the one side or servility on the other, men who were with him had a tendency to become courtiers. It was in vain that, so far as it had to do with their personal contentment, his manner placed men at their ease; there was some quality in him, or else some outward circumstance—it was partly, perhaps, the historic appeal of his maimed sword-arm—which was always enforcing remembrance, and preventing his fusion with other men

In truth, Lord Raglan's manner was of such a kind as to be —not simply ornament, but—a real engine of power. It swayed events. There was no mere gloss in it. By some gift of imagination he divined the feelings of all sorts and conditions of men; and whether he talked to a statesman or a schoolboy, his hearer went away captive. I knew a shy, thoughtful, sensitive youth, just gazetted to a regiment of the Guards, who had to render his visit of thanks to the military secretary at the Horse-Guards. He went in trepidation. He came back radiant with joy and wholesome confidence. Lord Fitzroy, instead of receiving him in solemn form and ceremony, had walked forward to meet him, had put his hand kindly on the boy's shoulder, and had said a few words so cheering, so interesting, and so free from the vice of being commonplace, that the impression clung to the lad, shaping his career for years, and helped to make him the man he was when he was out with his battalion in the winter of the first campaign. From the same presence the foremost statesman of the time once came away saying that the man in England most fitted by nature to be at the head of the Government was Lord Fitzroy Somerset, and he who so judged was himself a Prime Minister.

Marshal St. Arnaud and Lord Raglan brought together at the Tuileries.

The enemies of the Imperial Government in France had long made it a reproach against the English that they were joining in close alliance with the midnight destroyers of law and freedom; but when Lord Raglan came to Paris, when he went to the Tuileries, when he was presented by the Emperor to Marshal St. Arnaud, the notion that such things could be was a very torment to those of the Parisian malcontents who chanced to know something of the English General: 'You English are a 'robust, stirring people, and perhaps every man of you imag-'ines that he covers himself with dignity and grandeur by 'trampling upon the feelings of the rest of mankind; but sure-'ly those men wrong you who call you a proud people. Pride 'causes men to stand aloof, as we do, from that which is base; 'and if ever again we call you haughty islanders, you may si-'lence the calumny by reminding us of this 13th day of April, 'in the year of grace 1854. It was not enough that, for the 'sake of this silly war, you should ally yourselves body and 'soul to "Monsieur de Morny's Lawgiver," and that you should 'suffer him to drag you down into close intercourse with per-'sons whom the humblest of us here decline to know; but 'now—as though you really wished that your dishonor should 'be made signal in Europe—you send hither your General to 'be presented by this "French Emperor," as you call him, to 'his henchman, Mr. Le Roy St. Arnaud, and the man whom you 'choose out for this great public sacrifice is Fitzroy Somerset, 'the friend and the companion in arms of your Wellington. 'You say that Lord Raglan cares not with whom he associates, 'so that he is under the orders of the Queen whom he serves, 'and in the performance of a public duty; but because he in 'the loyalty, in the high-bred simplicity of his nature, is care-'less and forgetful of self, is that a reason why you should fail 'to be proud for him—why you should forget to be careful on 'his behalf? If the modesty of his nature hindered him from 'seeing the momentous significance of his contact with the 'people who have got into our palaces, ought you not to have 'interposed to prevent him from incurring the scene of to-day? 'We imagined that you knew how to honor the memory of 'your Wellington, and that after his death, when you looked 'toward Fitzroy Somerset, or spoke to him, or listened to his 'words, you looked, and spoke, and listened like men who re-'membered. Him, nevertheless, you now offer up. To have 'brought you down to this is a great achievement, the realiza-'tion of what they call here a "Napoleonic idea!" The pris-'oner of St. Helena is avenged at last. We are classic here, 'and we strike commemorative medals. You will soon see the 'honored image of your Fitzroy Somerset undergoing presen-'tation at the Tuileries. Already our artists have caught some 'glimpses of him, and they declare it is the coloring, the glow 'of the complexion which makes him look so English, and that 'in bronze he will be grandly Roman. Those noble lineaments 'of his, that upright manly form, nay, even the empty sleeve 'which speaks to you of your day of glory, will worthily sig-'nify what England was; and then the effigy of our counter-'feit Cæsar receiving the homage of a stainless Englishman, 'and joining him hand to hand with Mr. Le Roy St. Arnaud, 'this will show what England is. We hear that you are well 'pleased with the prospect of all this, and that—far from shrink-'ing—your "virtuous middle class," as you call it, is going into 'a state of coarse rapture. For shame!'

Lord Raglan, all unconscious of exciting this kind of sympathy in the heart of the angry Faubourg, had left England on the 10th of April, 1854, and on the following day both he and His Royal Highness the Duke of Cambridge were received in state at the Tuileries. The presence of a member of our Royal Family was welcome to the new Emperor. He understood its significance. The Parisians love to see a momentous idea so impersonated as to be visible to the eyes of the body, and when their monarch attained to be seen riding between the near kinsman of the English Queen and the appointed commander of her army in the field; when, on a bright spring day, he showed his guests some thirty thousand of his best troops in the Champ de Mars, and the scarlet of the ancient enemy sparkled gayly by the side of the blue and the gold, the people seemed to accept the scene as a fitting picture of the great alliance of the West. Almost for the first time in the history of France the accustomed cheers given to the Head of the State were mingled with cheers for England.

But now the time for concerted action had come; and though France and England were already allied by such bonds as are made with parchment and wax, it remained to be seen whether the great rivals could act together in arms. The conjuncture, indeed, drew them toward each other; but it was certain that the coherence of the union would greatly depend on one man. It might seem that he who had first sworn to maintain the French Republic, and had afterward destroyed it by stealth in the night time, would not be much trusted again by his fellow-creatures; but the alliance rested upon ground more firm than the trust which one prince puts in another. It rested—not indeed upon the common interests of France and England, for France, as we have seen, was suppressed, but—upon the prospect of personal advantage which was offered to the new French Emperor by an armed and warlike alliance with England. It being clear that the alliance was for his good, and that, for the time, he had really the control of France, the only remaining question was whether he would pursue what was plainly for his own advantage with steadiness and good sense. Upon the whole it seemed likely that he would; for, though he was not a man to be stopped by scruples, he did not discard the use of loyalty and faithfulness where loyalty and faithfulness seemed likely to answer his purpose; and there was a persistency in his nature which gave ground for hoping that, unless he should be induced to change by some really cogent reason, his steadfastness would endure. Moreover, as we have seen, he had the faculty of keeping himself awake to the distinction between the Greater and the Less; and he did not forget that for the time the alliance with England was the greater thing, and that most other objects belonged to the category of the Less. These qualities, supported by good humor and often by generous impulses, went far to make him an ally with whom (so long as he might find it advantageous to remain in accord with us) it would be possible, nay, easy, and not unpleasant to act.

Lord Raglan submitted to the publicity and ceremonial visits forced upon him during the days of the 11th and 12th of April,

Conference at the Tuileries. and at one o'clock on the 13th he had a private interview with the French Emperor at the Tuileries. The Emperor and the English General were not strangers to one another. They had been frequently brought together in London, and indeed it was by Lord Fitzroy Somerset that the heir of the first Napoleon—deeply moved by the historic significance of the incident—had been brought to Apsley House and presented to the Duke of Wellington. The Emperor showed Lord Raglan the draught of the instructions which he proposed to address to Marshal St. Arnaud.

It may be said that at this hour Lord Raglan began to have upon him the weight of that anxious charge which was never again to be thrown off so long as life and consciousness should endure. He had charge on behalf of England of the great alliance of the West; and since it happened that in this, the outset of his undertaking, he followed a method which characterized his relations with the French from first to last, there is a reason for now pointing it out. It seemed to him that in the intercourse of two proud and sensitive nations undertaking to act in concert, one of the chief dangers lay in that kind of mental activity which is generated in the process of arguing. He made it a rule to avoid and avert all needless discussion, and he regarded as needless—not only those discussions which spring out of abstract questions, but—many also of those which are generated by men's anxiety to provide for hypothetical conjunctures. He was very English in this respect, and he was no less English in the simple contrivance by which he sought to ward off the evil. Whenever there seemed to be impending a question which he regarded as avoidable, he prevented or obstructed its discussion by interposing for consideration some practical matter which was more or less important in its way, but not unsafe. And now, when there was perhaps some fear that questions of an embarrassing and delicate kind might be raised by the pondering Emperor, Lord Raglan kept them aloof by engaging attention to the choice of the camping-ground best suited for the two armies. He seems to have succeeded in confining all discussion to this one safe and practical subject.

When the Emperor at length brought his guest back into the outer room, there were there assembled Prince Jerome, the Duke of Cambridge, Marshal Vaillant the Minister of War, Marshal St. Arnaud, and Lord De Ros. The vital business of making arrangements best fitted to prevent collision between the armies was anxiously weighed. Marshal Vaillant, laborious, well instructed, precise, and rather, perhaps, fatiguing in his tendency to probe deep every question, strove hard to anticipate the eventualities likely to occasion difficulty in the relations of the two armies, and to force a clear understanding beforehand as to the way in which each question should be dealt with. This he endeavored to do by putting it to St. Arnaud in a categorical way[1] to say what solution he proposed for each of the imagined problems; but St. Arnaud, it then appeared, was hardly more fond than Lord Raglan was of hypothetical questions, for after a little while his endurance of Vaillant's interrogatories came to an end; and he answered impatiently, and in a general way, that when the conjunctures arose, they would be met as best they might by the concerted action of the Generals.

The period of the great French Revolution has gathered so much of the mellowness of age from later events, that it seems like a disturbance of chronology to be bringing into the joint-council of France and England, in the year 1854, a brother of the first Napoleon. Yet Prince Jerome was one of the speakers, and he spoke with sound judgment upon the great problem of how France and England should act together in arms. He spoke, as might be expected, with less sagacity when the subject of 'The Turks' floated up into notice. The whole French people and many even of the people of this country imagine that the wisdom and power of man are tested by his proximity to the newest stage of civilization, and from those whose minds are in that state the true worth of the Osmanli, whether in policy or in arms, must always be hidden. If he sustains reverses, their minds are satisfied, because in that case the sum of their knowledge seems to have come right; but his success disturbs their most deep-set notions of logical sequence; and now, after all Omar Pasha's achievements on the Danube, it seemed to be the impression of Prince Jerome and the French Marshals that the Turkish General would be a source of trouble and anxiety to the alliance. They looked upon the events which had been occurring as accidental and anomalous, and tending to produce a wrong conclusion. The Russians, as they well knew, had carried the industry of military preparation to the utmost verge of human endurance. The Turks had provided themselves with a powerful field artillery, had kept their old yatagans bright, and had cherished their ancient love of war; but for the rest, they had trusted much in Heaven. Yet during some six or seven months these pious, improvident, warlike men had been getting the better of drilled masses.

[1] The French verb 'poser' would describe Marshal Vaillant's labors. The English verb active 'to pose' would describe the effect upon the patient.

Their success seemed to carry a dangerous lesson; and the French Councilors thought it so important for the Turks to be broken in to the yoke of a newer civilization, that they even said it might be advantageous for Omar Pasha to undergo the discipline of a few wholesome reverses.[1]

From all he observed in the course of these interviews, Lord Raglan was led to believe in the stability of the Emperor's character, and the value he set upon the alliance.

Lord Raglan's departure for the East.

After a few days, the arrangements detaining Lord Raglan in Paris were complete, and he took his departure for the East.

The French and the English troops on the shores of the Dardanelles.

The joint occupation by French and English troops of the ground on the shore of the Dardanelles had yielded the first experience of the relations likely to subsist between the armies of the two nations when quartered near to each other. It quickly appeared that the troops of each force could be cordially good-humored in their intercourse with those of the other. Canrobert, Bosquet, and Sir George Brown, all destined to take prominent share in the coming events, made a kindly beginning of acquaintanceship amid the early difficulties and discomforts of Gallipoli; and upon the departure of Sir George Brown from the Dardanelles, there occurred one of those opportunities for the display of good feeling on which the French are accustomed to seize with a quickness, tact, and grace belonging to no other nation. Sir George Brown was to bring up with him to head-quarters two of the English regiments; and the French—spontaneously as it appeared, and from a simple impulse of good-will—came down to aid in the embarkation. They set themselves to the work with all that briskness and gay energy by which the French soldiery convert an operation of mere labor and industry into a cheerful and animating scene. The incident in itself was a small one; but, viewed as a sign of things to come, it had greater proportions. It was accepted at the time by Lord Raglan as a happy omen—an omen which seemed to promise that the alliance of the West would hold good.

Cordial intercourse between the two armies.

St. Arnaud's scheme for obtaining the command of the Turkish army.

But whilst the soldier was giving the best of sanctions to the great Alliance, the Marshal of France was putting it in jeopardy. M. St. Arnaud had not been long on the shores of the Bosphorus when he entered upon a tempting scheme of ambition. General

[1] Some might imagine that this hope must have been expressed in jest, but that is not the case. Incredible as it may seem, it is nevertheless certain that this view was gravely put forward.

Bosquet, dispatched to the head-quarters at Schumla, had brought back accounts, which the Marshal at first could hardly credit, of the good state and apparent effectiveness of the Turkish troops, and it was then perhaps that St. Arnaud first thought of the step which he afterward took. He conceived the idea of obtaining the command of the whole Turkish army. The effect which this united command would have upon the relations between the French and the English General was obvious. The English General, with his force of some twenty-five thousand men, had always foreseen that he was likely to be somewhat embarrassed in having to claim due consideration for a force which was less, by one half, than the army sent out by the French; but if Marshal St. Arnaud should be at the head, not only of his fifty thousand French, but of the whole force of Turkey, it would obviously become very hard, nay, even unfitting, for the English General to maintain an equality in council with one who, in this case, would command altogether nearly two hundred thousand men. Marshal St. Arnaud pressed his demand with the Ministers of the Porte at Constantinople, and he seems to have imagined that he had obtained their assent to his demand. If indeed they did really give a seeming assent to the proposed encroachment, they could hardly have meant it to take effect. They perhaps put their trust then, where they had put their trust before. They knew that Lord Stratford was at Therapia, and they might well believe that he would make the elaborate world go back into chaos before he would suffer the armies of the Caliph to pass like the contingent of some mere petty Christian State under the orders of a French Commander.

On the 11th of May Marshal St. Arnaud called upon Lord Raglan, and stated in the course of conversation that the Turkish Government had determined to place Omar Pasha's army under his (the Marshal's) command; and that he was then going to Reschid Pasha in order to have the matter finally settled. Lord Raglan merely said he believed the British Ambassador was not aware of the arrangement. On the 13th Marshal St. Arnaud sent to propose that Lord Raglan would meet him at Lord Stratford's, and intimated that he had an important communication to make. It was arranged that the English Ambassador should receive the Marshal alone, 'in or-'der,' as Lord Stratford almost cruelly expressed it, 'in order 'to make his acquaintance,' and that afterward Lord Raglan should join them.

It jars upon one's love of fair strife to see Marshal St. Arnaud brought in cold blood into the presence of the two men

St. Arnaud in the presence of Lord Stratford and Lord Raglan.

whom he ventured to encounter—into the presence of Lord Stratford, prepared and calmed by his foreknowledge of the intrigue; and of Lord Raglan, roused by his sense of the danger which threatened the alliance. But the interview took place. The Marshal went to the English embassy, and the operation of 'making his ac-'quaintance' was carried into full effect. Imagination may see the process—may see the light, agile Frenchman coming gayly into the room, content with himself, content with all the world, and charmed at first with the sea-blue depth of the eyes that lightened upon him from under the shadow of the Canning brow; but presently beginning to understand the thin, tight, merciless lips of his host, and then finding himself cowed and pressed down by the majesty and the graciousness of the welcome. For the welcome was such as the great Eltchi would be sure to give to one who (for imperative reasons of State) was to be treated as his honored guest, but who was also a vain mortal, pretending to the command of the Ottoman army, and daring to come with his plot avowed into the very presence of an English ambassador. Afterward Lord Raglan came into the room, and then the Marshal began upon the business in hand. He said he had required, and the Turkish Government had consented, that Omar Pasha should be placed under his orders; that a brigade of Turkish infantry and a battery of artillery should be incorporated into each of the French divisions; that fifteen hundred Bashi-Bazouks should be dismounted, that their horses should be turned over to the French troopers, and that the Bashi-Bazouks should be paid (it was not said by whom), and then be sent back to their homes.

If this proposal had been then for the first time made known to Lord Stratford, his fiery nature would scarcely perhaps have suffered him to hear with temper; but he had been prepared by Lord Raglan for what was coming, and he seemed all calm and gentleness. After hearing the proposal with benign attention, he quietly asked the Marshal whether he had cognizance of the tripartite treaty; and then turning to a copy of the treaty which happened—not at all by chance—to be lying within his reach, he read aloud the fourth article: an article which proceeds upon the assumption that the three armies would be under the orders of distinct commanders. The Marshal—ready perhaps to encounter the more obvious arguments against the expediency of the plan—was scarcely prepared for this quiet reference to the terms of the treaty. Lord Raglan then said that he thought a good deal of inconvenience might result from the adoption of the Marshal's plan—that Omar

Pasha was the ablest of the Turkish generals, that his services had been recognized by the grant of the rank of Generalissimo, and the title of Highness, and that to deprive him of the superior command, and to dismember his army at a moment when it was in presence of the enemy, would not only lower him in the estimation of those who looked up to him with confidence, but would probably induce him to throw up his charge in disgust, and declare that he would not suffer himself to be degraded.

But both Lord Raglan and the English Ambassador were gifted with the power which is one of the most keen and graceful of all the accomplishments of the diplomatist—the power of affecting the hearer with an apprehension of what remains unsaid. It is a power which exerts great sway over human actions; for men are more cogently governed by what they are forced to imagine than by what they are allowed to know. 'The Marshal,' Lord Raglan wrote, 'saw that our opinions 'were stronger than our expression of them.' He gave way. He immediately declared that, far from wishing to diminish the consequence of Omar Pasha, he was anxious to add to it, to uphold him to the utmost, and to increase his importance; and he added that he saw the propriety of deciding nothing until after a conference with Omar Pasha. By the time that St. Arnaud passed out of the Embassy gate, his enterprise was virtually abandoned.

His scheme defeated.

Some good, perhaps, resulted from the attempt to bring the Ottoman army under French command. Of all the faults tending to impair the value of Lord Raglan's advice to the home Government, there was none more grave than his want of power to appreciate warlike people belonging to an earlier state of civilization than that to which he had been accustomed in his latter years; and although nothing could ever soften his antipathy toward Turkish Irregulars of all kinds, and especially to the Bashi-Bazouks, he was by this incident drawn more than ever toward the Turkish Generalissimo, and he always thenceforth did his best to defeat any plan which tended to narrow the sphere of the Pasha's authority.

His scheme for obtaining the command of English troops.

So great was the elasticity of Marshal St. Arnaud's mind, that, far from remaining cast down under the discomfiture which he had undergone, he very soon entered upon a scheme yet more ambitious than the first. It seems he had become possessed with the idea that great achievements were within his reach, if only he could add to the powers which he already wielded the occasional command of English troops. He proposed that when French and

English troops were acting together, the senior officer, whether he chanced to be French or English, should take the command of the joint force; and although this proposal was so expressed that it might be regarded as applying only to the command of detachments, it was surmised that (M. St. Arnaud's military rank being higher than that of Lord Raglan) the control of the whole British force was the object really in view.

The experience of the conference at the British embassy had proved the good sedative effect of a dry document; and as the instructions addressed to the English General chanced to contain some words directing him to take no orders except from the Secretary of State,[1] the clause was happily put forward by Lord Raglan as an impediment to the proposed plan. Marshal St. Arnaud gave way, and thenceforth desisted from all farther prosecution of his scheme.

This also defeated.

So skillful was the resistance opposed to these enterprises of M. St. Arnaud, and the character of the Marshal was so free from all admixture of spite and bitterness, that their frustration did not create ill feeling. It was plain, however, that recurrence to projects of this sort would be dangerous to the alliance; and when the French Emperor knew that these schemes had been tried and defeated, he forbade all attempts to revive them.

Attempts of this kind checked by the French Emperor.

Hitherto, the cause which had been threatening the cohesion of the alliance was M. St. Arnaud's ambition. The next obstruction which Lord Raglan had to deal with was one of a very different kind. Checked, as is supposed, by the authoritative counsels sent out to him from Paris, Marshal St. Arnaud suddenly announced that, for some time to come, the French army could not be suffered to move toward the seat of the war.

St. Arnaud suddenly declines to move his army toward the seat of war.

The measures for sending up the British forces to Varna were in progress; and the Light Division had been already dispatched, when, at eleven o'clock at night, Colonel Trochu presented himself at the British head-quarters, and requested an immediate interview with Lord Raglan. The name of Colonel Trochu will recur in this narrative, for he was an officer of great weight in the councils of the French army. He had come from France so lately as the 10th of May, and, although his nominal office was simply that of first aid-de-camp to Marshal St. Arnaud, it was known that he came out fully charged with the notions and the wishes of the French Emperor. Col-

[1] The clause, I imagine, had been introduced in order to negative the supposition that the Ambassador at Constantinople was to have the control of the military operations.

onel Trochu was a cautious, thinking man, well versed in strategic science, and it was surmised that it was part of his mission to check any thing like wildness in the movements of the French Marshal.[1] He stated that he had been sent by Marshal St. Arnaud to request that Lord Raglan would postpone any farther movement toward Varna until the Marshal should have an opportunity of satisfying himself that any considerable portion of the French army was in a condition to take the field.

Up to this moment, no doubt had been entertained of the forwardness of the French preparations; and Lord Raglan, much astonished, expressed strong objection to the proposed delay.

Colonel Trochu replied that, upon his arrival in the Levant, he had gone to Gallipoli in order to see what degree of forwardness the preparations of the French army had really attained; and he had come, he said, to the conclusion that the French army was not as yet so equipped and provided as to render it practicable, with any thing like common prudence, to attempt operations against the enemy. He went on to justify his conclusion by details, showing the deficiencies under which the French army labored; he said that he had communicated the result of his inspection, and the opinion which he had formed to Marshal St. Arnaud, and that Marshal St. Arnaud, entirely adopting that opinion, had sent him to the English head-quarters in order that he might prevail upon Lord Raglan to suspend the intended movement.

Lord Raglan's disapproval of the proposed delay.

Lord Raglan observed that great inconvenience would result from the proposed suspension of the movement; that the movement was one actually proposed by the French and English commanders to Omar Pasha, and by him, as well as by the Turkish ministers, entirely approved; and that thus the French and the English commanders stood pledged to Omar Pasha and to the Porte, at a moment too when much anxiety existed for the fate of Silistria. Colonel Trochu admitted all this; but he again urged the necessity for delay.

The interview lasted till an hour after midnight, and Colonel Trochu's request was followed up on the ensuing day by written communications from the French Marshal. But the importance of these discussions was superseded by a farther and more perilous change in the French counsels.

At seven o'clock in the morning of Sunday, the 4th of June, Marshal St. Arnaud called upon Lord Raglan, and announced

[1] Modérer la fougue de M. le Marechal.

St. Arnaud's sudden determination to take up a defensive position in rear of the Balkan.

that he had determined upon an entirely new plan of operations for his army. Instead of moving his force to Varna, as had been agreed, he had resolved, he said, to send there only one division, and to place all the rest of his army in position—not in advance, but in rear of the Balkan range. He was to have his right resting on the sea at Bourgas. His head-quarters were to be at Aidos, and he hoped, he said, to be able to establish himself there by the third week of June. He invited Lord Raglan to conform to this plan, and to take up a position at Bournabat, a part of the proposed position which was the most remote from the sea.

Thus, at a time when the eyes of all Europe were upon Silistria and the campaign on the Danube, it was proposed that the armies of the Western Powers should take up a mere defensive —a timidly defensive—position, placing all Bulgaria, a part of Roumelia, and the whole range of the Balkan between them and the scene of conflict! What made the matter still more grave was this: that Marshal St. Arnaud did not come to consult. He had already adopted this almost incredible plan, and his troops were then actually in march for the new position.

Lord Raglan's determined resistance to this plan.

It might now indeed seem that those were right who had deemed the great alliance of the West to be impracticable. For all the purposes of the campaign the proposed plan would have caused the armies of the two Western Powers to become simply null. Lord Raglan at once declared his entire disapproval of it.

Tied perhaps to this singular plan by the counsels which Trochu had brought him, Marshal St. Arnaud, for the time, did not yield. But the English General, as I have already said, had a quality which made it difficult and painful for men to maintain a difference with him whilst they were in his presence. St. Arnaud was under this stress; and, as though he shrank from the ascendency of Lord Raglan, and sought a respite from the effort of having to oppose him in oral discussion, he imagined the idea of bending over a table and writing down what he had to say. This he did; and when the writing was finished, he left it with Lord Raglan. But the Marshal seems to have inwardly determined that Colonel Trochu, who had probably suggested this new plan of campaign, should himself be made to bear the pain of farther sustaining it; for he took his leave, saying that the Colonel should be sent to Lord Raglan on the following day.

In this curious paper, written by St. Arnaud in Lord Raglan's presence, the Marshal said the great advantage of the

French and English having only one division each at Varna, would be that they would not get entangled prematurely in hostile operations, for with such a small force no one could taunt the Western Powers for not marching to relieve Silistria, or for not giving battle to the Russians; whereas, argued the Marshal, if the Allies were present in greater strength, it was to be feared that they might suffer themselves to be carried away by the Turks. 'It is important,' said the Marshal, 'not to 'give battle to the Russians except with all possible chances 'of success, and the certainty of obtaining great results.' Then, after describing the supposed advantages of his intended position in rear of the Balkan, the Marshal reverted to his dread of being carried forward by the warlike Turks. 'We must 'not,' said he, 'lose sight of this; that we are here to aid the 'Turks—to succor them, to save them; but not by following 'their plans and their ideas. It is evident that Omar Pasha 'has no other idea but that of drawing on the allied army to 'give battle to the Russians and to relieve Silistria. The safe-'ty of Turkey is not in Silistria; and it is necessary to aid and 'succor the Turks in our own way.'

No one perhaps will now defend a plan of campaign which was to place the allied armies of the Western Powers in a position some hundreds of miles from the scene of any conflict, and to withdraw them from the very proximity of the Turk because of his warlike counsels. Still, such justice as is due must be rendered to the French strategists. France and England had sent to the East that portion of the two armies which consists of combatants; but neither of the Western Powers had hitherto constituted on the Dardanelles or the Bosphorus that vast accumulation of stores, of munitions of war, and means of transport which would enable it to live, to move freely, and to fight. Both of the two armies had the most of what for the moment they needed, but neither of them had hitherto any sufficing base of operations to rest upon. Both of the armies had means of subsistence for the next few days, and were so equipped as to be able to fight a battle on the beach; but neither army had, nor could have for many months, those vast warehouses of stores, and those immense means of land-transport, which could alone sustain regular and extended operations in the field. Therefore, if purely military rules were to govern, and if Russia were really the formidable invader of Turkey which the world had believed her to be, there would have been some rashness in pushing forward the combatants of the two armies toward the scene of conflict with a knowledge that for some time to come they would be unable to move freely in the field.

The true ground for overruling the hesitation of the French strategists lay in the now obvious fact that (to say nothing of the armies of France and England assembled on the Bosphorus with vast means of sea transport at their command) Russia, ill prepared for a great war in the South, driven out of the Euxine, threatened by Austria, and fiercely encountered and hitherto repulsed by the Ottoman forces, was not so formidable an invader of European Turkey as to deserve that her despairing struggles in the country of the Lower Danube should be encountered with all the resources of strategic prudence. Besides, the question was not purely a military one. It was certain that the mere presence of the French and the English forces in the neighborhood of the conflict would have a moral weight more than proportioned to their actual readiness for offensive operations. Finally, the question had been settled. The allied Generals, in their conference with Omar Pasha, had engaged to move their troops to Varna, and the honor of France and England stood pledged.

But if there was a semblance of military wisdom in the hesitation of the French to move up to Varna, there was none in their plan for the defensive line behind the Balkan at Aidos; for, if the want of means of land-transport threatened to hamper the force even in the advanced position of Varna, it is obvious that the same cause would have reduced the French and English forces to sheer uselessness if they had taken up a position at so vast a distance as Aidos is from the scene of the conflict. If the plan had been followed, no French nor English troops in that year would have seen the shape of a Russian battalion. Yet Marshal St. Arnaud, so far as concerned France, had determined thus to forfeit all military significance in the pending campaign, and had done so, and had begun to carry the plan into execution without consulting his English colleague.

How France was saved from this humiliation, and how the great alliance was preserved, will now be seen.

On the day following the interview with Marshal St. Arnaud, Colonel Trochu came, as had been agreed, to Lord Raglan's quarters. After repeating what Marshal St. Arnaud had stated the day before, namely, that Bosquet's Division was already in march for Adrianople, the Colonel pressed the advantages of the position which Marshal St. Arnaud had proposed to take up in rear of the Balkan.

Lord Raglan refuses to place any part of his army behind the Balkan.

Lord Raglan heard all, and then simply requested Colonel Trochu to inform Marshal St. Arnaud that he, Lord Raglan, objected to place any portion of Her Majesty's army in Roumelia.

Lord Raglan added that the movement which seemed to him the best was to advance to the front with a view to join Omar Pasha in an effort to relieve Silistria; and he said that if the Marshal were not prepared for such a movement, he (Lord Raglan) would keep his divisions on the Asiatic side of the Bosphorus, and hold them ready to embark at any moment for Varna.

St. Arnaud gives way, abandons his plan of a position behind the Balkan, and consents to move his army to Varna.

Firmness conquered. On the morning of the 10th of June, Colonel Rose came to the English head-quarters and announced that Marshal St. Arnaud now consented to abandon his plan of taking up a defensive position behind the Balkan, and that, reverting to the original determination of the Allies, he would assemble his army at Varna.

Thus the danger passed. Secrecy, it would appear, had been well maintained, and the world did not know that for all purposes of concerted military operations, the alliance of the Western Powers had lain in abeyance for five days.

The armies moved accordingly.

Leaving small detachments at Gallipoli, the French and the English armies were now moved up to Varna. General Bosquet's Division, however, was made to feel the consequences of the resolution adopted by the French strategists; for, this division having actually commenced its march toward Adrianople in furtherance of the then intended plan of taking up a position behind the Balkan, Marshal St. Arnaud, it seems, did not like to issue a countermand which would have disclosed to a sagacious soldiery his double change of counsels—nay, perhaps might have given them a glimpse of the almost ridiculous destiny from which they had been saved by Lord Raglan. So, whilst all the rest of the allied forces were gliding up to Varna by water, Bosquet's Division continued to follow the direction first given it, and was brought into Bulgaria by long, painful marches. If the warlike Zouaves, composing part of the division, had known that their long, toilsome movement in the midst of the great summer heats was the result of a plan for placing the French army in position at a distance of several hundreds of miles from the enemy, they would have solaced the labors of the march by tearing the repute of the schemer who contrived it, and making him the butt for their wit.

Bosquet's overland march.

The way in which St. Arnaud's schemes escaped publicity.

It is obvious that the premature disclosure either of Marshal St. Arnaud's ambitious scheme, or of his faltering counsels, would have been fraught with danger to the alliance; and since it used to happen in those days that tidings freshly intrusted to the English Cabinet were often disclosed to the world, it seems useful to show how it was that Lord Raglan was able to screen these transactions of Marshal St. Arnaud from the inquiring eye of the public. Apparently he did this by being careful in the choice of the time for making disclosures to the authorities at home. Except when there was a good reason for taking a contrary course, he liked to delay the communication of affairs involving danger until the danger was past. Thus, for instance, he would describe the beginning of an intrigue and also its final defeat at the same time; and the result was, that the end of the dispatch not only made the disclosure of the earlier part of it comparatively harmless, but even destroyed its value as an article of 'news;' for in proportion as people were greedy for fresh tidings, they were careless of things which ranged with the past, and the time was so stirring that the tale of an abandoned plan of campaign, or an intrigue already baffled and extinct, was hardly a rich enough gift for a Minister to carry to a newsman.

Thus were averted the early dangers which threatened the alliance; and thus, after resolving to take up a position some hundreds of miles distant from the nearest Russian outpost, the French Marshal gave way at last to Lord Raglan's ascendant, and was soon pushed forward to a camping-ground within hearing of the enemy's guns.

---

## CHAPTER XXX.

Tidings which kindled in England a zeal for the invasion of the Crimea.

THE closing events of the summer campaign in Bulgaria did so much to kindle that zeal which forced on the invasion of the Crimea, that it seems right to speak of them here; not with any notion of putting into the set form of "History" things which all Europe knew at the time in the most authentic way, but rather for the purpose of showing how the armies at Varna, and the statesmen and the people in England, were touched, were stirred, nay, were governed by the tidings which came from the Danube. Prince Paskievitch stood charged to execute with his own hand the plan of campaign which his Sovereign had persuaded him to design,[1] and accordingly, in the summer of the year 1854, he found himself marching on the Danube at the head of the Russian army, then engaged in at-

[1] See *ante*, p. 255.

tempting an invasion of the Ottoman Empire. He had insisted, as we have seen, that as the needful condition of a prosperous campaign, Silistria must fall by the 1st of May.[1] It was not before the middle of the month that he was able to appear before the place; but thenceforth he lost no time, and on the 19th he opened his first parallel.

Siege of Silistria.

The new defenses of the fortress had been planned by Colonel Grach, a Prussian officer in the service of the Porte. He had brought to the work a great deal of knowledge and judgment. He was still in the place, and he continued to lend the aid of his science to the garrison whenever he could do so without going out of his dwelling-house; but, adhering, it seems, to the bare terms on which he had engaged his services, he stiffly abstained from taking any other than a scientific part in the struggle.

Prince Paskievitch pressed the siege with a vehemence which seemed to disdain all economy of the lives of his soldiery, and, the place being weakly garrisoned, and seemingly abandoned to its fate, its fall was supposed to be nigh. To uphold the Sultan's cause three armies were at hand, but no one of them was moved forward with a view to relieve the place. Omar Pasha, shrewd and wary, was gathering the strength of the Ottoman Empire at Schumla, and it did not enter into his plan of campaign to smooth the path of the Russian General by going forward in strength to give him a meeting under the guns of the beleaguered fortress. On the other hand, France and England were rapidly assembling their forces in the neighborhood of Varna, but for want of sufficing means of land-transport they were not yet in a condition to take the field.

Day by day the two armies at Varna were moved by fitful tidings of a conflict in which, though it raged within ear-shot, they were suffered to take no part. At first, few men harbored the thought that—without deliverance brought by a relieving force—a humble Turkish fortress would be able to hold out against the collected strength of Russia and the most renowned of her Generals. Soon it was known that, of their own free will and humors, two young Englishmen, Captain Butler, of the Ceylon Rifles, and Lieutenant Nasmyth, of the East India Company's Service, had thrown themselves into the place, and were exercising a strange mastery over the garrison. On one of the hills overlooking the town there was a seam of earth which—as though it were a kind of low fence designed and thrown up by a peasant—passed along three sides of the slope

[1] See *ante*, p. 256.

in a doubtful, meandering course. This was the earthwork which soon became famous in Europe. It was called the Arab Tabia. The work was one of a slight and rude sort; but the ground it stood on was judged to be needful to the besiegers, and, at almost any cost of life to his people, Prince Paskievitch resolved to seize it. By diligent fighting on the hill-side, by sapping close up to the ditch, by springing mines which more than once blew in the counterscarp and leveled the parapet, by storming it in the daytime, by storming it at night, the Russians strove hard to carry the work; but when they sprang a mine, they ever found that behind the ruins the Turks stood intrenched; and whether they stormed it by day or by night, their masses of columns were always met fiercely, were always driven back with a cruel slaughter. Prince Paskievitch, the General commanding in chief, and General Schilders, who commanded the siege works, were both struck down by shot and disabled. On the side of the Turks, Mussa Pasha, who commanded the garrison, was killed; but Butler and Nasmyth, now obeyed with a touching affection and trustfulness by the Ottoman soldiery, were equal to the historic occasion which they had had the fortune and the spirit to seize. At one time they were laying down some new work of defense. At another, the two firm lads were governing the judgment of the Turkish commanders in a council of war. Sometimes, with ear pressed to the earth, they were listening for the dull blows of the enemy's underground pickaxes. Now and then they were engaged in dragging to his place under fire some unworthy Turkish commander; and once, in their sportive and English way, they were busy in getting together a sweepstakes, to be won by him who should name the day when Silistria would be relieved; but always when danger gathered in the Arab Tabia, the grateful Turks looked and saw that their young English guests were amongst them, ever ready with counsel for the new emergency, forbidding all thought of surrender, and even, it seems, determined to lay rough hands on the General who sought to withdraw with his troops from the famous earthwork.[1] It seemed that the presence of these youths was all that was needed for making of the Moslem hordes a faithful, heroic, and devoted soldiery. Upon ground known to be mined they stood as tranquilly as upon any other hill-side. 'It was 'impossible,' said Nasmyth's successor in the Arab Tabia—'it

[1] I take it that this is what was meant by Nasmyth's expression, "pecul-"iar inducement." The man upon whom the "peculiar inducement" was brought to bear was one whom Butler had dragged out bodily from his hiding-place.

'was impossible not to admire the cool indifference of the Turks 'to danger. Three men were shot in the space of five minutes 'while throwing up earth for the new parapet, at which only 'two men could work at a time so as to be at all protected; 'and they were succeeded by the nearest by-stander, who took 'the spade from the dying man's hands and set to work as 'calmly as if he were going to cut a ditch by the roadside.' Indeed, the childlike trust which these men were able to put in their young English leaders so freed them from all doubt and question concerning the wisdom of the orders given, that they joyfully abandoned themselves to the rapture of fighting for religion, and grew so enamored of death—so enamored of the very blackness of the grave, that sometimes in the pauses of the fight a pious Mussulman, intent on close fighting and blissful thoughts of Paradise, would come up with a pickaxe in hand, would speak some touching words of devotion and gratitude to Butler and Nasmyth, and then proudly fall to work and dig for himself the last home, where he charged his comrades to lay him as soon as he attained to die.

Omar Pasha not choosing to march to the relief of Silistria, but being unwilling to leave its defenders to sheer despair, sent General Cannon[1] (Behram Pasha he was called in the Turkish army) with a brigade of irregular light infantry, and instructed him to occupy some of the wooded ground in the neighborhood of the place, with a view to trouble the enemy and to encourage the garrison. General Cannon, however, learned on reaching the neighborhood of Silistria that the hopes of the garrison had already ebbed very low; and therefore, though without the warrant of orders, he resolved to throw himself into the place with his whole brigade. This, by means of a stratagem and a long, circuitous night-march, he was able to do. His achievement, as was natural, gave joy to the garrison; and turning to account the enthusiasm of the moment, he administered, as is said, a direful oath to the Pasha in command—an oath whereby the Turk swore that, happen what might, he would never surrender the place.

It was whilst General Cannon was in Silistria that Captain Butler received the wound of which he afterward died. The Russians had sapped up so close to the ditch that, if a man behind the parapet spoke much above a whisper, the sound of his voice used to draw the enemy's fire toward the nearest loophole or embrasure. Captain Butler, it seems, with a view

[1] General Cannon was an officer of our Indian army who had served with distinction in India, and in the force (the British Legion) which operated in Spain under the orders of General Evans.

to throw up a new work of defense, was reconnoitring the enemy's approaches through an aperture made in the parapet, and in consulting about his plan with General Cannon, he spoke loud enough to be heard by a Russian marksman, for the sound of his voice brought a rifle ball in through the loophole and struck him the blow from which (being weakened by toil and privation) he died before the end of the siege.

For some reason which he deemed to be imperative—stringent orders, perhaps, from Schumla—General Cannon marched out of the place with his brigade on the 17th of June, and at his request Nasmyth also went away for a time, in order to confer with Omar Pasha at the Turkish head-quarters; but meanwhile, Lieutenant Ballard, of the Indian army, coming thither of his own free will, had thrown himself into the besieged town, and whenever the enemy stirred, there was always at least one English lad in the Arab Tabia directing the counsels of the garrison, repressing the thought of surrender, and keeping the men in good heart.[1]

There was a part of the allied camp where the French and English soldiery could hear in a quiet hour the distant guns of Silistria. Day after day they listened for the continuing of the sound, and they listened keenly, for they were expecting the end, and there was nothing but the booming of the cannon to assure them that the fortress held out. On the 22nd of June, and during a great part of the night which followed it, they heard the low thunder of the siege more continuously than ever before; but on the dawn of the following day they listened, and listened in vain. The cannonade had ceased, and it was believed in camp that the place had been taken. The opposite of this was the truth. The siege had been raised. The event was one upon which the course of history was destined to hinge; for this miscarriage at Silistria put an end at once to all schemes for the invasion of the Sultan's dominions in Europe.

Whilst Europe was still in wonder at the deliverance of Silistria, the French and the English armies at Varna were greeted with tidings of yet another victory won by the Turks.

[1] The narratives of the siege of Silistria which appeared in the *Times* were given, as is well known, by Nasmyth himself, and by the officer who succeeded to him and to Butler in governing the counsels of the garrison and helping to defend the Arab Tabia. Therefore any other account of the siege which I might have founded upon the official materials in my possession would have been obviously inferior to the newspaper in point of authenticity. Accordingly, with the exception of two or three minor facts drawn from the correspondence which is in my possession, all I have said of the siege is taken from those journals of Nasmyth and his successor which were printed in the *Times* during the summer of 1854.

Hassan Pasha was at Rustchuk, with a large body of Turkish troops; and at Giurgevo, on the opposite bank of the river, General Soimonoff commanded twelve battalions of Russian infantry, with several squadrons of horse, and some guns. Both the Russian and the Turkish commanders desired that at this time there should be no conflict; and it might be thought that in this respect they would have their way; for, although the forces at Rustchuk and at Giurgevo were near to each other, the broad Danube rolled between them. But the Ottoman soldiery are of so warlike a nature that, when their enemy is at hand, they are oftentimes seized with a raging desire for the fight; and the one check which tends to keep down this passion is a sense of the incoherency which results from the want of good officers. But so ready and so deep is their trust in any of our countrymen who will take the trouble to lead them, that, if Turkish soldiers be camped within reach of the enemy, the coming amongst them of a few English youths supplies the one thing needed, completes the electric circle, and in general brings on a fight. Now it happened that besides General Cannon, who was on duty and in command of a Turkish brigade, seven young English officers had found their way to the camp of Hassan Pasha. Two of these, Captain Bent and Lieutenant Burke, were officers of the Royal Engineers; Meynell was a Lieutenant in the 75th Regiment; Hinde, Arnold, and Ballard (the last of them fresh come from Silistria) were officers of our Indian army; Colonel Ogilvy was General Cannon's aid-de-camp, but he gave his services freely, and, indeed, it may be said that, so far as concerns the part they took in the battle, every one of these seven young Englishmen was there of his own mere will.[1]

The battle of Giurgevo.

On the morning of the 7th of July it was observed that the Russians had struck their tents, and they were so posted that their numbers could not be descried from the right bank of the river. It was believed in the Turkish camp that Soimonoff had withdrawn the main part of his force; and it seems that what Hassan Pasha really meant to do was to execute a reconnaissance, and assure himself of the enemy's retreat. Be this as it may, he ordered, or consented, that the river should be crossed at two points; and General Cannon, embarking in boats with 300 riflemen, and speedily followed by a battalion

[1] The two engineer officers, Captain Bent and Lieutenant Burke, had been sent to the Turkish camp with instructions to advise and aid in the construction of military works; but of course they had not been ordered to lead the Turks into battle, and therefore I include them with the rest of the seven as men taking part in the battle without professional sanction.

of infantry under Ferik Bekir Pasha, succeeded in reaching the left bank of the river without encountering resistance. As soon as they had landed, the Turks tried to gain a lodgment upon a strip of ground where their front was covered by a long narrow mere or pool of water. Soon, however, they were attacked on their left flank by a body of Russian infantry, which issued from an earthwork placed above the western extremity of the mere. Cannon and Bent, with their riflemen, not only withstood this attack, but drove their assailants back into the fosse from which they had issued, and there, it seems, a good deal of slaughter took place. Afterward the riflemen were forced to give way, and fall back upon the main body of the troops which had effected their landing; but young Ballard led forward another body of skirmishers, and kept the enemy back. What was needed was, that the troops which had landed should intrench themselves; but they had come without gabions or sand-bags, and nothing as yet could be done toward gaining a firm lodgment. There was a good deal of confusion amongst the troops, and the enterprise seemed likely to fail, when Ali Pasha, who was a brave and an able officer, came over with fresh troops. He soon restored order, and the men began to throw up intrenchments.

Meanwhile two battalions, led on by Ogilvy, Hinde, Arnold, Meynell, and Burke, had crossed the river higher up, in detached bodies, and, although these small bands were left from first to last without re-enforcements, although they had to move flank-wise close under the guns of a Russian battery, which killed very many, and although they were sharply attacked and at one time hard pressed by the enemy's infantry, as well as by four squadrons of cavalry, the remnant of these venturesome men fought their way down along the river's bank, and at last made good their junction with the main body, then intrenching itself behind the mere. But before they attained to this, they had lost a great proportion of their comrades, and of their five youthful leaders they had lost three, for Burke, Arnold, and Meynell were killed.

Meanwhile fresh troops had been crossing the river at the point opposite to the landing-place first seized; and at length there was established, on the ground behind the mere, a force of some five thousand men.

Upon either flank of this body the Russian infantry came down in strong columns. Four times the attack was made, and four times the Turks, commanded or led on by Ali Pasha and General Cannon, by Bent, Hinde, Ogilvy, and Ballard, drove back their assailants with great slaughter. With pious and warlike cries, the Turks sallied over their new-made parapets, brought their bayonets down to the charge, forced mass after mass to give way, and fiercely pressed the retreat.

At sunset the action ceased. All night the Turks were intrenching themselves on the ground which they had gained, but, when the morning dawned, there was no sign that the enemy would hasten to renew the battle.

To keep a safe hold of the ground which had been won, it was necessary for the Turks to advance in the direction of their left front, and occupy a ridge which went by the name of the Slobenzie Heights; but Hassan Pasha dreaded the blame which might fall upon him if the movement should prove to be a wrong one. General Cannon pressed him hard. For some time in vain; but at length the Pasha yielded, upon condition that the English General would give him a written warranty certifying the wisdom of the step.

On the third day after the battle, Prince Gortschakoff came up with a force which was said to number some sixty or seventy thousand men. He had been set free by the raising of the siege of Silistria, and he now appeared upon one of the ranges of hills looking down upon Giurgevo from the northwest. It seemed that he meant to cover over the stain of the defeat sustained at Giurgevo by driving the Turks back into the river; but before he camped for the night the British flag was already in the waters beneath him.

Lieutenant Glyn and the young Prince Leiningen, both serving on board the 'Britannia,' had come up from the sea, with some gunboats and thirty seamen, together with a like number of sappers. Glyn quickly carried his gunboats into the narrow loop-stream which escapes from the main of the river above Giurgevo, and meets it again lower down. By this movement Glyn thrust his gunboats into the interval which divided the Russian army from the Turks. Gortschakoff, perhaps, overrated the force which had come with the British flag. At all events, he did not instantly move down to the attack, and, whilst he seemed to hesitate, the Turks and the English worked hard. Captain Bent and his sappers, with the aid of our seamen and the Turks, threw a bridge of boats across the main stream of the Danube. This done, it was plain that, if Gortschakoff were to attack, he would have to do not merely with the five thousand Turks already established on the left bank, but with the whole of the force which lay at Rustchuk. He resolved to avoid the encounter. Retreating upon Bucharest, he no longer disputed with the Turks for the mastery of the Lower Danube.

In this campaign on the Danube, those who fought for the cause of the Sultan were helped, it is true, by Fortune, by the anger and unskillfulness of the Czar, by the assured support of Austria, and by the impending power of England and France; but still there is one point of view in which their achievement was a great one. Military ascendency is so closely connected with military reputation, that to be the first to bring down the warlike fame of a great empire is to do a mighty work, and a work, too, which hardly can fail to change the career of nations. By the time that Prince Gortschakoff retreated upon Bucharest, people no longer thought of the Czar as they thought of him eight months before; and the glory of thus breaking down the military reputation of Russia is due of right, not to the Governments nor the armies of France or England, but to the warlike prowess of the Ottoman soldiery, and the ten or twelve resolute Englishmen who cheered, and helped, and led them.

Effect of the campaign of the Danube on the military ascendency of Russia.

The failure of the attempted invasion was almost instantly followed by the relinquishment of Moldavia and Wallachia. The Emperor Nicholas, as we saw, had been placed by Austria under the stress of a peremptory summons requiring him to withdraw from the Principalities, and, the demand being supported by powerful bodies of troops which threatened the flank of the intruding army, the Czar was schooled at last, and compelled to see that he must surrender his hold of the provinces which he had chosen to call his 'material guarantee.'

Thus, by the course of the events which followed it, the Czar's last defeat on the Danube was made to appear more signal than it really was. Of course men versed in war and in politics knew that causes of a larger kind than a few hours' fight at Giurgevo were bringing about the abandonment of the Principalities; but people who drew their conclusions from the mere advance or retreat of armies, and from the issue of battles, were left to infer that the once dreaded Emperor of the Russias was chased from the country of the Danube by the sheer prowess of the victorious Turks.

It is, therefore, very easy to believe that this discomfiture at Giurgevo was more bitter to the Czar than any of the disasters which had hitherto tried his fortitude. People knew, or affected to know, what the troubled man uttered in torment, and the words they put in his mouth ran somewhat to this effect:

The agony of the Czar.

'I can understand Oltenitza — I can even understand that 'Omar Pasha should have been able to hold against me his 'lines at Kalafat—I can partly account for the result of those 'fights at Citate—I can understand Silistria—the strongest 'may fail in a siege—and it chanced that both Paskievitch and 'Schilders were struck down and disabled by shot—but—but '—but—that Turks—mere Turks—led on by a General of Se-'poys and six or seven English boys—that they should dare to 'cross the Danube in the face of my troops—that, daring to at-'tempt this, they should do it, and hold fast their ground—that 'my troops should give way before them, and that this—that 'this should be the last act of the campaign which is ending 'in the retreat of my whole army, and the abandonment of the 'Principalities. Heaven lays upon me more than I can bear!'

Many men in the Anglo-French camp were fretted by the tidings of this last Turkish victory; for, besides that, with their natural and healthy impatience of delay, they were stung by the example of their Moslem ally, there was in the staff of the French and the English armies a pedantic dislike of wild troops. In this respect Lord Raglan had no breadth of view.

Lord Raglan's dislike of undisciplined combatants.

Far from understanding that the hardy, the fierce, the devout, the temperate Moslems of the Ottoman provinces were the rough yet sound material with which superb troops could be made, he always looked upon these brave men, but especially upon the genus which people called 'Bashi-Bazouks,' with an almost superstitious horror. He was so constituted, or rather he was so schooled down by long years of flat office labor, that it shocked him to see a man bearing no uniform, yet warlike, and armed to the teeth. Indeed, from Bulgaria he once wrote and complained quite gravely that every Turk he saw had the appearance of being a 'bandit;' and the prejudice clung to him; for, long after the period now spoken of, and even in the very hour when the fatal storm of the 14th of November was roaring through his port and his camp, he found time to sit at a desk and write down the Bashi-Bazouks.

This hatred of undrilled warriors was the more perverse, since England, above all other nations, was rich in men (men like Hodson, for instance, or Jacob) who knew how to make themselves the adored chiefs of Asiatic soldiers.

Importance to England of native auxiliaries.

Besides, it must be borne in mind, that when an English Government undertakes to wage war in a country beyond the seas without doing all it can to get soldierly aid from the natives, it does not merely neglect a slight or collateral advantage. On the contrary, it throws away its power of acting with efficient numbers, and is in danger of frittering away the nation's strength upon those (often ill-fated) schemes which go by the name of 'expedi-'tions.' Without our Portuguese auxiliaries there would have been no great Peninsular War, no successful invasion of France. Without the native soldiery of Hindostan there would have been no British India. Without the German auxiliaries who served under Wellington in his last campaign, he could not have given battle to Napoleon in the Netherlands, and the course of English history would not have run as it did. The truth is, that (especially at the beginning of a war) any body of troops which England brings together at one time and one place is in general so costly, and of so high a quality, but also so scant in numbers, that to use it, and use it singly for all the work of the campaign, is to consume and squander the precious essence of the nation's strength without making it the means of attaining any worthy result.

Therefore, whenever it is possible, a British force serving abroad and engaged in an arduous campaign ought to have by its side—not mere allies, for that is but a doubtful, and often a poor support to have to lean upon, but auxiliaries obeying the English commander, and capable of being trusted with a large share of the duties required from an army in the field. Nor is this an advantage which commonly lies out of our reach; for in most of the countries of the Old World the cost of labor is much lower than in England, and it is one of the prerogatives of the English, as, indeed, of all conquering nations, to be able to lead other races of men, and to impart to them its warlike fire. By beginning its preparations at the right time, and by bringing under the orders of some of our Indian officers a fitting number of the brave men who came flocking to the war from every province of the Ottoman Empire, our Government might have enabled their General to take the field with an army of great strength; with an army more fit for warlike enterprises than two armies—French and English—instructed to work side by side, and baffled by divided command.[1]

[1] The opinions which the Duke of Newcastle entertained on this subject were sound, and his efforts to give effect to them were vigorous; but he was thwarted by the curious antagonism which commonly shows itself at the beginning of a war—the antagonism between views really warlike and views which are only 'military.'

# CHAPTER XXXI.

The events on the Danube removed the grounds of the war.

By their own prowess, with the aid only of a moral support from their great allies and the actual presence of a few young English officers, the Ottoman soldiery had repelled the invasion; and, the defense of Turkey being accomplished in a way very glorious to the Sultan, and the deliverance of the Principalities being secured, it suddenly became apparent that the objects for which the Western Powers undertook the war had been already attained. And, since (by the mere act of declaring war against the Czar) the Porte had freed itself from the obnoxious treaties which heretofore entangled its freedom, the condition of affairs was such that a prudent statesman of France, or of England, or of the Ottoman empire might have well enough rested content. And in that condition of affairs the Emperor of Russia must have acquiesced; for, having now learned that he could not maintain an invasion of European Turkey, and being driven from the seas, he was cut off from all means of waging an offensive war against the Sultan except upon the desolate frontiers of Armenia, and the pressure of the naval blockade enforced against him by the Allies, together with the torture of seeing the Baltic and the Euxine placed under the dominion of their fleets, would have more than sufficed to make him sign a peace.

If France had been mistress of herself, or if England had been free from passion and craving for adventure, the war would have been virtually at an end on the day when the Russian army completed its retreat from the country of the Danube, and re-entered the Czar's dominions.

How came it to happen that, rejecting the peace which seemed to be thus prepared by the mere course of events, the Western Powers determined to undertake the invasion of a Russian province?

Helplessness of the French people.

France was still lying under the men who had got her down on the night of the 2nd of December; and it was in vain that her people at that time chanced to love peace better than war, for they had no longer a voice in state affairs. The French Emperor still wielded the whole strength of the nation, and, laboring to turn away men's thoughts from the origin of his power, he was very willing to try to earn for the restored Empire that kind of station and title which the newest of dynasties may acquire by signal achievements in war. It was still of great moment to him to remain in close friendship with England, and to use the alliance as an engine of war; but he observed that there was a spirit on this side of the Channel which—springing from motives very unlike his own—was nevertheless tending in the same direction, and therefore, to draw England in, he no longer needed to resort to those ingenious contrivances which he had employed against her in the foregoing year. All that he had to do was to encourage her desire to go on with the war, and, if necessary, to make his own plans yield to those of his ally. To do all this he was very able, for he had, as we have seen, at that time the power of keeping his mind alive to the difference between the greater and the less, and after he had once resolved to engage in alliance with England, he did not allow his main purpose to be baffled by differences on minor questions. Therefore now, when it became known that the Russian army was in full retreat, he was so willing to defer to English counsels, that virtually, though not in terms, he left it to the Queen's Government to determine what next step the Western Powers should take in the conduct of the war.

Course taken by the French Emperor.

England had become so eager for conflict that the idea of desisting from the war merely because the war had ceased to be necessary was not tolerable to the people. In the Baltic their hopes had been bitterly disappointed, and, as soon as it became clear that the defense of Turkey was a thing already accomplished, men longed to try the prowess of our land and sea forces in some enterprise against the Russian dominions. Already they had cast their eyes upon Sebastopol.

Desire of the English for an offensive war.

With a view to the conquest of empire on the Bosphorus, the ambition of Russia had taken advantage of the spacious port on the southwest coast of the Crimea, had made there a great arsenal, and furnished it with an enormous supply of warlike stores. And, having been warned a quarter of a century ago[1] that if he thus gathered his strength

Sebastopol.

[1] Dispatch from Count Pozzo di Borgo, dated the 28th of November, 1828-9. 'Although,' writes the Count, 'it may not be probable that we 'shall see an English fleet in the Black Sea, it will be prudent to make Se-'bastopol very secure against attacks from the sea. If ever England were 'to come to a rupture with us, this is the point to which she would direct her 'attacks, if only she believed them possible.'

in Sebastopol, he might have to count some day with the English, the Czar Nicholas had caused the place to be defended toward the sea by forts of great power. In the harbor, barred by these forts, his Black Sea fleet lay at anchor. Plainly it would be a natural and fitting consummation of a war in defense of the Sultan to destroy those very resources which the labors of years had gathered together against him. Moreover, the English, who hate the mechanic contrivances which prevent fair, open fighting, could hardly now bear that the vast sea-forts of Sebastopol should continue to shelter the Russian fleet from the guns of our men-of-war. Those who thought more warily than the multitude foresaw that the enterprise might take time; but they also perceived that even this result would not be one of unmixed evil, for if Russia should commit herself to a lengthened conflict in the neighborhood of Sebastopol, she would be put to a great trial, and would see her wealth and strength ruinously consumed by the mere stress of the distance between the military centre of the empire and the southwesternmost angle of the Crimea.

The longing of the English to attack it.

The more the English people thought of the enterprise, the more eager they became to attempt it; and it chanced that their feelings and opinions were shared and represented with great exactness by the Minister of War.

The Duke of Newcastle was a man of a sanguine, eager nature, very prone to action.[1] He had a good, clear intellect, with more of strength than keenness, unwearied industry, and an astonishing facility of writing. In the assumption of responsibility he was generous and bold even to rashness. Indeed, he was so eager to see his views carried into effect, and so willing to take all the risk upon his own head, that there was danger of his withdrawing from other men their wholesome share of discretion. He threw his whole heart into the project of the invasion; and if the Prime Minister and Mr. Gladstone were men driven forward by the feeling of the country in spite of their opinions and their scruples, it was not so with the Duke of Newcastle. The character of his mind was such as to make him essentially one with the public. Far from being propelled by others against his will, he himself was one of the very foremost members of the warlike throng which was pressing upon the Cabinet, and craving for adventure and

The Duke of Newcastle.

[1] I, of course, know that this view will not be assented to by those who found their opinion upon observation made in later years; but I am speaking of the summer of 1854, and I am very sure that the sentence to which this note has been appended is true.

glory. He easily received new impressions, and had nevertheless a quick good sense, which generally enabled him to distinguish what was useful from what was worthless. He seemed to understand the great truth that, without being military, the English are a warlike people, and that it is one of the great prerogatives of a nation gifted with this higher quality to be able to command other races of men, and to impart to them the fire of martial virtue. He also knew that, when England undertakes war against a great European power, she must engage the energies of the people at large, and must not presume to rely altogether upon the merely professional exertions of her small Peace Establishment. It was not from his default, but in spite of his endeavors, that, for several months, people lingered in the notion that our military system was an apparatus sufficing for war.

But the Duke had not an authority proportioned to the merits which a reader of his dispatches and letters would be inclined to attribute to him. Perhaps the very zeal with which he seized and adopted the ideas of the outer public was one of the causes which tended to lessen his weight; for he who comes into council with common and popular views, however likely it may be that he will get them assented to, can scarcely hope to kindle men's minds with the fire that springs from a man's own thought and from his own strong will. Moreover, it was by a kind of chance rather than by intentional selection that the Duke of Newcastle had become intrusted with the momentous business of the war; and, seemingly, it was only from this circumstance that the propriety of his continuing to hold the office was afterward brought into question by one of his principal colleagues.[1] But, whatever may have been the cause, it seems clear that there was a languor, not to say hollowness, in the support which the Duke got from his

[1] So Lord John Russell himself declared. What I have above called 'a 'kind of chance' was brought about in this way:—According to the practice which was in force up to the summer of 1854, the Secretary of State for the Colonies was also the 'Secretary of War.' Before the war, however, the public hardly observed, and, in fact, hardly knew this; because, in peacetime (thanks to the labors of the 'Horse-Guards,' the office of the Secretary *at* War, the Ordnance, and several other offices), the duties of the Colonial Secretary, in his character as Secretary of War, were very slight; and, there being no prospect of war when Lord Aberdeen's ministry was formed, the Duke of Newcastle was of course selected with a view to his qualifications for the administration of the Colonies, and not with any consideration, either one way or the other, as to his aptitude for the business of the War Department. When the rupture with Russia occurred, it became apparent that, unless a change were made, the minister who happened to be the Colonial Secretary would stand charged with the business of the war.

colleagues. They did not perversely thwart him in the business of the war,[1] but, on the other hand, they did not at all fasten themselves to his measures like men who would stand or fall with him. The Duke of Newcastle had not the gift of knowing how to surround himself with able assistants, and it was his misfortune to be without that precious aid which a Minister commonly finds in the permanent staff of his office. At the outbreak of hostilities, the little bevy of distinct public offices on which the military administration depended was in a condition unfit to meet the exigencies of war. The first Army Surgeon who applied for certain of the medical stores required on foreign service was met with no less than five official theories as to the functionary upon whom the demand should be made; and when, in the month of June, the scattered departments connected with the land service were gathered at last into one, the office thus newly formed was, after all, so ill constituted as to be wanting in some of the simplest appliances required for the transaction of business.

His zeal for the destruction of Sebastopol.

From the first, the Duke of Newcastle, resisting all proposals for operating against Russia on the side of Poland, had warmly shared the popular desire to invade the Crimea, and lay siege to Sebastopol. The Emperor of the French, steadily following his main policy, had long ago consented to look to this enterprise as next in importance to the defense of the Sultan's territory, and, in the early part of April, instructions to this effect had been given to the French and the English Generals.

It would seem, however, that at first the Duke of Newcastle was the only member of the Government who was fired with a great eagerness for the destruction of Sebastopol; and of himself he had not the ascendency which sometimes enables a Minister to bend other men to his purpose. Unless by the help of a mighty force pressing from without, he could not have brought the Cabinet of Lord Aberdeen to partake his zeal for the enterprise.

But—impending over the counsels of all the ostensible rulers—there was an authority not deriving from the Queen or the Parliament, which was destined to have a great sway over

[1] The rejection by the Cabinet of the Duke's proposal to ask for a vote adding 25,000 men to the army does not, in reality, displace the above statement, because the addition to which the Cabinet agreed, though falling short of the Duke's demand, was large enough to warrant the reception of all the recruits who could be obtained in the course of the year, and therefore the proposed vote for a number larger than what could be really obtained was a measure of general policy not tending in any direct way to increase the strength of the army.

events. It would be possible to elude the task, but it seems to me that a history would be wanting in fullness of truth if it failed to impart some conception of this other power.

Commanding power of the people when of one mind.

England was free; and although, whilst there was indifference or divided opinion in the country, the Government had very full latitude of action, yet, whenever it chanced that the feelings of the people were roused, and that they were known to be nearly of one mind, they spoke with a voice so commanding, that no Administration could safely try to withstand it.

But, the will of the nation being thus puissant, who was charged to declare it?

Means of forming and declaring the opinion of the nation.

In former times almost every body who could was accustomed to contribute in an active way to the formation of opinion. Men evolved their own political ideas and drew forth the ideas of their friends by keen oral discussion, and, in later times, by long, elaborate letters. But gradually, and following somewhat slowly upon the invention of printing, there came to be introduced a new division of labor. It was found that if a small number of competent men would make it their calling to transact the business of thinking upon political questions, the work might be more handily performed by them than by the casual efforts of people who were commonly busied in other sorts of toil; and as soon as this change took effect, the weighing of state questions and the judging of public men lapsed away from the direct cognizance of the nation at large, and passed into the hands of those who knew how to utter in print. What had been an intellectual exercise practised in a random way by thousands, was turned into a branch of industry, and pursued with great skill by a few. People soon found out that an essay in print—an essay strong and terse, but above all opportune, seemed to clear their minds more effectually than the sayings which they heard in conversation, or the letters they received from their friends; and at length the principle of divided labor became so complete in its application to the forming of political opinions, that by glancing at a newspaper, and giving swift assent to its assertions and arguments, many an Englishman was saved the labor of farther examining his political conscience, and dispensed from the necessity of having to work his own way to a conclusion.

Effect of political writings in saving men from the trou-

But to spare a man from a healthy toil is not always an unmixed good. To save a free-born citizen from the trouble of thinking upon questions of State is to take from him his share of dominion; and, although it be

ble of thinking. true that he who follows printed advice is under a guidance more skillful and dexterous than any he could have got from his own untutored mind, he is less of a man, and, upon the whole, is less fair, less righteous than one who in a ruder fashion contrives to think for himself. Just as a man's quality may in some respects be lowered by his habitual reliance on the policeman and the soldier who relieve him from the trouble and the anxiety of self-defense, so his intellectual strength and his means of knowing how to be just may easily become impaired if he suffers himself to walk too obediently under the leading of a political writer.

Want of proportion between the skill of the public writer and the judicial competence of his readers.

But the ability of men engaged in political writing grew even more rapidly than the power to which they were attaining, and after a while they so gained upon the ostensible statesmen that Parliament no longer stood alone as the exponent of opinion, and was obliged to share its privilege with a number of gifted men whose names it could hardly ever find out. Still, Parliament had valor and strength of its own, and, except in the matter of mere celebrity, it was a gainer rather than a loser from the wholesome rivalry forced upon it by its new and mysterious associate. It was the public which lagged. Men commonly take a long time to adapt themselves to the successive advances of civilization; and the people were backward in fitting themselves to deal with the increasing ability and the increasing knowledge of the public writer. They, indeed, hardly knew the true scope of the change which had been taking place; for, whilst the writer was a personage chosen for his skill, and acting with the force which belongs to discipline and organization, the readers were men straying loose; and for their means of acting in any thing like concert with one another, they were dependent in a great degree upon that very engine of publicity which was fast usurping their power. Moreover, these readers of public prints were slow to understand the new kind of duty which had come upon them. They were slow to see that it became them to look in a very critical spirit upon the writings of a stranger, unseen and unknown, who was not only proposing to guide them, but even to speak in their name; and they did not yet understand that they ought to read print—not perhaps in a captious spirit, but, to say the least, with something of the measured confidence which their forefathers had been accustomed to place in the words of princes and statesmen. The blessing conferred by print will perhaps be complete when the diligence, the wariness, and, above all, the courageous justice of those who read, shall be brought into fair proportion with the skill and the power of those who address them in print. Already a wholesome change has been wrought; and if in these days a man goes chanting and chanting in servile response to a newspaper, he misses the voices of the tens of thousands of fellow-choristers who sang with him five years ago. But certainly at the time of the Russian war the common discourse of an Englishman was too often a mere "Amen" to something he had seen in print.

For a long time there had remained to the general public a vestige of their old custom of thinking for themselves, because in last resort they were privileged to determine between the rival counsels pressed upon them by contending journalists; but several years before the outbreak of the war there had come yet another change. The apparatus provided by the Constitution for collecting the opinions of the people was far from being complete; and, notwithstanding the indications afforded by Parliament and by public writings, the direction which the nation's opinion had taken was a matter which could often be called in question. Some could say that the people desired one thing, and some, with equal boldness, that the people desired the contrary. Thence it came that the task of finding out the will of the nation, and giving to it a full voice and expression, was undertaken by private citizens.

The task of ascertaining and declaring the opinion of the country falls into the hands of a company.

Long before the outbreak of the war there were living in some of the English counties certain widows and gentlemen, who were the depositaries of a power destined to exercise a great sway over the conduct of the war. Their ways were peaceful, and they were not perhaps more turned toward politics than other widows and country gentlemen, but by force of deeds and testaments, by force of births, deaths, and marriages, they had become the members of an ancient firm or Company which made it its business to collect and disseminate news. They had so much good sense of the worldly sort, that instead of struggling with one another for the control of their powerful engine, they remained quietly at their homes, and engaged some active and gifted men to manage the concern for them in London. The practice of the Company was to issue a paper daily, containing an account of what was going on in the world, together with letters from men of all sorts and conditions who were seeking to bring their favorite subjects under the eye of the public, and also a few short essays upon the topics of the day. Likewise, upon paying the sum required by the Company, any person could cause whatever he chose to be inserted in the paper as an "advertisement," and the sheet containing these four descriptions of matter was sold to the public at a low rate.

Extraordinary enterprise was shown by the Company in the gathering of intelligence; and during the wars following the French Revolution they caused their dispatches from the Continent to reach them so early that they were able to forestall the Government of the day. In other countries the spectacle of a Government outdone in this way by private enterprise would have seemed a scandal; but the Englishman liked the thought that he could buy and bring to his own home as much knowledge as was in the hands of a Minister of State, and he enjoyed the success of his fellow-countrymen in their rivalry with the Government. From this time the paper gathered strength. It became the foremost journal of the world; and this was no sooner the case than the mere fact of its being thus foremost gave a great acceleration to its rise, for simply because it was recognized as the most public of prints it became the clew with which anxious man went seeking in the maze of the busy world for the lost, and the unknown, and all that was beyond his own reach. The prince who was claiming a kingdom, the servant who wanted a place, the mother who had lost her boy, they all went thither. Thither Folly ran hurrying, and was brought to a wholesome parley with Wisdom. Thither went righteous anger. Thither also went hatred and malice. And not in vain was all this concourse; for either the troubled and angry men got the discipline of finding that the world would not listen to their cries, or else they gained a vent for their passions, and brought all their theories to a test by calling a whole nation—nay, by calling the civilized world—to hearken and be their witness. Over all this throng of appellants men unknown sat in judgment, and—violently, perhaps, but never corruptly—a rough sort of justice was done. The style which Oriental hyperbole used to give to the Sultan might be claimed with more color of truth by the journal. In a sense it was the 'asylum of the world.'

Still, up to this point the Company occupied ground in common with many other speculators, and if they had gone no farther, it would not have been my province to notice the result of their labors. But many years ago it had occurred to the managers of this Company that there was one important article of news which had not been effectually supplied. It seemed likely that, without moving from his fireside, an Englishman would be glad to know what the bulk of his fellow-countrymen thought upon the uppermost questions of the day. The letters received from correspondents furnished some means of acquiring this knowledge, and it seemed to the managers of the Company that, at some pains and at a moderate cost, it would be possible to ascertain the opinions which were coming into vogue, and see the direction in which the current would flow. It is said that with this intent they many years ago employed a shrewd, idle clergyman, who made it his duty to loiter about in places of common resort and find out what people thought upon the principal subjects of the time. He was not to listen very much to extreme foolishness, and still less was he to hearken to clever people. His duty was to wait and wait until he observed that some common and obvious thought was repeated in many places, and by numbers of men who had probably never seen one another. That one common thought was the prize he sought for, and he carried it home to his employers. He became so skilled in his peculiar calling that, as long as he served them, the Company was rarely misled; and although in later times they were frequently baffled in their pursuit of this kind of knowledge, they never neglected to do what they could to search the heart of the nation.

When the managers had armed themselves with the knowledge thus gathered, they prepared to disseminate it, but they did not state baldly what they had ascertained to be the opinion of the country. Their method was as follows:—they employed able writers to argue in support of the opinion which, as they believed, the country was already adopting, and, supposing that they had been well informed, their arguments of course fell upon willing ears. Those who had already formed a judgment saw their own notions stated and pressed with an ability greater than they could themselves command; and those who had not yet come to an opinion were strongly moved to do so when they saw the path taken by a Company which notoriously strove to follow the changes of the public mind. The report which the paper gave of the opinion formed by the public was so closely blended with arguments in support of that same opinion, that he who looked at the paper merely to know what other people thought, was seized as he read by the cogency of the reasoning; and, on the other hand, he who imagined that he was being governed by the force of sheer logic, was merely obeying a guide who, by telling him that the world was already agreed, made him go and flock along with his fellows; for, as the utterance of a prophecy is sometimes a main step toward its fulfillment, so a rumor asserting that multitudes have already adopted a given opinion will often generate that very concurrence of thought which was prematurely declared to exist. From the operation of this double process it resulted of course that the opinion of the English public was generally in accord with the writings of the Company; and the more the paper came to be regarded as a true exponent of the national mind, the more vast was the publicity which it obtained.

Plainly, then, this printing Company wielded a great power; and if I have written with sufficient clearness, I have made it apparent that this was a power of more vast dimensions than that which men describe when they speak of "the power of the Press." It is one thing, for instance, to denounce a public man by printed arguments and invectives which are believed to utter nothing more than the opinion of the writers, and it is another and a graver thing to denounce him in writings which, though having the form of arguments, are (rightly or wrongly) regarded as manifestoes—as manifestoes declaring the judgment of the English people. In the one case the man is only accused, in the other he seems to stand already condemned.

But though the Company held all this power, their tenure of it was of such a kind that they could not exercise it perversely or whimsically without doing a great harm to their singular trade; for the whole scheme of their existence went to make them—not autocratic, but—representative in their character, and they were obliged by the law of their being to keep themselves as closely as they could in accord with the nation at large.

This, then, was the great English journal; and, whether men spoke of the mere printed sheet which lay upon their table, or of the mysterious organization which produced it, they habitually called either one or the other 'The Times.' Moreover, they often prefixed to the word such adjectives and participles as showed that they regarded the subject of their comments in the light of a sentient, active being, having a life beyond the span of mortal men, gifted with reason, armed with a cruel strength, endued with some of the darkest of the human passions, but clearly liable hereafter to the direst penalty of sin.[1]

On the Sabbath England had rest, but in the early morning of all other days the irrevocable words were poured forth and scattered abroad to the corners of the earth, measuring out honor to some, and upon others bringing scorn and disgrace.

[1] The form of speech which thus impersonates a manufactory and its wares has now so obtained in our language that—discarding the forcible epithets—one may venture to adopt it in writing, and to give *The Times* the same place in grammatical construction as though it were the proper name of an angel or a hero, a devil or a saint, or a sinner already condemned. Custom makes it good English to say 'The *Times* will protect him,' 'The *Times* is savage,' 'The *Times* is crushing him,' 'The blessed *Times* has put the thing right,' 'That d——d *Times* has done all the mischief.'

Where and with whom the real power lay, and what was its true source, and how it was to be propitiated—these were questions wrapped in more or less obscurity; for some had a theory that one man ruled, and some another, and some were sure that the Great Newspaper governed all England, and others that England governed the Newspaper. Philosophic politicians traced events to what they called 'Public opinion.' With almost the same meaning, women and practical men simply spoke of 'The Times.' But, whether the power of the great journal was a power all its own, or whether it was only the vast shadow of the public mind, it was almost equally to be dreaded and revered by worldly men; for plainly in that summer of 1854 it was one with England. Its words might be wrong, but it was certain that to tens of thousands of men they would seem to be right. They might be the collected voice of all these isles, or the mere utterance of some one unknown man sitting pale by a midnight lamp—but there they were. They were the handwriting on the wall.

Of the temper and spirit in which this strange power had been wielded, up to the time of the outbreak of the war, it is not very hard to speak. In general, 'The Times' had been more willing to lead the nation in its tendencies to improvement than to follow it in its errors; what it mainly sought was —not to be much better or wiser than the English people, but to be the very same as they were, to go along with them in all their adventures, whether prudent or rash, to be one with them in their hopes and their despair, in their joy and in their sorrow, in their gratitude and in their anger. So, although in general it was willing enough to repress the growth of any new popular error which seemed to be weakly rooted, still the whole scheme and purpose of the Company forbade it all thought of trying to make a stand against any great and general delusion. Upon the whole, the potentate dealt with England in a bluff, kingly, Tudor-like way, but also with a Tudor-like policy; for, though he treated all adversaries as 'brute folk' until they became formidable, he had always been careful to mark the growth of a public sentiment or opinion, and, as soon as he was able to make out that a cause was waxing strong, he went up and offered to lead it, and so reigned.

I have said that partly by guiding, but more by ascertaining and following the current of men's opinion, 'The Times' always sought to be one with the great body of the people; and since it happened that there was at this period a rare concurrence of feeling, and that the journal, after a good deal of experiment, had now at length thoroughly seized and embodied the soul of the nation, its utterance came with increasing force; and in proportion as the growing concord of the people enabled it to speak with more and more authority, power lapsed and continued to lapse from out of the hands of the Government, until at length public opinion—no longer content to direct the general policy of the State—was preparing to undertake the almost scientific, the almost technical duty of planning a campaign.

The opinion of the nation as declared by the Company demands the destruction of Sebastopol.

On the morning of the 15th of June, the great newspaper declared and said that 'The grand political and military objects of the war could not be attained as long 'as Sebastopol and the Russian fleet were in existence, but that if that central position of the Russian power in the south of the empire were annihilated, the whole fabric, which it had cost the Czars of Russia 'centuries to raise, must fall to the ground;' and moreover it declared, 'that the taking of Sebastopol and the occupation of 'the Crimea were objects which would repay all the costs of 'the war, and would permanently settle in our favor the principal questions in dispute, and that it was equally clear that 'those objects were to be accomplished by no other means, because a peace which should leave Russia in possession of the 'same means of aggression would only enable her to recommence the war at her pleasure.'

It was natural that some of the members of the Government should have qualms. They knew that Austria (supported for defensive purposes by Prussia) was at that time on the point of joining her arms to those of the Western Powers; and they could not but know that if the French and English armies were to be withdrawn from the main land of Europe in order to invade the Crimea, the wholesome union of the Four Powers would of necessity be weakened. The Prime Minister was he who loved peace so fondly that, though peace was no more, he had hardly yet been torn from her cold embrace; and though he lived under a belief that the military strength of the Czar was beyond measure vast, yet of the twelve months which Russia gave him for preparation he had only used three.[1] Having the heaviness of these thoughts on his mind, he saw it declared aloud that the country of which he happened to be the Prime Minister could not well do otherwise than invade the Russian dominions. To a prudent man the measure might

[1] Computing from the time when the Czar's determination to seize the Principalities was known to our Government. If the computations are to be made from the time when the hostile character of Prince Mentschikoff's mission became known, several months more would have to be added. See Lord Aberdeen's evidence before the Sebastopol Committee.

seem to be rash. To a good man, impressed with horror of war, it might even seem to be very wicked, for it was a violent revival of a war which, unless this new torch were thrown, would expire of its own accord. But the print was clear; like stern Anangkie it pressed upon feeble man's volition, for it was not to be construed away; and if an anxious Minister went back and looked again to see whether by chance he could find some loop in the wording, and whether possibly he might be able to fulfill his duty without besieging Sebastopol, he was met by the careful negation which taught him in four plain words that he could fulfill it 'by no other means.'

Before the seventh day from the manifesto of the 15th, the country had made loud answer to the appeal, and on the 22nd of June the great newspaper, informed with the deep will of the people, and taking little account of the fears of the prudent and the scruples of the good, laid it down that 'Sebastopol was 'the keystone of the arch which spanned the Euxine, from the 'mouths of the Danube to the confines of Mingrelia,' and that 'a successful enterprise against the place was the essential con- 'dition of permanent peace.' And although this appeal was founded in part upon a false belief—a belief that the siege of Silistria had been raised—it seemed as though all mankind were making haste to adjust the world to the newspaper, for within twenty hours from the publication of the 22nd of June, truth obeyed the voice of false rumors, and followed in the wake of 'The Times.'[1]

Of course there were those who saw great obstacles in the way of the proposed invasion, and they said that since Russia was a first-rate military Power, it must be rash to invade her territory, and to besiege her proudest fortress, without first gaining some safe knowledge of the enemy's strength. But the narrative then coming home in fragments from the valley of the Danube was heating the minds of the people in England.

When first England learned that the Turks were to be besieged in their fortress of Silistria by a great Russian army under the renowned Paskievitch, few believed that the issue was doubtful, or even that the contest could be long sustained. But as soon as it became known that day after day the military strength of the Czar was exerted against the place with a violent energy, and that every attack was fiercely resisted, and always as yet with success, our people began to give their heart to the struggle; and their eagerness rose into zeal when

[1] The siege, as we saw above, was raised early in the morning of the 23rd.

they heard that two young English travelers had thrown themselves into the fortress, were heading the Turkish soldiery, and were maintaining the conflict by day and by night.

The English were not of such a mettle as to be able to hear of tidings like these without growing more and more eager for warlike adventure. And in their hearts they liked the fact that the few young English travelers who helped to save Silistria and to turn away the war from the Danube were men who did these things of their own free will and pleasure, without the sanction of the public authorities; for our people are accustomed to think more highly of their fellow-countrymen individually than they do of our State machinery, and they can easily bear to see their Government in default, and can even smile at its awkwardness, if all the shortcomings of office are effectually compensated by the vigor of private enterprise. Nasmyth has passed away from us. I knew him in the Crimea. He was a man of quiet and gentle manners, and so free from vanity, so free from all idea of self-gratulation, that he always seemed as though he were unconscious of having stood as he did in the path of the Czar, and had really omitted to think of the share which he had had in changing the course of events; but it chanced that he had gone to the seat of war in the service of 'The Times,' and naturally the lustre of his achievement was in some degree shed upon the keen, watchful Company which had had the foresight to send him at the right moment into the midst of events on which the fate of Russia was hanging; for, whilst the State armies of France and England were as yet only gathering their strength, 'The Times' was able to say that its own officer had confronted the enemy upon the very ground he most needed to win, and helped to drive him back from the Danube in great discomfiture.

Thus day after day, in that month of June, the authority of the Newspaper kept gaining and gaining upon the Queen's Government, and if Lord Aberdeen had any remaining unwillingness to renew the war by undertaking an invasion of Russia, his power of controlling the course of the Government seems to have come to its end in the interval between the 23rd and the 27th of June. He continued to be the Prime Minister. His personal honor stood so high that no man attributed his continuance in office to other than worthy and unselfish motives; but, for those who lay stress upon the principle that office and power ought not to be put asunder, it was irksome to have to mark the difference between what the Prime Minister was believed to desire, and what he was now consenting to do.

The Government yields.

Parliament was sitting, and it might be imagined that there was something to say against the plan for invading a province of Russia at a moment when all the main causes of the dispute were vanishing; but the same causes which I have spoken of as paralyzing all resistance to the beginning of the war now hindered every attempt to withstand its renewal, for the orators who were believed to be tainted with the doctrines of the Peace Party were still lying under the ban which they had brought upon themselves by their former excesses of language. So now again in June, as before at the opening of the session, the counsels of these eloquent men were lost to the world. They became as powerless as the Prime Minister, and the cause which they represented was so utterly brought to ruin that the popular demand for an invasion, which carried with it the virtual renewal of an otherwise expiring war, had the sound of that voice with which a nation speaks when the people are of one mind.

No good stand made in Parliament against the invasion.

So now, in presenting to his colleagues this his favorite scheme of an enterprise against Sebastopol, the Duke of Newcastle was upheld — nay, was urged and driven forward — by forces so overwhelming, that scruples, and objections, and fears were carried away as by a flood; and when it was proposed in the Cabinet to go and fetch, as it were, a new war by undertaking this bold adventure, there was not one Minister present who refused to give his consent.

Forthwith the Duke of Newcastle announced the decision of the Government to the General commanding the English army in Bulgaria. He did this by a private letter written on the 28th of June,[1] and nearly at the same time he prepared the draught of a Dispatch[1] which was to convey to the English head-quarters, in full detail and in official form, the deliberate instructions of the Queen's Government. This paper was to be the instrument for meting out to the General in command the allowance of discretion with which he was to be intrusted. A Dispatch recommending the expedition, but leaving to the General in command the duty of determining whether it could be prudently undertaken, would not have been followed by any invasion of the Crimea; and that which brought about the event was — not the decision of the Cabinet already mentioned, but —the peculiar stringency of the language which was to convey it to the English head-quarters.[2] It therefore seems right to

Preparation of the instructions addressed to Lord Raglan.

[1] The contents of this will be given in another chapter.

[2] The truth of this statement will be shown, as I think, in a future chapter,

speak of what passed when the terms of this cogent Dispatch were adopted by Lord Aberdeen's Cabinet.

The Duke of Newcastle so framed the draught as to make it the means of narrowing very closely the discretion left to Lord Raglan; and it was to be expected that the Duke might wish his Dispatch to stand in this shape, because he was eager for the undertaking, and very willing to bear upon his own shoulders a large share of the responsibility which it entailed; but it is difficult to believe that all the other members of the Government could have intended to place the English General under that degree of compulsion which is implied by the tenor of the instructions. It is certain, however, that the paper was well fitted to elicit at once the objections of those who might be inclined to disapprove it on account of its cogency, for it confined the discretion to be left to the General with a precision scarcely short of harshness.

The Duke of Newcastle took the Dispatch to Richmond, for there was to be a meeting of the members of the Cabinet at Pembroke Lodge, and he intended to make this the occasion for submitting the proposed instructions to the judgment of his colleagues. It was evening, a summer evening, and all the members of the Cabinet were present when the Duke took out the draught of his proposed dispatch and began to read it. Then there occurred an incident, very trifling in itself, but yet so momentous in its consequences that, if it had happened in old times, it would have been attributed to the direct intervention of the immortal Gods. In these days, perhaps the physiologist will speak of the condition into which the human brain is naturally brought when it rests after anxious labors, and the analytical chemist may regret that he had not an opportunity of testing the food of which the Ministers had partaken, with a view to detect the presence of some narcotic poison; but no well-informed person will look upon the accident as characteristic of the men whom it befell, for the very faults, no less than the high qualities of the statesmen composing Lord Aberdeen's Cabinet were of such a kind as to secure them against the imputation of being careless and torpid. However, it is very certain that, before the reading of the paper had long continued, all the members of the Cabinet except a small minority were overcome with sleep.[1] For a moment the noise of a tumbling chair disturbed the repose of the Government; but presently the Duke of Newcastle resumed the reading of his draught, and then again the fated sleep descended upon

and, indeed, it is well enough proved by the tenor of Lord Raglan's reply to the dispatch.

[1] See Note in the Appendix.

the eyelids of Ministers. Later in the evening, and in another room, the Duke of Newcastle made another and a last effort to win attention to the contents of the draught, but again a blissful rest (not, this time, actual sleep) interposed between Ministers and cares of State, and all, even those who from the first had remained awake, were in a quiet, assenting frame of mind. Upon the whole, the Dispatch, though it bristled with sentences tending to provoke objection, received from the Cabinet the kind of approval which is often awarded to an unobjectionable sermon. Not a letter of it was altered; and it will be seen by-and-by that that cogency in the wording of the Dispatch, which could hardly have failed to provoke objection from an awakened Cabinet, was the very cause which governed events.

Instructions sent to the French commander.

The instructions addressed from Paris to the French commander did not urge him to propose the invasion of the Crimea, nor even to lend the weight of his opinion to the proposed enterprise, but they forbade him from advancing toward the Danube. If it should be clear that the English were willing to undertake the expedition to the Crimea, then the French Commander was not to be at liberty to hold back.[1]

---

## CHAPTER XXXII.

The Allies at Varna. Their state of preparation in the middle of July.

AT the time when the instructions from the Home Governments reached the camp of the Allies, the generals were preparing for an active campaign in Bulgaria, and Marshal St. Arnaud had around him, in the neighborhood of Varna, or moving thither, four strong divisions of infantry, with cavalry and field-artillery. He had no siege train.

Lord Raglan had around him four divisions of infantry, the greater part of a division of cavalry, and of his field-artillery seven batteries. He had also on board ship off Varna the half of a battering train, and the other half was nearly ready to be dispatched from England.

The French Marshal was receiving and expecting constant additions to his force, and Lord Raglan had been apprized that

[1] I deduce this conclusion in an inferential way, from the general tenor of the materials at my command, and not from any one document distinctly warranting the statement.

a reserve division of infantry under Sir George Cathcart would speedily reach the Bosphorus.

So long as the French and English forces remained camped in the neighborhood of Varna, their command of the sea-communication insured to them the arrival of the supplies which were sent to them; but the means of land-transport were not yet within their reach. It was estimated that, in order to move effectively in the interior, the English army alone would require pack-horses or mules to the number of 14,000. To obtain these was difficult, but not impossible; and, at the time to which we point, about 5000 had been collected. By a continuance of these exertions in Bulgaria, and by due activity in forwarding munitions and stores from England, it is probable that the English force, after a farther interval of about six weeks or two months, might have been prepared to move as an army carrying on regular operations; but of course this would only be true upon the supposition that the army should always march through countries yielding sufficient forage.

The preparations of the French were not, perhaps, quite so far advanced as our own; but it is probable that the two armies would have been found ready at about the same time for an active campaign in Bulgaria.

*Their command of the sea.*

The ships of the Allied Powers were at hand, and their fleets had dominion over all the Euxine home to the Straits of Kertch. They had the command of the Bosphorus, the Dardanelles, the Mediterranean, of the whole ocean; and of all the lesser seas, bays, gulfs, and straits, from the Gut of Gibraltar to within sight of St. Petersburg. The Czar's Black Sea fleet existed, but existed in close durance, shut up under the guns of Sebastopol.

*Information obtained by the Foreign Office as to the defenses of the Crimea.*

In the matter of gaining information respecting the enemy's resources, our Foreign Office had not been idle; and a great deal of material, bearing upon this vital business, had been carefully got together and collated. It resulted from these data, that, spread over vast space, Russia might nominally have under arms forces approaching to a million of men; but that the force in the Crim Chersonese, including the 17,000 men who formed the crews of the ships, did not at the highest estimate amount to more than 45,000; and that, although there were a few battalions which Russia might draw toward Sebastopol from her army of the Caucasus, she had no more speedy method of largely re-enforcing the Crimea than by availing herself of the troops then in retreat from the country of the Danube, and marching them round to Perekop by the northern shores of the Euxine.

No information obtained in the Levant.

Neither the ambassadors of France and England at Constantinople, nor any of their generals or admirals, had succeeded in obtaining for themselves any trustworthy information upon this vitally momentous business. For their failure in this respect more blame attaches upon the ambassadors than upon the military and naval commanders, because the ambassadors had been in the Levant during a period of many months, in which (since the war was impending, but not declared) they might have bought knowledge from Russian subjects without involving their informers in the perils of treason. The duty of gathering knowledge by clandestine means is one so repulsive to the feelings of an English gentleman, that there is always a danger of his neglecting it or performing it ill. Perhaps no two men could be less fit for the business of employing spies than Lord Stratford and Lord Raglan. More diligence might have been expected from the French, but they also had failed. Marshal St. Arnaud had heard a rumor that the force of the enemy in the Crimea was 70,000; and Vice-Admiral Dundas had even received a statement that it amounted to 120,000. But these accounts were fables. In point of fact, the information obtained by our Foreign Office approached to near the truth, and the Duke of Newcastle had the firmness—it was a daring thing to do, but it turned out that he was right—he had the firmness to press Lord Raglan to rely upon it. It was natural, however, that a general who was within a few hours' sail of the country which he was to invade, and was yet unable to obtain from it any, even slight, glimmer of knowledge, should distrust information which had traveled round to him (through the aid of the Home Government) along the circumference of a vast circle; and Lord Raglan certainly considered that, in regard to the strength of the enemy in the Crimea and the land defenses of Sebastopol, he was simply without knowledge.

Lord Raglan conceived that he was absolutely without any trustworthy information.

---

## CHAPTER XXXIII.

The instructions for the invasion of the Crimea reach the Allied camp.

ON the evening of the 13th of July Marshal St. Arnaud received a telegraphic dispatch from his Government. The dispatch had been forwarded by way of Belgrade, and was in cipher. The message came in an imperfect state. Part of it was intelligible, but the rest was beyond all the power of the decipherer. Yet the interpreted symbols showed plainly that the whole message, if only it could be read, would prove to be one of deep import. It forbade Marshal St. Arnaud from making any advance toward the Danube, and told him to look to the event of his army being conveyed from Varna by the fleet. This was all that could be deciphered. There were the mystic letters and figures which laid down, as was surmised, the destiny of the Allied armies, and no one could read. At night Colonel Trochu came to Lord Raglan's quarters, and communicated all that could be gathered from the telegraphic dispatch. The English General had just received the Duke of Newcastle's letter of the 28th, but had not yet broken the seal of it. Now, however, Lord Raglan opened the letter, and in a few moments he was able to give M. Trochu the means of inferring the matter contained in the illegible part of his dispatch. Apparently it was the desire of both the Home Governments that the Allied commanders should prepare to make a descent upon the Crimea, and lay siege to Sebastopol.

On the 16th of July the dispatch of the 29th of June was received at the English head-quarters; and a dispatch forwarded from Paris at nearly the same time reached the hands of Marshal St Arnaud.

The men who had to determine upon the effect to be given to the instructions.

Since the proposed expedition involved the employment of both land and sea forces, the duty of determining upon the effect to be given to the instructions from home devolved upon those who had the command of the Anglo-French armies and fleets. These were three: Marshal St. Arnaud (having Admiral Hamelin under his orders), Lord Raglan, and Vice-Admiral Dundas.

Marshal St. Arnaud.

Marshal St. Arnaud had not weight proportioned to the magnitude of his command. Reputed at first to be daring even to the verge of rashness, we have seen him so cautioned and schooled into strategic prudence as to have determined to place hundreds of miles of territory, and even the great range of the Balkan, between the French and the Russians; and now, within the last week, he had been almost reproved by his Government for want of enterprise. Colonel Trochu, admitted into consultation upon the most momentous affairs, seemed to wield great authority. At Constantinople and at Varna, no less than in Paris, the Marshal had been made the victim of unsparing tongues. Indeed at this time two of his divisional generals openly indulged in merciless invectives against their chief; and soldiers all know that a general officer thus setting himself against the commander-in-chief is never without a great following. Perhaps, as had been at first supposed, it may have been true that boldness and craving for adventure were the true lines of the Marshal's character; but, if that were so, his native ideas had been overlaid by much counsel and bent into unwonted shapes. After a while, as will be seen, his mind, fatigued by advice, and now and then broken down by bodily illness, began to lapse into a state which rendered him almost passive in very critical moments. Naturally, he had been cowed by the result of his endeavors to have his own way against Lord Stratford and Lord Raglan. He was without ascendency in the camp of the Allies.

Colonel Trochu was a student of the principles applicable to formal inland warfare, and it was to be expected that the more the obstacles to the proposed undertaking were canvassed, the more likely it would be that he would throw the weight of his scientific advice into the negative scale.

Upon the whole it resulted, from the composition of the various forces acting upon the mind of M. St. Arnaud, that, whatever opinion he might lean to, he was not strong enough to be able to act upon events. If the English should decide against the project, he would be well content, and perhaps much relieved. If, on the other hand, the English should press for its adoption, then the French Marshal would do his best to carry it to a good conclusion.

Admiral Hamelin.

The French fleet was commanded by Admiral Hamelin. It was understood that he disapproved the expedition, but he was under the orders of the chief who commanded the land forces.

Omar Pasha.

It was not at that time a part of the project to move any very large proportion of the Turkish army to the coast of the Crimea, and therefore the opinion of Omar Pasha would hardly become a governing ingredient in the counsels of the Allies. It was known, however, that he deprecated the proposed invasion.

Admiral Dundas.

The English fleet was commanded by Vice-Admiral Dundas. Most of the Vice-Admiral's latter years had been passed in political and official life, and it was by force of politics that he had now become troubled with the business of war; for his seat at the Admiralty Board, and his subsequent appointment in peace-time to the command of the Mediterranean fleet, were things which stood in the relation of cause and effect. He had not sought to return to scenes of naval strife, but the war overtook him in his marine retirement, converting his expected repose into anxious toil. He was an able, a steadfast, a genial man, and his square Scottish head, and his rough, shrewd, good-humored eyebrows, had grown gray in the faithful service of a political party. By nature he was so stout-hearted that he could afford to give free, manly counsel without the least dread lest men should say he was too cautious. His habits as a working subordinate member of Government, and perhaps also his natural temperament, inclined him to take a homely view of questions, a view recommended by what men term 'common sense.' I am sure, though I never heard him say so, that he believed the war to be extremely foolish, and that the less there was of it, the better it would be for the Whigs and for all the rest of mankind. He spoke and went straightforward. He thoroughly disapproved the project of invasion, and he said so in plain words. His opinion sprang—not from dread of peril to the forces which he himself commanded, but from anxiety—anxiety in every way honorable to him—for the safety of the English army. That that anxiety was altogether vain, or even that it was weakly founded, few men, speaking with the light of the past, will be ready to say. Still less will it be thought that the Vice-Admiral was wrong in giving bold expression to his views.

Admiral Dundas's command was of course independent of the general in command of the English army; but the feasibility of the sea transit was not at all in question,[1] and it was plain, therefore, that the decision would properly rest with those who were responsible for the direction of the land forces. So, although he held stoutly to his own opinion, the Vice-Admiral did not fail to give assurance that, if the decision of the Generals should be in favor of undertaking the expedition, they might rely upon the aid of the English fleet.

Lord Raglan.

There remained Lord Raglan: and now it is time to give the words of the instructions which had been addressed to him, as we have already seen, by the Secretary of State.

The private letter which was the forerunner of the detailed dispatch ran thus:—

The instructions addressed to him by the Home Government.

'Since I last wrote to you, events unknown to you at the 'date of these letters have been brought to us by 'the telegraph, and the raising the siege of Silistria, and the retreat of the Russian army across 'the Danube (preparatory probably to a retreat 'across the Pruth), give an entirely new aspect to the war, and

[1] Dundas, I think, said fairly and bluntly that he could undertake to land the army on the coast of the Crimea, but not to supply it, nor to bring it back.

'render it necessary at once to consider what shall be our next 'move.

'The Cabinet is unanimously of the opinion that, unless you 'and Marshal St. Arnaud feel that you are not sufficiently pre-'pared, you should lay siege to Sebastopol, as we are more than 'ever convinced that, without the reduction of this fortress and 'the capture of the Russian fleet, it will be impossible to con-'clude an honorable and safe peace. The Emperor of the 'French has expressed his entire concurrence in this opinion, 'and, *I believe*, has written privately to the Marshal to that ef-'fect. I shall submit to the Cabinet a dispatch to you on this 'subject, and if it is approved you may expect it by the next 'mail. In the mean time I hope you will be turning over in 'your own mind, and considering with your French colleague, 'what it will be safe and advisable to do.'[1]

So far as it related to the expedition which the Allies under-took, the promised dispatch was in these words:—

'*Secret.*

'War Department, 29th June, 1854.

'My Lord,—In my dispatch of the 10th April, marked "Se-'cret," I directed your Lordship to make careful inquiry into 'the amount and condition of the Russian force in the Crimea, 'and the strength of the fortress of Sebastopol.

'At the same time I pointed out to your Lordship that, 'whilst it was your first duty to prevent, by every means in 'your power, the advance of the Russian army on Constanti-'nople, supposing any such intention to exist, it might become 'essential for the attainment of the objects of the war to un-'dertake operations of an offensive character, and that the 'heaviest blow which could be struck at the southern extrem-'ities of the Russian empire would be the taking or destruction 'of Sebastopol. The events which have recently occurred, and 'which have become known to Her Majesty's Government by 'means of the telegraph from Belgrade—the gallant and suc-'cessful resistance of the Turkish army, the raising of the siege 'of Silistria, the retreat of the Russian army across the Dan-'ube, and the anticipated evacuation of the Principalities—'have given a new character to the war, and will render it 'necessary for you without delay to concert measures with 'Marshal St. Arnaud, and with Admirals Dundas and Hamelin, 'suited to the circumstances in which these events have placed 'the Allied forces.

[1] Private letter from the Duke of Newcastle to Lord Raglan, dated 28th June, 1854.

'The safety of Constantinople from any invasion of the Rus- 'sian army is now, for a time at least, secured, and the advance 'of the English and French armies to Varna and Pravadi has 'succeeded in its object, without their being called upon to 'meet the enemy in action.

'Any farther advance of the Allied armies should on no ac- 'count be contemplated. To occupy the Dobrutscha would 'be productive of no beneficial results, and would be fatally 'prejudicial to the health of the troops; and even if the Rus- 'sian army should not recross the Pruth, but continue in the 'occupation of the Principalities, it is the decided opinion of 'Her Majesty's Government that, for the present at least, no 'measures should be taken by you to dislodge them.

'The circumstances anticipated in my dispatch before re- 'ferred to have, therefore, now arrived; and I have, on the part 'of Her Majesty's Government, to instruct your Lordship to 'concert measures for the siege of Sebastopol, unless, with the 'information in your possession, but at present unknown in this 'country, you should be decidedly of opinion that it could not 'be undertaken with a reasonable prospect of success. The 'confidence with which Her Majesty placed under your com- 'mand the gallant army now in Turkey is unabated; and if, 'upon mature reflection, you should consider that the united 'strength of the two armies is insufficient for this undertaking, 'you are not to be precluded from the exercise of the discre- 'tion originally vested in you, though Her Majesty's Govern- 'ment will learn with regret that an attack from which such 'important consequences are anticipated must be any longer 'delayed.

'The difficulties of the siege of Sebastopol appear to Her 'Majesty's Government to be more likely to increase than di- 'minish by delay; and as there is no prospect of a safe and 'honorable peace until the fortress is reduced, and the fleet tak- 'en or destroyed, it is, on all accounts, most important that 'nothing but insuperable impediments—such as the want of 'ample preparations by either army, or the possession by Rus- 'sia of a force in the Crimea greatly outnumbering that which 'can be brought against it—should be allowed to prevent the 'early decision to undertake these operations.

'This decision should be taken solely with reference to the 'means at your disposal, as compared with the difficulties to 'be overcome.

'It is probable that a large part of the Russian army now 'retreating from the Turkish territory may be poured into the 'Crimea to re-enforce Sebastopol. If orders to this effect have 'not already been given, it is farther probable that such a 'measure would be adopted as soon as it is known that the 'Allied armies are in motion to commence active hostilities. 'As all communications by sea are now in the hands of the 'Allied Powers, it becomes of importance to endeavor to cut 'off all communication by land between the Crimea and the 'other parts of the Russian dominions.

* * * * * * *
* * * * * * *
* * * * * * *
* * * * * * *

'It is unnecessary to express any opinion, at this distance 'from the scene, as to the mode in which these operations 'should be conducted, or the place at which a disembarkation 'should be effected; and as the latter will, of course, be de-'cided with the advice and assistance of the French and En-'glish Admirals, it is equally unnecessary to impress upon your 'Lordship the importance of selecting favorable weather for 'the purpose, and avoiding all risks of being obliged by storms 'to withdraw from the shore the vessels of war and transports, 'when only a partial landing of the troops has been effected.

* * * * * * *
* * * * * * *
* * * * * * *
* * * * * * *

'I have only farther to express to you, on the part of Her 'Majesty's Government, their entire reliance in your judgment, 'zeal, and discretion; and their conviction that, while you will 'not expose the army under your command to unnecessary 'risk, you will not forget that to the gallantry and conduct of 'your troops their countrymen are now looking to secure, by 'the blessing of Providence, the great object of a just war, the 'vindication of national rights, and the future security of the 'peace of Europe.

'I have the honor to be, my Lord, your Lordship's obedient, 'humble servant, NEWCASTLE.

'General the Lord Raglan, G. C. B., &c., &c., &c.'

Extreme stringency of the instructions.

In common circumstances, and especially where the whole of the troops to be engaged are under one commander, it can not be right for any sovereign or any minister to address such instructions as these to a general on a distant shore; for the general who is to be intrusted with the sole command of a great expedition must be, of all mankind, the best able to judge of its military prudence; and to give him orders thus cogent is to dispense with his counsel.

But in this war, the united forces of France and England were under two commanders; and, besides, since the expedition was dependent upon naval co-operation, the admirals of the two fleets would necesarily be taken into council. It is true that the French admiral was under the orders of Marshal St. Arnaud, but there was no corresponding arrangement in regard to the English services, and our admiral's command was independent of the general commanding the land forces.

Considerations tending to justify this stringency.

Thus, it seemed to the Home Government that the question, if left to be decided on the shores of the Black Sea, would have to be weighed, not by one commander, but by a council of at least four, and to be actually decided by a council of not less than three; and it would scarcely be expected that such a body, deliberating freely, would come to that vigorous decision which might easily, perhaps, be attained by any one of them singly. On the other hand, the two Governments were perfectly agreed. Upon the whole, therefore, there was some ground for resolving to transmit to the camps at Varna the benefit of that concord which reigned between Paris and London, and to subject the generals and admirals to the overruling judgment of the authorities at home.

Again, the chief reason which makes it unwise to fetter the discretion of generals—namely, the superior knowledge which they are supposed to have of the enemy's strength and of the field of operations—was, in this instance, wanting; for the generals in the camp at Varna had absolutely no trustworthy information except what came to them from Paris or London; and, in their power of testing the statements which reached them in this way, they were below the Home Governments, for they did not so well know the sources from which the accounts were drawn.

Justice requires that these considerations should have their weight, for they tend, in some measure, to explain the extreme stringency of the instructions. The Minister who framed them had determined, with a boldness very rare in modern times, to take upon himself an immense weight of responsibility; and, having brought himself to this strong resolve, he rightly and generously did all he could to simplify the task of the general whom he ventured to direct, and to make the path of duty seem clear.

But Lord Raglan had a station in the allied camp which made it very difficult for the Home Government to take his

The power of deciding for or against the expedition becomes practically vested in Lord Raglan alone.

burden upon themselves by any mere bold form of words. He commanded the land forces, but he was clothed with a power of older date than the Queen's commission. He had been privy to the business of the wars which England waged in the great days; and, if he had seen how Wellington ordered affairs in the field, he had witnessed, too, his endurance, and helped him in the patient, unapplauded toil by which he prepared the end. Men serving under Lord Raglan were none of them blind to the distance which history herself interposed betwixt their general and themselves. There were none near the chief who would not feel bitter pain if they imagined that words or acts of theirs had thrown upon his face a shadow of displeasure. There were no men near him who would not fly with alacrity to execute his slightest wish. The ascendency of the English General over his own people could not but reach into the French camp. Upon the whole, Lord Raglan had so great an authority in the camp of the Allies, and amongst public men in England, that, if he had taken upon himself to resist the pressure of the Secretary of State, he would not have been left without support. On the other hand, if he should determine to follow the will of the Home Government, he would carry the French Marshal with him. So, in effect, the power of deciding for or against the expedition had passed from Paris and from London, and was all concentred in the English General.

Lord Raglan's deliberations.

Of the general officers in the English camp there was one whom Lord Raglan had always been anxious to have near at hand. This was Sir George Brown. He was a Scotsman, 66 years old, and had served with a great repute for his daring forwardness in some of the most bloody scenes of the Peninsular war. He was of an eager, fiery nature, and devoted to the calling of a soldier. After the peace of 1815 he began to hold office in the general staff of the army at the Horse-Guards, and in time he became adjutant-general. He now commanded the Light Division. His zeal, and his lengthened toils in the adjutant-general's office, had drawn him too far in a narrow path, and he overplied the idea of discipline, but he abounded in energy, and he was in many respects an accomplished soldier. He wrote on military subjects with clearness, with grace, and seemingly with a good deal of ease.

He requests the opinion of Sir George Brown.

After receiving the Duke of Newcastle's dispatch, Lord Raglan sent for Sir George Brown, and expressed to him a wish to have his opinion about it. He handed the paper to Sir George across the table, and then went on with his writing, leaving Sir George to consider its contents at his leisure. When he had read it, Lord Raglan asked him to give him his opinion. Before giving it, Sir George naturally inquired what information Lord Raglan had obtained in regard to the strength of Sebastopol, and what force he expected might be opposed to him in the Crimea.

Lord Raglan's answer was that he had no information whatever; that neither he nor Marshal St. Arnaud knew what amount of force the enemy had there; that they believed and hoped there might not be more than 70,000 men in the peninsula; but that, in fact, it had not been blockaded, and that no means had been taken to procure information, and that therefore they did not in reality know they might not be opposed by 100,000 men or even more.

Then Sir George Brown said, 'You and I are accustomed, 'when in any great difficulty, or when any important question 'is proposed to us, to ask ourselves how the Great Duke would 'have acted and decided under similar circumstances. Now, 'I tell your Lordship that, without more certain information 'than you appear to have obtained in regard to this matter, 'that great man would not have accepted the responsibility of 'undertaking such an enterprise as that which is now proposed 'to you! But, notwithstanding that consideration, I am of 'opinion that you had better accede to the proposal, and come 'into the views of the Government, for this reason, that it is 'clear to me, from the tenor of the Duke of Newcastle's letter, 'that they have made up their minds to it at home, and that, 'if you decline to accept the responsibility, they will send some 'one else out to command the army, who will be less scrupu- 'lous and more ready to come into their plans.'

Lord Raglan's determination.

This suggestion did not at all govern Lord Raglan's decision. At the time he disclosed no opinion of his own; but he soon made up his mind. His decision was governed by views which must be explained. He believed that the enterprise was one of a very hazardous kind, and was not warranted by any safe information concerning the state of the enemy's forces. Having that conviction, why did he not feel bound to assert it, notwithstanding the urgency of the Home Government? Lord Raglan was, as might be supposed, deeply imbued with reverence for the authority of the Duke of Wellington, and, rightly interpreted, that authority is surely the safest guide that an English general can follow. But there is a certain danger in the precepts of the Great Duke, unless when they are construed down to their right degree of significance by applying

The grounds on which it rested.

to them the splendid context of his deeds; for he was accustomed to use sayings founded on quaint and very literal readings of our English law, and the loyalty of his nature rose so high above the reach of all cavil, that the maxims which he uttered seemed to give a noble simplicity to the tenor of his public life, though in reality he rarely or never permitted them to derange his policy, still less to confuse him in the management of war. Naturally, therefore, men were in danger of being misled by a too narrow reading of his precepts. Now, one of the Duke's theories was, that an officer commanding an army on foreign service owed obedience to the Secretary of State—obedience close akin to that which a military subordinate owes to his military chief. If this precept were to be narrowly construed, a Secretary of State who conveyed the wishes of the Government to a general commanding forces abroad would be in danger of finding that he had shut out from his counsels the one man in all the world who could best advise him, and the relations of the Austrian generals with the old Aulic Council at Vienna would have to be adopted as a guide, instead of being valued as a warning. Against this doctrine, understood in its narrow sense, the Duke of Wellington's whole military career in Europe was an almost unceasing rebellion; and it would be hard to find an instance in which he suffered his designs to be bent awry by the military opinions of the Home Government. During the Peninsular war he did not surely pass his time in obeying the Home Government, but rather in setting it right, and in educating it, if so one may speak, for the business of carrying on war.[1]

It is known, however, that Lord Raglan accepted the Great Duke's precept without much qualification, and, when he applied it to the dispatch which had come to him from the Secretary of State, he saw, as he believed, where the path of duty lay. For now, in all its potency, the strange sleep which had

[1] The fierce, willful, and contemptuous way in which the Duke of Wellington dealt with a Secretary of State who ventured to think he might take him at his word, and make him obey his wish, must be familiar to every reader of the Dispatches; but I may refer to the specimen which will be found in Sir Arthur Wellesley's letter to Lord Castlereagh of the 5th of September, 1808. I mean the passage beginning, 'In respect to your wish that 'I should go into the Asturias, to examine the country and form a judgment 'of its strength, I have to mention to you that I am not a draughtsman.' It happened that just six days before, namely, on the 30th of August, Sir Arthur had addressed to the same Secretary of State his customary professions of obedience: 'I shall do whatever the Government may wish;' but he never thought of suffering himself to be hindered from penning an angry refusal on the 5th of September merely because he had used a submissive phrase on the 30th of August.

come upon the Cabinet on the 28th of June began to tell upon events. But for this, or some like physical cause, it could hardly have chanced that fifteen men, all gifted with keen intellect, and all alike charged with a grave, nay, an almost solemn duty, would have knowingly assented to the draught of a long and momentous dispatch, without seeking to wedge into it some of those qualifying words which usually correct the imprudence and derange the grammatical structure of writings framed in Council. A few qualifying words of this sort would have enabled Lord Raglan to act upon his own opinion. But the tranquil mood of the Cabinet on the evening of the 28th of June had prevented the mutilation of the dispatch; and it retained so perfectly all that bold singleness of purpose which characterized the mind of the framer, that it virtually directed the English General to undertake the invasion, unless it should happen that he had obtained fresh knowledge of the enemy's strength—fresh knowledge of such a kind as would enable him to controvert the statements sent out to him by the Home Government, and say distinctly that the Russian forces in the Crimea were too numerous to be encountered with common prudence by the Allied armies. Now, Lord Raglan had not succeeded in obtaining any information at all on the subject, and, therefore, the one circumstance which might have relaxed the stringency of the dispatch was entirely wanting. In the state of things which actually existed, the Duke of Newcastle's communication was little short of an absolute order from the Secretary of State. The English General determined to obey it.

It was thus that Lord Raglan persuaded himself into the belief that he would be justified in foregoing his own opinion, and acceding to the will of the Home Government; but perhaps, though he knew it not, he was under the power of a motive more heating than this bare process of the reason. There were sentences in the dispatch which seemed as though they were meant for the guidance of one not sufficiently prone to action. The writer seemed to have busied himself in closing the loops by which a general might seek to escape from the obligation of having to make the venture. In reality, as we have seen, the dispatch had been framed with a view of giving unanimity to a council of generals and admirals, but it reached its destination at a time when (for the purpose of this decision) the whole power of the camp at Varna was centred in the English General. Whether meant for the guidance of a council or not, the dispatch was addressed to one man, and that man was Lord Raglan. Some may deem it wrong, and may call it a plan of life too closely deriving from times of chivalry; but it is still the habit of the English gentleman to think that his personal honor is no part of the property of the state; and that even for what may seem the public good he ought not to do a violence to his self-respect. He has his code formed in the time of his boyish conflicts or of his early manhood; and if there be fire and strength in his nature, he will not depart from it merely because he has become responsible and mature in years. Lord Raglan was of the bodily nature of those whose blood flushes hot to the face under the sting of an indignant thought; and if mortal eyes could have looked upon him when he revolved the contents of the dispatch, they would have seen him turn crimson in poising the question whether he ought to resist the pressure of the Queen's Government, and to resist because of mere danger. What the Duke of Newcastle meant was to do all he reasonably could to enforce the invasion; and, so intending, he did honestly in making his order as peremptory as possible; but if in any times to come it shall be intended that an English General commanding on a foreign service is to exercise his judgment freely and without passion, the Secretary of State must not challenge him as Lord Raglan was challenged by the dispatch of the 29th of June.

His decision governed the counsels of the Allies.

Lord Raglan's decision governed the counsels of the Allied camp; for, although the staff of the French army[1] (including, as I believe, M. St. Arnaud himself) were adverse to the undertaking, the Marshal's instructions were so framed, that, if the English should be ready to go forward, he was virtually ordered to concur in the enterprise;[2] and we have seen that he had not such a weight in the French camp as would have enabled him to oppose any valid resistance to the wishes of his own Government and the determination of the English General.

In announcing his decision to the Home Government, Lord Raglan thus wrote to the Duke of Newcastle:—

He announces it to the Home Government.

'It becomes my duty to acquaint you that it was more in 'deference to the views of the British Government 'as conveyed to me in your Grace's dispatch, and 'to the known acquiescence of the Emperor Louis 'Napoleon in those views, than to any information in the pos- 'session of the naval and military authorities, either as to the 'extent of the enemy's forces, or their state of preparation, that 'the decision to make a descent upon the Crimea was adopted.

[1] This will be shown by the narrative in cap. 9, *post*.

[2] Lord Raglan had the advantage of knowing (by means of a communication from Lord Cowley) that the 'Emperor quite concurred in the views of 'the British Cabinet.'

'The fact must not be concealed that neither the English nor 'the French Admirals have been able to obtain any intelligence 'on which they can rely with respect to the army which the 'Russians may destine for operations in the field, or to the 'number of men allotted for the defense of Sebastopol; and 'Marshal St. Arnaud and myself are equally deficient in infor-'mation upon these all-important questions, and there would 'seem to be no chance of our acquiring it.'[1]

The Duke of Newcastle's reply to this dispatch was in full consistency with that fearless and unshrinking assumption of responsibility which had marked his instructions of the 29th of June.

The Duke of Newcastle's reply.

'I wish,' he writes,[2] 'that circumstances which are engross-'ing my attention this afternoon permitted my ex-'pressing to you the feeling of intense anxiety and 'interest which your reply of the 19th of July to 'mine of the 29th of June have created in my mind. I can 'not help seeing, through the calm and noble tone of your an-'nouncement of the decision to attack Sebastopol, that it has 'been taken in order to meet the views and desires of the Gov-'ernment, and not in entire accordance with your own opinions. 'God grant that success may reward you, and justify us!

The Queen's expression of feeling.

'I wrote to the Queen the moment I received your dispatch, 'and in answer she said, "The very important news '"which he conveyed to her in it of the decision '"of the generals and admirals to attack Sevasto-'"pol, have filled the Queen with mixed feelings of satisfaction '"and anxiety. May the Almighty protect her army and her '"fleet, and bless this great undertaking with success!"

'Let me add my humble aspirations and prayers to those 'of our good Queen. The cause is a just one, if any war is 'just, and I will not believe that in any case British arms can 'fail. May honor, victory, and the thanks of a grateful world 'attend your efforts! God bless you and those who fight un-'der you!'

---

## CHAPTER XXXIV.

Conference at the French head-quarters.

ON the 18th of July a conference took place at Marshal St. Arnaud's head-quarters. It was attended by the Marshal, by Lord Raglan, and by Admiral Hamelin, by Admiral Bruat (who was the second in com-

[1] 19th July. [2] Private letter to Lord Raglan, 3rd August, 1854.

mand of the French fleet), by Vice-Admiral Dundas, and by Rear-Admiral Sir Edmund Lyons, who was the second in command of the English fleet. It lasted four hours.

Perhaps most of the members of the conference imagined that they were met for the purpose of determining upon the expediency of undertaking the invasion; but Lord Raglan had already made up his mind, not merely to support the wish of his Government in the Allied camp, but to cause its actual adoption; and he was so constituted that he could bring the resources of his mind to bear upon the object in view with as much abundance and strength as if he had himself approved or even devised it. Clearly a discussion upon the expediency of undertaking the enterprise would have been fatal to it, for no member of the conference, except Lyons and (possibly) Bruat, could have conscientiously argued that the scheme was wise or even moderately prudent. How was it to be contrived that a council of war disapproving the enterprise should be prevented from strangling it?

Lord Raglan's way of eluding objections.

As almost always happened in conferences where Lord Raglan had the ascendant, the grand question was quietly passed over, as though it were either decided or conceded for the purpose of the discussion, and it was made to seem that the duty which remained to the council was that of determining the time and the means. The French had studied the means of disembarking in the face of a powerful enemy. Sir Ralph Abercrombie's descent upon the coast of Egypt in the face of the French army was an enterprise too brilliant and too daring to allow of its being held a safe example, for he had simply landed his infantry upon the beach in boats, without attempting, in the first instance, to bring artillery into action. It seems that hardly any stress of circumstances will induce a French general to bring his infantry into action upon open ground without providing for it the support of artillery. Naturally, therefore, the French authorities at Varna were impressed with the necessity of being able to land their field-guns in such a way as to admit of their being brought into action simultaneously with the landing of their battalions; and, having anticipated some time before that a disembarkation in the face of an enemy might be one of the operations of the war, they had already begun to make the boats required for the purpose. These were flat-bottomed lighters, somewhat in the form of punts, but of great size, and so constructed that they would receive the gun-carriages with the guns upon them, and allow of the guns being run out straight from the boat to the beach. It was understood that the building of these flat lighters would take about ten days, and it was determined that in the mean time a survey of the coast near Sebastopol should be made from on board ship, in order to determine the spot best suited for a descent.

Reconnaissance of the coast.

With a view to cover the reconnaissance and draw off the enemy's attention, the Allied admirals cruised with powerful fleets in front of the harbor of Sebastopol, and meanwhile the officers chosen for the service went northward along the coast in the 'Fury,' seeking out the best place for a landing. The officers who performed this duty were, on the part of the French, General Canrobert and Colonel Trochu, with one engineer and one artillery officer; and, on the part of the English, Sir George Brown, Lieut.-Colonel Lake, R.H.A., Captain Lovell, R.E., and Captain Wetherall, of the Quartermaster General's department. The 'Fury' was steered by no common hand.

In the moment when Lord Raglan determined to treat the instructions of the Government as imperative, and to put them in course for execution, he came to another determination (a determination which is not so mere a corollary from the first as men unversed in business may think): he resolved to carry the enterprise through. He knew that, though work of an accustomed sort can be ably done by official persons acting under a bare sense of duty, yet that the engine for conquering obstacles of a kind not known beforehand, when they are many, and big, and unforeseen, must be nothing less than the strong, passionate will of a man. If every one were to perform his mere duty, there would be no invasion of the Crimea, for a rank growth of hinderances springing up in the way of the undertaking would be sure to gather fast round it, and bring it in time to a stop.

Sir Edmund Lyons.

Amongst the English Generals there was no one who had given his mind to the enigma which went by the name of the 'Eastern Question;' but Sir Edmund Lyons had been for many years engaged in the animating diplomacy of the Levant. In Greece, the activity of the Czar's agents, or perhaps of his mere admirers, had been so constant, and had generated so strong a spirit of antagonism in the minds of the few contentious Britons who chanced to observe it, that the institutions called 'The Russian Party,' and 'The English Party,' had long ago flourished at Athens; and, since Sir Edmund Lyons had been accredited there for several years as British Minister, he did not miss being drawn into the game of combating against what was supposed to be the ever-impending danger of Russian encroachment. Long ago, therefore, he had been whetted for this strife; and now that the 'Eastern Question' was to be brought to the issue of a war in which he had part, he was inflamed with a passionate zeal. Resuming at once the uniform and the bearing of his old profession, he cast aside—if ever he had it—all semblance of diplomatic reserve and composure, and threw himself, with all his seaman's heart, into the business of the war.

Lord Raglan drew Sir Edmund Lyons into his intimate counsels. I know not whether this concord of theirs was ever put into words, but I imagine that at the least I can infer from their actions and from the tenor of their intercourse a silent understanding between them—an understanding that no lukewarmness of others, no shortcomings, no evasions, no tardy prudence, no overgrown respect for difficulty or peril, should hinder the landing of the Queen's troops on the coast of the Crimea. From the time that Lord Raglan thus joined Lyons to the undertaking he gave it a great momentum. To those within the grasp of the Rear-Admiral's energy it seemed that thenceforth, and until the troops should be landed on the enemy's shore, there could be no rest for man, no rest for engines. The 'Agamemnon' was never still. In the painful, consuming passion with which Lyons toiled, and even, as some imagined, in the anxious, craving expression of his features, there was something which reminded men of a greater name.

This was the officer who steered the 'Fury.' He carried her in so close to the shore that the coast could be reconnoitred with great completeness. The officers came to the conclusion (a conclusion afterward overruled, as we shall see, by Lord Raglan) that the valley of the Katscha was the best spot for a landing.

Rumored change in the plans of the Czar.

We saw that the Czar's withdrawal from the Principalities would deprive the German Powers of their main ground of quarrel with Russia, and that our plan of engaging in a great marine expedition against Crim Tartary would cause Austria and Prussia to despair of all effective support from the West, thus driving or tending to drive them into better relations with Nicholas. Before the 28th of July there were signs that this change was beginning to set Russia free from the straits in which she had been placed by the unanimity of the Four Great Powers; and tidings which reached the camp at Varna made it appear (though not with truth) that the Russian commander had not only suspended his retreat, but was commencing a fresh movement in advance. To deliberate upon this supposed change in the character of the war, a conference was held at the French

Second conference. head-quarters, and was attended by Marshal St. Arnaud, Lord Raglan, General Canrobert, Sir Edmund Lyons, General Martimprey, Sir George Brown, and Colonel Trochu. The French generals grasped this as an occasion for bringing about the relinquishment of an enterprise which they always had held to be rash. They submitted that the general instructions addressed to both of the Allied commanders made it their duty to provide in the first instance for the safety of the Ottoman territory, and that, until that object was secured, they were not warranted in attempting an invasion of a Russian province far distant from the threatened frontier of European Turkey; that the order to invade the coast of the Crimea had been framed by the Home Governments and acceded to by the Allied Generals upon the assumption that the armed intervention of Austria, then believed to be imminent, or, at the very least, a continuance of her menacing attitude on the flank of the Russian army, would preclude any attempt by the Czar to resume his war on the Danube; that that assumption now unfortunately turned out to be unfounded; and that the abandonment by Austria of the common cause made it the bounden duty of the Allied commanders to return to their defensive measures, because it was now plain that, if they quitted Bulgaria, Omar Pasha, without aid from any quarter, would have upon his hands the whole weight of the Russian army. Now then, supposing the premises to be conceded, the French counselors had made out good grounds for abandoning a resolution which, only a week ago, had been adopted by the Allied commanders.

The French urge the abandonment of the expedition against the Crimea.

Lord Raglan, however, was resolved that the enterprise should go on. From the moment he knew that the siege of Silistria had been raised, he never doubted that, for that year at least, the invasion of European Turkey was at an end. But he knew that clever men who have taken the pains to build up a neat logical structure do not easily allow it to be treated as unsound merely because it rests upon a sliding foundation. Without, therefore, combating the French arguments, he quietly suggested that the time which must needs elapse before the embarkation might throw new light on the probability of a renewed attack upon Turkey; and he proposed that, in the mean time, the preparations for the descent on the Crimea should be carried on with all speed. This opinion was adopted by every member of the conference. The preparations were carried on with increasing energy; and the theory that it was the duty

Lord Raglan's way of bending the French to the plans of the English Government.

of the Allied commanders to abandon the enterprise was never put down by argument, but left to die away uncontested.

Preparations.

Lord Raglan had been struck with the value of the French plan for landing artillery on flat lighters, and Sir Edmund Lyons and Sir George Brown were dispatched to Constantinople with instructions to do all they could toward supplying the British army with means which would answer the same purpose. They discovered that a platform resting upon two boats might be made to serve nearly as well as one of the French lighters. How they toiled the world will never know, for History can not pause to see them ransacking Constantinople and the villages of the Bosphorus in their search after carpenters and planks; but before the appointed time the whole work was done. This was not all. Sir Edmund Lyons and Sir George Brown propelled the arrangements for buying and chartering steamers, trampling down with firmness, perhaps one might say with violence, all obstacles which stood in the way. Of those obstacles one of the most formidable was what was called in those days the 'official fear of incurring responsibility.' Lyons and Sir George Brown taught men that in emergencies of this sort they should be pursued with the fear of not doing enough rather than with the dread of doing too much. 'I can not venture,' said a cautious official—'I can not venture to give the price.' 'Then I can,' said Sir George Brown; 'I buy it in my own name!' It is thus that difficulties are conquered. When the restless 'Agamemnon' came back into the Bay of Varna with Lyons and Sir George Brown on board, Lord Raglan was at the head of a truly British armament. He had the means, by steam power, and at one trip, to descend upon the enemy's coast, with all his divisions of infantry, with his brigade of light cavalry, and with the whole of his field artillery; and he would be enabled, if he landed in face of an enemy, to bring his guns into action, whilst his infantry formed upon the beach.

Ineffectual attempts of the Allies to deceive the enemy.

When the Allied commanders determined to execute the orders addressed to them, they saw the importance of endeavoring to veil their project from the enemy. With this view they tried to induce a belief that Odessa was to be the object of attack. But the measures which they took for this purpose were very slight and weak. To deceive the enemy by the mere spreading of a report, the first step for a General to take would be that of uttering the false word to some of his own people. That would be a difficult service for Lord Raglan to perform; and I do not believe that he ever could or ever did perform it.

Another contrivance for diverting the enemy's attention from the Crimea was that of endeavoring to alarm him for his Bessarabian frontier. Partly to attain this end, and partly, as was surmised, with the more ambitious object of striking a blow at some of the Czar's retiring columns, Marshal St. Arnaud moved no less than three divisions into the Dobrudja. But, in truth, all secrecy was forbidden to the Allies. The same power which dictated the expedition precluded its concealment. It was in a council of the whole people that England had resolved upon the enterprise; and what advantage there is in knowledge of an enemy's plans, that she freely gave to Russia. It might seem that for the Emperor of the French, who had shown that he was capable of the darkest secrecy in his own designs, it must have been trying to have to act with a Power which propounded her schemes in print. But, happily, he understood England, and knew something of the conditions under which she moves into action.

Fire at Varna.

On the 10th of August a fire broke out in the British magazines at Varna, and a large quantity of military stores was consumed.

Cholera.

But another and more dreadful enemy had now entered the camp of the Allies. From the period of its arrival in the Levant the French army had been suffering much from sickness. In the British army, on the contrary, though slight complaints were not unfrequent, the bodily condition of the men had been, upon the whole, very good; and so it continued up to the 19th of July. On that day, out of the whole Light Division, there were only 110 in hospital. But it seems that one of the omens which portend the visitation of a great epidemic is a more than common flush of health. With the French, the cholera first showed itself on board their troopships whilst passing from Marseilles to the Dardanelles. It then appeared among the French quartered at Gallipoli, and followed their battalions into Bulgaria. There, its ravages increased, and before the beginning of the last week in July it reached the British army. By the 19th of August our regiments in Bulgaria had lost 532 men. But it was amongst the three French divisions marched into the Dobrudja, and especially in General Canrobert's Division, that the disease raged with the most deadly virulence. In the day's march, and sometimes within the space of only a few hours, hundreds of men dropped down in the sudden agonies of cholera; and out of one battalion alone it was said that, besides those already dead, no less than 500 sufferers were carried alive in the wagons. On the 8th of August it was computed, by an officer of their staff, that out of the three French divisions which marched into the Dobrudja, no less than 10,000 lay dead or struck down by sickness.

If the cholera had been confined to the land forces, the Generals would not, perhaps, have allowed it to delay their embarkation; but it now reached the fleets. In a few days the crews were in such a state that all idea of attempting to embark the troops was, for the moment, quite out of the question; and on the 11th and 12th of August the Admirals put out from their anchorage, in the hope of driving away the disease with the pure breezes of the sea. But they had scarcely done this when, on board some of the ships, the mysterious pest began to rage with a violence rare in Europe. The 'Britannia' alone lost 105 men. The number of those stricken, and of those attending upon them, was so great, that it was impracticable to carry on the common duties of the ship in the usual way; and if the disease had continued to rage with undiminished violence for three days more, there would have been the spectacle of a majestic three-decker floating helpless upon the waves for want of hands to work her. This time of trial proved the quality of those who remained unstricken. There was a waywardness in the course of the disease, on board British ships, for which it is difficult to account. It spared the officers. On board British ships of war the seaman is accustomed to look to those who command him with a strong affectionate reliance; and now the poor sufferers, in their child-like simplicity, were calling upon their officers for help and comfort. An officer thus appealed to would go and lie down by the side of the sufferer, and soothe him as though he were an infant. And this trust and this devotion were not always in vain. Even against malignant cholera the officer seemed to be not altogether powerless; for partly by holding the tortured sufferer in his kind hands, partly by cheering words, and partly by wild remedies, invented in despair of all regular medical treatment, he was often enabled to fight the disease, or to make the men think that he did.

Almost suddenly the pestilence ceased on board the British ships of war. The dead were overboard, and the survivors returned to their accustomed duties with an alacrity quickened by the delight of looking forward to active operations against the enemy. Instinctively, or else with wise design, both officers and men dropped all mention of the tragedy through which they had passed.[1]

[1] I was for several days on board the 'Britannia' without once, I think, hearing the least allusion to the pestilence which just four weeks before had slain 105 of the ship's crew.

In a few days from the time when the cholera had been raging with its utmost fury the crews of the fleet were ready to undertake the great business of embarking the troops and landing them on the coast of the Crimea.

Weakly condition of the English soldiery.

In the camps of the Allied armies, at this time, the cholera had abated, but had not ceased. There were fevers, too, and other complaints. Grievous sickness fell upon that part of our camp which had been pitched in the midst of the beauteous scenery of the lake of Devna, but the whole English army at this time began to show signs of failing health. It appeared that, even of the men out of hospital and actually present under arms, hardly any were in the enjoyment of sound health; hardly any were capable of their usual amount of exertion.

This weakly condition of the men was destined to act, with other causes, in bringing upon the army cruel sufferings; and it may be asked whether, with the soldiers in this condition of body, it was right to undertake an invasion. The answer would be this:—the medical authorities thought, and with apparently good reason, that, for troops sickening under the fierce summer heats of Bulgaria, the sea voyage, the descent upon another and more healthy shore, and, above all, the animating presence of the enemy, would work a good effect upon the health of the men; and, although these hopes proved vain, they seemed at the time to rest upon fair grounds. And, after all, it is hard to say what other disposition of the troops would have united the advantages of being better and possible. To remain in Bulgaria, or to attempt to operate in the neighborhood of the Danube, was to linger in the midst of those very atmospheric poisons which had brought the health of the army to its then state; and, on the other hand, our people at home would hardly have borne to see the army sent back to Malta, and forced to recede from the conflict, for the bare reason that some of the men were in hospital, and that the rest—without being ill—were said to be in a weakly condition.

---

## CHAPTER XXXV.

Arrangements first made for the starting of the expedition.

OUR admiral had at his command the means for conveying the British force to the enemy's shore either in steam vessels or in sailing ships towed by steam power; and until the eve of the embarkation the

French believed that their resources would enable them to achieve a like result. So, at a conference of the four admirals, held on the 20th of August, it was arranged that the whole of the French and English armament should move from the coast at the same time under steam power; and the 2nd of September was looked forward to as the day when the armament might perhaps go to sea, but the exact time would of course depend upon weather and other circumstances beyond the reach of exact calculation.

On the 24th of August the huge operation of embarking the armies had already begun. The French embarked 24,000 infantry and 70 pieces of field artillery; but since they were straitened in their means of sea-transport, the number of horses they allotted to each gun was reduced from six to four. The French embarked no cavalry.[1] A large portion of the French troops were put on board ships of war,[2] and other portions were distributed among a great number of sailing vessels. Some of these were very small craft.

The embarkations.

Attached to the French army, and placed under the orders of Marshal St. Arnaud, there was a force of between 5000 and 6000 Turkish infantry. These men were embarked mainly or entirely on board Turkish vessels of war.

Sir Edmund Lyons was charged with the duty of embarking the English forces; and having first got on board our 60 pieces of field artillery, completely equipped, with the full complement of horses belonging to every gun, he proceeded with the embarkation of the 22,000 infantry and the full thousand of cavalry, which Lord Raglan intended to move from Bulgaria to the coast of the Crimea. To put on board ship a body of foot soldiers is comparatively a simple process, but the shipping of horses involves so heavy a cost, so great an exertion of human energy, that he who undertakes such a task upon any thing like a large scale must needs be a man in earnest. On the other hand, it was clear that for an invasion of the Crimea a body of cavalry was strictly needed. Therefore, a sagacious interpreter of warlike signs, who saw that the En-

[1] They took with them from 80 to 100 horsemen to perform escort duty; but of course I do not regard this as an exception to the statement that 'no cavalry was embarked.'

[2] Our naval officers are strongly opposed to the practice of putting troops on board ships of war. They are not the men to set their personal convenience against the exigencies of the public service, but they can not endure that the efficiency of a man-of-war should be for one moment suspended. It is well ascertained, too, that the presence of a great number of soldiers—men who for the time of the voyage are almost necessarily idlers—is injurious to the discipline of a ship.

glish General was embarking a thousand cavalry horses, and that the French were embarking none, would be led to conjecture that the English were resolved to make the descent, and that the French were not. It will be seen by-and-by that such a conjecture would have been sound.

The time necessary for embarking a given number of foot soldiers is small in proportion to that required for getting on board an equal number of troopers with their chargers. Nor is this all. The embarkation of infantry is not necessarily stopped by a moderate swell. The embarkation of cavalry is rendered very slow and difficult by even a slight movement of the sea, and is stopped altogether by a little increase of surf. The business of embarking the British cavalry was checked during some days by a wind from the northeast and its consequent swell, but afterward the weather changed, and the whole force was got on board without the loss of a man.[1]

Lord Raglan could not repress the feeling with which he looked upon the exertions of our naval officers and seamen. 'The embarkation,' he wrote on the 29th of August—'the 'embarkation is proceeding rapidly and successfully, thanks to 'the able arrangement of Rear-Admiral Sir Edmund Lyons, 'and the unceasing exertions of the officers and men under 'his orders. It is impossible for me to express in adequate 'terms my sense of the value of the assistance the army under 'my command derives from the Royal Navy. The same feel- 'ing prevails from the highest to the lowest—from Vice-Ad- 'miral Dundas to the youngest sailor, an ardent desire to co- 'operate by every possible means, is manifest throughout, and 'I am proud of being associated with men who are animated 'by such a spirit, and who are so entirely devoted to the serv- 'ice of their country.'

Failure of the French calculations in regard to their command of steam power.

Of course the French, unencumbered with cavalry, were on board before the English embarkation was complete; but the steam power at the command of the French fell short, and the necessity of a variation from the plan determined upon by the four admirals was now announced. On the 4th of September Admiral Hamelin and an officer on the staff of the French army informed Vice-Admiral Dundas that their resources would not, as they had expected, enable them to have their sailing transports towed by steamers.

[1] The French were not so fortunate, for a painful accident occurred in the course of their embarkation. One of their steam vessels ran down a boat laden with Zouaves. The men, encumbered by their packs, could do little to save themselves, and more than twenty were drowned.

No explanation was given of the failure which had thus suddenly crippled the French armament. The result was distressing at the time, for it was seen that the whole flotilla would be clogged by the slowness of the sailing vessels in which the French troops were embarked, and the fate of the enterprise was rendered more than ever dependent upon the accidents of weather. Marshal St. Arnaud grew restless.

---

## CHAPTER XXXVI.

Excitement and impatience of St. Arnaud.

WE have seen that the 2nd of September had been looked forward to as the time for the departure of the united armaments, and on that day, with military punctuality, Marshal St. Arnaud went to Baljik; but the wind and the waves are still undisciplined forces, and the French embarkations were not destined to be completed until the evening of the 4th. The Marshal, therefore, was kept waiting at Baljik, and meanwhile sickness began to make havoc with his troops, for they were densely crowded on board the transports.

He is induced to set sail without the English, taking with him all his sailing fleet and the troops on board them.

The marshal was much tortured by the anxiety which he had had to bear during these three painful days, and (possibly to calm his mind) Vice-Admiral Dundas seems to have suggested to him that, his sailing vessels not being provided with steam power to tow them, he might as well cause them at once to weigh anchor. By these causes, joined to his irritation at what he thought the backwardness of the English embarkations, the Marshal was induced to determine—not merely that he would act upon Dundas's suggestion, but—that he himself would wait no longer, and would put to sea on the 5th of September with his sailing fleet; so when, on the same morning, Lord Raglan reached Baljik, he was surprised by the intelligence that the Marshal had already sailed out on board the 'Ville de Paris.'

The naval forces of the Allies.

On the evening of the 6th the British armament was ready, and the arrangements for the voyage of the whole flotilla complete. The French fleet, already at sea, consisted of fifteen sail-of-the-line, with ten or twelve war-steamers, and the Turkish fleet of eight sail-of-the-line, with three war-steamers; but the French and the Turkish vessels were doing service as transports, and were so encumbered with troops that they could not have been brought into action with common prudence. It was upon the English fleet, therefore, that the duty of protecting the whole armada really devolved; and, supposing that the enemy were aware of the helpless state of the French and Turkish vessels laden with troops, and of the enormous convoy of transports which had to be protected, he might be expected to judge that it was incumbent upon him to come out of the harbor and assail the vast flotilla of transports; for under the guns of Sebastopol the Russians had fifteen sailing ships-of-the-line,[1] with some frigates and brigs, and also twelve war-steamers, though of these the 'Vladimir' was the only powerful vessel.[2] To encounter this force, and to defend from its enterprises the rest of the armada, the English had ten sail-of-the-line (including two screw-steamers), two fifty-gun frigates, and thirteen lesser steamers of war heavily armed.

Duty devolving on the English fleet.

The anxious duty of disposing and guiding the convoy was intrusted by Admiral Dundas to Sir Edmund Lyons, and, under Sir Edmund's directions, Captain Mends of the 'Agamemnon' framed the programme of the voyage. On the evening of the 6th the captains of transports were called by signal on board the 'Emperor,' and there Mends read to them the instructions which he asked them to obey. The captains thus addressed were not in the Queen's service, but they were English seamen, and their answer was characteristic. They were not flighty men. They respectfully asked for an assurance that in the event of death their widows would be held entitled to pensions; and, as to the question whether of their own free will they would encounter the chances of a naval action, they answered it with three cheers. It is not by the mere muster-roll of the army or the navy that England counts her forces.

Arrangements in regard to the English convoy.

With his force of horse, foot, and artillery, Lord Raglan had on board the transports (now all collected at Baljik)[3] the full number of ammunition-carts required for the first reserve of ammunition, the beasts required for drawing them, and sixty other carts, also provided with draught power. But, in order to move so large a force at one trip, it was found necessary to dispense with the bât horses of the army, and the force was not provided with means of land transport either for the tents of the men or for the bag-

The forces and supplies now on board.

[1] Some say sixteen.

[2] Unless the 'Bessarabia' be counted as a powerful steamer.

[3] At the time here spoken of there were two artillery transports lagging, but they were up in sufficient time.

gage of the officers. There were also on board large supplies of field ammunition, of food for the troops, and of barley and hay for the horses. In some of the horse transports there was an insufficiency of the forage required for the voyage. With that grave exception, all the arrangements seem to have been good. Due means had been taken for insuring, so far as was possible, the simultaneous transit, not only of our ships of war, but of the whole force which Lord Raglan had embarked, together with its vast appendage of warlike stores and provisions; for every sailing vessel, whether she were a ship of war or a transport, was towed by a sufficiently powerful steamer. None of our ships of war carried troops on board: they were all, therefore, ready for action.

Troops and supplies left at Varna.

In addition to the forces and the means of land transport which were actually on board, Lord Raglan had in readiness for embarkation the whole brigade of heavy cavalry, another division of infantry, a siege-train,[1] and some five or six thousand pack-horses. The sick remained in Bulgaria; and such of the men out of hospital as seemed to be in a very weakly state were left at Varna and employed in garrison duty.

Vice-Admiral Dundas, commanding the whole British fleet, had his flag on board the 'Britannia;' Lyons, in the 'Agamemnon,' had charge of the convoy. Each vessel had assigned to her the place she was to take when the signal for moving should be given.

Before night, the whole of the English flotilla, together with that part of the French and the Turkish flotilla which had the command of steam power, was assembled in Baljik Bay, and in readiness to sail on the morrow.

Departure of the English Armada and of the French steam vessels.

Men remember the beauteous morning of the 7th of September. The moonlight was still floating on the waters when men, looking from numberless decks toward the east, were able to hail the dawn. There was a summer breeze blowing fair from the land. At a quarter before five a gun from the 'Britannia' gave the signal to weigh. The air was obscured by the busy smoke of the engines; and it was hard to see how and whence due order would come; but presently the 'Agamemnon' moved through, and with signals at all her masts, for Lyons was on board her, and was governing and ordering the convoy. The

[1] The additional division of infantry (the 4th Division) was at Varna; the Scots Grays were on the Bosphorus; and the rest of the heavy cavalry in Bulgaria, where also the bât horses were left. The siege-train was on board off Varna.

French steamers of war went out, with their transports in tow, and their great vessels formed line. The French went out more quickly than the English, and in better order. Many of their transports were vessels of very small size; and of necessity, therefore, they were a swarm. Our transports went out in five columns of only thirty each. Then—guard over all—the English war fleet, in single column, moved slowly out of the bay.[1]

Here, then, and apart from the bodies of foot and artillery embarked by the French and the Turks, there was an armament not unworthy of England. Without combat, and by the mere stress of its presence, our fleet drove the enemy's flag from the seas which flowed upon his shores;[2] and a small but superb land force, complete in all arms, was clothed with the power of a great army, by the ease with which it could be thrown upon any part of the enemy's coast.[3]

Lord Raglan had not suffered himself to be disconcerted by the departure of Monsieur St. Arnaud, and the consequent severance of the Allied forces. No steamer was sent to re-knit his communications with the errant French Marshal.

---

## CHAPTER XXXVII.

WE have seen that Marshal St. Arnaud, under feelings of some vexation, put to sea on the morning of the 5th of September. He could not but know that, by his abrupt separation from the British fleet and army, he had offended against the English General. Upon reflection, he could not but grieve that he had done this. But he had put to sea, and had since

[1] I did not reach the fleet till some three days afterward, when it was anchored at the rendezvous, and my impression of the scene in the Bay of Baljik is derived partly from some MSS. which have been furnished to me, but partly, also, from what struck me as a very good account of it, which I saw in a printed book, by Mr. Wood, a spectator.

[2] I am justified in speaking of the English fleet as the force which kept the enemy's ships in duress; because, as we have seen, the French men-of-war were doing duty as transports, and were not, therefore, in a state for going into action.

[3] I, of course, speak here of the inherent power of such an armament, without reference to the fact that strictly-defined instructions had been addressed to Lord Raglan, and that the purport of these had become known to the enemy. The fixedness of the plan of campaign, and the publicity which it had obtained, reduced the power of the force to the level of its actual numbers and its intrinsic strength.

heard no tidings from the shore. No swift steamer had followed him with entreaties to stay his course. He was left free to pursue his voyage; and the voyage was growing more and more dismal.

'The Black Sea' is a truer name than the 'Euxine.' Now, as in old times (if the summer be hardly past), the voyager leaves a coast smiling bright beneath skies of blue and glowing with sunny splendor; yet, perhaps, and in less than an hour, the heavens above and the waters around him are dark with the gloom and threatening aspect belonging to the Northern Ocean.[1] Monsieur St. Arnaud encountered this change.

Marshal St. Arnaud at sea without the English.

The wind blew from its dark quarter. Every hour was carrying the Marshal farther and farther into the centre of the inhospitable sea, farther and farther from the English fleet, farther and farther from Lord Raglan. If he went on, there was no junction to look for except at an imaginary point marked with a pencil on the charts, but having no existence in the material world; and from the wind and the angry waves, no less than from his own fast cooling thoughts, he began to receive a distressing sense of his isolation. The struggle in his mind was painful, but it came to an end. 'I am nearly twenty leagues,' writes the Marshal, on the evening of the 6th, to Lord Raglan—'I am nearly twenty leagues northeast of Baljik, separated from the English fleet, and from the part of my own 'convoy which was to sail with the convoy of the English 'fleet. Admiral Dundas's last letter being worded condition'ally, so far as concerns his sailing this morning, I am not sure 'of not seeing increased, in great proportions, the distance 'which separates me from you, and then there is reason to 'fear circumstances of wind or sea which would render our 'junction difficult, and might compromise every thing defini'tively. In this painful situation I decide to invite Admiral 'Hamelin (on his declaration that he can not wait 'where he is) to return to meet the fleet and the 'convoy.' So the Marshal sailed back. Thus, happily, ceased the impulse which had threatened to sunder the fleets.

His anxiety.

He sails back.

Lord Raglan's answer was stern. He removed the grounds which the Marshal had assigned for his departure, and then pointed gravely to the true line of duty for the future. 'Thanks 'be to God,' he wrote, 'every thing now favors our enterprise. 'Very soon we shall reach the appointed rendezvous, and then

[1] The contrast between the climate of the Black Sea and that of the countries which surround it is one of the enigmas to which scientific men have applied their minds, but whether as yet with success I can not say.

Lord Raglan's reproof.

'we shall have an opportunity of showing that our 'manner of acting together remains unaltered, and 'that the sincerity of which you speak will continue, as at pres- 'ent, to be our guide and our mutual satisfaction.'[1]

Coming from Lord Raglan, this language was a reproof; but the result tends to show that it was happily adjusted to the object in view. Thenceforth there was no longer any tendency on the part of Marshal St. Arnaud to break away from his colleague. From the hour of the first conference at the Tuileries in the spring of the year, Lord Raglan's authority in the Allied counsels had been always increasing; and now, as we shall presently see, it gained a complete ascendant.

Its good effect.

Lord Raglan's increasing ascendency.

On the 8th the great flotilla, moving under steam, came up with the French and the Turkish sailing fleets which had left Baljik on the 5th of September. The French fleet was in double column, and tacking to eastward across the bows of the steam flotilla, but, upon being approached, the French ships backed topsails and lay to. Every one of the French vessels had kept its position beautifully, and, the moment the signal to lie to was given, it was obeyed with a quickness which was honestly admired by our seamen. The Turkish fleet also lay to; and, for a while, the whole armada of the Allies was gathered together. But the English fleet, being moved by steam, kept on to windward; and presently the French and the Turks began to sail off on opposite tacks. Between the fleets thus disparting, the English flotilla of transports passed through in five columns.

The whole Allied armada comes together at sea.

But the fleets are again parted.

The rendezvous was to be at a point forty miles due west of Cape Tarkan, and thither moved the three fleets with all their convoy.

There were in the French army several officers holding high command, and being otherwise men of great weight, who had become very thoughtful on the subject of the contemplated descent upon the enemy's coast. Personally, they were men quite as dauntless as those who gave no care to the business in hand, but, being versed in the study, if not in the practice of the great art of war, they had become strongly impressed with the hazardous character of the intended enterprise. It seems probable that up to this time they had relied upon the mature judgment and the supposed discreetness of Lord Raglan to

Step taken by French officers with a view to stop the expedition against Sebastopol.

[1] Translated from the French, in which the letter was written.

prevent what they regarded as a rash attempt. It might well seem natural to them that two Governments in the West of Europe, attempting to dictate an invasion of a Russian province at a distance of 3000 miles, would, sooner or later, be checked in their project by the generals commanding the forces; and, of course, they would have liked that the disfavor which unjustly attaches to military prudence should fall upon the English General rather than upon themselves or their own commander. But in the course of the 7th of September it became known to them that Lord Raglan was already at sea. They then knew, or rather they then recognized the fact, that the whole armada was really gliding on toward the enemy's coast, and the ferment their minds underwent now brought them to take a strange step.

Lord Raglan was on board the 'Caradoc,' and on the 8th of September, whilst the fleets lay near to one another, this vessel was boarded by Vice-Admiral Dundas. He came to say that a French steamer had conveyed to him the desire of the Marshal St. Arnaud to see Lord Raglan and the Vice-Admiral Dundas, and to see them on board the 'Ville de Paris,' because the Marshal himself was too ill to be able to move. It happened that the sea at this time was rough, and the naval men thought that it would be difficult for Lord Raglan, with his one arm, to get up the side of the three-decker in which the Marshal was sailing; Lord Raglan, therefore, deputed his military secretary, Colonel Steele, to accompany Vice-Admiral Dundas on board the 'Ville de Paris.'

Conference on board the 'Ville de Paris.'

The Vice-Admiral and Colonel Steele found the Marshal sitting up, but in a state of much suffering, and they were informed that he was very ill. He however sat at the conference, and the other persons present were Admiral Hamelin, Admiral Bruat, Admiral Count Buat Wiliaumez, Colonel Trochu, General Rose, Vice-Admiral Dundas, and Colonel Steele. The Marshal took no part in the discussion which ensued. It seems he could hardly speak.

St. Arnaud disabled by illness.

It was stated that the meeting had been summoned in order that a paper might be read to it. The document bore no signature, and Marshal St. Arnaud was no party to it; but it was stated that it emanated from General Canrobert, General Martimprey, and the principal officers of the French artillery and engineers; and it was said too that General Rose[1] had furnished some of the materials from which it was composed.

Unsigned papers read to the conference.

[1] Now Sir Hugh Rose, the officer spoken of as Colonel Rose in Chapter VII. He was at this time accredited as British Commissioner at the French

The document took it for granted that there were three places for landing which merited discussion—the Katscha, the Yetsa, and Kaffa; and it then went on to show the advantages and the drawbacks which would attend an attempt to land at each of those three spots. The objections to the landing at the Katscha were stated with so much force as to show that the framers of the document entirely disapproved it, and, indeed, they urged that any landing north of Sebastopol would be surely followed by disastrous results. The document also raised weighty objections to a descent upon the coast near the Yetsa. The only plan which was made to appear at all justifiable was that of a landing at Kaffa, and, although the difficulties attending even that operation were placed in a strong light, it was orally stated that the framers of the document considered that plan to be one nearly free from objection.

Now Kaffa was a sea-port in the eastern part of the Crimean peninsula, and divided from Sebastopol by many long marches over mountain roads. The autumn had already come. The landing at Kaffa implied an abandonment for that year at least of all attempts against Sebastopol. It was to attack Sebastopol forthwith, and in the year 1854, that the great flotilla, with all its precious freight, had been gathered together, and now, whilst the vast armada was moving toward the enemy's coast, there came from the men of weight and science in the French army this singular protest—for that is what it really was—against an enterprise already begun.

St. Arnaud leaves all to Lord Raglan.

Marshal St. Arnaud was in a painful strait. Being, as he knew, without ascendency in the French army, he apparently thought that the weight attaching to the combined opinion of all the protesting officers was too great to warrant him in meeting their interposition with reproof or inattention; yet, suffering as he did at the time under bodily anguish, he was ill able to go into the discussions thus strangely forced on by the remonstrants. He found a solution. He desired Colonel Trochu to say that he would concur in any decision to which Lord Raglan might come.

Conference adjourned to the 'Caradoc.'

The conference, therefore, was adjourned to the 'Caradoc,' and Lord Raglan and Sir Edmund Lyons were then present at it, together with all those who had met on board the 'Ville de Paris,' except only Marshal St. Arnaud.

Head-quarters. I have no reason for supposing that he intended to give any sanction to the step taken by the French Remonstrants; and I imagine that any materials which he may have put in their hands must have been confined to maps or statements showing the physical character of the country about to be invaded.

Thus, then, the ebullition of prudence which had broken out amongst the officers of the French army came under the arbitrament of the English General, and with him, and with him only, it rested to determine the movements of the whole Allied force.

The business of the conference was opened by Colonel Trochu. This officer, as we have already seen, was supposed to be better acquainted than any one else with the mind of the French Emperor, and his counsels, no longer bending in the direction of extreme caution, were now rather in favor of enterprise. The Colonel had possession of the document. He read it aloud, and, as he went on with the perusal, he commented upon every point; but he declared that he was no party to the contents of the paper, and that he did not share the anxieties[1] either of the army or the navy as to the disasters which might be expected to follow from a landing on the coast north of Sebastopol.

Thereupon Admiral Bruat repudiated the supposition of his being a party to the apprehensions attributed to the admirals. Lyons also repudiated it. Neither he nor Vice-Admiral Dundas had known before the conference that any such step as that of framing and presenting the remonstrance had been imagined by the French officers, and, as might be expected, they were both very sure that nothing of the kind had sprung from the British navy.

The inference which Lord Raglan drew from the document was, that it evinced 'an indisposition to the expedition amongst 'the officers who are supposed to be looked up to and to exer- 'cise influence in the French army,' and, 'in fact,' said he, 'we 'were told as much at the meeting here on Friday.'

These, then, were the 'timid counsels'[2] of which the French Emperor afterward spoke when he ascribed the glory of overruling them to Marshal St. Arnaud. If it was right, as most men will think it was, that these counsels should be overruled, there was merit due to St. Arnaud, but his merit lay, not in any personal resistance which he was able to oppose to his counselors (for he was helpless, as we have seen, from bodily illness), but in the sagacity and good sense which had led him to intrust the decision to his English colleague.

[1] 'Préoccupations.'

[2] 'Timides avis.' When this letter of the French Emperor first appeared, it was imagined that the imputation of giving 'timid' counsels was intended to be cast upon some of our Generals or Admirals; but the Duke of Newcastle, with a becoming spirit, determined instantly that this should not be suffered to pass; and the 'Moniteur' was afterward made to explain officially that the 'timides avis' were attributed by the Emperor, not to any Englishman, but to some unnamed officers in the French service.

Lord Raglan's way of dealing with the French remonstrants.

Lord Raglan's method of dealing with the protest of the French authorities was characteristic of himself and of the English nature. He did not much combat the objections set down in the paper, but he passed them by, and quietly lowered the debate from the high region of strategy to a question of humbler sort—a question as to what four steamers could be most conveniently employed for a reconnaissance on the enemy's coast.

So the conference which had been summoned to judge whether the enterprise against Sebastopol should not be brought to a stop, now found itself only deciding that the vessels sent on the reconnaissance should consist of one French steamer, together with the 'Agamemnon,' the 'Caradoc,' and the 'Sampson.'

His now complete ascendant.

But in truth the powers of the conference had silently passed into the hands of one man. Thenceforth the protest was dropped, for, if its framers had risen up against the notion of being drawn on into what they thought a rash venture by the mere effect of M. St. Arnaud's acquiescence, they were calmed when they came to know that the whole force at last had a leader. If still they held to their opinions, they did so in a spirit of cheerful deference which prevented them from throwing any farther obstacle in the way of the enterprise. The armada moved on.

The use he makes of his power.

Again and again it has happened that mighty armaments, including the forces of several states and people of diverse races, have been gathered and drawn into scenes of conflict by the will of one man; but in general, when such things have been done, the compelling mind has been brought to its resolve by the cogency of satisfied reason or by force of selfish desire. What was new in this enterprise was, that he who inexorably forced it on did not of himself desire it, nor deem it to be wise, nor even in a high degree prudent; and the power which had strength to bend the whole armada to the purpose of the invasion was—not ambition inflamed, nor reason convinced, but—the mere loyalty of an English officer refusing to stint the obedience which he owed to the minister of his Queen.

The English fleet at the point of rendezvous.

On the 9th the whole of the English fleet, with all its convoy, was anchored in deep water at the appointed rendezvous, a spot 40 miles west of Cape Tarkand.

Lord Raglan in person undertakes a reconnaissance of the coast.

Lord Raglan made haste to use the great powers with which he was now invested, and he determined to reconnoitre the coast with his own eyes. At four o'clock on the morning of the 10th General Canrobert, and the other French officers who were to attend the reconnaissance, came on board the 'Caradoc.' Lord Raglan had with him Sir Edmund Lyons, Sir John Burgoyne, and Sir George Brown. Not long after daybreak the 'Caradoc' neared Fort Constantine, and then approached the entrance of the harbor. It was a fair, bright morning, and the Sunday bells were ringing in the churches when Lord Raglan first saw the great forts, and the ships, and the glittering, cupola'd town. Afterward, the vessel being steered round off Cape Chersonesus, he could see two old Genoese forts, and ridges of hills dividing the great harbor from the southern coast of the peninsula. What he looked on was for him fated ground, for the Genoese forts marked the inlet of Balaclava, and the ridges he saw were the 'heights before Sebastopol.' But the future lay hidden from his gaze.

The 'Caradoc' was now steered toward the north, and the officers on board her surveyed the mouths of the Belbek, the Katscha, the Alma, and the Bulganak, and the coast stretching thence to Eupatoria. Of the sites thus reconnoitred General Canrobert thought the Katscha the one best fitted for a landing. Lord Raglan entirely disapproved of the Katscha, and he did not at all like the ground at the mouths of the other rivers; but when, moving on in the 'Caradoc,' he was off the part of the coast which lies six miles north of the Bulganak, he observed an extended tract of beach, which seemed to him to be the ground for which the Allies were seeking. Without generating a debate upon the subject, he nevertheless elicited so much of the opinion of those around him as he deemed to be useful. Then he declared his resolve. He said that the Allied armies should land at Old Fort.

He chooses the landing-place.

There are times when, to anxious, doubting mortals, no boon from Heaven is so welcome as the final resolve which is to govern their actions. It was so now. Debating ceased, and a happy alacrity came in its stead. That day, our fleet and the swarming convoy close gathered around had been still lying anchored in deep water at the point of rendezvous. To many, those long, peaceful Sabbath hours seemed to token a wanton delay—or worse than delay—some faltering in the great purpose of the Allies; but at night, the 'Caradoc' came in, and soon, though few could tell whence came the change, nor what had been passing, there flew from deck to deck a joyful belief—a belief that in some way—in some way not yet understood, the enterprise had gathered new force.

The French and Turkish fleets, less amply provided with steam power than the English, had fallen to leeward, but on the evening of the 11th they were anchored within thirty miles of the British fleet, and the communication was, of course, kept up by steam vessels.

During the whole of Tuesday the 12th, the French, Turkish, and English fleets were slowly drawing together and converging upon the enemy's coast. Before sunset the armed navies were all near together, and from their decks men could make out with glasses the low cliff to the north of Eupatoria. The English fleet anchored for the night. The French Admiral sent to intimate that he would not anchor, but go on all night, in the hope of being ready for the landing the next morning. Vice-Admiral Dundas saw that that hope was vain, because large portions of the French convoy were still so distant that there could be no landing on the following day. The French, it will be remembered, were without steam power for their transports, and the breezes were light. So, although every hour saw fresh clusters of vessels slowly closing with the fleet, the sea, toward the west, was always strewed with distant sails, and, before the hulls of those hove well in sight, the horizon got speckled again with sails more distant still. So the English Admiral anchored his fleet for the night.

The whole Armada converging on the coast of the Crimea.

The next morning, the 13th, the 'Ville de Paris,' under tow of the 'Napoleon' steamer, had come up, and, although so late as noon, some of the French ships of war, and very many of their transports, were still distant, they were under such breezes as promised to enable them to close before long with the fleets. So, virtually, the momentous voyage was over. The weather—and upon that, in such undertakings, the hopes of nations must rest—the weather had favored the enterprise. But the pest of modern armies had not relented. The cholera had followed the men into the transports. Many sickened on board the troop-ships whilst they were still off Varna or Baljik, and were carried back to die on shore. During the voyage many more fell ill, and many died.

But Marshal St. Arnaud, whose illness scarce three days before seemed bringing him fast to his end, was now almost suddenly restored, and, on the morning of the 13th, he was like a man in health. During the interval of five days in which the Marshal's illness had invested his English colleague with a supreme control, Lord Raglan had used to the full the occasion which Fortune thus gave him. In that time he had repressed the efforts of the French Generals who strove to bring the enterprise to a stop; he had committed the Allies to a descent upon the enemy's shores—on his shores to

St. Arnaud's sudden recovery.

The progress made by Lord Raglan during the Marshal's illness.

the north of Sebastopol; he had reconnoitred the coast, he had chosen the place for a landing, and meanwhile he had drawn the fleets on, so that now when men looked from the decks, they could see the thin strip of beach where the soldiery of the Allies were to land.

---

## CHAPTER XXXVIII.

Our ignorance of the country and of the enemy's strength.

CONCERNING the country which they were going to invade the Allies were poorly informed. Of Sebastopol, the goal of the enterprise, they knew little, except that it was a great military port and arsenal, and was deemed impregnable toward the sea. Respecting the province generally, it was known by means of books and maps that Crim Tartary, or 'the Crimea,' as people now called it, was a peninsula situate between the Black Sea and the Sea of Azof; and there was a theory—not perfectly coinciding with the truth—that the only dry communication with the main land was by the isthmus of Perekop. It was understood that the north of the peninsula had the character of an elevated steppe, that toward the south it was rocky and mountainous, and that the undulating downs which connected the steppe with the mountainous region of the south were seamed with small rivers flowing westward from the summits of the highland district. It was believed that the main of the inhabitants were Tartars, men holding to the Moslem faith. Of the enemy's forces in this country the Allies, in a sense, were ignorant; for, although the information which had come round to them by the aid of the Foreign Office was in reality well founded, they did not believe at the time that they could at all rely upon it, and therefore they were nearly as much at fault as if they had had no clew. They knew, however, that the peninsula was a province of Russia, that Russia was a great military power, that, so long as three months ago, the invasion had been counseled in print, and that afterward the determination to undertake it had been given out aloud to the world. From these rudiments, and from what could be seen from the decks of the ships, they inferred that, either upon their landing, or on some part of the road between the landing-ground and Sebastopol, they would find the enemy in strength.

But beyond this little was known; and the imagination of

This gives to the expedition the character of an adventure.

men was left to range so free that, although they were in the midst of their '19th century,' with all its prim facts and statistics, the enterprise took something of the character of adventure belonging to earlier ages. Common, sensible, fanciless men, men wise with the cynic wisdom of London clubs, were now by force turned into venturers, intent as Argonauts of old in gazing upon the shores of a strange land, to which they were committing their lives. From many a crowded deck they strained their eyes to pierce the unknown. They could not see troops. They saw a road along the shore. Now and then there appeared a peasant with a cart. Now and then a horseman riding at full speed. Neither peasant nor horseman seemed ever to pause in his duty that he might cast a glance of wonder at the countless armada which was gathering in upon his country. At the northern end of the bay there was a bright little town. Maps showed that this was Eupatoria.

Occupation of Eupatoria.

At noon, on the 13th, the English fleet had drawn near to this port of Eupatoria. There were no Russian forces there except a few convalescent soldiers; and, the place being defenseless, Colonel Trochu and Colonel Steele, accompanied by Mr. Calvert, the interpreter, were dispatched to summon it. The governor or head man of the place was an official personage in a high state of discipline. He had before his eyes the armed navies of the Allies, with the countless sails of their convoys; and to all that vast armament he had nothing to oppose except the forms of office. But to him the forms of office seemed all sufficing, and on these he still calmly relied; so, when the summons was delivered, he insisted upon fumigating it according to the health regulations of the little port. When he understood that the Western Powers intended to land, he said that decidedly they might do so, but he explained that it would be necessary for them to land at the Lazaretto, and consider themselves in strict quarantine.

On the following day the place was occupied by a small body of English troops. The few Russian inhabitants of the place, being mainly or entirely official personages, had all gone away, but the Tartar inhabitants remained; and although these men did not exhibit, as some might have expected, any eager or zealous affection for the allies of the Caliph, they seemed inclined to be friendly. Thoughtful men cared deeply to know whether between these natives and the Allies the relation of buyer and seller could be established; for it was of vital moment to the success of the expedition that the Allies should be able to obtain supplies of cattle and forage in the invaded country; and it was probable that much would turn upon the success of the first attempt to make purchases from the people of the country. The first experiment which was made in this direction elicited a curious proof of the difficulty which there is in causing mighty nations to act with the forethought of a single traveler. It was to be expected that, at the commencement of any attempted intercourse, the willingness of the natives to sell would depend upon their being tempted by the coins to which they were accustomed, because just at first they would not only be ignorant of the value of foreign money, but would also dread the consequence of being found in possession of coin plainly received from the invaders. Yet the precaution of bringing Russian money had been forgotten by the public authorities; and when Mr. Hamilton, of the 'Britannia,' was preparing to land, with a view of endeavoring to begin a buying and selling intercourse with the natives, he had nothing to offer except English sovereigns. It chanced, however, that there were two or three English travelers on board the flagship, and that these men (foreseeing the likelihood of their having to buy horses or make other purchases from the natives of the invaded country) had supplied themselves with some of the gold Russian coins called 'half imperials,' which were to be obtained without difficulty at Constantinople. The travelers —Sir Edward Colebrooke, I think, was one of them—advanced as many of these as they could spare to the public authorities; and Mr. Hamilton being thus enabled to land with a small supply of the magic half imperials, and being, besides, a good-tempered, humorous man, with a tendency to make cordial speeches in English to all his fellow-creatures alike, whether Russian, or Tartar, or Greek, he was able to make a merry beginning of that intercourse with the natives which was destined to become a fruitful source of strength to the Allied armies. The gains made by the first sellers soon drew fresh supplies into the place from the surrounding country; the commissariat afterward began its operations in the town, and in time a good, lasting market was opened to the invaders.

The whole Armada gathers toward the chosen landing-place.

After receiving the surrender of Eupatoria on the afternoon of the 13th, the assembled armada moved down toward the south. All day there were sailing vessels approaching from a distance, and closing at last with the French fleet, but before night (with the exception, it is believed, of two or three small lagging transports) the three fleets, and the host of vessels which they convoyed, were anchored near Old Fort in Kalamita Bay. The united armada extended in a line parallel with the coast, and in a direction, therefore, not far from north and south. The French and the Turkish fleets were on the south or right-hand side. The British fleet took the north, and formed the left of the Allied line.

---

## CHAPTER XXXIX.

The landing-place.

THE ground chosen by Lord Raglan for the landing of all the Allied forces is five or six miles north of the Bulganak River. It gained its name of 'Old Fort' from an indication appearing on the maps, rather than from any slight traces of the structure then remaining. Along this part of the coast the cliffs rise to a height of from 60 to 100 feet, and for the most part they impend too closely over the sea to allow much room for the beach. Near 'Old Fort,' however, the high grounds so recede that at first sight they appear to embrace a small bay or inlet of the sea, but upon a nearer approach it is perceived that the inner part of the seeming bay is a salt-water lake, and that this lake is divided from the sea by a low, narrow strip of beach. A little farther north the same disposition of land and water recurs, for there also another salt lake, called the Lake of Kamishlu, is divided from the sea by a low, narrow strip of beach a mile and a half in length. The first-mentioned strip of beach, namely, the strip opposite to Old Fort, was the one which Lord Raglan had chosen for the landing of all the Allied armies.

It was arranged that a buoy should be placed off the centre of the chosen ground to mark the boundary between the French and the English flotilla. The French and the Turkish vessels were to be on the south of the buoy, the British on the north; and in the evening and night of the 13th the ships and transports of the three nations drew in as near as they could to their appointed landing-places.

Step taken by the French in the night.

But in the night of the 13th there occurred a transaction which threatened to ruin the whole plan for the landing, and even to bring the harmony between the French and the English forces into grievous jeopardy. During the darkness, the French placed the buoy opposite—not to the centre, but—to the extreme north, of the chosen landing-ground; and when morning dawned, it appeared that the English ships and transports, though really in their proper places, were on the wrong side of the buoy, or, rather,

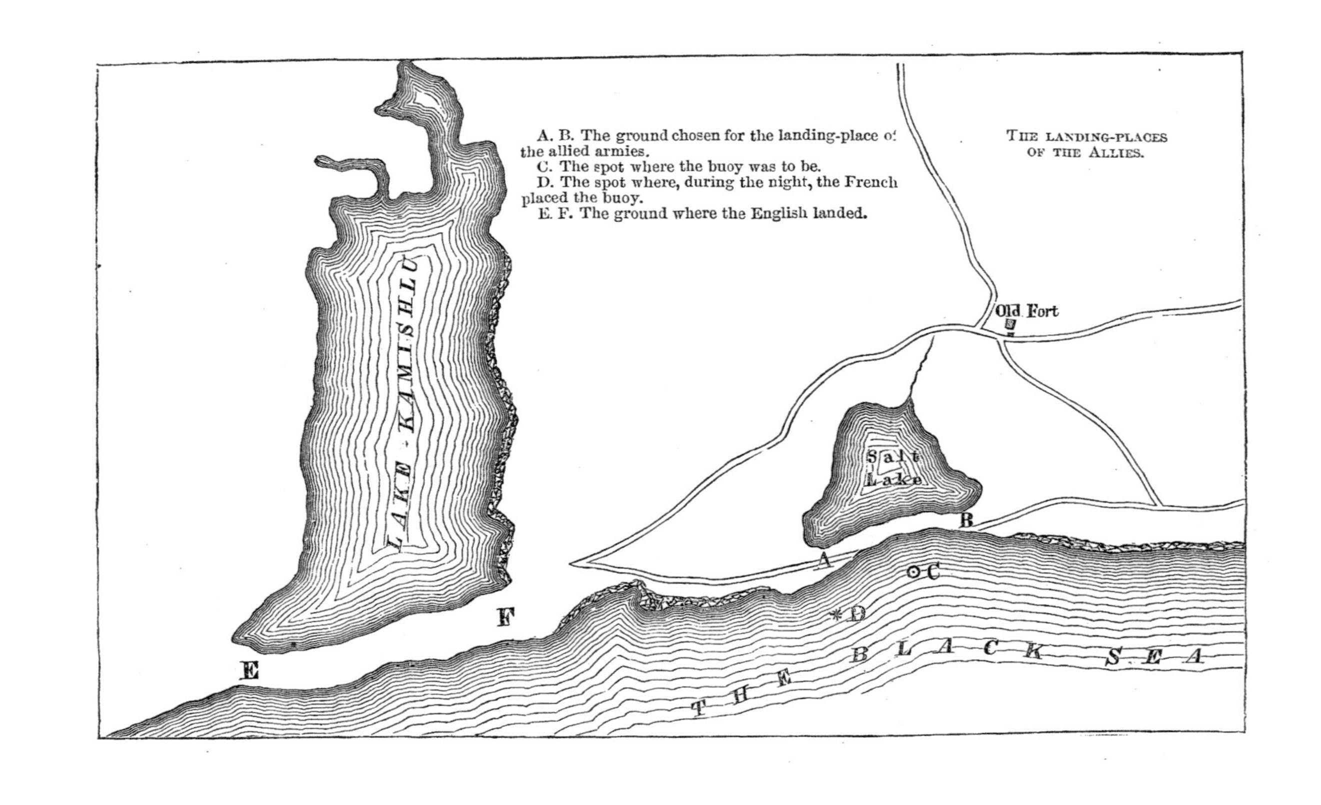
THE LANDING-PLACES OF THE ALLIES.
A. B. The ground chosen for the landing-place of the allied armies.
C. The spot where the buoy was to be.
D. The spot where, during the night, the French placed the buoy.
E. F. The ground where the English landed.
Old Fort
Salt Lake
LAKE KAMISHLU
A
B
C
D
E
F
THE BLACK SEA

that the buoy was on the wrong side of them. Whether the act which created this embarrassment was one resulting from sheer mistake on the part of our allies, or from their over-greediness for space, or from a scheme more profoundly designed, it plainly went straight toward the end desired by those French officers who had been laboring to bring the enterprise to a stop. For what was to be done? If the English, disregarding the altered position of the buoy, were to persist in keeping to their assigned landing-ground, their whole flotilla, their boats and their troops, when landed, would be hopelessly mixed up with the French, and what might be expected to follow would be ruinous confusion—nay, even perhaps angry and violent conflict between the forces of the Allies. To propose to move the buoy, or to get into controversy with the French at such a time, would be to delay and imperil the whole undertaking; and yet the boundary, as it stood, extruded the English from all share in the chosen landing-ground. It might seem that the whole enterprise was again in danger of failure; but again a strong will interposed.

This destroys the whole plan of the landing.

From the moment when Lord Raglan consented to undertake the invasion, he seems to have acted as though he felt that the belief which he entertained of its hazardousness was a reason why he should be the more steadfast in his determination to force it on. Nor was he without the very counsel that was needed for overcoming this last obstacle. Lyons, commanding the in-shore squadron of the British fleet, was intrusted with the direction of our transports and the whole management of the landing. Moving long before dawn in the sleepless 'Agamemnon,' he saw where the buoy had been placed by the French in the night time, and gathered in an instant all the perilous import of the change. He was more than a mere performer of duty, for he was a man driving under a passionate force of purpose. Without stopping to indulge his anger, he darted upon the means of dealing with the evil. He had observed that about a mile to the north of 'Old Fort' there was that strip of beach before spoken of, which divided the Lake of Kamishlu from the sea. There Lord Raglan and he now determined that the landing of the British forces should take place. It was true that this plan would sever the French from the British forces during the operation of landing, but the evil thus encountered was a hundred-fold less grave than the evil avoided; for, even in the face of an enemy, the separation of the French from the En-

Sir Edmund Lyons.

His way of dealing with the emergency.

New landing-place found for the English at Kamishlu.

glish would have been better than dispute or confusion; and, moreover, the observations of the previous day had led the Allies to conjecture that the enemy did not intend to resist the landing. The morning showed that this conjecture was sound; therefore, great as was the danger from which the Alliance had been delivered, it turned out in the result that the immense advantage of having two extended landing-places instead of one was not counterbalanced by any evil resulting from the severance of the two armies.

In point of security from molestation on the part of the enemy, both of the two landing-places were happily chosen. Both of them were on shores which allowed the near approach of the fleets, and placed the whole operation under cover of their guns. Also, both landing-places were protected on the inland side by the salt lakes, which interposed a physical obstacle in the way of any front attack by the enemy; and the access to the flanks of the disembarking armies was by strips of land so narrow that they could be easily defended against any force of infantry or cavalry. It is true that the line of disembarkation of either army could have been enfiladed by artillery placed on the heights; but then those heights could be more or less searched by a fire from the ships, and the enemy had not attempted to prepare for himself any kind of defense on the high ground.

Position of the English flotilla adapted to the change.

The necessity of having to carry the English flotilla to a new landing-place occasioned of course a painful dislocation of the arrangements which had already been acted upon by the commanders of the transports; but, after much less delay and much less confusion than might have been expected to result from a derangement so great and so sudden, the position of the English vessels was adapted to the change.

The cause and the nature of the change kept secret.

Meanwhile few of the thousands on board understood the change which had been effected, or even saw that they were brought to a new landing-ground. They imagined that it was the better method or greater quickness of the French which was giving them the triumph of being the first to land. Both Lord Raglan and Lyons were too steadfast in the maintenance of the alliance to think of accounting for the seeming tardiness of the English by causing the truth to be known; and even to this day it is commonly believed that the English army effected its landing at Old Fort.

The bend of the coast-line at Kalamita Bay is of such a character that a spectator on board a vessel close in-shore is bound-

Position of the in-shore squadrons.

ed in his view of the sea toward the south by the headland near the Alma; but if he stands a little way out to sea, the coast opens, and he then commands an unobstructed view home to the entrance of the Sebastopol harbor. So, whilst the in-shore squadrons approached the beach so closely as to be able to cover the landing, the bulk of the English fleet, commanded by Dundas in person, lay far enough out to be able to command the whole of the vast bay from Eupatoria to Sebastopol, keeping up an unbroken chain of communication from cape to cape, and always held ready to engage the Russian fleet if by chance it should come out and give battle.[1] Detached vessels reconnoitred the coast and practiced their gunners upon every encampment or gathering of troops which seemed to be within range. As though in the arrogant, yet quiet assertion of an ascendant beyond dispute, one solitary English ship, watching off the Sebastopol harbor, stood sentry over the enemy's fleet. Men had heard of the dominion of the seas, now they saw it.

Of the main English fleet.

The plan of the English disembarkation was imitated from the one adopted by Sir Ralph Abercromby when he made his famous descent upon the coast of Egypt; and it was based upon the principle of so ranging the transports and the boats as that the relative position of each company whilst it was being rowed toward the shore should correspond with that which it would have to take when formed upon the beach.[2]

Plan of the landing.

All the naval arrangements for the landing were undertaken by Sir Edmund Lyons; but, to dispose the troops on the beach—to gain a lodgment—to take up a position, and, if necessary, to intrench it—these were duties which specially devolved upon the Quartermaster-General. The officer who held this post was General Airey; and since it was his fate to take a grave part in the business of the war, and to share with Lord Raglan his closest counsels, it seems useful to speak here at once—not of the quality of his mind (for that will best be judged by looking to what he did, and

General Airey.

[1] It has been already explained that the French men-of-war were doing duty as transports, and were not, therefore, in a condition to engage the enemy. There were people who thoughtlessly blamed Dundas for not taking part with the in-shore squadron in the bustle of the landing. Of course his duty was to hold his off-shore squadron in readiness for an engagement with the Sebastopol fleet; and this he took care to do.

[2] The plans and the papers of instructions for the landing will perhaps be given in the Appendix; but I abstain from giving a detailed account of the operation, because it was not resisted by the enemy.

what he omitted to do), but rather—to speak of those circumstances of his life, and those outer signs and marks of his nature which any by-stander in the camp would be likely to hear of or see.

A strictly military career in peace-time is a poor schooling for the business of war; and the rough change which had once broken in upon Airey's professional life helped to make him more able in war than men who had passed all their lives in going round and round with the wheels. Airey was holding one of the offices at the Horse-Guards when he was suddenly called upon by his relative, Colonel Talbot, the then almost famous recluse of Upper Canada, to choose whether he and his young wife would accept a great territorial inheritance, with the condition of dwelling deep in the forest, far away from all cities and towns. Airey loved his profession, and what made it the more difficult for him to quit it was the favor with which he was looked upon by the Duke of Wellington. It chanced that he had once been called upon to lay before the Duke the maps and statements required for showing the progress of a campaign then going on against the Caffres, and the Duke was so delighted with the perfect clearness of the view which Airey was able to impart to him, that he instantly formed a high opinion of an officer who could look with so keen a glance upon a distant campaign, and convey a lucid idea of it to his chief. Airey communicated to the Duke of Wellington Colonel Talbot's proposal, and explained the dilemma in which he was placed. 'You must go,' said the Duke; 'of course you 'must go; it is your duty to go; but we will manage so that, 'whenever you choose, you shall be able to come back to us.' Airey went to Canada. It had been no part of Colonel Talbot's plan to smooth the path of his chosen inheritor. He gave him a vast territory. He gave him no home.

Isolated in the midst of the forest, and with no better shelter than a log hut half built, the staff officer, hitherto expert in the prim traditions of the Horse-Guards, now found himself so circumstanced that the health, nay, the very life of those most dear to him was made to depend upon his power to become a good laborer. He could not have hoped to keep his English servants a day if he had begun by sitting still himself and ordering them to do the rough work to which they were unaccustomed; so he worked with his own hands, in the faith that his example would make every kind of hard work seem honorable to his people; and, being endued with an almost violent love of bodily exertion, he was not only equal to this new life, but came to delight in it. Clad coarsely during the day, he was only to be distinguished from the other workmen by his greater activity and greater power of endurance. Many English gentlemen have done the like of this, but commonly they have ended by becoming altogether just that which they seemed in their working hours—by becoming, in short, mere husbandmen. It was not so with Airey. When his people came to speak to him in the evening, they always found him transformed. Partly by the subtle change which they were able to see in his manner, partly even by so outward a thing as the rigorous change in his dress, but most of all, perhaps, by his natural ascendant, they were prevented from forgetting that their fellow-laborer of the morning was their master—a master to whom they were every day growing more and more attached, but still their master. He therefore maintained his station. He did more; he gained great authority over the people about him; and when he bade farewell to the wilderness, he had become like a chief of old times—a man working hard with his own hands, yet ruling others with a firm command.

It was during a period of some years that Airey had thus wrestled with the hardships of forest life. At the end of that time Colonel Talbot died, and Airey, then coming home to England, resumed his military career. Those who know any thing of the real business of war will easily believe that this episode in the life of General Airey was more likely to fit him for the exigencies of a campaign and for the command of men than thrice the same length of time consumed in the revolving labors of a military department; nay, perhaps they will think that, next to a campaign, this manful struggle with the wilderness was the very work which would be the most sure to set a mind free from the habits, the by-laws, and the petty regulations of office.

Before the expedition left England, Lord Raglan had asked Airey to be his Quartermaster-General. Airey, preferring field-duty with the divisions, had begged that some other might be appointed, and Lord Raglan acceded to his wish; but when, on the eve of the departure of the expedition from Varna, Lord De Ros returned to England, the Quartermaster-Generalship was again pressed upon Airey in terms which made it unbecoming for him to refuse the burden. His loyalty and affectionate devotion to Lord Raglan were without bounds, and he imagined that he was always acting with a strict deference to the wishes of his chief. But then Airey was a man of great ardor, of a strong will; and having, also, a rapid, decisive judgment, he certainly accustomed himself to put very swift constructions upon Lord Raglan's words. No one ever used to see him in the pain of suspense between two opinions. Either he really knew with minuteness Lord Raglan's views, or else he was so prone to take a great deal upon himself that, in his zeal for the public service, he might almost be called unscrupulous. Men who were hesitating and trying to make out what was the path of their duty soon came to know that Airey was the officer who would thrust away their doubts for them, because, rightly or wrongly, whether with or without due authority, he used to speak in such a way as to untie or to cut every knot. He was himself, it would seem, unconscious of exercising so much power as he really did; but it is certain enough that those who complained of his ascendency were not very wrong in believing that he held a great sway; for though, being guileless and single-hearted, he always liked to receive his first impulsions from the chief, yet, when once he was thus set moving, his strong will used to burst into action with all its own proper force, and very much, too, in its own direction.

Notwithstanding this proneness to action, his manner had all the repose which is thought to be a sign of power. He did not in general speak at all until he could speak decisively; and he was more accustomed than most other Englishmen are to use that degree of precision and completeness of language which makes men content to act on it. Officers hesitating in the pain of suspense used to long to hear the tramp of his coming—used to long to catch sight of his eager, swooping crest (it was always strained forward and intent)—his keen, salient, sharp-edged features—his firm, steady eye—for they knew that he was the man who would release them from their doubts. He was gifted by nature with the kind of eloquence that it is good for a soldier to have. His oral directions to those in authority under him were models of imperative diction; but when he spoke of what he had seen, the vivid pictures he drew were marked with a sharpness of outline hardly consistent with a perfect freedom from exaggeration: they wanted the true English haze. He was too eager for action to be able to stand still weighing phrases; and I imagine that he did not even know how to try the exact strength and import of words in the way that a lettered man does. Upon the whole, his qualities were of such a kind as to make it impossible for him to be without great weight in the army. His friends would call him a man plainly fitted for high command; his adversaries would say that power in his hands was likely to be used dangerously; but all would alike agree that, whether for good or whether for evil, he had from nature the means of impressing his own will on troops.

The arrangements of the French were like those of the English; and at half past eight o'clock on the morning of the 14th of September, 1854, their first boat touched the shore. The English had made such good haste to retrieve the time spent in moving to their new landing-place, that very soon afterward their disembarkation began.

The first day's landing.

The morning was fine; the sea nearly smooth. The troops of the Light Division were in the boats, and the seamen were at their oars, expecting the signal. The signal was given, and instantly from along the whole of the first line of transports an array of boats freighted with troops—boats ranged upon a front of more than a mile—darted swiftly toward the shore. It was said that the boat commanded by Vesey of the 'Britannia' was the first to touch the beach. He was an officer who would do all man could to be foremost.

As soon as the boats had landed, the soldiers stepped ashore and began to form line upon the beach; but presently afterward they piled arms. There were some Tartar peasants passing along the coast-road with small bullock-wagons. The wagoners showed little or no alarm, and, knowing that they could not move off quickly with bullocks, they did not attempt to get away. Apparently they were not struck with any sense of unfairness when they saw that the English took possession of the wagons; and yet it could scarcely have been explained to them at that moment (as it afterward would be) that every thing taken by the English from private owners would be paid for at a just price. One of the wagons was laden with small pears, and the soldiers amused themselves with the fruit whilst the natives stood and scanned their invaders.

After a while, many of the battalions which had landed were ordered forward to occupy the hill on our right, and thenceforth, during all the day, the acclivity was sparkling with the bayonets of the columns successively ascending it. But what were those long strings of soldiery now beginning to come down from the hill-side and to wind their way back toward the beach? and what were the long white burdens horizontally carried by the men? Already? Already, on this same day? Yes. Sickness still clung to the army. Of those who only this morning ascended the hill with seeming alacrity, many now came down thus sadly borne by their comrades. They were carried on ambulance stretchers, and a blanket was over them. Those whose faces remained uncovered were still alive. Those whose faces had been covered over by their blanket were dead. Near the foot of the hill the men began to dig graves.

Zeal and energy of the sailors.

But, meanwhile, the landing went merrily on. It might be computed that, if every man in the navy had only performed his strict duty, the landing would have taken some weeks. It was the supererogation, the zeal, the abounding zeal, which seemed to achieve the work. No sailor seemed to work like a man who was merely obeying—no officer stood looking on as if he were merely commanding; and, though all was concert and discipline, yet every man was laboring with the whole strength of his own separate will. And all this great toil went on with strange good-humor, nay, even with thoughtful kindness toward the soldiers. The seamen knew that it concerned the comfort and the health of the soldiers to be landed dry, so they lifted or handed the men ashore with an almost tender care. Yet not without mirth; nay, not without laughter far heard, when, as though they were giant maidens, the tall Highlanders of the 42nd placed their hands in the hands of the sailor, and sprang by his aid to the shore, their kilts floating out wide while they leaped.

After midday the sea began to lose its calmness, and before sunset the surf was strong enough to make the disembarkation difficult, and in some degree hazardous. Yet, by the time the day closed, the French had landed their 1st, 2nd, and 3rd divisions of infantry, together with eighteen guns, and the English had got on shore all their infantry divisions, and some part of their field artillery.

Wet night's bivouac.

Some few of the English regiments remained on the beach, but the rest of them had been marched up to the high grounds toward the south, and they there bivouacked. At night there fell heavy rain, and it lasted many hours. The men were without their tents.[1] Lying in wet pools or in mud, their blankets clinging heavy with water, our young soldiers began the campaign. The French soldiery were provided with what they called dog-tents—tents not a yard high, but easily carried, and yielding shelter to soldiers creeping into them. It was always a question in the French army whether these tents gave the men more health and comfort than they could find in the open air.

Continuance of the landing.

The next morning was fine, but the surf had so much increased that for several hours the landing was suspended. After the middle of the day it became

[1] This was because there were no sufficing means of land transport for conveying the camp equipage toward Sebastopol. After the 14th the tents were landed, but they were afterward reshipped.

practicable, though still somewhat difficult, to go on with the work, and great efforts were made to land the English cavalry and the rest of the artillery, with the appertaining horses and equipages.

Unless a man has stood in the admiring crowd which gathers to see the process of landing one horse upon an open seashore; and unless, whilst he carries in his mind the labor and energy brought to bear upon this single object, he can imagine the same toil gone through again and again, and yet again, till it has been repeated many hundreds of times upon a mile and a half of beach, he will hardly know what work must be done before a general can report to his Government that he has landed upon an open coast with a thousand cavalry and sixty guns ready for the field. By labor never once intermitted (except when darkness or the state of the sea forbade it), and continued from the morning of the 14th until the evening of the 18th, the whole of the English land force, which had been embarked at Varna (together now with Cathcart's Division), was safely landed upon the enemy's coast.

Its completion;

by the English;

The result then was, that under circumstances of weather which were, upon the whole, favorable, and with the advantage of encountering no opposition from the enemy, an English force of some 26,000 infantry and artillerymen, with more than a thousand mounted cavalry, and sixty guns, had been landed in the course of five September days; and although the force thus put ashore was without those vast means of land transport which would be needed for regular operations in the interior, and was obliged to rely upon the attendant fleet for the continuance of its supplies, it was nevertheless so provided as to be able to move along the coast carrying with it its first reserve of ammunition, and food enough for three days.

The operation was conducted with an almost faultless skill, and (until a firm lodgment had been gained) it proceeded in the way that was thought to be the right one for landing in the face of the enemy. Though the surf was at times somewhat heavy, not a man was lost.

by the French;

With the French, who had no cavalry and a scanty supply of artillery horses, the disembarkation was a comparatively easy task; and if they had so desired it, the French might have been ready to march long before the English; but, knowing that their allies, having cavalry, would necessarily take a good deal of time, they were without a motive for hurrying, and, during the whole of the five days which the English took for their disembarkation, a like work was seen going on at the French landing-place.

The Turks did the work of landing very well; and, indeed, they quickly showed that they had an advantage over the French and the English in their more familiar acquaintance with the mode of life proper to warfare. They landed their camp equipage; for, with them, the carriage of tents is a very simple business. Two soldiers, one at each end, bear the pole of a tent between them, and the canvas is carried by others in turns. So early as the 15th, the first day after that on which the landing began, the Turks were comfortably encamped on the ground assigned to them; and whilst the young troops of France and England were still sitting wretched and chilled by the wet of their night's bivouac, the warlike Osmanlies seemed to be in their natural home. Soliman, who commanded them, was able to welcome and honor the guests who went to visit him in his tent as hospitably as though he were in the audience-hall of his own pashalic. He had all his tents well pitched; and his men, one could see, were still a true Moslem soldiery—men with arms and accoutrements bright, yet not forgetful of prayer. He had a supply of biscuit and of cartridges, and a good stock of horses, some feeding, some saddled, and ready for instant use. He was not without coffee and tobacco. His whole camp gave signs of a race which gathers from a great tradition, going on from father to son, the duties and the simple arts of a pious and warfaring life.

by the Turks.

---

## CHAPTER XL.

Deputations from the Tartar villages to the English head-quarters.

WHEN the people of the neighboring district came to see the strength of the armies descending upon their coast, the head men of the villages began to present themselves at the quarters of the Allies. The first of these deputations was received by Lord Raglan in the open air. The men were going up to headquarters when they passed near a group of officers on foot in blue frock coats, and they learned that the one whose maimed arm spoke of other wars was the English General. They approached him respectfully, but without submissiveness of an abject kind. Neither in manner, dress, appearance, nor language, would these men seem very strange to a traveler acquainted with Constantinople or any of the other cities of the Levant. They wore the pelisse or long robe, and, although their head-gear was of black lamb-skin, it was much of the same shape as the Turkish fez. They spoke with truthfulness and dignity, allowing it to appear that the invasion was not distasteful to them, but abstaining from all affectation of enthusiastic sympathy. They seemed to understand war and its exigencies; for they asked the interpreters to say that such of their possessions as might be wanted by the English army were at Lord Raglan's disposal. Pleased with the demeanor of the men, as well as with the purport of their speech, Lord Raglan told them that he would avail himself of some of their possessions, more especially their wagons and draught animals, but that every thing taken for the use of the English army would be paid for at a proper rate. Much to Lord Raglan's surprise (for he was not accustomed to the people of the East), the head man of the village resisted the idea of the people being paid, and anxiously pressed the interpreter to say that their possessions were yielded up as free gifts.

Result of exploring expeditions.

Pure ignorance of the invaded country gave charm to every discovery tending to throw light upon the character and pursuits of the inhabitants; and if our soldiery had found in the villages high altars set up for human sacrifices, they would scarcely have been more surprised than they were when, prying into the mysteries of this obscure Crim Tartary, they came upon traces of modern refinement and cultivated taste. In some of the houses at Kentugan there were pianos; and in one of them a music-book, lying open and spread upon the frame, seemed to show that the owner had been hurried in her flight. But the owners of these dwellings must have been official personages. The mass of the country people were Tartars.

In the villages there was abundance of agricultural wealth. The main want of the country was water; but Airey caused wells to be sunk.

The English system of payment for supplies rapidly began to bear its usual fruit, and the districts from which the people came in to barter with us were every day extending.

The English army, its absolute freedom from crime.

In their passage across the Euxine our battalions had not yet been followed by that evil horde who are accustomed to cling to an army, selling strong, noxious drinks to the men. Therefore our army was without crime.[1] It was with something more than mercy, it was with kindness and gentle courtesy, that the people of the villages were treated by our soldiery, and the interpreters had

[1] This statement, broad as it looks, is meant to be taken literally, and to be regarded as a statement taken from the right official source.

to strain the resources of the English tongue in order to convey a faint apprehension of the figures of speech in which the women were expressing their gratitude. Their chief favorites, it seems, were the men of the Rifle Brigade. Quartered for a day or two in one of the villages, these soldiers made up for the want of a common tongue by acts of kindness. They helped the women in their household work, and the women, pleased and proud, made signs to the stately 'Rifles' to do this and do that, exulting in the obedience which they were able to win from men so grand and comely. When the interpreter came, and was asked to construe what the women were saying so fast and so eagerly, it appeared that they were busy with similes and metaphors, and that the Rifles were made out to be heroes more strong than lions, more gentle than young lambs.

Kindly intercourse between our soldiery and the villagers.

A dreadful change came over that village. The Rifles were withdrawn. The Zouaves marched in. There followed spoliation, outrage, horrible cruelty. When those tidings came to Lord Raglan, he was standing on the shore with several of his people about him. He turned scarlet with shame and anger. The yoke of the alliance had wrung him.

Outrages perpetrated by the Zouaves.

In general, it would fall within the duty of light horse to sweep the face of the invaded territory and bring in supplies; but the French were without cavalry; and although the body of horse which we had landed was called 'the Light Brigade,' the Lancers, the Hussars, and the Light Dragoons of which it consisted were not of such a weight and quality, and were not so practiced in foraging, as to be all at once well fitted for this kind of service. Besides, it was plain that in advancing through the enemy's country the power of the invaders would have to be measured by the arm in which they were weakest, and a material loss in our small, brilliant force of cavalry might bring ruin upon the whole expedition. There was the Commissariat. The officers of that department were gentlemen taken from a branch of the Treasury; and although they could make requisitions on the military authorities with more or less hope of a result, they had no force of their own with which to act. The regimental officers were of course busied with their respective corps. Yet it was certain that the power of operating effectively with the English army would depend upon its obtaining a large addition to its existing means of land transport. In the result, it was the chief of one of the business departments of our Head-Quarter Staff who pressed forward into the gap, and succeeded in

The duty of sweeping the country for supplies.

achieving the work upon which, in a great degree, the fate of the campaign seemed likely to hinge.

Airey's quick perception of the need to get means of land transport.

From the first, General Airey had seen that the mere inert presence of armies in an invaded province is a thing very short of conquest. Conquest, he knew, must generally rest upon the success with which supplies can be drawn from the invaded province; and he never forgot that, unless the country could be made to yield means of land carriage, the Allies would have to creep timidly along the shore, tethered fast by the short string of carts with which they had come provided; therefore, even within a few minutes from the time when the landing began, he was already striving to gain—not the mere occupation of the soil—not the mere license of the troops to stand or lie down on the ground —but that hold, that military grasp of the country which would make it help to sustain the invasion. When only a few battalions of the Light Division had landed and were beginning to form on the beach, he rode up to the high ground on our right, and there, at some distance, he caught sight of a long string of wagons escorted by a body of Cossacks. Instantly he rode back to the beach, got Colonel Lysons to give him two companies of the 23rd Fusileers, and with these advanced quickly in skirmishing order. The Cossacks tried hard to save the convoy by using the points of their lances against the bullocks, and even against the drivers, but, the Fusileers advancing and beginning to open fire, the Cossacks at length retreated, leaving Airey in possession of just that kind of prize which the army most needed—a prize of some seventy or eighty wagons, with their oxen and drivers complete. Never ceasing to think it was vital to have more and more means of transport, Airey afterward dispatched the officers of his department in all directions to bring in supplies. Sending Captain Sankey to Tuzla and Sak, he thence got 105 wagons. Sending Captain Hamilton to Bujuk Aktash, to Beshi Aktash, to Tenish, and Sak, he got 67 camels, 253 horses, 45 cart-loads of poultry, barley, and other supplies, with more than a thousand head of cattle and sheep.[1] At a later date, and when the army was moving, he took 25 wagons from a village near the line of march. One day, moreover, it happened that Airey sent his aid-de-camp Nolan to explore for water, and, though he was without a cavalry escort, Nolan boldly cut in upon a convoy of 80 government wagons laden with flour, and seized the whole of it. In

His seizure of a convoy.

His continued exertions.

[1] In some, but not all of these expeditions, Sankey and Hamilton had cavalry escorts.

Their result. all some 350 wagons were obtained, with all their teams and with their Tartar drivers.

In general, the appropriation of the resources of the country is a business which ranges among mere commissariat annals; but in order to this invasion the seizing of means of land transport was a business hardly otherwise than vital. Even as it was, the army was brought to hard straits for want of sufficing draught power; and without the cattle and wagons which were seized whilst the troops were landing, the course of events must have been other than what it was.

Those Tartar drivers of whom I have spoken were a wild people, little fit, as it seemed, for the obedience and patient toil exacted from camp-followers; but the descent of the Allies upon the coast was the first military operation that they had witnessed, and, before their amazedness ceased, they found themselves unaccountably marshaled and governed, and involuntarily taking their humble part in the enterprise of the Western Powers. The Tartar drivers. Many of them wore the same expression of countenance as hares that are taken alive, and they looked as though they were watching after the right moment for escape; but they had fallen, as it were, into a great stream, and all they could do was to wonder, and yield, and flow on. There were few of those captured lads who had strength to withstand the sickness and the hardships of the campaign. For the most part they sank and died.

---

## CHAPTER XLI.

THERE were now upon the coast of the Crimea some 37,000 French and Turks,[1] The forces now on shore. with sixty-eight pieces of artillery, all under the orders of Marshal St. Arnaud; and we saw that 27,000 English, including a full thousand of cavalry, and together with sixty guns, had been landed by Lord Raglan. Altogether, then, the Allies numbered 63,000 men and 128 guns. These forces, partly by means of the draught animals at their command, and partly by the aid of the soldier himself, could carry by land the ammunition necessary for perhaps two battles, and the means of subsistence for three days. Their provisions beyond those limits were to be replenished

[1] 30,204 Frenchmen and 7000 Turks, according to the French accounts. Lord Raglan, I believe, thought that the French force was less, and put it at 27,600.

The nature of the operation by which the Allies were to make good their advance to Sebastopol.

from the ships. It was intended, therefore, that the fleets should follow the march of the armies, and that the invaders, without attempting to dart upon the inland route which connected the enemy with St. Petersburg, should move straight upon the north side of Sebastopol by following the line of the coast.

The whole body of the Allied armies was to operate as a 'movable column.'[1]

Comparison between regular operations and the system of the 'movable columns.'

Between an armed body engaged in regular operations, and that description of force which the French call a 'movable column,' the difference is broad; and there is need to mark it, because the way in which regular operations are conducted is not even similar to that in which a 'movable column' is wielded. It is, of course, from the history of continental wars that the principle of regular operations in the field is best deduced. A prince intending to invade his neighbor's territory takes care to have near his own frontier, or in states already under his control, not only the army with which he intends to begin the invasion, but also that sustained gathering of fresh troops, and that vast accumulation of stores, arms, and munitions, which will suffice, as he hopes, to feed the war. The territory on which these resources are spread is called the 'base of operations.' When the invading general has set out from this his strategic home to achieve the object he has in view, the neck of country by which he keeps up his communications with the base is called the 'line of operations;'[2] and the maintenance of this line of operations is the one object which must never be absent from his mind. The farther he goes, the more he needs to keep up an incessant communication with his 'base;' and yet, since the line is lengthening as he advances, it is constantly becoming more and more liable to be cut. Such a disaster as that he looks upon as nearly equal to ruin, and there is hardly any thing that he will refuse to sacrifice for the defense of the dusty or mud-deep cart-roads, which give him his means of living and fighting.

On the other hand, the commander of a 'movable column' begins his campaign by willfully placing himself in those very

[1] I make this endeavor to elucidate the true character of the operation for the purpose of causing the reader to understand the kind of hazard which was involved in the march along the coast, and also in order to lay the ground for explaining (in a future volume) the causes which afterward brought upon the army cruel sufferings and privations.

[2] This is generally, but not invariably, the same line as the one by which he has advanced.

circumstances which would bring ruin upon an army carrying on regular operations. He does not profess nor attempt to hold fast any 'line of operations' connecting him with his resources. He says to his enemy, 'Surround me if you will; 'gather upon my front; hover round me on flank and rear. 'Do not affront me too closely, unless you want to see some-'thing of my cavalry and my horse-artillery; but, keeping at 'a courteous distance, you may freely occupy the whole coun-'try through which I pass. I care nothing for the roads by 'which I have come. What I need whilst my task is doing, I 'carry along with me. I have an enterprise in hand. That 'achieved, I shall march toward the resources which my coun-'trymen have prepared for me. Those resources I will reach 'or else perish.' If an army engaged in regular operations were likened to an engine drawing its supplies by means of long pipes from a river, the principle of the 'movable column' would be well enough tokened by that simple skinful of water which—carried on the back of a camel—is the life of men passing a desert.

Each of the two systems has its advantages and its drawbacks. The advantages enjoyed by an army undertaking regular operations are:—the lasting character of its power, and its comparative security against great disasters. The general conducting an army in regular operations is constantly replenishing his strength by drawing from his 'base' fresh troops and supplies to compensate the havoc which time and the enemy—or even time alone—will always be working in his army; and if he meets with a check, he retires upon a line already occupied by portions of his force, already strewed with his magazines. He retires, in short, upon a road prepared for his reception, and the farther he retreats, the nearer he is to his great resources. The drawbacks attending this system are the great quantity of means of land transport required for keeping up the communication, and the eternal necessity of having to be ready with a sufficient force to defend every mile of the 'line of op-'erations' against the enterprises of the enemy.

The advantages of the 'movable column' are:—that its means of land transport may be comparatively small—may in fact be proportioned to the limited duration of the service which it undertakes; and that, not being clogged with the duty of maintaining a 'line of operations,' it has, in truth, nothing to defend except itself. But grave drawbacks limit the power of a 'movable column.' In the first place, it is an instrument fitted only for temporary use, because, during the service in which it is engaged, it has no resources to rely upon, except what it carries along with it. Another drawback is the hazard it incurs—not of mere defeat, but—of total extermination; for it is a force which has left no dominion in its wake, and if it falls back, it falls into the midst of enemies having hold of the country around, and emboldened by seeing it retreat.

Then, also, a movable column, even though it be never defeated in any pitched battle, is liable to be brought to ruin by being well harassed; and very inferior troops, or even armed peasants, if they have spirit and enterprise, may put it in peril; for, having the command of the country all round it, they can easily prepare their measures for vexing the column by day and by night. Again, the 'movable column' can not send its sick and wounded to the rear. It must either abandon the sufferers, or else find means of carrying them wherever it marches, and this, of course, is a task which is rendered more and more difficult by every succeeding combat. Again, if the 'movable 'column' is brought to frequent halts by the necessity of self-defense, there is danger that the operation in which it is engaged will last to a time beyond the narrow limit of the supplies which it is able to carry along with it.

In Algeria the French had brought the system of using small 'movable columns' to a high state of perfection; and there one might see a force complete in all arms, carrying with it the bread and the cartridges, and driving betwixt its battalions the little herd of cattle, which would enable it to live and to fight; one might see it bidding farewell for perhaps several weeks to all its communications, and boldly venturing into the midst of a wilderness alive with angry foes; but the Arabs and Kabyles, though not without some of the warlike virtues, were, upon the whole, too unintelligent and too feeble to be able to put the system of the 'movable column' to a test sufficing to prove that the contrivance would hold good in Europe.

Upon the whole, it may be acknowledged that, for operating in a country where the enemy is looked upon as at all formidable, the employment of a 'movable column' is a measure which will be likely to win more favor from those who love an adventure than from those who are acquainted with the art of war.

But, whichever of the two methods be chosen, it is of great moment to choose decisively, taking care that the operations are carried on in a way consistent with the principle of the system on which they proceed. A general conducting regular operations must be wary, circumspect, and resolutely patient. The leader of a 'movable column' must be swift, and, even for very safety's sake, he may have to be venturesome, for what would be rashness in another may in him be rigid prudence. The two systems are so opposite, that to confuse the two, or to import into the practice of one of them the practice applicable to the other, is to run into grave troubles and dangers. Yet this is what the Allies did. When the English Government committed to this enterprise a large proportion of their small, brilliant army, and appointed to the command of it a general mature in years and schooled by his long subordination to Wellington, they acted as though they meant that the army should engage with all due prudence in regular operations. When they ordered that this force should make a descent upon the Crimea without intending to prepare for it a base of operations at the landing-place, they caused it to act as a 'movable column.' It will be seen hereafter that from this ambiguity of purpose, or rather from this dimness of sight, the events of the campaign took their shape.

Again, it is right to see how far it be possible to change with the same force from one of the two systems to the other. Upon this, it can be said that an army engaged in regular operations may well enough be able to furnish forth a 'movable 'column;' but to hope that a 'movable column' will be able to gather to itself all at once the lasting strength of an army prepared for regular operations is to hope for what can not be. It is true, as we shall see hereafter, that by dint of great effort and the full command of the sea, the two mighty nations of the West were able in time to convert the remains of their 'movable column' into an army fitted for regular operations, but we shall have to remember that before the one system could be effectually replaced by the other, the soldiery underwent cruel sufferings.

The Allies were to operate as a 'movable 'column.'

The 63,000 invaders now preparing to march toward the south were the largest, and by far the best appointed force that the Powers of modern Europe had ever dared to engage in what (as distinguishing it from regular operations) may rightly be called an adventure. Their plan was to advance toward the north of Sebastopol, suffering the enemy to close round their rear, and intending to march every day to a new point of contact with the fleet. It was only at the mouths of the rivers that the cliffs between Old Fort and Sebastopol left room for any thing like a landing-place; and (except so far as concerned the mere interchange of signals) the land forces, whilst marching from the banks of one river to the banks of another, could not expect to be in communication with the fleets. Moreover, the Allied

Generals were still in ignorance of the numerical strength of the enemy whom they were thus to defy. All they knew was that, so far as concerned his numbers of brave, steady, highly-drilled troops, the Czar was reported to be the foremost potentate of the world; and that the publicity of the Allied counsels had given him a good deal of time for re-enforcing the garrisons of the invaded province.

It may be said that since the Allied armies were to be attended along the coast by their fleets, they were not in the strictest sense a 'movable column.' Each night, no doubt, they expected to be in communication with their ships, but, during each of the marches they were about to undertake, their dangers were to be in all respects the same as those which attend upon any other 'movable column;' for every morning they were to cast loose from the ties which connected them with their resources, as well as with their means of retreat, and were to ground their hopes of recovering their communications upon their power to force their way through a country held by the enemy. In short, the Allied armies were a 'movable column;' but a movable column which could hope to find means of succor, and, if necessary, of retreat, by fighting its way to a point of contact with the attendant fleets, and covering its withdrawal by a victory. There is the more need for showing this by dint of words, since it happened that the true nature of the expedition was obscured by the course of events. It passed for a measure more prudent than it really was, because Prince Mentschikoff, being willful and unskilled, did not take the right means for exposing its rashness.

Perilous character of the march from Old Fort.

The march now about to be undertaken by the invaders was of such a kind that an enterprising enemy who understood his calling might bring them to a halt whenever he chose; and, forcing them to try to convert their flank into a front, might compel them to fight a battle with their back to the sea-cliff: to fight, in short, upon ground where defeat would be ruin. When, therefore, on the 19th of September, 1854, the Allied armies broke up from their bivouacs and marched toward the south, they were engaging in a venturesome enterprise.

It seems that, although by human contrivance a whole people may be shut out from the knowledge of momentous events in which its armies are taking a part, there is yet a subtle essence of truth which will permeate into the mind of a nation thus kept in ignorance. To a degree which freemen can hardly imagine to be possible, the first Napoleon had succeeded in hiding the achievements of the English army from the sight of the French people; and since the French in after years were little tempted to gather up by aid of history the events which they had been hindered from learning in the form of 'news,' there was—not merely in the French army, but even in all France—a very scant knowledge of the way in which the two mighty nations of the West had encountered one another in the great war. Yet, now that the time had come for testing the faith which one army had in the prowess of the other, it suddenly appeared that a belief in the quality of the English soldier was seated as deep in the mind of the French army as though it were a belief founded upon historical knowledge. This will be understood by observing the relative place which the French commander was content to take in the order of march, and by looking at it in connection with what then promised to be the character of the impending campaign.

When once the invaders had landed and seized the coast-road, the one line of communication which the Russians could trust to for linking the garrison of Sebastopol to the main land was by the great road which passes through Bakshi Seräi and Simpheropol. It was vital to the Russian commander to be able to hold this road, for by that his re-enforcements were to come. On the other hand, he had to try to cover Sebastopol; but such was the direction in which the Allies were preparing to march upon the place, that by manœuvring with his back toward the great road passing through Simpheropol he could cling to his line of communication, and yet be able to come down upon the flank of the invading armies whilst they were marching across his front. In this way he would cover Sebastopol much more effectively than by risking his communications in order to place his army like a mere inert block between the invaders and their prey. Moreover he was known to be relatively strong in cavalry, and the country was of such a kind that the Allies advancing from Old Fort to the Belbec would have upon their left a fair undulating steppe such as horsemen exult to look upon. It was therefore to be expected that the whole stress of the task undertaken by the invaders would be thrown in the first instance upon that portion of the Allied force which might be chosen to form their left wing.

*The fate of the whole Allied army dependent upon the firmness of that portion of it which should take the left.*

In the armies of Europe the right is the side of precedence, and from the time that the Western Powers had begun to act together in Turkey, the French had always claimed, or rather had always taken, the right. Now it happened that both in Turkey and in the Crimea the side

*The French take the right.*

of precedence was the side nearest to the sea, whilst the left was the side nearest to the enemy. Lord Raglan had observed all this, but he had observed in silence; and, finding the right always seized by our Allies, he had quietly put up with the left. Yet he was not without humor; and now, when he saw that in this hazardous movement along the coast the French were still taking the right, there was something like archness in his way of remarking that, although the French were bent upon taking precedence of him, their courtesy still gave him the post of danger. This he well might say, for, so far as concerned the duty of covering the venturesome march which was about to be undertaken, the whole stress of the enterprise was thrown upon the English army. The French force was covered on its right flank by the sea, on its front and rear by the fire from the steamers, and on its left by the English army. On the other hand, the English army, though covered on its right flank by the French, was exposed in front, and in rear, and on its whole left flank, to the full brunt of the enemy's attacks. If the Russian General should act in any thing like conformity to the principles of the art of war, the whole weight of his attacks would have to be met in the first instance by the English alone; and, although the French would have an opportunity of acting as a reserve, they would do so under circumstances rendering it very difficult for them to retrieve any check sustained by their allies. In short, the French could not but know that, if the enemy should direct his enterprises against the left flank of the invaders, the least weakness on the part of the English might enable him to roll up the whole Allied force, involving French and English alike in one common disaster. Yet, so steadfast was the trust which the French reposed in the English, so unshaken the courage and good sense with which they committed themselves to the prowess of their ancient foe, that they never for an instant sought to meddle with the duty of covering the march from an attack on the left flank. They planned that the English should be there.

Their trustfulness and good sense.

On the morning of the 19th of September the Allied armies began their advance toward the south. On the right and nearest the sea the French army marched in a formation adopted by Marshal Bugeaud at the battle of Isly. The outline of the ground covered by their troops took the shape of a lozenge—a lozenge whereof the foremost apex was formed by the 1st Division, the angles on either flank by the 2nd and 3rd, and the rearmost point by the 4th Division. Within the mascle or hollow lozenge

The advance begun.

The order of march.

thus formed, there marched the Turkish battalions and those portions of the artillery and the convoy which were not specially attached to one or other of the divisions. Each French division[1] marched in two columns, consisting each of one brigade, and the artillery and incumbrances belonging to each division marched between the two brigades. Each brigade was in regimental column at sectional distance. The Allied fleets, slowly gliding along the coast, covered the French army on its right flank, and carefully reconnoitred every seam and hollow of the ground in front which could be reached by the eyes of men looking from the ships.

Since the English army was to advance in a way which left it open to the enemy in front, in rear, and on its left flank, Lord Raglan, of course, deemed it likely that he would be attacked in his march; and that upon smooth, open ground, his army would be called upon to defend both itself and its trailing convoy against the assaults of an enemy who was strong in the cavalry arm. But this task was rendered less hard than it would otherwise be by the quality of the English soldier, and the peculiar order of battle in which he loves to fight. He fights in line; and therefore, with his moderate force of infantry and artillery, Lord Raglan was able to resolve that, from whatever quarter the onset might come, he would be ready to meet it with a front of bayonets and field artillery extending along nearly two miles of ground.

In order to be able at a few minutes' notice to show a front of this extent either toward the south, the east, or the north, Lord Raglan kept each of his infantry divisions massed in close column, and he disposed his 1st, 2nd, 3rd, and light divisions in such a way that the whole body had both a front and a depth of two divisions. A body which moves in columns of this kind is said to be marching 'in grand divisions.'[2] The distances between the divisions were so arranged that, without dislocation, they could form line either in front or toward the flank. The artillery attached to each division marched on the right or seaward flank of the force to which it belonged.

[1] It was intended and ordered that the 1st and 4th French Divisions should affect a lozenge formation analogous to that which characterized the general order of march, but the direction was not practically attended to. No one knows better than an African General the art of enfolding the helpless portions of a column in battalions of infantry; but the French force being covered on all sides in the way already described, no elaborate precautions were needed.

[2] There are four or five different terms which have been used by experienced Generals in describing this disposition of troops, but the authority on which I place the most reliance sanctions the term used in the text.

The advance guard consisted of the 11th Hussars and the 13th Light Dragoons, under Lord Cardigan. In rear of the small infantry advanced guard, which followed the horsemen, there marched a detachment of the Rifles, in extended order. Then, on the right, came the 2nd Division, and, on the left, the Light Division: the 3rd Division marched in rear of the 2nd, and the Light Division was followed by the 1st Division. Of the 4th Division, the 63rd Regiment and two companies of the 46th had been left (with a squadron of the 4th Light Dragoons) to clear the beach at Kamishlu; but the remainder of the division, under Sir George Cathcart, marched in rear of the 1st Division. Along the left flank of the advancing columns, and at a distance from them of some 200 yards, were riflemen in skirmishing order, and a line of skirmishers from the same force closed the rear of the infantry. On the left flank, and nearly in the same alignment as the leading infantry divisions, was the 8th Hussars, and on the same flank, but in an alignment less advanced than the rearmost of the infantry columns, there was the 17th Lancers. The cattle and the baggage marched in rear of the 3rd Division, and so as to be covered, toward the left, by the 4th Division. Then followed the rear guard, and then a line of Rifles disposed at intervals in extended order. Last of all came the 4th Light Dragoons, under Lord George Paget.

The march.

Thus marched the strength of the Western Powers. The sun shone hotly as on a summer's day in England; but breezes, springing fresh from the sea, floated briskly along the hills. The ground was an undulating steppe, alluring to cavalry. It was rankly covered with a herb like southernwood; and when the stems were crushed under foot by the advancing columns, the whole air became laden with bitter fragrance. The aroma was new to some. To men of the western counties of England it was so familiar that it carried them back to childhood and the village church; they remembered the nosegay of "boy's-love" that used to be set by the Prayer-Book of the Sunday maiden too demure for the vanity of flowers.

In each of the close massed columns, which were formed by our four complete divisions, there were more than 5000 foot soldiers. The colors were flying; the bands, at first, were playing; and once more the time had come round when in all this armed pride there was nothing of false majesty; for already videttes could be seen on the hillocks, and (except at the spots where our horsemen were marching) there was nothing but air and sunshine, and, at intervals, the dark form of a single riflemen, to divide our columns from the enemy. But more warlike than trumpet and drum was the grave quiet which followed the ceasing of the bands. The pain of weariness had begun. Few spoke. All toiled. Waves break upon the shore; and though they are many, still distance will gather their numberless cadences into one. So, also, it was with one ceaseless, hissing sound that a wilderness of tall, crisping herbage bent under the tramp of the coming thousands. As each mighty column marched on, one hardly remembered, at first, the weary frames, the aching limbs which composed it; for—instinct with its own proper soul and purpose, absorbing the volitions of thousands of men, and bearing no likeness to the mere sum of the human beings out of whom it was made—the column itself was the living thing—the slow, monstrous unit of strength which walks the modern earth where empire is brought into question. But a little while, and then the sickness which had clung to the army began to make it seen that the columns, in all their pride, were things built with the bodies of suffering mortals.

Sickness and failing strength of many of the soldiers.

We saw that, before the embarkation, our troops had fallen into a weak state of health, and that, even of those who were free from serious illness, there were hardly any who had been able to keep their accustomed strength. It had been hoped that the voyage would bring back health and strength; but the hope proved vain; and Lord Raglan, knowing the weakly state of the men, had ordered that they should be allowed to enfold the few things they most needed in their blankets, and to land and march without their knapsacks. Yet now, before the first hour of march was over, the men began to fall out from their ranks. Some of these were in the agonies of cholera. Their faces had a dark, choked look; they threw themselves on the ground and writhed, but often without speaking and without a cry. Many more dropped out from mere weakness. These the officers tried to inspirit, and sometimes they succeeded; but more often the sufferer was left upon the ground. It was vain to tell him, though so it was believed at the time, that he would fall into the hands of the Cossacks. The tall, stately men of the Guards dropped from their ranks in great numbers. It was believed at the time that the men who fell out would be taken by the enemy; but the number of stragglers at length became very great, and, in the evening, a force was sent back to bring them in.

During the march the foot soldiers of the Allied armies suffered thirst; but early in the afternoon the troops in advance

The stream of the Bulganak. reached the long-desired stream of the Bulganak, and, as soon as a division came in sight of the water, the men broke from their ranks, and ran forward that they might plunge their lips deep in the cool, turbid, grateful stream. In one brigade a stronger governance was maintained. Sir Colin Campbell would not allow that even the rage of thirst should loosen the discipline of his grand Highland regiments; he halted them a little before they reached the stream, and so ordered it that, by being saved from the confusion that would have been wrought by their own wild haste, they gained in comfort, and knew that they were gainers. When men toil in organized masses, they owe what well-being they have to wise and firm commanders.

It was on the banks of this stream of the Bulganak that the Allied armies were to bivouac for the night.

---

## CHAPTER XLII.

EARLY in the afternoon, Lord Raglan, riding in advance of the infantry divisions, had reached the banks of the river, and, observing a group of Cossacks on the brow of the hill toward the south, he ordered the squadrons which Lord Cardigan had with him[1] to move forward and reconnoitre the ground. Lord Lucan was present with this portion of his cavalry force.

The affair of the Bulganak.

Where the post-road from Eupatoria to Sebastopol crosses the Bulganak, the ground on the south side of the river rises gradually for some hundreds of yards from the banks of the stream, then dips a little, then rises again, then dips rather deeply, and then again rises up to the summit of the ridge which bounds the view of an observer in the valley of the Bulganak.

Our reconnoitring squadrons went forward a great way into the lower dip, and when they were there it was perceived that, confronting them from the hill above, there was a body of cavalry 2000 strong. Our four squadrons halted and formed line. The Russian cavalry came forward a little, then halted, and, throwing out skirmishers, attempted some long, fruitless shots with their carbines. Our squadrons also threw out skirmishers.

But Lord Raglan, who had remained with his staff on the

[1] The 11th Hussars and 13th Light Dragoons.

northern side of the hollow, had now discerned the formidable body of cavalry which was confronting our four squadrons; and Airey, being gifted with a keen, far-reaching sight, was able to make out that the glitter which could be seen between the second crest and the summit was the play of the sun upon the points of bayonets, and that in the upper hollow there were several battalions. It was soon made plain that within a few hundred yards of our four squadrons the enemy was present with all three arms, and in some force. He had there, as we now know, about 6000 men of his 17th Division, two batteries of artillery, a brigade of regular cavalry, and nine sotnias of Cossacks.

Lord Raglan, whose army was still on its march, saw that he must take care to avoid provoking an action; but also he had to provide for the retreat of the four squadrons, which stood rooted in the centre of the lower hollow, so near to an overwhelming enemy's force of all arms, and so far from their supports, that they were in some danger. The problem was to extricate them, if possible, without getting into that sort of conflict which would be likely to bring about a serious engagement. Lord Raglan saw that what made the Russians hesitate was the steadiness, and the exact, ceremonious formation of the little cavalry force of four squadrons which tranquilly confronted them; and that, if he were to withdraw it before he had made arrangements for covering its retreat, it would be pursued and roughly handled by overwhelming numbers. He was anxious; for, small as was this little body of horse, it was a large proportion of his whole strength in the cavalry arm; but he saw that its safety would be best provided for by bringing up troops to its support, and allowing it in the mean time to remain where it was, confusing the enemy by its obstinate presence and its careful array. He ordered up in all haste the Light and the 2nd Divisions, the 8th Hussars, and 17th Lancers, and afterward the nine-pounder batteries attached to the Light Division. When our infantry divisions came up, they were formed in line, and the cavalry supports took a position in left rear of the advanced squadrons. All these operations the enemy suffered to take place without resistance; and when they were completed his opportunity was gone.

So, all being now in readiness, Lord Raglan wished that the four squadrons should forthwith retire; and the more so as he was apprehensive lest these horsemen, in their evident longing for a combat, should be tempted to charge the body of cavalry in their immediate front. Still, he was unwilling to embarrass Lord Lucan (close as he then was to the enemy) by an order too precise or imperative. In these circumstances, Airey galloped forward to give effect to Lord Raglan's wishes.

When Airey came up, he found that by communicating Lord Raglan's wishes without delivering a positive order he was supplying materials for a debate between Lord Lucan and his brigadier. Yet for a wordy debate the time and the place were ill fitted, for the four squadrons, as we have seen, were within but a little distance of overwhelming forces. There is some little obscurity as to the exact way in which Airey brought his will to bear; but he saw what was wanted, and he said the force must retire immediately, and by alternate squadrons. Though he spoke in terms which might have meant that he was only giving his own opinion, yet perhaps the decisiveness of his speech and manner led to the impression that he was delivering Lord Raglan's orders. Be this as it may, the result was quickly attained. Lord Lucan understood that he was to go forthwith to Lord Raglan. Lord Cardigan understood that the force was to retire immediately, and by alternate lines. The operation instantly commenced, and was conducted with excellent precision, for during the whole retreat there were always two squadrons out of the four which were showing a smooth front to the enemy.

The moment the withdrawal of our little cavalry force began, the enemy's artillery teams, unseen before, came bounding up from the hollow, and his guns, being quickly unlimbered, were soon in battery upon the ridge. With these he opened fire upon our retreating squadrons; but he saw that these horsemen, no longer isolated, were retiring upon ample supports of all arms. He did not, therefore, venture to pursue with his cavalry. Two men in our cavalry force were wounded, and four or five horses killed. The six-pounder guns attached to our cavalry replied to the enemy's artillery without good effect; but when our nine-pounder guns were brought into action, they caused the enemy's artillery to limber up and retire. They also, it seems, inflicted some loss upon the enemy's cavalry, for it was said that as many as thirty-five of his troopers were killed or wounded. The Russians were soon out of sight.

The slight combat thus occurring on the Bulganak was the first approach to a passage of arms between Russia and the Western Powers. The pith of what had happened was this: The Russians had been making a reconnaissance in force at a time when Lord Raglan was making a reconnaissance with only four squadrons; and, as the nature of the ground concealed the enemy's strength, our lesser force was exposed for some minutes to a good deal of danger; but the enemy, being slow to take advantage of fortune, had given the English General full time to extricate his squadrons by the use of the three arms. Lord Raglan was so well pleased with the success of this last operation, and with the steadiness shown by our cavalry, that even on the night of the Alma (when it might have been supposed that the impressions produced by the battle would have superseded the recollection of the previous day) he spoke with complacency of this affair on the Bulganak.

---

## CHAPTER XLIII.

Apparently dangerous situation of the English army.

WHEN this affair was concluded, Lord Raglan began to prepare for a contingency of graver import. The enemy, as it now appeared, had a force of all arms in the immediate neighborhood, and it was known that he had his whole field army within a few hours' march of the Bulganak. On the other hand, Lord Raglan was exposed to attack in front, left flank, and rear; and even on his right flank he was without immediate support, for the course of the day's march had thrown an interval of a mile between the French and the English armies. It was to be apprehended that the enemy, issuing during the night from his intrenched position on the Alma, would place himself in such a position as to be able to fall upon our army in front and flank at dawn of day. Lord Raglan, therefore, determined that the troops should bivouac in order of battle, and so as to be rapidly able to show a deployed front to the enemy either in front or flank. He placed the troops himself, fixing their exact position with minute care.

Lord Raglan causes it to bivouac in order of battle.

The first brigades of the 2nd and Light Divisions were drawn up in line parallel with the river, and some hundreds of yards in advance of it. The first brigades of the 1st and 3rd Divisions were placed in an oblique line, receding from the left of the Light Division, and going back to the river's bank. The troops, thus deployed, formed with the river a kind of three-sided inclosure, in which the principal part of the cavalry and the incumbrances of the army were infolded. The second brigade of each of the divisions already named was formed in column in rear of the first or deployed brigade. The 4th Division and the 4th Light dragoons were placed in observation on the northern side of the river. Finally, Colonel

Lagondie, one of the French Commissioners at our head-quarters, was requested to suggest to Prince Napoleon the expediency of his drawing his division somewhat more near to the English right.[1]

Our troops piled arms, and bivouacked in order of battle.[2] There was a post-house at the point where the road crossed the river, and there Lord Raglan passed the night.

The situation of our army seemed to be critical; but when morning dawned it appeared that the enemy, attempting nothing, had drawn off to his intrenched position on the Alma.

So the peril which the Allies had been encountering for the last twenty-four hours was now at an end; and the duty of carrying the position on the Alma might be regarded as easy, in comparison with that which would have devolved upon the invaders if our left flank had been briskly attacked on their march. It is common to attribute great results to careful design; but the truth is that the Allies owed their prosperous landing and their tranquil march to the forbearance of the Russian commander.

---

## CHAPTER XLIV.

### I.

Position on the Alma.

FOR an army undertaking to withstand the march of invaders who come along the shore from the north, the position on the left bank of the Alma is happily formed by nature, and is capable of being made strong. The river springs from the mountain range in the southeast of the peninsula, and its tortuous channel, resulting at last in a westerly course, brings it down to the sea near the headland called Cape Loukool. In that region the right or northern bank of the stream inclines with a very gentle slope to the water's edge; but on the south or left bank the river presses close against a great range of hills, and the rocky ground which forms their base, being scarped by the action of the river in its swollen state, gives a measure of the loud, red torrent thrown down in flood-times from the sides of the Tchatir Dagh. Yet, so long as it flows in its summer bed, the pure gray stream of the Alma, though strong and rapid even then, can be crossed

[1] Colonel Lagondie fulfilled his mission; but on his return, being a near-sighted man, he rode into the midst of a Cossack picket, and was taken prisoner.

[2] See the plan on p. 442.

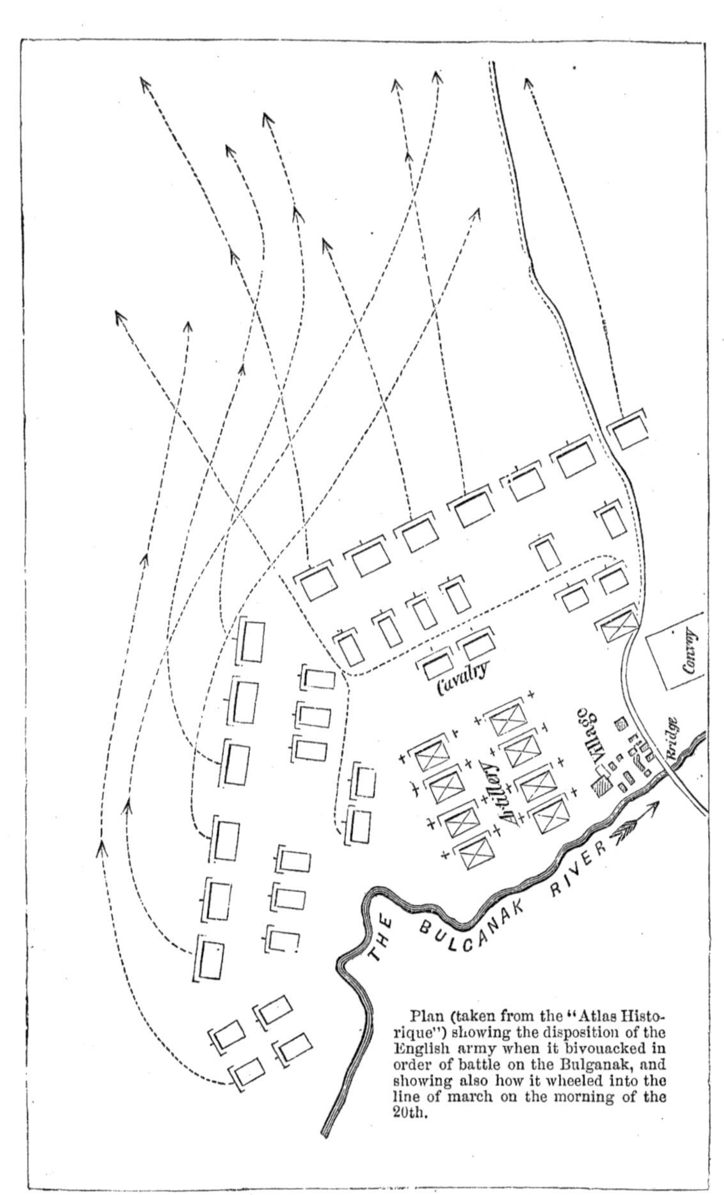

Plan (taken from the "Atlas Historique") showing the disposition of the English army when it bivouacked in order of battle on the Bulganak, and showing also how it wheeled into the line of march on the morning of the 20th.

in most places by a full-grown man without losing foot. There are, however, some deeps which would force a man to swim a few strokes; and, on the other hand, the river is passed in several places by easy and frequented fords. Near the village of Bourliouk, at the time of the action, there was a good timber bridge.

Along the course of the stream, on the north or right bank, there is a broad belt of gardens and vineyards, inclosed by low stone walls, and reaching down to the water; but on the left or south side there are few inclosures, for, in most places, the rock formation, which marks the left bank of the river, has its base so close down to the water's edge as to leave but little soil deep enough for culture.

The smooth slopes by which the invader from the north approaches the Alma are contrasted by the aspect of the country on the opposite bank of the river; for there the field is so broken up into hills and valleys—into steep acclivities and narrow ravines—into jutting knolls and winding gullies—that, with the labor of a Russian army, and the resources of Sebastopol at his command, a skilled engineer would have found it hard to exhaust his contrivances for the defense of a ground having all this strength of feature.

It is the high land nearest to the shore which falls most abruptly; for when a man turns his back to the sea, and rides up along the river's bank, the summits of the hills on his right recede from him more and more—recede so far that, although they are higher than the hills near the shore, they are connected with the banks of the stream by slopes more gently inclining.

The main features of the ground are these: first and nearest to the sea-shore there is what may be called the 'West Cliff,' for the ground there rises to a height of some 350 feet; and not only presents, looking west, a bluff buttress of rock to the sea, but also on its northern side hangs over the river so steep that a man going up along the bank of the stream has at first an almost sheer precipice on his right hand; and it is only when he all but reaches the village of Almatamack that he finds the cliff losing its severity. At that point the ground becomes so sloping and so broken as to be no longer difficult of ascent for a man on foot, nor even for country wagons. In rear—Russian rear—of the cliff there are the villages of Hadji-Boulat, Ulukul Tiouets, and Ulukul Akles.

Higher up the river, but joined on to the West Cliff, there is a height, which was crowned at the time of the war by an unfinished turret intended for a telegraph. This is the Telegraph Height. At top, the West Cliff and the Telegraph Height form one connected plateau or table-land; but the sides of the Telegraph Height have not the abrupt character which marks the West Cliff. They are steep, but both toward the river and toward the east they are much broken up into knolls, ridges, hollows, and gullies. At all points they can be ascended by a man on foot, and at some by wagons. These steep sides of the Telegraph Height are divided from the river by a low and almost flat ledge, with a varying breadth of from two to six hundred yards. The ledge was a good deal wooded at the time of the war, and on some parts of it there were vineyards or orchards.

To the east of the Telegraph Height the trending away of the hills leaves a hollow or recess, so formed and so placed that its surface might be likened to a huge vine-leaf; a vine-leaf placed on a gentle incline, with its lower edge on the river, its stem at the bridge, and its main fibre following the course of the great road which bends up over the hill toward Sebastopol. This opening in the hills is the main Pass; and through it (as might be gathered from what has just been said), the Causeway or great post-road goes up from the bridge.[1] Across the mouth of the Pass, at a distance of a few yards from the bridge, there are small natural mounds or risings of ground, having their tops at a height of about sixty feet above the level of the river. These are so ranged as to form, one with the other, a low and uneven but almost continuous embankment, running from east to west, and parallel with the river. The natural rampart thus formed controls the entrance to the Pass from the north, for it not only overlooks the bridge, but also commands the ground far and wide on both sides of the river, and on both sides of the great road. Behind, the ground falls and then rises again, till it mingles with the slopes and the many knolls and hillocks which connect it with the receding flanks of the Telegraph Height on the one side, and the Kourganè Hill on the other.

Still higher up the river, but receding from it in a south-easterly direction, the ground rises gradually to a commanding height, and terminates in a peak. This hill is the key of the position. It is called the Kourganè Hill. Around its slopes, at a distance of about 300 yards from the river, the ground so swells out as to form a strong rib—a rib which bends round

[1] In speaking of this opening as a 'Pass,' I have followed the example of one whom I regard as a great master of the diction applicable to military subjects; and it is not, of course, meant that there is any thing at all Alpine in the character of this range of low hills—hills less than 400 feet high.

Plan indicating, in a general way, the form of the opening called "The Pass," through which the Post-road, after crossing the Alma, bends up over the hills.

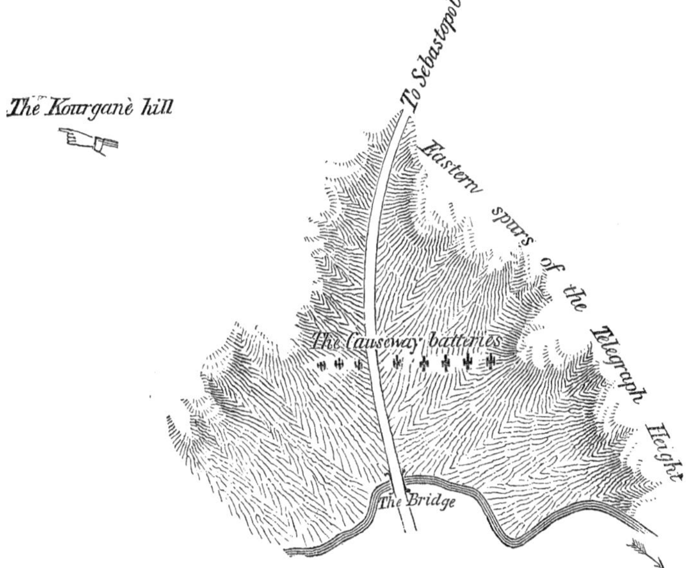

the front and the flanks of the bastion there built by nature, giving a command toward the southwest, the west, the northwest, and the northeast. Toward the west this terrace, if so it may be called, is all but joined to those mounds which we spoke of as barring the mouth of the Pass. Behind all these natural ramparts there are hollows and dips in the ground, which give ample means for concealing and sheltering troops; but from the jutting rib down to the bank of the river the slope is gentle and smooth like the glacis of a fortress. It was on this Kourganè Hill that Prince Mentschikoff established his head-quarters.

The immediate approach to the river from its right bank is every where gentle, but the ground on its south side is a good deal scarped by the action of the water; and all along that part of the river which flows opposite to the Kourganè Hill and the main Pass, the left bank rises almost vertically from the water's edge to a height of from eight to fifteen feet.

On the north bank of the river, and at a distance of about a mile from its mouth, there is the village of Almatamack. On the same bank, but more than a mile and a quarter higher up the stream, there stood at the time of the war a large white homestead. Yet a mile higher up the river, on the same bank, and nearly facing the mouth of the Pass, there stands the large straggling village of Bourliouk. The cottages and farm-buildings which skirt this village on its eastern side extend far up the river. From Bourliouk to the easternmost part of the position the distance is two miles.

To ascend the position from the north there are several frequented ways:

1. Close to the sea and to the mouth of the river there is a singular fissure in the rock, and through this a narrow way leads round, and up to the top of the cliff. This road was not traversed by artillery on the day of the battle, but it is believed that this was because the guns could not be brought across the river at the point where it flows into the sea.

2. From the ford at the village of Almatamack there is a wagon-road which leads up to the top of the plateau. It was practicable for artillery.

3. From the white homestead there is a road which crosses the river and goes up to the plateau; but, either because of the badness of the ford, or else the too rugged ascent beyond it, this road could not be used for artillery. The want of a road for their guns in this part of the field was the main cause which hampered the French army.

4. On the western side of the village of Bourliouk there is a

frequented ford across the river, and from that spot two wagon-roads forking off at no great distance from one another lead up to the Telegraph and the villages in its rear. The westernmost of these roads was found to be practicable for artillery.

5. Opposite to Bourliouk two almost parallel wagon-roads lead up from the bank of the river to the top of the plateau.

6. The Great Causeway, or post-road leading from Eupatoria, goes through the eastern skirts of Bourliouk, crosses the bridge, enters the Pass, and ascends by a gentle incline toward the low chain of mounds running across its mouth. After piercing that natural rampart, it bends into the southerly course which leads it to Sebastopol.

7. To the east of the main Pass there are other roads; but they are not farther spoken of here, because all the hill-side in that part of the field is more or less accessible to artillery.

Except at the West Cliff, every part of the position can be reached by men on foot.

In the rear—Russian rear—of the hills which form this position, the ground falls, and it rises again at a distance of two miles.

Down to the edge of the vineyards, the whole of the field on the north or right bank of the river is ground tempting to cavalry; and although the south side of the stream is marked, as we saw, by stronger features, still the summits of the heights spread out broad, like the English "Downs." Except the sheer sides of the cliff, and the steeps of the Telegraph Height, there is little on the higher ground to obstruct the manœuvres of horsemen.

From the sea-shore to the easternmost spot occupied by Russian troops, the distance for a man going straight was nearly five miles and a half; but if he were to go all the way on the Russian bank of the river, he would have to pass over more ground; for the Alma here makes a strong bend, and leaves open the chord of the arc to invaders who come from the north.[1]

[1] I am aware that in distances and in other material points this description of the position differs widely from the result of the hasty surveys which were made soon after the battle by English officers. The French Government plans bear such strong marks of having been made with great care and labor, that in general I have ventured to take them for my guide in preference to those of my own countrymen.

II.

Against any plan for occupying the whole of this range of hills by the forces of the Czar there were two cogent reasons: one was, that the summits of the West Cliff, and even of part of the Telegraph Height, were exposed to fire from the ships; the other, that the position was too wide for the numbers which were brought to defend it.

Mentschikoff's plan for availing himself of the position.

But the whole of the naval and military resources of the Crimea had been intrusted to the direction of Prince Mentschikoff. With him it rested to make head against the invasion; and it seems he had been so forcibly struck with the great apparent steepness of the West Cliff and the heights connected with it, that he thought it must be wholly inaccessible to troops. He conceived, therefore, that he might safely omit to occupy it, and might be content to take up a narrowed position, beginning on the eastern slopes of the Kourganè Hill, and terminating on the west of the Telegraph Height, at a distance of more than two miles from the sea.[1] By this course, as he thought, he would elude both of the obstacles which interfered with his hold of the position; for his extreme left would be comparatively distant from the shipping, and the whole ground occupied would be so far contracted that the troops which he had at his command might suffice to hold it. Upon this plan he acted. So, although the position of the Alma, as formed by nature, had an extent of more than five miles, the troops which stood charged to hold it had a front of only one league. Prince Mentschikoff rested upon the assumption that the whole of the ground which he proposed to leave unoccupied was inaccessible to troops; but if he had walked his horse into the road which was within half a mile of his extreme left, he would have found that it led down to a ford opposite to the village of Almatamack, and was perfectly practicable for artillery. His army had been on the ground for several days, yet, with a strange carelessness, he not only omitted to break up or to guard this road from Almatamack, but made all his dispositions exactly as though no such road existed.

His forces.

The forces brought forward to defend this position for the Czar were 3400 cavalry, 33,000 infantry, and 2600 artillerymen, making altogether 39,000 men,[2] with 106 guns.

[1] The Russian accounts estimate the distance at only two versts, but I adhere, as before stated, to the French plans.

[2] 39,017. See post, p. 450 et seq., where the details of the force are fully given.

Prince Mentschikoff commanded in person. He was a wayward, presumptuous man, and his bearing toward the generals under his command was of such a kind that he did not or could not strengthen himself by the counsels of men abler than himself.[1] In times past he had been mutilated by a round shot from a Turkish gun. He bore hatred against the Ottoman race; he bore hatred against their faith. He had opened his mission at the Porte with insult; he had closed it with threats. And now—a sequence rare in the lives of modern statesmen—he was out on a hill-side, with horse and foot, having warrant—full warrant this time, to adduce 'the last reason of kings.'

His personal position.

So far as regards the general scheme of the campaign, his conception, it seems, was this: he would suffer the Allies to land without molestation, because he desired that the defeat which he was preparing for them should be, not a mere repulse, but a crushing and signal disaster. He would not attack them on their line of march, because he liked better to husband his strength for the great position on the Alma. It seemed to him that there he could hold his ground against the invaders for three weeks, and his imagination was that, baffled for many days by the strength of his position, drawing their supplies from the ships with pain and uncertainty, and encumbered more and more every day with wounded men, the Allies would fall into evil days. In the mean time the troops, long since dispatched from Bessarabia, would begin to reach him by way of Perekop and Simpheropol; and, thus re-enforced, he would in due season take the offensive, inflicting upon the Western Powers a chastisement commensurate with their rashness.

His plan of campaign.

Prince Mentschikoff rested this structure of hope upon the assumption that he could hold the position on the Alma for at the least many days together, and against repeated assaults. Yet he took little pains to prepare the ground for a great defense.[2] On the jutting rib which goes round the front of the Kourganè Hill, at a distance of about 300 yards from the river, he threw up a breastwork, a work of a very slight kind, presenting no physical obstacle to the advance of troops, but sufficiently extended to be

His reliance on the natural strength of the position.

[1] I infer this from the fact that, the day before the action, General Kiriakoff, an officer of high reputation, was attempting indirect methods of calling Prince Mentschikoff's attention to the defectiveness of his arrangements.—*Kiriakoff's Statement.*

[2] I say this in the teeth of the English dispatches, and, I fear, of many written and oral statements from officers; but I am sure that every engineer who saw the ground will support my assertion.

capable of receiving the fourteen heavy guns with which he armed it.[1] This work was called the 'Great Redoubt.'[2] Prince Mentschikoff was delighted with this earthwork. 'Is not this a grand thing?' said he to General Kiriakoff the day before the action; 'see, it will do mischief both ways.' And he then pointed out how, whilst the face of the redoubt commanded the smooth slope beneath it, the guns at the shoulder of the work would throw their fire across the great road on either side of the bridge.

The means he took for strengthening it.

On the same hill, but higher up and more to his right, the Prince threw up another slight breastwork, which he armed with a battery of field-guns. This was the Lesser Redoubt.

The vineyards at some points were marked and cleared so as to give full effect to the action of the artillery; but, except the two redoubts, no field-works were constructed by the Russian General. Willful and confident, he was content to rest mainly upon the natural strength of the ground, the valor of his troops, and the faith that he had in his own prowess as a commander. He even omitted, as we have seen, to break up or to guard the wagon-road which led up from Almatamack to the left of his position. The Prince did not attempt to occupy the West Cliff; but some days before the action a battalion[3] and half a battery had been placed overlooking the sea in the village of Ulukul Akles, in order, as was said, to 'catch 'marauders,' or to prevent a descent from the sea in the rear of the Russian army; and the detachment remained in that part of the field until the time when the battle began.

On the ledge which divided the river from the steep, broken side of the Telegraph Height, Prince Mentschikoff placed four Militia[4] battalions, and supported them by three battalions of regular infantry,[5] placed only a hundred

Disposition of his troops.

[1] Twelve only, according to Prince Gortschakoff. The pieces were 32-pounders and 24-pound howitzers.

[2] The work was formed by cutting a shallow trench, and throwing up the earth in front of it. I follow the military authorities in calling these works "redoubts," because our people at home came to know of them under this description; but the term is not accurate, for they were open toward the rear.

[3] The No. 2 battalion of Minsk.

[4] I adopt this inaccurate term as the best I can find to describe these semi-regular troops, because to call them, as the Russians do, 'reserve battalions,' would tend to confuse, by suggesting the idea of 'reserves' in the ordinary sense. I thought at one time I might have called them 'depôt battalions,' but upon the whole it seemed to me that the term 'militia' would be less likely to convey a wrong notion than the term 'depôt.' They are troops regarded as very inferior in quality to troops of the line. The four battalions which I call 'militia' were the 'reserve' battalions of the 13th Division.—*Anitchkoff, Chodasiewicz.*

[5] Nos. 2, 3, and 4 of the Taroutine corps.—*Ibid.*

and fifty yards in their rear, and by a fourth battalion[1] drawn up in a neighboring ravine.[2] Farther still in rear, he held in hand as a reserve for his left wing the four battalions of the 'Moscow corps,' which had joined him that morning.[3] These, with two batteries of artillery,[4] were all the forces occupying that part of the position which was about to be assailed by the French.[5] Including the battalion and the half battery at Ulukul Akles, they consisted of thirteen battalions of infantry with twenty guns, and numbered altogether rather more than 10,000 men.[6] They formed the left wing of the Russian army, and were commanded by General Kiriakoff. The battalions were placed at intervals, checker-wise, and each battalion was massed in column of companies. A line of skirmishers was thrown out in front, but for want, as was said, of better ground to act upon, these skirmishers were kept within ten yards of the 'Militia' battalions. The two batteries of artillery were not at first so placed as to be of any use. No part of this force on the Telegraph Height was covered by intrenchments or by any kind of field-work.

Forces originally posted in the part of the position assailed by the French.

In the main Pass, facing the bridge, and destined to confront the 2nd Division of the English army, Prince Mentschikoff placed four battalions of light infantry,[7] with one battalion of rifles;[8] and three out of those five battalions had orders to advance and skirmish in the vineyards. The other two battalions were kept massed in column. Near the bridge was posted a battalion of sappers and miners.[9] Astride the great road, and disposed along the chain of hillocks which runs across the pass looking down on the bridge, the Prince placed two batteries of field artillery.[10] These two batteries, acting together, and compris-

Forces originally posted in the part of the position assailed by the English.

1 The No. 1 battalion of the same corps.—*Anitchkoff, Chodasiewicz.*

2 Chodasiewicz.

3 The battalions of the Moscow corps.—*Anitchkoff, Chodasiewicz.*

4 Viz., the Nos. 3 and 5 batteries of the 17th brigade of artillery.

5 The four batteries of the Minsk corps, with several guns, were afterward moved into this part of the ground, as will be seen by-and-by.

6

| | |
|---|---|
| Thirteen battalions of 750 each | 9,750 |
| One battery of position, 263 men | 263 |
| One light battery | 210 |
| Half of another light battery | 105 |
| | 10,328 |

Anitchkoff and Chodasiewicz, writing with opposite feelings and differing in many things, are strictly in accord as to the number of battalions posted in this part of the field.

7 The four battalions of the Borodino corps.—*Anitchkoff, Chodasiewicz.*

8 The 6th battalion of Riflemen.—*Ibid.*

9 Anitchkoff.

10 Light batteries Nos. 1 and 2 of the 16th Artillery brigade.—*Ibid.*

ing sixteen guns,[1] are here termed 'the Causeway batteries.' The force in this part of the field formed the centre of the line, and was under the command of Prince Gortschakoff.[2]

The right wing of the Russian army was the force destined to confront, first our Light Division, and then the Guards and the Highlanders. It was posted on the slopes of the Kourganè Hill. Here was the Great Redoubt, armed with its fourteen heavy guns;[3] and Prince Mentschikoff was so keen to defend this part of the ground, that he gathered round the work, on the slopes of the hill, a force of no less than sixteen battalions of regular infantry,[4] besides the two battalions of sailors,[5] and four batteries of field artillery.[6] The right of the forces on the Kourganè Hill rested on a slope to the east of the Lesser Redoubt,[7] and the left on the great road. Twelve of the battalions of regular infantry were disposed into battalion-columns posted at intervals and checker-wise on the flanks of the Great Redoubt. The other four battalions, drawn up in one massive column, were held as a reserve for the right wing on the higher slope of the hill. Of the four field-batteries, one armed the Lesser Redoubt, another was on the high ground

[1] Prince Gortschakoff says that these guns were eighteen in number.

[2] The Borodino corps formed part of General Kiriakoff's command; but the nature of the ground and the course which the action took prevented him from having it in his actual control, and Gortschakoff, in the absence of the General commanding in chief, was the General to whom the corps would have to look for guidance.

[3] Prince Gortschakoff puts the numbers of these guns at twelve. Chodasiewicz supposed that the redoubt was armed with the guns of the No. 2 battery of the 16th Artillery brigade; but the calibre of the gun and the howitzer now at Woolwich prove that the ordnance which armed the redoubt were not a part of the regular field artillery, but were brought from Sebastopol.

[4] The four battalions of the Kazan, or Prince Michael's corps, the four battalions of the Vladimir corps, the four battalions of the Sousdal corps, and the four battalions of the Uglitz corps.—*Anitchkoff*, *Chodasiewicz.*

[5] Chodasiewicz. Anitchkoff calls this force a half battalion only; but Chodasiewicz saw the two battalions in march with their four guns, and I accept his statement. Anitchkoff says that these men were thrown forward as skirmishers in the vineyards.

[6] The No. 2 heavy battery of the 16th Artillery brigade, the No. 3 battery of position of the 17th brigade of Artillery, and the No. 3 battery of position, half of the No. 3 light battery of the 14th Artillery brigade, and the half battery belonging to the sailors.—*Anitchkoff*, or *Chodasiewicz.* The latter supposes that some of these batteries were posted more toward the centre with the reserve battalions.

[7] It fired five guns only at the time when the Highlanders advanced; but it is believed that the three additional guns requisite to complete the battery were in the work at the beginning of the action. It was probably the No. 2 battery of the 16th Artillery brigade referred to in the former note.

commanding and supporting the Great Redoubt, and the remaining two were held in reserve.[1] General Kvetzinski commanded the troops in this part of the field. On his extreme right, and posted at intervals along a curve drawn from his right front to his centre rear, Prince Mentschikoff placed his cavalry—a force comprising 3400[2] lances, with three batteries of horse artillery.[3]

Each of these bodies of horse, when brought within sight of the Allies, was always massed in column.

Thus, then, it was to bar the Pass and the great road, to defend the Kourganè Hill and to cover his right flank, that the Russian General gathered his main strength; and this was the part of the field destined to be assailed by our troops. That portion of the Russian force which directly confronted the English army consisted of 3400 cavalry, twenty-four battalions of infantry, and seven batteries of field-artillery, besides the fourteen heavy guns in the Great Redoubt, making together 23,400 men[4] and eighty-six guns.

But besides this force, Prince Mentschikoff, at the commencement of the action, had posted across the great road leading down to the bridge a force of seven battalions of infantry,[5] with two batteries[6] of artillery. These troops he called his 'Great Reserve;' and they were, in fact, his last. Yet he held them so closely in rear of the battalions facing the bridge that they might be regarded as forces actually opera-

[1] Although I gather the numbers and descriptions of these forces from Russian authorities, I draw much of my knowledge of the way in which they were disposed from the observation of our officers; and it should be observed that the above statement applies to the state of the field at the time when the battle was going on, and not to the dispositions which Prince Mentschikoff may have made in the earlier part of the day.

[2] The Russian official authorities confess to but 3000. The force consisted of the brigade of Hussars, 6th division of cavalry, and two regiments of Cossacks of the Don.—*Chodasiewicz.*

[3] The No. 12 Light Horse battery, 6th brigade of Horse Artillery (*Chodasiewicz*), and two batteries of the Cossacks of the Don.—*Anitchkoff.*

[4]

| | |
|---|---|
| Twenty-four battalions at 750 each | 18,000 |
| Three heavy batteries at 263 each | 789 |
| Six light batteries at 210 artillerymen each | 1,260 |
| Cavalry | 3,400 |
| Men | 23,449 |
| Nine batteries at eight guns each | 72 |
| Heavy guns from Sebastopol in the Great Redoubt | 14 |
| Guns | 86 |

[5] The four battalions of the Volhynia corps, and three battalions, Nos. 1, 3, 4, of the Minsk corps.—*Anitchkoff, Chodasiewicz.*

[6] The No. 4 and No. 5 light batteries of the 17th brigade of Artillery. Chodasiewicz and Anitchkoff differ.

ting in support. Plainly, this disposition of his troops was governed by a keen anxiety to defend the great road and the Kourganè Hill, for it was so ordered that, to sustain the struggle there, it would cost him but a few moments to bring his last reserves into action; and, in truth, he committed himself so deeply to this, his favorite part of the battle-field, that, when he afterward endeavored to shift a portion of his reserves toward his left, he was unable to make their strength tell.

The numbers actually opposed to the French and the English respectively.

It will be seen, however, that in the course of the action the Prince took off to his left to use against the French three of the battalions belonging to his great reserve, and also moved in the same direction two light batteries, together with a few squadrons of Hussars, which formed, as it seems, his personal escort. So, omitting only from the calculation the change effected by moving those horsemen,[1] it would follow that the whole force which, sooner or later, confronted the French, was a force of 13,000 men[2] and thirty-six guns, and that the force which confronted the English was a force of 26,000 men,[3] with eighty-six guns.

Forces of the Allies.

The forces with which the Allied commanders prepared to assail this position were thus composed: There were some 30,000 French infantry and artillerymen,[4] with sixty-eight guns; and, added to this force, under the command of Marshal St. Arnaud, was the division of 7000 Turkish infantry.[5] With Lord Raglan, and present under arms, there was a force of fully 1000 cavalry, 25,000[6] infantry and artillery-

[1] I omit these horsemen from the calculation because I do not know their number. Anitchkoff calls the body "a portion of the Hussar brigade." The French official account says the force was one of eight squadrons. I imagine that an estimate putting it at 400 would not be far from the truth.

[2] Strictly, 12,998. This figure is attained by adding to the 10,328 before given, the three battalions taken from the Great Reserve (at 750 each), and the 420 artillerymen of the two light batteries which were moved during the action.

[3] Strictly, 26,029. This figure is attained by adding to the 23,449 before detailed the four battalions of the Great Reserve which were dealt with by English alone, and by subtracting the 420 artillerymen referred to in the preceding note.

[4] Précis Historique, p. 101-102, which gives 30,204 as the total, but that is a computation of the force embarked; and, since cholera was prevailing, the deductions from strength between the 7th and the 20th of the month must have brought the numbers below 30,000.

[5] Ib.

[6] The "morning state" which I have before me is of the 18th September, and it gives as present under arms (without including the cavalry, of which there was no "state") a total of 26,004 officers and men, and, deducting the 1600 men detached under Colonel Torrens, there remained 25,404 infantry and artillerymen.

men, and sixty pieces of field-artillery.[1] In all, the Allied armies advancing upon the Alma comprised near 63,000 men and 128 guns.

St. Arnaud, with 37,000 men and sixty-eight guns, and effectually supported by the fire of nine war-steamers,[2] was destined to confront a Russian force of 13,000 men and thirty-six guns. The English, with 26,000 men and sixty guns, had to deal with a Russian force comprising, so to speak, the same number of men, but having with it eighty-six guns.[3] Therefore the French had to do with somewhat more than one third of the Russian force; and the other two thirds of it—two thirds of it, speaking roughly—were left to the care of the English. St. Arnaud was to his adversaries in a proportion not very far short of three to one;[4] Lord Raglan was, so to speak, equal in numbers to his adversaries, and was inferior to them in point of artillery by a difference of twenty-six guns.

The tasks undertaken by the French and the English respectively.

That part of the position which was attacked by the French presented some physical obstacles to the advance of the assailants, but was not very strong in a military sense, and was defended by no field-works. The ground attacked by the English did not oppose great physical obstacles to the advance of the assailants, but it was intrenched, and, besides, was so formed by nature as to give great destructive power, and, by consequence, great strength to an enemy defending it with the resources of modern warfare. The French were covered and supported on their right by the sea and the ships; on their left by the English army.[5] The English had the French on their right, but they marched with their left flank quite bare. The French advanced upon heights well surveyed from the sea. Except in an imperfect way from maps, the English knew nothing of the ground before them. No spies or deserters had come in.

[1] The official "state" prepared for Lord Raglan gives two troops of horse artillery, and only seven batteries, but it omits the battery attached to the 4th Division.

[2] Official dispatch of Admiral Hamelin.

[3] In these calculations, as in those preceding them, the change effected by moving the horsemen of the escort is left unnoticed.

[4] Or, more strictly, 37 to 13.

[5] This sentence, perhaps, may help to elucidate the one which goes before it by showing what is meant when soldiers speak of "the strength of a position." In these days mere inert physical obstacles are commonly overcome or eluded; and the security of the defender depends not in general upon those geographical features which would make access difficult for travelers, but rather upon such a conformation of ground as will give him the means of doing harm to his assailants.

III.

Late in the evening on the 19th, Marshal St. Arnaud, attended by Colonel Trochu, rode up to the little post-house on the Bulganak in which Lord Raglan had established his quarters. He came to concert a plan of attack for the following day.

Conference the night before the battle between St. Arnaud and Lord Raglan.

From on board their ships, the French had long been busily engaged in surveying the enemy's position, and by this time they had gathered a good deal of knowledge of that part of the ground which lies near the sea-shore. They had ascertained, or found means of inferring, that the stream was fordable at its mouth, and they moreover assured themselves that at the time of their last observations the West Cliff was not occupied in strength by the enemy. Upon these important discoveries Marshal St. Arnaud based his plan of attack. He proposed that the war-steamers, closing in as nearly as was practicable, should move parallel with the land forces, and a little in advance; that under cover of their fire a portion of the French force should advance along the shore and seize the West Cliff; and that this movement should be followed up by a resolute, vigorous, and unremitting attack upon the enemy's left flank and left front.[1] M. St. Arnaud was at this time free from pain, and, knowing that now at last he had an enemy in his front, and that a great conflict was near at hand, he seemed to be fired with a more than healthy energy. Sometimes in English, sometimes in the rapid words of his own tongue, and always with vehement gesture, he labored to show how sure it was that the attack from his right centre would be fierce, unrelenting, decisive. Lord Raglan, cast in another mould, sat quiet, with governed features, restraining—or only, perhaps, postponing—his smiles, listening graciously, assenting, or not dissenting, putting forward no plan of his own, and, in short, eluding discussion. This method, perhaps, was instinctive with him; but, in his intercourse with the French, he followed it deliberately and upon system. He never forgot that to keep good our relations with the French was his great duty; and studying how best to avert the danger of misunderstandings, he had already made it his maxim that there was hardly any danger so great as the danger of controversy. Whether in any even small degree the English General had been brought to share the opinion

The French plan.

The part taken by Lord Raglan at the conference.

[1] The plan was like that of the great Frederick at Leuthen, but with the difference that the force advancing to turn the enemy's left was to be covered and supported by fire from the shipping.

entertained of M. St. Arnaud in the French capital and in the French army, the world will never know. Of a certainty, Lord Raglan dealt as though he held it to be a clear gain to be able to avoid intrusting the Marshal with a knowledge of what our army would be likely to undertake; but my belief is that this, his seemingly guarded method, was not so much based upon any thing which may have come to his ears from Paris or from the French camp, but rather upon his desire to ward off controversy, and upon his true native English dislike of all premature planning. He was so sure of his troops, and so conscious of his own power to act swiftly when the occasion might come, that, although he was now within half a march of the enemy's assembled forces, he did not at all long to ruffle his mind with projects—with projects for the attack of a position not hitherto reconnoitred.

M. St. Arnaud's plan for turning the enemy's left was to be executed by the French army, with the aid of the shipping; and the part which the English land forces should take in the action was a matter distinct. But for this, also, the French commander and his military counselors had carefully taken thought.

French plan for the operations of the English army.

To illustrate the operations which he proposed, M. St. Arnaud produced a rough map—a map slightly and rapidly drawn, yet traced with that spirit and significance which are characteristic of French military sketches. In this sketch Bosquet's Division and the Turkish troops were represented as effecting the turning movement on the enemy's left, and the 1st and 3rd French Divisions were shown to be so deployed and so placed, that in the order of attack assigned to them by the sketch, they would confront almost the whole face of the enemy's position, leaving only one or two battalions to be dealt with in front by the English troops.[1] So, to find some occupation for the English, the sketch represented our army as filing away obliquely, in order to turn the enemy's right flank. Of course this plan rested entirely upon the assumption that the enemy's front would be fully occupied (as represented in the sketch) by the French attack.

Lord Raglan's experience, or instinct, told him that no such plan as this could go for much until the assailing forces should come to measure their line with that of the enemy. So, without either combating or accepting the suggestion addressed to him, he simply assured the Marshal that he might rely upon

[1] See the fac-simile of this plan, taken from the 'Pièces Officielles' published by the French Government.

Reduced Plan of the "Projet" (untruly) stated to have been accepted by Lord Raglan.

Projet pour la Bataille de l'Alma.
Préparé le 19, au soir et exécuté le 20 Sept. 1854.

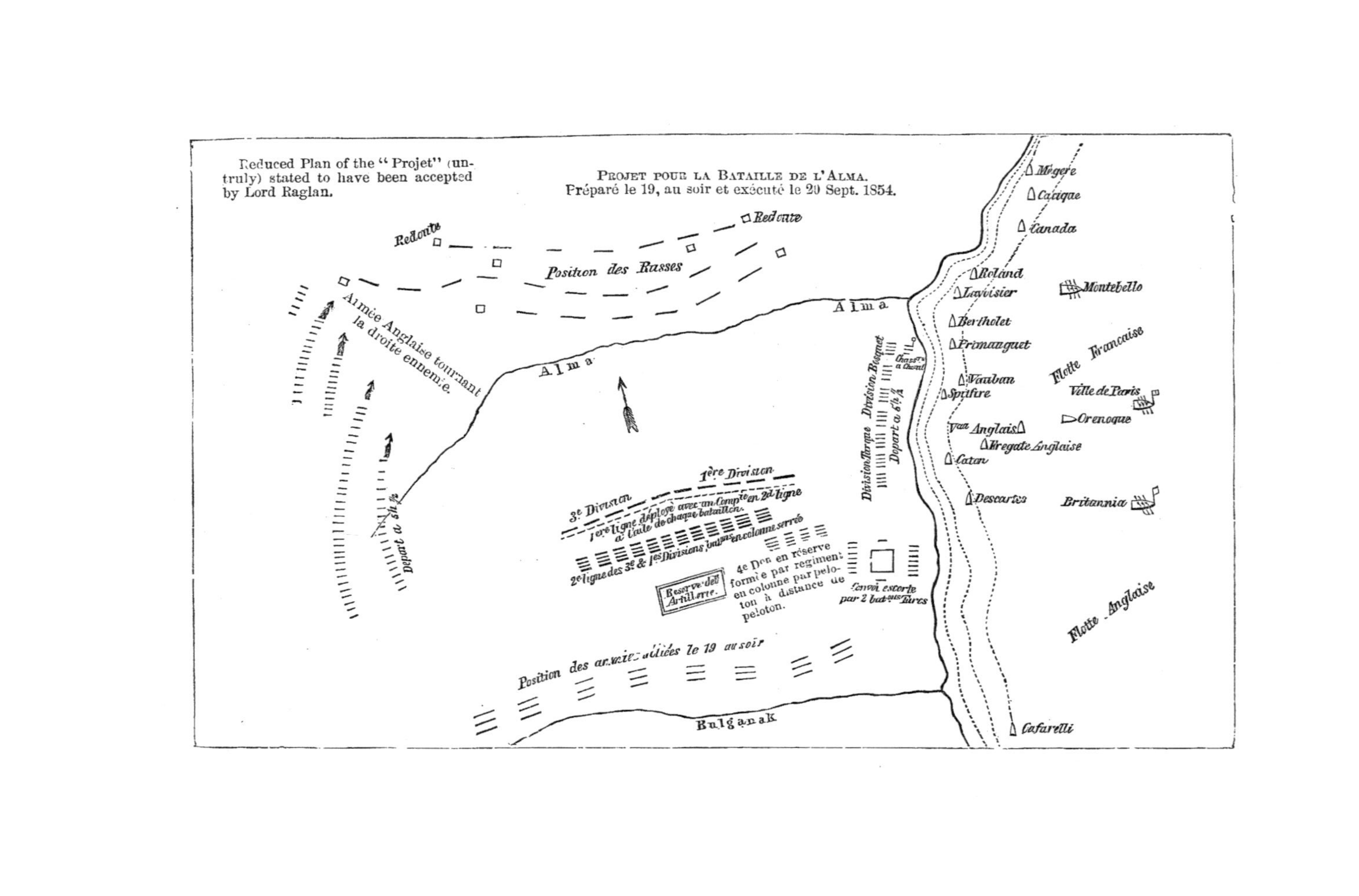

the vigorous co-operation of the British army. The French plan seems to have made little impression on Lord Raglan's mind. He foresaw, perhaps, that the ingenuity of the evening would be brought to nothingness by the teachings of the morrow.

St. Arnaud's demeanor.

Whilst the French Marshal was striving, in his vehement way, to convey an idea of the vigor with which he would conduct the attack, his appointed adviser, Colonel Trochu, whose mission it was to moderate the fire of his chief, thought it right to interpose with a question of a practical kind—a question as to the time and place for relieving the French soldiers of their packs. Instantly, if so one may speak, St. Arnaud reared, for Trochu had touched him with the curb; and in the presence, too, of Lord Raglan. He angrily suppressed the question of the packs as one of mere detail. Yet, on the afternoon of the morrow, that question of the packs was destined to recur, and to govern the movements of the whole French army.

Before the Marshal and Lord Raglan parted, it was agreed that Bosquet with his Division should advance at five o'clock in the morning, and that, two hours later, the rest of the Allied forces should begin their march upon the enemy's position.

Result of the conference.

This determination as to the time for marching was almost the only fruit which St. Arnaud drew from the interview. He had thought to engage his colleague in the plan contrived for the guidance of the English at the French head-quarters; but when he came to be in the presence of the English General, he unconsciously yielded, as other men commonly did, to the spell of his personal ascendency; and although he showed the sketch, and may have uttered, perhaps, a few hurried words to explain its meaning, he did not effectually bring himself to proffer advice to Lord Raglan. Either he altogether omitted the intended counsel, or else he so slurred it over as not to win for it any grave notice from even the most careful of listeners.

When the conference ended, Lord Raglan came out with his guests to the door of the hut. M. St. Arnaud mounted his horse, and was elate. But he was elate, not with the knowledge of having achieved a purpose, but rather, it would seem, from the sense of that singular comfort which anxious men always derived from the mere power of Lord Raglan's presence. Perhaps, when the Marshal reached his quarters, he began to see that, after all, there was a gulf between him and the English General, and that, notwithstanding his energy and boldness, he had been unaccountably hindered from passing it.

IV.

It had been determined that the troops should get under arms without bugle or drum.

Silently, therefore, on the morning of the 20th of September, 1854, the men of the Allied armies rose from their bivouac, and made ready for the march which was to bring them into the presence of the enemy. It was so early as half past five that Bosquet, with the 2nd French Division and the Turkish battalions, began his march along the coast; and at seven o'clock the main body of the French army was under arms, and ready to march. But the position taken up by the English for the defense of the Allied armies on the Bulganak had imposed upon Lord Raglan the necessity of showing a front toward the east; and for the Divisions so employed a long and toilsome evolution was needed in order to bring them into the general order of march.[1] At that time, too, there was a broad interval between our extreme right and Prince Napoleon's Division. Moreover, the line of the coast which the armies were to follow trended away toward the south west, forming an obtuse angle with the course of the stream (the Bulganak) on which the Allies had bivouacked; and in the movement requisite for adjusting the front of the Allied forces to the direction of the shore, the English marching upon the exterior arc had to undergo more labor than those who moved near the pivot on which the variation of front was effected.[2]

March of the Allies.

Causes delaying the march of the English army.

This was not all. The baggage-train accompanying our forces, though small in comparison with the incumbrances usually attending an army in the field, was large as compared with that of the French, and Lord Raglan (whose favorite anxiety was concerning his reserve ammunition) refused to allow the convoy to be stripped of protection. The oblique movement of the troops toward their right was tending to leave the convoy uncovered; and, in order that it should be again infolded as in the previous day's order of march, it was necessary to move it far toward our right. Lord Raglan insisted that this should be done; so on the morning of the long-expected battle, and with the enemy in front, St. Arnaud and the

[1] Those divisions had been posted nearly at right angles to the front line, and the segment in which the troops would have to wheel in order to get into the line of march would be nearly 90 degrees.

[2] Several military Reports and documents explain this, but the plan prepared by the French Government shows with admirable clearness the nature of the evolution which the English army had to perform. See the plan.

whole French army, and the English army too, chafed bitterly at the delay they had to endure whilst strings of bullock-carts were slowly dragged westward into the true line of march. Besides, the enemy's cavalry gave the English no leave to examine the ground toward which they were marching; and whilst the French, being next to the sea, could make straight for the cliff already reconnoitred from the ships, the English army advanced without knowledge of that part of the position which it was to confront, and was twice compelled to make laborious changes in the direction of its march. Therefore, for much of the delay which occurred there were good reasons; but not for all. Sir George Brown had been directed on the night of the 19th to advance on the morrow at seven o'clock, and he imagined—it is strange if he, of all men, with his great knowledge of such things, was wrong upon a point of military usage—he imagined that the order would be repeated in the morning, and he waited accordingly. Also the English troops moved slowly. Time was growing to be of high worth, and, from causes which justified a good deal—though not quite all—of their delay, the English at this time were behindhand.

In order that the operations of the day might be adjusted to the time which the English army required, orders were sent forward suspending for a while the advance of Bosquet's column; and at nine o'clock the main body of the French army came to a halt, and cooked their coffee. Whilst they rested, our troops, by moving obliquely toward their right, were slowly overcoming the distance which divided them from the French left, and were, at the same time, working their way through the angle which measured their divergence from the line of march.

Of those composing an armed force there are few who understand the hinderances which block its progress; and naturally the French were vexed by the delay which seemed to be caused by the slowness of the English army. They, however, conformed with great care to the tardiness of our advance, and even allowed our army to gain upon them; for, when the Allies reached the ground which sloped down toward the Alma, the heads of our leading columns were abreast of the French skirmishers.[1]

Meanwhile the Allied steamers had been seeking opportunities for bringing their guns to bear, and at 20 minutes past 10 they opened fire.[2] One or two of their missiles, though at a

[1] Lord Raglan was amongst those who observed this fact, and he stated it in a letter which is before me.

[2] Private MS. by Mr. Romaine, the Judge Advocate. I may here say gen-

very long range, reached some of those Russian battalions which stood posted in rear of the Telegraph.

At half past 11 o'clock the English right had got into direct contact with the French left, and our Light and 2nd Divisions were marching in the same alignment as the 1st and 3rd Divisions of our French Allies.

V.

The last halt of the Allies before the battle.

Twice again there were protracted halts. The last of these took place at a distance of about a mile and a half from the banks of the Alma. From the spot where the forces were halted the ground sloped gently down to the river's edge; and though some men lay prostrate under the burning sun, with little thought except of fatigue, there were others who keenly scanned the ground before them, well knowing that now at last the long-expected conflict would begin. They could make out the course of the river from the dark belt of gardens and vineyards which marked its banks, and men with good eyes could descry a slight seam running across a rising ground beyond the river, and could see, too, some dark squares or oblongs, encroaching like small patches of culture upon the broad downs. The seam was the Great Redoubt. The square-looking marks that stained the green sides of the hills were an army in order of battle.

That 20th of September, on the Alma, was like some remembered day of June in England, for the sun was unclouded, and the soft breeze of the morning had lulled to a breath at noontide, and was creeping faintly along the hills. It was then that in the Allied armies there occurred a singular pause of sound —a pause so general as to have been observed and remembered by many in remote parts of the ground, and so marked that its interruption by the mere neighing of an angry horse seized the attention of thousands; and although this strange silence was the mere result of weariness and chance, it seemed to car-

erally, to avoid repeated notes, that, whenever I speak of an event as happening at a time stated with exactness, I do so on the authority of Romaine. He was a man so gifted with long sight, as well as with power of estimating numbers, and, though a civilian, was so thoroughly apt for military business, that Lord Raglan used, at a later time, to call him 'the eye of the army.' During the action he rode an old hunter, steady enough to allow him to write without quitting his saddle; so, whenever he observed a change in the progress of the action, he took out his watch and pocket-book and made at the minute the memoranda on which I rely. I am therefore very certain that the spaces of time intervening between any two events spoken of in this precise way were exactly those which I give; but I have reason to think that the watches of men in the different camps had been differently set.

ry a meaning, for it was now that, after near forty years of peace, the great nations of Europe were once more meeting for battle.

Even after the sailing of the expedition the troops had been followed by reports that the war, after all, would be stayed; and the long, frequent halts, and the quiet of the armies on the sunny slope, seemed to harmonize with the idea of disbelief in the coming of the long-promised fight. But in the midst of this repose Sir Colin Campbell said to one of his officers, 'This 'will be a good time for the men to get loose half their car-'tridges;'[1] and when the command traveled on along the ranks of the Highlanders, it lit up the faces of the men one after another, assuring them that now at length, and after long expectance, they indeed would go into action. They began obeying the order. And with beaming joy, for they came of a warlike race. Yet not without emotion of a graver kind. They were young soldiers, new to battle.

VI.

Meeting between M. St Arnaud and Lord Raglan.

Lord Raglan now crossed the front of Prince Napoleon's Division in order to meet Marshal St. Arnaud, whose guidon was seen coming toward our lines.[2] The two commanders rode forward together, inclining toward their left. No one was with them. They rode on till they came to one of those mounds or tumuli, of which there were many on the steppe. From that spot they scrutinized the enemy's position with their field-glasses.

At this interview no change was made in that portion of the plan which determined that the French should turn the enemy's left; but the part to be taken by the English was still in question, and St. Arnaud threw out or revived the idea of a flank movement by the English on the enemy's right.[3] Lord Raglan, however, now gazed upon the real ground which the French counselors of the night before had striven to scan in their imaginations, and, having an eye for country, he must have begun to see the truth. He must have begun to see that the French, hugging the sea-shore, and pouring two fifths of their whole force against the undefended part of the opposite heights, would not only fail to confront the whole Russian

[1] The cartridges are delivered to each man in a packet, and, to avoid loss of time in presence of the enemy, a sufficient number should be 'shaken 'loose' before the troops are brought into action.

[2] They had met before at about half past nine, but the Russian cavalry had not then quitted the heights, and they were obliged to postpone their reconnaissance.

[3] Inferred from what follows.

army in the way promised by the sketch, but would, in reality, confront only a small portion of it, leaving to the English the duty of facing the enemy along two thirds of their whole front. Of a certainty he did not entertain for a moment the idea of making a flank attack, but it was not according to his nature to explain to men their errors, and it seems he spoke so little that St. Arnaud did not yet know what the English General would do;[1] but presently a general officer rode up and joined the two chiefs. Then the Marshal, closing his telescope, turned to Lord Raglan and asked him 'whether he would turn the 'position or attack it in front?' Lord Raglan's answer was to the effect 'that, with such a body of cavalry as the enemy 'had in the plain, he would not attempt to turn the position.'[2]

Whilst the chiefs were still side by side, it being now one o'clock, the advance sounded along the lines, and the French and the English armies moved forward close abreast. The Marshal then rode off toward his centre.

VII.

Bosquet's advance.

He divides his force.

The orders for the advance were sent forward to Bosquet, and, as soon as they reached him, he threw out skirmishers and moved forward in two columns. His right column was the brigade commanded by General Bouat. The left column was Autemarre's brigade. Each brigade, massed in column,[3] was followed by its share of the artillery belonging to the Division; and Bouat's brigade was followed by the whole of the Turkish Division except two battalions. Toward Bosquet's left, but far in his rear, there moved forward the 1st Division under Canrobert, and the 3rd Division under Prince Napoleon. These two divisions advanced in the same alignment. The 4th Division, under General Forey, marched in rear of the 1st and 3rd Divisions, and two Turkish battalions escorted the baggage.[4]

Disposition of the main body of the French army.

The formation of Canrobert's and Prince Napoleon's Divisions was upon two lines. The first brigade of each division was in front and deployed,[5] and the second brigade of each division followed the first brigade, and was massed in column.[6]

[1] Inferred from what follows.

[2] This disposes of the notion which seems to have been really entertained by many of the French—the notion that Lord Raglan stood engaged to turn the enemy's right.

[3] Regiments in column at section distance.

[4] Précis Historique mainly.

[5] Not deployed into 'line,' according to the English plan, but merely brought into a formation, which, leaving each battalion massed, places them all in the same alignment.

[6] Regiments in column at section distance.

The 4th French Division marched in the same order as the 1st and 3rd Divisions, except that its leading brigade was not deployed. The artillery of each division was infolded between its two brigades.

Of the English army.

On the immediate left of Prince Napoleon Sir De Lacy Evans marched, with the troops of his Division massed in battalion columns,[1] and was followed by the 3rd Division in column. The batteries belonging to each of these divisions marched on its right or inner flank.

Immediately on Sir De Lacy's left the Light Division, preceded by Norcott with a wing of the 2nd Rifle battalion in skirmishing order, moved forward, under Sir George Brown. The Division was massed in column,[2] and had the front and left flanks covered by riflemen in extended order. It was supported by the 1st Division, under the Duke of Cambridge, and that, in turn, was followed by the 4th Division,[3] under Sir George Cathcart. Sir George Cathcart, however, in accordance with a suggestion made by himself, was authorized to take ground to his left, and place his force in échelon to the 1st Division.[4]

The three great infantry columns thus composing the left wing of our army were covered in front, left flank, and rear by riflemen, in extended order, and by the cavalry. The battery belonging to each division marched on its right or inner flank.

But soon Major Norcott with his riflemen got on so far in advance as to provoke a fire from the Russian skirmishers, then swarming in the vineyards below, and some rifle balls shot from that quarter came dropping into the ground near the column formed by the Light Division. Almost at the same moment the artillerymen on the Russian heights began to try their range; and, although the air was so clear that our men could see and watch the flight of the cannon balls, thrown at so long a range, it seemed prudent for our leading divisions to go into line. Those divisions, therefore, were halted, and their deployment immediately began.

[1] In continuous battalion columns right in front at battalion distance. Sir De Lacy's touched Prince Napoleon's Division, and it was thought right to assimilate its order of march to that adopted by the Prince.

[2] In double column of companies from the centre.

[3] Minus the 63rd and two companies of the 46th, left, under the command of General Torrens, at the place of disembarkation. The force actually with Sir George during the action consisted of the 20th, 21st, and 68th Regiments, the 1st battalion of Rifles, and Townsend's battery.

[4] Sir George Cathcart marched with the head of his column (at quarter distance right in front) in line with the rear companies of the 1st Division.

The leading Divisions of the English army deploy into line.

In deploying, Sir De Lacy Evans, being pressed upon by Prince Napoleon's Division on his right, was compelled to take ground to his left, and to encroach upon a part of the space which Sir George Brown had expected to occupy with his Division.

The Light Division not on its right ground.

The deployment of the Light Division was effected by each regiment with beautiful precision;[1] but, unhappily, the division was not on its right ground.

Sir George Brown was near-sighted, and had not accustomed himself to repair the defect, as some commanders have done, by a constant and well-practiced use of glasses; and, on the other hand, the very fire and energy of his nature, and his almost violent sense of duty, prevented him from getting into the habit of trusting to the eyes of other men. For hours in the early morning the division had been wearied by having to incline toward its right. At half past eleven the effort was reversed, and the division then labored to take ground to its left. But, in that last direction, it had not taken ground enough. Lord Raglan, with his quick eye, had seen the fault, and sent an order[2] to have it corrected. Not content with this, he soon after rode up to the Division, and, failing to see Sir George Brown at the moment, told Codrington that the Division must take more ground to the left. Then, unhappily, when he had uttered the very words which would have thrown the British army into its true array, and averted much evil, Lord Raglan was checked by his ruling foible. He had already sent the order to the divisional general, and he could not bear to pain or embarrass him by pressing the execution of it upon one of his brigadiers. So he recalled his wholesome words;[3] the Division failed to take ground enough to the left; and, when the deployment was complete, Sir George Brown had the grief of seeing his right regiment (the 7th Fusileers) overlapped by the left—nay, even by the centre—of Pennefather's brigade.[4] The fault was not retrieved. It was fruitful of confusion.

The artillery attached to our two leading divisions was now also drawn up in line; and Sir George Brown reckoned that he alone showed a front extending to nearly a mile.

[1] The deployment was upon the two centre companies of the division. Whilst the movement was proceeding, one man, a sergeant, was killed by a rifle ball. This was probably the first death in our lines.

[2] Colonel Lysons, I think, carried it.

[3] I derive my knowledge from an officer who heard Lord Raglan's words.

[4] When the deployment took place, the 7th Fusileers was in rear of the 95th Regiment, and it afterward, as will be seen, marched through it.

At the same time the Duke of Cambridge, at Sir George Brown's request, altered the formation of his Division by distributing it into a line of columns.[1]

These changes having been completed, the English army resumed its march; and, the leading divisions coming more closely within range, and being a little galled by the enemy's fire, Sir George Brown halted, and tried the experiment of wheeling into open column. Afterward, however, he returned to his line formation, and in that order marched forward.[2]

The march continued.

VIII.

So now the whole Allied armies, hiding nothing of their splendor and their strength, descended slowly into the valley; and the ground on the right bank of the river is so even and so gentle in its slope, and, on the left bank, so commanding, that every man of the invaders could be seen from the opposite heights.

The Russian officers had been accustomed all their days to military inspections and vast reviews; but they now saw before them that very thing for the confronting of which their lives had been one long rehearsal. They saw a European army coming down in order of battle—an army arrayed in no spirit of mimicry, and not at all meant to aid their endless study of tactics, but honestly marching against them, with a mind to carry their heights and take their lives; and, gazing with keen and critical eyes upon this array of strangers, whose homes were in lands far away, they looked upon a phenomenon which raised their curiosity and their wonder, and which promised, too, to throw some new light on a notion they had lately been forming.

Spectacle presented to the Russians by the advance of the Allies.

The whole anxiety of Prince Mentschikoff had been for his right. If he could hold the Main Pass, and scare the Allies from all endeavor to turn his right flank, he believed himself safe; and it had been clear long ago that his conflict in this part of the field would be with the English. It was therefore the more useful to try to spread amongst the Russian troops an idea that the English, all powerful at sea, were thoroughly worthless as soldiers.

The working of this little cheat had been hitherto aided by

[1] 'A line of contiguous quarter-distance columns.'

[2] My knowledge respecting the movements and evolutions of our infantry divisions is derived mainly from original MSS. in my possession, written by Sir George Brown, the Duke of Cambridge, Sir De Lacy Evans, and Sir George Cathcart.

Notion which the Russian soldiers had been taught to entertain of the English army.

circumstance. With the force under Mentschikoff there were two battalions of Russian seamen; and these men, partly from their clumsiness in manœuvring, partly from their sailor-like whims, and partly, no doubt, from the mere fact of their being a small and peculiar minority, had become a subject of merriment to the soldiery of the regular land forces. The Russian soldiery, therefore, were prepared to receive the impression that the red-coats now discernible in the distance were battalions of sailors, men of no more use in a land engagement than their own derided seamen. This idea had fastened so well upon the mind of the Russian army that, before the battle began, it was shared by some of the more illiterate of the officers, and even, it was said, in one instance, by a general of division.

Surprise at the sight of the English array.

But the sight now watched with keen eyes from the enemy's heights was one which seemed to have some bearing upon the rumor that the English were powerless in a land engagement. The French and the Turks were in the deep, crowded masses which every soldier of the Czar had been accustomed to look upon as the formations needed for battle, but, to the astonishment of the Russian officers, the leading divisions of the men in red were massed in no sort of column, and were clearly seen coming on in a slender line—a line only two deep, yet extending far from east to west. They could not believe that with so fine a thread as that the English General was really intending to confront their massive columns.[1] Yet the English troops had no idea that their formation was so singular as to be strange in the eyes of military Europe. Wars long passed had taught them that they were gifted with the power of fighting in this order, and it was as a matter of course that, upon coming within range, they had gone at once into line.

Fire from the shipping.

Meanwhile the war-steamers—eight French and one English—had pushed forward along the shore in single file, moving somewhat in advance of the land forces; and now, at twenty-five minutes past one o'clock, the leading vessels opened fire against the four guns at the village of Ulukul Akles, and again tried the skill of their gunners upon the distant masses of infantry which occupied the Telegraph Height and the low flat ledge at its base. Convinced that his chief had been guilty of a grievous error in placing the Taroutine and the militia battalions on this low, narrow ledge, General Kiriakoff, who commanded in

Movement made without orders by the Taroutine and

[1] Chodasiewicz.

the 'Militia' battalions.

this part of the field, had tried by indirect means to procure a change of plan, but had not ventured to say any thing on the subject to Prince Mentschikoff himself. It is plain, however, that Kiriakoff's opinion getting abroad was adopted by the officers of these two corps; for first the militia battalions, and then the battalions of the Taroutine corps, without orders, and without having been assailed or touched (except perhaps by a chance shot or two at very long range from the shipping), began a retrograde movement, and slowly ascended the steep hill till they gained a more commanding position at no great distance from the Telegraph. No effort was made to check this seemingly spontaneous movement.[1]

IX.

Half past one o'clock. Cannonade directed against the English line.

At half past one o'clock a round shot from the opposite heights came ripping the ground near Lord Raglan, and it marked the opening of the battle between the contending land forces, for in the next instant the enemy began to direct a steady cannonade against the English line. At first no one fell, but presently an artilleryman riding in front of his gun bent forward his head, handled the reins with a convulsive grasp, and then, uttering a loud, inarticulate sound, fell dead. The peace of Europe had been so long, that to many men the sight was a new one; and of the young soldiers who stood near, some imagined that their comrade had fallen down in a sudden fit; for they hardly yet knew that for the most part in modern warfare death comes as though sent by blind chance, no one knows from whence or from whom.

Men of our leading divisions ordered to lie down. The First Division deployed into line.

Since the enemy's artillery fire had now become brisk, our leading infantry divisions were halted, and the men ordered to lie down. Soon afterward it was found that the 1st Division had also come within range, and it was then forthwith thrown into line. In preparing for this manœuvre, the Duke of Cambridge took care that ground should not be wanting. Both on his right and on his left he took more ground than had been occupied by the division which marched in his front. Whilst the Light Division in his front was jammed in and entangled with the 2nd Division, the Duke had the happiness of seeing his Guards and Highlanders well extended, and compe-

[1] General Kiriakoff's statement, confirmed by Romaine, who observed and noted the movement. The General thought the change of position requisite, but he admits that a retrograde movement of this kind just before the commencement of the battle, was a grave evil.

tent to act along the whole length of that superb line. The effect of this deployment was, that the extreme right of the Duke's line became a force operating in support to the 2nd Division, and that a part of his Highland Brigade, reaching much farther eastward than the extreme left of the Light Division, became in that part of the field the true front of the British line. When this manœuvre was completed, the men of the 1st Division lay down.

Sir Richard England ordered to support the Guards.

Observing the extent of ground occupied by the 1st Division, Lord Raglan at once saw that the 3rd Division would not have room to manœuvre in the same alignment with the Duke of Cambridge. He therefore ordered Sir Richard England to support the Guards. It was this or some other order sent nearly at the same time which, for some reason, good or fanciful, Lord Raglan chose to have carried quietly. The directions had been given, and the aid-de-camp was whirling round his charger in order to take a swift flight with the message, when Lord Raglan stopped him and said, 'Go quietly; don't gallop.' He seemed to like that whenever the enemy pointed a field-glass toward the English head-quarters, he should look upon a scene of tranquillity and leisure.

Our batteries tried their range, but without effect, and they ceased to fire, reserving their strength for the time when they would come to close quarters.

The batteries on the Telegraph Height did not yet open fire upon the French columns.

Lord Raglan conceived that the operation determined upon by the French ought to take full effect before he engaged the English army in an assault upon the enemy's heights; and perhaps, if the whole body of the Allies had been one people, under the command of one general, their advance would have been effected in échelon, and the left would have been kept out of fire whilst the effort on the right was in progress; but the pride of nations must sometimes be suffered to deflect the course of armies; and although there was no military value in any of the ground north of the vineyards, Lord Raglan, it seems, did not like to withhold his infantry whilst the French were executing their forward movement. Since our soldiers lay facing downwards upon the smooth slope which looked against the enemy's batteries, they were seen, every man of them, from head to foot by the Russian artillerymen, and they drew upon themselves a studious fire from thirty guns.

Thus the first trial our men underwent in the action was a trial of passive, enduring courage. They had to lie down, with

Fire undergone by our men whilst lying down.

no duty to perform, except the duty of being motionless, and they made it their pastime to watch the play of the engines worked for their destruction—to watch the jet of smoke—the flash—the short, momentous interval—and then, happily and most often, the twang through the air above and the welcome sound of the shot at length imbedded in earth. But sometimes, without knowing whence it came, a man would suddenly know the feel of a rushing blast and a mighty shock, and would find himself bespattered with the brains of the comrade who had just been speaking to him. When this happened, two of the comrades of the man killed would get up and gently lift the quivering body, carry it a few paces in rear of the line, then quietly return to their ranks, and again lie down.[1] This sort of trial is well borne by our troops. They are so framed by nature that, if only they know clearly what they have to do, or to leave undone, they are pleased and animated, nay, even soothed by a little danger. For, besides that they love strife, they love the arbitrament of chance, and a game where death is the forfeit has a strange, gloomy charm for them. Among the guns ranged on the opposite heights to take his life, a man would single out his favorite, and make it feminine for the sake of endearment. There was hardly, perhaps, a gun in the Great Redoubt which failed to be called by some corrupt variation of 'Mary' or 'Elizabeth.' It was plain that our infantry could be in a kindly humor whilst lying down under fire. They did not, perhaps, like the duty so well as an animating charge with the bayonet; but if they were to be judged from their demeanor, they preferred it to a church parade. They were in their most gracious temper. Often, when an officer rode past them, they would give him the fruit of their steady and protracted view, and advise him to move a little on one side or the other to avoid a coming shot. And this the men would do, though they themselves, however well their quickened sight might warn them of the coming shot, lay riveted to the earth by duty.

X.

The level posture of our infantry threw into strong prominence the figure of every mounted man who rode along their lines, but the group of horsemen composing or following the head-quarter staff was so marked by the white flowing plumes of the officers, that at a distance of a mile and a half it was a conspicuous object to the naked eye; and a Russian artillery-

[1] Casualties of this sort were going on here and there along our line, but the exact incident described in the text was observed in the 30th Regiment.

man at the Causeway batteries could make out with a common field-glass that, of the two or three officers generally riding abreast at the head of the plumed cavalcade, there was one, in a dark blue frock, whose right arm hung ending in an empty sleeve. In truth, Lord Raglan at this time was so often standing still, or else was riding along the line of our prostrate infantry at so leisurely a pace, that he and the group about him could not fail to become a mark for the Russian artillery. The enemy did not, as it seemed, begin this effort malignantly, and at first, perhaps, he had no farther thought than that of subjecting the English head-quarters to an ordinary cannonade, and forcing them to choose a more retired ground for their surveys.

Cannonade directed against Lord Raglan and his staff.

Still, as might be expected, the Russian artillerymen could not easily brook the conclusion that, whilst the English General chose to remain under their eyes, and within range, it was beyond the power of their skill to bend him from his path, or even, as it seemed, to break the thread of his conversation; so at length, growing earnest, they opened fire upon the group from a great number of guns; but in vain, for none of the staff at this time were struck. Failing with round shot, the enemy tried shells—shells with the fuses so cut as to burst them in the air a little above the white plumes. This method was tried so industriously and with so much skill, that a few feet over the heads of Lord Raglan and those around him there was kept up for a long time an almost constant bursting of shells. Sometimes the missiles came singly, and sometimes in so thick a flight that several would be exploding nearly at the same moment, or briskly one after the other, right and left, and all around. The fragments of the shells, when they burst, tore their shrill way down from above, harshly sawing the air; and when the novice heard the rush of the shattered missile along his right ear, and then along his left, and imagined that he felt the wind of another fragment of shell come rasping the cloth on his shoulders almost at the same moment, it seemed to him hardly possible that the iron shower would leave one man of the group untouched. But the truth is that a fragment of shell rending the air with its jagged edges may sound much nearer than it is. None of the staff were wounded at this time.

Some of the suite were half vexed and half angry, for they knew the value of their chief's life, and they conceived that he was affronting great risk without due motive, and from mere inattention to danger. The storm of missiles generally fell most thickly when Lord Raglan happened to be riding near the great road; for the enemy, having got the range of that point, always labored to make the bursting of his shells coincide with the moment when our head-quarters were passing. This soon came to be understood, and thenceforth, when the head-quarter group were going to cross the Causeway, they rode at it briskly as at a leap, and spanned it with one or two strides, thus leaving the prepared storm of shells to burst a little behind them. This effort of the Russian artillery against Lord Raglan and the group surrounding him lasted a long time, and was carried on upon a scale better proportioned to the destruction of a whole division than to the mere object of warning off a score of horsemen. If the fire thus expended had been brought to bear on Pennefather's brigade, it might have maimed the English line in a vital part of the field.

XI.

The Allies could now measure their front with that of the enemy.

The time was now come when the Allies could measure their front with the enemy's position. It will be remembered that the plan[1] proposed to Lord Raglan the night before by Marshal St. Arnaud rested upon the assumption that the whole of the enemy's forces except two or three battalions would be confronted by the French army, and that therefore the only opportunity for important service which the English army could find would be that of making a great flank movement against the enemy's right; but it had long become plain that only a portion of the Russian army would be met by the French, and that in providing a front to show against the main body of the Russian army there remained to the English an ample field of duty; and, now that the invading armies had come within cannon-shot range, it began to be seen that the entire front presented by the 1st and 3rd French Divisions, and by our 2nd and Light Divisions, would be only just commensurate with the length of the position which the Russian commander was occupying.

The bearing which this admeasurement had upon the plan which the French had proposed to the English.

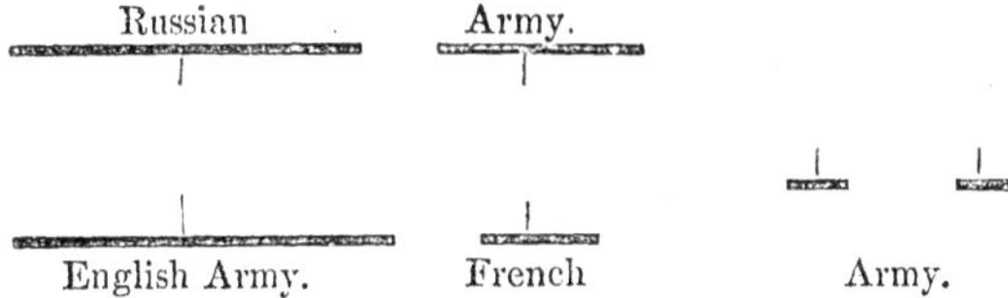


[1] See the *fac-simile*.

Of course, therefore, if Lord Raglan had not already rejected the French plan of a flank attack by our forces, it would have now fallen to the ground. It had never made any impression on his mind.[1]

The Allies were now so close to the enemy's position that the general of each of the five leading divisions could form a judgment as to the particular sphere of action which awaited him. To Bosquet the advance against the West Cliff had long ago been assigned. Canrobert faced toward the White Homestead and those spurs of the Telegraph Height which lie toward the west. Prince Napoleon confronted the centre and the eastern steeps of the Telegraph Height. Sir De Lacy Evans, with the 2nd Division, faced the village of Bourliouk; and it seemed at this time that his left would not reach farther up the river's bank than the bridge, for Sir George Brown had been reckoning that his first or right brigade would be charged with the duty of attacking the enemy's position across the great road, and that it would be his left, or Buller's brigade, which would assail the Great Redoubt.

The ground which each of the leading divisions had to assail.

The generals of the five leading divisions were thus directing their forces, and already the swarms of skirmishers thrown forward by the French, and the thinner chains of riflemen in advance of our divisions, were drawing close to the vineyards, and beginning their combats with the enemy's sharpshooters; but then, and with a suddenness so strange as to suggest the idea of some pyrotechnic contrivance, the whole village of Bourliouk, except the straggling houses which skirted it toward the east, became wrapped in tall flames.[2] No man could live in that conflagration; and

The village of Bourliouk set on fire by the enemy.

[1] I infer this from the fact that those with whom Lord Raglan was thoroughly confidential in such matters never heard him speak of it. Lord Raglan, as we saw, distinctly and finally rejected the plan at the close of his interview with St. Arnaud. It became a plan simply preposterous as soon as it was apparent that St. Arnaud would not confront any part of the Russian army except their left wing; for to make two flank movements, one against the enemy's left, and the other against his right, and to do this without having any force wherewith to confront the enemy's centre, would have been a plan requiring no comment to show its absurdity. The French accounts, whether official or quasi-official, have always persisted in saying that Lord Raglan had engaged, and afterward failed to make, a movement on the enemy's right flank. This is the only reason why the matter requires any thing like careful elucidation.

[2] The great number of haystacks, and the peculiar nature of the hay, were the causes which made the conflagration so instantaneously complete. The hay of that country is full of stiff, prickly stems, which resist compression, and so make ample room for air.

the result was that in one minute a third of the ground on which the English army had meant to operate was, as it were, blotted out of the field. If this firing of the village took place under the orders of the Russian commander, it was the most sagacious of all the steps he took that day, for his gravest source of care was the want of troops sufficing for the whole extent of the position at which he grasped, and therefore an operation which took away a large part of the battle-field was of great advantage to him. Our infantry were immediately thrown into trouble. The Light Division, as we saw, did not take ground enough on the left, and the firing of the village now cut short our front on the right. Sir De Lacy Evans, thus robbed of space, was obliged to keep his second brigade in rear of the first, and even then he continued to overlap the right of the Light Division.

The effect which this measure had in cramping the English line.

The smoke from the burning village was depressed, and gently turned toward the bridge by the faint breeze which came from the sea. There, for hours, in a long fallen pillar of cloud, it lay singularly firm and compact, obscuring the view of those who were near it, but not at all staining the air in any other part of the field.

XII.

The operations of the great column intrusted to General Bosquet now began to take effect. Bosquet was a man in the prime of life. Ten years of struggle and frequent enterprise in Algeria had carried him from the rank of a lieutenant to the rank of a general officer;[1] and he was charged on this day not only with the command of his own—the 2nd—Division, but with the command of the troops which formed the Turkish Contingent. The whole column under his orders numbered about 14,000 men. The Arabs and Kabyles of Algeria, though men of a fierce and brave nature and prone to petty strife, are so wanting in the power of making war with effect, that, as far as concerns the art of fighting, they can scarcely be said to have given much schooling to the bold and skillful soldiery of France; but the deserts, the broad solitudes, and the great mountain range of Northern Africa, have inured the French army to some of those military toils which are next in worth to the business of the actual combat; and for Bosquet, the hero of many a struggle in the passes of the Middle and the Lesser Atlas, it was no new problem to have to cross

General Bosquet.

[1] A brigadier; and now, at the time of the Crimean war, he was a general of division.

a stream and carry a body of troops to the summit of a hill with a steep-looking face.

In the morning he had ridden forward, escorted by a few Spahis, to reconnoitre the ground with his own eyes, and thus, and by the aid of the careful surveys effected by the naval men, he was able to assure himself, not only that the river could be passed at its bar, but that troops there crossing it would be likely to find the means of getting round and ascending to the summit of the cliff from the southwest. Examining also the face of the cliff farther inland, he saw that the broken ground opposite to the village of Almatamack could be easily ascended by foot soldiers; and he also, no doubt, perceived that the road leading up from the village (unless it should prove to have been effectually cut or guarded by the enemy), would give him a passage for his artillery. Upon these observations Bosquet based his plan. He resolved to march in person with Autemarre's brigade upon the village of Almatamack, there to cross the river, and afterward endeavor to ascend the plateau at the point where the road from Almatamack goes up between the West Cliff and the Telegraph Height; but he ordered General Bouat, with his brigade, and with the Turkish Contingent, to incline far away toward his right, to try to pass the river at its bar, and then to find the best means he could for getting his troops up the cliff.

His plan of operations.

The two bodies of troops under Bosquet's command began their diverging movement at the same time; and before two o'clock the swarms of skirmishers which covered the front of the columns were pushing their way through the village of Almatamack, and the vineyards on either side of it. A few moments more, and they were firing with a briskness and vivacity which warmed the blood of the many thousands of hearers then new to war. One of our officers, kindling a little with the excitement thus roused, and impatient, perhaps, that the French should be in action before our people, could not help drawing Lord Raglan's attention to the firing on our right. But the stir of French skirmishers through thick ground was no new music to Lord Fitzroy Somerset. Rather, perhaps, it recalled him for a moment to old times in Estremadura and Castile, when, at the side of the great Wellesley, he learned the brisk ways of Napoleon's infantry. So, when the young officer said, 'The French, my 'Lord, are warmly engaged,' Lord Raglan answered, 'Are 'they? I can not catch any return fire.' His practiced ear had told him what we now know to be the truth. No troops were opposed to the advance of Bosquet's columns in this part

Advance of Autemarre under Bosquet in person.

of the field; but it is the custom of French skirmishers, when they get into thick ground near an enemy, to be continually firing. They do this, partly to show the chiefs behind them what progress they are making, and partly, it would seem, in order to give life and spirit to the scene.

Advance of the detached force under Bouat.

When General Bouat reached the bank of the river, he found that the bar of sand at its mouth made it possible for his men to keep good their footing against the waves flowing in from the sea; and in process of time, with all his infantry, including the Turkish battalions, he succeeded in gaining the left bank of the river. He could not, however, carry across his artillery, and he therefore sent it back, with orders to follow the march of Autemarre's brigade.

When he reached the left bank of the river, Bouat found an opening in the cliff before him which promised to give him means of ascent. Into this opening he threw some skirmishers, and these, encountering no enemy, were followed by the main body of the brigade, and by the Turkish battalions. Pursuing the course thus opened to him, Bouat slowly crept forward with his column, and wound his way up and round toward the summit of the cliff. But it was only by marching with a very narrow front that he was able to effect this movement, and it was not until a late period of the action that he was able to show himself in force upon the plateau. Even then he was without artillery. The troops under his command had not an opportunity of engaging in any combat with the enemy, because they marched upon that part of the heights which the Russian General had determined to leave unoccupied.

Farther advance of Autemarre's brigade.

Meanwhile Bosquet, marching in person with Autemarre's brigade, traversed the village of Almatamack, forded the river at ten minutes past two o'clock, and immediately began to ascend the road leading up to the plateau. The road, he found, was uninjured, and guarded by no troops. His artillery began the ascent, and meanwhile the keen and active Zouaves, impatient of the winding road, climbed the heights by shorter and steeper paths, and so swiftly, that our sailors, looking from the ships (men accustomed to perpendicular racing), were loud in their praise of the briskness with which the Frenchmen rushed up and 'manned' the cliff. As yet, however, Bosquet had encountered no enemy.

Guns brought out against him from Ulukul Akles.

It has been seen that the position taken up by Prince Mentschikoff fell short of the sea-shore by a distance of more than two miles, and that he was not in military occupation of the cliff, now ascended by Bosquet with Autemarre's brigade; but also, it will be remembered, that at the village, in rear of the cliff, called Ulukul Akles, there had been posted some days before one of the Minsk battalions of infantry, with four pieces of light artillery, and that the detachment had there remained. These four guns were now brought out of the village, and, after a time, were placed in battery at a spot near the village of Ulukul Tiouets, and within range of the point where the Zouaves were beginning to crown the summit of the cliff. The 'Minsk' battalion was not brought into sight, but at some distance, on the cliff overlooking the beach, there could be seen some squadrons of horse.

Bosquet, after a momentary check, establishes himself on the cliff.

As soon as a whole battalion of Zouaves had gained the summit, they were drawn up and formed on the plateau. No shot was as yet fired by the enemy; and General Bosquet, with his staff, ascended a tumulus, or mound, on the top of the cliff, in order to reconnoitre the ground.

Meanwhile, his artillery was coming up, and the first two of his guns had just reached the summit, when one of the carriages broke down. This accident embarrassed the rest of the column, and whilst the hinderance lasted the enemy opened fire from his four guns.[1] The fire and the breaking down of the gun-carriage produced for the moment an ill effect upon the head of the French column, and one of its battalions fell back under the shelter of the acclivity. But this check did not last. The road blocked by the broken-down gun-carriage was quickly cleared, the guns were moved up rapidly, and swarms of skirmishers pressed up in all directions. Then the troops which were already on the summit moved forward, and lodged themselves upon a part of the plateau a little in advance of the steep by which they had ascended.[2]

Measures taken by Kiriakoff upon observing Bosquet's turning movement.

As soon as he began to hear guns in the direction of the West Cliff, Kiriakoff took from his reserves two of his 'Moscow' battalions, and posted them, the one low down, and the other higher up, on that part of the hill which looked down upon the White Homestead. He also drew from his reserve eight light pieces of artillery, and placed them in battery facing toward the sea, so as to command, though at a long range, the part of the plateau which Bosquet crossed by the Hadji road. Kiriakoff did not

[1] Half of the No. 4 battery of the 17th brigade of the Russian artillery.

[2] Sir Edward Colebrooke saw this operation from the deck of one of our ships of war, and describes it very well in his memorial. He was a skillful and very accurate observer of military movements.

take upon himself to make any other dispositions for dealing with the turning movement which threatened his left.

Horsemen on the cliff.

Amongst the French who were gaining the summit of the plateau, no one seems to have divined the reason why a little body of Russian horsemen should have made its appearance on the cliff overlooking the sea, nor why, without attempting hostile action, it had tenaciously clung to the ground. Those troopers were the attendants of a man in great trouble. They were the escort of Prince Mentschikoff.

XIII.

The effect of Bosquet's turning movement upon the mind of Prince Mentschikoff.

The enemy's survey of the Allied armies had been so carelessly made, and had been so little directed toward the sea-shore, that Bosquet, it seems, had already got near to the river before his movement was perceived. Prince Mentschikoff, with Gortschakoff and Kvetzinski at his side, had been standing on the Kourganè Hill, watching the advance of the English army, and giving bold orders for its reception; but presently he was told that a French division was advancing toward the unoccupied cliff on his extreme left. At first he was so shocked by the dislocation which his ideas would have to undergo if his left flank were indeed to be turned, that he had no refuge for his confusion except in mere disbelief, and he angrily refused to give faith to the unwelcome tidings.[1] For days he had been on the ground which he himself had chosen for the great struggle; but he was so certain that he had effectually learned its character by glancing at its general features, that he had not, it seems, had the industry to ride over it, nor even to find out the roads by which the villagers were accustomed to ascend the heights with their wagons.

He seemed to have imagined it to be impossible that ground so steep as the cliff had appeared to be could be ascended by troops at any point westward of the Telegraph Height; but when at length he was compelled to know that the French and the Turks were marching in force toward the mouth of the river, his mind underwent so great a revulsion, that, having hitherto taken no thought for his left, he now seemed to have no care for any other part of the position. In his place, a General, calm, skillful, and conscious of knowing the ground, might have seen the turning movement of the French and the Turks with unspeakable joy; but, instead of tranquilly regarding the whole field of battle under the new aspect which was given to

[1] Chodasiewicz.

it by this manœuvre, he only labored to see how best he could imitate the mistake of his adversary—how best he could shift his strength to the distant, unoccupied cliff which was threatened by Bosquet's advance. The nature of the ground enabled him to make lateral movements in his line without much fear of disturbance from the Allies; and, as soon as he saw that the French were detaching two fifths of their army in order to turn his flank, he wildly determined to engage a portion of his scanty force in a march from his right hand to his left—in a march which would take him far to the westward of his chosen ground. For this purpose he snatched two light batteries from his centre and his right, gave orders that he was to be followed by the four 'Moscow' battalions which were the reserve of his left wing, and by the three 'Minsk' battalions which formed part of his 'Great Reserves,' and then, with some squadrons of hussars, rode off toward the sea.

His measures for dealing with it. His flank march.

It was certain that a long time would elapse before the troops engaged in this vain journey could be expected to get into action with Bosquet; and meanwhile the power of the whole force engaged in the flank movement was neutralized. But that was not all. Prince Mentschikoff's mind was so strangely subverted by the sensation of having his left turned, that, although it must needs be a long time before he could be in force on the West Cliff, he could not endure to be personally absent from the ground to which he now fastened his thoughts. So when, with his Staff and the horsemen of his escort, he had got to the ground overlooking the sea, near the village of Ulukul Tiouets, and had seen the first groups of the Zouaves peering up on the crest of the hill, he still remained where he was. Whilst he sat in his saddle, the appearance of his escort drew fire from the shipping, and four of his suite were struck down. But the Prince would not move. It is likely that the fire assuaged the pain of his thoughts.

Mentschikoff on the cliff.

At this time, it would seem, he gave either no orders, or none of a kind supplying real guidance for his generals. Lingering upon the ground, without troops at hand, he impotently watched the progress of Autemarre's brigade. His light batteries soon came up; but neither these, nor the squadrons of hussars which formed his escort, were the best of implements for pushing back General Bosquet into the steep mountain road by which he had ascended; and, in the hands of Prince Mentschikoff, they were simply powerless. However, his guns,

His batteries at length coming up, there begins a cannonade between his and Bosquet's artillery.

when they came up, were placed in battery, and, Bosquet's guns being now on the plateau, there began a cannonade at long range between the twelve guns of the French and the whole of the light artillery which Prince Mentschikoff had hurried into this part of the field. At the same time the French artillery drew some shots from the distant guns which Kiriakoff had placed looking seaward on the Telegraph Height; and the annals of the French artillery record with pride that the twelve pieces which Bosquet brought up with him engaged and overpowered no less than forty of the enemy's guns. Nor is this statement altogether without something like a basis of truth, for the Russians had now thirty-six pieces of artillery on the West Cliff, or the Telegraph Height; and, though most of them at this time were so placed that their gunners could attempt some shots at a more or less long range against Bosquet's guns, the French artillerymen not only held their ground without having a gun disabled, but soon pushed forward their batteries to a more commanding part of the plateau.

Bosquet maintains himself.

By this time the seven battalions of infantry which Prince Mentschikoff had been moving flankwise were very near to the spot where their General had been eagerly awaiting them; but, just as he was about to have these troops in hand, the Prince seems to have come to the conclusion that, after all, he could do nothing in the part of the field to which he had dragged them. He was brought, perhaps, to this belief by seeing that the French and the Turks, who had been crossing the river at its mouth, were now beginning to show their strength toward the westernmost part of the cliff, for he may not have known that this force, being without artillery, could be easily prevented from advancing against his batteries on the open plateau. At all events, Prince Mentschikoff now thought it necessary to reverse his flank movement, and to travel back toward his centre with all the forces which he had brought from thence to his left.

Mentschikoff counter-marching.

But, when the Prince began this last counter-movement, he was already beginning to fall under the dominion of events in another part of the field.

Bosquet now stood undisturbed on the part of the plateau which he had reached. But he was not without grounds for deep anxiety. It did not fall to his lot on that day to be engaged in any conflict except with the enemy's artillery; but, from the moment when he began to establish himself on the plateau until toward the close of the action, he was in a dangerously isolated position; for he

Position of Bosquet on the cliff.

had no troops around him except Autemarre's brigade, and, until the action was near its end, he got no effective support either from Bouat on his right or from Canrobert on his left.

XIV.

As soon as Marshal St. Arnaud perceived that Bosquet would be able to gain the summit of the cliff, he tried to give him the support toward his left which his position, when he got established on the cliff, would deeply need; and he determined that the time was come for the immediate advance of his 1st and 3rd Divisions. Addressing General Canrobert and Prince Napoleon, and giving them the signal for the attack, he said, I am told, these words: 'With men such as you I have no orders 'to give. I have but to point to the enemy!'[1] Hitherto these two French Divisions had been nearly in the same alignment as the leading divisions of the English army; but now that they were ordered forward, leaving the English army still halted, the true character of the movement to be undertaken by the Allies was for the first time developed. Their array was to be what strategists call 'an order of battle in three échelons by the 'right, the first échelon making a turning movement.'[2]

St. Arnaud orders the advance of Canrobert and Prince Napoleon.

The order into which the Allies now fell.

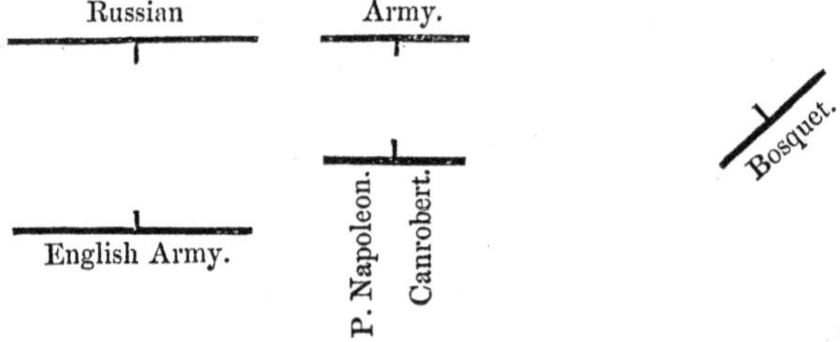


This disposition for the attack was not the result of any agreement made in words between Marshal St. Arnaud and Lord Raglan. It resulted almost naturally, if so one may speak, from Bosquet's turning movement, from the extent of the front which the enemy was now seen to present, and from the character of the ground. Just

Lord Raglan's conception of the part he had to take.

[1] I have this from an officer who assures me that he heard the words.

[2] 'Un ordre de bataille à trois échelons par la droite, le premier échelon 'attaquant par le flanc.' These are the words in which a staff officer present in the action, and very high in the French service, has described to me the advance of the Allies. See the diagram, a much better guide than mere words.

as the Marshal had kept back his 1st and 3rd Divisions till he saw that Bosquet could gain the height, so Lord Raglan, according to his conception at this time, had to see whether Canrobert and Prince Napoleon could establish themselves upon the Telegraph Height, before he endangered the continuity of the order of battle by allowing the English army to advance.

During the first forty minutes of the cannonade directed against the English infantry there had been no corresponding fire upon the French from the Telegraph Height; because the guns in that part of the field had been placed at first so low down on the hill-side that no use could be made of them, and the process of moving them to higher ground was tedious; but when Kiriakoff had at length established a couple of batteries upon the high ground near the Telegraph,[1] the fire of those guns, passing over the heads of the Taroutine and the militia battalions, began to molest the divisions which were led by Canrobert and Prince Napoleon.

Artillery contest between the Russian and the French batteries.

On the other hand, the artillery belonging to the divisions of Canrobert and Prince Napoleon came down to a convenient ground above the edge of the vineyards, and opened fire upon the columns of the 'militia' battalions, now posted much farther up than before on the opposite height. And with effect: for although the range did not admit of great slaughter, some men were struck, and the rest, though they did not yet move, began to be displeased with the ground on which they stood.[2]

The swarms of skirmishers which the French threw forward went briskly into the cover, forded the river, and then made themselves at home in the broken ground at the foot of the Telegraph Height. When the soldier is upon service of this kind, his natural character—neutralized in general by organization—is often seen to reassert itself. One man, prying eagerly forward, would labor to get shots at Russian sharpshooters still lingering near the river; another would sit down, take out his little store of food and drink, and be glad to engage with any one who passed him in something like cynical talk concerning the pastime of war. But, upon the whole, French skirmishers push on with great boldness and skill.

When the foremost ranks of Canrobert's massed battalions had entered the vineyards, each man got through as best he could, and rapidly crossed the river; and though during part of the advance the troops were

Canrobert's advance across the river.

[1] These were the batteries before spoken of as those from which shots at long range were attempted against Bosquet's artillery. [2] Chodasiewicz.

under the fire of the guns on the Telegraph Height, yet the nature of the acclivity before them was of such a kind that the farther they advanced (provided the heads of the battalions did not show themselves on the plateau above the broken ground) the better they were covered from fire. And, except some lingering skirmishers, they had no infantry opposed to them at this time; for the two 'Moscow' battalions which Kiriakoff had sent down toward the ford of the White Homestead were now, it seems, made to take part in the marches and counter-marches which Mentschikoff was directing in person, and there were then no other Russian columns in this part of the field.[1] So, when the head of Canrobert's Division gained the broken ground on the Russian side of the river, it was for the moment sheltered; but if it had then ascended above the broken ground so as to peer up over the crest, and face the open plateau at the top, it would not only have come under the fire of artillery, but would have before it the four battalions of militiamen, supported by the four Taroutine battalions.

His troops are sheltered from fire by the steepness of the hill-side.

For an army advancing to the attack, a rim of sheltered ground on the verge of the enemy's position is of infinite use, because it enables the assailants to make without hurry their final arrangements for the assault; but to troops which are not propelled by the decisive order of some resolute commander, such shelter as that is sometimes a snare, because it tempts men to hang back. In such a situation, the best troops will often abstain from going forward of their own accord, for it seems to officers and men that if they are to quit good shelter and go out into storm, they ought, at least, to know that the movement is one really intended, and is needful to the purpose of the battle. The duty of pressing forward to terminate the isolation of Bosquet rested primarily with the general of the 1st Division.

Duty attaching upon the commander of the First French Division.

General Canrobert was a man of whom great hopes were entertained. According to every test which could be applied by school and college examinations, he

General Canrobert.

[1] There is some ground for supposing that the second 'Moscow' battalion was for a while forgotten, and that, not receiving in due time the order to rejoin the other battalions of the corps, it was left alone in the ravine till it found itself opposed to Canrobert's whole Division. If this is the case, and if there resulted any thing which could be called a combat between the Russian battalion and the French Division, the statement that Canrobert was not met by any troops except skirmishers would have to be qualified. The statement of Chodasiewicz on this point receives no support from Kiriakoff, and that is the reason why I have not adopted it. Chodasiewicz did not belong to the 'Moscow' corps.

promised to be an accomplished general. To the military studies of his youth he had added the experience of many campaigns in Africa; and even in the French army, where brave men abound, his personal valor had become a subject of remark. He was so deeply trusted by his Emperor that he had become the bearer of a then secret paper which was to put him at the head of the French army in the event of St. Arnaud's death. He had the misfortune to have upon his hands the blood of the Parisians slain by his brigade on the 4th of December; but it was said—to his honor—that he, more than all the other generals employed at that time, had loathed the work of having to abet the midnight seizure of his country's foremost generals. His spirit, they say, had been broken by the pestilence which, some few weeks before, had come upon his Division in the country of the Danube; but the extremity of the grief to which he then gave way had so much to justify it in the appalling nature of the calamity which slew his troops, that it was not a conclusive proof of his being wanting in military composure. The most successful of respondents to school and college questions now had to undergo a new test. Commanding a fine French division, he had the head of his column close under a height occupied by the enemy, and this at a time when the isolated condition of a French brigade on his right seemed to make it a business of great moment for him to be able to bring support to his comrades.

But at the point where Canrobert faced the height, he found it impracticable to drag up artillery, and he was obliged to send his guns all the way down to the village of Almatamack, in order that they might there ford the river and ascend to the top of the plateau by the road which Bosquet had taken. This operation could not but take a long time; and what Canrobert was now called upon to determine was, whether he would wait until his artillery had completed its circuitous and difficult journey, or at once carry forward his infantry to the summit of the plateau, and engage the battalions there posted. He determined to wait. The maxims of the French army discourage the idea of bringing infantry into action upon open ground without the support of artillery; and Canrobert did not, it seems, conceive that the predicament in which Bosquet stood was a circumstance which dispensed him from the observance of a general rule. So, whilst he was thus waiting for his artillery, he did not deem it right to push forward his battalions on the open plateau, but he brought the head of his Division to a point high up on the steep, broken side of the hill,

Unable to get up his artillery, he is unwilling to advance, without it, upon open ground.

He posts his battalions on

the higher steeps of the Telegraph Height, close under the plateau.

and extended it, in single and double battalion columns, on either side of the track by which he had ascended. He spread himself more toward his left than toward his right, and did not move any of his battalions in such a way as to be able to give a hand to Bosquet.

The bulk of Prince Napoleon's Division still on the north bank of the river.

Prince Napoleon's Division hung back in the valley, and the bulk of it at this time was still on the north bank of the river.

Fire sustained by such of the French troops as are not forward enough to have shelter from the hillside.

Discouragement.

Although the head of Canrobert's Division, being under the heights on the Russian side of the river, was enjoying good shelter, the masses of troops which stood more toward the rear, including some of Canrobert's battalions and the great bulk of Prince Napoleon's Division, were exposed to the fire of the guns on the Telegraph Height. They suffered; and a feeling of discouragement began to spread.

Marshal St. Arnaud had understood the gravity of the danger which would result from any delay in the advance of his centre; but, to meet it, he used an ill-chosen safeguard. The way to send help to Bosquet was to give Canrobert due warrant to move up at once upon the plateau, whether with or without his artillery.[1] What the Marshal did, however, was

St. Arnaud pushes forward his reserves.

to order up his reserves, sending one brigade of his 4th Division to follow the march of Bosquet, and the other to support Canrobert. This last measure was actually a source of weakness rather than of strength, for, as far as numbers were concerned, Canrobert and Prince Napoleon were already in more than ample strength. With two superb divisions, numbering some 15,000 men, and having Bosquet and Bouat on their right with many thousands more, they were advancing upon a very narrow front; and the bringing

The ill effect of this measure upon the French troops.

up of fresh troops augmented the masses who came under the fire of the guns without at all propelling the leading divisions. So the evil lasted and increased. Inaction in the midst of a battle is hateful to the brave, impetuous Frenchman, and inaction under fire is intolerable to him. The troops toward the rear of the columns, not having the close presence of the enemy to animate them,

[1] If the objection to advancing on the plateau without artillery was, according to French ideas, insuperable, an effort, one would think, should have been made to push forward Prince Napoleon's Division. Prince Napoleon had in his front two roads leading up to the Telegraph, and one of these at the least was practicable (and was afterward used) for artillery.

and being without that shelter from the Russian guns which was enjoyed by the leading battalions, became discontented and uneasy. It was then that there sprang up among the French troops the ill-omened complaint that they were being 'massacred.'

Their complaint that they were being 'massacred.'

All this while, Bosquet was on the summit of the cliff with his one brigade, and his isolation, as we shall presently see, was becoming a source of great anxiety.

Anxiety on account of Bosquet.

Minute after minute aids-de-camp were coming to Lord Raglan with these gloomy tidings; and, in truth, the action was going on ill for the Allies. The duty of crowning the West Cliff had been fulfilled with great spirit and dispatch by a small body of men; but the step had not been followed up. Bouat, filing slowly round near the sea with some 9000 men, but without guns, was, for the time, annulled. Bosquet, with one brigade, stood halted upon the heights which he had climbed; and, though happily he had not been assailed by infantry, his advanced and isolated position had become a source of weakness to the Allies. Of the two French divisions, charged with the duty of attacking the front and western flank of the Telegraph Hill, the one had its foremost battalions high up the steep, and on the verge of the open ground at its top, whilst the other was all down in the valley; but (although in different ways, and for different reasons) these divisions were both hanging back; and no French force had hitherto attacked any part of the ground held by the enemy's formed battalions. Meanwhile the batteries still swept the smooth approach to the table-land where the Telegraph stood, and not only kept it free of all assailants, but, pouring their fire over the heads of their own soldiery, were able to throw plunging shots into the midst of Prince Napoleon's Division.

State of the battle at this time.

All this while the English army had been kept under the fire of the Russian artillery; and although the men had been ordered to lie down, the ground sloping toward the river yielded no shelter, and many had been killed and wounded.

At first our batteries replied; but, after a while, it had been ascertained that the advantage the enemy had in his commanding ground was too great to be overcome, and the English artillery had ceased to fire. Lord Raglan asked why this was: 'I observe,' said he, 'the enemy's six-pounders amongst us; 'why can not we send our nine-pounders amongst them?' But he was told that our fire had proved to be ineffectual, and that it was, therefore, discontinued. He seemed struck. Perhaps the answer which he had received became one of the grounds on which, a few minutes later, he resolved to change the face of the battle.

XV.

Opportunities offered to Mentschikoff.

For some time the course of the action had been offering to the Russian General an opportunity of striking a great blow; and, circumstanced as he was, it would have been easier for him to gain a signal victory before three o'clock than to stand on the defensive and hold his ground till sunset. The English forces, confronting, as they did, a position of great natural strength, and having their left on ground as open as a race-course, would have been hampered in every attempt to storm the Great Redoubt if their flank had been assiduously threatened, and now and then charged by the enemy's powerful cavalry. Therefore, if Mentschikoff, checking the English forces by a vigorous use of his horsemen, had undertaken, at this time, such an advance against Canrobert's Division as was afterward successfully executed by Kiriakoff, he would have found the French battalions quite soft to his touch, by reason of their want of artillery;[1] and Canrobert's retreat from the verge of the plateau would have occurred at a time when half the French army was so far from the true scene of conflict as to be unable to give the least help. Except by reckoning broadly upon the quality of the French and the British troops, or else upon the smiles of fortune, it is hard to see how the Allies could then have escaped a disaster.

But men move so blindly in the complex business of war that often, very often, it is the enemy himself who is the best repairer of their faults.

It was so that day. During the precious hour in which the Russian forces might have wrought a way to great glory, their cavalry were suffered to remain in idleness, and the battalions which formed the instrument afterward used for striking the blow were marching in vain from east to west and from west to east. The torpor and the false moves of the enemy countervailed the shortcomings of the Allies.

The battle, at this time, languished.

No combat of any moment was going on at this time. It is true that Major Norcott, with the left wing of the 2nd battalion of the Rifle Brigade, had gone into the vineyards in front of our Light Division, and by this time he had not only driven the enemy's riflemen

[1] I should not have ventured upon this sentence if it were not that I am warranted in doing so by what actually occurred a little later. See *post*.

from the inclosures, but had even stolen over the river higher up, and was opening fire on the left bank. But every where else the battle flagged. The men of our infantry divisions, though they were under the fire of thirty guns, still lay passive upon the ground. Our cavalry awaited orders. Our artillery declined to fire without being able to strike. The Russian and the French artillery continued engaged at long range. No French battalion advanced above the broken ground, though, covering their front and the left flank of their trailing columns, swarms of skirmishers were alive. Of these, some were firing to show where they were, some dueling with the Russian riflemen who yet remained in the valley; others ascended the knolls, and vexed any Russians they saw with long, careful shots; others, again, sat down, and contentedly took their rest.

This languishing of the battle seemed to promise ill for the Allies. They had undertaken to assault the enemy's left, and to that enterprise they stood committed, for they had drawn away from the real field of battle to the West Cliff some fourteen thousand men. Yet, since the moment when Bosquet began to ascend the cliff, more than forty minutes had elapsed, and nothing had yet been done to win a result from his movement, nor even to give him that support which he very grievously wanted. Both from Bouat on his right, and from Canrobert on his left, he was divided by a wide tract of ground.

Hitherto, then, the operations planned and undertaken by the French had not only done nothing toward carrying the position, but had even brought the Allies into danger.

Causes which had occasioned the failure of the French operations.

The causes of the miscarriage were the physical obstructions which hindered both Bouat and Canrobert from bringing up their guns with them, and the stiffness of the objection which prevents French generals from engaging their infantry on open ground without the support of artillery. According to the intended plan of operations, Bosquet, after gaining the cliff with his whole column of some 14,000 men, was to bring round his right shoulder in order to fall upon the flank of the Russians, and simultaneously with his appearance on the plateau a vigorous and resolute onslaught was to be made by the rest of the French army upon the front of the enemy's left wing. But Bosquet, as we saw, though he was personally present on the part of the plateau overhanging Almatamack, had only one brigade there, and whether he looked to Bouat on his right or to Canrobert on his left, he looked in either case to a general who, though he had masses of infantry, was without artillery, and he therefore looked in vain. In such circumstances, the utmost that Bosquet could be expected to do was to hold his ground, and this he did.

XVI.

For an hour and a half the Allies had lain under fire, without even beginning to assail the enemy's formed battalions. The only ground gained was that occupied by Bosquet. But Bosquet's achievement not having been followed up, his very success now threatened to bring disaster upon the Allies. When a French soldier is one of a body placed in a false position, he knows it, and comments on the fact; and the very force and vivacity of his nature make it difficult to keep him long upon ground to which he feels a scientific objection. A French aid-de-camp came in haste to Lord Raglan, and represented that unless something could be done to support or relieve Bosquet's column it would be 'compromised.' Gifted himself with the command of graceful diction, Lord Raglan was not without fastidious prejudices against particular forms of expression, and it chanced that he bore a singular hatred against the French word which we translate into 'compromised.' So he archly resolved to have the meaning of the word fully expanded into plain French, and he asked the aid-de-camp what would be the actual effect upon the brigade of its being 'com-'promised.'

A desponding account of Bosquet's condition is brought to Lord Raglan.

The answer was, 'It will retreat.'[1]

Was it time for the English General to take the battle into his own hands?

So long as Bosquet, with Autemarre's brigade, stood isolated upon the cliff, and Canrobert's and Prince Napoleon's Divisions remained hanging back in the vineyards and the broken ground below the Telegraph Height, an advance of our forces would plainly distort the Allied line in a hazardous way, and Lord Raglan had watched for the moment when the development of the expected French attack on the Telegraph Height would warrant him in suffering our infantry to go forward.

But he had hitherto watched in vain; and, not knowing how long the causes of the French delay might continue to operate, he resolved to depart from the scheme of action which had hitherto governed him, and to precipitate the advance of the English forces. It is true that whilst Bosquet stood halted on the cliff, whilst

Lord Raglan resolves to precipitate the advance of the English army.

[1] "Battra en retraite."

Canrobert abstained from assailing the Telegraph Height, and whilst Prince Napoleon's Division was still low down in the valley, the advance of the English forces against the Causeway and the Kourganè Hill would ruin the symmetry of the plan which the French had contrived; and if Bosquet should be obliged to retreat at a time when the English were hotly engaged in an attack upon the enemy's heights, the whole array of the Allies would be brought into peril. But the timely incurring of dangers is proper to the business of war; and, though the enemy had hitherto been torpid and indulgent, the cause of the Allies had fallen into such a plight that a remedy which involved heavy risks might nevertheless be the right one. And, so far as concerned his understanding with the French, Lord Raglan was freed from all care; for he had been already assured that Marshal St. Arnaud anxiously desired him to advance, and one aid-de-camp, as we have seen, had told him plainly that nothing less than a diversion by the English forces would prevent General Bosquet from retreating.

Grounds tending to cause, or to justify the resolve.

A man may weigh reasons against reasons, but sometimes, after all, it is the power of the imagination, or else some manly passion, which comes to strike the balance and lead him on to action. The motive of which Lord Raglan felt the most conscious was the simple and natural longing to cease from being passive. He could no longer endure to see our soldiery lying down without resistance under the enemy's fire.[1]

He had been riding slowly upon the ground between the Great Causeway and the left of the French army; but he now stopped his horse, and the cavalcade which had trailed in his wake whilst he moved then gathered more closely around him. There were altogether some twenty horsemen; and although with several of them Lord Raglan from time to time talked gayly, yet, so far as concerned the duty of taking thought how best to conduct the action, he was like a man riding in mere solitude, for it was not his custom to seek counsel, and the men around him so held their chief in honor that none of them would have liked to assail him with question or advice. Still, any one there could see that, besides Lord Raglan himself, there was one man of the Head-Quarter Staff whose mind was engaged in the business of the hour. We saw that Airey had already begun to wield great power in the English army. With the power was its burden. Whilst most of the other men on the Head-Quar-

Orders for the advance of the English infantry.

[1] This is the motive for accelerating the advance of the British troops which Lord Raglan avowed to me on the evening of the action.

ter Staff seemed to be merely spectators or messengers, there was care, vexing care on the lean, eager, imperious features of the Quartermaster-General. He was not simply impatient of the delay; he judged it to be a great evil.

It was to him that Lord Raglan now spoke some five words. Whatever it was that was said, it lit the face of the hearer, and turned his look of care into sunshine. The horsemen in the surrounding group rose taller in their saddles and handled their reins like men whose limbs are braced by the joy of passing from expectancy to action. Every man, whether he had heard the words or not, saw in the gladness of his neighbor's face that the moment long awaited was come.

Our infantry was to advance. The order flew; for it was Nolan—the impetuous Nolan—who carried it to the 2nd Division. A few moments later, and the order had reached the Light Division. The whole of the foremost English line, from the 47th Regiment on our right to the extreme left of the Light Division, rose alert from the ground, dressed well their ranks, and then, having a front of two miles with a depth of only two men, marched grandly down the slope.[1]

XVII.

Evans detaches Adams with two battalions, and with the rest of his Division advances toward the bridge.

Sir De Lacy Evans, commanding the 2nd Division, had before him the blazing village. In that conflagration no man could live, and in order to make good his advance on either side of the flames, he had split his force by detaching General Adams to his right with two regiments[2] and Turner's battery. With that force Adams, driving before him some Russian skirmishers, marched down toward the ford which divided the French and English armies. Evans himself, with four battalions and Fitzmayer's battery of field artillery, had to assail the defenses which Prince Mentschikoff had accumulated for the dominion of the Pass and the great road. Soon, however, Evans was a good deal strenghtened in the artillery arm; for an opportunity of rendering service in this part of the field was observed and seized by Captain Anderson with a battery belonging to the Light Division, and by Colonel Dacres with a battery belonging to the 1st Division. By the time that the infantry[3] had got down to near the inclosures, eighteen English

[1] Computing from the right of the 47th Regiment, the English front was a little short of two miles, but computing it from the ground on which Adams was advancing, the front was more than two miles in extent.

[2] The 41st and 49th.

[3] The 1st brigade, under Pennefather, and the 47th Regiment, belonging to Adams's brigade.

guns had begun to reply to the fire which the enemy was pouring upon Pennefather's brigade.

But Evans's task was a hard one; for, having on his right an impassable conflagration, and being cramped toward his left by our Light Division, he was forced to move along the unsheltered line of the Great Causeway upon a narrow and crowded front, and this under a converging fire of artillery; for with the sixteen guns of the Causeway batteries, and the flanking fire poured down from the left shoulder of the Great Redoubt, the enemy swept the main road and the bridge, and searched the fords both above and below it. And, whilst the enemy's batteries thus dealt with the more open approaches to the bridge, his infantry was strong in that part of the ground which could not be searched by round shot, for, posted in the covert on either side of the Causeway, Prince Mentschikoff had six battalions,[1] and besides these there was a great portion of the sixteen battalions posted on the slopes of the Kourganè Hill, which was near enough to be available for the defense of the Causeway as well as the Great Redoubt. Moreover, the enemy's reserves were so disposed as to be in close and easy communication with this part of the field. The Russian skirmishers at this time were swarming in the thick ground which belts the river.[2]

The conflict in which he became engaged.

Confronting these defenses, Evans strove to work his way forward; but, although the walls and inclosures on the skirts of the village here and there formed islands of shelter, the rest of the ground which had to be traversed was so bare, that every man of the force, as long as he stood there, came under the eyes of the Russian gunners; and their fire being therefore effective, Pennefather's brigade, though always moving forward a little, could only gain ground by degrees.

At times, when the balls were falling thickly, the men would shelter themselves as well as they could behind such little cover as the ground afforded; and when there came a lull, they would spring forward and find shelter more in advance. There were some buildings which afforded good cover against grape

[1] Viz., the four battalions of Borodino, the 6th battalion of 'riflemen,' and the battalion of sappers and miners. According to some accounts, there were only a few companies of the sappers and miners. There is some obscurity as to the operations of the Borodino corps. They were so placed as to become severed from the actual control of their divisional general, and they were covered, it seems, by the conflagration; but all accounts agree in stating that the Borodino corps was in the Pass and close to the great road.

[2] No less than three out of the above six battalions were thrown out as skirmishers.

and musketry, and some of the men, having gained this shelter by a swift rush across the open ground under very heavy fire, were slow to move out again into a storm of grape, canister, and musket balls. At a later time the enemy shattered the walls of these buildings with round shot, and some of our men were crushed or suffocated by the ruins. But those who died that poor death were men hanging back.

This kind of struggle did not, of course, allow the troops to adhere to their order of formation; but whenever any number of men got together upon ground which enabled them to extend, they quickly fell into line. And this they did notwithstanding that the groups thus instinctively hastening into their English formation were sometimes men of different regiments. Several times the men were ordered to lie down.

The 47th Regiment, pushing in between the river and the burning village, and afterward fording the stream a good way below the bridge, was better sheltered from the fire of the Causeway batteries than the regiments of Pennefather's brigade.

Colonel Stacy, of the 30th, persistently worked his men through the gardens and inclosures till at length he was able to cross the river and establish his regiment under cover of the steep bank on the Russian side of the stream. Thence for some time he maintained a steady fire against the gunners of the Causeway batteries.

The 95th, like the other regiments of the brigade, stole forward from one sheltering spot to another, and at one time three of its companies got divided from the rest of the corps, and united themselves in line with the 55th; but the whole regiment had been again got together when, the Light Division coming on, it appeared that its right regiment was overlapped by the 95th. Lacy Yea did not choose to stop, and, the 95th being halted at the time, he, with his 7th Fusileers, passed through it. But the 'Derbies' could not endure to be thus left behind, and soon the regiment rushed forward, bearing so strongly toward the left, that the fortunes of the corps thenceforth became connected with the exploits of Codrington's brigade.

The 55th Regiment, whilst advancing in line over open ground, came under so crushing a fire that it staggered; and though the line did not fall back, it was broken. But Colonel Warren soon rallied his regiment, and carried it forward. Afterward, when he reached a spot which yielded shelter to a man lying flat on the ground, he ordered his men to lie down, but he himself kept his saddle and remained steadfast in the centre of his regiment until the moment came when again he could lead it forward.

The kind of struggle in which Evans was engaged could not be long maintained without involving heavy loss. Major Rose, and Captain Schane, and Lieutenant Luxmore, were killed. Evans himself received a severe contusion, and almost all his staff were struck; for Percy Herbert, his Assistant Quartermaster-General, was dangerously hit, and Captain Thompson, Ensign St. Clair, and Captain A. M. McDonald were severely wounded. Of the officers of the 30th, 55th, and 47th regiments, Major Rose, Captain Schane, and Lieutenant Luxmore were killed. Colonel Warren was wounded, and so were Pakenham, Dickson, Conolly, Whimper, Walker, Coats, Bisset, Armstrong, Lieutenants Warren, Woollcombe, Philips, and Maycock. Pennefather's brigade alone lost in killed and wounded nearly one fourth of its strength.[1]

So long as the Causeway batteries swept the mouth of the Pass, Evans, with his three shattered battalions,[2] could do no more than maintain an obstinate and bloody combat in this part of the field, and gain ground by slow degrees. He was not yet able to push forward beyond the left bank of the river, and assail the enemy in the heart of his position across the great road.

XVIII.

On Evans's left, but entangled with some of his regiments, Sir George Brown moved forward with the Light Division. He had before him the Great Redoubt, armed with fourteen guns of heavy calibre, and this stronghold was flanked on the one side by the Lesser Redoubt with its eight guns, and on the other by the artillery and the infantry which guarded the Pass. Upon the slopes of the Kourganè Hill, and so posted as to look down into the Great Redoubt, there was a battery of field artillery, and in rear of this a battery and a half, besides the four guns of the sailors, were held in reserve.[3]

*Advance of the Light Division.*

*The task it had before it.*

Sixteen battalions of infantry[4] were posted upon the flanks or in the immediate rear of the Great Redoubt. Of this force, the four Kazan battalions, formed in two columns of attack,

[1] This, as well as all other statements which I make of casualties in the English army, is taken from the official returns.

[2] The 30th, 55th, and 47th Regiments. As to the 95th, see *post*.

[3] The details of these forces have been given already.

[4] The four Kazan, or Archduke Michael's, battalions, the four Vladimir battalions, the four Sousdal battalions, and the four Ouglitz battalions.

stood in front near to either shoulder of the Great Redoubt, and these were supported by the four battalions of the Vladimir corps. On the right—proper right—of these troops, but somewhat refused, there were two of the Sousdal battalions: more in advance, and so placed as to form the extreme right of the Russian infantry line, there were the two remaining battalions of the same corps. Besides the masses thus pushed forward, General Kvetzinski held in hand the four battalions of the Ouglitz corps as an immediate reserve, and posted them upon the higher slopes of the Kourganè Hill. Farther toward the rear (except, perhaps, whilst they were employed as skirmishers) there were placed the two battalions of sailors. On the extreme right, and massed in columns at intervals upon the eastern and southeastern slopes of the Kourganè Hill, there were the bulk of the Russian cavalry.[1] This force of horsemen was so placed that, whilst it covered the right and the right rear of the position, the Russian commander could, so to speak, swing it round, and hurl it against the flank of an enemy assailing his Great Redoubt. In few words, that Kourganè Hill, now about to be assailed by our Light Division, was defended by two redoubts, by forty-two guns, and by a force of some 17,000 men.

Again, the troops which defended the Causeway could aid the defense of the Kourganè Hill, and, moreover, the troops which Prince Mentschikoff called his 'Great Reserve,' were so placed that they might be regarded as operating in support of the troops in this part of the field.

It rested with the four Kazan battalions to make the first attack upon the English troops. This was to be done whilst our soldiery, after struggling through the fords, were gaining the top of the bank. The enemy's massive columns were to throw our men back into the channel of the river before they could find time to form.

The slope which led up from the top of the bank to the parapet of the Great Redoubt was almost as even as the glacis of a fortress; and, except to one who knew beforehand how unaccountably life and limb are spared in a storm of artillery fire, it seemed hard to understand that upon that smooth ground men would be able to live for many moments under round shot, grape, and canister from fourteen heavy guns.

Being on the extreme left of the Allied forces, Sir G. Brown had to stand prepared for an attack of cavalry on his flank. On our side of the river, home down to the edge of the vine-

[1] The whole of it, except the squadrons which Prince Mentschikoff took with him when he rode toward the sea.

yards, the broad and gently undulating downs, thickly clothed with elastic herbage, were all that horsemen could wish for, and even on the left bank, the ground in this part of the field was practicable for the evolutions of cavalry. Hardly ever in war did 3000 troopers sit still in their saddles under stronger provocation to enterprise, for they were upon fair ground, they were confronted by a body of horse which was in numbers but one third of their strength, and they gazed upon the naked flank of an infantry force advancing to the attack of a strong position. Therefore, the contingency which actually occurred—the contingency of the enemy's withholding his cavalry arm instead of lifting it against the open flank of the Allies, could not have been looked for beforehand, and can only be accounted for now by ascribing it to the eccentric forbearance of the Russian commander.[1]

Rightly, therefore—though the apprehension was not afterward justified by the event—the Light Division was carried into action with an idea that cavalry charges were to be expected on the flank; and the duty of preparing against enterprises of this sort pressed specially upon General Buller, because he commanded the left brigade.

Means for preparing a well-ordered assault were open to the assailants.

To storm a position thus held in strength by forces of all arms, and to answer at the same time for the safety of the whole of the Allied army against a flank attack, was a task of great moment; but, on the other hand, Sir George Brown was not without means for preparing a well-ordered assault, for the enemy was making no attempt to hold the vineyards in strength, and on the Russian side of the river, the bank, though very steep, and from eight to fifteen feet in height, was yet so broken, that a skirmisher seeking to bring his eye and his rifle to a level with the summit, would easily find a ledge for his foot. Here, then, was exactly the kind of cover which the assailants needed, for if this steep bank could be seized and lined for a few minutes by their skirmishers, it would enable their main body to recover its formation after passing through the inclosures and fording the river. But, in order to lay hold of the advantage thus offered by the nature of the ground, it was of necessity to take care that the advance of the Light Division should be amply covered by skirmishers. This was not done. The rifles under Norcott had long before scoured the

The Division not covered by skirmishers.

[1] Before the action there was a good deal of conversation amongst officers in the Light Division with respect to the way in which the expected charges of the Russian cavalry should be met, and it was then—then, perhaps, for the first time—that the idea of receiving the enemy's horse in line was broached.

vineyards; but they had swerved away toward their left, and, fording the river higher up, had left Codrington's brigade without any skirmishers to cover its advance. No other light infantry men were thrown forward in their stead, and the whole body went stark on, with bare front, driving full at the enemy's stronghold.

XIX.

The tenor of Sir G. Brown's orders for the advance.

Sir George Brown's right brigade, consisting of the 7th Fusileers, the 33rd and the 23rd Regiments,[1] was under General Codrigton. The left brigade, consisting of the 19th, the 88th, and the 77th Regiments, was commanded by General Buller. The orders which General Codrington received from Sir George were simply to advance with his brigade, and not to stop until he had crossed the river. A like order, it is believed, was given to General Buller. The Division still moved in line, and, after losing a few men from the fire of the enemy's artillery, it reached the boundary of the vineyards and gardens which belt the course of the river.

The advance through the vineyards,

In their eagerness for the conflict, the regiments strove to advance quickly; but it was a laborious task to traverse the gardens and inclosures, and many of those who had hitherto kept their knapsacks here laid them down. In a few minutes the whole of the Light Division of infantry, drawing along with it in its impetuous course the 95th Regiment, had forced a way into the vineyards. There our young soldiers found themselves, as they imagined, in a thick storm of shot and cannon balls; but it seems that missiles of war fly crashing so audibly through foliage that they sound more dangerous than they are.

The loss at this time was not great. Our men were in the belief that speed was required of them, and having before them no chain of skirmishers to feel the way and control the pace of the Division, they struggled forward with eager haste. In passing from one of the inclosures to another, part of the line came to the top of a vertical bank, revetted with stone, and forming a kind of 'sunk fence.' Standing there, the men observed that a violent gust of shot was beating in against the stone work at their feet; and it seemed to them that, the moment

[1] When I speak of several regiments in the same limb of the sentence, I generally follow the order in which they would be ranged, going from right to left. In a brigade consisting of three regiments, say *e. g.* of the 1st, 2nd, and 3rd Foot, the 1st would be posted at the right, the 2nd at the left, and the 3rd in the centre.

they sprang from the top of the fence to the lower vineyard, their legs would be shattered by a thousand missiles. For a moment they paused, as though for some guidance; but the guidance was such as is given by 'Forward! first company!' 'Second company, show them the way!' The first who leaped down stood unscathed in the vineyard below; the rest followed. Dangers shrink before the advance of resolute men. There was not much loss in that lower vineyard. The troops pressed on.

Amongst the vineyards there were here and there farm-cottages and homesteads; and since the obstructions which the men were encountering had destroyed their formation, it became possible for such as loved their safety more than their honor to linger in the shelter afforded by these buildings. Some few, they say, lingered.

The Division hurried forward with just such trace of its original line formation as could remain to it after rapidly passing through difficult inclosures. The river, though flowing in a swift current, was fordable by a strong man in most places, but it was of very unequal depth. General Codrington was seen riding quickly across at a point where the stream hardly flowed above his horse's fetlocks, and yet, almost close to him, the taller charger of another officer went down and had to swim. The soldiers rapidly waded across. Some few perished in the stream, and it was never known whether they fell from shot or from not being able to keep their footing in the current.

and over the river.

That part of Pennefather's brigade which was overlapped by the 7th Fusileers[1] had become entangled with the Light Division, and, at the moment of Codrington's advance, Hume of the 95th seized a color, and, dashing across the river, carried with him almost the whole of the regiment; but the men bore so much toward their left, that by the time they gained the foot of the bank on the Russian side of the river they had got blended—not (as might be supposed) with the right, but—with the left regiment of Codrington's brigade. They were destined to share the glory and the carnage which awaited the 23rd Fusileers.

At length the whole Light Division, together with the additional regiment which had strayed into its company, was upon the Russian side of the river; but as yet the troops only stood upon the narrow strip of dry ground at the water's edge, and such of them as were in the centre or toward the right

[1] *i.e.*, after the Fusileers had marched through the 95th.

were penned back by the rocky bank which rose steep and high over their heads. The soldiery were a crowd—a crowd shaped and twisted by the winding of the river's bank, yet with some remains of military coherence; for, although the inclosures and the fording of the river could not but destroy all formation, the men of every company had kept together as well as they were able.

Along the part reached by Codrington's brigade the left bank is lined with the enemy's skirmishers.

But a general who had omitted to line the bank with his own skirmishers might well expect to see it fringed with the enemy's rifles; and the strong wall which Nature had offered to the English as a cover for the formation of their battalions, was now, of course, held by the enemy's skirmishers. These light troops were in greatest force along the bank which faced the centre and the right of the Light Division. They came to the edge of the bank, fired down into the crowd of the redcoats, and then drew back for a pace or two that they might load in peace and be ready to fire again. They could kill and wound men in the crowd below without laying themselves open to fire.

Course taken by General Buller.

Toward the left of the Light Division the bank was less abrupt and also more free from the enemy's skirmishers. There, after passing the river, General Buller, who commanded the 2nd brigade, was able to form it at his leisure. He ordered the 77th Regiment to lie down under the cover afforded by the configuration of the ground, and, upon a slope somewhat sheltered from the fire of the enemy's artillery, he placed the 88th Regiment.[1] With these two regiments he remained long halted, not partaking in the subsequent advance of Codrington's brigade. His reason was, that, a large body of cavalry and infantry appearing on the plain to threaten his left, he thought it right to keep two regiments in hand until he should find himself supported by the near approach of the Highland brigade. He conceived that he ought to beware of outstripping the 1st Division by too great an interval; and, in truth, the duty which attached upon General Buller at this moment was one of a grave kind; for if the enemy should seize the moment of Sir George Brown's assault upon the Great Redoubt as his time for making a resolute attack with horse, foot, and artillery, upon the flank of our advancing troops, the safety of the whole Allied army would be challenged, and would be found to rest upon such dispositions as General Buller might have made for covering our left.

Nature of the duty attaching upon him.

[1] As to the 19th Regiment, see *post*.

Sir George Brown's order to Buller empowered him to advance until he was over the stream; but, that duty having been executed, the brigadier now found himself on the bank of a river, without, so far as I know, having any fresh orders to guide him, yet charged by circumstance with the duty of covering the flank of the whole Allied army at the moment of an assault upon the enemy's strong-hold. The business was a vital one; and the caution which Buller used at this time was required by the occasion.[1] For, to push forward the two regiments which formed the extreme left of the whole Allied front, and to march them against the enemy's strong-hold in a line, outflanked by the enemy's horse, and even, it would seem, by a portion of his foot, would have been to lay open—not Buller's brigade merely, but—the whole Allied army to the risk of a flank attack involving great disasters. In these circumstances it was Buller's duty to take up such a position as would enable him to cover the advance of Codrington's brigade and to sustain the shock of a flank attack. It was to that end that he kept in hand the 88th and the 77th Regiments.

XX.

The 19th Regiment.

Though forming part of Buller's brigade, the 19th Regiment was suffered, ere long, to associate itself with General Codrington's advance. So, with this and the other stray regiment[2] which clung to it, Codrington's brigade was swollen to a force of five battalions.

State of the five battalions standing crowded along the left bank of the river.

These five battalions were extended in a broken chain at the foot of the bank on the Russian side of the river, and were falling—especially toward the right—under the close fire of the skirmishers who crowned the top. In this strait some of our officers instinctively tried to clear the front by getting the men to mount part way up the bank and bring their rifles to a level with the summit. But, among the foremost, the general commanding the Division had forded the river. Sir George Brown was an officer whose career had begun, and begun with glory, in the great days under Wellington; but, whilst he was still in his early manhood, wars had ceased, and thenceforth for near forty years he had brought his strong energies to bear upon the kind of military business which used to be practiced by the English in peace-time. A long immer-

Sir George Brown.

[1] The way in which the 88th and the 77th Regiments were handled at a later period of the action was not the necessary result of the dispositions made at this time, and is a fit subject for distinct comments.

[2] The 95th. See *ante*.

sion in the Adjutant-General's department had led him to go even beyond other men in laying stress upon the value of discipline; but the practice of this sort of industry had not at all helped to school him for the command of a division in war-time; for in laboring after that mechanic perfection which, after all, is only one of many means toward an end, the end itself had been much forgotten by those who controlled our military system, and the business of war (as, for instance, the art of carrying a brigade in line through inclosures and thick grounds) had been little or never practiced in England.[1] To a military system which omits to anticipate and to deal with the common obstacles to be expected in a battle-field, war is a rough disturber; and, unless the industry of the barrack-yard is supported by other and better resources, it is liable to be turned to nothingness by even a gentle contact with reality. A belt of garden ground, a winding, though fordable stream, and an enemy hitherto inert, had sufficed to make Sir George Brown despair of being able to present his troops to the enemy in a state of formation. Great dislocation of military order was, of course, the necessary result of having to pass through inclosures and to ford a winding stream; so what the main body needed to have before it when it approached the left bank of the river was a swarm of skirmishers clearing its immediate front, and prepared to cover it during the process of forming anew. This cover, however, was wanting. Sir George Brown declared that to attempt any formation after the passage of the river would be impossible, and that he had "determined to trust to the spirit and individual courage of the "troops." Thus, on ground giving rare opportunity for the deliberate preparation of an attack, and under no great stress of battle, the Light Division—the "Light Division," whose very name carried with it a great inheritance of glory—was suffered to lapse into a mere throng of brave men. In this plight the five battalions had to advance under the guns of a powerful battery supported by heavy columns of foot.

But an officer honored with the command of British troops can always hope that, when his skill fails him, his men may still retrieve the day by sheer fighting; and to a commander frustrated in his evolutions, the prospect of a rude conflict with the enemy may offer the best kind of solace, and, perhaps, even a happy issue out of trouble. Of such comfort as was to be got from close fighting, there seemed to be fair promise in the Great Redoubt, and there Sir George Brown resolved to seek

[1] Sir Charles Napier, the conqueror of Scinde, used to press the importance of practicing troops in this way, but without success.

SECTION INTENDED TO CONVEY AN IDEA OF THE FORMATION OF THE GROUND BENEATH THE GREAT REDOUBT.

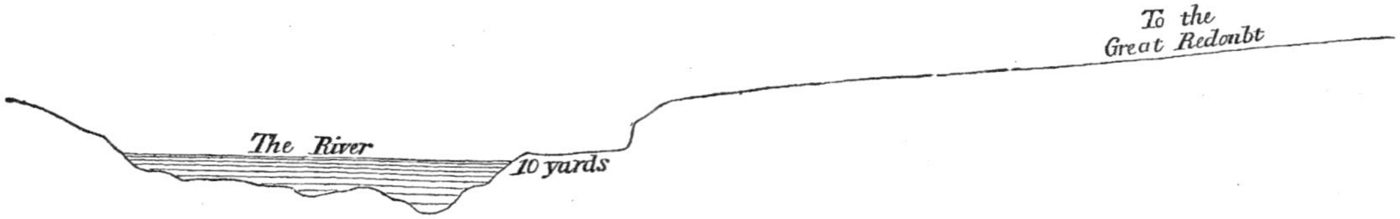

To the
Great Redoubt

The River

10 yards

*N.B.—This is not a section made from survey, and is not intended to be taken as a representation that such was the actual configuration of the ground. It is only meant to help the reader toward understanding the description given in the text.*

it. Eager to have, at the least, a forward place in the armed throng, he suffered agony lest the bank, very steep at the spot where he faced it, should be inaccessible to a mounted officer; but he soon found a place where a break in the stiffness of the acclivity left room for the two or three ledges which a horseman must find before he can reach the top. Then he quickly gained the open ground above. The Russian skirmishers were there. Schooled in habits of deep reverence for military rank, these men may have been startled, perhaps, by the sudden apparition of the flowing plumes which bespoke a general officer, and, what was worse, a general officer in a state of displeasure. It seems, too, there is something in the bearing of a fearless, near-sighted man which disturbs the reckonings of other people; for they see that his ways are not their ways, and they do not know but that he may be right in not fearing them, and that if they were not to be afraid of him, they themselves might be in the wrong. At all events, the enemy's skirmishers, omitting or failing to bring down the English General, suffered him to remain unhurt on the top of the bank. There, flushed and angry—he was angry perhaps with himself, or angry with the gardens and walls, and the perverse winding of a stream which had broken the cherished structure of his battalions—he sat on his gray charger full under the guns of the Great Redoubt, and the dun oblong columns of the enemy's infantry that flanked it on either side. However eagerly he might be longing to carry forward his Division, he was without the means of sending swift orders along his line.

But toward the right of Sir George Brown a movement corresponding with his determination had already begun. General Codrington, ordered to advance in line, and not to stop till he had crossed the river, had obeyed very swiftly, and the men of his brigade (in common with the 95th Regiment), having moved with a converging tendency during their passage through the vineyards and the river, were now thickly clustered under the left bank in a chain which took its bends from the winding of the stream. Codrington was at this time between the 33rd Regiment and the 23rd Fusileers. He strove to do something toward restoring the formation of his troops; but the crowd, jammed together, twisted into fantastic shape by the bends of the river's bank, and, standing helpless under the fire of the skirmishers shooting down into it from above, could hardly even try to perform an evolution requiring free space and time. And if for a moment it seemed possible that any approach to a formation under the bank could be effected, the hope was rudely destroyed; for,

General Codrington.

on ground lower down the river, a body of the enemy's light troops found for themselves a spot yielding them shelter, yet so placed that it enabled them to pour a flanking fire along the strip or ledge which divided the stream from the bank, and this at a part where the earth was alive with our devoted soldiery.

To keep the men under this fire for many minutes, and to keep them, too, standing all the time in unresisting masses, would be to lose a brigade. The only order received by General Codrington had been obeyed to the full. He had no time to seek guidance from his divisional general. Clearly there was come upon him one of those rare conjunctures in which a career is made to hinge upon the decision of a moment. General Codrington a few weeks before had been only a traveler[1] on a visit to the army in Bulgaria. He now commanded a brigade. His father was that admiral whose achievement at Navarino had been a link in the chain of events which now brought the son in arms for the Sultan's cause. And any one who loved our navy, even to jealousy of the land service, might persuade himself that the bright, ardent, straightforward glance, and the bold, decisive speech of the Coldstream officer, must have come by inheritance from a sailor. He had the close, tight lips bespeaking the obstinate man who lives a life undistracted by breadth and diversity of views. And much of what he seemed he was; a firm, plain soldier, not liable to be bent from the simple path by refined or complex views.[2] He could not see far without the help of the glass which he kept attached to his cap, but he was more alive to the world around him than near-sighted men often are. He had never before been in action. He could not suffer his troops to remain for another minute a helpless crowd under heavy fire. He knew not how he could withdraw them to any ground apt for manœuvring, and it was hardly possible for him to exert such a control over the crowd of soldiers hemmed in under the bank as would enable him to repair the evil by covering his brigade with skirmishers.

XXI.

Nelson, gliding into the Bay of Aboukir, told his assembled

[1] With the rank of colonel, but unattached.

[2] I of course know that an opinion attributing to General Codrington this manly simplicity of mind is liable to be challenged by those who remember the style of his dispatches. My answer is, that his dispatches do not indicate the man. His private letters do. They are written very simply, but with a good deal of power.

captains that if any one of them in the coming battle should chance to be disturbed by doubts about what he ought to do, he might find a good way out of trouble by closing with an enemy's ship.

Codrington resolves to storm the Great Redoubt.

And it was a solution of this sort which Codrington sought; for, with no authority except that which was cast upon him by the stress of the moment, he resolved to storm the Great Redoubt. And he resolved to do this instantly. His immediate power over the disordered masses around him was confined within the range of his voice, but, lifting himself a little in his stirrups, he spoke to the men in his clear, ringing voice, and ordered them (all who could hear him) 'to fix bayonets, get up the 'bank, and advance to the attack.'

His words to the men.

He gains the top of the bank.

Then also Codrington imagined that the need of the moment was a ready leader rather than a cool and placid general. Besides, this was his first battle; and perhaps—our army, and not the world, will understand him if so it was—he unconsciously felt that the foremost place was peculiarly befitting a Guardsman who commanded a brigade of the line. With the quickness of a man accustomed to hunting, he found a spot where the bank was practicable, and, facing it obliquely, his small white Arab, with two or three strides, carried him to the summit. From the spot which he thus reached the enemy's skirmishers had withdrawn;[1] and Codrington, with the few soldiers who had already been able to gain the top, was alone upon this part of the hill-side. Looking up the smooth, gentle slope, he had before him the Great Redoubt; but for the moment the mouths of the heavy guns which armed it remained black and silent. On his right front he saw a body of infantry massed in column. The men, in their long, gray, sombre coats, stood formed with great precision and rigidly still; but right and left of the mass there was a chain of skirmishers so placed on the flanks of the column as to be abreast of its front rank. The troops close in rear of the body in front could hardly be seen, for they were almost hidden by the dip of the ground, but the crest was fringed with sparkling light, and the light was light playing upon the bayonet points of battalions massed in the hollow.

Our troops were yearning to be commanded, and if the men, far and near, could have seen that the horseman on the small

[1] I imagine that they were withdrawn from this spot because it was under the guns—the guns of the Great Redoubt—from which the enemy was about to open fire on our troops.

white Arab above them was a general officer, they would have looked to every wave of his arm for a guiding signal; but Codrington had come to the East a mere traveler, and his simple forage cap had not the significance of the hat and the flowing plumes, which would have shown men far from the spot that a general officer was on the top of the bank. There were soldiers, however, who gained the top almost at the same moment as their leader. First one here and there, then knots, then bevies of men clambered up.

Hitherto the knowledge that there was to be an advance beyond the bank had been confined to the people who chanced to be near Sir George Brown or General Codrington; but those who heard the words or caught the meaning of the divisional general and the brigadier hastened to give effect to the will of their chiefs by sending their words along the line.

Lacy Yea and his Fusileers.

The 7th Fusileers, being on the extreme right of Codrington's brigade, was beyond the reach of his personal guidance; but Lacy Yea,[1] who commanded the regiment, was a man of an onward, fiery, violent nature, not likely to suffer his cherished regiment to stand helpless under muzzles pointed down on him and his people by the skirmishers close overhead. The will of a horseman to move forward, no less than his power to elude or overcome all obstacles, is singularly strengthened by the education of the hunting-field, and Lacy Yea had been used in early days to ride to hounds in one of the stiffest of all hunting counties. To him this left bank of the Alma crowned with Russian troops was very like the wayside acclivity which often enough in his boyhood had threatened to wall him back and keep him down in the depths of a Somersetshire lane whilst the hounds were running high up in the field some ten or fifteen feet above. His practiced eye soon showed him a fit 'shord' or break in the scarped face of the bank, and then shouting out to his people, 'Never mind 'forming! Come on, men! Come on, anyhow!' he put his cob to the task, and quickly gained the top.

On either side of him, men of his regiment rapidly climbed up, and in such numbers that the Russian skirmishers who had been lining it fell back upon their battalions.

The heaving of the crowd beneath the bank.

And now, in the masses still crowded along the foot of the bank there rose up that murmur of prayer for closer fighting which, coming of a sudden from men of Teuton blood, is the advent of a new and seemingly extrinsic power—the power ascribed in old times to the hand

[1] Pronounced Yaw.

of an Immortal. From the first company of the 7th Fusileers to the left of the 19th Regiment, the deep, angry, gathering sound was 'Forward!' 'Forward!' 'Forward!' The throng was heaved; and presently the whole 1st brigade of the Light Division, carrying with it the 19th and the 95th Regiments, surged up, and in numberless waves broke over the bank.

Effect of the converging tendency which had governed the troops.

That tendency to converge of which we have already spoken had contracted the front presented by the five regiments now on the crest of the bank to a fraction only of the line which they would have formed if they had been deployed in due order. The operation of taking ground and opening out into line is hardly one to be undertaken by a crowd of soldiery on ground which may be called the glacis of the enemy's fortress, and in the close presence of his formed battalions; but the 7th Fusileers, being on the extreme right of the brigade, and not being cramped at that time by any pressure from the regiments of the 2nd Division, was able to find space; and, though numbers of the regiment were wanting, and though many belonging to other corps were mixed up with the Fusileers, Lacy Yea, using violent energy, was able in some degree to make the men open out. But the silence which is the pride of the English army could not at that moment be preserved; for numbers of men, separated from their companies and their regiments, yet eager to follow the path of duty, were anxiously seeking advice from officers, and trying, in fact, to place themselves under such command as time and circumstances would allow. In this condition of things, the utmost that could be done was to give to the mass the rudiments of a line formation. Colonel Blake, with the 33rd, was able to make his regiment open out and form line.

Endeavors of the men to form line on the top of the bank.

In the other three regiments, too, the soldiers strove hard to put themselves in their English array; but on either flank space was wanting; and although these battalions, having now open ground before them, were no longer a helpless mass, their state was not such as to enable them to move at the will of a commander. They were an armed and warlike crowd.

The task they had before them.

The five regiments now gathered on the crest of the bank were the first body of Allied troops which moved up on that day to dispute with the enemy for ground which he held in strength. Both their right and their extreme left confronted the Russian infantry massed in columns upon either flank of the Great Redoubt; but the centre and left centre of this part of our assailing force stood right under the face of the work.

Although at this time there was in general no due formation, still the knotted chain into which the men of the five regiments found themselves extended was much more than long enough to outflank the Great Redoubt on either side; and the troops which formed the extreme left and the extreme right of our line were less exposed than the centre regiments to fire from the face of the work. But in order that he might at once crush those portions of our clustered force, the enemy, as we have seen, had massive columns of infantry posted on either flank of the redoubt. Two of these columns—columns formed of the Kazan corps—now moved down the hill.

The Right Kazan column advances against the 19th Regiment and some companies of the 23rd.

The column,[1] descending from the eastern flank of the work, marched against that part of our line which was formed by the 19th Regiment and some of the left companies of the 23rd. It had already come part way down the slope before any great number of the English had clambered up to the top of the bank; and our soldiers, it would seem, at that time might have been forced back into the channel of the river by a continued and resolute advance of the column; but when one by one, and in knots and groups, our men gained the top of the bank — when they saw the ground above spreading smooth and open before them, and the huge gray, square-built mass gliding down to where they were, then, happily for England and for the freedom of Europe—for on this, in no small measure, the common weal seems to rest—it came to be seen that now, after near forty years of peace, our soldiery were still gifted with the priceless quality which hinders them from feeling, in the way that foreigners feel it, the weight of a column of infantry. In their English way, half sportive, half surly, our young soldiers seemed to measure their task; and then—many of them still holding betwixt their teeth the clusters of grapes which they had gathered in the vineyards below—they began shooting easy shots into the big, solid mass of infantry which was solemnly marching against them. The column was not unsteady, but it was perhaps an over-drilled body of men unskillfully or weakly handled. At all events, those who wielded it were unable to make its strength tell against clusters of English lads who stood facing it merrily, and teasing it with rifle balls. Soon the column was ordered or suffered to yield, and since it fell back

The column is defeated, and retreats.

[1] A double battalion column, I believe, containing 1500 men. This Kazan corps, of which we shall see a great deal, is more commonly called in Russian accounts the 'Grand-Duke Michael's Regiment.' It was a regiment of 'Fusileers.'

to a spot where the ground was hollow, it lapsed nearly or quite out of sight. Then the 19th and the left companies of the 23rd, having thus ridded themselves of the infantry force in their front, began, as they advanced, to bend toward their right, and became a part of the force which was storming the Great Redoubt.

The Left Kazan column begins its fight with the 7th Fusileers.

But the other Kazan column[1]—the column coming down from the west flank of the redoubt—was a force of high mettle; and it now began that obstinate fight with the 7th Fusileers which was destined to last from the commencement of the infantry fight until almost the close of the battle.

XXII.

The storming of the Great Redoubt.

But between the two bodies of troops thus engaged on either flank with the enemy's infantry, the great bulk of Codrington's brigade, swollen by the accession of the 95th Regiment, was already moving up under the guns of the Great Redoubt. Codrington, indeed, had not waited for the moment when his whole brigade reached the top of the bank; for, having gathered some knots of men on either side of him, he rode forward gently a few paces, then waited until he gained some increase in numbers, and then again moved on, thus canvassing, as it were, for followers, and gradually carrying forward with him more and more of the troops. At first he got on slowly, for the bulk of our officers, having had no order to dispense with formation, they judged, when they gained the top of the bank, that they ought to strive to form line before they advanced, and they were laboring to that end; but when it came to be understood that an advance without formation was sanctioned by the generals or compelled by stress of events, the whole of the force, though clubbed and broken into clusters of men, began to move up the gentle slope of the hill.

For a little while, every gun in the great battery above remained dark and silent.

Amongst the Russians who were plying their field-glasses from the parapet of the Great Redoubt there was a question meet for debate:—'If the scarlet men of the sea were pre-'sumptuously bent upon storming the work, where was the 'great column of attack, and where the great column of sup-'port, and where the great columns of reserve which would 'have been formed for such an enterprise? Yet, if they had

[1] A double battalion column, I believe, containing 1500 men.

'no such purpose, why were so many men coming up under 'the guns, within grape-shot range? And, unless those En- 'glish were really attacking in force, why, in the name of the 'Holy Virgin and our own blessed Sergius,[1] why, riding for- 'ward even in front of the skirmishers, should there be that 'superb-looking horseman on the gray charger, whose visible 'rage, no less than his flowing plumes, clearly showed that he 'held high command?'

Upon the whole, it seemed that the advance of the red-coated soldiery was an irruption of skirmishers preparatory to an attack in force, but was an irruption so strong as to be worthy of all that artillery could do to crush it. So, the Russian sharpshooters having now, for the most part, fallen back, or moved aside out of the line of fire, the gunners in the Great Redoubt made ready to open fire upon our regiments with round shot, canister, and grape.

First one gun, then another, then more. From east to west the parapet grew white, and henceforth it lay so enfolded in its bank of silver smoke that no gun could any longer be seen by our men, except at the moment when it was pouring its blaze through the cloud. On what one may call a glaçis, at three hundred yards from the mouths of the guns, the lightning, the thunder, and the bolt are not far apart. Death loves a crowd; and in some places our soldiery were pressing on so close together, that when a round shot cut its way into the midst of them, it dealt a sure havoc.

There began a slaughter of our people. Some of the men struck down had got up a good way on the slope; others were so newly come to the top of the bank that they fell back dead and dying into the channel of the river; but all who were not struck down moved forward. Some of the clusters into which our men had gathered were eight or ten deep; and the round shot, tearing cruelly through and through, mowed down so many of our devoted soldiery that several times the crowd left standing was thinned.

But only for a moment; because that singular tendency which had begun with the advance into the vineyards was now setting in more strongly. Moving to the attack without being ordered to make toward any given spot, almost every officer and man (except those toward the flanks who were engaged with the enemy's infantry) had instinctively proposed to himself the same goal; and this goal was the Great Redoubt.

[1] The troops in and near the redoubt belonged to the 16th Division, and this Division carried with it a wooden image of the saint, solemnly intrusted to it by the Bishop of Moscow.

Upon the Great Redoubt, therefore, the regiments kept always converging; and in less time than it took the Russian artillerymen to sponge and load their guns, our people, inclining away from the flanks, and pressing in toward the centre, filled up every space cut clear by the shot; and this so constantly that, again, after a fall of many men, and again, and still again, there was always a flock ready for the slaughter. In the 'Derbyshire,'[1] Captain Eddington was shot in the throat and killed; Polhill was torn and slain with grape. The colonel was wounded, and Champion took the command of the regiment. He was a man of great gentleness and piety; and if he was not highly endowed with intellectual gifts, he was able to express the feelings of his heart with something of a poetic force. His mind was accustomed to dwell very much on the world that lies beyond the grave; and in the midst of this scene of carnage he gained, as it were, a seeming glimpse of the happy state; for when the younger Eddington fell at his side, Champion paused to see what ailed him, and, looking upon his young friend's pale face, he saw it suddenly clothed with a 'most sweet expression.' It was because death was on him that the blissful look had come. In the mind of Champion the sight had a deep import; for he was of the faith that God's Providence is special, and to him the beautiful smile on the features of 'the dead' was the smile of an immortal man gently carried away from earth by the very hand of his Maker.

Yet this piety of his was of no unwarlike cast. Nay, he was of so noble a sort that, though he had not willingly chosen the profession of arms, yet, when he prayed, he was accustomed to render thanks to his Creator for vouchsafing to make him a hardy soldier; and being, he said, very strong in the belief that he could die as piously on the battle-field as in 'a 'downy bed,' he pressed on content with his 'Derbies' to the face of the Great Redoubt.[2]

And now, whilst the assailing force was rent from front to rear with grape and canister poured down from the heavy guns above, another and a not less deadly arm was brought to bear against it; for the enemy marched a body of infantry into the rear of the breastwork, and his helmeted soldiers, kneeling behind the parapet at the intervals between the embrasures, watched ready with their muskets on the earthwork till they thought our people were near enough, and then fired into the crowd. Moreover, the troops on either flank of the redoubt began to fire obliquely into the assailing mass.

[1] The 95th.

[2] Champion's letters.

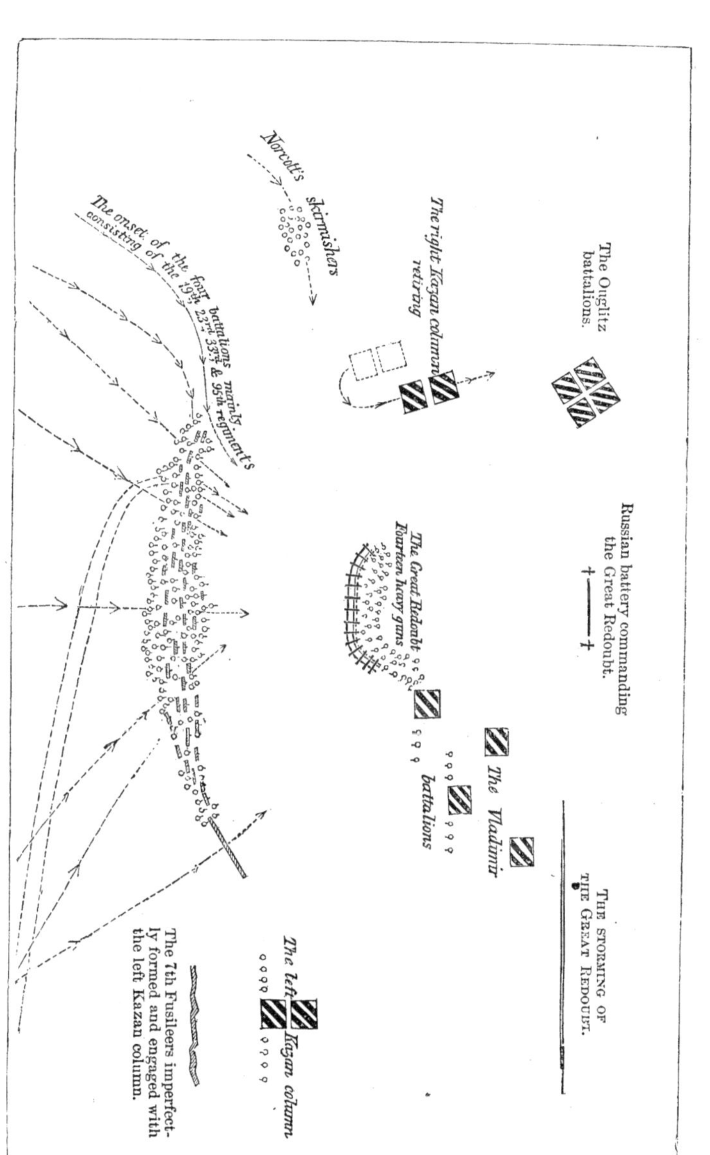

THE STORMING OF
THE GREAT REDOUBT.
The Ouglitz
battalions.
Russian battery commanding
the Great Redoubt.
The right Kazan column
retiring
Norcott's skirmishers
The onset of the four battalions mainly
consisting of the 19th, 23rd, 33rd & 95th regiments
The Great Redoubt
Fourteen heavy guns
The Vladimir
battalions
The left Kazan column
The 7th Fusileers imperfect-
ly formed and engaged with
the left Kazan column.

Then, for such of our men as were new to war, it became time to learn that the ear is a false guide in the computation of passing shot, and that amid notes sounding like a very torrent of balls, the greater part of even a crowded force may remain unhurt. The storm of rifle and musket balls, of grape and canister, came in blasts; and though there were pauses, yet, whilst a blast was sweeping through, it seemed to any young soldier, guided by the sound of the rushing missiles, that nowhere betwixt them, however closely he might draw in his limbs, could there be room for him to stand unscathed. But no man shrank. Our soldiers, still panting with the violence of their labor in crossing the river and scaling the bank, scarcely fired a shot, and they did not speak; but they every one went forward. The truth is, that the weak-hearted men had been left behind in the gardens and buildings of the village; the dross was below, and the force on the hill-side was pure metal. It was so intent on its purpose, that no one, they say, at this time was seen to cast back a look toward the 1st Division.

The assailants were nearing the breastwork, when, after a lull of a few moments, its ordnance all thundered at once, or, at least, so nearly at the same moment, that the pathway of their blast was a broad one; and there were many who fell; but the onset of our soldiery was becoming a rush. Codrington, riding in front of the men, gayly cheered them on; and all who were not struck down by shot pressed on toward the long bank of smoke which lay dimly infolding the redoubt.

But already—though none of the soldiery engaged then knew who wrought the spell—a hard stress had been put upon the enemy. For a while, indeed, the white bank of smoke, lit through here and there with the slender flashes of musketry, stood fast in the front of the parapet, and still all but shrouded the helmets and the glittering bayonets within; but it grew more thin; it began to rise; and, rising, it disclosed a grave change in the counsels of the Russian Generals. Some Englishmen—or many perhaps at the same moment—looking keen through the smoke, saw teams of artillery horses moving, and there was a sound of ordnance wheels. Our panting soldiery broke from their silence. 'By all that is holy! he is limbering up!' 'He is carrying off his guns!' 'Stole away! Stole away! Stole away.' The glacis of the Great Redoubt had come to sound more joyous than the covert's side in England.

The embrasures were empty, and in rear of the work long artillery teams—eight-horse and ten-horse teams—were rapidly dragging off the guns.

Then a small, childlike youth ran forward before the throng, carrying a color. This was young Anstruther. He carried the Queen's color of the Royal Welsh. Fresh from the games of English school life, he ran fast; for, heading all who strove to keep up with him, he gained the redoubt, and dug the butt end of the flag-staff into the parapet, and there for a moment he stood holding it tight and taking breath. Then he was shot dead; but his small hands, still clasping the flag-staff, drew it down along with him, and the crimson silk lay covering the boy with its folds; but only for a moment, because William Evans, a swift-footed soldier, ran forward, gathered up the flag, and, raising it proudly, made claim to the Great Redoubt on behalf of the 'Royal Welsh.[1] The colors, floating high in the air, and seen by our people far and near, kindled in them a raging love for the ground where it stood. Breathless men found speech. Codrington, still in the front, uncovered his head, waved his cap for a sign to his people, and then riding straight at one of the embrasures, leaped his gray Arab into the breastwork. There were some eager and swift-footed soldiers who sprang the parapet nearly at the same moment; more followed. At the same instant Norcott's riflemen came running in from the east, and the swiftest of them bounded into the work at its right flank. The enemy's still lingering skirmishers began to fall back, and descended—some of them slowly—into the dip where their battalions were massed. Our soldiery were up; and in a minute they flooded in over the parapet, hurrahing, jumping over, hurrahing, a joyful English crowd.

The cheer had not yet died away on the hill-side when from the enemy's battalions standing massed in the hollow there rose up—as though it had been wrung from the very hearts of brave men defeated—a long, sorrowful, wailing sound. This was the bitter and wholesome grief of a valiant soldiery not content to yield. For men who so grieve there is hope. The redoubt had been seized by our people; it was not yet lost to the Czar.

There was only one piece of ordnance remaining in the work. This was a brass 24-pound howitzer. At the sight of the piece (for our people were mainly of Anglo-Saxon blood), a characteristic desire to assert the claims of private ownership

[1] Afterward, there being a punctilio which governs those matters in our service, William Evans delivered the color to his superior, Corporal Soulbey, and Corporal Soulbey delivered it to Sergeant Luke O'Connor. Sergeant Luke O'Connor, though he soon got badly wounded, would not part with the honor of carrying the cherished standard, and he bore it all the rest of the day.

began to seize upon the crowd; and more than one man, so they say, scratched his mark upon the piece, that he might make it the peculiar trophy of himself or his regiment.

But there was a better prize than this within the reach of a nimble soldier;[1] for of the guns moving off toward the rear, there was one which, dragged by only three horses, had scarcely yet gained the rear of the redoubt. Captain Bell, of the Royal Welsh, ran up, overtook it, and pointing his capless pistol at the head of the driver, ordered him, or rather signed to him, to stop instantly and dismount. The driver sprang from his saddle and fled. Bell seized the bridle of the near horse, and he had already turned the gun round, when Sir George Brown riding up angry, and ordering him to go to his company, he of course obeyed, yet not until he had effectually started the horses in the right direction; for they drew the gun down the hill, and the capture became complete.[2]

Bell went back to his corps, and in truth his services there were soon about to be needed; for already Colonel Chester, commanding the regiment, had been killed, and Campbell, who then took the command, being afterwards struck down, the charge of the regiment devolved upon Bell.

Of the men of the five regiments which had moved forward from the top of the river's bank, many now lay upon the hill-side dead or wounded; and the 7th Fusileers, with fragments of other regiments, was still engaged with the enemy's infantry; but the greatest portions of four battalions,[3] and a wing of another battalion,[4] were now upon the ground which the enemy had made his strong-hold.

Yet the tendency to converge toward the redoubt as their goal had so closely compressed the assailing mass, that its front now hardly outflanked the parapet; and all the assailants of the redoubt were either within the work or closely gathered round it.

They were perhaps 2000 men, and their onset had for the moment so bewildered the enemy that, having close at hand

[1] When troops obtain possession of a gun left by the enemy in a field-work, they are not said to have 'taken a gun' in the true and highest sense of the phrase. It is only by the observance of this distinction that the Duke of Wellington can be said to have 'never lost a gun.' He surely, for instance, abandoned guns at Burgos; but because they were left by him in the works, and not taken from him in the field, the acquisition of them by the enemy was not a capture.

[2] The gun is now at Woolwich. The horses served for some time in our 'Black Battery.'

[3] The 33rd, the 'Royal Welsh' (or 23rd), the 'Derbies' (95th), and the 19th.

[4] 2nd battalion Rifle Brigade.

great masses of infantry, unbroken and scarcely touched—masses numbering full 10,000 bayonets—he nevertheless hung back, and for a while did little to molest our people in their occupation of the work. Our soldiery were well inclined to rest and make themselves at home; and Codrington, alighting from his horse, began to show the men how best to establish themselves on the ground they had won by lying down outside the parapet, and resting their rifles upon its top.

Thus the assaulting force had carried the great field-work which was the key of the enemy's position on the Alma; and if at this time the supporting Division had been half way up the hill, or even if it had been beginning to crown the banks of the river on the Russian side, the toils and perils of the day would perhaps have been over. But our men were only a crowd; and they, all of them, wise and simple, now began to learn in the great school of action, that the most brilliant achievement by a disordered mass of soldiery requires the speedy support of formed troops.

No supports yet coming up from the top of the river's bank.

Then—and then, as is said, for the first time—the men cast back a look toward the quarter from which they might hope to see supports advancing; but when they carried their eyes down the slope strewn thick with the wounded and the dead, they saw that, from the ground where they stood down home to the top of the river's bank, there were no succors coming.

## XXIII.

Where were the supports?

The Duke of Cambridge.

The Duke of Cambridge is the grandson of King George III., and a cousin of the Queen. At the outbreak of the war he was 35 years of age. He had made the most of such experience as could be gained by following the vocation of a military life in the British Isles. He understood the mechanism of our army system, and, so far as could be judged by the test of home service, he was a good and a diligent soldier. Nay, he had some qualifications for command which are not very common in England. He loved order, method, and organization. Long before the war it had been said that he was gifted with that faculty of moving troops which is one of the prime qualifications of a general officer; and the skill with which his superb Division had been now deployed seemed to give safe ground for saying that the flattering rumor was true. He was zealous and devoted to duty. He had the habit of exercising forethought. He was sagacious, and was more keenly alive than most other men of our land-service to passing and coming events. He had a good military eye.[1]

He was a great respecter of the public voice in England, and was even, perhaps, too ready to suffer himself to be swayed by light, transient breezes of 'opinion.' He had no dread of innovations, and the beard that clothed his frank, handsome, manly face was the symbol of his adhesion to a then new revolt against custom. He was much loved, for he was of a genial temper; and his rank was so well helped out by his hereditary faculty of remembering those with whom he had once conversed that —far from chilling his intercourse with other men—it enabled him to give happy effect to the kindliness of his nature. But, after all, what a general has to do is to try to overcome the enemy by exposing his own soldiery to all needful risks. At any fit time he must be willing and eager to bring his own people to the slaughter for the sake of making havoc with the enemy; and it is right for him to be able to do this without at the time being seen to feel one pang. Nay, however certain it may be that his gentler nature will overcome him on the morrow, it is well for him to be able to pass through the bloodiest hours of battle with something of a ruthless joy. The Duke of Cambridge was wanting in this kind of truculence; and, however careless of his own life (for he had the personal courage of his race), he was liable to be cruelly wrung by the weight of a command which charged him with the lives of other men. He was of an anxious temperament; and with him the danger was that, in moments when great stress might come to be put upon him, the very keenness of his desire to judge aright would become a cruel hinderance. Nor was he a man who who would be driven to burst his way though scruples and doubts by the impulse of any selfish ambition. Far from straining after occasions for acting on his own judgment, he would have liked, if he could, to receive a series of precise orders which would serve to guide him in every successive change. But a general of division must not expect to be long in a campaign without being thrown upon his own judgment. Lord Raglan had furnished the Duke with one order—an order 'to support the Light Division in its forward movement'

[1] A few words which fell from Lord Raglan in October, 1854, have caused me, perhaps, to speak with more confidence on this subject than I might otherwise venture to show. In that month—I believe on the 15th—Lord Raglan spoke to me of the exceeding anxiety of the Duke of Cambridge about the Inkerman position, and he said that in consequence of this pressure measures had been taken. Exactly three weeks afterward the very ground about which the Duke had been so anxious was the scene of the mighty onslaught which commenced the battle of Inkerman.

—and the Duke of Cambridge had begun to obey it by following the advance of the Light Division, and bringing his force home down to the inclosures; but, having thus come to the end of the open ground, he felt the want of some new sanction before he carried his Division into the vineyards. He knew that, for a while at least, the superb array of his Guards and Highlanders would be shattered by passing through inclosures, and he wished for another order from head-quarters before he submitted to see his beautiful line broken up. The order 'to 'support the Light Division' was becoming an imperfect guide, because that same Light Division had rushed headlong upon a task which was dissolving great part of it into a vast swarm of skirmishers. Were the Guards and Highlanders to do the like? Were they to do thus, although their efficacy as a force acting in support of the troops in advance was likely to depend upon their being able to come up in good order? The 1st Division was halted; yet the Light Division was moving rapidly forward.

Halt of the 1st Division before entering the vineyards.

Why was there this failure of concert between the Light and the 1st Division? Why was there no man there who could link the one division to the other by a few decisive words?

Lord Raglan had already given his orders, and at this moment, led forward by a golden chance, he was riding far away in another part of the field. Sir George Brown, already in the inclosures, and having no line of skirmishers to cover the advance of his battalions, was unable to govern the movements of his Division in such a way as to prevent it from getting too far in advance of the Guards and Highlanders; and afterward, when Sir George went forward in person with that part of his Division which stormed the Redoubt, he seems to have found no means of communicating with the Duke of Cambridge and pressing for the immediate support of the 1st Division.

Every moment was precious; for the men of the Light Division were moving down at a run through the vineyards, or wading across the river.

At the time of this halt the battalion of the Grenadier Guards was across the great road. Thither now from the west a horseman came galloping up. Of an actual order General Airey was not the bearer; but he was a man whose loyalty toward his chief made him always feel certain that what he himself saw clearly to be right was exactly what his chief desired to have done, and the result was that, in an emergency, he was able to speak with a weight which virtually brought to bear upon the matter in hand the whole power of

General Airey comes up.

Head-quarters. His keen eye had detected the halt of the 1st Division, and he saw also that the Light Division was pushing forward at a run. Another man would have gone round or sent to the commander of the forces for his opinion; but every moment of the lapsing time was bringing danger.

His exposition of the order to advance in support.

Airey rode straight up to General Bentinck,[1] and explained it to be Lord Raglan's meaning that the 1st Division should instantly continue its advance in support of the Light Division. 'Must we,' asked Bentinck, 'must we always keep within three hundred yards of the 'Light Division?' 'No,' said Airey, 'not necessarily at any 'fixed distance; that would not be possible. What his Royal 'Highness has to do is to support the Light Division by ad- 'vancing in conformity with its movements.' Then the 1st Division moved forward, and, breaking into the inclosures, began to work its difficult way through the vineyards.

The 1st Division resumes its advance.

The Division again stopped for a time.

Afterwards—but not, it seems, by any formal order to halt —the advance of the 1st Division was again stopped for a time: yet Codrington's brigade had then begun to rush forward. From the ground on which he was riding, Sir De Lacy Evans could see in profile the swift disordered advance of Codrington's brigade, and the stop to which the 1st Division had come. He understood the danger; and, comprehending at once that the advance of Codrington's brigade was a movement requiring instant support, he took upon himself to send a message conveying his opinion to the Duke of Cambridge.

Step taken by Evans.

Want of free communication along a line passing through inclosures.

But when a division of infantry extended in line is marched through gardens and walled inclosures, the power of the general commanding it must always be more or less thrown into abeyance, because the want of an unobstructed view and of free lateral communication makes it impossible for him to know what is going on along the whole line, or to send swift orders to the more distant companies. For a time his authority is necessarily dispersed among many; and if the force is moving deliberately and in face of an enemy, numbers of little councils of war will of necessity be going on here and there, in order to judge how best to deal with what seems to be the state of the battle in each field, each garden, each vineyard.

The right of the 1st Division was formed by the brigade of

[1] Lord Raglan had made an order specially providing that the bearer of an order for a divisional general should deliver it to the first brigadier whom he happened to find, to be by him transmitted to the divisional chief.

The Guards. 'Guards.' In its origin, the appellation given to the regiments called 'the Guards' imported that the personal safety of the sovereign was peculiarly committed to their charge. Princes have imagined that by specially ascribing this duty to a particular portion of their armed forces, rather than to the whole, and by granting some privileges to troops specially distinguished as their chosen defenders, they secure to themselves good means of safety in time of trouble, and that still, upon the whole, they do more good than harm to their military system by establishing a healthy spirit of rivalry between the favored body and the rest of the army. The danger is, that a corps thus set apart will come to be considered as a great reserve of military strength, and that, for that very reason, any disaster which it may sustain will be looked upon as more ruinous than a disaster of equal proportions occurring to other regiments.

With us, the corps of Guards numbers only seven battalions, distributed into three regiments, called the Grenadier Guards, the Coldstream, and the Scots Fusileer Guards; and each of these three regiments had sent one battalion to form the brigade of Guards now serving in the 1st Division. The officers of the corps enjoy some privileges tending to accelerate their advancement in the army. They are, for the most part, men well born or well connected; and, being aided by a singularly able body of sergeants and corporals, they are not so overburdened in peace-time by their regimental duties as to have their minds in the condition which too often results from monotonous labor. They have deeply at heart the honor of the whole brigade as well as of their respective corps, and the feeling is quickened by a sense of the jealousy which their privileges breed, or rather, perhaps, by the tradition of that ancient rivalry which exists between the 'Guards' and the 'Line.'

The men of the rank and file have some advantages over the Line in the way of allowances and accoutrements. They are all of fine stature. Without being over-drilled, they are well enough practiced in their duties; and whoever loves war, sees grandeur in the movement of the stately forms and the towering bearskins which mark a battalion of the Guards. It is true that these household troops are cut off from the experience gained by Line regiments in India and the Colonies; but, whenever England is at war in Europe, or against people of European descent, it is the custom and the pride of the Guards to take their part.

The force is deeply prized by the Queen, and the class from which it takes its officers connects it with many families of high station in the country. Its officers have so many relatives and friends amongst those who generate conversation in London, that when 'the Guards' are sent upon active service, the war in which they engage becomes, as it were for their sake, a subject of interest in circles which commonly yield only a languid attention to events beyond the seas. Grief for the death of Line officers is dispersed among the counties of the three kingdoms; and when they fall in battle, it is the once merry country-house, the vicarage, or the wayside cottage of some old Peninsular officer, that becomes the house of mourning. But by the loss of officers of the household regiments the central body of English society is touched, is shocked, is almost angered; and he who has to sit in his saddle and see a heavy slaughter of the 'Guards,' may be almost forced to think ruefully of fathers, of mothers, of wives, of sisters, who are amongst his own friends.

There was nothing in the history or traditions of the famous corps of 'the Guards' to justify the notion that they were to be more often kept out of the brunt of the battle than the troops of the line; and in this very war they were destined to encounter the hardest trials of soldiers, and to go on fighting and enduring until the glory of past achievements, the strange ascendency which those achievements had won, and a few score of wan men with hardly the garb of soldiers, should be all that remained of 'the Guards.' Still it is certain that the household battalions were more or less regarded as a cherished body of troops, and that the loss of the brigade of Guards would be looked upon as a loss more signal, and in that sense more disastrous than the loss of three other battalions of equal strength.

Now the enemy, whilst he dealt with the tumultuous onset of Codrington's brigade, had rightly enough given some of his care to the more ceremonious advance of the 1st Division; and, since the Guards confronted both the Causeway batteries and the Great Redoubt, they of course underwent for a time a fire of artillery, and some men were struck down.[1] The Grenadiers and the Scots Fusileers suffered the most. This loss did not occur as a consequence of any mistake: it was in the order of things that it should be. But, when men are new to war, and so placed in the battle-field as to be for the moment cut off from all knowledge of what is going on elsewhere, they are prone to imagine that a force which they see undergoing slaughter, yet having no immediate means of attack or resistance,

[1] Even when the Great Redoubt had been dismantled, and the Causeway batteries withdrawn, there were some guns in battery at more remote spots, which seem to have been brought to bear on the Guards.

must needs be the victim of some piece of forgetfulness or error; and when once this notion has got its lodgment in the brain of an officer, his next step probably is to try to avert what he fancies to be an impending disaster by venturing to disobey orders, or by counseling another to do so.

'The brigade of Guards will be destroyed,' said one adviser; and he asked whether it ought not to fall back a little in order to recover its formation?

Suggestion that the Guards should fall back in order to re-form.

These words were spoken by an officer not holding any high rank,[1] and they owe their whole importance to the answer which they elicited and the propulsion which thereupon followed.

He who answered the question was a veteran soldier, and it was with a deference no less wise than graceful that the Duke of Cambridge loved to seek and to follow his counsels.

Sir Colin Campbell.

Whilst Ensign Campbell was passing from boyhood to man's estate, he was made partaker in the great transactions which were then beginning to work out the liberation of Europe. In the May of 1808 he received his first commission—a commission in the 6th Foot—and a few weeks afterward—then too young to carry the colors—he was serving with his regiment upon the heights of Vimieira. There the lad saw the turning of a tide in human affairs, saw the opening of the mighty strife between 'Column' and 'Line,'[2] saw France—long unmatched upon the Continent—retreating before British infantry, saw the first of Napoleon's stumbles, and the fame of Sir Arthur Wellesley beginning to dawn over Europe.

He was in Sir John Moore's campaign, and at its closing

[1] I foresee that what I here say as to the obscure rank of the officer who made this suggestion will be regarded by some as inaccurate; and, indeed, I am aware that the belief of those who hold the contrary of this to be true is based upon grounds apparently strong. I did not hear the words myself; and all I can say is, that my statement is founded upon authority which makes me feel certain that I do rightly in making it; though I also think I am right in saying that I did not myself hear the words. If my statement as to the obscure rank of the officer is true, it follows, I think, that I am right in not disclosing his name, because (upon that supposition) his words had no sort of importance beyond that attributed to them in the text.

[2] In his most interesting and most valuable 'Life of the Duke of Wellington,' Mr. Gleig repeats the description of Vimieira, which the Duke once gave in his presence at Strathfieldsaye. The Duke's words are thus given by Mr. Gleig:—'The French came on on that occasion with great boldness, 'and seemed to feel their way less than I always found them to do after- 'ward. They came on, as usual, in very heavy columns, and I received them 'in line, which they were not accustomed to, and we repulsed them three 'several times.'

scene—Corunna. He was with the Walcheren expedition; and afterward, returning to the Peninsula, he was at the battle of Barossa, the defense of Tarifa, the relief of Taragona, and the combats at Malaga and Osma. He led a forlorn hope at the storming of St. Sebastian, and was there wounded twice. He was at Vittoria; he was at the passage of the Bidassoa; he took part in the American war of 1814; he served in the West Indies; he served in the Chinese war of 1842. These occasions he had so well used that his quality as a soldier was perfectly well known. He had been praised, and praised again and again; but since he was not so connected as to be able to move the dispensers of military rank, he gained promotion slowly, and it was not until the second Sikh war that he had a command as a general: even then he had no rank in the army above that of a colonel. At Chilianwalla he commanded a division. Marching in person with one of his two brigades, he had gained the heights on the extreme right of the Sikh position, and then bringing round the left shoulder, he had rolled up the enemy's line and won the day; but since his other brigade (being separated from him by a long distance) had wanted his personal control, and fallen into trouble, the brilliancy of the general result which he had achieved did not save him altogether from criticism. That day he was wounded for the fourth time. He commanded a division at the great battle of Gujerat; and, being charged to press the enemy's retreat, he had so executed his task that 158 guns and the ruin of the foe were the fruit of the victory. In 1851 and the following year he commanded against the hill-tribes. It was he who forced the Kohat Pass. It was he who, with only a few horsemen and some guns, at Punj Pao, compelled the submission of the combined tribes then acting against him with a force of 8000 men. It was he who, at Ishakote, with a force of less than 3000 men, was able to end the strife; and when he had brought to submission all those beyond the Indus who were in arms against the Government, he instantly gave proof of the breadth and scope of his mind, as well as of the force of his character; for he withstood the angry impatience of men in authority over him, and insisted that he must be suffered to deal with the conquered people in the spirit of a politic and merciful ruler.

After serving with all this glory for some forty-four years, he came back to England; but between the Queen and him there stood a dense crowd of families—men, women, and children—extending farther than the eye could reach, and armed with strange precedents, which made it out to be right that people who had seen no service should be invested with high command, and that Sir Colin Campbell should be only a colonel. Yet he was of so fine a nature that, although he did not always avoid great bursts of anger, there was no ignoble bitterness in his sense of wrong. He awaited the time when perhaps he might have high command, and be able to serve his country in a sphere proportioned to his strength. His friends, however, were angry for his sake; and, along with their strong devotion toward him, there was bred a fierce hatred of a system of military dispensation which could keep in the background a man thus tried and thus known.

Upon the breaking out of the war with Russia, Sir Colin was appointed—not to the command of a division, but of a brigade. It was not till the June of 1854 that his rank in the army became higher than that of a colonel.

Campbell was not the slave, he was the master of his calling, and therefore it was that he had been able to save his intellect from the fate of being drowned in military details. He knew that, although a general must have a complete mastery of even the smallest of such things, still they were only a part —a minute though essential part—of the great science of war. He understood the precious material whereof our army is formed. He heartily loved our soldiery; for he was a soldier, and had fellow-feeling with soldiers, and they had fellow-feeling with him. Instinctively they knew that together they might do great things—he by their help, they by his. Knowing the worth of their devotion and their bodily strength, he cherished them with watchful care; and they, on their part, loved, honored, and obeyed him with a faith that all he ordered was right. He set great store upon discipline, but it was never for discipline's sake that he did so (as if that were itself an end), but because he knew it to be one of the main sources of military ascendency. So, although the officers and soldiers serving under him got no more rest than was good for them, they were never vexed wantonly; and, in proportion as they grew in knowledge of their calling, they came to understand why it was that their chief compelled them to toil.

A bodily ardor for fighting may be more or less masked and hidden; but he to whom this great passion is wanting is without the quality of a general. For warfare is so anxious and complex a business that against every vigorous movement heaps of reasons can forever be found; and if a man is so cold a lover of battle as to have no stronger guide than the poor balance of the arguments and counter-arguments which he addresses to his troubled spirit, his mind, driven first one way and then another, will oscillate, or even revolve, turning miserably in its own axis and making no movement straight forward. Now it is a characteristic still marking the Scottish blood, that often — and not the less so when it flows in the veins of a gentle-hearted being—it is seen to fire strangely and suddenly at the prospect of a fight. Campbell loved warfare with a deep passion; and at the thought of battle his grand, rugged face used to kindle with uncontrollable joy.

'The brigade of Guards will be destroyed; ought it not to 'fall back?' When Sir Colin Campbell heard this saying, his blood rose so high that the answer he gave—impassioned and far-resounding—was of a quality to govern events.

Campbell's answer to the suggestion that the Guards should fall back.

'It is better, sir, that every man of Her Majesty's Guards 'should lie dead upon the field than that they 'should now turn their backs upon the enemy.' Doubts and questionings ceased. The Division went forward.

Advance of the 1st Division to the left bank of the river.

Sir Colin Campbell rode off to his left. His brigade at this time was not under a heavy fire, and he effected the operation of passing the river very simply; for, without attempting formal evolutions, each of his regiments, whilst it advanced, tried to keep up, as well as the nature of the ground would allow, the rudiments of its line formation, and when it gained the opposite bank its array was carefully restored. As soon as one of the regiments was duly formed on the Russian side of the river it was moved forward, and, since the ground presented more obstacles toward our left than toward our right, the brigade fell naturally, and without design, into direct échelon of regiments. The 42nd was in advance; on the left of that regiment there was the 93rd, somewhat refused; and on the left of the 93rd, but still farther refused, there came the 79th.

Meanwhile the Guards descended toward the bank with so much of the line formation as was permitted by the obstacles they had to overcome. Upon gaining the river's side, the Coldstream broke into open column of sections, in order to make the most advantage of the ford; and when it reached the opposite bank it preserved its column formation for a time, in order to march the more conveniently round an elbow there formed by the river. When this movement was complete, the color-sergeants went out to take ground, and the battalion opened out into line formation with all the precision and ceremony of a birthday review. On the right of this battalion, and moving with less deliberation, the Scots Fusileer Guards got through the inclosures and the river. On the right of that last corps there marched the battalion of the Grenadier Guards. The Grenadiers were a body of men so well instructed and so skillfully handled, that in working their way through the inclosures they were able to preserve all the essential elements of their line formation.[1] When they came to the bank, they looked for no ford, but, treating the river as a brook — as a brook which a soldier must pass without picking his way[2]— the battalion marched through it in line;[3] and though there were some points where a passage was easy, others where the soldiers had to wade deep, and some few, so they say, where the men were put to their swimming, still each file kept its place in the line with a near approach to exactness. At length —but after a painful lapse of time, for Codrington's disordered battalions were clinging all this while to the parapet of the Great Redoubt—the brigade of Guards stood halted, and forming anew under cover of the bank on the Russian side of the river. Their people were sheltered; but the heads of their colors, protruding a little above the top of the bank, could be seen by men looking down from the redoubt.

*Time was lapsing.*

But already there was nearly an end of the precious moments in which it was possible for the 1st Division to bring an effective support to the troops in the Great Redoubt.

*No support brought by the two battalions which remained under Buller.*

Nor did General Buller succeed in bringing his battalions to the rescue. We saw that the 19th regiment had slipped from his control, and joined with Codrington's brigade in storming the redoubt. The two battalions which remained in his power were the 88th and the 77th Regiments. He was in person with the 88th, some way above the bank of the river; and the 77th, under the orders of Colonel Egerton, was on the extreme left of the English infantry line. The 88th and the 77th were not at this time under fire; but before them, at somewhat long distances, there were heavy columns of Russian infantry; and the enemy's horsemen, though not, it seems, visible at this moment, were known to be hovering on the left front of the English line. Buller, however, had not yet apprehended that the Russians were preparing any enterprise against his left flank; and when he saw how matters

*The cause of this.*

[1] No less than seven of the officers serving with this battalion had acted as adjutants of the regiment, and to this circumstance the skill with which it was carried through the inclosures is in some measure ascribed.

[2] For very good reasons, soldiers in marching are called upon to go straight through brooks and pools of water without picking their way.

[3] With the exception of one (the 2nd) company, commanded by Prince Edward of Saxe-Weimar, which, happening to be near the bridge, filed over it.

stood in the redoubt, he rightly determined to advance at once with the two battalions which remained under his control. He therefore sent an order to Colonel Egerton, directing him at once to move forward with the 77th, and he himself prepared to advance at the same moment with the 88th.

Colonel Egerton was a firm, able man, and he felt the momentous importance of the duties attaching upon an officer who had charge of the extreme left of our infantry line; for it was obvious that a successful flank attack upon the one battalion which he commanded would bring into grievous jeopardy the whole array, English and French. The dips and hollows which marked the hill-side toward his left made it hard for him to see what the enemy was intending to do, and he failed to infer that the Czar's renowned forces were really abstaining from the enterprise which seemed to be almost forced upon them by the nakedness of our left wing, and by their strength in the cavalry arm. At the moment when Buller's order was brought to him, Colonel Egerton was so deeply impressed with a sense of the danger which he had to withstand in this part of the field, that—deliberately, and with a firmness which might have won him great praise, if the actual course of events had brought him his justification—he took upon himself a grave burden. He took upon himself to say that, in the circumstances in which he stood, he ought not to obey the order. This answer the aid-de-camp carried back to General Buller. Buller was a near-sighted man;[1] and being, it would seem, distrustful of what had been his own impression of the enemy's attitude, he acquiesced in Colonel Egerton's decision, allowed the 77th to remain where it was, and not only refrained from advancing with the 88th, but threw the regiment into square, as though it were about to be attacked by cavalry.

XXIV.

State of things in the Redoubt.

So when the men of Codrington's force looked back to whence they came, and when also they looked to their left rear, they saw they were alone — still alone—upon the hill-side. Then such of them as had the instinct of war began to understand that the blood of their comrades had been shed in vain.

For they were only clusters of men without the strength of

[1] It has already been said that Sir George Brown, who commanded the Division, and Codrington, who commanded its 1st brigade, were both of them near-sighted. The Light Division was the force which had to feel and fight its way to the key of the position, and it was an error to allow it to be carried into action by three near-sighted generals.

order, and masses of infantry, in a perfect state of formation, were heavily impending over them. The columns which were the nearest to them were in the dip behind the redoubt, and so placed that, without any danger to them, a Russian battery, which had been planted higher up on the side of the Kourganè Hill, could throw its fire into the site of the redoubt. The guns of this battery were soon brought to bear upon those of our soldiery who were within the redoubt; and this fire, after killing and wounding several men, drove the rest to seek cover by betaking themselves to the outer side of the parapet. This movement, though it wanted the sanction of orders, was scarcely wrong or unsoldierly; for, since the men were without formation, their duty became like the duty of skirmishers, and the parapet of the redoubt supplied that kind of shelter which the need of the moment demanded. Yet the movement looked like the beginning of a retreat, and Codrington strove to check it; for, being at the moment on the outside of the work, he for the second time put his horse at the parapet, and again entered the redoubt, with a hope that the men would follow him in once more. But this time his example was little observed; for almost every man being driven, by want of formation, to rely upon his own means of making a stand, was busied with the work of settling himself down, as well as he could, for a stubborn defense; and it was plain (as Codrington himself had been showing the men some few minutes before) that the best ground for making a stand was the foot of the parapet, on its outer side.

A battery on the higher slopes of the hill brought to bear on the men.

Our men lodge themselves outside the parapet.

When good infantry soldiers, in the immediate presence of a powerful enemy, are disordered, but still undaunted, the slightest rudiment of a field-work is of infinite value to it, not simply nor chiefly on account of the shelter which it affords, but rather because it gives a base and nucleus for that coherence which is endangered by the want of formation. If our men, then lying or kneeling along the foot of the parapet, had been well covered at the flanks, it would have been their duty to hold the ground firmly against even a great body of infantry attacking them in front.

But on either flank, as well as in front of the lengthened crowd of English soldiery which lay clustering about the parapet, the enemy's masses were gathered. On their right rear there was the double battalion column of the Kazan corps, still engaged with the 7th Fusileers. On their left and left front there were the two remaining battalions of the Kazan corps, and the four battalions of the Sousdal corps; but in their im-

The forces gathered against them.

mediate front, and posted in the hollow behind the redoubt, they had before them the four superb battalions of the Vladimir Regiment. These forces were supported by the four battalions of the Ouglitz corps, which stood massed in one column on a higher slope of the Kourganè Hill. The two battalions of sailors also were in this part of the field; and, besides the battery which armed the lèsser field-work, and the one which commanded the dismantled redoubt, there were two batteries of artillery held in reserve. Moreover, 3000 horsemen were close at hand on the enemy's extreme right. Thus (omitting the Kazan column, which was occupied with the 7th Fusileers) there was impending over our 2000 men, then kneeling or lying down by the parapet of the redoubt, a force of some 14,000 cavalry and infantry in a state of perfect formation, and supported by powerful batteries.

Warlike indignation of the Russian infantry on the Kourganè Hill.

And by this time there had sprung up amongst the Russian infantry on the slopes of the Kourganè Hill a sentiment of warlike indignation. Any Russian officer who had been standing on ground high enough to command a view of the river, must have seen that from the moment of their first onset on the left bank, the troops which stormed the redoubt were an isolated, and for the most part a disordered force; and even for some minutes after seeing them carry the work, he would be unable to make out that any supports moved up from the river were coming as yet to their aid. Naturally he would be shamed to think that many thousands of the once famous Russian infantry had been yielding up the Great Redoubt to a body which might almost be called a mere flush of skirmishers. Besides, it was known by this time in some of the Russian battalions that, of the pieces which had armed the redoubt, two were wanting, and to recover these there arose a burning desire. Unless the stain was to be lasting, it seemed clear that the redcoats still clinging to the dismantled redoubt must be driven at once down the hill.

Movement of the Ouglitz column.

Without, it seems, receiving any orders from head-quarters, or from the divisional commander, the great column formed of the Ouglitz battalions, and posted on the high ground above the redoubt, began to come swiftly down the hill; and for a few moments it came on, hot with zeal or anger, for the men of the front ranks fired vain, passionate shots whilst they marched, and young soldiers in the centre of the column kept shooting wildly into the air above them. Soon, however, this body was halted.[1]

[1] No mention is made of this movement in the Russian accounts, and I

But it was in the great Vladimir column that there sprang up the warlike spirit which was destined to bring the foot soldiery of Russia and of England into a closer strife. The column, as we have seen, was a mass composed of the four battalions of the Vladimir corps; and although it stood near to the English soldiery lying clustered along the outer side of the parapet, still, since it was in the dip behind the rear of the earth-work, it could not be perfectly seen even by such of our men as might be standing up, and could not be seen at all by those who were lying down or kneeling.

Advance of the Vladimir column.

For the honor of having led this high-mettled column against English infantry, two men contend. From the time when Prince Mentschikoff rode off toward the sea, Prince Gortschakoff had been left in command of the whole of the forces opposed to the English; and General Kvetzinski, who commanded the Division to which the Vladimir battalions belonged, was under Prince Gortschakoff's orders. Each of these generals says that (without knowing of the presence of the other) he gave orders for the advance of the column, and led it on in person. Their statements may perhaps be reconciled, for it is possible that Gortschakoff and Kvetzinski—the one riding with the left, the other with the right of the column—may have, both of them, done what they said they did. In that view of the matter, the coincidence would be accounted for by supposing that the resolve of each of the two Generals sprang from the same cause—sprang from the warlike anger which was heaving the mass. I am, however, inclined to believe that Prince Gortschakoff is mistaken in his statement;[1] and that the impulse which he gave to the Vladimir columns was after the movement now spoken of. Be this as it may, it is certain enough that—either alone, or jointly with Prince Gortschakoff—Kvetzinski led on the column.

These troops of the 16th Division had been touched with the warlike fire which a patriot priesthood can draw from Gospels, Epistles, and Psalms. With the baggage of the Division there was carried an image of the blessed Sergius; and when these troops were ordered to the south, the Archbishop of Moscow had taken care to whet them for the strife. "Chil-

imagine that it was a spontaneous movement soon stopped by orders from some one in authority. The movement was observed by English officers so placed as to command a view of this part of the field, and if I am guilty of any error, it is the error of ascribing the movement to the wrong corps.

[1] I found this belief upon a comparison of Prince Gortschakoff's statements with the known facts.

"dren of the Czar"—so ran the Primate's blessing—"Children "of the Czar our father, and Russia our mother, my warrior "brethren! The Czar, your country, the Christian faith, call "you to great deeds, and the prayers of the Church and coun-"try are with you. . . . Should it be the will of God that you "too face the foe, forget not that you are doing battle for the "most pious Czar, for our beloved country, for holy Church, "against infidels, against persecutors of the Christian faith—"persecutors of men united to us by ties of religion and of "blood—insulters of those who bow before the Holy Places, "sanctified by the birth, passion, and ascension of Christ. "Blessing and honor to him who conquers! Blessing and "happiness to him who, with faith in God, and love for his "Czar and country, offers up his life as a sacrifice! It is writ-"ten in the Scriptures, concerning those of olden times who "fought for their country, 'By faith were kingdoms conquer-"'ed' (Heb. xi., 33). Now by faith you too shall be conquer-"ors. Our most holy father Sergius whilome blessed our vic-"torious war against the enemies of Russia. His image was "borne in your ranks in the days of the Emperor Alexis, of "Peter the Great, and finally in the great war against twenty "nations in the reign of Alexander the First. That sacred "form journeys with you also as a token of his fervent and be-"seeching prayers to God on your behalf. Take unto your-"selves, moreover, the triumphal war-cry of the Czar and "prophet David, 'In God is my salvation and glory!'"[1]

The Vladimir column came on. It moved slowly, as though it were held in by some kind of awe or doubt. Still it moved, and without firing a shot; for the orders were not to fire, but to charge with the bayonet. Huge and gray, the mass crept gliding up the slope which divided it from our soldiery.

Our men, gathered round the parapet, were kneeling or lying down; and, being thus low, they could not see into the dip which lay at a little distance before them. But mounted officers, of course, could see farther, and even men on foot (especially those near to either flank of the redoubt), if they stood up for a moment to gain a wider view, could see a whole field of bayonet-points, ranged close as corn, and seeming to grow taller and taller. And though none of our men knew the strength of the column which was closing upon them, yet, sometimes from what he himself saw, but more commonly by hearsay, almost every man came to know that, toward the part of the parapet where he lay, there was a mass of Russian soldiery coming.

[1] Psalm li., 8; Eastern Papers, Part vii., p. 50.

Presently the head of the great Vladimir column approached the crest; and our men, whilst they lay with their rifles leveled across the parapet, and their eyes a little above its top, were face to face with the front rank of the mass.

Aspect of the column.

Before it confuses itself by hasty firing, a Russian column in good order is a solemn expression of warlike strength. With the hard, upright outlines of a wall, it is, in its color, a dark cloud; and the lowly beings who compose it are so merged in the grand unity of the mass, that, in the hour of battle, the aspect of it weighs heavy upon the imagination of anxious men. More, a hundredfold more than it is it seems to portend; and now, when the Vladimir column, three thousand strong and withholding its fire, emerged in silence from the hollow, when it slowly grew over the crest and rose up, at last, stark and square between the eyes of our soldiery and the light beyond, its power over the mind of a beholder was less the power of a substance than of a shadow—a shadow approaching—the dim, mighty shadow that is thrown forward by a military empire when it comes in great earnest to the front.

It is certain, however, that, whatever the cause be, some high quality of the soul, or only, after all, a certain hardness of temperament, our people in general are not impressed by the sight of massed infantry in the way that the nations of the Continent are; and, when our soldiers are formed in their English array, they can make merry with a mere column as a thing that is foreign, a thing with vast pretensions to strength, but helpless as a flock of sheep against firm men standing in line. Even now, though our men lay in clusters without formation, they were ready enough to begin shooting into the column; and those who first caught sight of the Russian helmets were going to deliver their fire, when suddenly they were checked by a voice which implored every man to stay his hand.

Confusing rumors amongst our soldiery.

When troops are about to be overpowered, confusing rumors flit round them; and if it happen that these rumors become the immediate causes of a default, they do not for that reason excuse it, because the very spreading of such tales is not the cause, but the effect of the bewildered state into which the troops are lapsing. The voice which had stayed the fire of our men was a voice crying out, "The column is French! the col- "umn is French! Don't fire, men! For God's "sake, don't fire!" The prohibition, repeated again and again, traveled fast along the line; and presently it was farther impressed, for a bugler of the 19th, under orders from a mounted officer, began to sound the "cease firing."

Unauthentic orders and signals to the men.

Our men, obeying the voice and the signal, withheld their fire and remained still. The belief that the column must be French was confirmed—and, indeed, it is likely that it had been caused—by observing that it delivered no fire; and although, if Kvetzinski's statements be accurate, the front rank men had their muskets brought down as though for a charge with the bayonet,[1] still the slow, formal movement of the approaching mass was so little like what the English regard as a 'charge,' that no one seems to have accounted for the silence of their firelocks by suggesting that the movement was intended for an attack with the bayonet. It seems that the column now halted,[2] as if from a suspicion of some snare, or perhaps from a dread of the unknown, for the men of the column could not see the stature of our men, but they saw forage-caps and a crowd of English faces of a fresh-colored hue very strange to their eyes, and they saw the muzzles of rifles leveled thickly across the parapet. From mistake on one side, and misgiving on the other, there had come to be a strange pause. Yet not along the whole line; for, either with a part of the Vladimir column, or else with some other body of troops, two or three of the companies of the 33rd were exchanging, at this time, a sharp fire. Obeying the light, simple motive which sometimes governs the soldier when his mind is a blank, the men of the column took the fancy of pouring the main volume of their shot toward the ground where the colors of the 33rd were upraised. The colors were new; and, as though the mere richness of their crimson folds were enough to draw the eye and the aim of the Russian musketeer, they were riddled, in two or three minutes, with numbers of balls. Of those who stood near them, a large proportion were struck down.[3]

Codrington, seeing that the fruits of the exploit performed by his brigade were going to be lost for want of supports, had already sent his aid-de-camp, Campbell, to press the advance of the Scots Fusileer Guards, the battalion most directly in his

[1] His expression, as rendered from the Russian into French, is "l'arme au "bras, prête à la baionette." This, I suppose, must mean that the front rank men had their bayonets "at the charge," and not merely "at the trail."

[2] The Russian accounts do not speak of this halt. They represent the whole advance of the column as a bayonet charge, and it seems quite true that the column really withheld its fire, but it would be a mistake to suppose that the forward movement of this body was marked with any of the swiftness or violence commonly associated with the idea of a "charge."

[3] I do not see any thing in the Russian narratives which I can identify with the combat in which a part of the 33rd was engaged, and I have not been able to say which of the Russian corps it was with which the 33rd was at this time exchanging fire.

rear. But the very moments then passing were the moments charged with the result, and there were no other and later moments that could ever be used in their stead.

It is said—but my faith in men's impressions of what passed at this minute is wanting in strength—it is said that one of the heavy columns which the enemy had on his extreme right was now seen to be marching upon the left flank of the English soldiery who lay clustered along the parapet of the redoubt,[1] and it seems there are grounds for believing that the left of our line was the spot where a conviction of the necessity of retiring was first acted upon. According to testimony which seems to be trustworthy, a mounted officer[2] rode up to the bugler of the 19th Regiment, and ordered him to sound the "retire." The man obeyed, and buglers along the whole line, from left to right, took up and repeated the signal.

A bugler sounds the 'retire.'

But the instinct of self-preservation, no less than the natural courage and tenacity of the soldier, made almost every man of the force very unwilling to abandon the ground; for it happened that at this time a brisk shower of missiles was passing over the heads of our men without doing them harm, and hearing how thickly the balls were raining into the ground behind them, they knew that a retreat would not only be an abandonment of ground dearly won, but also would bring them at once under a heavy fire. So strong was their conviction of the expediency of holding fast to the ground where they lay, that the sounding of the "retire" was believed to have originated in some error; and in order that they might determine what should be done, the officers of several regiments, but more especially of the 23rd, gathered into a group and began to consult together. Being firm, proud men, with a great self-respect, they did not, it seems, like to crouch for shelter under the parapet whilst they were exchanging counsel; so they conferred standing upright, but under so thick a flight of balls that several—nay, they say almost all of them, were struck down and killed.[3] However,

The troops had a double motive for remaining where they were.

Conference of officers at the parapet. Their fate.

[1] The Russian accounts do not confirm this belief.

[2] Afterward the bugler described the officer in a way which might have enabled a court of inquiry to identify him. He was not an officer of the regiment to which the bugler belonged, and he was not a general officer; and he did not deliver the order as coming from any one other than himself. The incident goes far to justify the opinion of officers who think that (unless it is strictly confined to the business of guiding skirmishers) the use of a bugle during an action is dangerous.

[3] I shall presently give the names of the officers who were killed in the 23rd, and the other regiments which stormed the redoubt, but I can not un-

those who survived continued to say that the sounding of the "retire" must have been a mistake, and that the force ought to hold its ground.

But then again, and from the same quarter as before, a bugle sounded the "retire;" and again, as before, the signal was taken up along the line. The repetition of the signal seemed to make it almost certain that the order must be authentic, but the troops were yet slow to persuade themselves that this was the case, and they still lingered at the parapet. Then a sergeant of the 23rd, standing upright in order to make himself better heard, told the men that they had twice heard the "retire" sounded, and that they must do their duty and obey. Whilst he spoke he was shot down and killed.

The 'retire' again sounded.

But it was now judged by officers and men that a signal twice made, and twice carried on along the line from regiment to regiment, was not to be neglected. The retreat began; and the men, quitting the shelter of the breastwork, fell back into open ground, and incurred the fire which was pelting into the slope beneath.

Our soldiery retreat from the Redoubt.

As the advance had been, so also the retreat was for the most part without order, but for the most part also it was not hurried. Our soldiers, in their retreat, took care to ply the enemy with fire; and they picked up and carried off with them those of our wounded officers and men whom they found lying wounded on the slope. Except in one place, the retreat was like the movement of skirmishers when they find themselves recalled to their battalions by sound of bugle. But a part of the retreating force, consisting mainly of the 23rd and the 95th, got heaped together in an unwieldy crowd, and became, as will be presently seen, the cause of a fresh disaster.

The enemy might have inflicted heavy loss upon the clusters of our soldiery then retreating down the slope, but there was some spell which bound him; for when the Vladimir column had moved forward as far as the parapet of the breastwork, it used a strange abstinence and halted, attempting no movement in pursuit. Of the two missing pieces of ordnance which the enemy had yearned to recover, one, they found, had disappeared,[1] and the other (the howitzer) was lying on the ground

dertake to say which of them fell at this time. In general it seems to be almost beyond the power of human testimony to fix the time and the spot at which an officer falls when he is killed in battle. The difficulty is occasioned—not by the dearth, but by the vast abundance of testimony—testimony all seeming to be perfectly trustworthy, yet strangely contradictory. It will be seen, however, that the number of officers killed in the 23rd was very great, and there is an impression that no small proportion of them met their death in the way above stated.

[1] This was the gun taken by Captain Bell.

dismounted, and was so unwieldy that Kvetzinski says his Vladimir men were unable to drag it away. It remained in the redoubt.

At the moment when this retreat began, the 1st Division had not yet emerged from the cover afforded by the river's bank; but General Codrington's message hurried the forward movement of the Scots Fusileer Guards. The battalion climbed to the summit of the bank, formed line, and advanced.

But whilst this battalion moved forward, the remnant of the men who had stormed the redoubt were coming down the hill, and some of them were huddled in a throng, and bearing toward the left companies of the Scots Fusileer Guards. Therefore the Scots Fusileer Guards received in their advance much of the fire directed against our retreating soldiery, and many were struck down; still the onward movement was maintained, and the Grenadiers on the right, and the Coldstreams on the left of this battalion were now also moving up. But at last the advancing line of the Scots Fusileers and the crowd descending from the redoubt came into bodily contact, and this so roughly, that the retreating crowd, by its sheer weight, broke through the left companies of the Scots Fusileers and destroyed their formation. The weight of the retreating throng at that one spot was so great and so unwieldy, that a soldier of the Scots Fusileers was thrown, it is said, to the ground, and got his ribs fractured. The left companies of the Scots Fusileer Guards, being thrust out of line by physical pressure, fell back in disorder.

At a later moment, some of the men who were retreating, but retreating in less heavy clusters, came down upon the Grenadier Guards. The Grenadiers neatly opened their ranks for the discomfited soldiery, and afterward formed up again, soon recovering their perfect array.

Losses of the regiments which stormed the work.

During this conflict, the four regiments which stormed the redoubt had undergone cruel slaughter. In the 23rd Regiment, besides Colonel Chester, Wynn, Evans, Conolly, Radcliffe, Young, Anstruther, and Butler, and 3 sergeants, were killed; and Campbell, Hopton, Bathurst, Sayer,[1] and Applethwaite, and 9 sergeants, were wounded. Of the rank and file, 40 were killed and 139 wounded.

In the 33rd, Lieutenant Montague and 3 sergeants were killed; and Colonel Blake, Major Gough, Captain Fitzgerald, Wallis, Worthington, Siree, and Greenwood, and 16 sergeants

[1] Sayer was one of those struck down by that salvo-like discharge which preceded the dismantling of the redoubt.

were wounded.[1] Of the rank and file, 52 were killed and 172 were wounded.

In the 95th, Dowdall, Eddington, the younger Eddington, Polhill, Kingsley, Braybrooke, and 3 sergeants, were killed; and Hume, Reyland, Wing, Sargent, Macdonald, Gerard, Braybrooke, Brooke, Boothby, Bazalgette, Gordon, and 12 sergeants, were wounded. Of the rank and file, 42 were killed and 116 wounded.

In the 19th, Stockwell and Wardlow were killed; and Cardew, Saunders, M'Gee, Warden, and Currie, and 4 sergeants, wounded. Of the rank and file, 39 were killed and 170 wounded.

In the Rifles there were 11 killed and 38 wounded, and most of those casualties occurred in the left wing. So, of the four line battalions and the four companies of Rifles which had stormed the redoubt, there was a loss, in killed and wounded, of about 100 officers and sergeants, and 800 men.

XXV.

Cause which paralyzed the Russians in the midst of their success.

But what was the spell which bound the Czar's commanders? and why did they throw back the gifts which seemed to be brought them by the fortune of battle?

When our storming force under Codrington was ascending the glacis in a crowd—in a crowd torn through and through by grape and canister—how came it that the enemy could suddenly make up his mind to stop the massacre, and dismantle his Great Redoubt?

When the remnant of our storming force was flocking back down the hill, why did the enemy spare from destroying it, and bring to a halt his triumphant Vladimir column?

Having several thousands of troops between the Causeway and the Kourganè Hill, why did the Russian Generals suffer Lacy Yea still to keep his stand on open ground with one disordered battalion?

We saw that when Mentschikoff, disturbed by the report of Bosquet's flank movement, rode off in great haste toward the sea, Prince Gortschakoff was left in command of all that part of the Russian army which confronted the English. Kvetzinski,

[1] Colonel Blake would not report his wound, lest the account should alarm his wife and family. His horse was struck in three places. Siree, though badly wounded, insisted upon remaining out on the hill-side all night, in order that men in a worse condition should be first attended to. Wallis was badly wounded, but he tied a handkerchief round the place, and remained with his regiment to the close of the battle. Worthington died from the amputation which was necessitated by the wound he received.

the brave and able general who commanded the division on the Kourganè Hill, was under the orders of Prince Gortschakoff, and as long as the absence of the commander-in-chief was protracted, Gortschakoff was the officer who had to answer for the defense of the Pass and of the whole position thence extending to the extreme right of the Russian army. Every part of the ground thus committed to Prince Gortschakoff's care was precious, but the Kourganè Hill was the key of the whole position on the Alma. There, and there only, the ground had been intrenched. There, and there only, heavy guns had been planted. That barren hill had become the very gage for which the Great Powers of the West and the Czar of All the Russias were to join in a strife computed to last many days. Prince Mentschikoff himself had so judged it. Establishing his head-quarters on the slope overlooking the Great Redoubt, and so disposing his troops that, whilst standing there, he could exercise an immediate personal control over more than two thirds of his whole force, he had intended that every movement of this part of the field should be under his own eyes. It might well be deemed certain that any one of Prince Mentschikoff's lieutenants, intrusted during the absence of his general with this great charge, would be tenacious of the ground. As a general in high command, he would act upon the knowledge that the hill was vital to the whole position. As an officer commanding troops placed in a fortified work, he would be taught by the punctilio of his profession to hold his intrenchments, even at great sacrifice, until the weight of his charge should be taken from him by an order from the commander of the forces.

But there was a whim of the Emperor Nicholas which tended to weaken and disperse the authority of any man in command of his army. Longing always to make Wellington an example for his generals, but mistaking the gist of the saying that "the Duke never lost a gun," Nicholas gave his commanders to understand that the loss of a piece of ordnance would be likely to bring them into disgrace.[1] The result of such an intimation was just what a more sagacious prince would have easily foreseen. The commander who received

[1] The sense in which it can be said that Wellington "never lost a gun," has been referred to in a former note. The fact of the Duke never having lost a gun in action is a superb and summary proof that his career was uncheckered by the loss of a battle; but his avoidance of the loss of guns was not the cause, but the effect and the proof of his ascendency in war. The Duke would have scorned the notion of risking the loss of a battle for the sake of keeping his guns safe.

the warning took good care to hand it down—to hand it all down the steps of the military hierarchy; and every general of division, every brigadier, nay, every artillery officer who commanded a battery, was evidently made to understand that, happen what might, he must not lose a gun. In other words, every such officer, rather than run the risk of losing a gun, was empowered to resolve upon the abandonment of a fortified position, and even to commence a retreat, which might carry with it the retreat of the whole army.

It was, therefore, very natural that the anxiety which had seized upon the mind of Prince Mentschikoff should not only extend to Prince Gortschakoff and to General Kvetzinski, but also to the artillery officers who commanded the Causeway batteries and the guns in the Great Redoubt. Now, from the moment when Prince Mentschikoff rode off toward the sea, he had never reappeared in the Pass or on the Kourganè Hill, he had sent no good tidings, and apparently had dispatched no orders or directions of any kind.[1] With every moment the just grounds for alarm were increasing, and when the foremost division of the British army sprang to their feet and rapidly advanced along their whole line, the Russian generals and commanders of batteries had to cast in their minds and see how far their desire to hold fast a position very precious to the army and to the honor of the empire could be made to consist with the absolute safety of a few pieces of ordnance. They were about to be assailed by the English army. But this was not all they had to look for. The continued detention of Prince Mentschikoff in that part of the position which confronted the French gave ground for the fear that an evil crisis must there be passing. The fear would be that Bosquet's turning movement against the Russian left was producing its full effect, and that the tide of war, rolling up along the line of the Russian position, had set in from west to east.

If men were filled with this dread—a dread well justified by inference fairly drawn at the time, though not by actual facts—it would be to the Telegraph Height that they would bend their inquiring eyes, and there they would gaze with minds prepared to learn that the French, marching eastward, had doubled up the Russian left wing, and were coming to ground from which they would look down triumphantly into the flank of the Causeway batteries. Suddenly, to men thus expectant

[1] I think I might have almost ventured to leave out the "apparently;" for, although the narratives of Gortschakoff and Kvetzinski do not in terms declare that they received no orders, the tenor of their statements is all but equivalent to actual assertion.

of a dreaded calamity, there was presented a sight well fitted to confirm their worst fears—nay, even to make them imagine that the whole tenor of their duty was changed. For one of the high knolls jutting up from the eastern slopes of the Telegraph Height, and closely overlooking the Russian reserves, became crowded all at once with a gay-looking group of horsemen, whose hats and white plumes showed that they were staff officers. What made the apparition seem the more fatal was that it was deep in the very heart of the Russian lines, and even somewhat near to the ground where Prince Mentschikoff had posted his reserves. It could be seen that the horsemen wore coats of dark blue. They were exactly on the ground where the van of the French army might hope to be if it had achieved a signal victory over the left wing of the Russian army. It was hardly to be imagined possible that the Allies could have a numerous staff in that part of the field without being there in great strength. Even a tranquil and cautious observer of the apparition could hardly have failed to infer that the French, carrying all before them, had marched through and through from west to east, and made good their way into the centre—nay, almost into the rear of the Russian position. Oppressed by this belief, Russian officers would be led to think that if they stood bound to provide against the possibility of losing their guns, the time they had for saving them was beginning to run very short.

Apparition of horsemen on a knoll in the midst of the Russian position.

The divisional general who was in command on the Kourganè Hill does not allege that he had any authority from Prince Gortschakoff or from the commander of the forces to remove the guns which armed the Great Redoubt. What he says is that the defeat of the Kazan battalions by the English troops left the battery exposed, and necessitated its withdrawal.[1] General Kvetzinski, however, was the master of sixteen prime battalions, of which twelve were at this time untouched.

[1] This is what Kvetzinski says:—'During this time masses of English 'troops were directing their steps toward the regiment of the Grand-Duke 'Michael (the "Kazan" regiment). The batteries of our first lines began 'firing violently. Shells and missiles worked their bloody way through the 'lines of the enemies, but they immediately re-formed their lines, and under 'cover of a strong line of bayonets, and their battery then standing behind 'the smoking ruins of Bourliouk, they hastened to force their way over the 'ford in order to reach the breastwork. The "Kazan" regiment bravely met 'them, but, tormented by the destroying fire of the enemy, and having lost a 'frightful amount of men, was obliged to give way under the superior num- 'bers of the enemy. The battery, being thus left exposed, was obliged to 'move.'

At the time when the order must have been given for the removal of the guns, the defeat which one of his 'Kazan' columns had sustained was nothing which, in the eyes of a man so firm as he was, would seem to justify despair.[1] Yet to remove these guns was to abandon the key of the position on the Alma. It is hard to imagine that Kvetzinski could have brought himself to take such a step without trying resistance, unless he had been in some measure governed by an inculcated dread of losing guns, and also by what he wrongly imagined to be the state of the battle on the other side of the Causeway. Be this as it may, it is certain that within some fifteen minutes from the time when the horsemen were first seen on the knoll the Great Redoubt was dismantled.

The riders whose sudden appearance on the knoll thus scared and misled the enemy were a group of perhaps eighteen or twenty Englishmen. How came it that they were sitting unmolested in their saddles, and contentedly adjusting their field-glasses in the heart of the Russian position?

The road which Lord Raglan took when he ordered the advance of his infantry.

At the time when Lord Raglan dispatched to his leading divisions the final order to advance, he was riding between the French and the English armies, and was close to a road or track which led down toward a ford below the burning village. Impelled by his desire for a clear view of the coming struggle, and guided only by Fortune or by the course of the track, he rode down briskly into the valley, followed close by his staff, but leaving our troops in his rear. He soon reached, soon passed through the vineyards, and gained the bank of the river.

The stream at this spot flowed rapidly, breaking against a mass of rock, which so far dammed it back as to form on the upper side of it a pool about four feet deep. One of the staff rode into the stream at that point, and his horse nearly lost his footing. Lord Raglan, almost at the same moment, took the river on the right or lower side of the rock, and crossed it without any trouble. Though he was parted at this time from his own troops, there were several French soldiers near him. They were a part of the chain of skirmishers which covered the left flank and left front of Prince Napoleon's Division. They seemed to be engaged with some of the enemy's sharpshooters, whom they were able to discern through the foliage;

[1] Up to the time when Kvetzinski dismantled the Redoubt, the only defeat which the Kazan corps had sustained was the one inflicted upon two of its battalions by the 19th Regiment and the left companies of the 23rd. See *ante*. The defeat of the other two battalions—the battalions engaged with Lacy Yea—had not then occurred.

for they were sheltering themselves behind vineyard walls, watching moments for firing, and receding in order to load, or cautiously peering forward. They looked surprised when Lord Raglan, with the group which followed him, rode down and passed them. More than one of them, sagacious and curious, paused in his loading, and stood gazing, with ramrod half down, as though he were trying to make out how it accorded with the great science of war that the English General and his staff should be riding through the skirmishers, and entering, without his battalions, into the midst of the enemy's dominions.

Though they were unseen by our officers, the Russian sharpshooters, who had been exchanging shots with the French riflemen, were not far away. Of this they gave proof. Leslie dropped out of his saddle and fell to the ground. His startled horse making a move much as though he were blundering at a grip, the fall seemed at first sight like a fall in hunting; but a rifle ball had entered Leslie's shoulder. Nearly at the same time Weare, another of the staff, was struck down. There was not a heavy fire, but the Russian sharpshooters had been patiently dueling with the French skirmishers, and, of course, when they saw Lord Raglan and his plumed followers, they seized the occasion for easier shooting, and tried to bring down two or three of the gay cavalcade.

After gaining the left bank of the river, Lord Raglan at first got parted from most of those who had followed him, for he took a track intô a kind of gulley toward his right, and there for a moment he had no one very near him except one man, who had crossed the stream next after him; for the rest of the horsemen, when they reached the dry ground, had borne rather toward their left. Some one, however, from that quarter cried out, "This seems a better way, my lord," and Lord Raglan, then turning, rejoined the rest of the staff, and took the path recommended. I do not know who the officer was who advised this road. He has possibly forgotten the counsel which he gave; but if he remembers it, and sees how the issue was governed by taking the path which he chose, he may suffer himself to trace the gain of a battle, with all its progeny of events, to his few hurried words.

The brown bay Lord Raglan rode was of course well broken to fire, and he had been quiet enough during the earlier part of the action; but now, suddenly, his blood rose, and for all the rest of the day he was so eager that he would hardly suffer his rider to use a field-glass from the saddle. The truth is, that in other times he had been ridden to hounds in England,

and, although he had long stood careless of all that was done by the Causeway batteries, yet when he and his rider and the horsemen around him cantered down into the valley—when they plunged into the river—when they briskly dashed through it, and began to gallop up the steep, broken ground on the Russian side, the old hunter seemed to think of the chase and great days in the Gloucestershire country.

But it was not "Shadrach"[1] alone who felt the onward impulse. They say that there lurks in the men of these isles a vestige of Man the Hunter and Man the Savage, and that this, after all, is the subtle leaven which, in spite of the dangerous inroads of luxury, still keeps alive the warlike spirit of the people, and the freedom which goes along with it. It was not right—nay, if it were not that success brings justification, it would have been scarcely pardonable—that a general, charged with the care of an army, should be under the guidance of feelings akin to the impulses of the chase; but what one has to speak of is not of what ought to have been, but what was. By the stir and joyous animation of the moment Lord Raglan was led on into a part of the field which he would not have sought to reach in cold blood. He would have regarded as nothing the mere difference between the risk of being struck by shot in one part of the field and the risk of being struck by shot in another; but he knew that in general it is from a point more or less in rear of battalions actually engaged that a chief can exercise the most constant and the most extended control over his army; and an ideal commander would not suffer himself to ride to so forward a spot as to run the risk of losing the government of his troops for many minutes together in the critical period of an action; but the horseman who now rode his hunter across the valley of the Alma and indulgently gave him his head was not an ideal personage, but a man of flesh and blood, with many very English failings. "*Avant tout je suis gentilhomme Anglais,*" was the preface of the fierce message sent by the then foremost man of the world to the king of France,[2] and certainly in the nature of that "*gentilhomme Anglais*" the willfulness is so firmly set that no true sample of the breed can be altered, and altered down to suit a pattern. The state must dispense with his services or take him as he is.

Body and soul, Lord Raglan was so made by nature that, though he knew how to be prudent enough in the orders he gave to officers at a distance, yet, when he was in the saddle,

[1] The name of the horse.

[2] To Louis the XVIIIth in the summer of 1815, shortly after his second restoration.

directing affairs in person, and there came to be a question between holding back and going forward, his blood always used to get heated, and, like his great master, he had so often been happy in his choice of time for running a venture, that his spirit had never been cowed. Having once begun to ride forward, he did not restrain himself. And surely there was a great fascination to draw him on. The ground was of such a kind that with every stride of his charger a fresh view was opened to him. For months and months he had failed to tear off the veil which hid from him the strength of the army he undertook to assail; and now, suddenly in the midst of a battle, he found himself suffered to pass forward between the enemy's centre and his left wing. As at Badajoz, in old times, he had galloped alone to the drawbridge and obtained the surrender of St. Christoval, so now, driven on by the same hot blood, he joyously rode without troops into the heart of the enemy's position; and Fortune, still enamored of his boldness, was awaiting him with her radiant smile. For the path he took led winding up—by a way rather steep and rough here and there, but easy enough for saddle-horses—and presently in the front, but some way off toward the left, he saw before him a high, commanding knoll, and, strange to say, there seemed to be no Russians near it. Instantly, and before he reached the high ground, he saw the prize and divined its worth. He was swift to seize it. Without stopping—nay, even, one almost may say, without breaking the stride of his horse, he turned to Airey, who rode close at his side, and ordered him to bring up Adams's brigade with all possible speed. Then, still pressing on and on, the foremost rider of the allied armies, he gained the summit of the knoll.

Lord Raglan's position on the knoll.

I know of no battle in which, whilst the forces of his adversary were still upon their ground, and still unbroken, a general has had the fortune to stand upon a spot so commanding as that which Lord Raglan now found on the summit of the knoll. The truth is, that the Russian commander had not troops enough to occupy the whole position, and the part which he neglected was, happily, that very one into which Lord Raglan had ridden. During the earlier part of the day a battalion had been posted in the ravine close under the knoll; but, in an evil hour for the Czar, the battalion had been removed,[1] and the enemy having no other troops in the immediate neighborhood, and having no guns in battery which commanded the summit of the knoll, the English

[1] The No. 1 Taroutine battalion, Chodasiewicz.

General, though as yet he had no troops with him, stood unmolested in the heart of the enemy's position—stood between that wing of the Russian army which confronted the French, and that much larger portion of it which confronted the English, but so far in advance as to be actually in the close neighborhood of the Russian reserves. The knoll was not, indeed, so situated as to command a distant view toward our right, and the view toward the front was obstructed by the features of the ground; but, looking to his left, or, in other words, looking eastward and up the valley of the river, Lord Raglan commanded nearly the whole ground destined to be the scene of the English attack.[1]

But more; he looked upon that part of the Russian army which confronted ours; he saw it in profile; he saw down into the flank of the Causeway batteries which barred the mouth of the Pass; and beyond, he saw into the shoulder of the Great Redoubt, then about to be stormed by Codrington's brigade.[2] Above all, he saw, drawn up with splendid precision, the bodies of infantry which the enemy held in reserve. They were massed in two columns.[3] The formation of each mass looked close and perfect as though it had been made of marble, and cut by rule and plumb-line. These troops, being in reserve, were of course some way in rear of the enemy's batteries and his foremost battalions; but they were only 900 yards from the eye of the English General; for it was Lord Raglan's strange and happy destiny to have ridden almost into the rear of the position, and to be almost as near to the enemy's reserves as he was to the front of their array.

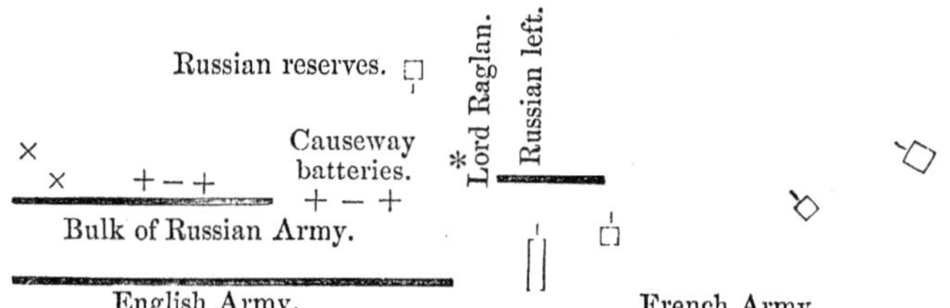


All this—now told with labor of words—Lord Raglan saw at a glance, and at the same moment he divined the fatal perturbation which would be inflicted upon the enemy by the

[1] *i. e.*, that attack the first stages of which have been already described.

[2] As already narrated. It will be remembered that Codrington's brigade was joined in the storming by the 19th and 95th Regiments.

[3] See former note as to the probable number of the troops in these columns, and the corps to which they belonged.

mere appearance of our Head-Quarter staff in this part of the field. The knoll, though much lower than the summit of the Telegraph Height, stood out bold and plain above the Pass. It was clear that even from afar the enemy would make out that it was crowned by a group of plumed officers; and Lord Raglan's imagination being so true and so swift as to gift him with the faculty of knowing how in given circumstances other men must needs be thinking and feeling, it hardly cost him a moment to infer that this apparition of a few horsemen on the spur of a hill was likely to govern the enemy's fate. It would not, he thought, occur to any Russian general that fifteen or twenty staff officers, whether French or English, could have reached the knoll without having thousands of troops close at hand. The enemy's generals would therefore infer that a large proportion of the Allied force had won its way into the heart of the Russian position. This was the view which Lord Raglan's mind had seized when, at the very moment of crowning the knoll, he looked round and said, 'Our presence here will 'have the best effect.' Then, glancing down as he spoke into the flank of the Causeway batteries, and carrying his eye round to the enemy's infantry reserves, Lord Raglan said, 'Now, if we had a couple of guns here!'[1]

Lord Raglan desires to have a couple of guns brought up to the top of the knoll.

His wish was instantly seized by Colonel Dickson[2] and one or two other officers. They rode off in all haste.

The rest of the group which had followed Lord Raglan remained with him upon the summit of the knoll, and every one, facing eastward and taking out his glass, began to scan the ground destined to be assailed by the English troops.

The Light Division had not then begun to emerge from the thick ground and the channel of the river; but presently some small groups, and afterward larger gatherings of the red-coats appeared upon the top of the river's bank on the Russian side, and at length—seen in profile by Lord Raglan—there began the tumultuous onset of Codrington's brigade against the Great Redoubt.[3]

Meantime he watches the progress of the battle.

Lord Raglan knew that the distance between him and the scene of the struggle at the redoubt was too great to allow of his then tampering with it; for any order that he might send would lose its worth in the journey, and tend to breed confusion. And it was not in his

[1] I heard him say so, and say so immediately upon crowning the knoll.

[2] Colonel Dickson of the Artillery. It was the happy accident of his being with Lord Raglan as chief of the staff of interpreters which gave him the opportunity of rendering the services narrated in the text.

[3] See *ante*.

way to assuage his impatience by making impotent efforts. Nor would he even give vent to his feeling by words or looks disclosing vexation. He had so great a power of preventing his animal spirits from drooping that no one could see in his glowing countenance the faintest reflection of the sight which his eyes took in. His manner all the time was the manner of a man enlivened by the progress of a great undertaking without being robbed of his leisure. He spoke to me, I remember, about his horse. He seemed like a man who had a clew of his own, and knew his way through the battle.

Watching the onslaught of Codrington's brigade, Lord Raglan had seen the men ascend the slope and rush up over the parapet of the Great Redoubt. Then moments, then whole minutes—precious minutes—elapsed, and he had to bear the anguish of finding that the ground where he longed to see the supports marching up was still left bare. Then—a too sure result of that default—he had to see our soldiery relinquishing their capture and retreating in clusters down the hill.

Moreover, at that moment affairs were going ill with the French. The appearance of our head-quarters on the knoll had been marked by our Allies as well as by the enemy; for now a French aid-de-camp, in great haste, came climbing up the knoll to seek Lord Raglan. He seemed to be in a state of grievous excitement; but perhaps it was the violence of his bodily exertion which gave him this appearance, for he had quitted his horse in order the better to mount the steep, and he rushed up bareheaded to Lord Raglan, but so breathless from his exertions that for a moment he could hardly articulate; and when he spoke, he spoke panting. He persisted in remaining uncovered. What he came to ask was that Lord Raglan would give some support to the French; and as a ground for the demand, he urged that the French were hardly pressed by the enemy. 'My Lord,' he said, 'my Lord, my Lord, we have before us eight battalions!'[1] One could see, or imagine that one saw, what was passing in Lord Raglan's mind. He was pained by thinking that, either from mental excitement or from the violence of his bodily exertion, the officer should seem discomposed; but what tormented him most was the sight of the young man standing bareheaded, for to tell him to be covered would be to assume that the bared head was an obeisance meant to be rendered to himself. Bending in his saddle, Lord Raglan turned kindly round toward

*A French aid-de-camp on the knoll.*

*His mission.*

*Lord Raglan's way with him.*

[1] 'Milord, milord, nous avons devant nous huit bataillons.' I heard him say those words.

his right—toward the side of his maimed arm—and his expression was that of one intent to assuage another's pain, but the sunshine of the last two days had tanned him so crimson, that it masked the generous flush which used to come to his face in such moments. He did not look at all like an anxious and vexed commander who had to listen to a desponding message in the midst of a battle. He was rather the courteous, lively host entertaining a shy, youthful visitor, and trying to place him at his ease. In his comforting, cheerful way, he said, 'I 'can spare you a battalion.'[1] But it was something of more worth than the promise of a battalion that the aid-de-camp carried back with him. He carried back tidings of the spirit in which Lord Raglan was conducting the battle. At a time when the French were cast down, it was of some moment to them to learn that the English head-quarters, strangely placed as they were in the midst of the Russian position, were a scene of robust animation, and that Lord Raglan looked and spoke like a man who had the foe in his power.

XXVI.

Causes of the depression which had come upon the French.

It is now time to speak of the events which had been bringing the French army into a state of increased depression. We saw that General Kiriakoff, commanding the Russian left wing, had charge of the Telegraph Height, and confronted the Divisions of Prince Napoleon and Canrobert, having also on his left and left front, though at greater distances, the two separated brigades of Bosquet's Division and the five battalions of Turks. The infantry force remaining under Kiriakoff's orders had been reduced by Prince Mentschikoff's abstraction of the 'Moscow' troops to a force of only nine battalions; and afterward, when the second 'Moscow' battalion rejoined the rest of the corps, the infantry force remaining under Kiriakoff consisted only of the four 'Taroutine' and the four 'Militia' battalions. The part which these 'Taroutine' and 'Militia' battalions had been taking in the battle may be told in a summary way. They did not attack the French, and no French infantry attacked them; but, since they were kept massed in battalion columns upon slopes which faced

Operations on the Telegraph Height.

[1] 'Je puis vous donner un bataillon.' I heard Lord Raglan make that answer. Lord Raglan, I imagine, meant to fulfill the promise by detaching one of the two battalions about to arrive under Adams; but by the time that force came up the course of events rendered it unnecessary to send the promised aid. However, Sir Richard England afterward moved into the close neighborhood of Prince Napoleon's Division.

toward the French, they were exposed to a good deal of artillery fire at long range, and were from time to time forced to shift their ground. The 'Militia' battalions were troops of inferior quality; and, finding at last that wherever they stood they were more or less galled by artillery, they dissolved.[1] So, although he was supported by Prince Mentschikoff in person, with 'the column of the eight battalions' of which we shall presently speak, yet, in his own hands, Kiriakoff had only four battalions of sound infantry with which to show a countenance to thirty thousand Frenchmen and Turks. But both of Bosquet's brigades were distant. Canrobert indeed was on the verge of the plateau, and had so spread out his battalions as to have them in readiness for an encounter. Nay, seeing that he had no enemy before him except on his left front, he had somewhat brought round his right shoulder, and was fronting toward the Telegraph, but he was still without his artillery, and was therefore hanging back cautiously on the steep ground close below the smooth cap of the hill.

Backwardness of the 3rd French Division.

Prince Napoleon's Division at this time was in the bottom of the valley, close to the river; and, indeed, of the whole force which the Prince at this time had around him, there were only two battalions which had hitherto forded the stream.[2] To the hopes which the French army had of being able to take a great part in the action, this backwardness of one of their finest divisions was almost ruinous; and it is natural enough that a divisional general, whose rank gave him shelter from the ordeal of a fair military investigation, should, for that very reason, be made to suffer the more bitterly from the stings which men robbed of their freedom are accustomed to plant with the tongue.

Prince Napoleon.

Resembling the first French Emperor in outward looks, Prince Napoleon was also very like his uncle, not apparently in his main objects, but in the character of his intellect; for he had that rare and exceeding clearness of view which man is able to command when he can separate things essential from things of circumstance, and keep the two sets of thoughts so clean asunder as to be able to go to the solution of his main problem with a mind unclouded by details —unclouded by even those details which it is vital for him to master and provide for, though he refuses to let them mix with

[1] Chodasiewicz.

[2] The battalion of the 19th Chasseurs, and one of the battalions of the Marine Corps. The 2nd Zouave Regiment had also crossed, but this, it will presently be seen, was not a part of the force which Prince Napoleon 'had 'around him.'

the elements from which he fetches out his conclusion. And although one can not help knowing that the most cruel of all the imputations which can be brought against a soldier has long been kept fastened upon Prince Napoleon, I may say that such knowledge as I have hitherto chanced to gain of his career has not yet enabled me to infer that he is a man of lower grade than his uncle in the matter of personal courage.

The mishaps which befell him.

Before the delinquency of the 3rd French Division on the day of the Alma is accepted as one of the grounds which entitle the world to ratify its harsh judgment against Prince Napoleon, men ought, in all fairness, to know the mishap which befell the Division, and to understand the considerations which rendered this same mishap a much more grave evil than it might seem to be at first sight.

The materials from which the bulk of the French army is taken.

The French are so military a people that, when a great national sentiment is once aroused, the very children are ready to seize their little muskets and fall into columns of companies; but, in the mean time, and until the mighty nation is challenged, the great bulk of the French peasantry are perhaps more homely, more rustic, more unadventurous than most of the people of Europe. From these quiet millions of people many tens of thousands of small, sad, harmless-looking young men are every year torn by the conscription, and immense energy—energy informed with the traditions of an ancient and ever warlike nation—is brought to bear upon the object of turning these forlorn young captives into able soldiers. All that instruction can achieve is carefully done; but the enforced change from rural life to the life of barracks and camps seems not to be favorable to the animal spirits of the men; for although, when seen in masses or groups working hard at their military duties, they always appear to be brisk, and almost merry, their seeming animation is the result of smart orders—the animation of a horse when the rowels on either side are lightly touching his flanks; and during the hours whilst they are left to themselves, the French soldiers of the line engaged in campaigning are commonly depressed and spiritless.[1] Of course, this want of lustiness in the French army is superbly masked by all the resources of military pomp and all the outward signs which seem to show the presence of vigor, dispatch, and warlike ardor; but the material of which the line regiments are composed must always keep a good deal of its original nature, and whoever glances at the rising steps of French officers successful in Africa will

[1] I rest this upon what I have seen of the French army in Africa, in the Crimea, and on board ship.

find that they have climbed to eminence, not by leading troops of the line, but by obtaining, in the critical part of their career, the command of choice French regiments, or, failing that, the command of troops of foreign race.[1] These choice French regiments are not composed of materials at all like those which supply the line. On the contrary, they number in their ranks many thousands of bold, adventurous men, who take service in the army of their own accord, and it is in these choice regiments that France sees the true expression of her warlike nature. Of all these choice regiments, the 'Zouaves' are the most famous; and each of the three foremost Divisions of the French army on the Alma had in it a regiment—a regiment with its two war battalions—belonging to the corps of the Zouaves. What the spear-head is to a spear, that its Zouave Regiment was to each of these three Divisions.[2]

The great difference between their choice regiments and the rest of their troops.

Each Division, therefore, is furnished with a Zouave or other choice regiment.

Prince Napoleon is abandoned by his Zouave regiment.

Prince Napoleon's Division comprised 9000 men, and of these some 2000 were men of the 2nd Regiment of Zouaves. Whether this regiment was impatient of the supposed slowness with which Prince Napoleon had hitherto advanced, whether it was governed by its contempt of line regiments, and a fierce resolve to have no neighborship with any other than Zouave comrades, or whether there were other causes which shaped its movements, I have not learned; but what happened was this:—The regiment, after fording the river, broke away from the unfortunate Division to which it belonged, marched off toward its right front, began to climb the height, and never stopped until it had coolly ranged itself close alongside of the 1st Zouave Regiment—a regiment which formed the left of Canrobert's array. With Canrobert's Division, instead of with Prince Napoleon's, the regiment continued to act until the close of the battle. Before men are hard upon a divisional general for his seeming backwardness in an action, they ought to allow for the misfortune which left him, indeed, the master of some 7000 men, but robbed him of the warlike corps on which he must have relied as the element for giving life and fire to his masses. For, if one might recur to the image already used, one would say that the spear-head had flown off, and that what remained in the

[1] *i. e.*, of the Foreign Legion, or of the native African levies.

[2] I have borrowed this expressive image from one of our veteran commanders, who used it once in conversation as a means of illustrating the kind of power which even a large body of our native Indian troops is accustomed to derive from the presence of one or two English battalions.

hands of Prince Napoleon was only the wooden shaft. Justice, in this regard, is the more needful, since it would plainly be unfitting and impolitic for Prince Napoleon to say in his defense that, with 7000 French troops around him, he was still reduced to helplessness by the want of his Zouave Regiment.

Also St. Arnaud was riding with this Division, and he therefore was answerable for its place in the field.

There is another consideration which alone would seem to free Prince Napoleon from almost all the blame founded upon the backwardness of his Division. In the midst of that very Division Marshal St. Arnaud was all this time riding; and it is obvious that, by being thus present with a force which was hanging back out of its place, the officer who commanded the whole French army brought full upon his own shoulders the weight of the blame which might otherwise be thrown upon the divisional general.

D'Aurelle's brigade thrusts itself forward in advance of Prince Napoleon;

But the eloping of his Zouave Regiment was not the only mishap which befell Prince Napoleon. We saw that D'Aurelle's brigade—a brigade forming part of the 4th or Reserve Division—had been ordered to support Canrobert. Of the motives which governed the leader of this brigade I know nothing. Perhaps, whilst he was low down in the bottom of the valley, he lost his conception of the distance (the lateral distance from east to west) which separated him from the Division he was ordered to support. At all events, what he did was this:—Having his whole brigade in a close, deep, narrow column, he pushed forward and jammed it into a steep road exactly in front of Prince Napoleon's foremost battalion. He thus made it impossible for Prince Napoleon to get into action by that road,[1] and put him in the plight of a man left behind—in the plight of a general who commands one of the Divisions intended to be foremost, and yet is left planted with his force in the rear of troops meant to act as reserves. Nor did D'Aurelle's brigade do any the least good by thus thrusting itself into the road in advance of Prince Napoleon; for, either because of the nature of the ground or from some other cause, the brigade never spread itself out so as to be capable of fighting.

but in an order which incapacitates it from any immediate combat.

Always in deep column with narrow front, it hung back, clinging fast to the steep part of the hill, and remaining unseen by Kiriakoff, who moved freely across its front, as though there were no such force on the hill-side. Upon the whole, the result was, that, taken together, D'Aurelle's brigade and Prince Napoleon's mutilated

[1] There was another road by which the Prince could, and by which, at a later period, he did ascend.

Division were a column of near 12,000 men which might be said to be in mere order of march during all the critical period of the battle; for, with a depth of nearly a mile, the column had a front of only a few yards. Thus disposed, the 12,000 men who formed the column were not, of course, in a state which allowed of their attempting to engage an enemy inclined to make a stand against them; and they were, it would seem, very helpless for purposes of mere self-defense.[1] Indeed, it is hard to see how they could have escaped a great disaster, if a bold Russian officer who knew the ground had come down with a few score of light infantry men upon the flank of D'Aurelle's brigade. Apparently Kiriakoff's abstinence from all enterprises of this sort, and the quiet confidence with which he afterward manœuvred on the plateau, were both owing to the steepness of ground which hindered him from perceiving the small, slender head of D'Aurelle's column.

Helplessness of the deep column which was formed by D'Aurelle's Brigade and Prince Napoleon's Division.

Upon the whole, then, Kiriakoff, though handling no forces except his two batteries, his four Taroutine battalions, and his fast dissolving militiamen, was not at this time out of heart. His artillery, sweeping down the smooth cap of the Telegraph Height, both on its northern and northwestern sides, commanded the only ground by which Canrobert could advance; and, firing over the heads of the Taroutine battalions, effectually kept him down. Moreover, it still tormented all those masses of French infantry which, though approaching the Telegraph Height, were yet so low down as not to have come in for the shelter which the steepness of the hill-side afforded.

Condition of Kiriakoff on the Telegraph Height.

And now we shall see the cause of the stress which had been put upon the French army by that incubus of the 'eight battalions' of which the aid-de-camp spoke. We left Prince Mentschikoff countermarching from west to east with the seven battalions which he had under his personal orders. The detached battalion of the 'Moscow' corps had been afterward called in, and its junction brought up the whole body to eight battalions. With this force gathered in mass, and standing halted on the right rear of the Telegraph, Prince Mentschikoff was preparing to make an onslaught upon the head of Canrobert's Division; but just as he was going to move, he abandoned the idea of leading the column in person. The cause of this change is obvious. Evidently Prince Ments-

The 'column 'of the eight 'battalions.'

[1] See the plan showing the way in which Prince Napoleon's Division and D'Aurelle's brigade were disposed. It is taken from the official French plan of the 'Atlas de la Guerre d'Orient.

Plan (taken from the French official Atlas) showing what (at the time of the advance of the Column of the eight battalions against Canrobert) were the respective positions of Marshal St. Arnaud, of D'Aurelle's brigade, of Prince Napoleon's Zouaves, and of the rest of the Prince Napoleon's division which remained with him when his Zouave battalions had gone off.

*Canrobert's troops*..........................

*Prince Napoleon's*..........................

*D'Aurelle's brigade (a brigade belonging to Forey's division)*..............

*Marshal St. Arnaud and his escort*............

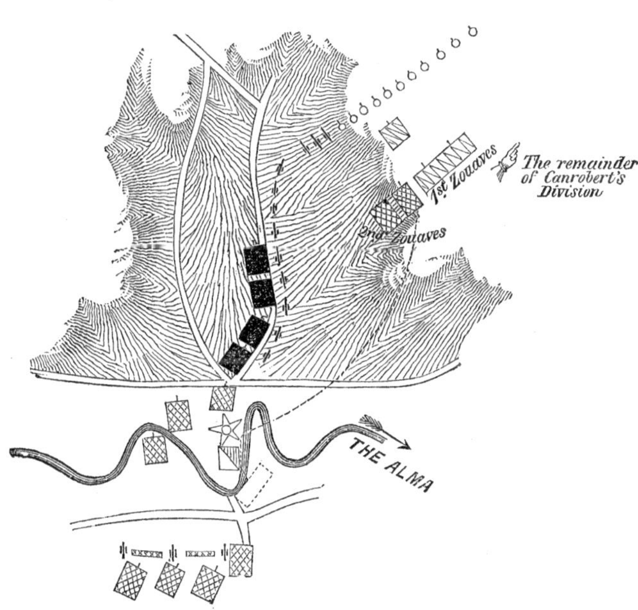

chikoff was called off to another part of the field by tidings of what the English were doing.

Kiriakoff is invested with the charge of this column.

Kiriakoff had had a horse shot under him, and was standing on foot near one of his 'Taroutine' battalions when Prince Mentschikoff rode up, and (apparently suppressing the tidings which forced him to quit this part of the field) gave Kiriakoff the charge of the great 'column of the eight battalions' which had been amassed for the purpose of an attack upon Canrobert's Division. The Prince then rode off, and was not again seen or heard of in this part of the field. Of course it follows that he went as straight as he could toward that part of his position which was undergoing the assault of the English.[1]

He marches it across the front of D'Aurelle's brigade.

Kiriakoff instantly took a fresh horse, and rode to the ground —ground on the right rear of the Telegraph— where the 'column of the eight battalions' awaited him. This vast column he disposed in a solid body,

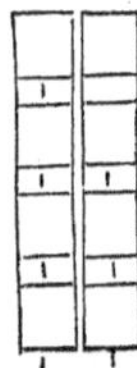

with a front of two and a depth of four massed battalions. When all was ready he began to move it flankwise from east to west. Plainly hindered by the ground from seeing the head of the column which was formed by D'Aurelle's brigade and Prince Napoleon's Division, he dealt with the French as though they had no such force near; for with that heavy column of his which trailed, as we have seen, to a depth of four battalions, he marched straight across the front of D'Aurelle's brigade. He marched in peace. Nay, so far were the French from looking upon his hazardous movement in the light of a gift offered them by Fortune, that it was the dread apparition of this vast Russian column which had sent the panting aid-de-camp to the side of Lord Raglan's stirrup.

Bending afterward more toward the north, Kiriakoff ad-

[1] I say 'it follows,' because Prince Mentschikoff was a brave man, incapable of quitting one of the two scenes of battle except for the purpose of going to the other. In the mention which they make of Prince Mentschikoff's presence in different parts of the field, the narratives of the Russian divisional generals leave a chasm of several important minutes. This chasm, as will be seen at a later page, I try to fill up by conjecture.

And then advances upon the right centre of Canrobert's Division.

vanced upon the right centre of the ground on which Canrobert had spread his battalions. Canrobert's troops did not long stand their ground; for when Kiriakoff, advancing and still advancing, was nearly at last within musket-shot of his foe, the French no longer bore up under the weight that is laid upon the heart of a Continental soldier by the approach of a great column of infantry. Kiriakoff conceives that he inflicted a sheer defeat upon his foe. 'Canrobert's Division,' he writes, 'could not 'resist our charge. Hastily taking off their batteries, they be-'gan to descend the hilly bank.'[1] On the other hand, the French say nothing of this reverse. Perhaps the truth lies intermediately between the broad assertion of Kiriakoff and the unfaithful silence of the French; for what seems the most likely is, that Canrobert, being still without his artillery, was for the moment resolved to decline the combat, and that with that view, and of his own free will, without waiting to be put under stress of actual fight, he drew his troops down to a steeper part of the hill-side. Be this as it may, it is certain that, under the pressure of Kiriakoff's great column, the head of Canrobert's Division fell back.[2]

The head of Canrobert's Division falls back.

Along almost their whole array at this time it seemed to fare ill with the Allies. Still close to the sea-shore, Bouat, with one French brigade and 5000 Turks, was without artillery, and was therefore holding back from the plateau, far away from any scene of strife. Following the same barren track, General Forey, with Lourmel's brigade, was marching to the sea-shore, and was annulled. Bosquet, with his one brigade on the plateau, had long been isolated, and was not so near to any Russian battalion as to be able to engage it with his infantry. Canrobert was undergoing the check which we have just seen. The unwieldy column formed by D'Aurelle's brigade and by Prince Napoleon's Division — a column with a front of only a few yards, and the depth of a mile, was in an order adapted for the march, but not for fighting, and, its small slender crest being kept close down out of sight, had failed to exert that pressure which—

State of the battle at this time.

[1] Kiriakoff's narrative. It will be observed that his statement clashes with the passage in which I say that Canrobert was without his guns. I have relied upon the detailed statements supplied to me from French sources, and if I am right in doing so, it follows that Kiriakoff must have been mistaken in supposing that he saw the French carrying off their guns.

[2] Upon this point Kiriakoff's narrative is confirmed by Romaine. Writing from his saddle, and at the very minute of witnessing the event, he recorded it in these words:—'French centre falling back.' Romaine's saddle-notes.

Plan (taken from the French official Atlas) showing the advance of the "Column of the eight Battalions" against Canrobert's Division.

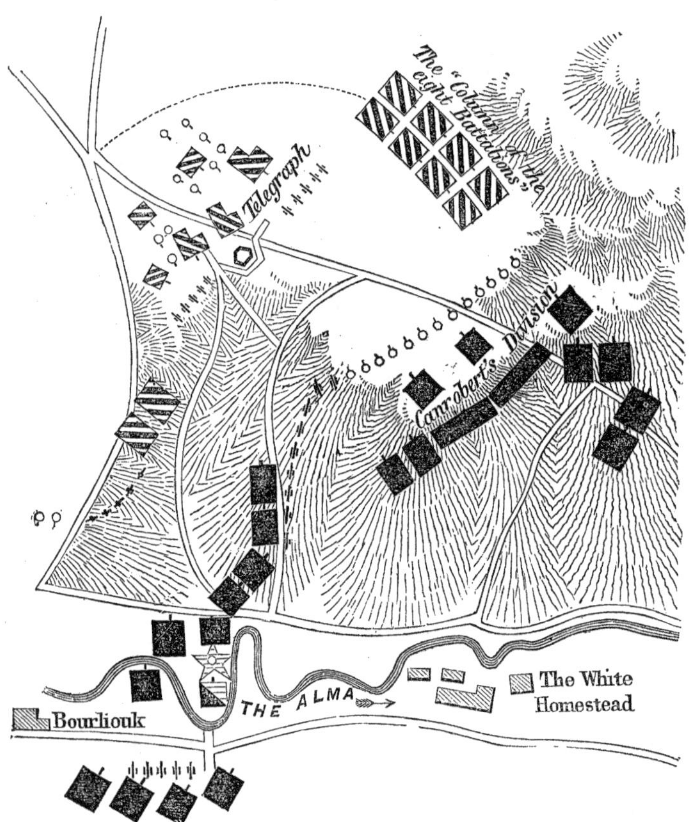


*N.B.—Those parts of the above plan which show the position of the "Column of eight Battalions" and of the French troops are believed to be nearly accurate, but the other parts of the plan are not to be relied upon.*

even without firing a shot—may be inflicted by the known presence of a great body of troops. And the forces thus palsied were nothing less than the whole French army, including even their reserves. Much, of course, might always be hoped from the bravery and the swift invention of the warlike French; but apart from that vast though undefined resource, and apart from what fortune might do for him, Marshal St. Arnaud was without the means which would enable him to bear up against any grave disaster, and hinder it from becoming sheer ruin.

The fortunes of the English had been checkered, and it might be said that at this moment their prospects were a good deal overcast. Evans, still repressed by the commanding fire of the Causeway batteries, and having but three battalions to fight with, was sustaining a hard conflict. Codrington's people had been forced to relinquish their hold of the Great Redoubt; and the shattered remains of the battalions which stormed the work were descending the slope of the hill, and breaking down by their bodily weight the left wing of a battalion of Guards. Finally, General Buller, on our extreme left, was in an attitude of mere defense. It is true that the Great Redoubt had been dismantled, that (with the exception of the centre battalion of the Guards) our supports had not yet tried their prowess, and that the bare apparition of our Head-Quarter Staff on the knoll was putting a heavy stress on the enemy. It is true, also, that there was one English regiment still fighting with a Russian column. All else had of late gone ill.

XXVII.

This was the condition of things when, having been hurried down to the ford, and dragged through the river, and up over steep, rugged ground, the two guns, for which Lord Raglan had prayed, were brought up at length to the summit of the knoll. They were guns belonging to Turner's battery, and they were already crossing the river when Dickson came upon them. The two pieces were soon unlimbered; and one of them—for the artillerymen had not all been able to keep pace—was worked by Dickson with his own hands. The guns were pointed upon the flank of the Causeway batteries. Every one watched keenly for the result of the first shot. The first shot failed. Some one said: 'Allow a little more 'for the wind;' and the words were not spoken as though they were a quotation from 'Ivanhoe,' but rather in a way showing that the speaker knew

The two guns which Lord Raglan had called for are brought to the top of the knoll. Their fire enfilades the Causeway batteries, and causes the enemy to withdraw his guns.

something of artillery practice. The next shot, or the next shot but one, took effect upon the Causeway batteries. It struck, they say, a tumbril which stood just in rear of the guns.

It presently became a joyful certainty that the Causeway batteries, exposing their flank to this fire from the knoll, could not hold their ground; and in a few moments a keen-eyed officer, who was one of the group around Lord Raglan, cried out with great joy, 'He is carrying off his guns!' And this was true. The field-pieces which formed the Causeway batteries were rapidly limbered up, and dragged to another ground far up in the rear.[1]

It plows through the enemy's reserves, and drives them from the field.

With the two great columns of infantry, which constituted the enemy's reserves, it fared no better. After not more than two failures, the gunner got their range, and our nine-pounders plowed through the serried masses of the two Russian columns, cutting lanes through and through them. Yet for some minutes the columns stood firm. And even when the still increasing havoc at length overruled the punctilio of those brave men, it seemed to be in obedience to orders, and not under the stress of any confusing terror, that the two great columns gave way. They retreated in good order.

Our gunners then tried their pieces upon the Vladimir battalions, and although the range was too great to allow of their striking the column, they impressed Kvetzinski with a contrary belief. He was sure that these troops were reached by the guns on the knoll; and it will be seen by-and-by that this his belief was one of the causes which helped to govern his movements.

The Ouglitz column was stopped in its advance.

This was the time when the great column of the Ouglitz corps, being fired, as it seemed, with a vehement spirit, was still marching down from the higher slopes of the Kourganè Hill with a mind to support the Vladimir battalions, and enable them to press the retreat of our soldiery then coming down in clusters from the Great Redoubt; but the disasters which Lord Raglan had that moment inflicted upon the enemy by the aid of the two guns on the knoll made it natural for the Russian Generals, who saw what was done, to stop short in any forward movement. The Ouglitz column, as we before saw, was stopped in the midst of its eager

[1] Kiriakoff says that these guns were dragged off by the men of the Borodino corps. I do not think that there were any observers on the knoll who saw guns dragged from the field by infantry; but there were features in the ground which prevented their seeing into the line of retreat as effectually as they had seen into the batteries.

So also was the Vladimir. advance; and, for want of the support which these troops had been going to lend, the triumphant Vladimir column was brought to a halt on the site of the Great Redoubt.

So, here was the spell which now for several minutes had been governing the battle. The apparition of a score of plumed horsemen on this knoll may have had more or less to do with the resolve which led Kvetzinski to dismantle the Great Redoubt; but, at all events, this apparition, and the fire of Lord Raglan's two guns, had enforced the withdrawal of the Causeway batteries; had laid open the entrance of the Pass; had shattered the enemy's reserves; had stopped the onward march of the Ouglitz battalions; and had chained up the high-mettled Vladimir in the midst of its triumphant advance.

XXVIII.

Progress hitherto made by Evans.

On and near the great road leading down to the bridge, Evans had been continuing his difficult struggle. He still shared with the flames the possession of the village; still held the vineyards below it; and a part of his small force had succeeded, as already shown, in crossing the river, and establishing itself under the bank on the Russian side; but beyond the ground thus gained Evans had not yet been able to push; for the Causeway batteries were so well placed and so diligently served that they closed the mouth of the Pass.

He hears the guns from the knoll, and presently sees their effect upon the Causeway batteries.

The force around Evans was scant, but in other times he had commanded an army, and whilst he watched the efforts of the only three battalions[1] remaining near him, he was alive to the progress of the action in other parts of the field. He had just witnessed the onset of Codrington's brigade; and he was sitting in his saddle, tormented with the grief of observing that, for want of supports, the storming of the Great Redoubt was likely to be all in vain, when suddenly he heard the report of a nine-pounder gun sounding from a very new quarter—sounding from somewhere among the knolls and broken ground on his right front, and in the heart of the Russian position. The fire was repeated. Evans keenly watched the Causeway batteries in his front. And not in vain, for again the nine-pounder was heard, and there followed that sort of change in the Russian batteries which seemed to show that

[1] The 47th, the 30th, and the 55th. The 95th, as we saw, was carried forward in the rush of Codrington's brigade, and Evans's second brigade (with the exception of the 47th regiment) was in another part of the field.

they were under fire—under fire coming flankwise from the west. Again and again the fire of the nine-pounder was repeated. The sound came from a quarter to which it was to be expected that the French might have reached; but some, they say, fancied and said, 'That is an English gun!' A busy change began to stir in the Russian batteries. Presently, though the smoke of the burning village lay heavy in this part of the field, our people could make out what the change was. It was one of great moment to the Allies; for the enemy was limbering up, and beginning to carry off the sixteen guns which up to this minute had barred the mouth of the Pass. The great road lay open.

He at once advances.

Evans understood the battle. He acted instantly. He saw that, though he was weak, yet the moment had come for the advance of his three battalions.

The 47th Regiment had to ford the river below the bridge, and at a part where the water was deep. It encountered a good deal of difficulty in crossing. Some men were drowned, but the rest gained the bank on the Russian side of the stream, and moved forward. Evans rode across the stream at a point between the 47th and Pennefather's brigade.

Pennefather pressed forward. Colonel Stacy needed no order to advance. Understanding the business of war, he had already gained a lodgment for his battalion[1] under the farther bank of the river, and he was plying the Russian artillerymen with rifle fire when he observed that the enemy's batteries suddenly slackened their fire. He inferred the change that was coming, and at once caused his men to spring up the bank, formed them carefully on the top, and then, having his battalion in a beautiful line, marched straight up toward the site of the Causeway batteries. Colonel Warren moved up his battalion[2] in the same direction. The enemy had partly destroyed the bridge.[3]

From first to last, the enemy, so far as I know, had done but little with the two formed battalions of his Borodino corps which had been posted in this part of the field;[4] and he now began to draw in the multitude of skirmishers which had hith-

[1] The 30th Regiment. [2] The 55th Regiment.

[3] He imagined that his battalion of sappers and miners had destroyed it, but this was an error. Except to the parapet, which was removed, not much harm was done to the bridge.

[4] General Kiriakoff says, as we have already mentioned, that the Borodino battalions dragged away the guns of the Causeway batteries, but I can not find any other distinct statement of things done by the regiment in the course of the battle.

The enemy does not farther resist this advance with his infantry.

erto swarmed in the valley.[1] He did not engage his infantry in farther endeavors to bar the mouth of the Pass, nor even show one of his battalions in this part of the great road; but upon the hillocks, a good way in rear of the ground just abandoned by the Causeway batteries, he again established his guns; and from this new position, though not with great effect, he opened fire upon our advancing troops.

Evans joined by Sir Richard England in person, who now has with him thirty guns.

To this fire Evans was now able to reply with a strong force of artillery, for Sir Richard England rode up, proposed to accompany him in the advance, and offered to place both his batteries at Evans's disposal. So the two divisional generals rode forward together, having with them altogether some thirty pieces of field artillery.[2]

Moreover, the Division of Sir Richard England was following him into the Pass, and would soon bring a welcome support to Evans's three battalions.[3]

Sir Richard England's dispositions for bringing support to Evans.

But some minutes elapsed before these supports could come up, and, by reason of the disasters which had befallen our soldiery at the Great Redoubt, the three battalions which Evans had with him were for some time almost alone upon the enemy's ground. Yet not utterly; for on the western slope of the Kourganè Hill one English battalion—Lacy Yea, with his 7th Fusileers—was still holding its ground, still engaged with a mass of the enemy's infantry. That stand that Lacy Yea had been making was a hinge on which a good deal might turn. If he should

[1] Three battalions, it seems, viz., two out of the four Borodino battalions, and the No. 6 rifle battalion, were employed as skirmishers.

[2] *i.e.*, with the three batteries belonging respectively to the 1st, the 2nd, and the Light Divisions.

[3] Apparently Sir Richard England did not know of the disaster which befell the Scots Fusileer Guards in time to be able to adapt his measures to that event. Of course, if he had known it in time, he would have been anxious to put a literal interpretation upon the order 'to support the Guards,' and would have moved a part of his force toward the chasm which had been wrought in the centre of the Household brigade. I took pains to make out the exact movements of the 3rd Division, but in vain; for those who would be the most likely to know, differ broadly the one from the other. By farther trouble I might have dispelled this obscurity; but the Division was not engaged to an extent greater than might be inferred from its losses (one killed and seventeen wounded), and therefore I have desisted from farther endeavors. It may be safely said, however, that after receiving the order to support the Guards, Sir Richard England held his Division in hand, sending portions of it to give support where he deemed it to be needed; and that when Pennefather's brigade crossed the river, it was followed by the whole or by the bulk of the 3rd Division.

hold his ground a few minutes more, he would cover from the enemy's masses the left flank and left front of Evans's three battalions, and at the end of that time the supports would be up. Evans was an old commander, who knew how to read the signs of a battle, and he was able to see and understand that the enemy, almost in the very moment of his success at the Great Redoubt, was palsied by the guns still sounding from the knoll, and was losing his freedom of action. He resolved to stand firm in the Pass; and he established his thirty guns near the site of the batteries which had just been withdrawn by the Russians. For some minutes his position was rather critical; and he had to trust much to the hope that Lacy Yea and his Fusileers would be able to hold their ground.

Evans's situation in the mean time.

XXIX.

It was between the Great Causeway and the slopes of the Kourganè Hill that Lacy Yea, with his 7th Fusileers, had long been maintaining an obstinate conflict. Long ago, as we saw, he had crossed the river, had brought his men to the top of the bank, and was trying to form them, when there came down marching upon him a strong Russian column—a column of two battalions, and numbering 1500 men. These battalions belonged to the corps which was sometimes called the Regiment of the Grand-Duke Michael, and more often the Regiment of Kazan. Like the English corps to which they stood opposed, these battalions were 'Fusileers.' Soon the column was halted.

Protracted fight between the 7th Fusileers and the left Kazan column.

It was then that for the first time in that war the soldiery of the Western Powers were brought so near to a body of Russian troops as to be able to scrutinize its material. The men of the column were of high stature and strictly upright, with broad, plain, whitish faces, all seemingly cast in a common mould, and very similar the one to the other. The long gray overcoat, worn alike by all the officers and men of the Russian forces, and reaching down to the ankles, gave no clew to distinguish this mass from any other of the Czar's battalions; but spiked helmets, glittering with burnished plates of brass, led some of the English to imagine that the column formed part of the Emperor's guard.[1] The body was formed

[1] The notion was ill founded, there being none of the Imperial Guard in the Crimea. I supposed at one time that the helmet imported the presence of heavy infantry, and that the flat round forage-cap with which Crimea men are so familiar, denoted a light infantry regiment. This, however, is not, it seems, the case. The regiment of Kazan was a light infantry regiment.

with great precision in close column with a front of only one company; but a chain of skirmishers, thrown out on either flank in prolongation of the front rank, sought to combine with the solid formation of the column some of the advantages of an array in line.[1] The steady men were in the front and on the flanks of the column; and the constant firing in the air which went on in the interior of the solid battalions showed that that was the place assigned to the young soldiers. The column stood halted at a distance of, perhaps, some fifty yards from the knotted chain of soldiery which represented the 7th Fusileers.

Lacy Yea was so rough an enforcer of discipline that he had never been much liked in peace-time by those who had to obey him; but when once the 7th Fusileers were in campaign, and still more when they came to be engaged with the enemy, they found that their chief was a man who could and would seize for his regiment all such chances of welfare and glory as might come with the fortune of war. Before many months were over, they learned that although other regiments might be dying of want, yet by force of their Colonel's strong will there was food and warmth to be got for the 7th Fusileers; and still sooner, they came to know that the fiery nature of their chief was the quality which would help them to have dominion over the enemy. Thenceforth the strong man was a king beloved by his people.

Lacy Yea had not time to put his Fusileers in their wonted array, for the enemy's column was so near, that forthwith, and at the instant, it was necessary to ply it with fire; but what man could do, he did. His very shoulders so labored and strove with the might of his desire to form line, that the curt red shell-jacket he wore was as though it were a world too scant for the strength of the man and the passion that raged within him; but when he turned, his dark eyes yielded fire, and all the while from his deep-chiseled, merciless lips, there pealed the thunder of imprecation and command. Wherever the men had got clustered together, there—fiercely coming—he wedged his cob into the thick of the crowd—the 'rooge,' he would call it in his old Eton idiom of speech—and by dint of will tore it asunder. Though he could not form an even array, yet he disentangled the thickest clusters of the soldiery,

[1] The advantages of this hybrid formation were strongly urged about the middle of the last century by General Lloyd, an Englishman. General Lloyd was an officer in the service of Russia, and it seems probable that the formation of which he was a vehement advocate may have been adopted in the Russian service in consequence of his advice.

and forced the men to open out into a lengthened chain approaching to line formation. Numbers of the Fusileers were wanting, and on the other hand there were mingled with the battalion many of the soldiery of other regiments. With a force in this state, Yea was not in a condition to attempt a charge or any other combined movement. All he could hope to be able to do was to keep his people firm on their ground, to hinder them from contracting their front or gathering into heavy clusters, and then leave every man to make the best use he could of his rifle.

Continental generals would not easily believe that upon fair open ground there could be a doubtful conflict between, on the one side, a body of fifteen hundred brave, steady, disciplined soldiers, superbly massed in close column, and, on the other, a loose knotted chain of six or seven hundred light infantry men without formation. Yet the fight was not so unequal as it seemed. A close column of infantry has only small means of offense, and is itself a thing so easy to hurt that every volley it receives from steady troops must load it with corpses and wounded men. Tested strictly in that way—tested strictly by its small means of hurting people, and the ease with which it can be hurt—the close column is a weak thing to fight with; and yet it has power over the troops of most nations, because its grandeur well fits it for weighing upon the imaginations of men.

But Lacy Yea and his islanders were not so fashioned by nature, nor so tamed down by much learning, as to be liable to be easily coerced in any subtle, metaphysical way; and although the shots of individual soldiers and small knots of men had not, of course, the crushing power which would have been exerted by the fire of the 7th Fusileers when formed and drawn up in line, still, the well-handled rifles of our men soon began to carry havoc into the dark gray oblong mass of living beings which served them for their easy target. And though seemingly the front rank of the compact mass yearned to move forward, there was always occurring in the interior some sudden death or some trouble with a wounded man, which seemed not only to breed difficulty in the way of an advance, but also to make the column here and there begin to look spotted and faulty. The distance was such as to allow of a good deal of shooting at particular men. Once, Yea himself found that he was singled out to be killed, and was covered by a musket or rifle; but the marksman was so fastidious about his aim, that before he touched the trigger a quick-eyed English corporal found time to intervene, and save his colonel's life by shooting the careful Russian in the midst of his studies. 'Thank you, my 'man,' said Lacy Yea; 'if I live through this, you shall be a ser-'geant to-night.'

Whilst this long fight went on, it sometimes happened that the fire and impatience of one or other of the Fusileers would carry a man into closer quarters with the column. Of those who were spurred by sudden impulses of this kind, Monck was one. He sprang forward, they say, from his place on the left of the Fusileers, and saying, 'Come on, 8th company!' rushed up to the enemy's massed battalions, ran his sword through a man in the front rank, and struck another with his fist. He was then shot dead by a musket fired from the second rank of the column. Personal enterprises of this kind were incidents varying the tenor of the fight; but it was by musket or rifle ball, at a distance of some fifty yards, that the real strife between the two corps was waged.

It was not always against the enemy that Lacy Yea was laboring. He came to know or imagine that some of his Fusileers had remained behind in the valley finding base shelter. That this should be, and that even for a few minutes this should pass, was to him not tolerable; and in the fiercest heat of his strife with the column, one of his best officers was sent back, that he might turn the drove out of their sheds, and force them to come instantly into the presence of the enemy—into the presence—more terrible still—of their raging colonel.

The fight lasted. When Codrington's people were scarce beginning their rush toward the face of the Great Redoubt, the 7th Fusileers—rudely and hastily gathered, but contriving to hold together—were beginning this battle of their own. When the storming battalions came down, the regiment was fighting still. When the despondency of the French army was at its worst; when the head of Canrobert's Division was pushed back down the hill by the 'column of the eight battalions;' when along the whole line of the Allies there was no other regiment fighting, Lacy Yea and his people were still at their work. When Evans, having crossed the river, was leading his three battalions to the site of the Causeway batteries, it was the 7th Fusileers that stood fighting alone on his left; and nearly at the very time when disaster befell the centre of the brigade of Guards, Lacy Yea and his Fusileers were gathering at last the reward of their soldierly virtue.

For by this time death and wounds, making cavities and compelling small changes in the great living mass, had injured the symmetry of the spruce Russian column. As a piece of mechanism, it was no longer what it had been when the fight began; but the spirit of the brave and obedient men who composed it was still high. The cohesion of the mass was not yet destroyed; but it was endangered, and had come to depend very much upon the personal exertions of officers.

Lacy Yea observed that every now and then, when a part of the column was becoming faulty, a certain man always on foot, but of vast towering stature, would stride quickly to the defective spot, and exert so great an ascendency, that steadiness and order seemed always to be restored by his presence. The gray overcoat common to all shrouded the rank of every Russian officer, and since this man was not on horseback, there was nothing to disclose his station in the corps save the power which he seemed to wield. What its colonel was to the 7th Fusileers, that the big man seemed to be to the Russian column; and it was not, I think, without a kind of sympathy with him; it was not, one would believe, without a manly reluctance that Yea ordered his people to shoot the tall man. He did, however, so order, and he was quickly obeyed. The tall man dropped dead, and when he had fallen there was no one who seemed to be the like of him in power.

The issue of this long fight of the Fusileers was growing to be a thing of so great moment, or else the sight of it was become so heating, that Prince Gortschakoff now resolved to take part in it bodily. So, deputing Colonel Issakoff, then acting as his Chief of the Staff, to represent him in his absence, he rode down to the column, and strove to lead it on to a charge with the bayonet. But he could do nothing; for, because of the disorder already beginning, and the loss of great numbers of its officers, the heart was nearly out of the column. So, giving orders for the battalions to keep up their fire, he rode away to his right, and left the column still engaged with Yea and his Fusileers.[1]

Portions of the column—mainly those in the centre and in the rear—became discomposed and unsettled. Numbers of men moved a little one way or another, and of these, some looked as though they stepped a pace backward; but no man as yet turned round to face the rear. However, though the movement of each soldier, taken singly, was trifling and insignificant, yet even that little displacement of many men at the same time was shaking the structure. Plainly, the men must

[1] What Prince Gortschakoff says was this:—'I first rode toward the Fu- 'sileers, who were standing firm under a very heavy fire, although losing a 'large amount of men. I first tried to lead them on (à la baionette), but, 'finding that they could not re-form immediately for a charge, and had lost 'nearly all their officers, I left them with orders to continue their feu de 'bataillons.'

be ceasing to feel that the column they stood in was solid. The ranks, which had been straight as arrows, became bent and wavy.

The Russian officers well understood these signs. With drawn swords, moving hither and thither as actively as they could in their long, gray, melancholy coats, they seemed to become loud and vehement with their orders, their entreaties, their threats. Presently their gestures grew violent, and more than one officer was seen to go and seize a wavering soldier by the throat. But in vain; for, seemingly by some law of its own nature rather than under any new stress of external force, the column began to dissolve. The hard mass became fluid. It still cohered; but what had been, as it were, the outlines of a wall, were becoming like the outlines of a cloud. First some, then more, then all turned round. Moving slowly, and as though discontent with its fate, the column began to fall back.

Defeat of the column.

The 7th Fusileers bought this triumph with blood. In killed and wounded it lost twelve officers, and more than two hundred men. Monck, we before saw, was killed; and Hare, Watson, Fitzgerald, Persse, Appleyard, Coney, Crofton, Carpenter, and Jones, were wounded. For some time one of the colors of the regiment was missing, but it did not at any time fall into the hands of the enemy. It was safe in the charge of some soldiers belonging to the Royal Welsh.[1]

A regimental officer engaged in a general action can not often at the time compute the relative importance of the duty which he is performing; but on the morrow of the battle, or even perhaps much later, he may learn that the fortune of the day was hinging upon the conduct of his single regiment. Lacy Yea was a simple-hearted, straight-going man, with a wholesome ardor for fighting, and a great care for the honor and welfare of his regiment, but not looking far beyond it. Around him the battle had been flowing and ebbing. With the watching of those changes he did not much vex his mind. He hardly, perhaps, remarked them. He was too busy with the fight to be able to contemplate the battle. Except when he yearned to unearth the people whom he believed to be skulking, and to have them dragged before him, he thought of nothing but that the corps he commanded should stand fighting and fighting till it got the victory. He went through with his resolve, and hardly knew at the time the full worth of his

[1] The color, I believe, was found lying upon the ground, but how that came to happen I do not know, and I have not thought it necessary to find out, because the color was never for a moment "lost."

constancy. He hardly knew that, whilst he fought, the whole of the English front line—first on his left hand, and then on his right—had been getting the support it grievously needed from the tenacity of his 7th Fusileers.[1]

It is arranged that the defeated column is to be pressed by the Grenadier Guards.

It was plainly right that the defeated column should be pressed in its retreat by troops in a state of formation; and Yea, looking back, perceived that the Guards were now at hand. Troubridge went to the Grenadiers; saw one of its officers; told him of the defeat of the Russian column, and of the condition of the 7th Fusileers; and asked whether it would not be well that the Grenadier Guards should come up and clinch the defeat of the retiring column. Colonel Hood was referred to, and he at once consented to do as was proposed.

Sir George Brown—his gray so wounded that men saw the blood from afar—now chanced to ride to the part of the hill-side where Troubridge was passing. After telling him of the defeat of the Russian column, and of the state of the 7th Fusileers, Troubridge asked him whether the Fusileers should go on, or allow the Guards to pass them.[2]

Sir George said, 'Let the Guards go on. Collect your men, 'and afterward resume the advance.'

## XXX.

State of the field in this part of the Russian position.

When it was nearly abreast of the Great Redoubt, the column just defeated by Lacy Yea's Fusileers was able to rally, and again show a front to the English;[3] for it had on its right the great Vladimir column, which still stood halted near the parapet of the Great Redoubt. On the right rear of the Vladimir men there was a double-battalion column, formed out of the Kazan corps.[4] On the right of that last column, but still farther held back,

[1] See plan. When Codrington's people were storming the redoubt, they were covered on their right by the fight which Yea was there maintaining. When they had to fall back, it was still that stand of the Fusileers which covered their flank. When Evans advanced with his three battalions, there was nothing but the 7th Fusileers to cover his left.

[2] At this time, and whilst he was still speaking with Sir George Brown, Troubridge observed the sight, which will be referred to in a future page, as fixing the order in which events followed one another in different parts of the field.

[3] After their defeat, the two battalions which composed the column seem to have parted from one another. The two bodies into which it resolved itself remained bravely lingering on the hill-side, though, having lost most of their officers, they were in a helpless condition.

[4] The column defeated by the 19th Regiment, and by some of the men of the 23rd.

there was another double-battalion column, formed of the Sousdal corps; and next to these, but much more in advance, and standing on the extreme right of the whole of the Russian infantry, there were posted the two remaining battalions of the Sousdal corps. Somewhere in this part of the field, but operating, it would seem, as skirmishers, and not perhaps bringing any very material accession of strength, there were the two battalions of sailors. As an immediate reserve, or rather as a support for all these forces, the four Ouglitz battalions were kept in hand on the higher slopes of the Kourganè Hill, and were still, as before, massed in column. At some distance on the extreme right of the Russian position, the enemy's cavalry stood posted as before, confronting from afar, but never provoking, the horsemen of our Light Brigade. After allowing for casualties, and especially for the heavy losses sustained by the column which engaged our 7th Fusileers, it may be conjectured that these Russian forces on the Kourganè Hill amounted to some 15,000 men. Except the Kazan battalions, none of these troops had been hitherto engaged in hard fighting, for the triumphant Vladimir column had not yet encountered formed troops. Nearly all the Russian artillery had been taken away from the front, and, except that there were five pieces of ordnance not yet withdrawn from the Lesser Redoubt, the enemy had no guns now remaining in battery. The impending struggle was a fight — a sheer fight — of infantry.

The Scots Fusileer Guards advance up the slope.

Disaster which befell its left companies.

The advance of the Guards had an ill beginning. We saw that whilst the Grenadiers and the Coldstream were still forming under the bank or completing their passage of the river, the centre battalion of the brigade—the battalion called the 'Scots Fusileer Guards' —had been hurried forward by the appeal from the troops then still clinging to the redoubt, had incurred the fire of the Vladimir column, and had afterward encountered a heap of our men retreating, which broke the formation of its left companies by sheer bodily force, and compelled them to fall back in disorder. The remnant of the battalion thus maimed was at the moment without support; for directly in its rear there were no formed troops coming up, and of the two battalions on its right hand and on its left, neither one nor the other had hitherto come up abreast of it. On the other hand, the force to which the remnant of this English battalion stood opposed was that majestic Vladimir column which had just been driving our Light Infantry men from the parapet of the redoubt. Numbering perhaps some four or five hundred men, these remains of what had been the centre battalion of the Guards stood drawn up in line upon a smooth, open slope, and were met by a hitherto victorious column, which was nearly three thousand strong. Still, for some time the maimed battalion pushed forward, and, when afterward it came to a halt, a hard effort was made to hold the ground. But in vain. Either the overwhelming weight of the column in its front, or the mishap encountered by the left companies of the English battalion, or some other cause of evil had destroyed its principle of cohesion; for this right wing now followed the fate of the left one, got into disorder, and fell back. For a time, the whole battalion of the Scots Fusileer Guards was in confusion near the bank of the river.

Situation in which the remnant of the battalion stood.

It falls back in disorder.

This disaster, and the hard struggle maintained by those who sought to avert it, inflicted loss upon the Scots Fusileer Guards. Lord Chewton and 3 sergeants were killed. Colonel Dalrymple, Colonel Berkeley, Colonel Hepburn, Colonel Haygarth, Astley, Bulwer, Buckley, Gipps, Lord Ennismore, and Hugh Annesley,[1] and 13 sergeants, were wounded; and of the rank and file, 17 were killed and 137 wounded.

When Colonel Hood consented to move forward his battalion against the column just defeated by Lacy Yea, he at once caused his men to ascend the bank which had hitherto sheltered it; and, as soon as the battalion was on the top, its left wing began to incur a good deal of the fire of the Vladimir column. Burgoyne, carrying one of the colors, was wounded; and the charge of the colors then devolving on Lieutenant Robert Hamilton, he also, in the next minute, was struck down by shot; but he quickly rose from the ground, recovered his hold of the standard, and was able to carry it to the end of the battle. Under this fire the battalion dressed its ranks with precision, and marched forward in beautiful order. This it kept till its left wing encountered some of the clusters of men coming down from the Great Redoubt. Then, as we saw before, the battalion opened its ranks for the passage of the retreating soldiery, and afterward formed up anew. This done, it marched on.

The Grenadier Guards ascend to the top of the bank, and there dress their ranks under fire.

Their march up the slope.

[1] It happened to me afterward to see and wonder at the high courage and composure with which Annesley bore his dreadful wound. A musket-shot had entered his jaw, and passed, tearing its way through the mouth. The wound was of such a kind that it seemed as though nothing but death could be of use to him. Yet he was not only uncomplaining, but able to think and act for others.

Meanwhile, General Codrington had been laboring to bring together the remnant of his brigade. Sergeant O'Connor, of the 23rd, still bore the color which he had been carrying with loving care through the worst stress of the fight. The missing color of the 7th Fusileers, now committed to the honor of the 23rd, was borne by Captain Pearson. Around these two standards Codrington rallied such men as he could gather, and made them open out and form line two deep. The body thus formed numbered about 300 men, and Codrington was going to move it forward and place it on the left of the Grenadier Guards, in order to fill up a part of the chasm which had been wrought in the Household Brigade by the discomfiture of its centre battalion.[1] But it occurred to him—for he was himself a Guardsman, and he knew the feelings of the corps—that to place soldiers of the Line abreast of the Grenadiers, and in the room of the broken regiment, might give pain to a battalion of the Guards; so he sent to the Grenadiers to know if they would like troops to come up to fill the empty space. The answer was a proud one. It was also, perhaps, a rash answer;[2] for the Vladimir column—vast and strong, with a sense of the power it had just put forth—was impending over the left front of the Grenadiers, and confronting the interval which the defeat of the centre battalion left empty. However, the answer was 'No!' and the Grenadiers, with their left flank stark open, but in beautiful order, contentedly marched up the slope.

Codrington rallies some of the men of the Light Division, and proposes to place them in the chasm left by the centre battalion of the Guards.

His proposal rejected by the Grenadier Guards.

Continued advance of the 1st Division.

A little later, and at a moment when the Grenadiers were halted on the slope, with the Vladimir column impending over their left flank, Major Home of the 95th, and an ensign of the same corps, came bearing the colors of their regiment, and having with them eight men. Home, accosting Colonel Hamilton, who commanded the left wing of the Grenadiers, said that the eight men then following the colors of the 'Derbyshire' were all that remained together, and that he wished to take part with the Grenadiers in continuing the fight. Colonel Hamilton, assenting, told Home to fall in on the left of the Grenadiers. Afterward, other men of the 'Derbyshire' came up and joined their colors. A few moments

Afterward some men of the 95th Regiment, and a rallied company of the Scots Fusileer Guards, come and advance on the left of the Grenadiers.

[1] The Scots Fusileer Guards. See *ante*, p. 572.

[2] It would be so, if the emergency was one in which three or four hundred men, hastily gathered from several broken regiments, were likely to do good. Upon the contrary supposition, the answer, of course, was a wise one.

later, Colonel Berkeley came up, bringing with him a company of the Scots Fusileer Guards, which he had been able to rally, and he also was requested to place himself on the left of the Grenadiers.

On the left of the Grenadiers there was that chasm which had been wrought in the brigade of Guards by the defeat of its centre battalion; and on the left of the chasm there stood the 'Coldstream.' This battalion of the Guards confronted the centre and right of the great Vladimir column, and was drawn up in line with beautiful precision. Because of the position of the ground on which it advanced, it had been much less exposed to fire and mishaps than either of the other battalions of the brigade, and it had not been pressed forward, as each of the two other battalions had been, to meet any special emergency occurring on its front. Therefore it was that it fell to the lot of the Coldstream to become an almost prim sample of what our Guards can be in the moment which precedes a close fight. What the best of battalions is when, in some Royal Park at home, it manœuvres before a great princess, that the Coldstream was now on the banks of the Alma, when it came to show its graces to the enemy. And it was no ignoble pride which caused the battalion to maintain all this ceremonious exactness; for though it be true that the precision of a line in peace-time is only a success in mechanics, the precision of a line on a hill-side, with the enemy close in front, is the result and the proof of a warlike composure. And it ought to be remembered—though our knowledge of the final result makes it hard to go back into the dark, trying dimly to measure the worth of deeds done in the hour of trial—it ought to be remembered that the undertaking of the troops in this part of the field was not an undertaking to swell the tide of victory, but to retrieve a disaster.

The Coldstream.

Happily it is then, just then, after the discomfiture of troops in front, that English soldiery advancing in support attain their highest glory. For by nature they are so constituted that the misfortune of their comrades carries no alarm into their ranks. It only heats their blood, rousing, as it seems, a sentiment akin to anger; and when they have thus been wrought upon, they are sterner men for a foe to have to do with than they are when all has gone well.

The temper of English soldiery advancing in support after a check sustained by their comrades.

The Duke of Cambridge was with this battalion, for its left was nearly in the centre of the troops over which his command extended. With it also there was a visitor whose presence showed the strength of the tie between the officer and his regiment. Colonel Steele had broken loose from his duty at Head-quarters, and was riding with his own beloved 'Cold-'stream.'[1]

Advance of the Highland brigade.

Farther to the left, and in the same formation, the three battalions of the Highland brigade were extended. But the 42nd had found less difficulty

than the 93rd in getting through the thick ground and the river, and, again, the 93rd had found less difficulty than the 79th; so, as each regiment had been formed, and moved forward with all the speed it could command, the brigade fell naturally into direct échelon of regiments, the 42nd in front. And although this order was occasioned by the nature of the ground traversed and not by design, it was so well suited to the work in hand that Sir Colin Campbell did not for a moment seek to change it.

These young soldiers, distinguished to the vulgar eye by their tall stature, their tartan uniforms, and the plumes of their Highland bonnets, were yet more marked in the eyes of those who know what soldiers are by the warlike carriage of the men, and their strong, lithesome, resolute step. And Sir Colin Campbell was known to be so proud of them, that already, like the Guards, they had a kind of prominence in the army, which was sure to make their bearing in action a broad mark for blame or for praise.

From the time when General Buller had judged it right to abstain from bringing his force to the support of his comrades in the Great Redoubt, the two battalions which remained under his control had stood halted near the bank of the river, and one of them — the 88th — was still formed in a hollow square, as though expecting a charge of cavalry. Sir Colin Campbell conceived that this attitude of the 88th was unsuited to the time and the place, and not knowing that General Buller in person was directing the regiment, Sir Colin, in some anger, took upon himself to request, nay, almost to command, that the hollow square should be instantly changed into line formation. When the ranks of the Highlanders came up to

[1] He was military secretary to Lord Raglan.

this part of the ground, and still went on continuing their advance, a man of one of the halted regiments—a man speaking—perhaps in a coarse, cynic spirit, perhaps in the deep, honest bitterness of his heart—cried out, 'Let the Scotchmen go 'on! they'll do the work!' Then the Highlanders marched through, leaving General Buller and his two battalions in their rear.

It was upon Sir Colin Campbell now, as on General Buller a short time before, that there devolved the anxious duty of securing the Allied armies from any flank attack which might be undertaken against them at a moment when our troops were engaging the enemy in front; and Sir Colin at one moment judged that with the battalion which formed his extreme left he ought to stand ready to show a front in any direction. He therefore sent Sterling to direct that the 79th should go into column.[1]

But, seen in the dim field of battle, an enemy's force bears marked on its front faint, delicate, momentous signs, analogous to those which, in speaking of a man or a woman, are called 'expressions of countenance;' and it is given to men who know and love the business of war to be able to read those signs. Sir Colin Campbell well understood that the enemy ought to assail his left flank with a storm of horse, foot, and artillery; and, to deal with any such onslaught, he at first took care to stand ready; but when he came to ride forward and gain higher ground, the old soldier was able to divine that with all their three thousand lancers, and all their columns of infantry, the Russians would venture nothing against his flank. He therefore recalled his order to the 79th, and allowed it to go forward in line.

Including the chasm which divided the Grenadier Guards from the Coldstream, the whole line in which the Duke of Cambridge now moved forward to the attack of the Kourganè Hill was more than a mile and a half in length.[2] It was only

[1] It is from a body of troops massed in column that the greatest variety of manœuvres can be quickly and safely evolved. When a battalion extended in line is called upon to change its front, the radius of the segment in which it must wheel is of course very long.

[2] The 1st Division was upon a greater front than had been covered by the 47th Regiment, Pennefather's brigade, and the Light Division; yet it did not cover a foot more of ground than was right. We before saw the effect produced by trying to put ten battalions upon ground which was now found to be not more than enough for six. It is hardly necessary to say that a knowledge of the quantity of ground covered by a single battalion in a barrack-yard would not give a sufficient clew for getting at the extent of ground which was covered by six battalions drawn up in line upon a field of battle.

two deep; but its right regiment was supported by a part of Sir Richard England's Division; and Sir George Cathcart was on its left rear with the part of his Division then on the field. On the extreme left and left rear of the whole force, there was the cavalry under Lord Lucan.

The nature of the fight now about to take place on the Kourganè Hill.

These troops were going to take part in the first approach to close strife which men had yet seen on that day between bodies of troops in a state of formation deliberately marshaled against each other.[1] The slender red line which began near the bridge, and vanished from the straining sight on the eastern slopes of the Kourganè Hill, was a thread which in any one part of it had the strength of only two men. But along the whole line from east to west these files of two men each were strong in the exercise of their country's great prerogative. They were in English array. They were fighting in line against column.

After the rupture of the peace of Amiens, Sir Arthur Wellesley, being then in India, became singularly changed, growing every day more and more emaciated, and seemingly more and more sad. He pined; and was like a man dying without any known bodily illness, the prey of some consuming thought. At length he suddenly announced to Lord Wellesley his resolve to go back to England; and when he was asked why, he said, 'I observe that in Europe the French are fighting in 'column, and carrying every thing before them, and I am sure 'that I ought to go home directly, because I know that our 'men can fight in line.' From that simple yet mighty faith he never swerved; for, always encountering the massive columns of infantry, he always was ready to meet them with his slender line of two deep. With what result the world knows.[2]

Sir Colin Campbell was free to take ground to his left, and he took it amply, contriving to outflank, or almost to outflank, the enemy's infantry array.

[1] The French had not been engaged in any conflicts of this sort; for, though the head of Canrobert's Division confronted formed troops for a moment at a distance of a few hundred yards, it dropped back, as we saw, without fighting. Evans's struggle had been in thick ground, not allowing regular array. Codrington's people (including Lacy Yea's Fusileers as well as the stormers of the redoubt) had had hard fighting, and against troops in perfect order, but they had gone through their struggles without the advantage of being themselves in a state of formation.

[2] An account of Sir Arthur Wellesley's pining sickness, his "wasting away," as he himself described it, is given in published accounts of men who remarked it (in Malcolm's book, I think, or Monro's), and his disclosure of the motive which caused him to return to Europe was preserved and handed down by Lord Wellesley. What I have ventured to do is to seem to connect the pining sickness with the mighty resolve which was destined to change the fate of the world.

Long years had passed since the close of those great wars, and now, once more in Europe there was going to be waged yet again the old strife of line against column.

Looking down a smooth, gentle, green slope, checkered red with the slaughtered soldiery who had stormed the redoubt, the front-rank men of the great Vladimir column were free to gaze upon two battalions of the English Guards, far apart the one from the other, but each carefully drawn up in line; and now that they saw more closely, and without the distractions of artillery, they had more than ever grounds for their wonder at the kind of array in which the English soldiery were undertaking to assail them. 'We were all astonished,' says Chodasiewicz—yet he wrote of what he saw when the English line was much less close to the foe than the Guards now were—'We were all astonished at the extraordinary firmness with 'which the red-jackets, having crossed the river, opened a 'heavy fire in line upon the redoubt. This was the most ex'traordinary thing to us, as we had never before seen troops 'fight in lines of two deep, nor did we think it possible for 'men to be found with sufficient firmness of morale to be able 'to attack, in this apparently weak formation, our massive columns.' But soon the men of the column began to see that though the scarlet line was slender, it was very rigid and exact. Presently, too, they saw that even when the Grenadiers or the Coldstreams began to move, the long line of the black bearskins still kept a good deal of its straightness, and that here on the bloody slope, no less than in the barrack-yard at home, the same moment was made to serve for the tramp of a thousand feet.

## XXXI.

Beginning on our right hand with the Grenadier Guards, and going thence leftward to the Coldstream, and, lastly, to the Highland brigade, we shall now see what manner of strife it was when at length, after many a hinderance, five British battalions, each grandly formed in line, marched up to the enemy's columns.

Advancing upon the immediate left of the ground already won by Pennefather's brigade; the Grenadiers were covered on their right, but their left was bare; and it was in that direction—in the direction of their left front—that the Vladimir battalions stood impending. The Grenadiers were marching against the defeated, but now rallied column, which had fought with the 7th Fusileers, when Prince Gortschakoff, having just ridden up to the two left battalions of

Prince Gortschakoff's ad-

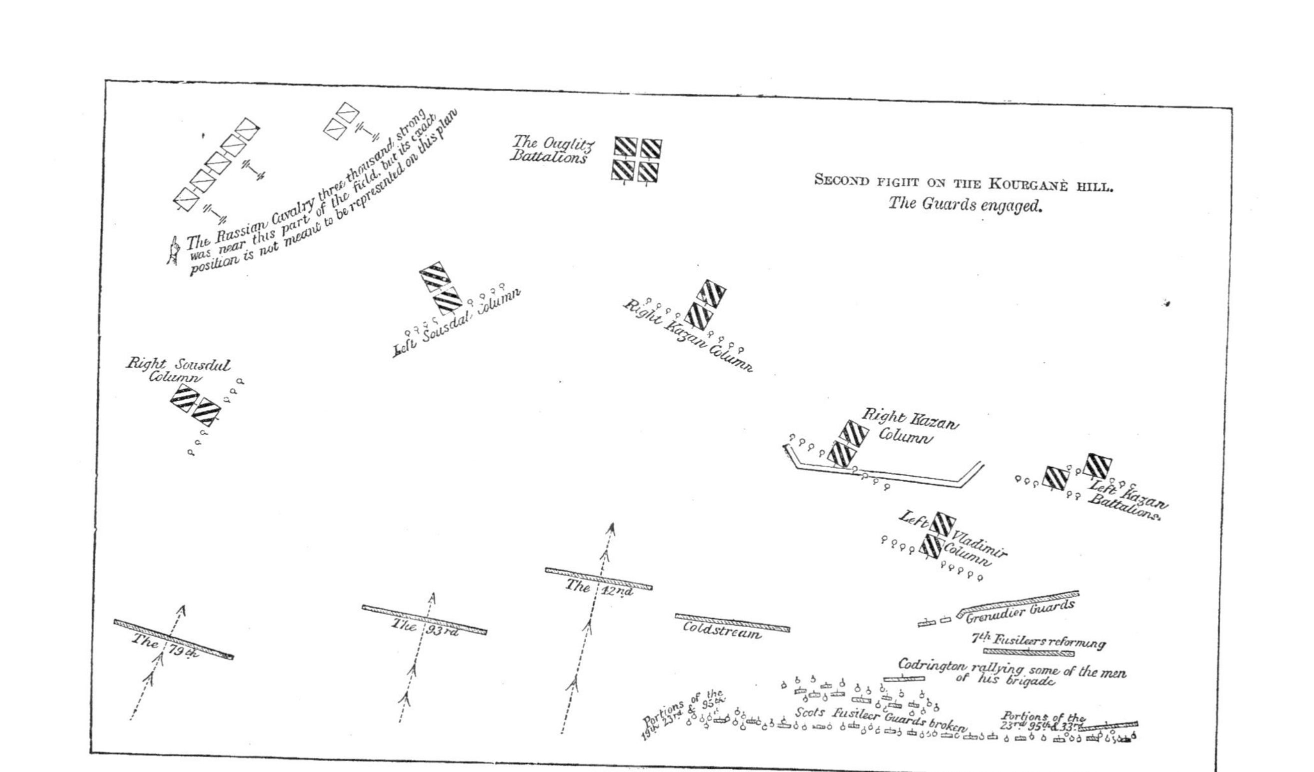
SECOND FIGHT ON THE KOURGANÈ HILL.
The Guards engaged.
The Russian Cavalry three thousand strong was near this part of the field, but its exact position is not meant to be represented on this plan
The Ouglitz Battalions
Left Sousdal Column
Right Kazan Column
Right Sousdul Column
Right Kazan Column
Left Kazan Battalions.
Left Vladimir Column
The 79th
The 93rd
The 42nd
Coldstream
Grenadier Guards
7th Fusileers reforming
Codrington rallying some of the men of his brigade
Portions of the 19th 23rd & 95th
Scots Fusileer Guards broken
Portions of the 23rd 95th & 33rd

vance with a column of the Vladimir corps.

the Vladimir, undertook to lead them forward. First sending his only unwounded aid-de-camp to press the advance of any troops he could find, the Prince put himself at the head of the two left Vladimir battalions, and ordered them to charge with the bayonet.[1] The Prince then rode forward a good deal in advance of his troops, and his order for a bayonet charge was so far obeyed, that the column, without firing a shot, moved boldly down toward the chasm which had been left in the centre of our brigade of Guards. The northwest angle of this strong and hitherto victorious column was coming down nearer and nearer to the file—the file composed of only two men—which formed the extreme left of the Grenadiers.

Colonel Hood's manœuvre.

Then, and by as fair a test as war could apply, there was tried the strength of the line formation, the quality of the English officer, the quality of the English soldier. Colonel Hood first halted, and then caused the left subdivision of the left company to wheel—to wheel back in such a way as to form, with the rest of the battalion, an obtuse angle. The manœuvre was executed by Colonel Percy (he was wounded just at this time) under the directions of Colonel Hamilton, the officer in command of the left wing. In this

[1] I must acknowledge that I do not gather from the Russian accounts any distinct mention of this separation of the great Vladimir column into two columns of two battalions each. Prince Gortschakoff's narrative speaks of the column with which he moved as 'the battalions of the Vladimir regiment 'standing on the left of the epaulement' (the breastwork), and this is an expression which might either apply to two battalions which had been separated from the other two, or it might apply to all the four battalions of the corps. I have, however, found it so impracticable to reconcile this last interpretation with known facts, that I have adopted the former one. Upon this point I am not in terms helped by Kvetzinski's narrative; but as he himself was clearly with *some* of the Vladimir battalions all this time, and as he had no knowledge of the fact that Gortschakoff had made a charge with battalions of the same corps, it seems to follow as a necessary consequence that at this time the four battalions had been divided into two columns. A concurrence of circumstances leads me to infer that this was the case, and that one of the columns, as I have stated, was toward the right and the other toward the left of the redoubt. At first sight it may seem odd that Kvetzinski, the divisional general, should not know what was being done with two of his battalions posted at only a small distance from the column with which he rode; but the truth is that Gortschakoff, having for the time the supreme command in this part of the field, and being (as is evident from his own account) in a high state of excitement, rode up to the Vladimir battalions, which he found near the (Russian) left of the earthwork, and, so to speak, snatched them without saying a word to the general commanding the Division. After all, the movement which he made in advance was only a slight one; and for that reason, perhaps, it was hardly looked upon as severing the troops taking part in it from those which remained with Kvetzinski.

way, whilst he still faced the column which he had originally undertaken to attack, Colonel Hood showed another front, a small, but smooth, comely front, to the mass which was coming upon his flank. His manœuvre instantly brought the Vladimir to a halt; and to those who—without being near enough to

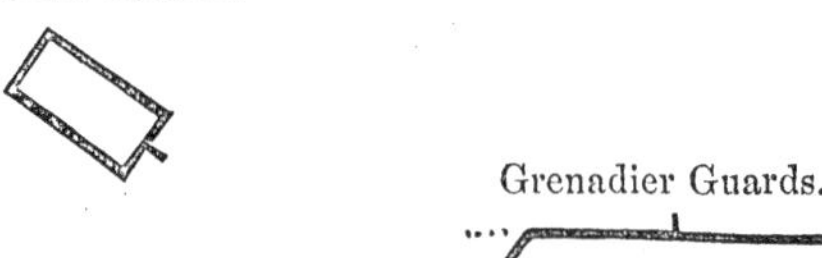


hear the giving and the repeating of the orders—still were able to see Colonel Hood thus changing a part of his front and stopping a mighty column by making a bend in his line, it seemed that he was handling his fine, slender English blade with a singular grace; with the gentleness and grace of the skilled swordsman, when, smiling all the while, he parries an angry thrust. In the midst of its pride and vast strength of numbers, the Vladimir found itself checked; nay, found itself gravely engaged with half a company of our Guardsmen; and the minds of these two score of islanders were so little inclined to bend under the weight of the column, that they kept their perfect array. Their fire was deadly, for it was poured into a close mass of living men. It was at the work of "file firing" that the whole battalion now labored.

*Its effect.*

On the left of the interval wrought by the displacement of the centre battalion of the Guards, the Coldstream, drawn up in superb array, began to open its smart, crashing fire upon the more distant battalions which formed the right wing of the Vladimir force.

*The Coldstream.*

We shall see the share which other Russian and other British troops were destined to have in governing the result of the struggle; but if, for a moment, we limit our reckoning to the troops which stood fighting at this time, it appears that the whole of the four Vladimir battalions and the lessened mass of the left Kazan column were engaged with the Grenadiers and the Coldstream. In other words, two English battalions, each ranged in line, but divided the one from the other by a very broad chasm, were contending with six battalions in column. And, although of these six battalions standing in column there were two which had cruelly suffered, the remaining four

*The Grenadiers and the 'Coldstream' engaged with six battalions in columns.*

had hitherto had no hard fighting, and were flushed with the thought that they stood on ground which they themselves had reconquered.

But, after all, if only the firmness of the slender English line should chance to endure, there was nothing except the almost chimerical event of a thorough charge home with the bayonet which could give to the columns the ascendency due to their vast weight and numbers; for the fire from a straitened, narrow front could comparatively do little harm, whilst the fire of the battalion in line was carrying havoc into the living masses. Still, neither column nor line gave way. On the other hand, neither column nor line moved forward. Fast rooted as yet to the ground, the groaning masses of the Russians and the two scarlet strings of Guardsmen stood receiving and delivering their fire.

The stress which a line puts upon the soldiery of a column.

But meanwhile, on the part of the English, another mind, as we shall see by-and-by, was bringing its strength to bear upon this part of the battle.

If the English method of array puts a grievous stress upon the soldiery of Continental masses, its pressure is not less hard upon the mind of a general who has the suffering columns in his charge. It not only shocks him by the sight of a great slaughter of his people occurring in small spaces of ground; it not only forces upon him a sense of being outflanked, but sometimes, it even seems, oppresses him with a belief that he is overwhelmed by mighty numbers. General Kvetzinski was with the right Vladimir column. He was a brave, able man, and we have already seen something of what the relative numbers were with which the Russians and the English were fighting; but it seems that the spectacle of the immense front presented by the English army broke down the General's sense of his own comparative strength, and put upon him the belief that he was cruelly outnumbered. Even the sight of the wide chasm there was between the two battalions of the Guards did not lift the weight from his heart. 'The enormous forces,' said he—'the enormous forces 'of the enemy made our position a very dangerous one.'

And upon a general who has charge of columns.

Impressions as wrought upon the mind of Kvetzinski by the English array.

It was near the eastern shoulder of the redoubt that he sat in his saddle. Every moment he had been growing more anxious, for, besides the troubles that were besetting his front, he could not but know that Pennefather's brigade was established in the Pass, and the apparition of our Head-Quarter Staff on the knoll, followed quick by Turner's guns, had cheated him into the notion that the whole French army was marching straight eastward into the English field of battle. Nay, he imagined that the guns on the knoll were throwing a flanking fire into the left of his Vladimir battalions;[1] and, indeed, it would seem that these battalions were really struck—not by cannon on the knoll, but—by some guns just put in battery on one of the spurs overlooking the Pass.[2] But now, when he looked to his right; when he looked slantwise down to the east of where the Coldstream stood ranged, he saw an array of tall plumes, having eight times the front of one of his own battalion columns; looking a little farther eastward, he saw another array which, though it was not yet so near, was like to the first, and was moving. Again, when he looked still farther eastward, he saw yet another array coming up, and though it was less near than the first, and even less near than the second, it was like to either of them in the greatness of its front, and the towering plumes of the men. Kvetzinski could see that, taken together, these three lines of plumed soldiers had a front some twenty times broader than one of his battalion columns, and (still, it seems, suffering himself to infer vast numbers from mere extent of front) he began to have that torturing sense of being outnumbered and outflanked which weighed upon the memory and forever replenished the diction of the

[1] He was wrong in this. Turner's guns tried their range against the columns on the Kourganè Hill, but found the distance too great. The passage in which Kvetzinski speaks of the state of things in the direction of 'the 'knoll' is this:—'From the left the French, having forced our left wing fore-'posts, were hurrying to the rescue of their allies, whose efforts were begin-'ning to flag before the unheard-of and unparalleled heroism of the brave 'Vladimirtzi. The French battery, having taken up its position on the left 'wing of our side' (this so called "French battery" was Turner's battery on the knoll), 'began to fire sideways on the fast thinning ranks of our gallant 'regiment. Their reserve were hastening to cut off our retreat.' I have already shown how all but inevitable it was that Kvetzinski and all other Russians on the Kourganè Hill should make this mistake, should suppose that the group of plumed officers in blue frocks who crowned the knoll betokened the presence of the French army in that part of the field, and that Turner's guns were a French battery. If amongst the French or their friends there are any men so constituted as to wish to keep the benefit derived from this mistake, their best course will be to quote this passage from Kvetzinski, and to suppress the explanation which shows how his error arose. For the sake of fairness, and not without a foresight of the wrongful use which may be made of the passage, I give what I believe to be a close and accurate translation from the Russian words in which it was written.

[2] I rest this belief entirely upon the authority of Colonel Hamley's soldierly narrative, 'The Campaign of Sebastopol,' p. 31. Colonel Hamley was himself in the artillery, and all that he says respecting the operations of the arm to which he belonged has of course a peculiar value. The guns were some of those thirty pieces of ordnance which Evans and Sir Richard England had just brought into the Pass.

warlike Psalmist. It seemed to him that the enemy 'increased 'upon him to trouble him;' that 'the nations compassed him 'round about;' that they 'came round about him like water;' that they 'kept him in on every side; yea, that they kept him 'in on every side.' This anxiety was all wrongly based. Far from having his whole array outflanked toward the east to any woeful extent, Kvetzinski had a column on his extreme right which fairly enough confronted the extreme left of the English infantry; and, far indeed from being outnumbered, he was fighting this fight of the Kourganè Hill with a strength of nearly three against two; but it followed, from the difference between his and his enemy's manner of fighting, that each of his columns, taken separately, was widely outflanked, and he was becoming an example of what must happen to the commander of columns when (without exerting his weight by trying to charge home with the bayonet) he strives to set his dense masses against troops standing firmly in line.

The sight of a battalion advancing upon his right front convinces him that he must move.

Presently he saw that the array of plumed soldiers which had stood ranged next to the Coldstream was moving—was moving up—was moving swiftly; and he knew that the nearest of the columns which he had on his right was so far from the ground where he stood, and so hindered, too, by the intervening dip of the ground, as to be unable to engage the new-comers before the moment when (unless he retreated) they would reach the flank of his right Vladimir battalions. On the other hand, he could not, in common prudence, stand still and wait to be turned by the battalion now gliding up the slope on his right; for, brave as were his Vladimir men, a huge, massive Russian column was not the delicate weapon with which he could try to imitate Colonel Hood, showing a front at once on two sides. Therefore it became but too clear to him that the columns along the redoubt must move to some ground other than where they were. And this almost instantly, for the bending plumes did not cease from coming.

Meantime the columns along the redoubt are becoming distressed by their fight with the Grenadiers and the Coldstream.

But, also, all this while the columns along the redoubt were more and more feeling the stress that was put upon them by the fire and the array of the Guards. Just after the moment when the Vladimir men were brought to a halt by Colonel Hood's manœuvre, Prince Gortschakoff, still riding at the head of the column, was violently thrown to the ground. He had received no wound from the shot which caused his fall, but his charger was killed by it; and, there being no other horsemen near, he was obliged to remain on foot. It would seem that the concussion of the fall may have clouded his judgment. At all events, after this accident he walked away toward a column which he saw coming down in support.[1] On his road he passed through the site of the Great Redoubt, and there found General Kvetzinski. The Prince, walking up to the divisional general, told him that he had had his horse shot under him, and that all the field-officers of the regiment[2] he commanded had been killed. It is not stated that the two Generals, thus meeting at a critical moment, took occasion to consult about the way in which they should fight out the battle. When their conversation had ended, Prince Gortschakoff walked up the hill-side, going on toward the column which he wanted to meet.[3]

The shot which dismounted Prince Gortschakoff, his departure from the ground where the Vladimir stood, the spruce beauty of the slender red line which had brought it to bay, and the steadiness of the fire with which the brave column had been plied for now several minutes — all these were causes which helped to distress the left Vladimir battalions; and although it was the turning movement on the right of the Russian columns which made it a thing of sheer need to move, and to move at once,[4] still it would seem that General Kvetzinski's measures for dealing with the new emergency were forestalled by what he presently saw on his left front; and the event which was destined to put its actual and direct governance upon this part of the battle was the still pending fight between the left Vladimir battalions and the Grenadier Guards.[5]

Continuance of the fight between the Grenadier Guards and the left Vladimir column.

The Grenadiers, when we left them just now, were busy with their rifles along their whole line, and were making good use of that delicate bend in the formation of their leftmost company which enabled them to pour their fire into the heart of the Vladimir column then hanging on their flank. The reckoning of him who puts his trust in column is mainly based on the

[1] The four Ouglitz battalions.

[2] Meaning, I imagine, the Kazan Fusileers.

[3] All this is told by Prince Gortschakoff himself with simplicity and apparent truthfulness. It is plain that his fall had shaken and confused him.

[4] Kvetzinski says: 'The decisive moment I had been fearing and expect-'ing had arrived: the English moved higher up in three lines, and threat-'ened to turn our right wing.'

[5] 'The left wing,' he says, 'began to falter, leaving my left side exposed.' I understand him to be speaking of troops on the immediate left of the column with which he was riding, and not of any troops on the left of the whole Division which he commanded, because the retreat of the troops in the Pass had taken place before the time of which he is speaking.

notion that its mere grandeur of aspect will give it a clear ascendant as soon as it is seen at all near; and when the English line had once delivered its fire, the front-rank men of the column were not without grounds for making sure that their next glimpse of the red-coats would be a glimpse of men in retreat; for to have come forward to within a distance convenient for musket-shots, and to have once delivered their fire, this was surely the utmost in the way of close fighting that files of only two men each would attempt against masses. But when, though only a little, the smoke began to lift, the gleams that pierced it were the light that is shed from bayonet points and busy ramrods—gleams twinkling along the line of the two ranks of soldiery, who still, as it seemed, must be lingering in their strange array; and whenever the smoke lifted clear, there—steadfast as oaks disclosed by rising mist—the long avenue of the Bearskins loomed out, and so righteously in place as to begin to enforce a surmise that, after all, the files of the two men each might be minded to stand where they were, ceremoniously shooting into the column, and filling it minute by minute with the tumult of men killed or wounded. And though it was but a few of the men planted close in the massive columns who could thus from time to time look upon the dim forms of the soldiery who dealt the slaughter, yet the anxiousness of those who could gain no glimpse of the Bearskins was not for that reason the less. Nay, it was the greater; for he who knows of a present danger through his reading of other men's countenances, or by seeing his neighbors fall wounded or killed around him, is commonly more disturbed than he who, standing in the front, looks straight into the eye of the storm.

Still, up to this time it was only from the extreme left of the Grenadiers' line that fire was poured into the column. A harder trial was awaiting the Vladimir men. Colonel Hood had hitherto wielded his line as though he judged it right to deal carefully with the left Kazan battalions still lingering on his front; and up to the last, he did not think himself warranted in disdaining their presence; for he could not know that their loss in officers had made them so helpless as they were; but he now saw enough to assure him that his real foe was the left Vladimir column on his flank. Thither, therefore (though he would not altogether avert his line from the defeated troops in his front), he now determined to bend the eyes and the rifles of a great portion of his battalion. So he wheeled forward his battalion upon its left, or in other, and perhaps the more expressive form of military speech, he 'brought forward 'his right shoulder.' Still respecting the presence of the defeated Kázan troops, he did not carry this manœuvre so far as to place his battalion bodily on the flank of the Vladimir column, but he carried it far enough to make the column a mark for the troops which formed his left wing. The Vladimir was

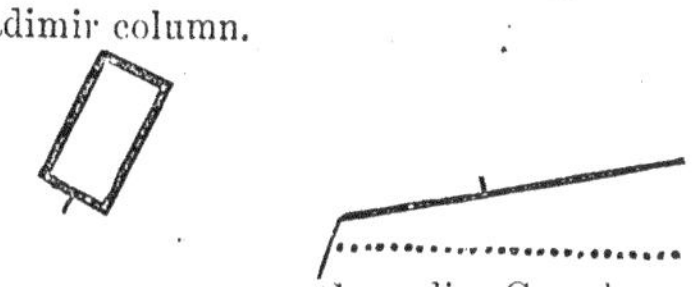

Vladimir column.

Grenadier Guards.

wrapped in fire: was wrapped in that fire which is hardly tolerable to soldiery massed in column—fire poured upon its flank. Even this, for some minutes, the brave Vladimir bore.

If the voice of the English soldier is heard loud in fight, his shout may be the shout of triumph achieved, or else—and then it is of a thousand-fold higher worth—it may be the like of what used to foretoken the crisis of the old Peninsular battles, when, late in the day, the voice of 'the Light Division' was heard—the almost inspired utterance by which the soldier, growing suddenly conscious of an overmastering power, declares and makes known his ascendant. Of two things happening in a field of battle at nearly the same time, it is often hard to say which was the first, and yet upon that narrow priority of a few moments there may depend the question of which event was the cause and which the effect. What people know is, that there was an instant when the Vladimir column was seen to look hurt and unstable, and that, either at the same instant, or the instant before, or the instant after, the Grenadiers were hurrahing on their left, hurrahing at their centre, hurrahing along their whole line. As though its term of life were measured, as though its structure were touched and sundered by the very cadence of the cheering, the column bulged, heaving, heaving. 'The line will advance on the centre! The men may advance firing.' This, or this nearly, was what Hood had to say to his Grenadiers. Instant sounded the echo of his will. 'The line will advance on the centre! Quick march!' Then, between the column and the seeing of its fate, the cloud which hangs over a modern battle-field was no longer a sufficing veil; for although, whilst the English battalion stood halted, there lay in front of its line that dim, mystic region which divides contending soldiery, yet the Bearskins, since now they were marching, grew darker from east to west, grew taller, grew real, broke

Defeat of the left Vladimir

column, and of the left Kazan battalions.

through. A moment, and the column hung loose. Another, and it was lapsing into sheer retreat. Yet another, and it had come to be like a throng in confusion. Of the left Kazan troops there was no more question. In an array which was all but found fault with for being too grand and too stately, the English battalion swept on.[1]

Kvetzinski's oblique movement of retreat with the right Vladimir column.

Seeing that, before many moments were over, the Grenadiers would be up in the redoubt, Kvetzinski conceived that his retreat by the great road was already cut off, and he ordered that the right Vladimir column —the column with which he was present—should move from the field obliquely, avoiding the English right. This was a path which would take the column along the eastern skirts of the Kourganè Hill, and bring it toward the spot where the right Kazan column stood posted. Kvetzinski, still firm and soldierly, charged a few of his men with the duty of covering his retreat; and, intrusting the command of this little rear-guard to Ensign Berestoffsky, gave orders that the march should be leisurely. He was not ill obeyed; but the movement was hardly one which could be executed with all the accustomed dignity of Russian troops in retreat, for the column had to move slantwise across the front of the battalion which was swiftly ascending the hill, and, if it were to lose many moments, the plumed soldiery would be on its flank.

The Duke of Cambridge is master of the Great Redoubt.

The left wing of the Grenadiers was quickly in the part of the battery where lay the dismounted howitzer, and, on the opposite or eastern shoulder of the work, the Duke of Cambridge, riding up with the Coldstreams, stood master of the Great Redoubt.

Kvetzinski is wounded and disabled.

In its retreat, the right Vladimir column was still plied with the fire of the Coldstream. General Kvetzinski had his horse shot under him; and presently afterward he was so wounded in the leg as to be unable to move on foot. The soldiers around formed a litter for him with their muskets, and the brave man, causing his bearers to march with the rear guard, continued to give his orders to Ensign Berestoffsky. Presently, however, he was again struck by shot, and, indeed, he was now almost shattered, being wounded in two of his limbs and in the side. To the last he had comported himself as a good soldier.

[1] The criticism alluded to in this sentence was that of a French officer who witnessed the advance of the Guards. After speaking of it with enthusiastic admiration, he ended by saying that it was 'too majestic'—'trop majestueux.'

XXXII.

But whose was the mind which had freshly come to bear upon this part of the fight, and what was the plumed array which, threatening Kvetzinski on his right front, forbade him from farther tarrying on the line of the Great Redoubt? Before the moment when the Guards and the columns began their fight, Sir Colin Campbell was sitting in his saddle by the left of the Coldstream, and talking from time to time with the Duke of Cambridge. The veteran was watching for his time. And although the ground before him favored the concealment of troops, yet his skill in the reading of a field of battle had enabled him to see, or in some way know or divine that what forces the Russians had on the right of the Great Redoubt were all more or less held back. So, if he could swiftly move up a battalion to the crest which rose straight before him, he would be on the flank of the position from which the Vladimir confronted the Guards before any other battalions could come down to engage him. Upon descrying his advance, the Russians, he thought, would see the instant need of abandoning their struggle with the Guards; but if by chance, or because of their obstinacy, they should fail to do so, then, as soon as he could reach the ground he longed for, he would bring round the left shoulder, turn full toward the west, and roll up the Muscovite columns before their supports could come down to save them. This was what he thought might be done, and the keen, perfect weapon with which to do it had come fresh into his hand. The other battalions of the Highland brigade were approaching; but the 42nd — the far-famed 'Black Watch' — had already come up. It was ranged in line. The ancient glory of the corps was a treasure now committed to the charge of young soldiers new to battle; but Campbell knew them, was sure of their excellence, and was sure, too, of Colonel Cameron, their commanding officer. Very eager—for the Guards were now engaged with the enemy's columns — very eager, yet silent and majestic, the battalion stood ready.

Sir Colin Campbell's conception of the part he would take with his brigade.

The 42nd was at his side.

Before the action had begun, and whilst his men were still in column, Campbell had spoken to his brigade a few words—words simple, and for the most part workmanlike, yet touched with the fire of warlike sentiment. 'Now, men, you are going into action. Remember this: Whoever is wounded—I don't care what his rank is—whoever is wounded must lie where he falls till the bands-

Sir Colin Campbell and the Highland brigade.

'men come to attend to him. No soldiers must go carrying 'off wounded men. If any soldier does such a thing, his name 'shall be stuck up in his parish church. Don't be in a hur-'ry about firing. Your officers will tell you when it is time 'to open fire. Be steady. Keep silence. Fire low. Now, 'men'—those who know the old soldier can tell how his voice would falter the while his features were kindling—'now, men, 'the army will watch us; make me proud of the Highland 'brigade!'[1]

Their engagement with several Russian columns.

It was before the battle that this, or the like of this, was addressed to the brigade; and now, when Sir Colin rode up to the corps which awaited his signal, he only gave it two words. But because of his accustomed manner of utterance, and because he was a true, faithful lover of war, the two words he spoke were as the roll of the drum: 'Forward, 42nd!' This was all he then said; and, 'as a steed that knows his rider,' the great heart of the battalion bounded proudly to his touch.

Sir Colin Campbell went forward in front of the 42nd, but before he had ridden far he saw that his reckoning was already made good by the event, and that the column which had engaged the Coldstream was moving off obliquely toward its right rear. Then, with his staff, he rode up a good way in advance, for he was swift to hope that the withdrawal of the column from the line of the redoubt might give him the means of learning the ground before him, and seeing how the enemy's strength was disposed in this part of the field. In a few moments he was abreast of the redoubt, and upon the ridge or crest which divided the slope he had just ascended from the broad and rather deep hollow which lay before him. On his right, he had the now empty redoubt; on his right front, the higher slopes of the Kourganè Hill. Straight before him there was the hollow, or basin, just spoken of, bounded on its farther side by a swelling wave or ridge of ground which he called the 'inner crest.' Beyond that, whilst he looked straight before him, he could see that the ground fell off into a valley; but when he glanced toward his left front, he observed that the hollow which lay on his front was, so to speak, bridged

[1] Of course, the memory of those who unexpectedly found themselves hearing Sir Colin's address to his brigade can supply but an imperfect record of the words which were uttered; and perhaps, if the impressions of any great number of the hearers were compared, few or none would be found to be closely similar. I think, however, that the address given in the text is not grossly wide of the truth. At all events, I can answer for the substantial accuracy of the injunction against quitting the ranks in order to carry off wounded men.

over by a bending rib which connected the inner with the outer crest—bridged over in such a way that a column on his left front might march to the spot where he stood without having first to descend into the lower ground. More to his left, the ground was high, but so undulating and varied that it would not necessarily disclose any troops which might be posted in that part of the field.

Confronting Sir Colin Campbell from the other side of the hollow, the enemy had a strong column—the two right battalions of the Kazan corps—and it was toward this body that the Vladimir column, moving off from the line of the redoubt, was all this time making its way. The Russians saw that they were the subject of a general officer's studies; and Campbell's horse at this time was twice struck by shot, but not disabled. When the retiring column came abreast of the right Kazan column, it faced about to the front, and, striving to recover its formation, took part with the Kazan column in opposing a strength of four battalions—four battalions hard-worked and much thinned—to the one which, eager and fresh, was following the steps of the Highland General. Looking toward his left front, and along the natural bridge or viaduct which has just been spoken of, Sir Colin Campbell saw another column much heavier than either of the two which confronted him. This heavy column was composed of two battalions of the Sousdal corps, and it was of greater size and strength than the Vladimir and the Kazan columns, because it was as yet untouched. A column formed of the two remaining Sousdal battalions—battalions also untouched—was on the extreme right of the enemy's infantry position, but so placed that at this moment it could not be seen by Campbell. On the higher slopes of the Kourganè Hill, the four Ouglitz battalions stood impending over the scene of the coming fight, and these battalions were also untouched. With three battalions Sir Colin Campbell was about to engage no less than twelve;[1] but the three were in line, and the twelve were massed in five columns.

[1] Taking the eight untouched Russian battalions at 6000, and supposing the four thinned battalions to have been reduced by one third, *i. e.*, from 3000 to 2000, the Russian force here engaging would be 8000; and if the numbers of the Highland brigade be put at 2500, it results that the numbers of the Russians were to those of Sir Colin as 16 to 5, or rather more than 3 to 1. If it be thought fairer to exclude the Ouglitz column (on the ground that its soldiery did not actually exchange fire with the Highlanders, and might therefore be regarded as counterbalanced by the force under Cathcart), the numbers of the Russians actually engaging Sir Colin Campbell would be to the Highland brigade in a proportion of exactly two to one. This comparison of numbers is given in order to convey a true idea of the nature of the

Few were the moments that Campbell took to learn the ground before him, and to read the enemy's mind; but, few though they were, they were all but enough to bring the 42nd to the crest where their General stood. The ground they had to ascend was a good deal more steep and more broken than the slope close beneath the Redoubt. In the land where those Scots were bred, there are shadows of sailing clouds skimming straight up the mountain's side, and their paths are rugged, are steep, yet their course is smooth, easy, and swift. Smoothly, easily, swiftly, the 'Black Watch' seemed to glide up the hill. A few instants before, and their tartans ranged dark in the valley. Now their plumes were on its crest. The small knot of horsemen who had ridden on before them were still there. Any stranger looking into the group might almost be able to know—might know by the mere carriage of the head—that he in the plain, dark-colored frock, he whose sword-belt hung crosswise from his shoulder, was the man there charged with command; for in battle men who have to obey sit erect in their saddles; he who has on him the care of the fight seems always to fall into the pensive, yet eager bend which the Greeks—keen perceivers of truth—used to join with their conception of Mind brought to bear upon War. It is on board ship perhaps more commonly than ashore that people in peace-time have been used to see their fate hanging upon the skill of one man. Often landsmen at sea have watched the skilled, weather-worn sailor when he seems to look through the gale, and search deep into the home of the storm. He sees what they can not see; he knows what, except from his lips, they never will be able to learn. They stand silent, but they question him with their eyes. So men new to war gaze upon the veteran commander, when, with knitted brow and steady eyes, he measures the enemy's power, and draws near to his final resolve. Campbell, fastening his eyes on the two columns standing before him, and on the heavier and more distant column on his left front, seemed not to think lightly of the enemy's strength; but in another instant (for his mind was made up, and his Highland blood took fire at the coming array of the tartans) his features put on that glow which, seen in men of his race—race known by the kindling gray eye, and the light, stubborn,

fight in which the Highland brigade took part; but it would be a mistake to use it as a warrant for any thing like vaunting over a brave enemy; for after the retreat of the Vladimir from the Great Redoubt, and the shot which disabled Kvetzinski, the divisional general, a comparison of the mere numbers which took part in the succeeding fight could not justly be put forward as a means of showing the relative prowess of the combatants.

crisping hair—discloses the rapture of instant fight. Although at that moment the 42nd was alone, and was confronted by the two columns on the farther side of the hollow, yet Campbell, having a steadfast faith in Colonel Cameron and in the regiment he commanded, resolved to go straight on, and at once, with his forward movement. He allowed the battalion to descend alone into the hollow, marching straight against the two columns. Moreover, he suffered it to undertake a manœuvre which (except with troops of great steadiness and highly instructed) can hardly be tried with safety against regiments still unshaken. The 'Black Watch' 'advanced firing.'[1]

But whilst this fight was going on between the 42nd and the two Russian columns, grave danger from another quarter seemed to threaten the Highland battalion; for, before it had gone many paces, Campbell saw that the column which had appeared on his left front was boldly marching forward, and such was the direction it took, and such the nature of the ground, that the column, if it were suffered to go on with this movement, would be able to strike at the flank of the 42nd without having first to descend into lower ground.

Halting the 42nd in the hollow, Campbell swiftly measured the strength of the approaching column, and he reckoned it so strong that he resolved to prepare for it a front of no less than five companies. He was upon the point of giving the order for effecting this bend in the line of the 42nd, when, looking to his left rear, he saw his centre battalion springing up to the outer crest. But almost in the same moment he saw, or in some way divined, that this battalion, in its exceeding ardor for the fight, was coming up wild and raging. He instantly rode to his left.

The 93rd, in the Crimea, was never quite like other regiments, for it chanced that it had received into its ranks a large proportion of those men of eager spirit who had petitioned to be exchanged from regiments left at home to regiments engaged in the war. The exceeding fire and vehemence, and the ever-ready energies of the battalion, made it an instrument of great might, if only it could be duly held in, but gave it a tendency to be headlong in its desire to hurl itself upon the enemy.

In a minute this fiery 93rd came storming over the crest, and, having now at last an enemy's column before it, it seemed to be almost mad with warlike joy. Its formation, of course, was

[1] We saw that Colonel Hood, with the Grenadier Guards, 'advanced firing,' but at that moment he had already brought the column which he attacked to the verge of its ruin.

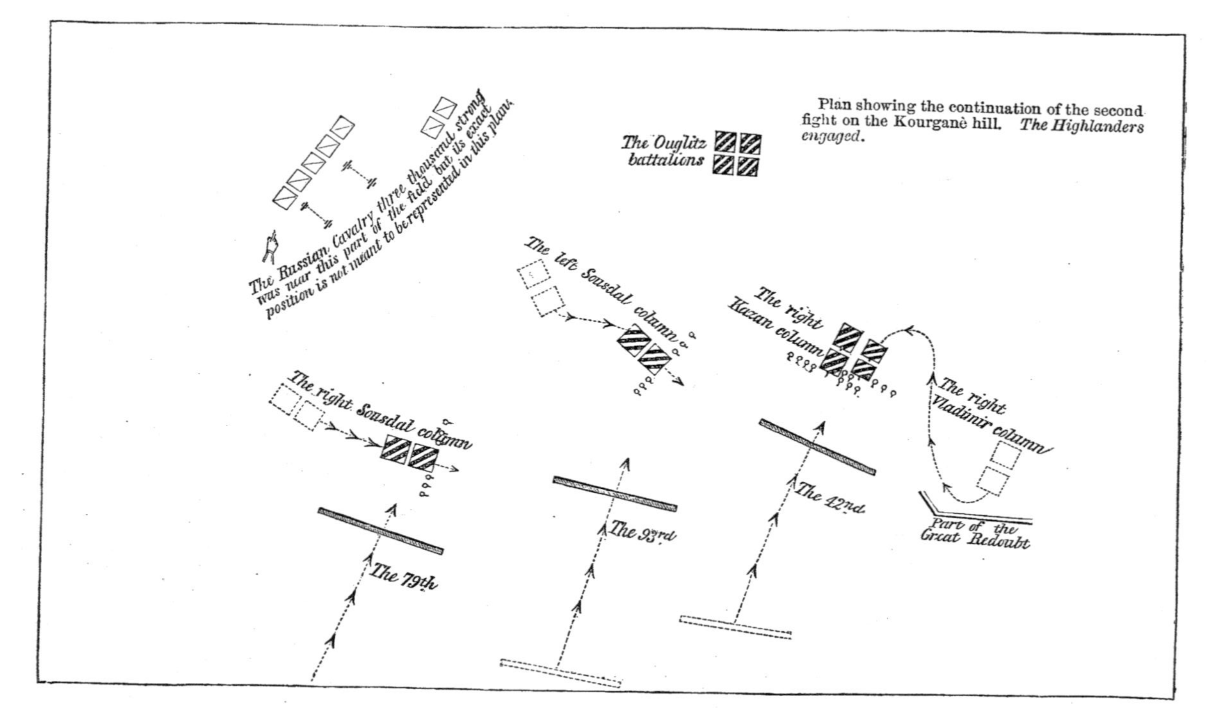


Plan showing the continuation of the second fight on the Kourganè hill. *The Highlanders engaged.*

disturbed by the haste and vehemence of the onset; and Campbell saw that, unless the regiment could be halted and a little calmed down, it would go on rushing forward in disordered fury, at the risk of shattering itself against the strength of the hard, square-built column which was solemnly coming to meet it.

But he who could halt his men on the bank of a cool stream when they were rushing down to quench the rage of their thirst, was able to quiet them in the midst of their warlike fury. Sir Colin got the regiment to halt and dress its ranks. By this time it was under the fire of the approaching column.

Campbell's charger, twice wounded already, but hitherto not much hurt, was now struck by a shot in the heart. Without a stumble or a plunge, the horse sank down gently to the earth and was dead. Campbell took his aid-de-camp's charger; but he had not been long in Shadwell's saddle, when up came Sir Colin's groom with his second horse. The man, perhaps, under some former master, had been used to be charged with the 'second horse' in the hunting-field. At all events, here he was; and if Sir Colin was angered by the apparition, he could not deny that it was opportune. The man touched his cap, and excused himself for being where he was. In the dry, terse way of those Englishmen who are much accustomed to horses, he explained that, toward the rear, the balls had been dropping about very thick, and that, fearing some harm might come to his master's second horse, he had thought it best to bring him up to the front.

When the 93rd had recovered the perfectness of its array, it again moved forward, but at the steady pace imposed upon it by the chief. The 42nd had already resumed its forward movement. It still advanced firing.

There are things in the world which, eluding the resources of the dry narrator, can still be faintly imaged by that subtle power which sometimes enables mankind to picture dim truth by fancy. According to the thought which floated in the mind of the churchman who taught to All the Russias their grand form of prayer for victory, there are 'angels of light' and 'angels of darkness and horror,' who soar over the heads of soldiery destined to be engaged in close fight, and attend them into battle.[1] When the fight grows hot, the angels hover

[1] This is part of the Russian prayer for victory:—'O Lord! . . . . . . 'hear us this day praying for these troops that are gathered together. Bless 'and strengthen them, and give them a manly heart against their enemies. 'Send them an Angel of Light, and to the enemies an Angel of Darkness 'and Horror, to scatter them, and place a stumbling-block before them, to 'weaken their hearts and turn their courage into flight.'

down near to earth with their bright limbs twined deep in the wreaths of the smoke which divides the combatants. But it is no coarse, bodily help that these Christian angels bring. More purely spiritual than the old Immortals, they strike no blow, they snatch no man's weapon, they lift away no warrior in a cloud. What the Angel of Light can bestow is valor, priceless valor, and light to lighten the path to victory, giving men grace to see the bare truth, and, seeing it, to have the mastery. To regiments which are to be blessed with victory the Angel of Light seems to beckon, and gently draw his men forward. What the Angel of Darkness can inflict is fear, horror, despair; and it is given him also to be able to plant error and vain fancies in the minds of the doomed soldiery. By false dread he scares them. Whether he who conceived this prayer was soldier or priest, or soldier and priest in one, it seems to me that he knew more of the true nature of the strife of good infantry than he could utter in common prose. For, indeed, it is no physical power which rules the conflict between two well-formed bodies of foot.

The mere killing and wounding which occurs whilst a fight is still hanging in doubt, does not so alter the relative numbers of the combatants as in that way to govern the result. The use of the slaughter which takes place at that time lies mainly in the stress which it puts upon the minds of those who, themselves remaining unhurt, are nevertheless disturbed by the sight of what is befalling their comrades. In that way, a command of the means of inflicting death and wounds is one element of victory. But it is far from being the chief one. Nor is it by perfectness of discipline, nor yet by a contempt of life, that men can assure to themselves the mastery over their foes. More or less, all these things are needed; but the truly governing power is that ascendency of the stronger over the weaker heart which (because of the mystery of its origin) the churchman was willing to ascribe to angels coming down from on high.

The turning moment of a fight is a moment of trial for the soul and not for the body; and it is, therefore, that such courage as men are able to gather from being gross in numbers can be easily outweighed by the warlike virtue of a few. To the stately 'Black Watch' and the hot 93rd, with Campbell leading them on, there was vouchsafed that stronger heart, for which the brave, pious Muscovites had prayed. Over the souls of the men in the columns there was spread, first the gloom, then the swarm of vain delusions, and at last the sheer horror which might be the work of the Angel of Darkness.[1] The two

[1] See the next note.

lines marched straight on. The three columns shook. They were not yet subdued. They were stubborn; but every moment the two advancing battalions grew nearer and nearer, and although—dimly masking the scant numbers of the Highlanders—there was still the white curtain of smoke which always rolled on before them, yet fitfully, and from moment to moment, the signs of them could be traced on the right hand and on the left in a long, shadowy line, and their coming was ceaseless.

But, moreover, the Highlanders being men of great stature, and in strange garb, their plumes being tall, and the view of them being broken and distorted by the wreaths of the smoke, and there being, too, an ominous silence in their ranks, there were men among the Russians who began to conceive a vague terror—the terror of things unearthly; and some, they say, imagined that they were charged by horsemen strange, silent, monstrous, bestriding giant chargers.[1] The columns were falling into that plight—we have twice before seen it this day—were falling into that plight, that its officers were moving hither and thither with their drawn swords, were commanding, were imploring, were threatening, nay, were even laying hands on their soldiery, and striving to hold them fast in their places. This struggle is the last stage but one in the agony of a body of good infantry massed in close column. Unless help should come from elsewhere, the three columns would have to give way. But help came. From the high ground on our left another heavy column—the column composed of the two right Sousdal battalions—was seen coming down. It moved straight at the flank of the 93rd.

So now for the third time that day a mass of infantry, some fifteen hundred strong, was descending upon the naked flank of a battalion in English array; and, coming as it did from the extreme right of the enemy's position, this last attack was aimed almost straight at the file—the file of only two men—which closed the line of the 93rd.

But some witchcraft, the doomed men might fancy, was causing the earth to bear giants. Above the crest or swell of ground on the left rear of the 93rd, yet another array of the tall, bending plumes began to rise up in a long, ceaseless line, stretching far into the east, and presently, in all the grace and beauty that marks a Highland regiment when it springs up the side of a hill, the 79th came bounding forward. Without

[1] It was from the poor wounded prisoners that our people gathered the accounts of the impression produced upon their minds by the advance of the Highlanders.

a halt, or with only the halt that was needed for dressing the ranks, it sprang at the flank of the right Sousdal column, and caught it in its sin—caught it daring to march across the front of a battalion advancing in line. Wrapped in the fire thus poured upon its flank, the hapless column could not march, could not live. It broke, and began to fall back in great confusion; and, the left Sousdal column being almost at the same time overthrown by the 93rd, and the two columns which had engaged the 'Black Watch' being now in full retreat, the spurs of the hill and the winding dale beyond became thronged with the enemy's disordered masses.

Defeat of the four Russian columns.

Then again, they say, there was heard the sorrowful wail that bursts from the heart of the brave Russian infantry when they have to suffer defeat; but this time the wail was the wail of eight battalions; and the warlike grief of the soldiery could no longer kindle the fierce intent which, only a little before, had spurred forward the Vladimir column. Hope had fled.

After having been parted from one another by the nature of the ground, and thus thrown for some time into échelon, the battalions of Sir Colin's brigades were now once more close abreast; and since the men looked upon ground where the gray remains of the enemy's broken strength were mournfully rolling away, they could not but see that this, the revoir of the Highlanders, had chanced in a moment of glory. Knowing their hearts, and deeming that the time was one when the voice of his people might fitly enough be heard, the Chief touched or half lifted his hat in the way of a man assenting. Then along the Kourganè slopes, and thence west almost home to the Causeway, the hill-sides were made to resound with that joyous, assuring cry which is the natural utterance of the northern people so long as it is warlike and free.[1]

Descending into the hollow where the vanquished troops flooded down, the waves of sound lit upon the throng and touched it, some imagined, as a breath of air touches a forest, lightly stirring its numberless leaves. And in truth it might be that, even in this the hour of turmoil and defeat, the long-suffering Muscovites were stirred with a new thought; for they never before that day had heard what our people call "cheers," and the sound is of such a kind that it startles men not born to freedom.

[1] Many of our people who had heard the cheers of the Highlanders were hindered from seeing them by the bend of the ground, and they supposed that the cheers were uttered in charging. It was not so. The Highlanders advanced in silence.

The three Highland regiments were now re-formed, and Sir Colin Campbell, careful in the midst of victory, looked to see whether the supports were near enough to warrant him in pressing the enemy's retreat with his Highland brigade. He judged that, since Cathcart was still a good way off, the Highlanders ought to be established on the ground which they had already won; and, never forgetting that all this while he was on the extreme left of the whole infantry array of the Allies, he made a bend in his line, which caused it to show a front toward the southeast as well as toward the south.

Stand made by the Ouglitz battalions.

The great column of the four Ouglitz battalions was still on the rise of the hill beyond the hollow. It was a force 3000 strong, was as yet untouched, and was glowing with the same fire and zeal as when it had come down in anger to support the attack upon Codrington's brigade. From the high and commanding ground where the column stood posted, its officers had been able to see and understand the numerical proportions of the combatants more clearly than any man could who was toiling in the smoke of the fight. Looking down from the slope, they had had to endure to see the gathered masses of their fellow-countrymen giving way to the slender lines of the red-coats; and, not bearing to think that their Czar and his famed infantry were to be coerced by means so small and delicate, they became inflamed with a great indignation against their own people for being defeated; and presently the whole column came down the hill, undertaking nothing less than to stay the ebb of the tide. It thrust itself full against the retreating masses, and angrily strove to drive them back into the fight.

The enemy's neglect of other measures for covering the retreat.

But the Highland brigade now again opened fire, and the enemy, being left very helpless, and having no guns in battery wherewith to attempt a stand, the Ouglitz column was forced to turn. It went part way up to its old ground in order to be able to cover the retreat of the vanquished masses.

The enemy's brave and devoted infantry, already abandoned by their ordnance, were now deserted in their great need by the Russian cavalry. Those horsemen, near 3000 strong, had been so palsied by orders or want of orders, or by some failure of spirit or capacity, that, although they were confronted by only a third of their number of horse, they had not only abstained from all challenge, but had twice borne to look upon the open flank of a slender infantry line ascending to carry the heights, they themselves standing still all the while on the pleasant slopes of the hill; and now, when the faithful soldiery might well look for charges of horsemen to cover the retreat, their cavalry still remained idle, though it lingered for a while on the field.[1]

Our cavalry, long impatient of the restraint imposed upon it by the commander of the forces, had crossed the river without Lord Raglan's authority; and although the nature of the ford and the upset of a gun-carriage had caused a good deal of delay, they reached the top of the hill soon after the Highlanders had crowned it. With Lord Lucan's sanction, three guns of the horse artillery, under Captain Maude, were placed in battery, and three guns of Captain Brandling's troop, which came up at the time, were established on the right of the 42nd. The fire of these six guns told cruelly upon the enemy's retreating masses; and the like being done by other English batteries on the west of the Kourganè Hill, the slaughter was so great that, of those who fell, very many fell upon their comrades, making in some places small banks of slain or wounded men; but where the round shot plowed into columns still keeping something of their old coherence, there the men so fell that there were—but I care not to speak any more of the slaughter that is wrought by cannon when the infantry strife is all over.

*Slaughter of the retreating masses by artillery.*

Of the four Russian Generals who took part in this fight of the Kourganè Hill, three were wounded, and nearly all the field-officers, together with very many officers of humbler grade who were on duty with the enemy's infantry in this part of the field, were either killed or wounded. The brave Vladimir and the Kazan corps suffered dreadful losses. The loss of the four Kazan battalions alone was put at no less than seventeen hundred.[2]

*Losses sustained by the enemy on the Kourganè Hill:*

This achievement by the Guards and the Highland brigade was so rapid, and was executed with so steadfast a faith in the prowess of our soldiery and the ascendency of Line over Column, that in vanquishing great masses of infantry, 12,000 strong,[3] and in going straight through

*by the Guards and Highlanders.*

[1] At an early period of the action, symptoms of this backwardness of the Russian cavalry had been sagaciously detected by the practiced eye of Sir George Cathcart. Being on our extreme left, he had narrowly watched the enemy's horsemen, and, even before the deployment of the 1st Division, he had found himself able to assure Lord Raglan that nothing serious was likely to be attempted by the enemy's cavalry on the right bank of the river. This message was carried, I think, by Captain Elliot. It was of great value to Lord Raglan.

[2] Chodasiewicz, p. 76. The estimate was not official, and was made under the influence of the despondency created by the retreat. It seems probable, therefore, that it exaggerated the loss.

[3] This figure is got at by first taking at their usual strength the 18 battal-

with an onset which tore open the Russian position, the six battalions together did not lose 500 men.[1]

Is it then with slight loss, is it thus in a swift march of a few hundred paces on a hill-side, and with all this seeming ease and grace, that the last of the work is done whereby nation gains the mastery over nation?

Well, the truth is that, before it comes to a struggle like this, a State waging war may have to bear cruel losses—losses at sea, losses by pestilence and famine; losses also inflicted by the enemy before he consents to give battle with his infantry upon open ground; and it might happen to a nation to have to go through a campaign without coming once to the strife for which her people are fitted; but when at last, after many an obstacle vanquished, after many a tormenting delay, the English array of two deep is suffered to reach open ground and there measure its strength with gross columns, then the annals of our country have taught us that, unless there be an almost overwhelming disparity of numbers, there ought to be no misgiving about what will be the end of the fight.[2]

ions which were on the Kourganè Hill, and then deducting 2500 (a very ample deduction) for losses which these troops sustained before the advance of the Guards.

[1] The exact number seems to be 438, and of this loss a large proportion was occasioned by the disaster which befell the Scots Fusileer Guards. Besides the casualties occurring to officers, which have been mentioned elsewhere, Cust of the Coldstream, and Abercrombie of the 93rd, were killed, and Baring of the Coldstream was wounded.

[2] The power which a nation may have of fighting in line depends, perhaps, mainly upon the constitutional temperament of its people, but in some degree, also, upon the question whether the high quality of its soldiery is fairly spread through the bulk of its army. No nation can expect to be able to fight in line if the prowess of its people is so abundantly gathered into the choice regiments as to leave the rest of the army in a condition of recognized inferiority. In Sir George Cathcart's book there is an interesting statement both of the causes which deprived the French of the power of fighting in line, and of the manner in which the predicament was met by the genius of Dumouriez. The system which Dumouriez contrived as a makeshift was attended with success so brilliant, that it was not only acted upon by France herself throughout the revolutionary war, but was adopted by all the Continental Powers which came into conflict with her; and, until the English displayed to them once more the line formation, Bonaparte and the other imitators of Dumouriez were encountered by nothing but their own system—their own system worked out with inferior ability, and with means to which the system was ill adapted. Dumouriez's system is the one still used by France, and still rendered necessary by the manner in which the French army is constituted. A French general goes into action probably with a strong proportion of cavalry, but certainly with a very powerful artillery. He also has several Zouave, Chasseur, or other choice regiments, well fitted for skirmishing, and for close, bold fighting in villages, inclosures, and broken ground; but a great part of the rest of his army consists of masses—the fruit

XXXIV.

On the western slopes of the Kourganè Hill, no step, that I know of, was taken for covering the withdrawal of the defeated troops; and if in the minds of Russian officers in that part of the field there yet remained any notion of trying to govern the retreat, their last hope was blasted by the new and ominous sign which then started full into view. On the fatal knoll, whence evil seemed always to come to the army of the Czar, there took place a sudden change. The horsemen with the white plumes were withdrawn from sight, and in a minute the knoll was surmounted with a scarlet arch. The arch was an arch built of English troops ranged in line across the summit, and thence on either side stretching down the steep shoulders of the knoll. And this arch of formed troops rose up in the heart of what had been the Russian position. Moreover, it faced toward the southeast, plainly showing that it was in the mind of the red-coats to cross the higher part of the Pass, and spring upon the flank of the troops which were retiring along the Great Causeway.

The scarlet arch on the knoll.

Then, perhaps, if not long before, the most hopeful of the Russian officers who looked from the Pass or from the western slopes of the Kourganè Hill would be constrained to acknowledge that their army had fallen under the mastery of that gracious-looking horseman, long seen on the knoll, who managed his charger and his field-glass with one hand and a half empty sleeve. And, indeed, the mastery was now so complete that, to any poor Muscovite soldier who was simply moving from the field with all the speed he had, his officers could hardly say with truth that they knew any better strategy than his.

It will be remembered that when Lord Raglan, after crossing the river, gained his first joyful glimpse of the knoll, he ordered up Adams's brigade in all haste. The force encountered some trouble in passing the river; but it was keenly urged forward, and, the moment it gained the summit of the knoll, Lord Raglan, with his own eye and voice, caused it to be drawn

of the conscription—masses which may be so displayed as to give an appearance of impending strength, but which he well knows must not be placed in any very trying situation. Thus provided and thus clogged, he tries to make such a use of his artillery and of his choice regiments as shall *avert any extended conflict between formed battalions.* If he can do that (he did so in the Italian campaign of 1859, but at the horrible cost of sacrificing his choice regiments), he will have a very good chance of winning the battle. His difficulties, however, are likely to be increased by the progress of modern invention, for the new artillery is making it hard for him to know where to place the less impetuous part of his army.

up in line. In order to make way for it on the top, the Head-Quarter Staff moved aside, and Lord Raglan so placed the line that it fronted toward the southeast.

If the battle at this time had been hanging in doubt, Lord Raglan, placed as he was with these two battalions in his hand, could hardly have failed to make them the means of governing the result, for their advance would have threatened to roll up the enemy's line from its centre to its extreme right. As it was, the force became that scarlet bow on the knoll which seemed to present to the enemy the alternative of sheer flight or captivity.

Lord Raglan, however, perceived that the cogency with which these battalions would act in hurrying the retreat depended rather upon their mere appearance in this part of the field than upon any real power that they had of intercepting the enemy; for, though the enemy might judge them to be very near, they were parted from him by deep hollows, and it was plain that if they were moved forward before the knowledge of their presence had sufficiently spread, they would in a great measure lose their weight, because, in crossing the hollow which divided them from the line of the retreat, they would necessarily drop out of sight. So, in order that the aspect of the force might sink into the enemy's heart, Lord Raglan kept it formed upon the summit of the knoll for two or three minutes. He then moved it toward the southeast.

Retreat of the last Russian battalions which had hitherto stood their ground.

Nearly at this time the column of the Ouglitz battalions began to fall back. Then there was no part of the Russian army in this part of the field which was not in full retreat.

Final operations of the artillery.

The guns of Turner's battery were limbered up and pushed forward to a commanding spot farther up in the Pass, and thence, at long range, they continued to pour their fire upon the enemy's retreating troops. In the performance of this duty they were aided by a French battery. Afterward, Lord Raglan sent an aid-de-camp with orders to cause the guns to advance to a more commanding ground, which he had observed on their left front. The English battery advanced accordingly, but the officers in command of the French battery declined to move forward. It was at this time that Walsham was killed. He was the last officer who fell that day. Besides Walsham, our artillery corps lost two officers killed, namely, Dew and Cockrell; and of the rank and file, nine were killed and twenty (besides one sergeant) were wounded.

Their losses.

XXXV.

Lord Raglan now descended the knoll whither Fortune, in her wild and puissant government of human events, had happily chosen to lead him. Bending his steps toward the ground just won by the Duke of Cambridge's Division, he rode across the main causeway.

Lord Raglan crossing the Causeway:

At that very time, as I make it,[1] there was riding toward Lord Raglan, and riding, too, along the same road, though at a distance of some few hundred yards, a man confounded and troubled, who had helped to bring great woe on his country.

Prince Mentschikoff riding down toward him.

Clearly wanting in many, nay, perhaps in most, of the qualities which make an able commander, Prince Mentschikoff was still a brave man. It could not but be that his heart was in the cause. A momentous battle had been raging. Of one of the contending armies he was the Commander-in-Chief. He was in full health. He yearned to be acting. Yet, from the moment when he intrusted to Kiriakoff the great column of the eight battalions, his mind had given no impress to events.

In order to see how this came to be possible, it must be remembered, first, that the tract of ground over which Prince Mentschikoff watched was somewhat broad, and, secondly, that all the decisive fighting of that day was condensed into a narrow period of time. The Allies had been advancing upon a front of five miles; and all the fights in which the combatants had engaged with their ranged battalions took place, as I reckon it, within a period of some thirty-five minutes. Now, if any man used to the saddle, and acquainted, also, with a country of open downs much divided by hollows and ravines, will fasten his mind upon any two hilltops or other landmarks which he knows to be five miles asunder, and will then imagine a number of brief events to be happening, first in one part of this extended tract and then in another, but all within little more than half an hour, he will be able to understand how it might be possible for the Russian General to be eagerly riding from east to west and from west to east, yet always being so luckless as never once to strike in upon the ground where the event which he yearned to witness and to control was swiftly passing. It was not, I am sure,

The part which he had been taking in the battle.

[1] The General who describes his meeting with Prince Mentschikoff shows the stage to which the battle had reached at the time when the meeting took place; and it seems to me that that was just the stage in which the battle was when Lord Raglan crossed the great road. This is my only ground for supposing that the two incidents occurred simultaneously.

from any neglect or delinquency that Prince Mentschikoff came to be annulled during all the heavy stress of the battle.

We left the Prince handing over to Kiriakoff the charge of the great column of the eight battalions, and it is only by conjecture that I can form an idea of what became of him during the critical period of several minutes which then immediately followed. He would not have abandoned the personal command of the column which he had eagerly gathered together for a great enterprise, unless he had been dragged away by tidings of what was happening in the English part of the field. Thither, therefore, he would ride, and he would ride, no doubt, with the knowledge (for that was what his last tidings must have taught him) that the English had stormed and carried the Great Redoubt. But he would have to cross the great road, and before he got thither he would see, and would see, one may imagine, with unspeakable astonishment, that the columns which formed his "great reserves" were no longer in their place. Finding that they were retiring or had already retired, and knowing nothing of the way in which Lord Raglan had driven them from the field by the use of his two guns on the knoll, the Prince would be likely to ride in the direction which the reserve columns took, very eager to find some man upon whom to vent his anger. The minutes it took him to ride after the reserves to seek out the cause of their retreat, and to come back to the front, would be those very minutes in which the position held by the centre and the right of the Russian army was falling into the hands of the English.

Prince Mentschikoff's reappearance in the English part of the field.

This, I repeat, is only a conjectural mode of filling the chasm which is left open by the Russian narrators; but the spot where the Prince is found when he reappears to the eye of History is exactly the one in which those who adopt my surmise would expect to see him riding; for it was by the great road, where his reserves had been posted, that Prince Mentschikoff came back into that part of the field with which the English had dealt. When last he saw it, the position, immensely strong by nature, was held in the gripe of powerful batteries and battalions standing rigid as granite. Since that time, it is true, some hours had passed, but it was only a few minutes before that he had been the assailant in the other part of the field, placing a mighty column in the hands of Kiriakoff with orders to make an onslaught upon Canrobert's Division. Now—he gazed and gazed again, being slow to understand—being slow to let in the belief that the gray, rolling masses which approached him were the ruins of two thirds of his army. But presently he came upon a sight hardly less strange, hardly less shocking to him than his retreating soldiery. He met on the road a lone man—a lone man on foot, walking away from the field. He looked, and came to make out that this lone pedestrian was Prince Gortschakoff—Prince Gortschakoff, the chief to whom he had intrusted the command of the whole centre and the whole right wing of his army. 'What is this?' 'What is the matter?' 'Why 'are you on foot?' 'Why are you alone?' These, as was natural, were the questions hurled at Prince Gortschakoff by his troubled, amazed commander. 'My horse,' said Gortschakoff, 'was killed near the river. I am alone, because all the 'aids-de-camp and officers of my Staff have been killed or 'wounded: I have received six shots;' and then, in a spirit scarce worthy of historic moments, scarce matching with the greatness of the disaster which his overthrow had brought upon a proud and mighty empire, Prince Gortschakoff showed the rents which shot had made in his clothes.[1]

His meeting with Gortschakoff.

At this time, so far as I know, Prince Mentschikoff used none of the means by which, though forced to retreat, skilled commanders can make themselves feared. On the very road where he stood, the Czar's faithful infantry—infantry famous for its heroism in the trying hour of a retreat—was left to extricate itself from the field by brute flight. It would seem that Prince Mentschikoff's authority—already for some time neutralized by the mischances which, all the day long, had been throwing him into the wrong part of the field—now slipped from out of his hands. He had no longer a grasp of his army. A little later he was seen borne along with the ebb, a dismal unit in the throng. Endued with a high spirit, and having a good deal of the pride which a man may justly take in his country so long as it is warlike and honest, he broke out into a loud, angry cry, 'It is a disgrace,' he said, 'for a Russian soldier to retreat!' An officer, hearing his words, and being maddened, partly by the defeat, and partly, as they say, by strong drink—fiercely answered his general, and told him to his face, in the hearing of the soldiery, that if he had ordered the men to stand they would have held their ground.[2] To this depth of wretchedness Prince Mentschikoff fell in the nineteenth month from the time when, in the name of a mighty empire, and under the gaze of all Europe, he came

He does not at this time effect any operation for covering the retreat.

He is carried along with the retreating masses.

[1] It is Prince Gortschakoff himself who gives this account of his meeting with Prince Mentschikoff.

[2] Chodasiewicz.

down into the Bosphorus with commission to trample upon the Ottoman State.

XXXVI.

The array of the English army on the ground they had won.

Meantime Evans, still on our right front, had been rejoined by the two regiments detached under Adams. The Scots Fusileers had resumed their place in the centre of the brigade of Guards. The Light Division, re-formed, had followed the advance of the Duke of Cambridge. Sir Richard England, pushing forward toward his right front, had taken up ground on one of the eastern spurs of the Telegraph Height. At the opposite extremity of our line Cathcart had established himself on the left rear of the Highland brigade. Facing almost due south, pushed forward to the reverse of the slopes which made the strength of the Russian position, and ranged upon a front of two miles, the British infantry looked down upon the enemy's retreating masses.

Operations of the English cavalry.

At this time Lord Raglan sent the Adjutant-General with his orders to the cavalry. Those orders, however, did not authorize the operations by which it is usual for horsemen to gather in the fruits of a victory. A commander, even in battle, must not forget the campaign. The Western Powers were invading a province of Russia, with forces which had to march through an open country. Their pretension to wage such war as that depended upon their having at their command all the three arms of the service. Therefore the strength of the arm in which they were the most weak was the measure of their power as invaders. The French, as we saw, had no cavalry, and the English had rather more than a thousand sabres and lances. With such a force thrown forward to intercept the enemy's retreating masses, many prisoners, together perhaps with some guns, might have been taken; and it was to be expected that blows of this kind would aggravate the despondency of the beaten army. But Lord Raglan judged that no practicable capture of trophies or prisoners was worth the risk of losing a material part of his small, brilliant cavalry force. He therefore declined to let his horsemen push forward without the support of a powerful artillery; and the orders he sent by the Adjutant-General directed that the cavalry should escort the foot batteries to the front. In delivering this instruction, Estcourt cautioned Lord Lucan, and told him 'that the cavalry were 'not to attack.'

Lord Cardigan, with one half of the cavalry force, was directed to escort the guns which were to go to the right, whilst Lord Lucan in person went forward with the rest of the cavalry, and escorted the guns advancing on our left. Lord Lucan, riding in advance of the guns with a squadron of the 17th Lancers, came upon many of the enemy's stragglers in retreat, and he ordered the horsemen who were with him, supported by another squadron, to pursue and take prisoners. A troop of the 11th Hussars had been ordered (it was said by Lord Raglan himself) to do the same thing, and the 17th had already taken a great many prisoners, when the operation was stopped by special orders from Lord Raglan. What Lord Raglan had meant was, that the troopers employed in taking prisoners should be spread out as skirmishers; and when he saw that they were acting in serried ranks, and were going on far in advance, he became anxious lest some of the enemy's guns should be brought to bear upon them, and occasion him a loss in that one description of force with which the Allies were scantily provided. He therefore sent, first one and then another Staff officer to the commander of the cavalry, with orders to give up the pursuit of prisoners, and return to the duty of escorting the guns. Thereupon Lord Lucan recalled the troopers in advance, and the prisoners they had taken were set free.

XXXVII.

Progress of a French artillery train along the plateau from east to west.

It will be remembered that at the time when the head of the French Division was pushed back by the 'great 'column of the eight battalions,' Canrobert was still without his artillery. But these batteries, having been sent down to Almatamack, and having there crossed the river, had at last been brought up to the plateau, and (along with some guns belonging to Bosquet's Division) they were now traveling eastward. In the part of the field where Bosquet stood, and from which this long train of artillery had commenced its eastward journey, there was no enemy at hand, and even when the guns had come to within a short distance of the ground in front of Canrobert's right wing, there was no Russian battalion which could be seen by the French artillerymen; for the train was moving along a hollow which, so long as a man rode low down, was deep enough to hinder him from seeing far either on his right hand or on his left. But some of the officers who were with the guns now thought it was time to obtain a wider view of the ground, and they therefore rode part way up the slope which overhung the ravine toward their right.

Officers riding with the train descry the 'column of the

'eight battal- 'ions.' Before they had yet got quite up to the flat ground above the ravine, they suddenly stopped; for—monstrous, immense, and obtruded before them on the plateau, at a distance of only a few hundred yards, they saw a gray, oblong-cut block—saw what in one moment they knew to be a mass of Russian infantry—a mass of unwonted size—standing rigidly built in close column. This was the great 'column of 'the eight battalions'—the dumb, gliding phantasm of the Telegraph Height, whose bare aspect had given strange speed to the breathless French aid-de-camp on the knoll, and had just been constraining the head of Canrobert's Division to fall back and drop under the crest. With that warlike swiftness of thought which is natural to the French in the hour of battle, the officers who caught sight of this apparition darted straight upon the perception of what ought to be done. Some of the guns were brought up to a part of the slope from which—without being easily seen—they could throw their fire into the column.[1]

Suddenly Kiriakoff found that his close mass of eight battalions was cruelly rent by shot and shell coming from the west. Without stopping to find out by calm scrutiny the quarter whence the fire really came, Kiriakoff hastily accepted the belief that it came from the sea; and, in order to place his troops out of the reach of the ships, he began to move off his column in an inland, or easterly direction, taking nearly the same route as that by which he had advanced.[2] Whilst he thus

The column is torn by artillery fire.

Kiriakoff moves it.

[1] See the plan. It is taken from a sketch which was made for me by a French officer who was present with the artillery thus brought to bear on the column.

[2] At one time the French stated (see Ducasse, 'Preçis Historique') that the retreat of this great column was the result of a fight with their infantry, but no such representation is now persisted in, for the French official statement (agreeing in that respect with Kiriakoff) says fairly that what forced the column to retreat was, not any sort of combat with the French inafntry, but the fire of the batteries mentioned in the text. After describing the advance of the great Russian column, the official French statement says:—'Déjà 'cette colonne était parvenue à 150 mètres de la droite du 7° de ligne, et la 'situation devenait très critique lorsque les deux batteries de la division Can- 'robert (qui avaient été forceés d'aller passer au gué d'Almatamak), et les 'deux batteries de la division Bosquet arrivent au galop sur le champ de 'bataille, ouvrent un feu terrible contre la colonne Russe, lui font éprouver 'des pertes considerables *et la forcent à la retraite.'—Atlas Historique et Topographique de la Guerre d'Orient.* The only words in this official statement which might produce a wrong impression are those which describe the guns as coming up at a gallop. When the train was traveling along the hollow, it no doubt moved as fast as it properly could; but when the guns were brought part way up the slope, and unlimbered and placed in battery, the

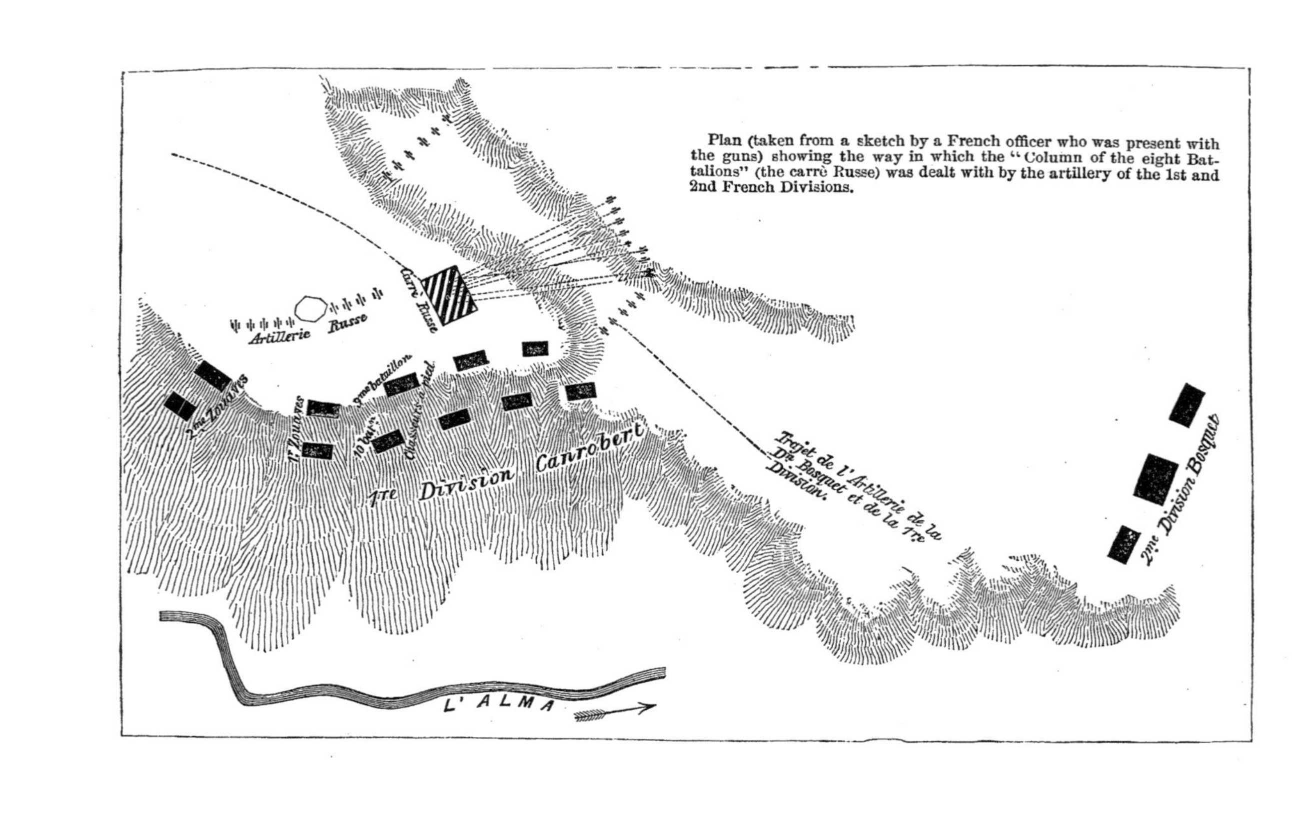


Plan (taken from a sketch by a French officer who was present with the guns) showing the way in which the "Column of the eight Battalions" (the carrè Russe) was dealt with by the artillery of the 1st and 2nd French Divisions.

marched, shot and shells continued to cut their way into the midst of his hapless column, inflicting a dreadful slaughter. This trial—the trial of men who have to march under a shattering fire without being able to strike one blow at their slayers—was borne by the Russian soldiery with a great fortitude.

Its demeanor.

Order was maintained; and, torn as it was from moment to moment, the column marched grandly. Along with the column there were two batteries; but, far from helping to cover its retreat, these guns were suffered to become a burden; for, several of the horses having been wounded or killed, the task of dragging off the cannon was thrown upon soldiers. It would seem, however, that the natural awe with which Canrobert's troops had looked upon the advance of the huge column was not lifted off from their minds when first they saw it withdrawing; for no French infantry moved forward to press the retreat of the eight battalions. 'The French,' says

It is not followed by the French, and is halted on the right rear of the Telegraph.

Kiriakoff, 'did not follow us. I am ignorant of the 'reason why. Maybe they did not want to stand 'between the fire of their ships and our regiments. 'Maybe the sight of the two bodies of Hussars, 'headed by Colonel Wailinovich, may have checked 'them.[1] In fact, I can not explain their conduct.' By pursuing his easterly march for some time, Kiriakoff brought his column out of the artillery fire which had been tearing it, and he came at last to halt upon a spot on the right rear of the Tele-

The part this great column had taken in the battle.

graph. Although it was the destiny of this 'column of the eight battalions' to be able to put a great stress upon the French army, and afterward to be cruelly shattered by cannon, yet from first to last the

operation was performed so skillfully and, so to speak, so stealthily, that Kiriakoff never made out the quarter whence destruction came, and imagined that his column was rent by the gunnery of the ships. My knowledge of the exact way in which these guns were brought to bear upon the hapless column is derived from a French officer who was present with the guns, and who took part in seizing the occasion which was presented by the sudden discovery of the column. When an account of an infantry fight with 'the column 'of the eight battalions' had once gone out to the world, it may seem strange that the story should be afterward repudiated by any French personages writing or drawing officially; but, besides that there is really a strong, honest leaning toward truth in the 'Atlas Historique,' it is obvious that the French artillery officers, whose skill and quickness had shattered the great column and driven it from the field, might justly and most cogently call upon the authorities to withdraw the falsehood which gave to French infantry the credit justly due to French gunners.

[1] The translation I have says 'annoyed them,' but I gather from the context that the word I have ventured to substitute more accurately represents the General's meaning.

body which thus did and thus suffered was without an occasion for firing a shot.

XXXVIII.

Moved from west to east along the top of the plateau, the French guns which had dealt with the column were now once more in battery, and upon ground from which they threw a flanking fire in the direction of the troops which still remained on the slopes in front of the Telegraph Height. The only infantry forces which had been placed in that part of the field were the four Taroutine, and the four 'Militia' battalions; but, supposing that the breaking-up of the 'Militia' battalions was by this time virtually complete, Kiriakoff had no infantry on the whole Telegraph Height except the four Taroutine battalions, and the stricken, the bleeding column which he had just withdrawn from the front. Yet at this time, though Kiriakoff evidently did not know of the proximity of many of the French battalions which were hanging back close under the plateau, there were in reality some thirty thousand Frenchmen and Turks standing on ground from which, in a period of only a few minutes, they might close in both upon his front and his left flank. Without apprehending the extent to which he was encompassed, Kiriakoff came to see that the troops he had in front of the Telegraph must not be left standing under a cross-fire of artillery. He had not in his own hands the means of repelling or silencing the guns which were pouring their fire from the west along the summit of the plateau; and, being without orders, and even, it seems, without tidings, he tried to find a clew for the guidance of his conduct by learning the course which the battle was taking in the English part of the field. Hitherto his glances in that direction had brought him no comfort. Even so early as the time when he pushed back the head of Canrobert's Division, he had found that the English were gaining the ascendency over the centre and right wing of the Russians. 'When,' he writes—'when 'the first success of the enemy had been stopped on the left 'wing, in the centre[1] and the right wing[1] the turn of affairs 'was beginning to be against us. I can not judge the particu-'lars of that part of the battle, being fully occupied by doing 'my own duty, and I could not observe as well the events on 'my right; but thus far I could see that the enemy had taken

A flanking fire from the French artillery is poured upon the troops on Telegraph Height.

Condition of things in that part of the field.

The result of what Kiriakoff had hitherto observed in the English part of the field.

[1] *i.e.*, those portions of the Russian army which were opposed to the English.

'up a strong position on the left bank of the Alma.' This, at the moment of his success against Canrobert, had been Kiriakoff's perception of the course which events were taking in the English part of the field; and now, when he looked once more to where the red-coats were moving, he saw that in that part of the field the battle was lost to the Czar. He saw, not only that the Causeway batteries had been withdrawn, and that upon their site English regiments were established (apparently he had seen that before[1]), but that Mentschikoff's infantry reserves were in retreat; and that, looking eastward along the Russian side of the river as far as his eye could reach, he was unable to see the end of the slender red line which marked the advance of the English supports. Even if he did not observe or understand the ominous silence of the Great Redoubt, he could not fail to see that the withdrawal of the Causeway batteries and of the infantry reserves was not only an abandonment of the great 'position on the Alma,' but was also a retreat with which it was his obvious duty to conform. For that reason, he first ordered his troops to retire to a part of the Great Post-road which lay on the right rear of his position; and when he got to that spot, he found that the victory won by Lord Raglan was by that time so well assured as to oblige him to continue his retrograde march, and conform at once to the movements of the seven-and-twenty battalions then yielding to their English assailants.

He now sees that in that part of the field the English have won the battle.

He conforms to the movement of the troops retreating before the English.

'Impossible'—writes Kiriakoff, after speaking of the direction in which French artillery had been brought to bear upon his troops in front of the Telegraph—'impossible to leave the 'left wing thus exposed to a cross-fire, and I could not send or 'wait for orders from the Commander-in-Chief. The right 'wing[2] having already begun a very decisive movement of 'retreat, I commanded the march toward the main road, on 'either side of which I ranged the troops. This road was be-'yond the height where our principal reserves had stood. Then 'I became aware that our right wing[2] was indeed retreating; 'and, wishing to conform as much as possible with their move-'ments, I ordered a second march toward a height beyond the 'road.[3] . . . The enemy did not follow us.'[4]

[1] When he said that the English 'had taken up a strong position on the 'left' [*i. e.*, the Russian] 'bank of the river.'

[2] *i. e.*, troops opposed to the English.

[3] If full faith be given to this testimony of Kiriakoff, it is of course conclu-

[4] See next page.

His retreat is not molested by French infantry.

In their retreat the Taroutine battalions—the troops which marched in what was then the rear of Kiriakoff's force—were plied with the fire of cannon, but were not at all vexed by French infantry.[1]

XXXIX.

Great conflux of French troops toward the Telegraph.

When Kiriakoff's battalions had withdrawn, Canrobert's Division and D'Aurelle's Brigade—that brigade followed close by Prince Napoleon—moved straight upon the Telegraph. This took place at the moment when, in the English part of the field, our Grenadier Guards were stepping up from the river's bank to engage the enemy's columns.[2] The two Zouave Regiments, which stood side by side on the left front of Canrobert's force, and, almost at the same moment, the 39th Regiment of the Line—the regiment which formed the head of D'Aurelle's column—pushed

sive of the question as to where the Russian retreat began, for he speaks as an eye-witness of the retreat which had taken place in front of the English, and he was the actual ordainer of the retrograde movement which he deemed to be the necessary consequence of the defeat which his countrymen had sustained at the hands of the English. It may be said that it was for his interest to make this statement, and that therefore he is not an impartial witness. This is true; but, besides that his character for honor and high spirit places him above the suspicion of gross and intentional misstatement, it happens that his account is corroborated in the most distinct terms by Anitchkoff, an apparently impartial narrator. Anitchkoff, when he wrote, was an officer on the General Staff of the Russian army, writing under circumstances which gave him considerable means of knowing the truth, and which made it his duty to hold the balance evenly between Gortschakoff, Kiriakoff, and Kvetzinski. Yet in clear words he corroborates Kiriakoff. After speaking of the centre and right wing of the Russians, the troops with which the English had been dealing—and of their retreat 'to the former position two versts 'to the south,' he adds immediately these words: 'Whither they were' [remark the word presently coming] 'whither they were followed by the left 'wing, who had withstood and repelled the attack of the whole of the four 'French Divisions until the moment of the general retreat.'

[4] Kiriakoff does not himself say that he made any of the arrangements commonly resorted to by a general who has to withdraw his troops from the enemy's presence; but the French authorities say for him that he covered his retreat with a powerful artillery. The whole tenor of Kiriakoff's memorial leads to the impression that, at the time of his retreating from the Telegraph Height, there was no French infantry near enough to induce him to take the usual means for covering his retreat. It is probable, however, that, without any express orders from their divisional general, officers commanding Russian batteries may have found and seized opportunities of using their guns.

[1] Chodasiewicz. This writer was a field-officer in the Taroutine corps, and his statements (almost all of them valuable) are an excellent authority in all that relates to the operations of his own regiment.

[2] See, in the Appendix, the grounds on which I rest this statement.

swiftly forward toward the Telegraph; and some of the more active men of these soldiery, running on in advance of their comrades, successively planted the colors of their three Regiments on the stump of the unfinished pillar, or on the scaffolding which the builders had placed there. It is said that while he was in the very act of thus uplifting the colors of his regiment, Lieutenant Poitevin, of the 39th, was struck by a shot and killed.

When soldiers in battle break loose from the guidance of their commanders, they so feel the need of a purpose that a tree, a house, or a windmill—any object, in short, which stands out plain in the landscape, may have power to draw men toward it; and when a conflux like this has once set in, the eddy soon begins to run strong. First three or four eager and venturous men, then clusters, then scores, then hundreds, then thousands of panting soldiers were thronging from several quarters upon a single point. There could not but be a great turmoil. Joy, warlike ardor, the instinctive longing of the young soldier in his first battle to keep on discharging his musket, and perhaps (with some) the sight of the body of Lieutenant Poitevin—all these were causes much more than enough to account for abundance of firing on the part of the French troops; and when the mound of smoke thus generated was once piled up, the soldiers would be likely to continue firing into it for some time. Besides, the French artillery at this period was playing upon the enemy's retreating battalions, and, on the other hand, it may be believed that the Russians were covering their retreat by a more or less diligent use of their ordnance. It is probable that this fire of the Russian artillery took effect at a time when the heads of the French columns had already thronged up to the Telegraph, for it is certain that several of the Zouaves were there struck down; and although it is made plain that no Russian infantry were intentionally placed at the Telegraph with orders to make a stand, there is no difficulty in supposing that a knot of Russian soldiers may have been lingering about near the scaffolding of the turret, and may have remained long enough to have an opportunity of firing into the heads of the great columns which were converging upon the spot, and provoking a fire in return. In that way, though the Russian accounts show no trace of it, there was, perhaps, a farewell interchange of shots.

Turmoil and supposed fight at the Telegraph.

Be this as it may, it is certain that (from the causes already shown) there was much of the appearance of a real fight at the Telegraph, and, until the Russian narratives brought other light to bear, it was believed that the French and the Russian infantry had met in fierce strife at this spot. On the other hand, the enemy's accounts represent that Kiriakoff's troops withdrew quietly from the Telegraph Height, without being even annoyed by French infantry, and without making or trying to make a defensive stand either at the pillar of the Telegraph, or on any ground near it; and unless all the Russian narrators, though speaking with very different and even opposite feelings, have united to join in an unaccountable[1] perversion of the truth, it must now be held certain that the impetuous Zouaves, no less than their despised and peaceful comrades of the line, were precluded by sheer want of opponents from the means of engaging in that dreadful scene of hand-to-hand fighting and slaughter which, under the description of 'the 'combat at the Telegraph,' has found a place in French annals.[2]

At length the state of the smoke allowed men to see that there were no Russians near. Then the close of what resembled a fight was joyfully hailed as a victory.

From the time when the bulk of the French advanced to the banks of the river, Marshal St. Arnaud had placed himself in the midst of Prince Napoleon's battalions; and, the Prince's Division having been kept low down in the bottom during the critical period of the battle, it must have been hard for a man who remained jammed down with those troops to get a fair view of what was going on;[3] but the Marshal, it seems, now galloped up to the Telegraph, and sharing, no doubt, in the belief that there had been a hot fight there, and inferring also that the fight had been won by the thousands of eager Zouaves whom he saw thronging round the pillar, he turned, it is said, to these his most trusted soldiery, and said to them, 'I thank you, my Zouaves!'

Marshal St. Arnaud.

Canrobert's and Prince Napoleon's Divisions, with D'Aurelle's brigade betwixt them, were then massed about the Telegraph upon a very small space of ground.

[1] I say 'unaccountable' because, if the French story were true, the stand which must have been made at the Telegraph by Kiriakoff's infantry would have been an achievement so heroic, that, far from disowning, or concealing, or forgetting it, every good Russian would have made it his pride and his boast.

[2] The narratives which French historians have given of this supposed fight, together with my reasons for excluding their stories from my text, will be found in the Appendix.

[3] See the plan (taken from the 'Atlas Historique'), which shows the Marshal's position.

XL.

At this time two messengers came in haste from different parts of the English field of battle. They both came with the same object. The first of these was an aid-de-camp sent straight from Lord Raglan to the nearest French troops he could find. The other was Colonel Steele, who came charged with the request which General Airey, from another part of the field, had taken upon himself to address to Marshal St. Arnaud. Whilst the Russian battalions were retreating before the English infantry, Lord Raglan in one part of the field, and Airey in another, had, almost at the same moment, observed the same opportunity, and fastened upon the same mode of seizing it. Each of them had seen that masses of the retreating infantry were moving in such a direction and through a gorge which so straitened their movements, that their retreat could be cut off or turned into a ruinous disaster by the immediate advance of a few battalions pushing forward from the left of the French line, and bearing toward the great road.

Opportunity of cutting off some of the enemy's retreating masses.

Vain endeavors of Lord Raglan and of Airey to cause the requisite advance of French troops.

When Lord Raglan's aid-de-camp reached the Telegraph, he found that the troops he came upon had just halted, two hundred yards in front of the building, and that the column with which he sought to find the Prince was under a good deal of excitement. Used to the silence of English troops, the aid-de-camp was a good deal struck with the effect produced by thousands of soldiers in heavy masses talking all at the same time. The aid-de-camp was accompanied by Vico, the French commissioner accredited to the English head-quarters. Vico conveyed Lord Raglan's wishes to the general commanding the brigade, and was told in answer that the troops would advance. This, however, they did not do.

The similar request which Colonel Steele addressed to St. Arnaud was met by a refusal. The Marshal excused himself for declining to advance by saying that his troops had left their knapsacks in the valley below.

Marshal St. Arnaud was able to remain all day on horseback; and it does not appear that the state of his health at this time was such as to hinder him from using his intellectual powers; but he did not place himself in a part of the field from which a general could hope to be able to govern events. And from the time when he dispatched his ill-devised orders to the 4th Division, I have not been able to perceive that his mind at all touched the battle.

St. Arnaud. The extent to which his mind was brought to bear on the battle.

XLI.

Situation of Forey with Lourmel's brigade.

General Forey, perhaps, had hoped that in the presence of the enemy he might be able to cover over the mark which his reputation contracted on the 2nd of December, on the day when, along with Maupas's commissaries of police, he suffered himself to be publicly used as the assailant and the jailer of the unarmed Legislature of France; but if by chance this man shall be brought some day to his account, it will not be by an appeal to the memory of the Alma that he will be able to avert his punishment. With Lourmel's brigade,[1] as we saw, he had followed the steps of Bouat, marching off to the peaceful sea-shore, and becoming null in the battle. When D'Aurelle was already at the Telegraph, Forey, with Lourmel's brigade, had but just crossed the river at its very mouth, and was more than two miles distant from the nearest of the enemy's forces. But with the exception of this annulled brigade under Forey, and the two Turkish battalions which had been left to guard the baggage, the whole of the French and Ottoman troops were now ranged upon the plateau of the Telegraph Height. Their array was upon ground less advanced than that taken up by the English. It fronted toward the east.

The rest of the French army arrayed upon the plateau.

XLII.

The position taken up by Kiriakoff.

When Kiriakoff's movement of retreat had brought him to the ridge which lay at a distance of nearly two miles in rear of the Telegraph, he forthwith took up a position, and once more showed a front to the Allies. Having with him not only his own artillery, but that also which Prince Mentschikoff had brought from the centre at the commencement of the action, and being in company at this time with some of the cavalry, he was able to complete the semblance of something like a defensive stand by placing thirty guns in battery, and covering his left front with several squadrons of hussars. By this wise and soldierly attitude Kiriakoff masked the confusion into which the rest of the Czar's army had been thrown, and caused the Allied commanders to believe that they had still a formidable enemy in their front.

The effect produced upon the Allies by his soldierly attitude.

[1] This Lourmel was one of those who acted against Paris in the massacres of the 4th of December, and although he was only a colonel at that time, it is still proper to keep the December badge upon him, because it was the known character of the colonels commanding regiments which had caused the President to bring them and their regiments to Paris with a view to use them.

Not only did Kiriakoff thus face round, but he even caused the body of cavalry which he had on his left to move forward; and it happened that this advance of the Russian Hussars brought them down to a spot which was near the ground where Lord Cardigan rode with his squadrons. It seems, however, that there was an intervening bend or rise in the formation of the ground, which prevented these two hostile bodies of cavalry from being visible the one to the other.

He moves forward some cavalry.

Lord Raglan, with some of his staff, had ridden forward to this part of the field. He met the advance of the enemy's squadrons with an almost cold gaze. The joyous animation with which, from the summit of the knoll, he had watched the changeful battle—this had passed. He wore the look—men came to know it too well before he died—the look which used to show that he was feeling the stress of the French alliance, and dissembling the pain of his anger.

Lord Raglan's vexation.

XLIII.

The world was old enough to know that, in order to be made to yield its natural fruits, a victory ought to be followed up; and that, in general, a victorious army is made to press on in pursuit until nightfall or other good cause makes it prudent or needful to halt. But the maps of this Crim Tartary gave no indication of the existence of any fresh water between the Alma and the Katcha—a stream some seven or eight miles distant. It seemed that unless the troops which might be pushed forward could reach the Katcha, and reach it, too, in strength enabling them to establish themselves on its banks, they would have to bivouac on the hills without the means of allaying the rage of thirst. Except at the mouth of the Alma, or at the mouth of the Katcha, the nature of the coast did not allow free communication between the Allied armies and the ships. It was half past four o'clock. Soon after six the sun would set. Since morning the soldiery of both armies had toiled under a burning sun. They were very weary; and many of them—indeed almost all the English—were in a weakly state of health. These were reasons which made it needful for the Allies to effect their farther pursuit of the enemy by preconcerted arrangements. They were not, I think, reasons which warranted a protracted halt of the whole of the Allied armies on the heights of the Alma. Lord Raglan had been swift to see what ought to be done by the Allies, and not less swift to determine what he himself could offer to do. He deemed that the Allies ought

Question as to the way in which the retreat should be pressed.

Lord Raglan's opinion. His plan.

to push forward instantly with such portions of their force as were the least wearied. We have seen the share which the English soldiery had had in the work of the day; but, compared with the troops of the 1st, the 2nd, and the Light Divisions, Sir Richard England's Division was fresh. With that force of infantry, together with the whole of his cavalry and horse artillery, Lord Raglan desired to press forward; but he required that a portion of the French army should take part in this movement, for he did not understand that the rout of the enemy's forces was so complete and irremediable as to put them in the power of one English division of infantry and a thousand horsemen. Besides, he well knew that (even though the aid should be given for mere form's sake and not for actual use) there was a political reason which forbade him from pressing forward without making sure that his advance would be accompanied by a portion of the French army; for it was nearly certain that an English General advancing on the afternoon of a battle, and leaving his sensitive allies in the rear, would so mortify the French people as to put the alliance and even the ruler who contrived it in grievous peril.

It is proposed to the French.

Accordingly, General Airey proposed to General Martimprey, the chief of the French Staff, that the whole of our cavalry, together with one English division of infantry, and such portion of the French army as the Marshal might think fit, should move forward and press the enemy's retreat.

They decline to move.

The answer was that any farther advance of the French on that day was 'impossible;' and the necessity of returning to where the knapsacks had been laid was once more used as the reason which forbade all forward movement. Men may fairly surmise that a sterner method than that which Lord Raglan took would have served his purpose better, and that if he had simply ordered his cavalry and Sir Richard England's Division to advance, M. St. Arnaud would have been compelled to follow. But to act upon such a speculation as that would have been hardly consistent with the duties imposed upon the English General. Lord Raglan, it is true, was a soldier acting against an enemy in the field. But he was something more. He was a diplomatist specially charged with the care of that fragile structure on which the war was resting. He was charged with the care of the French alliance. Except on grounds of paramount cogency, he had no right to break loose from the fetters by which his Queen's Government had thought fit to bind their country.

Question whether a sterner method with the French might have answered better.

XLIV.

Lord Raglan watched the advance of the Russian cavalry until he saw it come to a halt. Then it seemed—he was used of old to read such signs—it seemed that he regarded this movement and this halt of the enemy's horse as a kind of farewell gesture which marked the end of the battle; for, turning his horse's head, he slowly rode back to the ground where his infantry stood.

The close of the battle.

When our soldiers observed the approach of the Head-Quarter Staff, they looked eagerly into the group that they might see if amongst the plumed horsemen the Chief himself were coming; and the moment they got a sure sight of the frock with the half empty sleeve, it came into their hearts to offer to their General that which is of other worth than vulgar treasures, nay, that which in common times the world can not give. They brought him the greeting which a proud soldiery can bestow upon their chief in the hour of victory and upon the field of battle. Begun at first by one corps, taken up by the next, and then by the next again, the cheers flew on from regiment to regiment, and tracked the chief in his path, till all along, from the spurs of the Telegraph Height to the easternmost bounds of the crest which had been won by the Highland brigade, those desolate hills in Crim Tartary were made to sound like England. And the sound traveled back to the plateau on which the French were halted, and descended also the slopes where our dead and wounded lay thick. There many a red-coat, so wounded that the roar of artillery and the tramp of battalions had become to him mere idle sounds, would yet find his heart stirred anew by the English cheers on the heights, and would raise himself on his arm and strive so to use his last strength that, in the swelling tumult of the voices above, his own faltering 'hurrah!' might be one.

The cheers which greet Lord Raglan.

But, pensive and intent on sad thoughts, Lord Raglan now rode down into the valley, recrossed the river, and entered the village of Bourliouk. The flames had been extinguished; and in some of the farm-buildings less burnt than the rest, there lay many wounded officers, Amongst the painful scenes in those barns and sheds Lord Raglan passed a long time, giving tender care to the sufferers. Yet of the sunlight of that day there were nearly two hours remaining. There was a routed enemy in front; and beyond, there was the mighty prize for which the invaders were come.

He rides back to Bourliouk and visits the wounded.

Ambition lends strength and momentum to the purposes of a general. Lord Raglan gave his heart to wounded men. A commander wrapped in self, and burning for fame, would have risked a breach of the French alliance, would have hardened his heart, and, killing perhaps some few of his people with cruel fatigue, would have drunk of the Katcha that night. If he had done thus, the reconnaissance of the next morning would have brought him some knowledge of hardly less worth than a victory.

The Allied armies bivouac on the ground they have won.

The Allied forces bivouacked on the ground which they had won. The French were on the Telegraph Height. The English head-quarters were established on the left bank of the river, near the road leading up from the bridge, and almost on the site of that Causeway battery which, until it was touched by the mastering key, had barred the mouth of the Pass.

Colonel Torrens's force comes up in the evening. Lord Raglan in his marquee.

In the evening our army was joined by Colonel Torrens with the troops which had been left at Kamishlu to clear the beach; and, at about nine o'clock, whilst Lord Raglan was dining in his little marquee with only one man for his guest, Torrens came to report his arrival. A third cover was laid for him. He had made a forced march, and was in bitter pain because his great haste had not availed to bring him up in time for the battle. With kind, frank, thoughtful words, Lord Raglan strove to soothe him.

## XLV.

Continuation of the Russian retreat.

The position which Kiriakoff had taken up was not held for many minutes. To any calm man who looked from that ridge toward the north it must have been plain that the Allies were making no movement in pursuit. But—for thus powerful and thus wayward is the imagination of man in his fears — the Russians were no sooner in safety than vague terrors were assailing their minds, and panic began to drive them.

When the Russian soldiery have no longer an enemy near them, their retreat degenerates into a disorderly flight.

The brave soldiery who had stood superbly firm when shot were tearing their ranks, were scared by phantom thoughts, and the square-built, hard, rigid battalions which had checkered the hill-sides on the Alma now dissolved into shapeless masses. Even when, after accomplishing several miles of retreat, the troops at length reached the hill-sides which looked down on the banks of the Katcha, they had no belief that the Allies would suffer them to drink of its waters in peace; and the army of the Czar degenerating into a helpless throng, officers, men, horses, guns, tumbrils, carts laden with stores, carts laden with the wounded, all pressed into a gorge leading down to the ford; and then the disorder was so complete, and the masses which choked the gorge were so dense and helpless, that it seemed as though a small force of cavalry and horse artillery would have sufficed to make the whole army prisoners or bring it to utter ruin.

When they had crossed the Katcha, the bulk of the troops still hurried on, though with no idea of the direction they were to take, except that their course ought to be a prolongation of the line of the retreat already accomplished.

But presently even that poor clew failed them; for some got to imagine that, instead of falling back upon Sebastopol, they were to make for Baktchi Seräi. Then darkness came; and, there being no landmarks, the army was as a child that has lost its way at night in a trackless moor. Sometimes the masses were bent in their course by a voice shouting out, 'To the 'right;' and then again they would swerve the other way under the impulse of a cry, 'To the left.' All idea of bearings was so utterly lost, that even in their flight the fugitives could no longer be sure that they were retreating; for they did not know but that they might be marching all the while toward an enemy. Afterward the uselessness of this wild movement in the dark got to be understood; and, shouts for a halt becoming general, the masses at length stood still.[1]

All this while the Allied armies were quietly bivouacking upon the banks of the Alma, at a distance of several miles from the enemy; and the Staff of the Russian army having ascertained that no pursuit was going on, mounted officers and Cossacks were sent to announce to the wandering battalions that the Katcha was the rendezvous. But some of the messengers, having received these directions before they crossed the river, carried on the very words intrusted to them with the servile exactness of a Chinese copyist, and told the troops which had long ago forded the stream, and were thence marching southward, that they were to 'go on to the Katcha.' Orders thus conveyed led to a belief that the stream already passed was not the Katcha; and, although in reality the troops had over-

[1] One day at Balaclava I had some conversation with Lord Raglan respecting the panic which seized the Russian army on the banks of the Katcha, and he told me that he thought the panic may have been occasioned by the appearance of his patrols; but I have never heard from any other source that our cavalry patroled to the neighborhood of the Katcha on the evening of the battle; and I imagine that Lord Raglan must have spoken rather from what he inferred than from what he knew.

stepped the place of rendezvous, they imagined that they had not yet reached it.

Thus confusion was prolonged; but the halt began, after a time, to produce good effects. The officers called for men who could undertake to find the way back to the Katcha. Some were found. These acted as guides; and at midnight the wearied troops regained the river. For about two hours they rested; but then—by panic, it is believed, in the first instance, and afterward by orders which the panic engendered—the army was hastily roused, and thrown once more into full retreat. It moved upon Sebastopol.[1]

XLVI.

Losses of the French.

In this action the French lost three officers killed;[2] and, on grounds which he deemed, and (privately) stated to be, to his mind 'conclusive,' Lord Raglan came to the belief that their whole loss in killed was 60, and their number of wounded 500.[3] The English army lost 25 officers and 19 sergeants killed, and 81 officers and 102 sergeants wounded; and of rank and file, 318 killed and 1438 wounded, making, with the 19 who were missing, and who are supposed to have been buried in the ruins of the houses in the village, a total loss of 2002. The loss of the Russians in killed and wounded was officially stated at 5709, and it is believed that later and more accurate computations would carry the loss up to a much higher

Of the English.

Of the Russians.

[1] My knowledge respecting the enemy's retreat to the Katcha is mainly derived from Chodasiewicz; but on the 23rd of September the peasantry of the village of Eskel, on the banks of the Katcha, described to me the scene of panic which they had witnessed in the night of the 20th.

[2] St. Arnaud's Dispatch.

[3] The French official accounts state the total loss of their army in killed and wounded at 1339 (or, according to M. St. Arnaud's dispatch, 1343), but those statements have not obtained such credence as to induce me to place the figures in the text. Lord Raglan, I know, believed not only that the French returns were grossly erroneous, but that they were intentionally falsified; for, in the same letter in which he states it to be 'impossible' their accounts could be true, he also speaks of the 'pains' which the French authorities took to make him believe them. On the other hand, I think it right to say that I am acquainted with the grounds on which Lord Raglan based his low estimate of the French losses, and that, not thinking them quite so conclusive as he did, I have abstained from hazarding a positive statement on the subject. The field of battle did not give indication of considerable losses by the French; and I recollect that, the morning after the battle, a French soldier told me that he estimated the whole loss of his people at fifty (une cinquantaine). As an actual estimate of the losses, of course, his statement was of no worth, but it went toward showing what was the first impression of the French army as to the extent of the carnage.

number. Except the Russians left wounded on the field, there were scarcely any prisoners taken by the Allies; and by the Russians none. Amongst the wounded Russians left on the field and taken by the English there were two general officers. Great quantities of small arms were left upon the ground; but of prouder trophies there were few. The French captured a small four-wheeled open carriage, in which a clerk had been traveling with a quantity of office forms and papers. The English had the gun taken by Captain Bell, and the howitzer abandoned by the enemy in the Great Redoubt.[1]

The trophies of victory were scanty.

## XLVII.

Question whether the attack upon the position of the Alma could have been avoided.

Whether it was wise to assail the enemy on the very ground where he sought to make his stand, is a question depending upon the measure of respect which was due from an Anglo-French army to a Russian force one third less in numbers. On the inland or eastern flank of the position on the Alma the country was open, and therefore it was possible for the Allies to avoid all encounter with the enemy on his chosen strong-hold by taking ample ground to their left, and boldly marching round him. If a man so resolute as Marshal Pelissier had been then at the head of the French army, this perhaps is what he would have proposed to do. At all events, this is the way in which, under like circumstances, he would now undertake to deal with a Russian army. But then he judges things by the light of what has since passed, and especially by the light of his own great achievement. To have undertaken so daring a flank movement as this in the presence of an unhumbled and confident foe, would have implied a steadfast faith in the excellence of the whole Allied army, and a somewhat early perception of that want of nimbleness and enterprise on the part of the Russians which was afterward found to be characteristic of their field operations. Those who know how heavily—even down

[1] On the following day the French quietly came with an artillery team, and were going to carry off one of the guns taken by the English. An English officer caught them in the act, and prevented them from executing their purpose. This enterprising attempt was the more curious, since it happened that the gun was more than a mile distant from the ground on which the nearest of the French troops had been moving. Apparently it was calculated that any Englishman who chanced to observe the French drivers would assume that they were acting under authority from Lord Raglan, and that, when once the gun was in the French lines, the transcendent importance of the alliance, and of a cordial feeling between the two armies, would be relied on as grounds which might prevent the English General from reclaiming it.

to the day of the Alma—the thought of the Moscow campaign still weighed upon the mind of the French, will hardly wonder that Marshal St. Arnaud and his advisers should have shrunk from the idea of lending the flank of the French army to the enterprises of a foe who had still a great warlike repute, and whose numbers were imperfectly known. Besides, since the French had taken the right, the success of any such plan, and with it the honor and safety of the whole Allied force, would have been made to depend upon the stability of the French troops alone, rather than upon the prowess of the whole Allied army. Even if Marshal St. Arnaud had desired to make the venture, there is no reason for believing that Lord Raglan would have consented to move into the interior, with a French army marching on his right between him and the enemy.[1] To have done so would have implied great confidence in the steadiness of the French army.

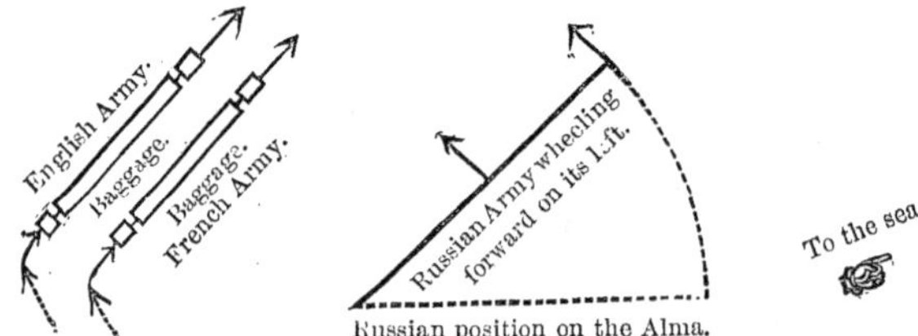


The course actually taken.

But, whatever be the worth of a plan for turning instead of attacking the Russian position on the Alma, it is certain that Marshal St. Arnaud and his advisers thought it would be more prudent to choose the course which they actually took to possess themselves of the unoccupied ground which lay between the Russian position and the sea-shore, to pit the rest of the French forces against Prince Mentschikoff's left, and to leave to Lord Raglan the duty of dealing with the enemy's centre as well as with his left wing.

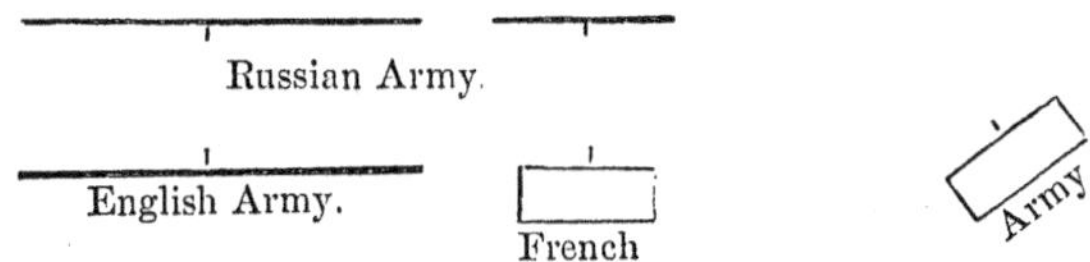


[1] The first diagram above will perhaps convey some idea of the nature of the hazard which would have been incurred by venturing upon a flank march.

XLVIII.

Summary of the battle.

Told summarily, the battle of the Alma was this:—The French seized the empty ground which divided the enemy from the sea, and then undertook to assail the enemy's left wing, but were baffled by the want of a road for Canrobert's artillery, and by the exceeding cogency of the rule which forbids them from engaging their infantry on open ground without the support of cannon. Their failure placed them in jeopardy; for they had committed so large a proportion of their force to the distant part of the West Cliff and the sea-shore, that for nearly an hour they lay much at the mercy of any Russian general who might have chosen to take advantage of their severed condition. But, instead of turning to his own glory the mistake the French had been making, Prince Mentschikoff hastened to copy it, wasting time and strength in a march toward the sea-shore, and a countermarch back to the Telegraph. Still, the sense the French had of their failure, and the galling fire which Kiriakoff's two batteries were by this time bringing to bear on them, began to create in their army a grave discontent, and sensations scarce short of despondency. Seeing the danger to which this condition of things was leading, and becoming, for other reasons, impatient, Lord Raglan determined to order the final advance of the English infantry, without waiting any longer for the time when Canrobert and Prince Napoleon should be established on the plateau. So the English infantry went forward, and in a few minutes the battalions which followed Codrington had not only defeated one of the two heavy 'columns of attack' which marched down to assail them, but had stormed and carried the Great Redoubt. From that moment the hill-sides on the Alma were no longer a fortified position; but they were still a battle-field, and a battle-field on which, for a time, the combatants were destined to meet with checkered fortune; for, not having been supported at the right minute, and being encompassed by great organized numbers, Codrington's disordered force was made to fall back under the weight of the Vladimir column, and its retreat involved the centre battalion of the brigade of Guards. Nearly at the same time, Kiriakoff, with his great 'column of 'the eight battalions,' pushed Canrobert down from the crest he had got to, obliging or causing him for a time to hang back under the cover of the steep. At that time the prospects of the Allies were overcast. But then the whole face of the battle was suddenly changed by the two guns which Lord Raglan had brought up to the knoll; for not only did their fire extirpate the Causeway batteries, and so lay open the Pass, but it tore through the columns of Prince Mentschikoff's infantry reserves, and drove them at once from the field. This discomfiture of the Russian centre could not but govern the policy of Kiriakoff, obliging him to conform to its movement of retreat; and he must have been the more ready to acknowledge to himself the necessity of the step he was taking, since by this time he had suffered the disaster which was inflicted upon his great 'column of the eight battalions' by the French artillery. He retreated without being molested by the French infantry, and took up a position at a distance of two miles from the Alma. Meanwhile, after a sheer fight of infantry, the whole strength that the enemy had on the Kourganè Hill was broken and turned to ruin by the Guards and the Highlanders. Thenceforth the slaughter that is wrought by artillery upon retreating masses was all that remained to be fulfilled.

## XLIX.

Question how far the Allies were entitled to take glory to themselves.

The trophies, we saw, were scanty. But was there a gain of that priceless spoil which one nation takes from another, when it proves itself the better in arms? The Western Alliance had the ear of Europe, and it awarded to itself an unstinted measure of glory. Was this glory honestly taken?

The Allies were more than 60,000, and the strength of the Russians fell short of that by one third. This was a disparity which made it unbecoming for the Great Alliance of the West to indulge in the language of a boisterous triumph. But, besides that the strength of the ground went some way toward making the conflict equal, the very faults and shortcomings of the Allies had the effect of putting a heavy stress upon some portions of their united army; for, by sending two fifths of his army to the sea-shore, and by crowding the remainder of it upon a narrow front, the French Marshal placed Prince Gortschakoff and General Kvetzinski upon a numerical equality with their English foes; and, the Russian artillery being vastly more powerful than ours, and the ground being intrenched and singularly strong by nature, the Russians were in circumstances which tended to give them a great advantage over their English adversaries. Besides, though our forces were equal in numbers to the part of the Russian army with which they had to deal, yet it happened that, in each distinct infantry fight, the English battalions were almost always confronted by masses far greater in numerical strength. Justly, therefore, there may be rendered to some of the components of the Allied army a part of the glory which History must refuse to the aggregate host.

At three o'clock, as we saw, the battle had been suffered to lapse into such a condition that there was then bitter need of a general, and of troops so placed in the field, and so inclined toward the practice of close fighting, as to be able to restore—to restore, as it were, by sheer force—the waning fortune of the day. How the occasion was met, this History has shown. I narrate, and soldiers will comment. They must judge, and say whether for simplicity's sake it be better to pile up a heap of praise, and distribute it, like a cargo of medals, amongst all the French, English, and Turks who heard the sound of the guns; or, in a harsher and more careful spirit, to part off the troops which fought hard from the troops which scarce fought at all, and to show by whose ordering it was that the course of the battle was governed.

I have been eager to acknowledge the valor and the steadiness of the Russian infantry. If I had caused it to appear that, upon the whole, Marshal St. Arnaud and the troops he commanded had done marvels on the day of the Alma, I should have been helping to prolong a belief in that which I know to be false, and should be even running counter to what, with good reason, I hold to be the opinion of the French army;[1] but I have tried to do careful justice to those who were then our allies by marking and commending the warlike quality which was displayed by their artillerymen, as well as by their keen, bold, active skirmishers. Of my own countrymen I have hardly once suffered myself to speak in words of praise. I have only told what they did.

## L.

Those three sunny hours of the 20th of September were the time, and the only time, when a French and an English army stood abreast in an open pitched battle;[2] and therefore it is

[1] I speak in great measure from knowledge acquired long subsequently to the battle, but the conviction of which I speak was not long to show itself in the French army. Writing three days after the battle, and speaking of the conviction which was produced upon the English army by the fact that Marshal St. Arnaud had not 'kept moving on after he had turned the enemy's 'left,' Lord Raglan says: 'I have reason to believe that the same feeling is 'prevalent amongst the officers of the French army.' For any one who was not in the Crimea during the month which followed the battle of the Alma, it would be difficult to form a conception of the state into which the repute of the French army had fallen. Later events (and the first of these was the brilliant charge of two squadrons of the Chasseurs d'Afrique at Balaclava) showed that the warlike spirit of France was not extinct in her army.

[2] The English at Inkerman were valiantly aided by a body of French troops;

that, when many generations shall have passed away, mankind will still gaze and gaze upon a barren hill-side in Crim Tartary, comparing the demeanor of the two great rivals of the West whilst they fought side by side on the Alma. Yet, if people shall end this comparison without making honest allowance for the ban I am going to speak of, they will do a wrong to the warlike repute of France.

Cause of any shortcomings on the part of the French army.

It would be unjust to look upon the action between Marshal St. Arnaud and the Russian left wing as a fair sample of what a French army can do. That glance at the things done in Paris which helped us to understand the origin of the Anglo-French alliance, will now serve to teach us the cause of any shortcomings which may be attributed to the army commanded by Marshal St. Arnaud.[1] We saw something of a strange decree, which enacted that services rendered by military men in their operations against Frenchmen should hold good as titles to advancement in the same way as though they were deeds done in war against the foreigner.[2] Incredible as it may seem, that decree was long observed to the full;[3] and the shameful principle which it involved was made to weigh heavily upon France during several of the months which followed the landing at Old Fort. Indeed, the principle, though partly waived for a time in 1855, was found to be still in dire operation long after the close of the Russian war. Just as in a later year the French Emperor intrusted to a scared and bewildered literary man the command of a whole French army in Italy, so now he committed the honor of the flag—committed it almost exclusively—to men who had shared with him in the adventure which put France under his feet. His reckoning was that, whether it were led by honorable and skilled commanders, or were tossed and flung into action by him and his December friends, a French army engaged in a short, brisk war against a Continental state would always be likely to push its way to more or less of success; and that if it should chance to do this under the leadership, or apparent leadership, of him and his friends, he and they would become similar to heroes. If they could attain to be thus thought of for a time, they might hope that for a still longer period they would enjoy the immunity and the thousand rewards which nations are accustomed to lavish upon victorious commanders.

but that great fight was not one of which it could be said that a 'French and an English army stood abreast in an open pitched battle.'

[1] *Ante*, cap. 14. [2] *Ibid.*, Decree of 5th December, 1851.

[3] It was carried to the length of making Magnan and St. Arnaud Marshals of France.

This was the principle which governed the choice of the man to whose charge, on the day of the Alma, the honor of the French arms was left. He who commanded the army was St. Arnaud, formerly Le Roy, the person suborned by Fleury. Under him, in the Crimea, there were four Divisions of French infantry. He who commanded the 1st of these Divisions was Canrobert. This officer, as I have said, was not without honest titles to military distinction; but, whilst he had a professional repute which would have earned him the approval of even the most loyal of monarchs, he had also the qualification which entitled him to the favor of the French Emperor. He had commanded one of the brigades which operated against the gay boulevards on the 4th of December. The 2nd Division was commanded by Bosquet. Bosquet was a man without a stain; but he was the only French General of Division at the Alma who could say that he did not owe his command to the December plot; and, since it happened that he was left isolated with only one brigade during the whole time when the issue of the battle was pending, his presence at the Alma was only an imperfect exception to what was, as it were, the general rule. He who commanded the large detached force of some 9000 men[1] which first crossed the river at its mouth was General Bouat; and Bouat, it seems, was an officer who earned his command by exploits against Parisians in the boulevard, the rue St. Denis, or the neighborhood of the Nouvelle France.[2] He who commanded the 3rd Division was Prince Napoleon. He who commanded the 4th Division was Forey; and no man could come within the principle of selection more clearly than he did, for it was he of whom I spoke when I said that he had suffered himself to be used as the assailant and the jailer of an unarmed Legislature. There were, besides, the Lourmels, the Espinasses, and numbers of others, no doubt, whose names could be easily found in their Emperor's list of worthies. Therefore it is that the part which was taken by Marshal St. Arnaud and his troops in the battle of the Alma was no fair sample of what could be done by a French army. It was only a sample of what a French army could manage to do when it labored under the weight of a destiny which ordained that all its chiefs should be men chosen for their complicity in a midnight plot, or else for acts of street slaughter.[3] Because they had perpetrated an extensive massacre of their

[1] One of Bosquet's brigades, and the whole of the Turkish Contingent except the two battalions left to guard the baggage.

[2] With the 33rd Regiment.

[3] Prince Napoleon's complicity was only, as I am inclined to believe, a

unarmed fellow-countrymen, there was no certainty, perhaps, that they might not be men firm and able in honest war against the foreigner; but also there was no such close similarity between what these men had done in Paris, and what they were meant to do in the Crimea, as to warrant the notion of intrusting to them almost exclusively the honor of the French flag. There was a salient point of difference between the boulevards and the hill-sides of the Alma. The Russians were armed.

No! The Power which fought that day by the side of England was not, after all, mighty France—brave, warlike, impetuous France. It was only that intermittent thing which to-day is, and to-morrow is not. It was what people call 'The 'French Empire.'

LI.

Effect of the battle upon the prospects of the campaign.

The Battle of the Alma seemed to clear the prospects of the campaign, and even of the war. It confirmed to the Allies that military ascendency over Russia which had been more than half gained already by the valor of the Ottoman soldiery. It lent the current sanction of a victory to the hazardous enterprise of the invasion. It ended the perils of the march from Kamishlu, and made smooth the whole way to the Belbec. It established the Allies as invaders in a province of Russia. It did more. Upon condition that they would lay instant hands on the prize, it gave them Sebastopol.

complicity after the fact; but it is, of course, clear enough that he owed his command entirely to the Coup d'Etat.

# NOTES TO FOURTH EDITION.

---

Page 40. In note 2, Sir George Larpent should be Mr. Larpent.

Page 49. '*should be strictly executed.*'—June, 1850.—'Eastern Papers,' part i, p. 2.

Page 50. '*said our Foreign Secretary.*'—In his dispatch of the 28th of January, 1853.

Page 53. '*Prince Garari.*'—So spelled in the official dispatches; but it has been suggested, and probably with truth, that the person meant was Prince Gagarin, one of the secretaries or attachés of the Russian Legation at Constantinople.

Page 91. '*For almost two years Sir Stratford Canning had been absent from* '*Constantinople.*'—No; not nearly so long. It was not till June, 1852, that his absence from Constantinople began.

Page 127.—Instead of note 1, the author gives the following:—'Even if 'the Governments of France and England were not *in honor bound* to pro- 'tect the Sultan,' etc.—Lord Clarendon to Lord Cowley. 'Eastern Papers,' part ii. p. 321.

Page 133. Instead of note 1, the following:—Count Mensdorf, I believe, was an honest soldier, too high-spirited to be capable of shrinking from what he understood to be his duty; but he had had little of the training needed for a diplomatist, and (as is often the case with the representatives of Austria at foreign Courts) he was not kept well informed of the policy which his Government was pursuing. It was not in deference to his own tastes or wishes that he accepted the mission to St. Petersburg. An illustration of the courtier-like attitude assumed by the French Envoy will be found in the note to p. 496.

Page 157. '*he hit upon a general officer who was christened, it seems, Jacques Arnaud Le Roy.*'—Giving in a formal way its list of the new Ministry of the 27th of October, the 'Annuaire,' an authority favorable to the Elysée, has these words: 'A la guerre, Jacques Arnaud le Roy de St. Arnaud,' p. 352.

Page 161. '*they might soon be called upon to act against Paris and against the* '*Constitution.*'—Granier de Cassaignac, p. 392. There, the 26th is the day of the month which the historian mentions, but he gives Thursday (which fell on the 27th) as the day of the week when the meeting took place.

Page 161. Instead of note 1, the following:—'All the generals embraced 'each other, and from that moment it might be said with certainty that 'France was going to come out of the abyss.'—Ibid. p. 392. The names of the twenty-one generals will be found ibid. p. 393.

Page 163. '*vowed anew that his duty was to maintain the Republic.*'—'My duty is to baffle their perfidious projects, *to maintain the Republic*, and 'to save the country,' etc.—'Annuaire,' App. p. 60.

Page 163. Instead of note 1, the following:—The proclamation to the army contained this passage: 'In 1830, as in 1848, they treated you as 'conquered men. After having spurned your heroic disinterestedness, they 'disdained to consult your sympathies and your wishes, and yet you are the '*élite* of the nation. To-day, in this solemn moment, I desire that the 'army may make its voice heard.'—Granier de Cassaignac, vol. ii. p. 404. A copy of the proclamation will also be found in the 'Annuaire' for 1851. This last publication (which must be distinguished from the 'Annuaire 'des Deux Mondes') gives an account of the events of December, written in a spirit favorable to the Elysée; but the Appendix contains a full collection of official documents.

Page 165. '*the announcement of measures not hitherto disclosed.*'—'The 'Assembly,' he wrote, 'has been dissolved amid the applause of the whole 'population of Paris.'—Circular to the Prefects.

Page 165. '*striking some of them with the butt-ends of their muskets.*'—The names of nine of these are given in the 'Recueil,' p. 64, ; and besides these, the seizure of MM. Daru and De Blois is stated.—Ibid. pp. 6, 7.

Page 165. '*rode through some of the streets of Paris.*'—Fleury rode in front of the cortége, waving his sword and trying to get the people in the streets to cheer.

Page 167. '*assembled at the Mayoralty of the 10th arrondissement.*'—'Recueil d'Actes Officielles,' p. 60. In that and in pp. 61-3, the names of 220 Deputies are given.

Page 167. '*President and his accomplices.*'—'Recueil d'Actes Officielles,' pp. 37, 45. The report of the proceedings of the Assembly is from the short-hand-writer's notes.—See ibid. p. 35.

Page 167. '*One of the Vice-Presidents.*'—Namely, M. Vitet. Through all those last moments of the struggle between law and force, M. Vitet's demeanor was admirable for its firmness and dignity. Of this I am assured by one of the most eminent of the many statesmen who were there present.

Page 167. '*any Deputies offering resistance.*'—It was in the second of the two written orders produced that the prison of Mazas was designated. It is given, 'Recueil d'Actes Officielles,' p. 57.

Page 167. Instead of note 2, the following:—The order rendered into English was in these words: 'Commandant! *In consequence of the orders 'of the Minister of War*, cause to be immediately occupied the Mayoralty 'of the 10th arrondissement, and cause to be arrested, if necessary, such of 'the representatives as shall not instantly obey the order to disperse. '(Signed) The General-in-Chief Magnan.'—Ibid. p. 57.

Page 167. '*collared by officers of police and led out.*'—Ibid. p. 60. M. Benoist d'Azy was one of the Vice-Presidents, and the other Vice-President collared by the soldiery was M. Vitet.

Page 168. '*It was now only two o'clock in the afternoon.*'—Ibid. p. 12; but the procès-verbal makes it later—viz., twenty minutes past three o'clock. Ibid. p. 60.

Page 168. '*raised to two hundred and thirty-five.*'—According to the 'Recueil' the number was 232.—La Vérité, 'Recueil d'Actes Officielles,' p. 64. The difference is occasioned by including, or not including, M. Daru, and M. de Blois, and one other.

Page 169. '*Into these the two hundred and thirty-five members of the Assem-'bly were thrust.*'—Not all in one batch, but in three. The last batch was so large a one, that the prison-vans had to be reinforced by some omnibuses;

and some few of the Deputies were left behind for a time in the barrack.—Ibid. p. 15.

Page 169. '*Benoist d'Azy.*'—One of the Vice-Presidents of the Assembly. Among the Deputies thrown into the prison there was also M. Vitet, another of the Vice-Presidents.

Page 169. Instead of note 1, the following:—The facts mentioned in the above paragraph are not, I believe, controverted in any important point. A full account of what passed will be found in the well-known letter of M. de Tocqueville (now printed in the collection of his letters), and in the 'Re-'cueil' above quoted, pp. 13, 14, 60 *et seq.*

Page 170. '*the Judges were driven from the bench.*'—The 'Annuaire' says triumphantly that two Commissaries of Police 'interrupted this fresh 'attempt at legal resistance,' p. 373.

Page 170. Instead of note 1, the following:—It seems that in his mission to the Elysée the process-server was accompanied by the President of the Court.—Ibid. 'Bulletin Français,' p. 27.

Page 174. Instead of note 3, the following:—Several of their letters to this effect appeared from time to time in the English journals; but M. Léon Faucher (who had been a few weeks before a member of the Cabinet) addressed his indignant protest straight to the President:—

'MONSIEUR LE PRESIDENT,—It is with a painful surprise that I see my 'name figuring among those of the members of a Consultative Commis-'sion which you have just been instituting. I did not think I had given 'you any right to offer me this insult [*de me faire cette injure*]. The serv-'ices I have rendered to you in the belief that they were services rendered 'to the country, entitled me perhaps to expect from you a very different 'treatment. At all events my character deserved more respect.'—'Re-'cueil,' p. 24.

Page 180. '*calmly seen by this English officer.*'—Another English officer, who was in that part of the Boulevards which is at the corner of the Rue de Grammont, writes to me thus:—'Having been in Paris during the *coup* '*d'état*, and having been a spectator and nearly a victim when the French 'troops fired against harmless people on the Boulevards, and having been 'standing, until forced to leave it, on the balcony of my club at the corner 'of the Rue de Grammont—which club was struck thirty-seven times, six 'balls entering the drawing-room—I can vouch for the correctness of your 'description of it.'—Letter dated 9th March, 1863.

Page 184. To note 1, the author adds:—In the 'Quarterly Review' of April, 1863, p. 527, it is stated that M. Xavier Durrieu says 'he saw *some-*'*thing of the kind* from his prison window,' but that his 'words, as given by 'Mr. Kinglake in a note, do not quite bear out the somewhat exaggerated 'statement in the text.' Since a statement like this has been ventured upon by a respectable publication, it seems right to give a translation of the above passage: 'Several times, when the gate was shut, the sergeants of police 'threw themselves like tigers on the prisoners, whose hands were fastened 'behind their backs. They knocked them down with loaded clubs. They 'left them with their throats gurgling upon the flag-stone, where several of 'them expired. . . . It was so—neither more nor less; we saw it from the 'windows of our cells, which looked out on the court.' The writer adds:—'A chaque prison son genre de supplice et de mort: on fusillait à Mazas, au 'Champ de Mars, et dans les divers postes de la ville. A la Préfecture de 'Police, on tuait à coup de casse-tête.' 'At each prison there was its own 'kind of punishment and of death: they shot people at Mazas, on the 'Champ de Mars, and at the different posts (military posts) of the town. 'At the Prefecture of Police they killed people with loaded clubs.'

*Page 188. 'French citizens to be shot by platoons of infantry in the night of 'the 4th and the night of the 5th of December.'*—I find that what I, in my caution, thus speak of as a 'question' has been recorded as a proved fact in the 'Edinburgh Review.' The article referred to is known to have been written by a gentleman who was in Paris at the time of the *coup d'état*, who was gifted more than most men with the power of seeking for truth in an impartial spirit, and who enjoyed great opportunities of informing himself concerning the events which had been passing in the French capital. The article asserts, in plain, unqualified terms, that 'hundreds' were 'put to death in 'the court-yards of the barracks, or in the subterraneous passages of the 'Tuileries.'—'Edinburgh Review' for April, 1852. Still, the writer did not see the prisoners shot with his own eyes, and I persist in my inclination to treat it as a 'question,' whether these alleged executions did or did not take place in the nights of the 4th and 5th of December.

Page 190. '*should be dismissed.*'—'You will immediately dismiss the 'juges de paix, the mayors, and the other functionaries, whose concurrence 'may not be assured, and appoint other men in their stead. To this end, 'you will call upon all the public functionaries to give you in writing their 'adhesion to the great measure which the Government has just adopted.' Morny's Circular to the Prefects. 'Annuaire,' Appendix, p. 67.

Page 194. Instead of note 1, the following:—Decree of 8th December, inserted in the *Moniteur* of the 9th. It is also in the 'Annuaire,' pp. 75, 76. The transportation was to be to a penal colony in Algeria or Cayenne, and was to be for a period of five years at the least, and ten years at the most (Articles 1 and 2). The order for transportation was to be an act of administration. In other words, every body whom the police authorities chose to designate as having belonged to a secret society was made liable to be transported without trial. This decree was superscribed *Liberty, Equality, Fraternity.* I observed that, within forty-eight hours from the time when they thus got France down—viz., on the 10th of December—the brethren of the Elysée began their 'concessions' to railways and other companies. Thenceforth, as might be expected, 'concessions' went on at a merry rate. See whole lists of them in the Appendices to the 'Annuaire.' Those who know how vast have been the sums expended by our public companies in obtaining 'Private Acts of Parliament,' may form some idea of the importance of the patronage in this direction which the brethren got into their hands.

Page 195. Instead of note 2, the following:—Granier de Cassaignac, vol. ii. p. 438. To meet the cost of these wholesale transportations an extraordinary credit was opened on the 28th of January. It is only the title of the decree, and not the sum fixed, which is given in the 'Annuaire,' Appendix, p. 95.

Page 196. '*has been done to living men.*'—I have not ventured to speak of the number of these hapless sufferers farther than to use the phrase, 'the 'two thousand men whose sufferings are the best known;' but the conductors of the 'Edinburgh Review,' who were armed with a great deal of trustworthy information on the subject, conceived themselves warranted in venturing upon the following words:—'All that is known, is that about three 'thousand two hundred have since disappeared from Paris; they may have 'been killed in the Boulevards, and thrown into the large pits in which those 'who fell on that day were promiscuously interred; they may have been 'among the hundreds who were put to death in the court-yards of the barracks, or in the subterraneous passages of the Tuileries; they may be in the 'casements of Fort Bicêtre, or in the bagnes of Rochefort, or they may be at 'sea on their way to Cayenne. . . . We have already stated that the 'number of persons undergoing or sentenced by these cruelties is believed 'to exceed ten thousand. *A hundred thousand more* are supposed to be in the 'vaults and casemates which the French dignify with the name of prisons, 'often piled, crammed, and wedged together so closely that they can scarce- 'ly change their positions.'—'Edinburgh Review,' vol. xcv. p. 319.

Page 198. '*within forty-eight hours from the receipt of a dispatch of the 3rd of December.*'—'Annuaire,' Appendix, p. 67. M. St. Arnaud's circular to the Generals of Division ordered that the vote of the soldiers be taken within forty-eight hours, and also said, 'The President reckons on the sup- 'port of the nation and of the army; and, so far as concerns your Division, 'on the energy of your attitude, the prompt and severe repression of the 'slightest attempt at disturbance.'—Ibid.

Page 198. '*nearly eight millions.*'—7,439,216, against 640,737 noes.—'Annuaire,' Appendix, p. 95.

Page 199. '*should pay him tribute and obey.*'—The free way in which the purse of France was laid open by the success of the *coup d'état* may be in some measure gathered from the long catalogue of decrees opening supplementary and extraordinary credits, which is given in the Appendix to the 'Annuaire,' pp. 95 *et seq.* As was mentioned in a former note (*ante*, p. 297), the 'concessions' to railway and other companies began so early as the 10th of December. See the Appendix to the 'Annuaire.'

Page 202. Instead of note 2, the following:—Decree of the 5th, inserted in the *Moniteur* of the 7th December: 'Lorsq'une troupe organisée aura 'contribuée par des combats à rétablir l'ordre sur un point quelconque du 'territoire, ce service sera compté comme service de campagne.'—Article 1, 'Annuaire,' Appendix, p. 70.

Page 206. '*made merry with what they saw.*'—It was not in this spirit that the Press of free England dealt with France. In the journal which most carefully made it its study to give utterance to English opinion, the leading article said, 'Speaking within the limits of historical truth, and 'upon the evidence of many eye-witnesses of these events, we affirm that 'the bloody and treacherous deeds of the 4th of December will be remem- 'bered with horror in the annals even of that city which witnessed the mas- 'sacre of St. Bartholomew and the Reign of Terror.'—*Times*, Dec. 8, 1851.

Page 207. '*in the Cathedral of our Lady of Paris.*'—I have thought fit to speak of the deeds which are the subject of this chapter, without, in general, undertaking to judge and formally say whether they were pardonable, or wicked, or good; for it seemed to me that there was a native expressiveness in the facts which would enable them, as it were, to speak for themselves without the interpreter's help. But at a time when these things were fresh in men's minds, no such cold abstinence as mine was to be expected from the periodical press of a free country. After the events of the 2nd of December, it became the peculiar duty of the conductors of those journals which are published at intervals giving time for full investigation and for the formation of a deliberate judgment, not only to make a careful gathering of the facts which had been happening on the other side of the Channel, but also to pronounce upon the men who had just been stifling France the judgment of a nation still blessed with the power of free speech. It was in no doubtful, balancing words that this duty was fulfilled. Of the knowledge with which the 'Edinburgh Review' was soon able to arm itself, and of the unshrinking firmness with which it delivered its judgment, some samples have been given in foregoing notes. The 'Quarterly Review' summed up its account of the things done to France in these words:—'All the in- 'stitutions of the country overthrown—all constitutional authority dissolved '—all legality abrogated—the streets of Paris a human slaughter-house—

'innocent strollers and spectators on public walks and from drawing-room 'windows wantonly massacred—hundreds of the most honorable and emi-'nent men of the nation imprisoned like felons, some of them handcuffed—'thirty-three departments in a state of siege—and, as the Bonapartist advo-'cates are forward to admit, half the surface of the country reeking with 'blood and fire! . . . All the mischief, whatever it may be, is chargeable 'to no other cause but Louis Napoleon's perjury to the Constitution, and 'his treason to the State.'—'Quarterly Review' for December, 1851.

Page 231. '*the Sultan was placed in a state of war with the Emperor of* '*Russia.*'—A writer in the 'Edinburgh Review' imagined that the state of war began on the 4th of October—the date of the Declaration ('Edinburgh 'Review,' No. 240, p. 328); but that is a mistake. It was Lord Stratford who devised the plan of a contingent declaration of war ('Eastern Papers,' part ii. p. 198); and he, of all men living, would be the least likely to be wrong as to the time when the state of war began. Reporting to the Home Government the effect of the decision of the Great Council as conveyed to him by Reshid Pasha, Lord Stratford writes, that 'Omar Pasha will be 'instructed to re-summon Prince Gortschakoff by letter to evacuate the 'Principalities within fifteen days from the receipt of his letter; *that the* '*Prince's refusal will be considered as tantamount to a declaration of war on the* '*part of Russia;* that hostilities will be declared *thereupon* by the Porte; that 'all persons now here in the employment of Russia will *then* be requested 'to withdraw; and, finally, that all merchant vessels under Russian colors 'will also be required to leave the port of Constantinople.'—('Eastern 'Papers,' part ii. p. 151.) After the 4th of October, and at a time when the Edinburgh Reviewer supposed the state of war to have begun, the Turkish Government was sending to Prince Gortschakoff the summons devised by Lord Stratford—a summons which the Sublime Porte described as '*the* '*last expression of its pacific sentiments.*'—(Ibid. p. 154.) The Edinburgh Reviewer was kept in his error by a notion that the postponement of hostilities applied only to 'hostilities *on the Danube;*' but if he had glanced at Lord Stratford's dispatch of the 21st of October, he would have seen that—not only on the Danube, but—*on the Asiatic frontiers* the attack was to be '*immediately after the expiration of the fifteen days.*'—(Ibid. p. 198.) At one time the Turkish Ministers set up a theory that, as Prince Gortschakoff's answer (dated the 10th of October) was virtually a refusal, the term offered by the summons was brought to a close on that day—the 10th (ibid. p. 198); but the very fact that they were discussing with Lord Stratford this question about the state of war beginning *on the* 10*th*, shows conclusively that neither they nor Lord Stratford had any notion of its having begun, as the Edinburgh Reviewer supposed, on the 4th of October.

Page 238. Instead of note 1, the following:—'Eastern Papers,' part ii. p. 114. In the opinion of Lord Stratford, this violent and inevitably perturbing measure was unnecessary. After saying that he had been content with the plan of calling up three steamers from each of the squadrons, he writes:—'I am still of opinion that assistance thus limited would have *an-* '*swered every purpose*, unless, indeed, the Ottoman squadron had taken 'part against the Sultan, which was a very extreme case to suppose. *I* '*wished to save Her Majesty's Government from any embarrassments likely to* '*accrue from a premature passage of the Dardanelles* by Admiral Dundas's 'squadron, and at the same time to take precautions adequate to the ap-'pearance of danger. I did not form my opinion in this respect without 'taking the opinion of Her Majesty's senior officer in command in the 'Bosphorus.'—Ibid. p. 188.

Page 245. '*He resigned his office.*'—This statement was formally denied by a respectable journal; but it may be verified by any one who has an opportunity either of addressing a question to some surviving member of Lord Aberdeen's Cabinet, or of consulting Hansard's debates. After speaking of the resignation of Lord Palmerston, and calling it 'the resignation of my 'noble friend the Secretary of the Home Department,' Lord Aberdeen, the then Prime Minister, went on to say, 'I myself informed Her Majesty 'of the resignation at Osborne.'—'Hansard,' vol. cxcvi. pp. 93, 94.

Page 248. To note 2 the author adds:—That which, in the above note, I treated as a fair inference from the dates, is now a proved truth; for the evidences which establish it have been brought to light and given to the public by a writer in the 'North British Review' of April, 1863. At the time in question, the *Morning Post* was Lord Palmerston's known organ. Combating the assertion that Lord Palmerston's dislike to a large measure of Reform was the cause of his resignation, his journal said:—'We are 'convinced that Lord Palmerston has not approved of the sluggish policy 'pursued in the Eastern question.' — *Morning Post*, 19th December, 1853. On announcing his resumption of office, the same journal said:— 'The present Ministerial crisis is therefore at an end. The vacillating 'policy pursued in the East is abandoned.'—Ibid., 26th December, 1853. The truth stands thus:—Before the time when Lord Aberdeen's Government was called upon to deal with the state of things brought about by the disaster of Sinope, the discussions in the Cabinet on the subject of a new Reform Bill had elicited so strong a difference of opinion between Lord Palmerston and the majority of the Cabinet, that, whenever the time might come for decisive action upon that subject, or even for a formal and final decision, Lord Palmerston's resignation was to be expected; but, as Lord Aberdeen said, the 'provisions of the measure had not been finally settled,' and therefore the moment which might necessitate Lord Palmerston's resignation had not yet come, when, on Monday the 12th of December, the news of Sinope reached London. Of course a Cabinet was forthwith summoned. It met on Wednesday the 14th of December, but rose from its sitting without having agreed to meet the disaster of Sinope by the adoption of any new and hostile measure. Lord Palmerston instantly resigned; but knowing, of course, that it would be inconvenient to disclose to Europe prematurely a difference of opinion between public men on what was hardly less than a question of Peace or War, he took up the heretofore suspended question of Reform, and put forward his difference of opinion on that subject as the ground of his resignation. There was nothing in this which he would be likely to think wrong, for his difference of opinion on Reform was a real one, acknowledged to be broad enough to warrant his resignation; and, as the moment when he might choose to give full effect to this difference of opinion had remained undefined, there was nothing to prevent him from fixing upon Wednesday evening the 14th of December as well as any other time; but as he had then just come from the Cabinet which had been deliberating upon the news from Sinope, without consenting to adopt in consequence any fresh measure of hostility to Russia, no one having any knowledge about Lord Palmerston would doubt that the inert way in which the Cabinet of the 14th sought to deal with the disaster of Sinope, and the instant resignation which followed, were in the relation of cause and effect. It does not follow that, in any unworthy sense, 'Reform' was a mere pretext: it was a ground—an apparently sufficing ground for resignation *at any convenient time;* but the reason why Lord Palmerston's resignation went in *on that particular Wednesday evening, or on the following morning,* was the way in which the Cabinet had just been dealing with the disaster of Sinope.

Perhaps a statement of the facts and the dates in a tabular form will make their significance yet more clear:—

| | |
|---|---|
| Monday the 12th.......................... | The news of Sinope reaches London. |
| Wednesday afternoon, the 14th............ | The Cabinet sits. |
| The evening of the same Wednesday, or on the following morning...... | Lord Palmerston sends in his resignation. |
| Thursday the 15th........................ | Lord Aberdeen announces Lord Palmerston's resignation to the Queen at Osborne. |
| Friday the 16th.......................... | Lord Palmerston's resignation announced in the *Times*. |
| Saturday the 17th........................ | Dispatch from Lord Clarendon to Lord Stratford intimating that, notwithstanding the disaster of Sinope, 'no special instruc-'tions as to the manner in which they [the 'Admirals] should act, appear to be neces-'sary.' |
| Sunday the 18th.......................... | The Government receive the French proposals. |
| Tuesday the 20th......................... | The Government on that day had not yielded to the pressure of the French Government, and was still adhering to its comparatively pacific policy. See Lord Clarendon's Dispatch to Lord Stratford of that day, 'Eastern Papers,' part ii. p. 320. |
| Thursday the 22nd........................ | The Cabinet meets and yields to the pressure, adopting the French proposals. |
| Saturday the 24th........................ | Lord Clarendon writes:—Her Majesty's Government do not disguise from themselves that it [the course then resolved upon] may at no distant period involve England and France in war with Russia. |
| Same day................................. | Lord Palmerston withdraws his resignation. |
| Monday the 26th.......................... | The *Times* and the *Morning Post* announce Lord Palmerston's return to office. |

Page 250.—'*forced upon the acceptance of Lord Aberdeen's Cabinet by the 'Emperor of the French.*'—Commentators have denied that Lord Aberdeen's Cabinet was pushed from the paths of peace by the urgency of the French Government. With proofs of what I have said about this, the volume, I think, abounds; but for those who like to see facts and dates put closely together, it may be convenient to glance at the following statement of the way in which the lever acted upon England between Tuesday the 20th and Saturday the 24th of December:—

| | |
|---|---|
| Tuesday, 20th December.................. | Our Government having just determined that no special instruction to the Admirals were necessitated by the disaster of Sinope ('Eastern Papers,' part ii. p. 304), and having up to this day resisted the French proposals, Lord Clarendon is able to write of 'the *unabated desire for peace* by which 'the British Government will be animated' [*i. e.*, peace between Turkey and Russia], to assure Lord Stratford that the course which he was 'taking with a view to *the 'adoption by* the Porte of *pacific coun-'sels* is in accordance with the wishes of 'Her Majesty's Government as being cal-'culated to *prepare the Porte to give a fa-'vorable reception to the proposals which 'have been forwarded from Vienna.*'—'Eastern Papers,' part ii. p. 320. |
| Thursday, 22nd December................ | The Government no longer resists the pressure applied (some of the words inflicting the pressure are given in the text), and adopts the French proposals. |

| | |
|---|---|
| Saturday, 24th December.................. | Lord Clarendon announces to Lord Cowley the adoption by our Government of the French proposals, and adds:—'Her Majes-'ty's Government have not hesitated to 'adopt the course which the honor and 'dignity of the country prescribe; but at 'the same time they do not disguise from 'themselves that it may at no distant pe-'riod *involve England and France in war* '*with Russia*.'—Ibid. pp. 221, 222. |

Thus, in the interval of three clear days between Tuesday the 20th and Saturday the 24th, there is a transition from peaceful language, and from obviously strong hopes of even ending the then existing war between Turkey and Russia, to a very close prospect of a new war—a war involving England and France; and the three days' interval in which this momentous change took place was marked by but one event—by the determination of the Cabinet (on Thursday the 22nd) to adopt the French proposals.

Page 295. '*and now at length was broken.*'—A writer in one of the Reviews said that the state of war did not begin until the declarations of the Western Powers were issued; but that is a mistake. What brought the Western Powers into a state of war, was the Czar's refusal to answer the summons; for the moment that refusal was given, it became, in the mind of the Western Powers, as enounced by the express words of their summons, a constructive declaration of war by Russia. The English summons had these words: 'The British Government, having exhausted all 'the efforts of negotiation, is compelled to declare to the Cabinet of St. 'Petersburg, that if . . . [see the summons at length in the Appendix] 'the British Government consider *the refusal or the silence* of the Cabinet 'of St. Petersburg *as equivalent to a declaration of war*.'—'Eastern Pa-'pers,' part vii. p. 61.

Page 305. '*slaughter of the Turks at Sinope.*'—So far as concerns Count Mensdorf's personal presence in the Cathedral, this is a mistake, for he was absent on leave, and in an almost dying state. Austria's 'shameful 'presence' at the 'Te Deum' was in the person of her Secretary of Legation.

Page 306. '*will long be remembered against her.*'—So far as concerns Colonel Rochow's personal presence in the Cathedral, this is a mistake, for he was absent on leave. Prussia's 'shameful presence' at the 'Te 'Deum' was in the person of her Secretary of Legation.

Page 308. '*baffled by the prostrations of his French colleague.*'—For those who have not had ample means of becoming acquainted with the doubleness which characterizes the French Emperor's habits of action, it will be hard to believe in the extent to which his Envoy at St. Petersburg was suffered to carry his adulation of the Czar. At the very time when the French Emperor was pushing our Government into the adoption of a measure of vengeance barely short of flagrant war, his Envoy, M. Castelbajac, though he could not actually attend the public thanksgivings for Sinope in the Cathedral, did nevertheless permit himself to wait on the Chancellor, Count Nesselrode, and tender his congratulations for the slaughter of the Turks at Sinope, and the sinking of their ships. It is believed that he expressly desired to tender these his congratulations to the Czar 'as a Christian, a soldier, and a gentleman.'

Page 316. '*he entered the military profession.*'—That is, in an active way, as an officer serving with troops. It must not be inferred from the words in the text, that in the interval between September, 1835, and November, 1836, his name was (for the second time) out of the Army List.

He seems to have been employed at that time in the 'Gymnase Militaire' ('Lettres du Maréchal de St. Arnaud,' vol. i. p. 92). Considering that he had attained to the rank of a full lieutenant in a French regiment, that he had been on General Bugeaud's Staff and in high favor, and that he had been intrusted with duties of an important and delicate nature, it is obvious that his removal to such a corps as the 'Foreign Legion,' under orders for Africa, with no higher rank than that which he had previously held in a French regiment, was a descent — a descent and a change so abrupt and decisive as to warrant me in speaking of it as the commencement of a fresh career. The editor of the 'Letters' speaks of the death of M. St. Arnaud's first wife in terms implying that that was the event which caused him to seek for service in Africa (ibid.). It may be easily imagined that the grief caused by this event was one of the motives which made him long to change his career; but it would seem that other circumstances must have contributed to reconcile him to a step which placed him in the 'Foreign Legion' with the mere rank of a lieutenant.

Page 323. '*being about to depart for the expedition against Copenhagen.*'—Lord Fitzroy Somerset was not introduced to Sir Arthur Wellesley until just as he was starting for the Peninsula. Sir Arthur Wellesley and Lord Fitzroy Somerset sailed in the same ship, and they worked together at the Spanish language.

Page 349. '*with some gunboats.*'—The gunboats were lying in this part of the river before Lieutenant Glyn and Prince Leiningen came up, but were placed at the disposition of Lieutenant Glyn. It was by land that Glyn and the Prince, with their seamen and sappers, traveled to the Turkish camp.

Page 349. '*divided the Russian army from the Turks.*'—In stating, and stating truly, that no gunboats came up the Danube, one of the commentators used language which might seem to throw doubt on the above narrative of Lieutenant Glyn's operations. So proof may be useful. In a letter now before me, Lieutenant (now Captain) Glyn writes: 'He [Omar 'Pasha] immediately threw across a large force, and ordered me to hold 'the creek between Slobenzie and the town of Giurgevo with gunboats, 'which was done; otherwise the Russians would have turned the position 'of Slobenzie.'

Page 376. '*I believe.*'—I need hardly say that the underscoring represented by these statistics appears in the original note.

Page 378. The first break, indicated by asterisks, is thus filled up in the fourth edition:—'This would be effectually done by the occupation of the 'Isthmus of Perekop; and I would suggest to you that, if a sufficient 'number of the Turkish army can now be spared for this purpose, it would 'be highly important that measures should be taken without delay for 'sending an adequate force to that point, and associating with the troops 'of the Sultan such English and French officers as would assist, by their 'advice, in holding permanently the position. With the same object, im'portant assistance might be rendered by Admiral Dundas, if he has yet 'been able to obtain any vessels of a light draught which would prevent 'the passage of Russian troops to the Crimea through the Sea of Azov.'

The second break on the same page is also filled up by the following paragraphs:—

'I will not, in this dispatch, enter into any consideration of the opera'tions which it would be desirable to undertake in Circassia or the coast 'of Abasia. The reduction of the two remaining fortresses of Anapa and 'Sujak Kaleh would be, next to the taking of Sebastopol, of the greatest 'importance, as bearing upon the fortunes of the war; but not only is 'their fall of far less moment than that of Sebastopol, but the capture of 'the latter might possibly secure the surrender of the Circassian fortresses.

'In the event, however, of delay in undertaking these operations being 'inevitable, and the transports being in consequence available for any oth-'er service, I wish you to consider, with his Highness Omar Pasha and 'Marshal St. Arnaud, whether some part of the Turkish army might not 'be conveyed by steam from Varna, and, by a combined movement with 'the forces of General Guyon and Schamyl, so entrap the Russian army in 'and around Tiflis as to compel its surrender to superior numbers.'

Page 380. '*He was a Scotsman, 66 years old.*'—No; only 64, I am told, at that time.

Page 381. '*more ready to come into their plans.*'—One of the commentators—a commentator in the *Times* newspaper—imagined that this piece of counsel was the work of the author's 'ingenious' fancy, and remonstrated with him for carrying his love of ridicule to the extreme length of putting 'unmitigated nonsense' in the mouth of a 'gallant and sensible' old soldier like Sir George Brown.—*Times* newspaper, 9th February, 1863. I have only to say that the words attributed to Sir George Brown in the text are copied, without the change of a word, from a written narrative of the conference, which was handed to me by one of the two conferring Generals.

Page 381. '*did not at all govern Lord Raglan's decision.*'—All who were acquainted with Lord Raglan's nature will acknowledge, I think, that his mind would have refused to harbor, for one instant, the notion submitted to him by Sir George Brown—the notion of engaging his army in an imprudent undertaking from an apprehension of finding himself superseded in the command by some one less scrupulous and more ready to come into the plans of the Government.

Lord Raglan's inclination to single out Sir George Brown as a one man to consult with upon affairs of the highest grade of importance did not, I think, increase after this conference; and it will be seen that, very soon after the battle of the Alma, the desire to take close counsel with Sir George Brown had lost its force.

Page 390. '*as well as one of the French lighters.*'—I believe that the merit of making this discovery, and of the irresistible energy by which it was carried into effect, belonged to Mr. Roberts, late a Master in the Navy. See the forcible exposition of Mr. Roberts's services, and of his cruelly frustrated hopes, in the little work called 'The Service and the Reward,' by Mr. George John Cayley.

Page 392. To the note at the bottom, the author adds:—I understood that number to be the one officially given; but according to the Report of Dr. Rees, the surgeon of the 'Britannia' (which has been kindly brought to my notice by Mr. Robarts, a midshipman at the time of the war on board the same ship), the number of deaths from cholera was even greater, amounting to no less than 139 out of 985. Out of the first 60 cases, 55 died; and of those, 50 were dead within the first 20 hours; two-thirds of the crew were ill.

Page 408. '*from the summits of the highland district.*'—A great body of most valuable information respecting the Crimea had been imparted to the English public by General (then Colonel) Mackintosh, and the Colonel had also addressed important reports on the same subject to the military authorities. What I intend to indicate in the text is, not that the means of knowledge were wanting, but that they had not been extensively taken advantage of.

Page 411. '*to mark the boundary between the French and the English flo-*

'*tilla.*'—Captain Mends, Sir Edmund Lyons's flag-captain, thought proper to write a letter to a newspaper on the 18th of March, 1863, saying, 'It might 'suffice for me simply to say that I remember nothing about a buoy;' but on the 5th of the following April he did me the honor to address a letter to me, in which he said, 'It would seem there was a buoy.'—See the correspondence on the subject in the Appendix, Note VII.

Page 413. '*from all share in the chosen landing-ground.*'—See the extract from Lord Raglan's private letter on this subject, which is given in the next foot-note.

Page 413. '*landing of the British forces should take place.*'—The conductors of the *Times* newspaper took upon themselves to deny the truth of my statement about the buoy, and this so confidently, that they permitted their print to sum up and say, 'In short, the whole story is a sick man's 'dream.' Since this denial was uttered so confidently by a respectable newspaper, and was supported (during a period of more than a fortnight) by the testimony of Captain Mends, it seems right to give an extract from the private letter in which Lord Raglan narrates the facts to the Duke of Newcastle:—

Extract from Lord Raglan's Narrative of the Landing, addressed as a Private Communication to the Duke of Newcastle, the Secretary of War, and dated 'Camp above Old Fort Bay, September 18, 1854.'

'The disembarkation of both armies commenced on the morning of the '14th.

'It had been settled that the landing should be effected in Old Fort 'Bay, and that a buoy should be placed in the centre of it to mark the 'left of the French and the right of the English; but when the "Agamem-'"non" came upon the buoy at day-light, Sir Edmund Lyons found that the 'French naval officer had deposited it on the extreme northern end, and 'had thus engrossed the whole of the bay for the operation of his own army. 'This occasioned considerable confusion and delay, the English convoy 'having followed closely upon the steps of their leader, and got mixed with 'the French transports; but Sir Edmund Lyons wisely resolved to make 'the best of it, and at once ordered the troops to land in the bay next to 'the northward.'

I may add that all the many accounts which I have seen of the movements and counter-movements of the ships and the transports on the early morning of the 14th of September tally perfectly with the above statement by Lord Raglan. In saying this, I include Captain Mends's letter to the newspaper. See the Appendix. It will be seen that the facts which he describes in the fourth and fifth paragraphs of that letter are exactly those which would naturally result from the discovery and the change of plan which Lord Raglan communicates to the Minister of War.

I may add that Sir George Brown was on board the 'Agamemnon;' that he was personally cognizant of the change which Lord Raglan described; that many years ago he recorded what occurred in language tallying perfectly with Lord Raglan's account; and, finally, that he (Sir George Brown) is still alive.

Page 414. '*the change which had been effected.*'—In this number was Captain Mends, Sir Edmund Lyons's flag-captain. See his letter to the newspaper in the Appendix.

Page 418. '*as to untie or to cut every knot.*'—An illustration of this way of his (which was supplied to me after the publication of the third edition) will be found in the note for page 425, farther on.

Page 419. '*was the first to touch the beach.*'—The question as to which of the English boats was the first to land has excited more interest than it apparently deserves; for the landing did not take place in face of the enemy. Perhaps one of the causes which led men to look at the question with something more than mere curiosity, was the surprise of finding that, notwithstanding all the charges of want of zeal which had been brought against Admiral Dundas, a boat from his flag-ship (the 'Britannia') was said, after all, to have been the first to land.

According to one opinion, Captain Dacres, with the gig of the 'Sanspa-'riel,' was the first to reach the shore; and there are antecedent reasons for supposing that this would be likely to be the case; for, besides that Captain Dacres was (as the work of that and the four following days showed) an officer of great zeal and ability, he had been intrusted with the naval command on the beach (he was beach-master), and would of course be anxious to reach the shore as soon as possible. It seems that there got to be, as it were, a kind of race between the 'Britannia' boat and the gig of the 'Sanspariel,' and a race, too, which was a very close one; for although the 'Britannia' boat, laden with troops, could not match its speed with the gig, it had a start just long enough to make up for the superior swiftness of its rival. Captain Dacres never doubted that he, with the gig of the 'Sanspariel,' was the first to land; but amongst those who were on board the 'Britannia' boat (and I speak now of soldiers as well as sailors) the belief was that that was the boat which won.

On both sides the statements are positive, and on one side they are also circumstantial. They are also rather interesting; and I would have given them here, if it were not that I am unwilling to place men in an attitude of direct conflict with one another upon an unimportant matter of fact.

If Vesey, with the 'Britannia' boat, was the first to land, Colonel Lysons of the 23rd Fusileers must have been the first man of the land service who touched the shore. If, on the other hand, Dacres, with the gig of the 'Sanspariel,' landed first, Sir George Brown, I think, must have been the first English officer of the land service who reached the shore of the Crimea.

Page 420. '*with the whole strength of his own separate will.*'—When it is seen that I conceive myself warranted in applying this language to the exertions of the navy at the time of the landing, it may be asked whether there was not some one man who had the merit of giving a right direction to the zeal and energy of the seamen thus toiling on the beach? There was. The officer who commanded on the beach was Captain Dacres; and I believe one might safely echo the words of him who once said to Captain Dacres, 'The 14th of September was *your day*.' Both Dundas and Lyons were doing all that was right; but, so far as concerns the vast operation going on upon the beach, their wisdom lay in the wise trustfulness with which they committed the business to a fit man, and then left him alone, undisturbed and unfretted by orders. I believe that during the four days and four nights which followed the commencement of the landing, Captain Dacres never received any orders from Sir Edmund Lyons.

Page 425. '*he rode,*' etc.—General Airey's duties as Quartermaster-General made it necessary that his charger should be landed at the earliest possible moment, but I am not quite certain whether he was on horseback when this incident occurred. My impression was that he was already in his saddle, but according to Colonel Lysons's recollection, he was on foot.

Page 425. '*he rode back to the beach.*'—Or rather to the ridge which overlooked it, for it was there that Colonel (then Major) Lysons was standing with a company of the 23rd Fusileers in extended order.

Page 425. '*to give him two companies.*'—Only one company, it seems.

Page 425. '*with their oxen and drivers complete.*'—After the publication of the third edition, I received from Colonel Lysons a more detailed narrative of this incident than is given in the text. He says: 'Shortly after land-'ing, Sir George Brown ordered me to extend the company that was with 'me along the top of the ridge which overlooked the landing-place. While 'there, General Airey came up to me, and, pointing to a line of arabas 'which was moving across the plain some way off, asked if I could take 'them. I answered, "Yes, but Sir George had ordered me to stay where I '"was." The General (Airey) then began to write on a piece of paper to 'ask leave to send me from my post; but on looking up, and seeing that 'the wagons were already far off, he exclaimed, "We shall lose them if '"you don't go at once. I will take the responsibility on myself." So 'away I went in skirmishing order. On approaching a hillock, which 'screened the arabas from our view, I saw the long lances of some Cos-'sacks waving in the air. Fearing they might attack us, I closed my men 'to the centre on the march; but as we cleared the top of the rising 'ground, these gentlemen (the Cossacks) galloped off to the arabas, on 'which we had gained considerably. A few minutes after I saw the Cos-'sacks making the drivers unyoke their bullocks, that they might drive 'them away from us. Knowing they would beat me at that game, I de-'sired three old soldiers to fall out of the ranks and fire at the Cossacks. 'The first shot fell short. On the second being fired, I saw one of the 'Russians jump up from his saddle as though he was hit, . . . and forthwith 'the whole party scampered away over the plain. The drivers then came 'running to us, and kneeling down and embracing our knees. I made them 'yoke their bullocks again, and took the train back and handed them over 'to General Airey. On our way back we passed Sir George Brown.'

We saw that (supposing the 'Britannia' boat to have been the first to touch the beach) Colonel Lysons was the first English soldier who landed in the Crimea, and the above incident enabled him also to say not only that the first shot fired by our soldiery was fired under his orders, but that the first prize taken from the enemy was taken by him—was taken by him in derogation of the standstill commands which had been given him by Sir George Brown, but in obedience to the boldly-ventured order by which General Airey unleashed him.

Page 435. '*with a squadron of the 4th Light Dragoons.*'—No; only one troop.

Page 437. '*In one brigade a stronger governance was maintained.*'—I ought not to cause it to be understood that in one brigade *only* this stronger governance was maintained. In General Codrington's, and probably in several other brigades, the discipline was proof against the rage of thirst.

Page 440. '*this affair on the Bulganak.*'—In speaking of the affair of the Bulganak, Lord Raglan's dispatch says: 'In the affair of the previous day, 'Major-General, the Earl of Cardigan, exhibited the utmost spirit and 'coolness, and kept his brigade under perfect command.'—Published Dispatch of the 23rd of September, 1854.

Page 444. '*This hill is the key of the position.*'—This assertion was denied by a commentator in the 'Quarterly Review,' who professed to write with military knowledge. It may therefore be well to give here the following extract from Lord Raglan's published dispatch: 'The high pinnacle 'and ridge before alluded to *was the key of the position*, and, consequently, 'there the greatest preparations had been made for defense.'—Published Dispatch of the 23rd September, 1854. Probably no living man is a better judge of what is the true 'key' of a position than Sir John Burgoyne. Now, I have before me a manuscript in his handwriting, which he wrote at the time, and while he was still on the banks of the Alma. In that paper he says: 'The high pinnacle and ridge on the right' [he is speaking of the Russian right, and the Kourganè Hill] 'was *the key of the position* if at-'tacked in front.'

Page 450. To note 1, the author adds:—A commentator in the 'Quar-'terly Review' says, The author 'mistakes in asserting tha it was armed 'with fourteen heavy guns. We believe that its armament consisted of six 'or eight, not guns of position, but field-guns and howitzers.' As to the number of the guns, the author relies upon several English observers for the supposition that it amounted to fourteen, and upon high Russian authority—namely, Prince Gortschakoff himself—for the supposition that the number was not less than twelve.—See *post.* That the two captured guns now at Woolwich are guns of position, and not mere field-pieces, as the Quarterly Reviewers imagined, will be seen from the following report of a competent officer, dated from Woolwich:—'The calibres of the guns taken at the Alma 'were as follows:—

'Brass shot-gun..................................................4.82 inches.
" howitzer..................................................6.12 "

'These calibres indicate, I believe, that the shot-gun was a 24-pounder, and 'the howitzer a 32-pounder.'

Page 457. To note 1, the author adds:—My justification for saying (in the corner of the plan) that it was '*untruly* stated to have been accepted by 'Lord Raglan,' will be found in succeeding pages.

Page 463. To note 2, the author adds:—When the Marshal got near, he was cheered by the English soldiery. Pleased with the compliment, he lifted his hat, and said (speaking in English and with only a slight accent)—'Hurrah for Old England!'

Page 465. '*preceded by Norcott.*'—In both of the places where it occurs in this page, the name of Lawrence should be substituted for that of Norcott. It was on the flank of the Division that Norcott was moving with the left wing of the 2nd Rifle battalion.

I may here say that I was led into the error of omitting Colonel Lawrence's name in this and in several other places by what I must call the erroneous wording of Sir George Brown's Report to Lord Raglan. I say 'erroneous' because, though Sir George Brown does not, in terms, deny that the right wing of the 2nd battalion of Rifles was fighting in front of his Division, he suppresses all mention of its achievements, and this in a dispatch which gives a prominent place to the operations of the left wing under Major Norcott. In excuse for the error into which I was led by trusting too implicitly to Sir George Brown's Report, I may say that Lord Raglan also trusted to it, and was obviously misled by it into the adoption of the same mistake; for although we now know that Lawrence and the men of the right wing were among the foremost of those who stormed the redoubt, Lord Raglan—seeing no mention of this in Sir George Brown's Report, and observing that Sir George specially spoke of Major Norcott's wing as taking part with the 23rd Regiment in the capture of the redoubt—was induced to speak of the aid given by Major Norcott and the left wing of the Rifles, without speaking at all of the right wing, which was also taking a foremost part in the storming of the redoubt, under the orders of Colonel Lawrence.

Page 466. To the last word of the sentence, 'Lord Raglan, with his 'quick eye, had seen the fault, and sent an order to have it corrected,' append the following note:—

I know, from one whose strict and absolute truthfulness makes me as sure of what I am saying as if I had myself heard the words, that the late Duke of Wellington said of Lord Fitzroy Somerset, 'By G—d, he has a 'better eye for placing troops than any man I know!' Allied, perhaps, to the faculty which makes a man skillful in placing troops, there is in some men that instinctive power which people call 'an eye for country.' With this also, and in an uncommon degree, Lord Raglan was gifted.

Page 488. '*It is true that,*' etc.—Here should come these words: 'Colonel 'Lawrence with the right, and . . .'

Page 488. '*had gone into the vineyards in front.*'—During the march, as was shown in a former note, Major Norcott had been on the flank of the Division; but when the battle opened, he began to operate in front of Buller's brigade.

Page 490. '*it would be "compromised."*'—Exactly the same pressure had just been applied by the French Marshal to Sir De Lacy Evans. In his published letter of the 28th of June, 1855, Evans writes: 'On the arrival of the '2nd Division in front of the village of Bourliouk, which, having been pre- 'pared for conflagration by the Russians, became suddenly for some hundred 'yards an impenetrable blaze, Major Claremont came to me in great haste, 'to say from the Marshal, that a part of the French army, having ascended 'the heights on the south of the river, became threatened by large bodies 'of Russians, and might become compromised unless the attention of the 'enemy were immediately drawn away by pressing them in our front. I made 'instant dispositions to conform to this wish, sending at the same time, as 'was my duty, an officer of my Staff (Colonel Herbert) to Lord Raglan, who 'was then a short distance in our rear, for his Lordship's approval, which 'was instantly granted.' From the recurrence of the word 'compromised,' and from the coincidence in point of time, one is led to infer that the message given in the text and the message conveyed to Lord Raglan through General Evans may have been one and the same. There is nothing that I know of to interfere with this conclusion, if it be supposed that Major Claremont was accompanied by a French aid-de-camp, who rode first to General Evans, and from him to Lord Raglan.

Page 492. '*who carried it to the 2nd Division.*'—My authority for this statement is the journal of poor Nolan, now lying before me. There, after stating that 'a general advance was ordered,' he says: 'To the 2nd 'Division I carried the order myself, and in riding forward with the advanced 'brigade had my horse shot under me by a round-shot.' On the other hand, General Evans, I think, conceives that he got his warrant to advance when Colonel Herbert returned to him with the message that Lord Raglan granted his request to be allowed to accede to the prayer of the French Marshal. And again, Colonel Lysons (who was Assistant Adjutant-General of the 2nd Division) stated that he carried the order, and he adds this spirited record of the emotion which impressed the fact upon his memory: 'I could not be mistaken 'on this point; I so well remember the excitement I felt as I galloped back 'to the 2nd Division, and then went on to the right of the Light Division, 'passing the order along the line; and I shall never forget the excited look 'of delight from each face as I repeated the words, "The line will advance!"' It is evident that both Nolan's and Colonel Lysons's statements are correct; and I conceive that the impression which each of them entertained, as well as the impression entertained by General Evans, may be reconciled by supposing that the return of Colonel Herbert to Evans's side preceded the arrival of the formal orders, and that (either intentionally, or else from some mistake) the carriage of the formal order was intrusted to two Staff officers.

Page 492. '*and Fitzmayer's battery of field artillery.*'—Fitzmayer commanded both this and Turner's battery; the Captain of this battery was Franklin.

Page 496. '*before they could find time to form.*'—After speaking of the disposition of the Russian infantry on the banks of the river, Prince Gortschakoff writes: 'These arrangements had been taken with a view to the 'unavoidable disorders among the enemy's lines when crossing the river, and 'in order to throw the Allies backward by a violent shock. Orders had 'been issued to that effect by Prince Mentschikoff, and severally reported to 'the commanding generals under me, and by me.'

Page 497. '*The Rifles under Norcott.*'—Should read 'The Rifles under 'Lawrence and Norcott.'

Page 498. '*to cover its advance.*'—Both the wings of this Rifle battalion had inclined to their left at the time of crossing the river; and it is strictly accurate to say that the battalion, *taken as a whole*, did just what was stated in the text. The two wings, however, were not under the same commander, and therefore it may be well to repeat that the right wing—the wing under Lawrence—was the wing which had had to advance in front of Codrington's brigade. Lawrence found himself so baffled by the smoke of the burning village, that he inclined away to his left, leaving Codrington's front uncovered, and got at last to the front of the 19th Regiment.

Page 498. '*driving full at the enemy's stronghold.*'—Sir George Brown's omission to cause skirmishers to be thrown out from the regiments of Codrington's and Buller's brigades seems to have been caused by his imagining that the necessity of the step would be effectually superseded by the operations of the Rifle battalion. The event proved his error; but one would have thought that it might have been perceived beforehand; for, however well an independent body of riflemen may be led, and however important a share it may be likely to have in governing the result of a battle, there is no safe ground for anticipating that its operations will supply the place of skirmishers thrown out from the formed battalions. Indeed, it may be said that the more able and enterprising the leader of an independent body of light-infantry men may be, the less his force will be likely to fulfill the peculiar duty of companies thrown out from the formed battalions, and kept in close relation with them by the link of that obedience which a captain owes to his colonel.

Page 499. '*The troops pressed on.*'—The author here adds the following paragraph:—

'And by this time the 2nd battalion of the Rifle brigade 'had not only driven the enemy's riflemen from the inclos- 'ure, but had already crossed the stream; for Colonel Law- 'rence, with the right wing, advancing in front of the 19th 'Regiment, had brought his men straight across the river as 'though it were only a brook; and Major Norcott, with the 'left wing, had stolen over the river higher up, and was 'opening fire on the left bank.'

To which he appends this note:—The expression 'stolen over the stream 'higher up,' is not, in its origin, mine, but Sir George Brown's. Before the 88th and 77th Regiments reached the bank of the river, Major Norcott's left wing (then operating in front of those two regiments) inclined to its left for the sake of a ford which crossed the river somewhat higher up; and that is the reason for retaining the statement, though it now stands in a page which connects it with a later part of the battle than that in which Sir George Brown placed it. Sir George imagined (I have his Report before me) that Major Norcott had crossed the stream before the orders came for the advance of the Light Division, and I accepted Sir George's account as accurate in this respect; but I was wrong in doing so. Colonel Norcott writes: 'At length 'the line came up, and without a moment's pause I threw Fyer's and Errol's 'companies,' etc.; and he *then* goes on to describe his passage of the river.

Page 500. '*also more free from the enemy's skirmishers.*'—Because our riflemen, as we saw, were operating in this part of the field. The whole of the 2nd battalion of Rifles was operating in the front or left front of Buller's brigade.

Page 500. '*appearing on the plain to threaten his left.*'—The absence of Prince Mentschikoff in a distant part of the field was probably the cause of the enemy's want of enterprise in not pressing with any degree of vigor upon the open flank of the English army. The only approach to any actual movement against the flank of the Light Division at the time of its advance from the river was one perceived and checked by Major Norcott. Norcott, having crossed the stream, had thrown forward his two right companies to a ridge in advance of the bank, and with his two remaining companies was occupying the precincts of a farmstead which offered him a point of *appui* for his left flank. While he was thus posted, he saw some sixty or seventy Cossacks coming down from the south-east by a road which led to the farm, and close following these he perceived the head of a column of infantry. Norcott immediately withdrew his two right companies from the ridge, and prepared to make a stand at the farm. To aid him in this undertaking, he requested Captain Colville (who had come into this part of the field with one of Colonel Lawrence's companies) to draw up his men in line across the road leading down to the farm. Seeing these preparations for their reception, the horsemen, and the column of infantry which had been following them, turned about and withdrew.

Page 501. '*Though forming part of Buller's brigade, the 19th Regiment,*' etc.—Having Lawrence on its front with the right wing of the 2nd Rifle battalion.

Page 502. '*laying stress upon the value of discipline.*'—One of the commentators said that the above account of the career of Sir George Brown from 1815 to 1854 was inaccurate; but he was wrong. The commentator's error was occasioned—not by any want of knowledge about Sir George Brown's career, but—by misreading the passage. The account given in the text is right as it stands.

Page 504. '*sudden apparition of the flowing plumes.*'—Instead of 'the flow-'ing plumes,' I ought to have been content to say 'the hat;' for, adopting the evidently authentic information on this subject which was obtained by the conductors of the 'Quarterly Review,' I have come to the conclusion that, at this time, Sir George Brown's hat was without its plumes.

Page 505. Instead of note 1, the following:—He had come out in command of the 1st battalion of the Coldstream; but the brevet of the 20th of June (which reached him at Varna in the following month) deprived him for the time of all military occupation by raising him to the rank of Major-General. Greatly distressed by a change which seemed to rob him of his opportunity of seeing active service before the enemy, General Codrington pressed to be allowed to remain serving with the army in any capacity; but the opportunity of granting his prayer did not occur until nearly two months afterward, and during the interval he was without any military occupation, so he traveled in the country of the Balkan. On the 1st of September he was appointed to the command he now held—the command of the 1st brigade of the Light Division.

Page 507. '*had come to the East a mere traveler.*'—See the correction in the preceding note for p. 505.

Page 509. '*line which was formed by the 19th Regiment,*' etc.—Having Lawrence's Rifles on its front.

Page 509. '*which was solemnly marching against them.*'—The column, it seems, was also under a flanking fire poured into it by some of the riflemen whom Major Norcott had posted at the farmstead on the extreme left of the English line.

Page 510. '*Then the* 19*th.*'—With Lawrence's Rifles in front of it. Major Norcott's two right companies were extended along the ridge above the river's bank, and were lying down, when Colonel Lawrence, advancing in person with his wing of the Rifle battalion, rode through them. It was through a part of Fyers's company that Colonel Lawrence rode.

Page 511. '*no less than his flowing plumes.*'—Instead of 'his flowing 'plumes,' I should have been content to say 'his general's hat.'

Page 515. Instead of note 1, the following:—It almost always happens that incidents occurring in a battle are told by the most truthful by-standers with differences more or less wide. One of the eye-witnesses of the above-mentioned incident, whose impressions wear all the appearance of being accurate, has given me the following account of it: Young Anstruther, he says, rushed forward just as is mentioned in the text, and being shot dead, he fell clasping the color in the way above described; but the spot of ground where he fell was short of the redoubt by some thirty or forty yards. At the moment when Anstruther fell, Sergeant Luke O'Connor (the centre sergeant), who had been keeping close up with the color, was also struck down by a shot which wounded him in the breast. Then, as is told in the text, William Evans gathered up the color, but in the next moment Sergeant Luke O'Connor became aware that, bad as his wound was, it would not prevent him from springing to his feet. So rising up quickly, he asserted his right as sergeant to the honor of carrying the color. He accordingly received it from the hands of William Evans, carried it up to the breastwork, and planted it on the parapet, laying claim to the Great Redoubt on behalf of the Royal Welsh. And after this, notwithstanding his wound, O'Connor persisted in refusing to part with the honor of carrying the color. Lieutenant Granville, and also, I think, some other officers of the regiment, observed that O'Connor was growing weak from the effect of his wound, and pressed him to go to the rear; but, setting at naught all these counsels, O'Connor persisted in his determination to carry the cherished standard until the close of the battle. He received the thanks of Sir George Brown and General Codrington on the field; and, for having done what is above told, he was decorated with the Victoria Cross. He was also promoted. He is now a captain in that same devoted regiment with which he had the glory of serving on the day of the Alma.

Page 515. '*more followed.*'—Among the foremost of these was Major Norcott with some of his riflemen. After the moment when Colonel Lawrence with his wing pushed forward through Major Norcott's right companies, Major Norcott moved so far westward that he entered the redoubt—not, as might have been expected, at its (proper) left shoulder, but toward its right. The effect of the movements made by these two wings of the Rifle battalion was, that their respective positions were in a manner reversed; for when the redoubt was seized, the right wing of the Rifle battalion was heading the extreme left of the storming force; and, on the other hand, the left wing had inclined a good way to the right.

Page 515. '*At the same instant Norcott's riflemen.*'—'Lawrence's riflemen' should here be substituted for 'Norcott's.' Both Lawrence and Ross, his adjutant, were dismounted when within a few yards of the work by a discharge of grape—grape discharged from the field-battery on the higher slope of the Kourganè Hill. Lawrence rolled almost under the breastwork.

It may be remembered that, in the published dispatch, Lord Raglan spoke of the capture of the redoubt as an operation 'materially aided by 'the advance of four companies of the Rifle brigade under Major Norcott, 'who promises to be a distinguished officer of light troops.' The omission of Colonel Lawrence's name in a dispatch containing that sentence, was obviously occasioned by what (in the sense indicated in a former note) I have ventured to call the 'erroneous wording' of Sir George Brown's Report to Lord Raglan. My omission of Colonel Lawrence's name in the text was brought about by the same cause.

Page 515. '*This was a brass 24-pound howitzer.*'—It appears by a former note that the calibre of this howitzer is 6.12—a calibre which indicates, I believe, a 32-pounder.

Page 516. '*Colonel Chester . . . had been killed.*'—No; it was some minutes later that Colonel Chester fell.

Page 516. '*four battalions, and a wing.*' Instead of 'a wing' read 'the whole.'

Page 520. '*by advancing in conformity with its movements.*'—At this moment the Duke of Cambridge rode up, and to him Airey repeated it to be Lord Raglan's meaning that the Division should instantly 'push on.' H.R.H. then gave orders for the immediate advance of the Division, and Clifton, I think, was the aid-de-camp who carried the order to Sir Colin Campbell.

Page 520. '*conveying his opinion to the Duke of Cambridge.*'—Evans sent the message by Colonel Steele, who chanced to be near him at the time. Steele was Military Secretary, and he seems to have fulfilled his mission in a way which caused it to be understood that the message he brought was an order from Lord Raglan.

Page 520. To the sentence in which it is stated that General Evans, com'prehending at once that the advance of Codrington's brigade was a move'ment requiring instant support, took upon himself to send a message convey'ing his opinion to the Duke of Cambridge,' append the following note:—

In reference to the above statement, the conductors of one of the Reviews deemed it fitting and wise to profess to know the limit of what was remembered upon this subject by H.R.H. the Duke of Cambridge; for in the number of their journal which appeared in the beginning of April, they ventured upon the following assertion: 'The Duke of Cambridge and his Staff have 'no recollection of the receipt of these orders.' But only a few hours later, General Evans, in a letter of the 3rd of April addressed by him to one of the newspapers, not only contradicted the contradiction hazarded by the 'Review,' but stated that on the 9th of February (and therefore several weeks before the publication of the Review) His Royal Highness had 'frankly' and 'repeatedly' acknowledged the facts. After citing the words of the *Review*, General Evans writes:—'Herein there is a mistake. The Duke of Cam'bridge and his Staff did forget, it is true, all about this matter until my 'reply of February 7th reached him. His Royal Highness's rejoinder of 'February 9th very frankly (and I may say repeatedly) acknowledges the 'facts: "I have a perfect recollection," he says, "of Colonel Steele coming '"to me," etc. "Your explanation clears up that point." "I see nothing '"very particular in this incident, only I could not recollect the fact." 'Again, on the 14th, His Royal Highness says: "My only object was to '"clear up a mystery which Mr. Kinglake's book had raised in my mind '"as to a message being sent to me by you, of which I had no recollection '"whatever, but which your letter fully explained."'

Page 527. After the conclusion of the paragraph in the middle of which this page commences, the author adds another (not in the first edition), as follows:—

His (Sir Colin Campbell's) brigade at this time was not under a heavy fire, and he effected the operation of passing the river very simply; for, without attempting formal evolutions, each of his regiments, while it advanced, tried to keep up, as well as the nature of the ground would allow, the rudiments of its line-formation; and when it gained the opposite bank, its array was carefully restored. As soon as one of the regiments was duly formed on the Russian side of the river, it was moved forward; and since the ground presented more obstacles toward our left than toward our right, the brigade fell naturally, and without design, into direct échelon of regiments. The 42nd was in advance; on the left of that regiment there was the 93rd, somewhat refused; and on the left of the 93rd, but still farther refused, there came the 79th.

Page 528. To note 1, the author adds:—Experience has shown that by the use of glasses, and by a judicious use of the eyes of other men, an officer may do much to compensate for the defect of near-sightedness; and of the truth of this, both General Codrington and General Buller were instances more or less strong. But when near-sightedness is combined with an unconsciousness of the defect, it of course becomes very dangerous. People who served in the Light Division will smile at the idea of my taking the trouble to prove that which every body knew—namely, that Sir George Brown was extremely near-sighted; but the fact has been gravely contradicted by a commentator in the *Quarterly Review* who wrote under the instructions of Sir George Brown himself, and it does not always do to attempt to establish a truth by speaking of it as 'notorious;' so perhaps a succinct proof may be useful. I can give it thus:—We know that in the gorge or opening through which the great road runs, Evans was operating with Pennefather's brigade and the 47th Regiment; and he was there engaged in so hard a struggle that Pennefather's brigade lost a fourth of its strength. Yet incredible as it may seem, Sir George Brown imagined that he, with his right brigade, *was in the occupation of the whole of that ground.* In the Report, in his own handwriting, now lying before me, he writes:—'My 1st brigade itself *completely filled the whole mouth of the gorge or valley* '*through which the road runs.*' Obviously, the cause of this extraordinary misstatement by Sir George Brown was near-sightedness—near-sightedness combined with so imperfect a consciousness of the defect as to cause him to rely with undue confidence on his own uncorrected impressions.

Page 533. '*began to sound the "cease firing."*'—At this moment—for so an eye-witness tells me—Colonel Chester was still living. He was sitting in his saddle close to the redoubt, and when he saw the soldiery beginning to catch the belief that the approaching column was French, he eagerly strove to undeceive them. Enforcing his words by gesture, he was impatiently moving his uplifted sword, as though he would say to those who might see without being able to hear, 'No! no! nonsense! the column is not French—'it is an enemy's column. Fire into it! fire into it!' While he was thus speaking, and thus making signs to his people, he was struck first by one shot, and then almost instantly by another. Upon receiving the first shot, he seemed to put his hand to the wound, but when the second shot struck him he dropped from his horse and fell dead.

Page 537. '*formed line, and advanced.*'—But it seems in an imperfect way, for the advance was urgently hurried. The left-flank company had got separated, and from that circumstance it escaped the confusion which involved the main body.

Page 537. '*broke through the left companies of the Scots Fusileers.*'—That is to say, through the left companies of the main body. The left-flank company, as before mentioned, had got separated.

A commentator in the *Quarterly Review*, who had suffered himself to receive, in an indiscriminate way, the impressions of Sir George Brown, said I was 'wrong in having asserted that the Fusileers, in their tumultu- 'ous advance, encountered a heap of our men running away from the re- 'doubt. The fugitives from the redoubt were clean out of the way when the 'Fusileer Guards pushed forward.'

Is there any truth—any semblance of truth—in this denial? We will see.

General Bentinck, who was personally present with the Fusileer Guards when they began their advance, wrote in his Report the day next after the battle: 'The intrenchment partially won by the Light Division was lost, 'and at the moment *some confusion was occasioned by the regiment obliged to* '*abandon it retiring through the Scots Fusileer Guards, and thereby putting* '*their left wing out of line.* The battalion retired for a short time, re-formed, 'and returned to its post. In this partial movement to the rear, a severe 'loss was sustained by the Scots Fusileer Guards.'—Holograph Report by General Bentinck. Colonel (now General) Ridley commanded one of the wings of the Fusileer Guards, and he has orally confirmed to me the truth of the statement.

Colonel Percy commanded the left-flank company of the Grenadiers, and was therefore so placed as to be able to see what happened to the Fusileer Guards. He writes:—'*The repulsed regiment came down violently upon them* '*and broke their line.* If the Russians alone had come down upon them, 'they would have been received with the bayonets.'

Captain Annesley, an officer of the Fusileer Guards, two days after the battle, made this entry in his journal:—'Then the 23rd *came down in one* '*mass right on top of our line.* Their disorder was caused by the Colonel 'and both Majors being killed, and no one knowing who to look to for or- 'ders. However it was, *they swept half my company clean away, and a great* '*many of the next one to it.*'—Extracted from the original MS.

Of the officers of the Fusileer Guards with whom I have conversed on the subject, the one who was the least impressed with the extent of the confusion thus wrought was Lord Listowel; but it is only in regard to the *extent* of the mischief that he differs from the other eye-witnesses. I hear that Colonel Sir Charles Hamilton (who commanded the battalion), Colonel Jocelyn, Colonel Francis Seymour, and others, all agree in stating that the line of the Fusileer Guards was broken by the bodily pressure of the retreating troops of the Light Division. With the exception of Sir George Brown, I do not remember to have heard of any one present at the battle who held a contrary belief.

Page 537. '*and destroyed their formation.*'—For the battalion was hurrying forward so impatiently as to be unable to open its ranks in the usual way.

Page 537. '*and got his ribs fractured.*'—I have heard that this man's name was Hesketh.

Page 538. '12 *sergeants were wounded.*'—Colonel Webber Smith also (whose name was omitted by mistake in the text) received two gunshot wounds, and a hardish contusion besides.

Page 538. '*most of those casualties occurred in the left wing.*'—I am not sure that that was the case. I have not before me the materials for showing the proportions in which the two wings suffered.

Page 538. '*the four companies of Rifles.*'—Instead of 'the four compa- 'nies of Rifles,' read 'the battalion of Rifles.'

Page 562. To note 2, the author adds:—While the 55th was approaching the Alma, General Pennefather wished to form line; but after forming two or three groups which were immediately struck down by the enemy's shot, Pennefather allowed the 55th Regiment to follow Colonel Warren. Colonel Warren instantly crossed the river, and formed the regiment in line under cover of a spur or rising ground at the base of the hills. When the line had been formed, it moved forward, General Pennefather leading in front. At that time the line of the 55th was parallel with the river.

Page 564. '*these battalions were "Fusileers."*'—The English MS. translation from the Russian original on which I founded this statement, spoke of the Kazan battalions as 'Fusileers;' but I believe that this was an error, and that the word should have been translated 'Chasseurs.'

Page 568. '*lead it on to a charge with the bayonet.*'—This statement is founded, as will be seen below, upon a narrative written by Prince Gortschakoff himself; but it interested me to hear, as I lately did from an officer in the 7th Fusileers, a statement coinciding exactly (so far as it goes) with the Prince's narrative. Sir Thomas Troubridge, who was the Major commanding the right wing of the 7th Fusileers, told me he remembers that after the fight between the column and the 7th Fusileers had been going on a long time, he saw a horseman, with some mounted followers—evidently, as he conceived, a General and his Staff—ride down and join the column.

Page 568. To note 1, the author adds:—When Prince Gortschakoff had ridden off, the column was subjected, as I now know, to this farther stress: Colonel Warren with the 55th extended in line—a regiment belonging to Evans's Division—was advancing up the Pass when he saw on his left front the column which was engaged with the 7th Fusileers. Colonel Warren instantly caused his regiment to bring forward their right shoulders, and in fact to wheel upon their centre, very much as a company wheels. This manœuvre was performed under fire from the column, and the change of front was carried to the length of bringing the battalion into a line almost perpendicular to the line of its former front, and almost parallel with the flanks of the Russian column. When the manœuvre was complete, the 55th opened fire upon the flank of the Russian column.

Page 569. '*the column began to fall back.*'—It seems that, at the moment when the discomfiture of the column became evident, the 55th received orders (probably from General Pennefather) to 'cease firing and charge.' Thereupon the officers went forward in front, 'stopping the firing,' and meanwhile the column gliding off, and afterward betaking itself to a more rapid retreat, escaped a good deal of the slaughter which would have been inflicted upon it if the fire of the 55th had not been stayed by the order to charge.

Page 569. '*and Hare,*' etc.—Hare died of his wounds a few hours after the battle.

Page 569. '*and Jones, were wounded.*'—Add to this list of wounded, Lieutenant Hibberd and Adjutant Hobson.

Page 570. To note 1, the author adds:—It has been declared that no such fight as is above described took place; that the 7th Fusileers was not separately engaged with any Russian column on the day of the Alma; and that, far from maintaining, and maintaining victoriously, the struggle which I have described, this 7th Fusileers fell back in the midst of the fight, retreating through the Grenadier Guards. This notion has been propounded —not by a common gatherer of the many contradictory stories which battles are apt to breed, but—by General Sir George Brown, the officer commanding the Division to which the 7th Fusileers belonged. Under these circumstances, I have thought it right to give in the Appendix (Note VIII.), first, a copy of the statement on this subject which is understood to be based on Sir George Brown's instructions, and then the series of proofs by which I undertake to refute it.

Page 572. '*got into disorder, and fell back.*'—But the immediate cause which brought about the retreat of this small and disordered body of men was, after all, the word of command. See the more detailed account given in the Appendix, Note IX. The state of increased disorder into which the battalion fell was not before, but *after* the delivery of the command to retire. The retreat of the Fusileer Guards was pressed, but not with great vigor, by Russian skirmishers pushing forward in advance of the Vladimir column; and the column itself was tempted, as it were, by the movement of retreat, to come down below the redoubt, and advance in pursuit. Colonel Hood, who was on the immediate right of the Fusileer Guards, speaks of them as 'beaten back, and pursued.'—Private letter, 21st September, 1854.

Page 572. '*was in confusion near the bank of the river.*'—The main part of the battalion was rallied upon ground just in advance of the road which runs parallel with the bank of the river. Judging from the French map, this road would seem to be about 150 yards above the water's edge; and that space, therefore, would about represent the distance between the river and the ground on which the main part of the battalion was rallied.

In this note I have ventured to say that the main part of the battalion of the Fusileer Guards was rallied *in advance of the road running parallel with the river.* The *Quarterly Review*, however, in an article written with the aid of instructions from Sir George Brown, has made the following statement:—'The men of the Light Division who had been driven out of the 'Redan *were lying in an irregular line with the Fusileer Guards under the* '*bank.*' That, for some little time after the check they had sustained, many of the men of the Fusileer Guards were lingering about under the bank, I have never doubted; but it is new to me to hear that, taken as a whole, the centre battalion of the Guards — the *Quarterly Review* calls the body, simply without subtraction or qualification, 'the Fusileer Guards' —was content to be deliberately lying down under the bank at this period of the battle, and there joining with the light-infantry men in keeping up 'a heavy fire upon the space between themselves and the work.' If this passage is an accurate representation of Sir George Brown's assertion, Sir George is at variance with every one of the officers who have spoken to me on the subject. Deliberately, and in a careful, detailed way, Colonel (now General) Ridley has assured me that, immediately after the check sustained by the battalion of the Fusileer Guards, it was rallied and re-formed under his own eyes in advance of the road above spoken of, and that thenceforth it took part in the advance of the Guards without afterward retreating a step, and, of course, without afterward falling back under the bank. General Ridley's statement tallies perfectly with the Report which H.R.H. the Duke of Cambridge addressed to Head-quarters the day next but one after the battle, for the Duke there says that the Fusileer Guards re-formed '*with* '*the greatest alacrity.*'—Holograph MS. Report of the 22nd September, 1854, by H.R.H.

Page 572. '*inflicted loss upon the Scots Fusileer Guards.*'—Some of the officers who were pained by the above account of the operations of the Scots

Fusileer Guards, did me the honor to request an interview with me, in order that they might have an opportunity of submitting to me their view of the matter. I was of course most ready to accede to this request, and some interviews accordingly took place. With much care we went together over the passages in question, discussing them, paragraph by paragraph, sentence by sentence, and sometimes almost word by word. The result was that, at the close of the discussion, those who had been the most pained by the narrative did not at all maintain that any one sentence was wrong, but they stated to me many *additional* facts which they thought it would be well for the repute of the regiment to have stated. They, in short, seemed to think that an account upon a somewhat larger scale than the one I had adopted would put the conduct of the battalion in a better light. I gladly acceded to this view, and the 3rd edition gave the new facts which had been imparted to me in notes at the foot of the page; but it now occurs to me that I shall still better carry out the object in view if, instead of breaking up the additional matter into several foot-notes, I put into a connected form the more minute narrative which I am now enabled to give. Accordingly, this more minute narrative will be found in the Appendix, Note IX. I think it will be found that the difference between the account here appearing and the account appearing in the Appendix, is a difference resulting entirely, or almost entirely, from the difference of the scale.

Page 572. '*When Colonel Hood,*' etc.—Colonel Hood had not failed to seize the precious opportunity which was offered to his battalion by the sheltering steepness of the bank. In a private letter he writes:—'Under 'the steep bank of the river, we closed in to our centre; and to this ma-'nœuvre our after-success was mainly attributable.'

Page 572. '*and marched forward in beautiful order.*'—'We formed in 'perfect and compact order on the top of the bank, and then advanced 'steadily up the intrenched position.'—Colonel Hood, private letter.

Page 572. '*and afterward formed up anew.*'—'Our 6th and 7th compa-'nies opened out to let them pass, and closed up as coolly as if in Hyde Park.' —Colonel Hood, private letter.

Page 573. '*through the worst stress of the fight.*'—Notwithstanding his wound. See *ante.*

Page 573. '*to fill up a part of the chasm.*'—Of course it is not intended that this word 'chasm' (which occurs in several places) should be taken as indicating that the Scots Fusileer Guards were not on the ground, but merely that, for the moment, the main body of the battalion had lost its formation, and was re-forming upon an alignment very little in rear of that on which the Grenadiers were standing.

Page 573. To note 1, the author adds:—The term 'Household Brigade' is so habitually applied to the Household *Cavalry*, that although the three battalions of Guards at the Alma were 'Household' battalions, and although they formed a 'brigade,' it would have been better to avoid the expression used in the text.

Page 573. '*contentedly marched up the slope.*'—It was in disobedience to the contingent orders he had received that Colonel Hood thus advanced with the Grenadiers. In his journal he writes:—'Last order received by me was 'from Captain Fielding, Brigade-Major (when battalion was lying down 'under cannonade and shelling)—"The Brigadier desires you to conform '"to any movements on your left."' Now the movement on Colonel Hood's left, to which, by the words of General Bentinck's orders, he thus found himself told to conform, was the retreat ot the Fusileer Guards. In other words, there had occurred an event which placed Colonel Hood under orders to retire. Therefore it was that, immediately after the sentence above quoted, he wrote in his journal these words:—'Thank God I dis-'obeyed!!! Advanced steadily in line.'

Page 574. '*Colonel Berkeley came up.*'—It seems that Colonel Dalrymple was the officer whose name should have here appeared, instead of that of Colonel Berkeley, who, it seems, was wounded. Colonel Dalrymple, from the first, had kept the right-flank company together, and now, with General Bentinck's sanction, he formed it on the left of the Grenadiers.

It is still maintained by an eye-witness that the text as it stands is right; but if it is true that Berkeley brought up some men of the Scots Fusileers, it is certain that Colonel Dalrymple did the like with his company.

Page 576. After the paragraph ending with the sentence:—'Then the 'Highlanders marched through, leaving General Buller and his two battal-'ions in their rear,' the author in the third edition added several new paragraphs with notes, which are here transcribed as follows:—

[1] 'The brigade of Guards will be destroyed,' said one ad-

[1] When the incident now about to be narrated took place, the state of things in this part of the field was as follows:—The 88th, while still formed in square, was retreating, and the 77th, though extended in line, was also falling back. Whilst this was the condition of the troops under Buller, the soldiery who had been forced to relinquish the redoubt were spread along the lower part of the slope firing powerless shots toward the earth-work. It seemed to Sir Colin Campbell that this discomfiture of Sir George Brown's troops was fast involving the fate of the battle, and that it was a thing of great need to show, and to show at the very instant, a steady and well-formed battalion ranged frank and fair on the slope. With this intent he was carrying forward the 42nd, and placing it in advance of the alignment which the Coldstream was taking up on his right. The 42nd had just been taking ground to its left, and was still in the formation which had been resorted to for effecting the change—that is, it was in open column of companies, 'right in front,' and facing westward, but was preparing to wheel into line. So far as concerned all this part of the field, the fight was in its crisis. The Staff of the 1st Division were near the left, or left front of the Coldstream, and not far from the ground where the grenadier company of the 42nd stood ranged. It was then that there occurred the incident described in the text.

An officer of the Coldstream informs me, of what I certainly did not know before, namely, that an order 'to retire' passed along the line of his battalion, and that the buglers, too, sounded 'the retire.' With the information which I at present possess, I must decline to speak of this order as one which came from an authentic source; but that it passed along the line in the way above described I am unable to doubt. The order, however, was met by the battalion with loud and general cries of 'No! no! —it must be a mistake!' 'Retire!—No! no!' This popular opposition to the notion of retiring was probably re-enforced (though I have not yet heard the fact stated) by proper orders from the divisional general, for the Duke of Cambridge was present in person with this battalion. At all events the opposition was completely successful, for the battalion kept its ground, and did not, as I believe, make any, the least, movement in retreat. It is true that, in his journal, Colonel Hood (who commanded the Grenadier Guards) wrote:—'Scots Fusileers and Coldstream!!—retired by command!' but he was mistaken in supposing that the retreating movement which he observed on his left extended so far as to include the Coldstream. The Coldstream was not advancing at the moment, but it did not retire.

viser; and he asked whether it ought not to fall back a little in order to recover its formation?

These words were spoken by an officer not holding any high rank,[2] and they owe their whole importance to the answer which they elicited and the propulsion which thereupon followed.

He who answered the question[3] was a veteran soldier, and it was with a deference no less wise than graceful that the Duke of Cambridge loved to seek and to follow his counsels.

Whilst Ensign Campbell was passing from boyhood to man's estate, he was made partaker in the great transactions which were then beginning to work out the liberation of Europe. In the May of 1808 he received his first commission—a commission in the 6th Foot; and a few weeks afterward—then too young to carry the colors—he was serving with his regiment upon the heights of Vimieira. There the lad saw the turning of a tide in human affairs; saw the opening of the mighty strife between 'Column' and 'Line;'[4] saw France, long unmatched upon the Continent, retreating before British infantry; saw the first of Napoleon's stumbles, and the fame of Sir Arthur Wellesley beginning to dawn over Europe.

He was in Sir John Moore's campaign, and at its closing scene—Corunna. He was with the Walcheren expedition; and afterward, returning to the Peninsula, he was at the battle of Barossa, the defense of Tarifa, the relief of Taragona,

[2] I foresee that what I here say as to the obscure rank of the officer who made this suggestion will be regarded by some as inaccurate; and, indeed, I am aware that the belief of those who hold the contrary of this to be true is based upon grounds apparently strong. I did not hear the words myself; and all I can say is, that my statement is founded upon authority which makes me feel certain that I do rightly in making it; though I also think I am right in saying that I did not myself hear the words. If my statement as to the obscure rank of the officer is true, it follows, I think, that I am right in not disclosing his name; because (upon that supposition) his words had no sort of importance beyond that attributed to them in the text.

[3] He answered the question the moment he heard its purport told to him. He had not himself heard it fall from the lips of the officer with whom it originated.

[4] In his most interesting and most valuable 'Life of the Duke of Wel-'lington,' Mr. Gleig repeats the description of Vimieira, which the Duke once gave in his presence at Strathfieldsaye. The Duke's words are thus given by Mr. Gleig:—'The French came on, on that occasion, with great 'boldness, and seemed to feel their way less than I always found them to 'do afterward. They came on, as usual, in very heavy columns, and I re-'ceived them in line, which they were not accustomed to, and we repulsed 'them three several times.'

and the combats at Malaga and Osma. He led a forlorn hope at the storming of St. Sebastian, and was there wounded twice; he was at Vittoria; he was at the passage of the Bidassoa; he took part in the American war of 1814; he served in the West Indies; he served in the Chinese war of 1842. These occasions he had so well used that his quality as a soldier was perfectly well known. He had been praised and praised, again and again; but since he was not so connected as to be able to move the dispensers of military rank, he gained promotion slowly, and it was not until the second Sikh war that he had a command as a general: even then he had no rank in the army above that of a colonel. At Chilianwalla he commanded a division. Marching in person with one of his two brigades, he had gained the heights on the extreme right of the Sikh position, and then bringing round the left shoulder, he had rolled up the enemy's line and won the day; but since his other brigade (being separated from him by a long distance) had wanted his personal control, and fallen into trouble, the brilliancy of the general result which he had achieved did not save him altogether from criticism. That day he was wounded for the fourth time. He commanded a division at the great battle of Gujerat; and, being charged to press the enemy's retreat, he had so executed his task that 158 guns and the ruin of the foe were the fruit of the victory. In 1851 and the following year he commanded against the hill-tribes. It was he who forced the Kohat Pass. It was he who, with only a few horsemen and some guns, at Punj Pao, compelled the submission of the combined tribes then acting against him with a force of 8000 men. It was he who, at Ishakote, with a force of less than 3000 men, was able to end the strife; and when he had brought to submission all those beyond the Indus who were in arms against the Government, he instantly gave proof of the breadth and scope of his mind as well as of the force of his character; for he withstood the angry impatience of men in authority over him, and insisted that he must be suffered to deal with the conquered people in the spirit of a politic and merciful ruler.

After serving with all this glory for some forty-four years, he came back to England; but between the Queen and him there stood a dense crowd of families—men, women, and children—extending farther than the eye could reach, and armed with strange precedents which made it out to be right that people who had seen no service should be invested with high command, and that Sir Colin Campbell should be only a colonel. Yet he was of so fine a nature that, although he did not always avoid great bursts of anger, there was no ignoble bitterness in his sense of wrong. He awaited the time when perhaps he might have high command, and be able to serve his country in a sphere proportioned to his strength. His friends, however, were angry for his sake; and along with their strong devotion toward him there was bred a fierce hatred of a system of military dispensation which could keep in the background a man thus tried and thus known.

Upon the breaking out of the war with Russia, Sir Colin was appointed—not to the command of a division, but of a brigade. It was not till the June of 1854 that his rank in the army became higher than that of a colonel.

Campbell was not the slave, he was the master of his calling, and therefore it was that he had been able to save his intellect from the fate of being drowned in military details. He knew that although a general must have a complete mastery of even the smallest of such things, still they were only a part—a minute though essential part—of the great science of war. He understood the precious material whereof our army is formed. He heartily loved our soldiery; for he was a soldier, and had fellow-feeling with soldiers, and they had fellow-feeling with him. Instinctively they knew that, together, they might do great things—he by their help, they by his. Knowing the worth of their devotion and their bodily strength, he cherished them with watchful care; and they, on their part, loved, honored, and obeyed him with a faith that all he ordered was right. He set great store upon discipline, but it was never for discipline's sake that he did so (as if that were itself an end), but because he knew it to be one of the main sources of military ascendency. So, although the officers and soldiers serving under him got no more rest than was good for them, they were never vexed wantonly; and in proportion as they grew in knowledge of their calling, they came to understand why it was that their chief compelled them to toil.

A bodily ardor for fighting may be more or less masked and hidden; but he to whom this great passion is wanting is without the quality of a general. For warfare is so anxious and complex a business, that against every vigorous movement heaps of reasons can forever be found; and if a man is so cold a lover of battle as to have no stronger guide than the poor balance of the arguments and counter-arguments which he addresses to his troubled spirit, his mind, driven first one way and then another, will oscillate, or even revolve, turning miserably on its own axis, and making no movement straight forward. Now, it is a characteristic still marking the Scottish blood, that often—and not the less so when it flows in the veins of a gentle-hearted being—it is seen to fire strangely and suddenly at the prospect of a fight. Campbell loved warfare with a deep passion; and at the thought of battle his grand, rugged face used to kindle with uncontrollable joy.

'The brigade of Guards will be destroyed; ought it not to 'fall back?'[5] When Sir Colin Campbell heard this saying,[6] his blood rose so high that the answer he gave—impassioned and far-resounding—was of a quality to govern events.

'It is better, Sir, that every man of Her Majesty's Guards 'should lie dead upon the field than that they should now 'turn their backs upon the enemy!'[7] Doubts and questionings ceased.[8] Sir Colin Campbell rode off to his left.

Page 576. '*He therefore sent Sterling,*' etc.—Colonel Douglas's narrative of the part which the 79th took in the battle is to the effect that no order was brought him by any officer of the brigade except Shadwell; but it also appears from his statement that he has no recollection of having received from any one the order stated in the text.

Page 578. '*but their left was bare.*'—By reason of the retreat of the Scots Fusileer Guards.

Page 580. '*left in the centre of our brigade of Guards.*'—'I saw a heavy 'mass of Russians in column in pursuit.'—Private letter from Colonel Hood. In another letter he says, 'the Russian column then passed out in pursuit.'

Page 580. '*and then caused.*'—Or allowed.

Page 580. '*in command of the left wing.*'—It seems that at the moment of the halt, a mounted officer not belonging to the battalion rode up to near where the left-flank company was, and used the word 'retire!' Then Percy, looking at the Vladimir column, and seeing in an instant what ought not to be done, inferred, or professed to infer, that the manœuvre which the conjuncture required was the one which the mounted officer must mean. 'Retire!' he said. 'What the devil do they mean? They must 'mean "dress back."' Percy then, aided by Neville, his senior subaltern, began causing the subdivision to 'dress back' in such a way as to make it face toward the Vladimir column; and this, it quickly appeared, was exactly what Colonel Hood desired, for he rode up and told Percy to go on with the operation.

Page 581. '*kept their perfect array.*'—Dalrymple, with the right-flank

---

[5] As to the comparatively subordinate rank of the officer with whom this suggestion originated, see note *ante.*

[6] Respecting the way in which he came to hear its purport, see note *ante.*

[7] Then, speaking apart to the Duke of Cambridge, and counseling him to go straight on with the Guards, Sir Colin Campbell undertook to turn the redoubt by marching up instantly with the 42nd.

[8] The advance was continued.

company of the Scots Fusileer Guards, seems to have done good service at this conjuncture; for, wheeling back his left, in conformity with the bend effected by Colonel Hood in the line of the Grenadiers, he poured some fifteen volleys into the Vladimir column.

Page 581. '*drawn up in superb array.*'—But from ground less advanced than that which the Grenadiers had reached.

Page 583. To note 2, the author adds:—I think that the shot which struck the column were thrown from guns belonging to Franklin's battery.

Page 587. '"*brought forward his right shoulder.*"'—'I brought up my 'right shoulder.'—Private letter from Colonel Hood, dated the day after the battle. One of the characteristics which can hardly fail to interest any one who has had the advantage of reading Colonel Hood's letters, is the exceeding modesty which makes him continually seek to ascribe all merit to others rather than to himself. Thus, although, in hurriedly writing the six words above quoted, he chanced to use the first person, he hastened, in a subsequent letter from the banks of the Alma, to give the whole merit of the manœuvre to the battalion. He writes, '*Instinctively* our men brought right 'shoulders forward.'

Page 587. '*fire poured upon its flank.*'—'Instinctively our men brought 'right shoulders forward, and commenced file-firing with such coolness and 'accuracy that the effect was instantaneous. They [the Russians] were 'checked perceptibly with astonishment at the telling nature of our flank-'fire.' *N.B.* The word which I have written 'perceptibly' seems in the original to have the syllable 'im' at its commencement, but I imagine that the word as I have written it was the one intended.

Page 587. '*the brave Vladimir bore.*'—Speaking, of course, roughly, Colonel Hood puts this period of Russian endurance at 'five minutes.'—Private letter, 21st Sept., 1854.

Page 587. '"*The line will advance on the centre!*"'—In this and in the sentence presently following where it occurs, the word 'on' should be replaced by the word 'by.'

Page 587. '"*The men may advance firing.*"'—'Unsupported I would not 'charge, but made my men advance, firing steadily.'—Private letter from Colonel Hood, 21st Sept., 1854.

Page 588. '*like a throng in confusion.*'—'In five minutes the Russian col-'umn faltered, then turned, then ran.'—Private letter from Colonel Hood, 21st Sept., 1854.

To note 1, the author adds:—Speaking of this advance of his Grenadiers, Colonel Hood writes:—'I am told the effect was great, and *this common-'sense manœuvre of a line against a dense column is my only merit.* It was 'done at Waterloo effectively, and on the Alma yesterday. I hope due 'credit will be done to my fine fellows, for it was a proud sight to see them 'behave so well; and what an honor to command such a body of men! . . . 'The battalion has been the admiration of French, English, and Russians.' —Private letter, 21st September, 1854. See in a note at the foot of a later page an account of the thanks publicly addressed to Colonel Hood and the Grenadiers at the close of the battle.

My numerous quotations from the private journal and private letters of Colonel Hood correspond so closely with the tenor of this part of the narrative that the reader will be likely to say,' 'That journal and those letters 'were evidently the authority on which the author based his account of the 'operations of the Grenadier Guards.' It is, however, a fact, that I never saw the journal nor the letters, and never knew any thing of their tenor, until after the publication of the first and second editions of this book.

Page 588. '*where lay the dismounted howitzer.*'—Respecting the theory—a theory propounded by the *Quarterly Review*—that it was Sir George Brown who caused the Grenadier Guards to enter the redoubt, see Appendix, Note VIII.

Page 588. '*stood master of the Great Redoubt.*'—Considering that H.R.H. the Duke of Cambridge commanded the Division to which the Grenadiers as well as the Coldstream belonged, and that the Coldstream (with which His Royal Highness was personally present) advanced to the proper right of the redoubt at a moment not very much later than that at which the Grenadiers entered the work at its western extremity, I thought it a fair and not untruthful use of language to say, that His Royal Highness, 'riding up with the Coldstream, stood master of the Great Redoubt.' But I see that, according to Sir George Brown, as represented by the 'Quarterly Review,' the interval between the final advance of the Grenadiers and the final advance of the Coldstream was so great as to exclude the Coldstream, and, with it, H.R.H. the Duke of Cambridge, from the honor of being actual partakers in the movement which effected the recapture of the redoubt; and, moreover, it is represented by the same authority, that the final advance of the Coldstream did not take place at all *until after a conference, which Sir George Brown thought proper to hold with H.R.H. the Duke of Cambridge and with General Bentinck*—a conference held *after the time when (according to the 'Quarterly Review') Sir George Brown had caused the redoubt to be occupied by a detachment from the Grenadier Guards.* The statement made on this subject by the *Quarterly Review* with the apparent (or transparent) authority of Sir George Brown, is given in the Appendix, Note XI., together with the few words of comment which I have chosen to add. From these, and from any other materials at his command, the reader may judge whether the above sentence of the text, in which I connect the Duke of Cambridge and the Coldstream with the recapture of the redoubt, is worded in terms which should be qualified by bringing to bear on them the testimony of Sir George Brown.

Page 589. '*could come down to engage him.*'—'The immediate object being 'to turn the redoubt, while the attack in front was made by the Guards.'—Original MS. Report, dated 'Bivouac on the River Alma, 22nd September, '1854,' and signed 'C. Campbell, Major-General.'

Page 590. '*Sir Colin Campbell went forward.*'—Riding quite alone. He did not choose his staff to be with him at this time, for he knew that a group of officers would be likely to draw more fire than a single horseman.

Page 590. '*Then, with his staff.*'—It was not till the 42nd had come up that he was rejoined by his staff.

Page 593. '*marching straight against the two columns.*'—'This flank move-'ment was completely successful. . . . The 42nd, being the leading regi-'ment, gained the heights first, and found a large body of Russian troops, 'which had just quitted the central redoubt, endeavoring to form in its 'front, with another large body already posted there. The 42nd continued 'to advance, firing, in line.'—The MS. quoted at page 589.

Page 593. '*was boldly marching forward.*'—'On reaching the crest of the 'hill on the enemy's side, *another mass was met advancing* to support the re-'tiring enemy.'—The MS. quoted at page 589.

Page 593. '*springing up to the outer crest.*'—'As these troops [the Russian 'column mentioned in the last note] came on, the 93rd arrived most op-'portunely.'—The MS. quoted at page 589.

Page 597. '*It moved straight at the flank of the 93rd.*'—'While the 93rd 'was still engaged, another body of Russians from their extreme right '*moved down direct on the flank of the 93rd.*'—The MS. quoted at page 589.

Page 598. '*of a battalion advancing in line.*'—I fear that the form of expression which I have used in the above sentence may be read as indicating a greater swiftness of movement than the actual truth would warrant. It is quite true that the 79th caught the Russian column in the act of marching across its front, and instantly attacked it. This, however, it did—not by a charge with the bayonet, but (as is rightly shown by the next sentence of the text) by pouring its fire into the flank of the advancing column.

Page 598. '*began to fall back in great confusion.*'—Speaking of the column which the enemy was moving flankwise from his extreme right, Sir Colin Campbell, in the same MS., says:—'At this moment the 79th arrived, and 'opened fire upon them, causing them to retreat in great confusion.'

Page 598. '*enemy's disordered masses.*'—'The 42nd continued to ad- 'vance, firing, in line, and drove these troops before them in confusion, and 'caused them great loss. *Their resistance was stubborn.*'—The MS. quoted at page 589.

Page 598. '*had chanced in a moment of glory.*'—'Thus the three regi- 'ments of the Highland brigade were formed in line on the inner crest of 'the enemy's position, having driven all the large bodies of troops which 'were posted there down into the valley.'—The MS. quoted at page 589.

Page 599. '*strove to drive them back into the fight.*'—After speaking (as shown in the former notes) of the defeat of the Russian columns with which his brigade had been fighting, Sir Colin Campbell says that they 'were 'driven down into the valley upon a mass of troops which were placed in 'reserve on the heights in their rear, and an attempt was made by this reserve 'to move in advance, forcing forward the retiring troops.'—The MS. quoted at page 589.

Page 599. '*the Ouglitz column was forced to turn.*'—'But fire being again 'opened, this reserve returned to its position, evidently with a view to cover 'the men who had been driven by the three Highland regiments.'—The MS. quoted at page 589.

Page 599. '*cover the retreat of the vanquished masses.*'—The conductors of the 'Quarterly Review' have thought fit to print in their publication the following words:—'The Coldstreams took their place on the left of the 'Grenadiers, and shared in the battle. *But the battle was already dying out.* 'The Grenadiers had carried all before them; the Redan was empty, and, 'stealing away in a direction to their own right, *the Russian columns were in* '*full retreat.* It was at *this juncture* that Sir Colin Campbell and his High- 'landers made their appearance. Pushing past Buller, Sir Colin's battal- 'ions, coming up in échelon, *arrived just in time to see the enemy in full flight,* 'and fired on them as each battalion got within range, *which, however, to the* '*more forward of the three, was never a close range.*'—'Quarterly Review,' No. 226, p. 567. In answer to this statement, I only say that I refer people to the extracts which I have given in the foregoing pages from the original Report by Sir Colin Campbell, now lying before me. The Report is official, and addressed to the Assistant Adjutant-General of the Division. It is dated, as I have said, 'Bivouac on the River Alma, 22nd September, 1854,' and is signed 'C. Campbell, Major-General.'

Page 603. '*which was not in full retreat.*'—It was at this time that H.R.H. the Duke of Cambridge summoned Colonel Hood to his side in order to have his thanks conveyed to the Grenadiers. Colonel Hood writes:— 'The Duke of Cambridge, after the Russians were beaten back, came and 'called me to the front to shake me by the hand, and convey his thanks 'to the gallant Grenadiers. This was most gratifying. It is true, I had 'the honor to command, but they command themselves!'

Page 616. To note 2, the author adds:—See also now the 'farther note' in the part which forms Note XIII. of the Appendix.

# APPENDIX.

## I.

### PAPERS SHOWING THE DIFFERENCE WHICH LED TO THE RUPTURE OF PRINCE MENTSCHIKOFF'S NEGOTIATION.

*Draft of Note proposed by Prince Mentschikoff to be addressed to him by the Porte.**

La Sublime Porte, après l'examen le plus attentif et le plus sérieux des demandes qui forment l'objet de la mission extraordinaire confiée à l'Ambassadeur de Russie, Prince Mentschikoff, et après avoir soumis le résultat de cet examen à Sa Majesté le Sultan, se fait un devoir empressé de notifier par la présente à son Altesse l'Ambassadeur la décision Impériale emanée à ce sujet par un Irade suprême en date du (date Musulmane et Chrétienne).

Sa Majesté voulant donner à son auguste allié et ami l'Empereur de Russie un nouveau témoignage de son amitié la plus sincère, et de son désir intime de consolider les anciennes relations de bon voisinage et de parfaite entente qui existent entre les deux Etats, plaçant en même temps une entière confiance dans les intentions constamment bienveillantes de Sa Majesté Impériale pour le maintien de l'intégrité et de l'indépendance de l'Empire Ottoman, a daigné apprécier et prendre en sérieuse considération les représentations franches et cordiales dont l'Ambassadeur de Russie s'est rendu l'organe en faveur du culte orthodoxe Greco-Russe professé par son auguste allié ainsi que par la majorité de leurs sujets respectifs.

Le Soussigné a reçu en conséquence l'ordre de donner par la présente note l'assurance la plus solennelle au Gouvernement de Russie, que représente auprès de Sa Majesté le Sultan son Altesse le Prince Mentschikoff, sur la sollicitude invariable et les sentiments généreux et tolérans qui animent Sa Majesté le Sultan pour la sécurité et la prospérité dans ses états du clergé, des églises, et des établissements religieux du culte Chrétien d'Orient.

Afin de rendre ces assurances plus explicites, préciser d'une manière formelle les objets principaux de cette haute sollicitude, corroborer par des éclaircissements supplémentaires que nécessite la marche du temps, le sens des Articles qui dans les Traités antérieurs conclus entre les deux Puissances ont trait aux questions religieuses, et prévenir enfin à jamais toute nuance de malentendu et de désaccord à ce sujet entre les deux Gouvernements, le Soussigné est autorisé par Sa Majesté le Sultan à faire les déclarations suivantes:

1. Le culte orthodoxe d'Orient, son clergé, ses églises, et ses possessions, ainsi que ses établissements religieux, jouiront dans l'avenir sans aucune atteinte, sous l'égide de Sa Majesté le Sultan, des privilèges et immunités qui leur sont assurés *ab antiquo*, ou qui leur ont été accordés à différentes reprises par la faveur Impérial, et dans un principe de haute équité participeront aux avantages accordés aux autres rites Chrétiens, ainsi qu'aux Légations Etrangères accréditées près la Sublime Porte par Convention ou disposition particulière.

* This was the last demand made by the Prince.

2. Sa Majesté le Sultan ayant jugé nécessaire et équitable de corroborer et d'expliquer son firman souverain revêtu du hattihoumayoum le 15 de la lune de Rebiul-Akhir 1268 (10 Février, 1852), par son firman souverain du
et d'ordonner en sus par un autre firman en date du
la réparation de la coupole du Temple du Saint Sépulcre, ces deux firmans seront textuellement exécutés et fidèlement observés, pour maintenir à jamais le *status quo* actuel des sanctuaires possedés par les Grecs exclusivement ou en commun avec d'autres cultes.

Il est entendu que cette promesse s'étend également au maintien de tous les droits et immunités dont jouissent *ab antiquo* l'église orthodoxe et son clergé tant dans la ville de Jérusalem qu'au-déhors, sans aucun préjudice pour les autres communautés Chrétiennes.

3. Pour le cas où la Cour Impériale de Russie en ferait la demande, il sera assigné une localité convenable dans la ville de Jérusalem ou dans les environs pour la construction d'une église consacrée à la célébration du service divin par les ecclésiastiques Russes, et d'un hospice pour les pélerins indigents ou malades, lesquelles fondations seront sous la surveillance spéciale du Consulat-Général de Russie en Syrie et en Palestine.

4. On donnera les firmans et les ordres nécessaires à qui de droit et aux Patriarches Grecs pour l'exécution de ces décisions souveraines, et on s'entendra ultérieurement sur la régularisation des points de détail qui n'auront pas trouvé place tant dans les firmans concernant les lieux saints de Jérusalem que dans la présente notification.

Le Soussigné, etc.

### *Reshid Pasha to Prince Mentschikoff.**

(Translation.)

The statement made by Prince Mentschikoff, in his written and verbal communications, concerning the doubts and want of confidence entertained by the Porte with regard to His Majesty the Emperor's good intentions, has been seen with great regret. His Majesty the Sultan has perfect faith and confidence in His Majesty the Emperor, and highly appreciates the great qualities and spirit of justice which animate his august ally and neighbor, and it is a great honor for me to proclaim that it has always been His Majesty the Sultan's desire to consolidate and strengthen the friendly relations happily subsisting between the two countries.

With reference to the religious privileges of the Greek churches and clergy, the honor of the Porte requires that the exclusively spiritual privileges granted under the Sultan's predecessors, and confirmed by His Majesty, should be now and henceforward preserved unimpaired and in force; and the equitable system pursued by the Porte toward its subjects demands that any spiritual privilege whatever granted henceforward to one class of Christian subjects should not be refused to the Greek clergy. It would be a cause of much regret that the fixed intentions of His Majesty the Sultan in this respect should be called into question.

Nevertheless, the imperial firman now granted to the Greek Patriarchate, confirming the religious privileges, is considered to afford a new proof of His Imperial Majesty's benevolent sentiments in this respect, and the general promulgation thereof must afford every security, and remove for ever from His Imperial Majesty's mind all doubts for the future respecting the religion which he professes, and it is with pleasure that I perform the duty of making this declaration.

In order that there should be no alteration respecting the Shrines at Jeru-

* This was the last offer made by the Porte to Prince Mentschikoff.

salem, it is formally promised that for security in the future thereon the Sublime Porte will take no step concerning them without the knowledge of the French and Russian Governments. An official note has been addressed to the French Embassy also to this purpose.

The Sultan consents that a church and hospital should be built at Jerusalem (for the Russians); and the Porte is ready and disposed to conclude a Sened, both on this subject and concerning the special privileges of the Russian monks at that place.

---

## II.

THE 'VIENNA NOTE,' WITH THE PROPOSED TURKISH MODIFICATIONS, SHOWING THE POINTS OF THE DIFFERENCE, WHICH WAS FOLLOWED BY WAR BETWEEN RUSSIA AND TURKEY.

*Copy of the Vienna Projet de Note, as modified by the Sublime Porte.*

[The Turkish modifications are shown by printing in italics the words which the Porte rejected, and placing the words which it proposed to substitute in the foot-note.]

Sa Majesté le Sultan n'ayant rien de plus à cœur que de rétablir entre elle et Sa Majesté l'Empereur de Russie les relations de bon voisinage et de parfaite entente qui ont été malheureusement altérées par de récentes et pénibles complications, a pris soigneusement à tâcher de rechercher les moyens d'effacer les traces de ce différend.

Un iradé suprême en date du                     lui ayant fait connaître la décision Impériale, la Sublime Porte se félicite de pouvoir la communiquer à son Excellence M. le Comte de Nesselrode.

Si à toute époque les Empereurs de Russie ont témoignés leur active sollicitude pour *le maintien des immunités et privilèges de l'Eglise Orthodoxe Grecque dans l'Empire Ottoman, les Sultans ne se sont jamais refusés à les consacrer** de nouveau *par des* actes solennels qui attestaient de leur ancienne et constante bienveillance à l'égard de leurs sujets Chrétiens.

Sa Majesté le Sultan Abdul-Medjid, aujourd'hui régnant, animé des mêmes dispositions et voulant donner à Sa Majesté l'Empereur de Russie un témoignage personnel de son amitié la plus sincère, n'a écouté que sa confiance infinie dans les qualités éminentes de son auguste ami et allié, et a daigné prendre en sérieuse considération les représentations dont son Altesse le Prince de Mentschikoff s'est rendu l'organe auprès de la Sublime Porte.

Le Soussigné a reçu en conséquence l'ordre de déclarer par la présente que le Gouvernement de Sa Majesté le Sultan restera fidèle *à la lettre et à l'esprit des stipulations des Traités de Kainardji et d'Andrinople, relatives à la protection du culte Chrétien,*† et que Sa Majesté regarde comme étant de son honneur de faire observer à tout jamais, et de préserver de toute atteinte, soit présentement, soit dans l'avenir, la jouissance des privilèges spirituels qui ont été accordés par les augustes aïeux de Sa Majesté à l'Eglise Orthodoxe de l'Orient, qui sont maintenus et confirmés par elle; et, en outre, à faire participer dans un esprit de haute équité le rit Grec aux avantages *concédés aux autres rits Chrétiens par Convention ou disposition particulière.*‡

* Le culte et l'Eglise Orthodoxe Grecque, les Sultans n'ont jamais cessé de veiller au maintien des immunités et privilèges qu'ils ont spontanément accordés à diverses reprises à ce culte et à cette Eglise dans l'Empire Ottoman, et de les consacrer.

† Aux stipulations du Traité de Kainardji confirmé par celui d'Andrinople, relatives à la protection par la Sublime Porte de la religion Chrétienne, et il est en outre chargé de faire connaître.

‡ Octroyés ou qui seraient octroyés aux autres communautés Chrétiennes sujettes Ottomanes.

Au reste, comme le firman Impérial qui vient d'être donné au patriarcat et au clergé Grec, et qui contient les confirmations de leurs privilèges spirituels, devra être regardé comme une nouvelle preuve de ses nobles sentiments, et comme, en outre, la proclamation de ce firman, qui donne toute sécurité, devra faire disparaître toute crainte à l'égard du rit qui est la religi•n de Sa Majesté l'Empereur de Russie; je suis heureux d'être chargé du devoir de farie la présente notification.

---

## III.

PAPERS SHOWING THE CONCORD EXISTING BETWEEN THE FOUR POWERS AT THE TIME WHEN FRANCE AND ENGLAND WERE ENGAGING IN A SEPARATE COURSE OF ACTION.

### *Protocol of a Conference held at Vienna, February* 2, 1854.

(Translation.)

Present: The Representatives of Austria, France, Great Britain, and Prussia.

The Representatives of Austria, France, Great Britain, and Prussia, have met together in conference to hear the communication which the Austrian Plenipotentiary has been good enough to make to them of the propositions submitted by the Cabinet of St. Petersburg in reply to those which he had undertaken, on the 13th of January, to forward to the Imperial Government, and which were sanctioned by the approval of the Powers represented in the Conference of Vienna. The document which contains them is annexed to the present Protocol.

The Undersigned, after having submitted the above-mentioned propositions to the most careful examination, have ascertained that, in their general character and in their details, they so essentially differ from the basis of negotiation agreed upon on the 31st of December at Constantinople, and approved on the 13th January at Vienna, that they have not considered them to be such as should be forwarded to the Government of His Imperial Majesty the Sultan.

It consequently only remains for the Undersigned to transmit the annexed document to their respective Courts, and to wait till they shall have taken their final resolutions.

(Signed) BUOL-SCHAUENSTEIN.
BOURQUENEY.
WESTMORLAND.
ARNIM.

### *The Earl of Westmorland to the Earl of Clarendon.*—(*Received February* 13.)*

Vienna, February 8, 1853.

My Lord,—I have just left the Conference to which Count Buol had this morning invited me, in conjunction with my colleagues. Upon our assembling, he stated that he had no proposal to make to us, but, in consideration of the perfect union existing amongst us upon the Eastern Question, he thought he was forwarding our common objects by communicating the dispatches he had addressed to Count Esterhazy, for the purpose of being submitted to Count Nesselrode.

Count Buol then read to us these dispatches. The first gave an account of the proposal brought forward by Count Orloff, that the Emperor of Aus-

* *i. e.* just one fortnight before England dispatched the hostile summons which brought her into a state of war.

tria should, in conjunction with Prussia, take an engagement with the Emperor of Russia for the maintenance of a strict neutrality in the war now existing with the Porte, and in which the Maritime Powers seemed likely to take part. Count Buol, in his dispatch, develops in the clearest and most distinct language the impossibility of the adoption by the Emperor of any such engagement. He states, with all courtesy to the Emperor Nicholas, the obligations by which the Austrian Government is bound to watch over the strict maintenance of the principle of the independence and integrity of Turkey—a principle proclaimed by the Emperor Nicholas himself, but which the passage of the Danube by his troops might, by the encouragement of insurrections in the Turkish Provinces, endanger. Count Buol, therefore, states that he can not take the engagement proposed to him. The second dispatch to Count Esterhazy relates to the answer which has been returned to the proposals for negotiations transmitted by Count Buol with the sanction of the Conference on the 13th ultimo.

In this dispatch, Count Buol states with considerable force the disappointment felt by the Emperor at the want of success which had attended his recommendation in favor of the Turkish propositions. He enters very fully into the subject, and renews the expression of the Emperor's most anxious desire that the Emperor Nicholas may still adopt the proposals which had been submitted to him.

The last dispatch is one in which Count Buol replies to the reproach which was addressed to the Imperial Government, that by its present conduct it was abandoning the principles upon which the three Governments of Russia, Austria, and Prussia, had hitherto acted for the maintenance of the established interest and independence of the different States of Europe, and that, by so doing, it was endangering the established order of things in Europe, and the security at present existing.

The answer of Count Buol to this reproach is very firmly and clearly stated.

It is impossible for me to give your Lordship a more detailed account, before the departure of the messenger, of these dispatches; but I must add, that they met with the entire approbation of the members of the Conference, that they were looked upon as most ably drawn up, and that while using every courteous and friendly expression toward the Emperor Nicholas, they most clearly pointed out the present position which the Austrian Government would maintain with the view of upholding the principles they had proclaimed, and the engagements which they had taken for their support.*

*Protocol of a Conference held at Vienna, March* 5, 1854.†

(Translation.)

Present: the Representatives of Austria, France, Great Britain, and Prussia.

The undersigned, Representatives of Austria, France, Great Britain, and Prussia, having again met in Conference on the summons of the Austrian Plenipotentiary, the annexed document which had been communicated to the Cabinet of Vienna by the Envoy of Russia, and which contains the preliminaries of the Treaty to be concluded between Russia and the Porte, was read to them, the Court of Austria being requested by the Cabinet of St. Petersburg to apply for the support of the two Maritime Powers in order to obtain the acceptance of these preliminaries by the Sublime Porte.

* The rest of the dispatch relates only to a suggestion for an arrangement which came to nothing, and is therefore omitted.

† *i. e.* whilst messengers were carrying the hostile summons from Paris and London to St. Petersburg.

After mature deliberation, the Plenipotentiaries of France and Great Britain, taking as the basis of their examination the previous documents which had received the sanction of the four Powers, established the existence of radical differences between those documents and the proposed preliminaries.

1. Inasmuch as the evacuation of the Danubian Principalities, which is fixed to take place after the signature of the preliminaries, is made to depend on the departure of the combined fleets not only from the Black Sea, but from the Straits of the Bosphorus and of the Dardanelles, a condition which could only be admitted by the Maritime Powers after the conclusion of the definitive treaty.

2. Inasmuch as the document now under consideration tends to invest with a form strictly conventional, bilateral, and exclusively applicable to the relations of the Porte with Russia, the assurances relative to the religious privileges of the Greeks—assurances which the Porte has only offered to give to the five Powers at the same time and in the form of a simple identic declaration. The assurances, in fact, once inserted in the preliminary Treaty, must then needs be reproduced in the definitive Treaty, and would be accompanied moreover by an official note confirmatory of the said privileges exclusively addressed to the Court of Russia, a note which, in its turn, would be considered as annexed to the Treaties, that is to say, as having the same force and the same effect.

3. Inasmuch as the preliminaries communicated to Vienna are by implication withheld from any discussion in Conference upon the modifications considered necessary to make them correspond with the original text of the Acts which had received its assent, and inasmuch as the conclusion of the definitive Treaty contains no greater reservation for its inspection and interference.

4. Inasmuch as whilst the propositions of the Porte expressly require the revision of the Treaty of 1841, so as to make Turkey participate in the guarantees of the public law of Europe, this condition is passed over in silence.

The Plenipotentiaries of Austria and Prussia, appreciating the force of the observations offered by the Plenipotentiaries of France and of Great Britain, recognized in like manner on their part the remarkable differences pointed out between the Russian draft of preliminaries and the Protocols of the 13th of January and 2nd of February.

In consequence, the Conference unanimously agreed that it was impossible to proceed with those propositions.

(Signed) BUOL-SCHAUENSTEIN.
BOURQUENEY.
WESTMORLAND.
ARNIM.

*Protocol of a Conference held at Vienna, April* 9, 1854.*

(Translation.)

Present: The Representatives of Austria, France, Great Britain, and Prussia.

At the request of the Plenipotentiaries of France and of Great Britain, the Conference met to hear the documents read which establish that the invitation addressed to the Cabinet of St. Petersburg to evacuate the Moldo-Wallachian provinces within a fixed time having remained unanswered, the state of war already declared between Russia and the Sublime Porte is in actual existence equally between Russia on the one side, and France and Great Britain on the other.

This change which has taken place in the attitude of two of the Powers

* *i. e.* the very day before the treaty of alliance between England and France.

represented at the Conference of Vienna, in consequence of a step taken directly by France and England, supported by Austria and Prussia as being founded in right, has been considered by the Representatives of Austria and Prussia as involving the necessity of a fresh declaration of the union of the four Powers upon the ground of the principles laid down in the Protocols of December 5, 1853, and January 13, 1854.

In consequence, the Undersigned have at this solemn moment declared that their Governments remain united in the double object of maintaining the territorial integrity of the Ottoman Empire, of which the fact of the evacuation of the Danubian Principalities is and will remain one of the essential conditions; and of consolidating in an interest so much in conformity with the sentiments of the Sultan, and by every means compatible with his independence and sovereignty, the civil and religious rights of the Christian subjects of the Porte.

The territorial integrity of the Ottoman Empire is and remains the *sine quâ non* condition of every transaction having for its object the re-establishment of peace between the belligerent Powers; and the Governments represented by the Undersigned engage to endeavor in common to discover the guarantees most likely to attach the existence of that Empire to the general equilibrium of Europe; as they also declare themselves ready to deliberate and to come to an understanding as to the employment of the means calculated to accomplish the object of their agreement.

Whatever event may arise in consequence of this agreement, founded solely upon the general interests of Europe, and of which the object can only be attained by the return of a firm and lasting peace, the Governments represented by the Undersigned reciprocally engage not to enter into any definitive arrangements with the Imperial Court of Russia, or with any other Power, which would be at variance with the principles above enunciated, without previously deliberating thereon in common.

(Signed) BUOL-SCHAUENSTEIN.
BOURQUENEY.
WESTMORLAND.
ARNIM.

*Treaty of Alliance, Offensive and Defensive, between Austria and Prussia.*

(Translation.)

His Majesty the Emperor of Austria and His Majesty the King of Prussia, penetrated with deep regret at the fruitlessness of their attempts hitherto to prevent the breaking out of war between Russia, on the one hand, and Turkey, France, and England, on the other;

Mindful of the moral obligations entered into by them by the signing of the last Vienna Protocol;

In the face of the military measures ever gathering on both sides around them, and of the dangers resulting therefrom for the general peace of Europe;

Convinced of the high duty which on the threshold of a future pregnant with evil, is imposed, in the interest of the European welfare, on Germany, so intimately united with the States of the two High Parties;

Have determined to ally themselves in an offensive and defensive alliance for the duration of the war which has broken out between Russia, on the one hand, and Turkey, France, and England, on the other, and have appointed for the conclusion of it the following Plenipotentiaries:

His Majesty the Emperor of Austria, the Baron Henry de Hess, his actual Privy Councilor, &c., &c.; and the Count Frederick de Thun-Hohenstein, his Chamberlain, actual Privy Councilor, &c., &c.;

And His Majesty the King of Prussia, the Baron Othon Theodore de

Manteuffel, his President of the Council of Ministers, and Minister for Foreign Affairs, &c., &c.

The same having exchanged their full powers found to be in good order, have agreed upon the following points:

ARTICLE I.

His Imperial Apostolic Majesty and His Majesty the King of Prussia guarantee to each other reciprocally the possession of their German and non-German possessions, so that an attack made on the territory of the one, from whatever quarter, will be regarded by the other as an act of hostility against his own territory.

ARTICLE II.

In the same manner, the High Contracting Parties hold themselves engaged to defend the rights and interests of Germany against all and every injury, and consider themselves bound accordingly for the mutual repulse of every attack on any part whatsoever of their territories; likewise also in the case where one of the two may find himself, in understanding with the other, obliged to advance actively for the defense of German interests. The agreement relating to the latter-named eventuality, as likewise the extent of the assistance then to be given, will form a special as also integral part of the present Convention.

ARTICLE III.

In order also to give due security and force to the conditions of the offensive and defensive alliance now concluded, the two great Great German Powers bind themselves, in case of need, to hold in perfect readiness for war a part of their forces, at periods to be determined between them and in positions to be fixed. With respect to the time, the extent, and the nature of the placing of those troops, a special stipulation will likewise be determined.

ARTICLE IV.

The High Contracting Parties will invite all the German Governments of the Confederation to accede to this alliance, with the understanding that the federal obligations existing in virtue of Article 47 of the final Act of Vienna will receive the same extension for the States who accede as the present Treaty stipulates.

ARTICLE V.

Neither of the two High Contracting Parties will, during the duration of this alliance, enter into any separate alliance with other Powers which shall not be in entire harmony with the basis of the present treaty.

ARTICLE VI.

The present Convention shall be ratified as soon as possible by the High Contracting Sovereigns.

Done at Berlin, April 20, 1854.*

(L.S.) HENRY BON. DE HESS.
(L.S.) F. THUN.
(L.S.) BON. OTH. THEOD. MANTEUFFEL.

(Translation.)

*Additional Article to the Offensive and Defensive Alliance between Austria and Prussia of April* 20, 1854.

According to the conditions of Article II. of the Treaty concluded this day

* *i. e.* ten days after the date of the Anglo-French alliance.

between His Imperial Majesty the Emperor of Austria and His Majesty the King of Prussia for the establishment of an offensive and defensive alliance, a more intimate understanding with respect to the eventuality when an active advance of one of the High Contracting Parties may impose on the other the obligation of a mutual protection of the territory of both, was to form the subject of a special agreement to be considered as an integral part of the Treaty.

Their Majesties have not been able to divest themselves of the consideration that the indefinite continuance of the occupation of the territories on the Lower Danube, under the sovereignty of the Ottoman Porte, by Imperial Russian troops, would endanger the political, moral, and material interests of the whole German Confederation as also of their own States, and the more so in proportion as Russia extends her warlike operations on Turkish territory.

The Courts of Austria and Prussia are united in the desire to avoid every participation in the war which has broken out between Russia, on the one hand, and Turkey, France, and Great Britain, on the other, and at the same time to contribute to the restoration of general peace. They more especially consider the declarations lately made at Berlin by the Court of St. Petersburg, to be an important element of pacification, the failure of the practical influence of which they would view with regret. According to these declarations, Russia appears to regard the original motive for the occupation of the Principalities as removed by the concessions now granted to the Christian subjects of the Porte, which offer the prospect of realization. They therefore hope that the replies awaited from the Cabinet of Russia to the Prussian propositions, transmitted on the 8th, will offer to them the necessary guarantee for an early withdrawal of the Russian troops. In the event that this hope should be illusory, the Plenipotentiaries named, on the part of His Majesty the Emperor of Austria, Freiherr Baron von Hess and Count Thun, and on the part of His Majesty the King of Prussia, Baron Manteuffel, have drawn up the following more detailed agreement with respect to the eventuality alluded to in the above-mentioned Article II. of the Treaty of Alliance of this day:

*Single Article.*

The Imperial Austrian Government will also on their side address a communication to the Imperial Russian Court with the object of obtaining from the Emperor of Russia the necessary orders that an immediate stop should be put to the farther advance of his armies upon the Turkish territory, as also to request of His Imperial Majesty sufficient guarantees for the prompt evacuation of the Danubian Principalities; and the Prussian Government will again, in the most emphatic manner, support these communications with reference to their proposals already sent to St. Petersburg. Should the answer of the Russian Court to these steps of the Cabinets of Vienna and Berlin—contrary to expectation—not be of a nature to give them entire satisfaction upon the two points aforementioned, the measures to be taken by one of the Contracting Parties for their attainment, according to the terms of Article II. of the Offensive and Defensive Alliance signed on this day, will be on the understanding that every hostile attack on the territory of one of the Contracting Parties is to be repelled with all the military forces at the disposal of the other.

But a mutual offensive advance is stipulated for only in the event of the incorporation of the Principalities, or in the event of an attack on or passage of the Balkan by Russia.*

* Of course the contemplated march of Austrian troops into the Principalities (though

The present Convention shall be submitted for the ratification of the High Sovereigns simultaneously with the above-mentioned Treaty.

Done at Berlin, the 20th of April, 1854.

(Signed) HESS. (Signed) MANTEUFFEL.
THUN.

*Protocol signed at Vienna on the 23d of May,* 1854, *by the Representatives of Austria, France, Great Britain, and Prussia.*

(Translation.)

Present: The Representatives of Austria, France, Great Britain, and Prussia.

The Undersigned Plenipotentiaries have deemed it conformable to the arrangements contained in the Protocol of the 9th of April, to meet in conference in order to communicate reciprocally and record in one common Act the Conventions concluded between France and England on the one hand, and between Austria and Prussia on the other, upon the 10th and 20th of April of the present year.

After a careful examination of the aforesaid Conventions, the Undersigned have unanimously agreed:

1. That the Convention concluded between France and England, as well as that signed on the 20th of April between Austria and Prussia, bind both of them, in the relative situations to which they apply, to secure the maintenance of the principle established by the series of Protocols of the Conference of Vienna.

2. That the integrity of the Ottoman Empire, and the evacuation of that portion of its territory which is occupied by the Russian army, are and will continue to be the constant and invariable object of the union of the four Powers.

3. That, consequently, the Acts communicated and annexed to the present Protocol correspond to the engagement which the Plenipotentiaries had mutually contracted on the 9th of April, to deliberate and agree upon the means most fit to accomplish the object of their union, and thus give a fresh sanction to the firm intention of the four Powers represented at the Conference of Vienna, to combine all their efforts and resolutions to realize the object which forms the basis of their union.

(Signed) BUOL-SCHAUENSTEIN.
BOURQUENEY.
WESTMORLAND.
ARNIM.

*Convention between His Imperial Majesty the Emperor of Austria and the Ottoman Porte. Signed at Boyadji-Kevy, June* 14, 1854.

(Translation.)

His Majesty the Emperor of Austria, fully recognizing that the existence of the Ottoman Empire within its present limits is necessary for the maintenance of the balance of power between the States of Europe, and that, specifically, the evacuation of the Danubian Principalities is one of the essential conditions of the integrity of that Empire; being, moreover, ready to join, with the means at his disposal, in the measures proper to insure the object of the agreement established between his Cabinet and the High Courts represented at the Conference of Vienna:

undertaken with a view to expel the Russian forces) could not be 'a mutual offensive advance.' The clause defines the circumstances in which the two great German sovereigns should be bound to attack Russia, and does not cast any obscurity upon that part of the treaty which provided for the event in which 'one of the two may find himself in understanding with the others obliged to advance actively for the defense of German interests.'

His Imperial Majesty the Sultan having on his side accepted this offer of concert made in a friendly manner by His Majesty the Emperor of Austria;

It has seemed proper to conclude a Convention, in order to regulate the manner in which the concert in question shall be carried into effect.

With this object, His Imperial Majesty the Emperor of Austria and His Imperial Majesty the Sultan have named as their Plenipotentiaries, that is to say:

His Majesty the Emperor of Austria, M. le Baron Charles de Bruck, Privy Councilor of His Imperial and Royal Apostolic Majesty, his Internuncio and Minister Plenipotentiary at the Sublime Ottoman Porte, Grand Cross of the Imperial Order of Leopold, Knight of the Imperial Order of the Iron Crown of the first class, &c.;

And His Imperial Majesty the Sultan, Mustapha Reshid Pasha, late Grand Vizier, and at present his Minister for Foreign Affairs, decorated with the Imperial Order of Medjidié of the first class, &c.;

Who, after having exchanged their full powers, found to be in good and due form, have agreed upon the following Articles:

ARTICLE I.

His Majesty the Emperor of Austria engages to exhaust all the means of negotiation and all other means to obtain the evacuation of the Danubian Principalities by the foreign army which occupies them, and even to employ, in case they are required, the number of troops necessary to attain this end.

ARTICLE II.

It will appertain in this case exclusively to the Imperial Commander-in-chief to direct the operations of his army. He will, however, always take care to inform the Commander-in-chief of the Ottoman army of his operations in proper time.

ARTICLE III.

His Majesty the Emperor of Austria undertakes by common agreement with the Ottoman Government to re-establish in the Principalities, as far as possible, the legal state of things such as it results from the privileges secured by the Sublime Porte in regard to the administration of those countries. The local authorities thus reconstituted shall not, however, extend their action so far as to attempt to exercise control over the Imperial army.

ARTICLE IV.

The Imperial Court of Austria farther engages not to enter into any plan of accommodation with the Imperial Court of Russia which has not for its basis the sovereign rights of His Imperial Majesty the Sultan, as well as the integrity of his Empire.

ARTICLE V.

As soon as the object of the present Convention shall have been obtained by the conclusion of a Treaty of Peace between the Sublime Porte and the Court of Russia, His Majesty the Emperor of Austria will immediately make arrangements for withdrawing his forces with the least possible delay from the territory of the Principalities. The details respecting the retreat of the Austrian troops shall form the object of a special understanding with the Sublime Porte.

ARTICLE VI.

The Austrian Government expects that the authorities of the countries temporarily occupied by the Imperial troops will afford them every assistance and facility, as well for their march, their lodging or encampment, as for their subsistence and that of their horses, and for their communications. The Austrian Government likewise expects that every demand relating to the requirements of the service shall be complied with, which shall be addressed by the Austrian commanders, either to the Ottoman Government, through the Imperial Internunciate at Constantinople, or directly to the local authorities, unless more weighty reasons render the execution of them impossible.

It is understood that the commanders of the Imperial army will provide for the maintenance of the strictest discipline among their troops, and will respect, and cause to be respected, the properties as well as the laws, the religion, and the customs of the country.

ARTICLE VII.

The present Convention shall be ratified, and the ratifications shall be exchanged at Vienna in the space of four weeks, or earlier, if possible, dating from the day of its signature.

In faith of which, the respective Plenipotentiaries have signed it and set their seals to it.

Done in duplicate, for one and the same effect, at Boyadji-Keuy, the fourteenth of June, one thousand eight hundred and fifty-four.

(L.S.) V. BRUCK. (L.S.) RESHID.

---

## IV.

*Note to Page 200.*

The condition of the French Emperor on the day of Magenta was publicly seen; but on the day of the great battle which was soon afterward fought on the Mincio he avoided the criticism of multitudinous eye-witnesses, and great pains were taken to make France and Europe believe that the Emperor, on the day of Solferino, was not only in a state to be able to give useful orders, but was actually present in a part of the field where there was dreadful danger. 'The Emperor Napoleon,' said the *Moniteur*, 'was, so to speak, superior to himself: every where he was seen, always 'directing the battle; every one about him shuddered at the danger which 'incessantly threatened him; he alone seemed to be ignorant of it.' These efforts caused people in England to believe a good deal of what was represented to them; but in France their success was hindered by a practical difficulty which the French Emperor had brought upon himself by his odd love of dresses and imitative display. In the ride he took on the day of Solferino, he had chosen to be followed—not only, as might have been expected, by a numerous staff, but also by a cavalry escort, with beautiful new dresses and decorations, which went by the name of the 'Cent 'Gardes'—'The Hundred Guards.' All these horsemen—the whole Imperial staff, and the cavalry escort—covered altogether a good deal of ground—ground as broad and as long as many a whole street; and if they had really intruded themselves into any part of the field where there was what may be called 'fighting,' then, humanly speaking, they must have undergone dreadful carnage. It so happened, however, that of all this acreage of horsemen not one was killed, and only one of the 'Cent Gardes' was even touched—said by some to have been struck in a part of his dress, and warranted by the *Moniteur* to have been hit in the actual body.—*Moniteur*, 29th June, 1859. Here then, was the practical difficulty. It had to be represented that a large mass of horsemen had been moving about all day in the thick of a most bloody battle, and yet had remained unscathed. In this stress the *Moniteur* did not hesitate. It resorted to the theory of preternatural agency. It declared that the protection which the Deity threw around the Emperor *was extended to his suite.* 'La protection dont Dieu l'a couvert s'est etendue à son état-major.'—*Moniteur*, 29th June, 1859.

Paris laughed her laugh; and thenceforth it seems to have been understood by the more prudent of the Imperialists in France that the subject of their master's demeanor on the day of Solferino was one which they might advantageously drop.

The process of dispelling a falsehood sometimes generates a wrong notion —a notion that the exact opposite of the falsehood so dispelled is the truth. I must guard against this. The French Emperor at Solferino conducted himself in exact accordance with what I have said in the text. 'He did not so give way to fear as to prove that he had less self-control in 'moments of danger than the common run of peaceful citizens; but he 'showed that though he had chosen to set himself heroic tasks, his tempera- 'ment was ill-fitted for the hour of battle and for the crisis of an adven- 'ture.'

---

## V.

### LORD CLARENDON'S DISPATCH DEMANDING THE EVACUATION OF THE PRINCIPALITIES.

*The Earl of Clarendon to Count Nesselrode.*

Foreign Office, February 27, 1854.

M. LE COMTE,—As the ordinary channels of communication between England and Russia have been closed by the recent interruption of diplomatic relations between the two Courts, I am under the necessity of addressing myself directly to your Excellency on a matter of the deepest importance to our respective Governments and to Europe.

The British Government has for many months anxiously labored, in conjunction with its allies, to effect a reconciliation of differences between Russia and the Sublime Porte, and it is with the utmost pain that the British Government has come to the conclusion that one last hope alone remains of averting the calamity which has so long impended over Europe.

It rests with the Government of Russia to determine whether that hope shall be realized or extinguished; for the British Government, having exhausted all the efforts of negotiation, is compelled to declare to the Cabinet of St. Petersburg, that if Russia should decline to restrict within purely diplomatic limits the discussion in which she has for some time past been engaged with the Sublime Porte, and does not, by return of the messenger who is the bearer of my present letter, announce her intention of causing the Russian troops under the orders of Prince Gortschakoff to commence their march with a view to recross the Pruth, so that the Provinces of Moldavia and Wallachia shall be completely evacuated on the 30th of April next, the British Government must consider the refusal or the silence of the Cabinet of St. Petersburg as equivalent to a declaration of war, and will take its measures accordingly.

The messenger who is the bearer of this letter to your Excellency is directed not to wait more than six days at St. Petersburg for your reply; and

I earnestly trust that he may convey to me an announcement on the part of the Russian Government that by the 30th of April next the Principalities will cease to be occupied by Russian forces. I have, etc.,

(Signed) CLARENDON.

---

## VI.

*Note respecting the torpor of the English Cabinet on the evening of the* 28*th of June*, 1854.

When a man has been set to sleep by a document, he commonly imagines that he was awake all the time, and that he "heard every word." A firm impression of that sort is one of the known phenomena of sleep in a chair; and it is obvious, therefore, that any of those who slept the sleep of which I have spoken may honestly contradict the statement in the text, without, however, being entitled to expect that their contradiction will have any weight. But, though the accuracy of the statement will be denied—and denied in perfect good faith—by those who slept, it will not, I am sure, be questioned by any of those who remained awake. Of course the deliberations of a Cabinet ought to be kept secret; but sleep is not deliberation, and there is no rule or principle which precludes a Minister from describing any natural phenomenon which he may have observed at a Cabinet meeting.

I own that to me the assenting disposition of those who remained awake (for they were anxious, careful, laborious men) is harder to account for than the condition of those who were in a complete state of rest; and I incline to the solution which I have spoken of as likely to be offered by the analytical chemist, because his theory (that of a narcotic substance having been taken by some mischance) would account for a torpor which affected all more or less, though in different ways and in different degrees.

That I am right in the view I take as to the inexorable stringency of the Dispatch, is shown, I think, clearly enough by the effect which it instantly had upon the minds of the two men who first saw it when it reached the camp—namely, Lord Raglan and Sir George Brown. Lord Raglan's letter of the 19th of July (p. 385) shows clearly that he submitted to act with soldierly readiness under instructions which he looked upon as imperative, or, at all events, violently cogent; and Sir George Brown gives his interpretation of the Dispatch (p. 381) with a bluntness which precludes all doubt about the light in which he regarded it. The Government, he considered, were resolved that at all hazards the expedition should proceed; and if Lord Raglan should not consent to lead it, he thought they would instantly send out some one else who would.

It may be said that this sleep of the Cabinet is one of those things which, however true they may be, it is better not to disclose. Certainly no one is obliged to go and state a thing thoughtlessly or without a purpose merely because it happened. But I have to account for a great transaction—the invasion of a Russian province. I ascertain that this invasion was caused, and caused entirely, by the peculiar wording of a dispatch. But why was it that a dispatch so worded received the approval or the tacit assent of a Cabinet? It would be unfaithful for me to stop short at that point in the chain of causation unless I were brought to a stop by the want of knowledge, or by the want of a right to disclose what I know. It so happens, however, that neither of these excuses is available to me. I know the truth, and I learned it under circumstances which gave me a full right to disclose it.

# VII.*

## CORRESPONDENCE RESPECTING THE PLACING OF THE BUOY BY THE FRENCH IN THE NIGHT BETWEEN THE 13TH AND 14TH OF SEPTEMBER.

### *First Letter.—Captain Mends on the subject of the Buoy.*

TO THE EDITOR OF THE 'TIMES.'

SIR,—May I ask the insertion in your columns of the following remarks? As I have been referred to by many as to the truth of Mr. Kinglake's statement, in his 'Invasion of the Crimea,' 'that the landing of our army 'at Old Fort was materially delayed by the willful misplacement of a buoy 'by the French,' I feel called upon, in justice to the French naval service, to state the facts which came under my own observation; and here I desire to observe that, during two years of very close intercourse with that service, their whole conduct, so far from being such as to bring our harmony into grievous jeopardy, was that of chivalrous, loyal allies.

As I am the officer who, by the direction of Sir Edmund Lyons, planned the whole of the details connected with the embarkation, transfer, and landing of the army, *it might suffice for me simply to say that I remember nothing about a buoy;* that Mr. Bower, the master of the 'Agamemnon,' who conned the ship under my orders, *remembers nothing about a buoy;* and that Captain Spratt (who then commanded the 'Spitfire,' and, as the senior surveying officer, was usually intrusted with such delicate and important duties) *remembers nothing about a buoy;* but I will not take upon myself to state positively that there was no buoy in question, as it is not impossible that Sir Edmund Lyons may have entered upon a confidential agreement with the French Admiral that the duty of placing a buoy on the coast selected by the Allied Admirals and Generals during the final reconnaissance on the 10th should be kept in the hands of the French, to be laid by them during the night preceding the landing, in order to prevent so significant a mark of the designed locality becoming known to the enemy; but it is passing strange that Sir Edmund Lyons, in whose confidence I was, and who had intrusted the whole of the arrangements to me, should have given me no instructions relative to it if he attached importance to it.

The 'Agamemnon,' having weighed from Eupatoria at 1 A.M., accompanied by the 'Sanspareil,' 'Triton,' and 'Spitfire,' and followed by all the transports, was the advance ship, by a long way, of the Allied flotilla. Sir Edmund Lyons, in his eager desire to be in the van, pushed on to the southward of the beach, behind which lay Lake Kamishli, the southernmost of the three lakes marked on the maps, until we arrived off the rocky headland lying between two shallow bays, within which lay the beaches, one having Lake Kamishli at the back of it (being that on which the British ultimately landed), the other and more southern beach (on which the French landed) having no lake behind it, and being circumscribed in its limits.

When off the Point, Sir Edmund Lyons, who was anxiously scanning the coast, desired me to stop the engines; while thus hove-to, with the ship's head brought round to the N.E., or in-shore, the French Admiral, heading his fleet, came up, and, passing close to us, hailed to say we were too far to

* The publication of the above correspondence as an 'Addendum' to the second volume takes place with the assent of Captain Mends. For the purpose of indicating passages which seem to me to be among the most important in regard to the question of fact, I have taken the liberty of causing some portions of Captain Mends's letters to be printed in italics.

the southward; upon which a conversation ensued between Sir Edmund Lyons and the French Admiral from the poops of their respective ships until the onward movement of the French ship terminated it, whereupon a French naval officer came on board immediately with a message from his Admiral to Sir E. Lyons to say that we were too far to the southward, the Point off which we then were being the line of demarcation between the armies. During this short suspense I called the attention of Sir Edmund to the approach of the transports, and pointed out that they would fall into confusion if he did not quickly decide upon his anchorage, as the 'Spit-'fire' and 'Triton,' the two steamers told off to anchor as the points within which our flotilla had been instructed to bring up, were looking to the 'Agamemnon' for position. Sir Edmund instantly gave me orders to steer back to the northward of the Point, and close in with the beach as near as possible. Meanwhile the 'Agamemnon's' boats had been hoisted out and the artillery rafts put together, so that on the moment of anchoring, which we did about half-past six, we were ready to commence the operation of landing, which Sir E. Lyons desired to do at once; but Sir George Brown, who was on board the 'Agamemnon,' wished to await the decision of Lord Raglan, who was approaching on board the 'Caradoc.' The French had by this time many men landed, for seeing no prospect of opposition they began to disembark as fast as their ships got to the anchorage. As soon as the 'Caradoc' closed, Lord Raglan came on board the 'Agamemnon,' and after a short consultation Sir Edmund Lyons desired me to make the signal to land, and we commenced immediately.* Thus it will be seen that the French were the cause of no serious delay, as British transports had never arrived at the Point, to the southward of which a buoy is said to have been placed. If the choosing of the beach was left in the hands of the French, they certainly gave us the advantage of position, our landing-place having the lake at the back, and being less circumscribed.

Had it been decided to land both armies in the bay selected by the French, the space on the beach would not have sufficed for the work, and serious confusion would have ensued, whilst the anchorage would have been too limited for the assembling of so many vessels.

I am, Sir, your obedient servant,

(Signed) W. R. MENDS, Captain, R.N.

United Service Club, Pall Mall,
March 18.

*Second Letter.—Mr. Kinglake to Captain Mends.*

12 St. James's Place, April 4, 1863.

SIR,—I have the honor to enclose an extract from that part of Lord Raglan's private letter to the Secretary of War which relates to the affair of 'the buoy.'

Since the appearance of your letter to the newspaper, you have probably received some communications on the subject; and if there be any thing in those communications, or in the enclosed extract from Lord Raglan's letter, which is calculated to modify the impression under which you thought it your duty to come forward and question my statement, I feel certain that you will take the course which your own sense of fairness must dictate.

I have the honor to be, Sir, your obedient humble servant,

(Signed) A. W. KINGLAKE.

CAPTAIN MENDS, R.N., etc., etc., etc.

* A careful reader will observe that all the movements backward and forward, and the conferences here described, are exactly such as might have been expected to occur upon the supposition that Lord Raglan's account, as given in the next page, is strictly accurate.

*Enclosure accompanying Mr. Kinglake's letter.*

INVASION OF THE CRIMEA.

*The placing of the Buoy by the French in the night between the 13th and 14th of September, 1854.*

Captain Mends having stated (in a letter which he thought proper to address to the editor of a newspaper) that he remembers nothing about a buoy, it may be convenient for readers of the book which was the subject of Captain Mends's remarks, to have before them the words in which Lord Raglan described the transaction.

Extract from Lord Raglan's Narrative of the Landing, addressed as a Private Communication to the Duke of Newcastle, the Secretary of War, and dated 'Camp above Old Fort Bay, September 18, 1854.'

'The disembarkation of both armies commenced on the morning of the '14th.

'It had been settled that the landing should be effected in Old Fort Bay, 'and that a buoy should be placed in the centre of it to mark the left of the 'French and the right of the English; but when the "Agamemnon" came 'upon the buoy at daylight, Sir Edmund Lyons found that the French naval 'officer had deposited it on the extreme northern end, and had thus en-'grossed the whole of the bay for the operation of his own army. This oc-'casioned considerable confusion and delay, the English convoy having fol-'lowed closely upon the steps of their leader, and got mixed with the 'French transports; but Sir Edmund Lyons wisely resolved to make the 'best of it, and at once ordered the troops to land in the bay next to the 'northward.'

*Third Letter.*—Captain Mends to Mr. Kinglake.*

3 Broomfield Crescent, Harrow Road, W.,
5th April, 1863.

SIR,—In reply to your communication of the 4th instant, enclosing an extract from Lord Raglan's private letter to the Secretary of War, which relates to the affair of the 'buoy,' I have the honor to acquaint you that, since writing my letter to the *Times* of the 18th ult., I have heard nothing which is calculated to modify the impression under which I wrote it; for though *it would seem there was a buoy*, and though I differ from Lord Raglan, whose memory I so highly respect, I aver that not the slightest inconvenience, confusion, or delay, was occasioned to the disembarkation of the British by any act of the French. I never heard of the buoy until I saw your book; and I feel satisfied that were Sir Edmund Lyons alive, he would be one of the first to do justice to the chivalrous conduct of his colleague, Admiral Bruat, whose heart and soul were in the success of the undertaking, and whose example was cordially followed by every officer under his command; that, *in my opinion, wherever the buoy was placed, none but the most upright motives prompted the act*, and the most sound practical reasons warranted the selection of the spot.

I have the honor to be, Sir, your obedient humble servant,

(Signed) W. R. MENDS.

A. W. KINGLAKE, Esq., M.P., etc., etc., etc.

* It seems right to say that this copy has been carefully compared with the original, and found to be strictly correct. In the original, the words 'by any act of the French' are underscored.

## VIII.

*Note respecting the operations of the 7th Fusileers.*

Written, it would seem, with the help of information deriving from Sir George Brown,* the *Quarterly Review* has this statement:—

'While this was going on upon the left of Codrington's brigade, the 'right, consisting of the 33rd and 7th, gallantly attacked the Russian infantry 'which protected the battery and the Redan. The battle was not fought, 'however, as Mr. Kinglake would have us believe. Lacy Yea and his 'gallant Fusileers did just as well, but not one whit better, than Colonel 'Blake and his equally gallant 33rd. The personal exploits of Lacy Yea, 'Mr. Kinglake's particular protégé, are about as authentic as those of 'Homer's heroes, and so is the long fight maintained by him and his men 'against five or six times their number of Russian troops. The two regi-'ments went forward together, Codrington leading them on.† They drove 'back the Russians and planted themselves on the brow of the height, from 'which the enemy retired; and they remained there, partially engaged, till 'the Russians rallied and advanced to recover the Redan. Symptoms of 'unsteadiness then began to show themselves, and no wonder. A mass of 'Russian troops came toward them in front. They saw their comrades 'driven out of the Redan upon their left; they distrusted their own ability 'to keep the advanced position which they had won, and *they wavered.* 'Sir George Brown observed this from the point where he was, trying to 'rally the 19th and 23rd in their retreat: *he rode over to the height and did 'his best to stop the 33rd and 7th; but they would not attend to him.* It has 'been said that a bugle sounding the retreat misled them. For this the 'evidence is, to say the least of it, very incomplete; but whether by sound 'of bugle or not, *they turned round and moved back*, slowly and doggedly, 'just as the Grenadier Guards came upon the ground and were formed and 'ready for action.

'Having opened *to let the 7th and 33rd pass*, the Grenadiers re-formed line 'and advanced against the Russian columns in their immediate front. Sir 'George Brown went with the Grenadier Guards.'—'Quarterly Review,' No. 226, p. 566.

Thus, according to Sir George Brown and the *Quarterly*, the 7th Fusileers and the 33rd Regiment advanced side by side up the slope, attacked 'the Russian infantry which protected the battery and the Redan,' and obtained a temporary success, but then, under pressure of an advancing column, 'wavered,' and fell back,—fell back in such a state that, when the divisional General tried to stop them, 'they would not attend to him,' and, continuing to fall back, retreated through the Grenadier Guards.

On the other hand, my statement is that Lacy Yea and his 7th Fusileers did not move up at all with the rest of the brigade to the line of the Great Redoubt, because, at the very moment of ascending the river's bank, they encountered a heavy Russian column, with which they remained long engaged; that, at last, they defeated the column; and that, when they had done so, Sir Thomas Troubridge was sent to suggest that the enemy's retreat should be pressed by an advance of the Grenadier Guards.

Now, of these perfectly dissimilar accounts, which is the true one?

Without referring to the means by which (as a sagacious reader will infer)

* The grounds on which I infer this will be found at the commencement of Note X. *post*, p. 689.

† This was a mistake of Sir George's. Codrington was not with the 7th Fusileers. He, as we saw, led the 23rd, and the other troops with them, straight into the redoubt.

I gathered my first impressions of what the battalion did, I must say, in the outset, that at the battle of the Alma Sir Thomas Troubridge was a field-officer, on duty with the right wing of the regiment; that, from the beginning to the end of the engagement between the 7th Fusileers and the column, he, Sir Thomas Troubridge, was personally present; that he witnessed the defeat of the column with his own eyes; that he himself carried the message which suggested that the Grenadier Guards should advance in pursuit; that he, Sir Thomas Troubridge, is living—is living in London and holding office at the Horse-Guards; and, finally, that he has over and over again assured me of the substantial truth of my narrative so far as it concerns what he saw of the operations of the 7th Fusileers.

Colonel Yea did not live to hear it imputed to his 7th Fusileers,—to hear it imputed to them by their divisional General,—that they had given way at the sight of an enemy's column, and had retreated in such a state that they 'would not attend to him;' but some of Lacy Yea's simple, truthful letters have been laid before me.

In a letter addressed to Lord Vivian, and dated the 27th of September, 1854, Lacy Yea describes the passage of the river at the Alma, and then writes:—'I had to deal with the 32nd Regiment*—I should suppose of 'some distinction, as they wore Wellington boots, pulled high up over their 'trowsers, and grand-looking helmets, and had kits which were beautiful, 'and which my men eagerly put on; there was not one of them who 'would not have made a front rank for me. One of the men said they had 'been marched from Moscow, through Odessa, here. . . . There was 'an unlucky check in the 23rd, which caused a similar retrograde in their 'supporters, the Fusileer Guards, which cost an enormity of lives in both 'regiments. *I never stopped until we drove our birds clean off the ground,* 'having commenced with them after emerging from the deep banks of the 'river, within fifteen yards of their skirmishers.'

Shortly afterward, Colonel Yea wrote to his sister, Mrs. Cholmley Dering:—

'Jeffries being ordered home suddenly, I take the opportunity of sending 'you, to take care of, a helmet ornament belonging to one of the regiments '(Russian) to which my regiment was opposed at Alma. It was the sharp-'shooters belonging to that regiment, which I found within fifteen yards 'when I rode up the bank out of the river. *We—that is, the 7th—were sole-'ly engaged against this regiment without help, and a pretty thrashing we gave 'them.*'

Colonel Aldworth writes the following letter to Sir Thomas Troubridge:—

'May 3, 1863.

'My dear Sir Thomas,—I write in reply to your inquiry as to what oc-'curred on the right of the 7th Royal Fusileers at the Battle of the Alma, 'after crossing the river.

'I was, as you know, in command of the right company of the regiment, 'and can confidently state that the right wing of the regiment *did not at 'any time fall back.* We were opposed to a heavy Russian column, *which 'had come down the hill and halted in our immediate front,* throwing out nu-'merous skirmishers. The Guards did not pass us *until this column had 'turned, and was in full retreat.* I can not say much about the left wing, 'having seen but little of it during the engagement, owing to the smoke, and 'my position on the extreme right. Yours sincerely,

(Signed) 'R. W. ALDWORTH, Col.,
'Lt.-Col. Commanding 1st Battalion
'7th Royal Fusileers.'

* Two battalions of the Kazan corps. Their accoutrements were marked '32nd.'

Of Colonel Aldworth Sir Thomas Troubridge thus writes:—'The steadi-'ness with which the men held their ground on the right, under a very 'heavy fire, was in great measure due to the example and coolness of this 'officer.'

Nor is it only from the officers of the 7th Fusileers that the proof of what the battalion did at the Alma is to be found. The regiment next on the right of Colonel Lacy Yea's Fusileers was the 55th. The 55th was commanded at the Alma by Colonel, now General, Warren. In a memorandum by him, now lying before me, there is this passage:—

'Sir John [Pennefather] allowed the 55th Regiment to follow Colonel 'Warren, who crossed the river and formed the regiment in line under the 'cover of a spur of the heights of the Alma, up which they advanced in 'line (Major-General Pennefather leading in front the battalion which was 'parallel to the Alma); then, having ascended this spur, they formed them-'selves in presence of a column of Russians who fired into them. This col-'umn of Russians *was at that time engaged with a part of the Light Division* '*under Colonel Yea*, and the 55th were directed by their Colonel to bring for-'ward their right shoulders and make a wheel to the left. . . . With 'this accession to Colonel Yea's force, *the Russians in a short time disappear*-'*ed*, leaving many on the ground.'

A writer, who seems to have inquired a good deal about what was passing at the time when Sir George Brown imagined that the 7th Fusileers 'would not attend to him,' has undertaken the somewhat intricate task of showing how Sir George Brown fell into his error. He thus writes:—

'But we are not only able to free the 7th Fusileers from the effects of Sir 'George Brown's wondrous narrative. We can do more: we can explain to 'Sir George Brown how it was that—honestly, quite honestly—he fell into 'his error. Mr. Kinglake states that, when the 7th Fusileers had defeated 'the left Kazan column, it was not thought wise for the victors to advance 'in pursuit themselves, but to leave that duty to the Grenadier Guards. 'The 7th Fusileers, therefore, at the moment of its victory, remained halted. 'Mr. Kinglake also represents that the defeat of this left Kazan column 'took place "nearly at the very time when disaster befell the centre of the '"brigade of Guards."—(Page 567, first edition.) Attention to this, re-en-'forced by information from officers present, soon discloses the cause of Sir 'George Brown's mistake. In their retreat, some of the Fusileer Guards 'passed through the left companies of the 7th, and these companies becom-'ing entangled with the defeated soldiery, and having on their left front a 'fresh, a heavy, and a victorious column of the enemy's infantry (the Vladi-'mirs), were far from being in a state for any aggressive movement, and 'were in great need of the support which they got when the Grenadiers 'passed through them. It was from what he saw there—from what he saw 'at the extreme left of the regiment—that Sir George Brown formed the 'notion which he has imparted to the *Quarterly*. If he had ridden along 'the line to Lacy Yea's right wing, he would have seen that, notwithstand-'ing the critical state of its left companies, the regiment (taken as a whole) 'was almost in the very moment of achieving its final victory over the left 'Kazan column. If he had stooped to the use of a glass, and had conde-'scended to recognize for a moment the existence of one of Evans's bat-'talions, he would have seen the Kazan column slowly retiring, and would 'have been surprised to observe that, on ground where he imagined there 'were none but his own Light Division regiment, Colonel Warren, with his '55th, was not only well in advance, but had wheeled on his left, and was 'pouring his fire into the flank of the enemy's column. Far from doing 'this, and far from informing himself of the truth by subsequent inquiry,

'Sir George Brown has remained for nearly nine years under the impres-'sion produced on his mind by a glance at the extreme left of the 7th; and 'because at this time he saw the 33rd and the 7th close together, and in 'nearly the same line, he seems to have inferred that from first to last they 'had been acting together.'—Pamphlet by an 'Old Reviewer,' published by Harrison, Pall Mall.

---

# IX.

*Note respecting the operations of the Scots Fusileer Guards at the Battle of the Alma.*

Just as in the corner of a sheet containing the delineation of a whole kingdom, some city or district which forms a part of it is often set out upon a scale more extended than the one that is used for the principal map, so here I am going to record what I judge to be the result of the late discussion about the Fusileer Guards, by repeating the narrative of their operations after passing the Alma, but repeating it with rather more minuteness of detail than readers will find in the text.

We saw that, at the time of passing the river, the left-flank company got parted from the rest of the battalion. That separation lasted during the period of the struggle which followed; and when, therefore, in this Note, I speak of the Scots Fusileer Guards in general terms, it must be understood that I mean to designate that body of seven companies which remained together, when the left-flank company had got parted from the rest of the battalion.

At the moment when the troops which had stormed the redoubt began to retreat, the 1st Division had not yet emerged from the cover afforded by the river's bank; but General Codrington's message hurried the advance of the Scots Fusileer Guards. The battalion climbed up the bank, formed line with a good deal of haste, and began to move forward.

At this time, there were numbers of stragglers of the Light Division standing about near the bank of the river; but in front of the left centre of the Fusileer Guards there was a large disordered body (men chiefly, I believe, of the 23rd and 95th Regiments), who had just let go their hold of the redoubt. These men had faced about to the front, and were firing in the direction of the great column of the Vladimir corps then halted within the redoubt. The moment the heads of the Fusileer Guards rose clear of the ground which till then had been giving them shelter, the men found themselves under a flight of the enemy's missiles, and the higher they marched, the more they incurred the fire which seemed to be directed against the light-infantry men in their front. Many of the Fusileer Guards were struck down. Still, their onward movement was maintained.

Suddenly, the parapet of the redoubt became thickly lined with Russian soldiery; and, in the next instant, the fire of the enemy's musketry came heavily pouring down into the confused body of light-infantry men who had been hitherto making a stand in front of the Fusileer Guards. The crowd of light-infantry men which received this fire gave way; and in another instant it was coming down in a mass toward the left centre of the Fusileer Guards. Perhaps the haste with which the Fusileer Guards had been pushed forward was one of the causes which hindered them from meeting the emergency by a fitting manœuvre. It does not appear that any step was taken to make the battalion open out. So, presently, the descending crowd came into bodily contact with the Fusileer Guards; and this so heavily, that the crowd broke through a great part of the left wing of the advancing battalion. The weight of the retreating throng at that one spot was so great and so unwieldly, that a soldier of the Scots Fusileer Guards was thrown, it is said, to the ground with such force as to break his ribs. The part of the Scots Fusileer Guards which had thus been thrust out of line by physical pressure was, of course, in a state of confusion.

The remnant of the battalion thus maimed was, at the moment, without support; for, directly in its rear, there were no formed troops coming on; and of the two battalions on its right hand and its left, neither one nor the other had hitherto come up abreast of it. On the other hand, the force which our Fusileer Guards undertook to attack was that majestic Vladimir column which had just been defeating Sir George Brown. With a strength of no more than perhaps some four or five hundred men, the remnant of what had been the centre battalion of the brigade of Guards was advancing all alone, not merely against a breastwork thick lined with Russian soldiery, but also against a hitherto victorious column which was nearly 3000 strong. Still, the maimed battalion pushed on; but by this time it had so far lost its symmetry that it had come to be, as it were, two sides of a triangle—two sides of a triangle whereof the salient pointed straight to the front. At the foremost point or apex thus formed, Lindsay was carrying the Queen's color; and it would seem that the swiftness of his onward movement, and the eagerness of those who were near him to keep up with the color, may have been the cause which refracted the line. There was a good deal of impetuosity at this time, and it would seem that the conception of what was the needful thing to do was—not so much to labor after the restoration of complete order, but rather—to carry the redoubt, and break down the great column by a rush; for in the midst of such shouts as 'For-'ward, Guards! Forward, Guards!'—Hugh Annesley was heard cheering thus—the bent and irregular line pressed on; and in a few moments it had got so far up the slope as to be within some thirty or forty yards of the work. Then numbers of the Russians burst out over the parapet, and some, it is said, came straight on, with their bayonets down 'at the charge.' The Queen's color was in danger; for it was not to be imagined that these few companies of the Fusileer Guards could maintain themselves long against the overwhelming weight of the column in their front. But the immediate cause which brought about the retreat was, after all, the word of command. I believe that the order to retire which was now about to reach the battalion was given by the authority of General Henry Bentinck, the officer commanding the brigade. It was delivered to the line by the Adjutant of the Fusileer Guards. With pistol in hand—for some of the Russian soldiery were coming close down—Drummond, the Adjutant of the battalion, rode up, and gave the order to retire. By these words, as I gather, the battalion was stopped; but it did not instantly obey the command to retire. There was a reluctance to fall back; and it would seem that the feeling which caused this reluctance was not altogether a false instinct; for, however imperative the necessity for retreating may have been, the order had come too late to avert the impending disaster; and it is likely enough that, being, as they were, in the close presence of a powerful enemy, our men may have fancied there must needs be some mistake in an order which directed them to go about at a moment when no due arrangements had been made for covering the retreat. Be this as it may, the Adjutant (as it was his duty to do) repeated the order. It seems he repeated it thrice; and the last time he was no longer content to say, 'The battalion will retire!' for he told it with force that it 'must.'

I know of no means that were taken for covering the retreat. If any were tried, they failed; for, the moment the battalion obeyed the word of command, it lapsed into a state of disorder, and then fell back in confusion. Seeing this, the soldiery thrown out by the Russians in advance of their great column pushed forward with increasing boldness, and the Queen's color was now in greater danger than ever. But borne by a resolute officer, and surrounded by resolute men, it was guarded with care to the last, and kept safe from the enemy's touch.* At one moment, the foremost of the assailants were so close, that a soldier of the Fusileer Guards received a wound in the hand from a bayonet. It was then that the Fusileer Guards suffered the chief part of their losses.† By its retreat, the battalion seemed, as it were, to draw the enemy forward; for the great Vladimir column, which had hitherto stood halted within the redoubt, now broke out over the parapet, and began to glide down the slope. For a little while, the column went on in pursuit; but then (as is shown in the text) it was checked, and brought to a halt by the advance of the Grenadier Guards.

For some time a great part of the Fusileer Guards remained in confusion on the lower part of the slope; but Dalrymple's, and also, I think, Jocelyn's companies, were rallied so quickly as to be enabled to partake of the fight which engaged the Grenadier Guards; and, before long, the main part of the battalion had not only been re-formed in advance of the road running parallel with the river, but was briskly resuming its place in the centre of the brigade of Guards.‡

* It was for his resolute defense of the color at this juncture that Lindsay received the Victoria Cross.

† The casualties are given in the text; but (because the statement tends to confirm, in some points, the account I have given) I will here show the number of casualties which occurred among the non-commissioned officers and men of each company:

| | |
|---|---|
| No. 1 Company | 18 |
| No. 2 do. | 25 |
| No. 3 do. | 17 |
| No. 4 do. | 23 |
| No. 5 do. | 33 |
| No. 6 do. | 25 |
| No. 7 do. | 19 |
| No. 8 do. | 6 |

‡ It would seem as though this were meant to be denied by the journal which follows Sir George Brown's impressions; for the *Quarterly Review* has these words:—'The Fusileer 'Guards rushed forward to take the Redan, but failed. Some of them got up to the parapet 'and clung to it, but not a man entered the work, while the great body, retreating, got in-'termixed with the 23rd Regiment, *along with whom they lay down behind the broken* '*bank, from which it was found impossible for a considerable space of time to move them.*' And also: 'The *Coldstreams* took their place on the *left of the Grenadiers*' [the place properly belonging to the Scots Fusileers], 'and shared in the battle. But the battle was already 'dying out.'—No. 226, p. 567. I can hardly imagine that the statement really intended to be made is such as the words seem to import; and until it is repeated in plainer terms, and supported by the testimony of some officer present at the time, I need not, I think, do more than say that, according to the Report of H.R.H. the Duke of Cambridge, the Scots Fusileer Guards re-formed 'with *the greatest alacrity*' (Holograph Report by H.R.H., now lying before me); and that, according to the Report of General Henry Bentinck (Holograph Report, also before me), the battalion, after having 'retired for a short time, re-formed, and *return-* '*ed to its post*.'

## X.

*Note respecting the theory that it was Sir George Brown who caused the Grenadier Guards to enter the Great Redoubt at the Alma.*

It would be perverse to disturb the wholesome privilege of anonymous publication by saying in print, and on the faith of common rumor, or even of sound external evidence, that such or such a paper was written by such or such a man. But, in order to the enjoyment of the privilege, the writing must not be so worded as to force the reader to perceive its source. It must not show by its tenor that it comes from any given man. The moment it does so, it speaks with all the weight of the informant whose guidance it discloses, and then, of course, the shield being dropped, people may either bend under the authority of the personage thus thrust upon the public attention, or else take leave to deal with him as though he were the avowed author of assertions which are nominally, not really, anonymous.

Now the *Quarterly Review* has given so minute an account of where Sir George Brown was riding on the day of the Alma, and of what he saw, and of how he reasoned, and of how he conferred, and how he advised, that an uninspired writer could hardly have learned so much unless he derived his knowledge with more or less directness from Sir George Brown himself. Either, therefore, such an account must be a fiction, or else it must be based upon instructions directly or indirectly obtained from Sir George Brown; and, the notion of treating it as a fiction being forbidden by the respectable character of the publication, it follows that the *Quarterly's* account of Sir George Brown's actions comes upon the world with all the weight and authority of Sir George Brown himself.

Again, and still without listening to a word of rumor, I can produce a clew which shall very soon trace to Sir George Brown one of the most striking of the assertions put forward by the *Quarterly Review*. In flat contradiction to the written narratives of Lord Raglan, of General Evans, and of General Pennefather, and setting at naught the belief which I conceive to be unquestioned in the whole English army by any number greater than one, the *Quarterly Review* has undertaken to say that Sir George Brown, with Codrington's brigade, 'filled the whole mouth of the Pass extending 'on both sides of the Eupatoria road,'—in other words, that it filled the whole of that very ground on which the world believed that—not Brown, but—Evans, with Pennefather's brigade, had fought a hard fight.

Now perhaps we might get at the authority which supported the Reviewers in making this strange assertion, if only we could find out the name of the man in the English army who sincerely believed it to be true. I can help the search. It so happens that that very notion of Sir George Brown's having filled the whole mouth of the Pass with his 1st brigade was entertained by Sir George Brown himself. It was one of the most curious and interesting parts of the dream that was dreamed by Sir George on the day of the Alma. That he did truly believe this (incredible as it may seem) I know from his own official, but hitherto unpublished, Report now lying before me, in his own handwriting, and dated the 23rd of September, 1854. The very belief so strangely entertained by Sir George Brown in September, 1854, is not only adopted in its entirety by the writer of April, 1863, but is repeated in almost the same words. The two statements shall stand side by side:—

| SIR GEORGE BROWN. | THE 'QUARTERLY REVIEW.' |
|---|---|
| 'My first brigade itself' [Codrington's brigade] 'completely filled the whole mouth of 'the gorge or valley through which the road 'runs.'—MS. unpublished Report of 23rd September, 1854, in the handwriting of Sir George Brown. | 'General Codrington's brigade (the right 'brigade of the Light Division) filled the whole 'mouth of the Pass, extending on both sides 'of the Eupatoria road.'—'Quarterly Review,' No. 226, p. 560. |

Even if that curious statement by Sir George Brown had chanced to be one that can be assented to by mankind in general, the recurrence of it in words so closely similar to his would have warranted a surmise that the two sentences may have had a common origin; but supposing it to appear that the statement first made and afterward recurring was a sheer mistake, surmise would change into proof. If an author were to state in his book that the Allies at Waterloo were commanded by the Duke of Wellington, no one would be able to detect in such an assertion the guidance of another man's mind, because the similarity of the statement to any older one of the same import is sufficiently accounted for by the fact that both are true; but if we were to find an old number of the *Quarterly Review* asserting, and asserting in earnest, that the Allies at Waterloo were commanded by the Prince Regent of England in person, we should instantly see that, whoever might be the nominal propounder of such a statement, its real and virtual author was the late King George the Fourth—the one man who believed it to be true. So, when it is remembered that this statement of Sir George Brown's is very wide of what other people believe, the adoption of the belief in a later writing gives proof, irresistibly cogent, that both statements were the offspring of the same honest, erring mind.

I must add, that even if Sir George Brown had been able to say that he never made any direct communication to any body at all connected with the *Quarterly Review*, his assertion, though carrying, of course, the most perfect conviction of its truth, would still fall short of what is needed for disentangling him; because it so happens that, before the publication of the *Review*, Sir George Brown thought it right to circulate a MS. (authenticated by his initials) in which he gave his version of the part he sincerely believed he had taken in the Battle of the Alma. Sir George can not know, nor even, perhaps, believe, that the MS. thus circulating did not fall into the hands of an admirer, who saw in it a treasure of historic proof, took it straight to the managers of the *Quarterly Review*, and caused them to fancy it must be accurate by showing that it was really genuine.

Thus, then, I am obliged to connect Sir George Brown with the account which is given of his actions in the *Quarterly Review*. For some little time, indeed, after the appearance of the Reviewers' narrative, it seemed possible that something might be written or said which would relieve me from the necessity of treating Sir George Brown as the person to be refuted. Sir George, one imagined, might perhaps take some means of declaring that the Reviewers had made an inaccurate use of their instructions. But time has rolled on; and at length it can be said (in defense of the *Review*, though in aggravation of the responsibility which is attaching upon Sir George Brown), that Sir George has allowed three months to pass away without publicly repudiating the curious statement which his organ lately gave to the world. Of course, a man is not in general to be held answerable for acquiescing in the accounts which strangers, deriving no information from himself, may choose to give of his actions; but I have shown, I think, that Sir George and the *Quarterly* can not stand thus clear asunder; and when we find, first, that Sir George Brown has circulated a MS. containing an account of what he imagines he saw, and what he imagines he did, at the Battle of the Alma; next, that one of the mistaken statements adopted by the *Review* was addressed by Sir George Brown in his own handwriting to the English head-quarters; next, that the *Review* (a publication of unimpeached respectability) is so worded as to all but disclose its informant; next, that having thus displayed its title to be deemed authentic, the *Review* proceeds to attribute to Sir George Brown a series of striking achievements; and that, finally, after an interval of three months, Sir George Brown allows a fresh number of the *Review* to appear without a word of disavowal or modest remonstrance,* then, I think, we can hardly fail to see that the narrative given by the *Review* acquires the kind of interest which belongs to autobiography. We recur to the pages; and whenever we can find the name of 'Sir George Brown,' we put in before it the significant 'Ego,' which gives an interesting, nay, an almost humorous, authenticity to the whole story. Whether the story be true or not, that is another question; and, to solve it, one may be obliged to compare Sir George Brown's impressions (as indeed shall be presently done) with the impressions of other people; but until Sir George Brown shall come forward and impute to the journal which reproduces his ideas an erroneous use of the information supplied to it, one is warranted in attributing the kind of authenticity above pointed out to every thing concerning Sir George which the *Quarterly Review* has narrated. Add to this great merit of 'authenticity' the well-known fact that Sir George Brown's honor and truthful intent are above the reach of all cavil, and then we come to understand the kind of interest which attaches to the Reviewers' story. Then, as we light upon each shining deed ascribed to Sir George Brown, we are able to say,—'This is in-'deed curious. True or not, here is a story which is really believed to be 'true by the very officer—a General of Division—who is represented to have 'been the principal actor—nay, rather, to have been the almost sole actor—'in these stirring scenes. No doubt this is all very new. No doubt there 'are many who think that Lord Raglan, the Commander of the Forces, had 'something to do with governing the issue of the battle. Perhaps, also, 'General Evans may still persist in maintaining that he existed on the day 'of the Alma; nay, that he fought a hard fight on that day, and lost the 'fourth of a brigade upon ground which Sir George Brown declares to have 'been wholly occupied by himself.† Again, the 7th Fusileers may main-'tain that, almost at the moment when, according to the recipient of Sir 'George Brown's ideas, they neglected to "attend to" Sir George,‡ and, on 'the contrary, "turned round and moved back,"§ they (the 7th Fusileers) 'were not only standing fast, but were in the very act of defeating a Rus-'sian column. Again, those who knew the worth of Colonel Hood may im-'agine that, in the crisis of the fight, he and his Grenadier Guards must 'have known how to find the redoubt without the guidance or "request"‖

* This circumstance leads me to infer that the Reviewers may have followed Sir George's instructions with a more confiding exactness than I ventured to believe probable when I wrote the foot-note at p. 588 (See Notes to Fourth Edition).

† 'My 1st brigade itself *completely filled the whole mouth of the gorge or valley through* '*which the road runs.*'—(Holograph Report, now before me, by Sir George Brown.) The ground thus described as '*completely filled*' by Sir George's troops was exactly that on which Evans was operating with Pennefather's brigade. In this Holograph Report of the 22nd of September, 1854, Evans says that he operated with four of his regiments and one of his batteries '*to the left of the conflagration*, to endeavor to force by that direction *the* '*passage of the river and the bridge*;' and Lord Raglan, in his published Report, spoke of Pennefather's brigade as '*connected with the right of the Light Division*,' an expression which exactly confirms Evans's statement. General Pennefather writes to the same effect. So does General Warren. I never heard the name of any man except Sir George Brown who imagined that his, Sir George's, right brigade 'filled the whole mouth of the gorge.'

‡ *Quarterly Review*, No. 226, p. 566. § Ibid. ‖ Ibid. p. 567.

'of Sir George Brown. Yet again, the friends of the Duke of Cambridge 'may continue to think that His Royal Highness brought up the Cold-'stream from the river's bank a good bit before the "dying out" of the 'battle,* and that he did this without waiting to be "briefly conferred '"with"† by Sir George Brown. Yet again, the Scots Fusileer Guards 'may deny that "they lay down behind the broken bank, from which it '"was found impossible, for a considerable space of time, to remove them," 'and may maintain that, even if Sir George Brown did really assume the 'practical command of the Guards by "requesting" and "briefly confer-'ring," he could not have placed the Coldstream in the interval "on the '"left of the Grenadiers,"‡ because (after the temporary check which they 'had undergone) they, the Scots Fusileer Guards, were swift to resume their 'place in the centre of the brigade. Finally, the men of the Highland 'Brigade may maintain that, instead of coming up only "just in time" to 'see the Russians "in full flight,"§ they did really engage in that "stub-'"born" contest with the enemy's columns, which their chief, Sir Colin 'Campbell, described and officially reported the second day after the battle.‖ 'People may say all these things. They may labor to maintain that Sir 'George Brown must have been mistaken, and that he could not have really 'performed the achievements which his admiring *Quarterly* attributes to 'him; but whether Sir George performed them or not, there remains this 'curious and interesting fact—he sincerely believes that he did.'

Such being the kind of interest, if not actual importance, which attaches to the account of the battle as given in the *Quarterly Review*, it would seem that, at worst, I am erring on the safe side when I not only treat it as serious, but quote, and refute its statements.

But now for the passage which is to be the special subject of comment in this Note. After having stated (in a passage before quoted, Appendix, Note VIII.) that two of the regiments of Sir George Brown's Division persisted in retreating, notwithstanding Sir George's efforts to prevent them, also that they would not 'attend to him,' and that they 'turned round and moved 'back'**—the *Review* goes on:—'Having opened to let the 7th and 33rd 'pass, the Grenadiers re-formed line, and advanced against the Russian 'columns in their immediate front. *Sir George Brown went with the Gren-'adier Guards;* and when they arrived abreast of Redan, he *requested the 'commander of the battalion to detach a party from his left and to reoccupy that 'work.*'

Now, Sir George Brown commanded the Light Division—the Division which, under his guidance, had had the misfortune to be defeated;†† and he had no authority over the Grenadiers, or any other of the regiments belonging to the 1st Division. Yet the theory is, that Sir George abandoned his troops—troops said to be in such a state that they 'would not attend to 'him'—and that, joining himself to a regiment with which he had nothing to do, and imagining his judgment to be more sound or more swift than that of Colonel Hood (Colonel Hood was one of the very ablest of the officers then serving with the English army), he took upon himself to 'request' the Colonel to reoccupy the redoubt. This story, of course, supposes that,

* *Quarterly Review*, No. 226, p. 567.
† Ibid.; and see the next Note (VI.) of this Appendix.
‡ *Quarterly Review*, No. 226, p. 567.
§ Ibid.
‖ MS. Report now before me, signed 'C. Campbell.'
** *Quarterly Review*, No. 226, p. 566.
†† The only regiment of Sir George Brown's which did not undergo defeat was the 7th Fusileers, and Sir George had so little to do with the victorious fight which rendered the fate of that regiment an exception to the fate of the Division, that until this summer he did not even believe in it; and but for me, I imagine, he would hardly have known it now.

taken as a body, the battalion of the Grenadier Guards moved up in a direction which brought it clear of the redoubt, and that it continued its advance without marching through the work; for, otherwise, it could not have been said that the recapture of the redoubt was effected by a request 'to *detach* a 'party' for the purpose. So, if I show that the advancing battalion marched up right through the redoubt, there at once is an end of the story which seeks to mutilate my account of Colonel Hood's achievement by ascribing the recapture of the work to Sir George Brown.

Now, as it happens, I can not only prove that the advancing line of the Grenadier Guards marched bodily through the redoubt, but am even enabled to show the exact point in the line of the battalion which impinged upon the howitzer then remaining within the work. Writing on another question, and before this theory about Sir George Brown and the redoubt had been propounded to the world, Colonel Percy (who commanded at the Alma the left-flank company of the Grenadier Guards) addressed to me a letter, of which the following is an extract:—

'With regard to the gun in the redoubt, *the right of the 8th company and 'the left of the 7th company, in advancing, were exactly opposite to the gun.* I 'halted my men about five paces off the rampart for fear of there being 'some mine, [and] clambered over, *aiding myself by the gun.* Colonel 'Pakenham, since killed, clambered over at the same moment, and scratch-'ed the number of the company (No. 7) on the carriage with his sword, say-'ing to me afterward (almost directly) "that he had done so that the gun '"might not be claimed by others." I replied, "I wished I had thought '"of doing so too." As the Russians had left the gun after the repulse of 'the first line, the gun was clearly the prize of the Grenadier Guards.'

Again, Sir Charles Russell was another of the officers of the Grenadier Guards who was with the left-flank company of the battalion; and I find that, in the admirably clear private journal which he has been so kind as to intrust to me, there is contained this passage:—'The gallant Light Di-'vision, quite cut up, were falling back upon us, and impeding our fire, 'but still we moved steadily toward the battery. The Fusileers on our left 'received a partial check, and (the colors and a few men of the 95th having 'formed on our left) *we entered the battery close to the brass gun, and poor 'Pakenham made a mark on it as he passed.** We still pushed on, and it was 'not till the hurried retreat of the enemy put them beyond the reach of our 'Miniés, that we halted. Too much can not be said of Colonel Hood's gal-'lantry; and by his admirable coolness and unerring judgment he took his 'regiment through action as few have done.'

These narratives of Colonel Percy and Sir Charles Russell are accounts —not of what happened to any detached 'party,' but—of the advance of that superb and unbroken line of the Grenadier Guards, whereof their company formed the left;† and unless these two officers were under some delusion,—some delusion strangely common to both—nay, common, I am sure, to every survivor of the battalion,—the notion of Sir George Brown's having recaptured the redoubt, by causing Colonel Hood to 'detach a party' for the purpose, must be looked upon, either as the mistake of Reviewers straying loose from Sir George's guidance, though their words all but purport to follow it, or else as the genuine production of a mind much confused, which refracted the lights it received, and connected its impressions of what went on at the Alma with wrong people, wrong times, and wrong places.

* Pakenham, as we before saw, was with the 7th Company.

† Sir Charles Russell has been so good as to assure me once again, both orally and in writing, that at the Alma the line of the Grenadier Guards 'was never broken, either by 'detaching companies or otherwise.'

I will add (though, after the proofs I have given, it is hardly worth while to do so), that neither in Colonel Hood's private journal, nor in any of his letters known to his family, is there any, the least, mention either of his having received any 'request' or other communication from Sir George Brown, or of his having recaptured the redoubt by detaching 'a party' for the purpose.

Of course, when one sees a man of Sir George Brown's unquestioned honor and truthfulness submitting to have it said of him—and that by what would seem to be his own chosen organ of publicity—that it was he who taught Colonel Hood and his Grenadier Guards the way to retake the redoubt, one strains after some counter-theory that will account for an honest mistake. The very best counter-theory I can frame for the purpose has the fault of being weak and far-fetched; but, weak and far-fetched as it is, I offer it to the attention of Sir George Brown.

Long after the recapture of the redoubt, and when the Grenadier Guards were far in advance of the work, it occurred to some officers in the regiment (who were anxious that their corps should not lose its fairly-won trophy) to send back a man—not a 'party'—with directions to stand sentry over the brass howitzer then remaining within the redoubt. After a moment's hesitation, Colonel Hood acceded to the suggestion, and a man—he volunteered for the service—went back and stood sentry over the howitzer.

Now, supposing that Sir George Brown imagined the redoubt to be before him instead of behind him; that, being unacquainted with the actual state of the battle, he believed the already recaptured redoubt to be still awaiting recapture; and, finally, that he was anxious to put Colonel Hood in the way of effecting an operation which had been performed some minutes before—then the fact of a man having been really sent back to look after the howitzer, and so, in a sense, to 'reoccupy' the empty redoubt, would be enough to supply that small element of truth which is conducive—nay, almost necessary—to the growth of a modern fable.

Be this as it may, I must persist in asking my countrymen to believe that the recapture of the Great Redoubt was effected—not by a 'party' detached from Colonel Hood's regiment at the 'request' of Sir George Brown, but—by a self-sufficing chief and an undivided battalion—by Colonel Hood, advancing in person at the head of his Grenadier Guards.

---

## XI.

*Note respecting the statement in the text that 'the Duke of Cambridge, riding 'up with the Coldstream, stood Master of the Great Redoubt.'*

I conceived that the above sentence was a fair and not untruthful use of language, partly because H.R.H. the Duke of Cambridge commanded the Division to which the Grenadier Guards belonged, but partly also because I believed that the 'Coldstream' (with which His Royal Highness was personally present) had marched up to the redoubt—not quite simultaneously with the Grenadiers, yet—so soon after them that the advance of these two battalions of the Guards might be fairly regarded as one movement. But armed, as they would make it appear, with information which must needs come from Sir George Brown, and unchecked as yet by any public complaints against their accuracy on the part of Sir George, the conductors of the *Quarterly Review* are still leaving unretracted the narrative which they gave to the world more than three months ago. In it there is this paragraph:—

'Having opened to let the 7th and 33rd pass, the Grenadiers re-formed 'line and advanced against the Russian columns in their immediate front. 'Sir George Brown went with the Grenadier Guards; and when they ar- 'rived abreast of the Redan, he requested the commander of the battalion 'to detach a party from his left and to reoccupy that work. There was no 'risk in this; neither could the flank of the Grenadiers be said at this 'juncture to be exposed, because the men of the Light Division, who had 'been driven out of the Redan, were lying in an irregular line with the 'Fusileer Guards under the bank, and kept up such a heavy fire on the 'space between themselves and the work as compelled the enemy's masses, 'which had occupied the work, to halt, and finally to withdraw. Protected 'on the left by this fire, the Grenadiers moved forward, till, having crossed 'the swell of ground from which Codrington's brigade had retreated, they 'found themselves confronted by the Russian columns. Upon these they 'opened such an effective and well-sustained fire as soon told. The enemy 'wavered and gave ground; but in proportion as the Grenadiers pressed 'upon them, their own flank became exposed, and they were in danger of 'getting involved in a contest single-handed with a very superior force of 'the enemy. Seeing this, Sir George Brown *rode back* across the front of 'the Redan, and, rounding the corner of the hill, *came upon the Coldstream* '*Guards* in line and *under the steep ground*, and with their right somewhat 'thrown forward. *He conferred briefly with the Duke of Cambridge and* '*General Bentinck, both of whom were beside the Coldstreams, and the whole* '*immediately advanced.* The Coldstreams took their place on the left of the 'Grenadiers and shared in the battle. *But the battle was already dying out.* 'The Grenadiers had carried all before them; the Redan was empty; and, '*stealing away in a direction to their own right, the Russian columns were in full* '*retreat.*'

Now, if it were really to be proved to me that, after the time when the Grenadier Guards were abreast of the redoubt, the Duke of Cambridge, with the Coldstream, was still down below, under the steep ground near the river, and that there he and the Coldstream remained until a general officer, who had already been up with the Grenadiers abreast of the redoubt (and who had already provided for the reoccupying of the 'work' by a detached party), was able to ride back, to pass 'across the front of the Redan,' to 'round the corner of the hill,' to come at last to the Coldstream as they stood ranged 'under the steep ground,' and there to confer 'briefly' with H.R.H. the Duke of Cambridge and General Henry Bentinck; finally, if it were to be proved to me that the advance of the Duke of Cambridge and the Coldstream was the result of the 'brief' conference thus held, and that, by that time, the battle was already 'dying out,' the redoubt 'empty,' and the Russian columns 'stealing away' 'in full retreat,'—then indeed I should be forced to qualify the words by which I ventured to connect the Coldstream and the name of His Royal Highness the Duke of Cambridge with those moments of actual strife and glory which preceded the time of mere triumph.

But happily I conceive that I am not yet brought to this; and I will say why.

In the first place, the *Quarterly's* narrative of what Sir George Brown did at the Alma has not been expressly adopted by Sir George; and although, I fear, I must grant, both that Sir George Brown was the founder of the singular creed which inspired a part of the narrative, and that, after an interval of more than three months, he has not yet publicly disavowed the achievements which it attributes to him, still it is yet possible that when Sir George shall see all the bearings of the account which describes his actions, he will hold it his duty to come forward and correct the story.

But, in the next place, I have to say that, even if Sir George Brown shall do the reverse of this, and shall actually undertake to ratify all that the *Review* has said of him, he will be ratifying a narrative which I have shown to be wild as a dream in five of its chief assertions, and which therefore is likely enough to prove equally wild in this one.

For the present, however, I do not undertake to refute this curious account of the spot where Sir George Brown (on his return from the recapture of the redoubt) is represented to have found the Duke of Cambridge, General Henry Bentinck, and the Coldstream Guards. I leave this story to be dealt with by those who can speak from their personal knowledge of the state to which the battle had got when Sir George Brown is stated to have ridden back from abreast of the redoubt, and to have held the brief conference which was followed by the advance of the Coldstream. To what may be addressed to me, whether for or against the story, I shall listen, I hope, with due care; but in the mean time, and until the account shall be confirmed, I must decline to cut down the words by which I assign to the Duke of Cambridge and the Coldstream—not a mere share in a battle 'al-'ready dying out,' but—a real and timely participation in the 'brilliant ad-'vance' of the Guards.*

This is the last of the Notes elicited by the narrative of the Alma contained in the *Quarterly Review*. If Sir George Brown shall say that he has made no written nor oral communication about the Alma to any body connected as a contributor or otherwise with the *Quarterly Review*, and that he has never circulated a MS. which could have furnished ingredients for the publication, then I will gladly unsay every word which tends to connect him with the narrative contained in the *Review*. In the mean time, however, the narrative given in the *Review* is speaking, as it were, with what seems to be the transparent authority of Sir George Brown; and, this being so, I must for the present permit myself to regard Sir George as an officer who has connected himself (in the way I have indicated) with the periodical press. Sir George Brown has taken part in gainsaying my account of the Alma, and is now in turn doing me the honor to sit and undergo a few comments.

---

## XII.

*Note respecting the order of time in which certain events occurred at the Battle of the Alma.*

It may be remembered that when Sir Thomas Troubridge had just delivered the message which was followed by the immediate advance of the Grenadier Guards, he met Sir George Brown, and from him received his directions as to the course to be taken by the 7th Fusileers. Now it happened that, while Troubridge was still in conversation with Sir George Brown, he observed that a movement was taking effect on the Telegraph Height; and, drawing out his field-glass, he presently saw the left of the French army moving fairly up toward the Telegraph. The fact of his seeing this at

* In his published dispatch, Lord Raglan calls the movement 'a brilliant advance of the 'brigade of Foot-Guards under Major-General Bentinck.'

the time of his interview with Sir George Brown has happily fixed the exact point which had been reached by the progress of events in the English part of the field at the moment when the French army made good its advance from the cover of the steep hill-sides to the smooth plateau above. It has shown in a summary way—and the conclusion exactly agrees with inferences deducible from other grounds—it has shown that the advance of the French to the smooth plateau leading up to the Telegraph was after the storming and the dismantling of the Great Redoubt; was after the withdrawal of the Causeway batteries; was after the retreat of the enemy's reserves; was after the overthrow of the column long engaged with Lacy Yea's Fusileers; and was exactly simultaneous with the movement which brought our Grenadier Guards into their final engagement with the enemy's columns.

---

## XIII.

*Note respecting the truth of the accounts which represent that a great and terrible fight took place near the Telegraph on the day of the Alma.*

In the beginning of the year 1855 the Baron de Bazancourt was sent to the theatre of war by the French 'Minister of Public Instruction,' and the 'Mission' with which the Baron went charged was that of writing a history of the Crimean expedition. He was accredited to the then French Commander-in-chief by the Minister of War, and he seems to have been freely supplied with all such materials for getting at the truth as could be found in the military journals of the French army, and in the statements voluntarily made to the historian elect by officers who had themselves directed the operations which they undertook to describe.* Closely translated, the Baron's account of the supposed fight at the Telegraph runs thus. After speaking of the point where the building of the Telegraph stands, he says:—'It is 'there that the battle is; it is there that there are the efforts of attack and 'defense. On all sides we crown the plateau; but the considerable Russian 'forces massed behind the Telegraph, the sharp-shooters sheltered in this 'partly-built tower, and the batteries placed right and left, decimate our 'troops. Already the 1st Zouave Regiment and the 1st battalion of the 'Chasseurs of the 1st Division, and on their left the 2nd Zouaves of the 3rd 'Division, shelter themselves behind the undulations of the plateau, and 'were keeping up a sustained fire against the Russians, when two batteries 'of the reserve, led by Commandant La Boussinière, came to oppose artillery 'to artillery. The battery of Captain Toussaint quitted the road in order 'to arrive more rapidly by a movement toward its left, just in front of the 'Telegraph; the Zouaves themselves help to drag the guns up the last ac'clivities. They are soon placed, and open their fire, to which the Zouaves 'of the two divisions and the foot Chasseurs add a redoubling of fire. Four 'Russian guns quickly limber-up and withdraw. But the fire of the enemy's 'masses and that of the artillery placed in the rear of the Telegraph cause us 'serious losses. This position of expectancy could not long be maintained; 'an impetuous charge of the Russian cavalry on this point was imminent.

'Colonel Cler, who knows the war-tried and resolute troops which he com'mands, comprehends that he can not save them from utter destruction but 'by one of those sacrifices which snatch victory. For an instant he hesitates 'between a charge with the bayonet against the great front of the Russian

* See his Preface, p. vi.

'square, and an attack on the tower of the Telegraph, the centre and culminating point of the enemy's line. It is upon this last plan that he decides; and, going forward in advance of the angle formed by the regiments, and putting his horse into a gallop, he cries out, "To me, my Zouaves! To the tower! to the tower!"

'All precipitate themselves at the same time—that is, the 2nd Zouaves, the 1st Zouaves with Colonel Bourbaki at their head, the foot Chasseurs, the 39th Regiment, which comes up with Colonel Beuret and General d'Aurelle.

'It is a human torrent which nothing stops. Colonel Cler comes the first to the tower; all have followed him; all arrive ardent, impetuous, irresistible. The struggle was short, but it was one of those bloody, terrible struggles in which man fights body to body with his enemy, in which the looks devour each other [où les regards se dévorent, whatever that may mean], in which the hands grapple each other, in which arms dashed against arms are made to yield sparks of fire.* Dead and dying are heaped together, and the combatants trample upon them and smother them.

'The Russians received this formidable shock on the points of their bayonets; they ask each other if these are indeed but men [si ce sont des hommes] who thus dare to rush upon death; they fight, but soon they stagger, and these formidable masses, menaced on all sides by the two divisions, which advance in close columns, become broken, and operate their retreat.

'Colonel Cler seized the eagle of his regiment, which he plants on the tower to the cry of, "May the Emperor live!" Sergeant-major Fleury, of the 1st Zouaves, rushes upon the upper scaffolding of this partly-built building and balances the flag, which sinks with the intrepid non-commissioned officer, struck in the forehead by a ball. The flag of the 1st Zouaves also floats on this glorious trophy, which a fragment of shell breaks at the staff [flotte aussi sur ce glorieux trophée qu'un éclat d'obus brise a la hampe]; Lieutenant Poitevin, ensign-bearer of the 39th, precipitates himself in his turn outside his battalion, and comes in the midst of a rain of projectiles to plant on the tower of the Telegraph the eagle of his regiment; a bullet strikes him full in the breast, and stretches him lifeless. Every one among all these intrepids seemed to have in himself the enthusiasm of death.'

That is the account which M. de Bazancourt gives, and he does not seem to have found himself cramped by the officially admitted fact that in the whole battle the French only lost three officers killed. One of these, Lieutenant Poitevin, was struck, as we saw, after the Telegraph was carried, and when the Russians were operating their retreat; but in the actual fight, terrific and murderous as M. de Bazancourt represents it to have been, it does not appear that any French officer was either killed, wounded, or hurt.

It would seem that in 1856 the feeling of the French army respecting the story of the supposed fight at the Telegraph was not in such a state as to favor any thing like a repetition of M. de Bazancourt's description, for in that year M. du Casse published his *Preçis Historique;* and, although he describes some portions of the battle at considerable length, he disposes of the capture of the Telegraph in terms which do not necessarily denote any kind of infantry fight, and in only eight words.† 'The Telegraph, the key of the position, is carried.' 'Le Télégraphe clef de la position est enlevé.'

If the accounts given by the French had ended there, it might have been

* I have observed this phenomenon in fights upon the stage.

† He adds an account of the planting of the flags on the Telegraph; but his narrative of the *taking* of the Telegraph is, as I have said, in eight words.

inferred that they wished quietly to repudiate the bloody narrative of M. de Bazancourt, and to drop the notion of saying that there was really a great fight at the Telegraph; but the official *Atlas* of the French Government renews the story; for, in the plan which illustrates this period of the battle, it places the Taroutine and the 'Militia' battalions close in front of the Telegraph and around it; and the letter-press narrative accompanying the plans has these words:—'Le Général Canrobert lance sa division sur les défenseurs du Télégraphe; après un combat opiniâtre, auquel prend part le '39° de ligne de le brigade d'Aurelle de la 4e division, les Russes sont 'chassés de leur position, et les drapeaux des 1er et 2e de Zouaves et du 39° 'de ligne flottent successivement sur le Télégraphe.'

That the three flags were hoisted on the Telegraph no one doubts; but the question is whether those triumphant demonstrations were preceded by any thing like a serious fight. The difficulty of believing this is occasioned by the tenor of the Russian accounts. General Kiriakoff was naturally anxious to show that he had made an obstinate stand; and it may be imagined that if the heroic struggle described by M. de Bazancourt had really occurred, General Kiriakoff's narrative would have put it in full relief. He, however, says not a word of any such struggle. In one part of his narrative he speaks of the Taroutine and the 'Militia' battalions as being so far in advance, and so low down, that the batteries near the Telegraph fired over their heads; and at a later period of his narrative, without having said a word about any intermediate operation, he says that these battalions were under a cross-fire of artillery, and that, for that reason, and because the troops opposed to the English were already in full retreat, he 'commanded 'the march toward the main road.' He does not say a word of the bloody struggle with infantry in which the French represent his troops to have been engaged.

At first sight, it does not seem highly probable that upon the very summit of a smooth hill-top, where there was nothing to offer cover for the body of even one man, a few battalions (already dispirited by the passive endurance of artillery fire to which they had been condemned) should be ordered to make a stand against the 30,000 Frenchmen and Turks who were converging upon that very point from the west, as well as from the north; and if Kiriakoff had resorted to such a measure, it is all but incredible that his careful and almost minute narrative of his operations should have omitted all mention of an exploit strange in itself, and, if only it were true, redounding very much to the glory of his troops. Not only, however, does Kiriakoff appear to have been ignorant of any such fight, but the whole tenor of the narrative in which he describes what he did is inconsistent with the notion that any thing of the kind could have passed. According to his statement, he was a divisional general left without orders; he saw his troops suffering under a cross-fire of artillery; he knew (though apparently in an imperfect way) that overwhelming masses of French troops were more or less near to the verge of the plateau; and being thus circumstanced, and seeing, moreover, that the English had already carried the position, he thought it time to withdraw his battalions from the line of the artillery fire; but, from first to last, he never was challenged or vexed by the near approach of any French infantry. Such is his account. But this is not all. Both Kiriakoff and the official French statement of the *Atlas de la Guerre d'Orient* agree in representing that, after the check which it had given to Canrobert's Division, the great 'column of the eight battalions' had been kept together and moved a good way in the rear of the Telegraph, without ever engaging in any kind of struggle with infantry. Now, except the troops composing that column, the only battalions of Russian infantry which were at any time in this part of the field were the Taroutine and the 'Militia' battalions; and accordingly these are the troops which the French official *Atlas* places in array at the Telegraph. Now the 'Militia' battalions, we saw were inferior troops, and had dissolved. There remained the Taroutine battalions; and if any stand had been really made at the Telegraph, these must have been the troops which made it. It happens, however, that an intelligent and highly instructed field-officer of that corps has written an apparently complete account of every part of the battle of which he was competent to speak; and if any of Kiriakoff's forces, but still more if any of the Taroutine battalions had made the stand alleged, it is quite incredible either that Major Chodasiewicz, who was present with the Taroutine corps, should have remained ignorant of the fact, or that, knowing it, he should have omitted to state the truth. If any of the Taroutine battalions had been engaged in a fight of this sort, it would have been for them the grand, the all-absorbing event of the day; for it certainly was not their fate to be brought into conflict with French infantry in any other part of the field, and they would not have failed to remember an obstinate and bloody fight of the kind described by the French. But Chodasiewicz, though he minutely describes the way in which the Taroutine battalions were galled in their retreat by the fire of artillery, does not say a word of any kind of fight at the Telegraph between French and Russian infantry. Yet his was the very regiment which, if the French story were true, must have borne the brunt of the alleged fight.

Upon the whole, I have conceived that these authentic and trustworthy narratives of General Kiriakoff and Major Chodasiewicz* forbid me to admit into my text any statement similar to the account given by M. de Bazancourt, or even to that contained in the *Atlas de la Guerre d'Orient;* but those who are so constituted as to wish to incline the ear to a teacher duly prepared for them by the French Emperor's 'Minister of Public Instruction,' will find in the above quotation from M. de Bazancourt the sort of guidance they like.

---

## XIV.

*Note containing an Extract from a Letter addressed by Colonel Napier, the Historian of the Peninsular War, to Lord Fitzroy Somerset.*

If the foregoing volume has begun to disclose to its readers the entireness of Lord Raglan's devotion to the public service, his more than common swiftness of action, his subtle understanding of the feelings of other men, and his tenderness for their honest pride, it may be interesting to hear, that some thirty years before the time I write of, these very qualities had been ascribed to Lord Fitzory Somerset by the Historian of the Peninsular War. In a letter of October, 1824, which is now before me (but which I never saw until long after the publication of this book), Napier wrote:—

'My Dear Lord Fitzroy,—The rapidity with which you have fulfilled '——'s desires would be extraordinary, coming from any other quarter, but 'your accurate knowledge of every thing that does or has belonged to the 'army enables you to *do* before others can *think*. You are well aware, from 'the long acquaintance you have had with my opinions, that I am no flat-'terer, and that I am not disposed to express sentiments which I do not

* Anitchkoff was an officer of the staff, whose narrative is based on accounts taken from various Russian sources, and he says not a word of any fight at the Telegraph, or of any other combat which could have been confounded with it.

'feel. I would certainly rather have my feelings judged of by my actions 'than by my words; but I should be wanting both to you and myself if I 'failed to express my admiration of the unabated warmth with which you 'assist real merit, uninfluenced by any consideration but the services of the 'individual. Neither has the delicacy with which you have upon several 'occasions kept back all appearance of personal protection been unobserved 'by myself, or those numerous claimants who have at different times found 'a sure friend in you when they could find none elsewhere.'

When I see Napier writing that Lord Fitzroy Somerset could *do* before others could *think*, I am reminded of a singular instance of the uncommon swiftness with which his mind worked. One day in the Peninsula, and at a time when the Head-quarter's Staff were moving along the road, there was brought an intercepted dispatch, but it was in cipher—in a cipher unknown. Lord Fitzroy Somerset took up the paper, and, still riding on with the rest of the Staff, began to bend his mind to the letters and signs. Before he quitted his saddle he had pierced the secret, had found out the key, and had read the dispatch.

---

## XV.

*Note respecting the following Plans of the Battle of the Alma.*

The plan of the country, as shown by these Maps, is taken from the French official *Atlas Historique*, but with some slight changes, exaggerating in some degree the natural features of the ground, in order to make some of the slopes and hollows more easily apparent. The signs purporting to indicate the positions of the troops have been made by myself; but it is not intended that any thing seen in the Plans should be regarded as varying, or in any way qualifying, the description contained in the foregoing chapters; and it must not be understood that the positions of the troops are asserted to have been at any two moments such as they are represented to be in these two Plans. The object of the Plans is not to assert any one of the facts thereby appearing to be indicated, but merely to aid the reader in his endeavors to follow the statements contained in the text.

END OF VOL. I.

www.ingramcontent.com/pod-product-compliance
Lightning Source LLC
LaVergne TN
LVHW021047110826
845150LV00001B/2
* 9 7 8 1 4 2 5 5 6 9 0 9 9 *